Sociology

Exploring the Architecture of Everyday Life

Twelfth Edition

David M. Newman
DePauw University

Los Angeles | London | New Delhi
Singapore | Washington DC | Melbourne

FOR INFORMATION:

SAGE Publications, Inc.
2455 Teller Road
Thousand Oaks, California 91320
E-mail: order@sagepub.com

SAGE Publications Ltd.
1 Oliver's Yard
55 City Road
London EC1Y 1SP
United Kingdom

SAGE Publications India Pvt. Ltd.
B 1/I 1 Mohan Cooperative Industrial Area
Mathura Road, New Delhi 110 044
India

SAGE Publications Asia-Pacific Pte. Ltd.
3 Church Street
#10-04 Samsung Hub
Singapore 049483

Printed in the United States of America

Library of Congress Cataloging-in-Publication Data

Names: Newman, David M., author.

Title: Sociology : exploring the architecture of everyday life / David M. Newman, DePauw University.

Description: Twelfth Edition. | Thousand Oaks : SAGE Publications, [2018] | Revised edition of the author's Sociology, [2017] | Includes bibliographical references and index.

Identifiers: LCCN 2017044463 | ISBN 9781506388205 (pbk. : alk. paper)

Subjects: LCSH: Sociology.

Classification: LCC HM585 .N48 2018 | DDC 301—dc23
LC record available at https://lccn.loc.gov/2017044463

Acquisitions Editor: Jeff Lasser
Content Development Editor: Sarah Dillard
Editorial Assistants: Adeline Wilson & Tiara Beatty
Production Editor: Nevair Kabakian
Copy Editor: Tammy Giesmann
Typesetter: C&M Digitals (P) Ltd.
Proofreader: Barbara Coster
Indexer: Sheila Bodell
Cover Designer: Candice Harman
Marketing Manager: Kara Kindstrom

This book is printed on acid-free paper.

SUSTAINABLE FORESTRY INITIATIVE
Certified Chain of Custody
Promoting Sustainable Forestry
www.sfiprogram.org
SFI-01268
SFI label applies to text stock

18 19 20 21 22 10 9 8 7 6 5 4 3 2 1

• Brief Contents •

• Detailed Contents •

• Preface to the Twelfth Edition •

It was the first day of the fall semester several years ago. I had just finished making the final adjustments to an earlier edition of this book, which was due to be published the following January. I felt pretty good about myself, like I'd just accomplished something monumental. Let's face it; being able to call yourself *an author* is pretty cool. Even my two sons were impressed with me (although not as impressed as the time we went to a professional hockey game and I leaped out of my seat to catch an errant, speeding puck barehanded). I walked confidently into the first meeting of my Introduction to Sociology class eager to start teaching wide-eyed, first-year students a thing or two about sociology.

In my opening comments to the class that day, I mentioned that I had just written this book. The panicked look in students' eyes—a curious combination of awe and fear—calmed when I told them I wouldn't be requiring them to read it that semester. I told them that the process of writing an introductory text helped me immensely in preparing for the course and that I looked forward to passing on to them the knowledge I had accumulated.

The next day after class, one of the students—a bright-eyed, freshly scrubbed 18-year-old—approached me. The ensuing conversation would leave a humbling impression that lasts to this day:

Student: Hi. Umm. Professor Newman . . . I called my parents last night to, like, tell them how my first day in college went. I think they were, like, more nervous than I was. You know how parents can be.

Me: Yes, I sure do. I'm a parent myself, you know.

Student: Yeah, whatever. Anyway, I was telling them about my classes and my professors and stuff. I told them about this class and how I thought it would be pretty cool. I told you you had written a book. I thought that would impress them, you know, make it seem like they were getting their money's worth and everything.

Me: Well, thanks.

Student: So, they go, "What's the book about?" [He laughs sheepishly.] I told them I really didn't know, but I'd find out. So, like, that's what I'm doing . . . finding out.

Me: Well, I'm glad you asked. You see, it's an introductory sociology textbook that uses everyday experiences and phenomena as a way of understanding important sociological theories and ideas. In it I've attempted to . . .

Student: [His eyes, which were already glazed over with boredom, suddenly jumped back to life.] Wait, did you say it was a textbook?

Me: Why, yes. You see the purpose of the book is to provide the reader with a thorough and useful introduction to the sociological perspective. I want to convey . . .

Student: [Quite embarrassed now] Oh . . . Professor Newman, I'm really sorry. I misunderstood you. I thought you had written a real book.

Real book. *Real* book. *Real* book. Those words rang in my head like some relentless church bell. At first, I tried to dismiss this comment as the remark of a naïve kid who didn't know any better. But the more I thought about it, the more I realized what his comment reflected. The perception that textbooks aren't *real* books is widespread.

A couple of years ago, I heard a radio ad for a local Red Cross book drive. The narrator asked listeners to donate any unused or unwanted books *as long as they weren't textbooks.* Yep, that's what he said. A torn copy of *The Cat in the Hat*? Fine, they'll take it. A grease-stained owner's manual for a Ford Fusion? Sure, glad to have it. A 2003 guidebook on how to use Myspace? What a lovely addition to the collection. Textbooks? No way!

Sadly, these sorts of perceptions are not altogether undeserved. Textbooks hover on the margins of the literary world, somewhere between respectable, intellectual monographs on trailblazing research and trashy romance novels. Traditionally, they've been less than titillating: thick, heavy, expensive, and easily discarded for a measly five bucks at the end-of-semester "book buy-back."

My goal—from the first edition of this book to the current one—has always been to write a textbook that reads like a *real* book. In the previous 11 editions, I tried to capture simultaneously the essence and insight of my discipline and the reader's interest. From what reviewers, instructors, and students who've read and used the book over the years have said, I think I've been fairly successful. While no Hollywood movie studio has expressed interest in turning this book into a movie (yet!), people do seem to like the relaxed tone and appreciate the consistent theme that ties all the chapters together. Many instructors have commented on how the book enables students to truly understand the unique and useful elements of a sociological perspective. Take that, Red Cross!

Features of the Twelfth Edition

To my sons—who believe that I have nothing important to say about anything anyway—continually revising this book has always been clear evidence of my incompetence. Back when he was in middle school, my younger son once asked me, "Why do you keep writing the same book over and over? My English teacher made me rewrite a book report on *To Kill a Mockingbird* because I answered some questions wrong. Is that what's going on here, Dad? Is your publisher making you write the book again because you made too many mistakes?" I told him no and that I'd make him read the whole book—cover to cover—if he continued to ask such questions. He stopped . . . although to this day, he's still not convinced I have anything useful to say.

Despite his concerns, sociology textbooks do need to be revised regularly and frequently to be of any use. No book can be of lasting value if it remains static, locked into a particular style and content. So I keep my ears and eyes open, always looking for some new example or current issue to include in the book. My office overflows with stacks of books, newspaper clippings, photocopied journal articles, Post-it notes, and shreds of paper napkins containing scribbled ideas that I write to myself at the breakfast table when I come across something interesting. I've even been known to send myself e-mails at 3:00 in the morning so as not to forget the great idea that came to me in the haziness between sleep and wakefulness.

One thing I've learned over the years is that when revising a book, it's a lot easier to add new material than it is to cut out the old stuff. But simply inserting bits and pieces here and there tends to make books fat and unwieldy. So I've tried to streamline this edition wherever possible. I've replaced outdated material with new material where appropriate, revised all the statistical information, condensed or deleted some sections, and changed the order of others.

Here are some of the specific changes I've made to enhance the features that worked so well in the previous editions.

Updated Examples and Statistical Information

As in the first 11 editions, I've peppered each chapter with anecdotes, personal observations, and accounts of contemporary events that serve as illustrations of the sociological points I'm making. Many of the examples you will read are taken from today's news headlines; others come from incidents in my own life.

It would be impossible to write an introduction to the discipline of sociology without accounting for the life-altering occurrences—wars, natural disasters, school shootings, political upheavals, court decisions, economic meltdowns, the latest Kardashian escapade—that we hear about every day. So throughout this book, I've made a special effort to provide some sociological insight into well-known contemporary events and trends, both large and small. In doing so, I intend to show you the pervasiveness and applicability of sociology in our ordinary, everyday experiences in a way that, I hope, rings familiar with you.

As you will see, it is impossible to understand what happens to us in our personal lives without taking into consideration broader social and historical phenomena. Several specific recent developments have had—and will continue to have—a dramatic impact on sociological thought and on people's everyday lives: the political changeover brought about by the 2016 election, trends in the global economy, the stream of fatal encounters between police and unarmed people of color, and the continued dramatic growth of communication technology, particularly ever-present social networking sites:

- As I'm writing this preface, the new Trump administration has been in office for one year. How will it shift global politics, the course of the nation, and the rhythm of our everyday lives after 8 years of a Democratic administration?

- When the economy suffers (or improves), everyone—from tycoons to unemployed welfare recipients—experiences some kind of alteration in her or his day-to-day routine. It's been quite a challenge to keep up with the most current information on joblessness, hiring trends, home foreclosures, spending patterns, and so on.

- Each new incident of racially or ethically connected violence—whether at the hands of law enforcement, hate groups, or lone assailants—alters the trajectory of race relations in this country.

- And how can we analyze the sociology of everyday life without acknowledging the powerful role online social networking has had in shaping the way we learn, work, relate to others, and ultimately define ourselves?

Thus, you will see references to these—and many other—developments throughout the book to illustrate the interconnections between private life and massive historical occurrences.

I also want to call your attention to the fact that many extended examples of sociological theories and concepts throughout the book focus on some aspect of health, illness, and medicine. I have done this for two reasons. First of all, no matter who we are or where we come from, all of us must deal with health matters from time to time. Our own physical and mental well-being is perhaps the most personal and immediate thing in our lives. At the same time, whenever we seek medical attention—whether in a doctor's office, a local pharmacy, or a hospital—or try to figure out how to pay for it, we enter a massive health care system that can sometimes feel immensely bureaucratic and *im*personal.

And as medical costs continue to rise, changes to our health care system—both proposed and enacted—will dominate economic forecasts, newspaper headlines, and legislative action for years to come. Second, students taking the Medical College Admissions Test now must take a course in sociology. And so these health care-related examples will provide such students with applications and illustrations that are directly relevant to their needs and, hopefully, make them better doctors in the future.

I've also tried to provide the most current statistical information possible. I've updated all the graphic exhibits and, in the process, changed some of them from statistical tables to more readable charts and graphs, making trends and relationships more obvious. Much of the new statistical information is drawn from the most recent data from sources such as the U.S. Census Bureau, the Population Reference Bureau, the Centers for Disease Control and Prevention, the National Center for Education Statistics, the U.S. Bureau of Labor Statistics, the U.S. Bureau of Justice Statistics, and the Pew Research Center.

Updated "Sociologists at Work" and "Micro-Macro Connections"

In the previous 11 editions, I provided many in-depth features that focused either on a specific piece of sociological research or on some issue that illustrates the connection between the everyday lives of individuals and the structure of their society. These extended discussions link social institutions to personal experiences and provide insight into the methods sociologists use to gather information and draw conclusions about how our world works.

Instructors and students alike have found these features very useful in generating classroom discussion. The features that I've thoroughly updated from previous editions focus on topics such as suicide, the vocabulary of war, family privacy, smartphone usage, cultural influence on emotions, children's toys, dual-earner households, clergy sexual abuse, the cultural impact of antidepressants, same-sex marriage, the global health divide, interracial identity, residential segregation, racial mistrust of medical research, sexual harassment in the military, dangerous media images of eating disorders, intergenerational conflict, and the shifting politics of immigration. In addition, I've also added a few new features on the effect of clothing on the way we think, the mismatch between perceptions and the reality of wealth inequality, cultural appropriation of race and ethnicity, and online privacy.

Teaching Resources and Website to Accompany the Book and Companion Reader

SAGE edge™ **edge.sagepub.com/newman12e**

SAGE edge offers a robust online environment you can access anytime, anywhere, and features an impressive array of free tools and resources to keep you on the cutting edge of your learning experience.

SAGE edge for Students provides a personalized approach to help students accomplish their coursework goals in an easy-to-use learning environment.

Mobile-friendly **eFlashcards** strengthen understanding of key terms and concepts

Mobile-friendly practice **quizzes** allow for independent assessment by students of their mastery of course material

Video and multimedia content that enhances student engagement and appeals to different learning styles

EXCLUSIVE! Access to full-text **SAGE journal articles** that have been carefully selected to support and expand on the concepts presented in each chapter

SAGE edge for Instructors supports teaching by making it easy to integrate quality content and create a rich learning environment for students.

Test banks provide a diverse range of prewritten options as well as the opportunity to edit any question and/or insert personalized questions to effectively assess students' progress and understanding

Editable, chapter-specific **PowerPoint®** **slides** offer complete flexibility for creating a multimedia presentation for the course

EXCLUSIVE! Access to full-text **SAGE journal articles** have been carefully selected to support and expand on the concepts presented in each chapter to encourage students to think critically

Video and multimedia links include original SAGE videos that appeal to students with different learning styles

Lively and stimulating **chapter activities** can be used in class to reinforce active learning. The activities apply to individual or group projects.

A course cartridge provides easy LMS integration

A Word About the "Architecture of Everyday Life"

I chose the image of architecture in the subtitle to convey one of the driving themes of this book: Society is a human construction. It is not "out there" somewhere, waiting to be visited and examined. It exists in the minute details of our day-to-day lives. Whenever we follow its rules or break them, enter its roles or shed them, work to change things or keep them as they are, we are adding another nail, plank, or frame to the structure of our society. In short, society—like the buildings around us—couldn't exist were it not for the actions of people.

At the same time, however, this structure that we have created appears to exist independently of us. We don't usually spend much time thinking about the buildings we live, work, and play in as human constructions. We see them as finished products, not as the processes that created them. Only when something goes wrong—the pipes leak or the walls crack—do we realize that people made these structures and people are the ones who must fix them. When buildings outlive their usefulness or become dangerous to their inhabitants, people must renovate them or, if necessary, tear them down.

Likewise, society is so massive and has been around for so long that it *appears* to stand on its own, at a level above and beyond the toiling hands of individual people. But here, too, when things begin to go wrong—widespread discrimination, environmental degradation, massive poverty, lack of affordable health care, escalating crime rates—people must do something about it.

So the fascinating paradox of human life is that we build society, collectively "forget" that we've built it, and live under its massive and influential structure. But we are not stuck with society as it is. Human beings are the architects of their own social reality. Throughout this book, I examine the active roles individuals play in designing, building, maintaining, renovating, or tearing down society.

A Final Thought

One of the greatest challenges I have faced in three decades of teaching sociology is trying to get my students to see the personal relevance of the course material, to fully appreciate the connection between the individual and society. The true value of sociology lies in its unique ability to show the two-way connection between the most private elements of our lives—our characteristics, experiences, behaviors, and thoughts—and the cultures, groups, organizations, and social institutions to which we belong. The "everyday life" approach in this book uses real-world examples and personal observations as a vehicle for understanding the relationship between individuals and society.

My purpose is to make the familiar unfamiliar—to help you critically examine the commonplace and the ordinary in your own life. Only when you step back and examine the taken-for-granted aspects of your personal experiences can you see that there is an inherent, sometimes unrecognized organization and predictability to them. At the same time, you will see that the structure of society is greater than the sum of the experiences and psychologies of the individuals in it.

It is my conviction that this intellectual excursion should be a thought-provoking and enjoyable one. Reading a textbook doesn't have to be boring or, even worse, the academic equivalent of a painful trip to the dentist (although I personally have nothing against dentists). I believe that one of my responsibilities as a teacher is to provide my students with a challenging but comfortable classroom atmosphere in which to learn. I have tried to do the same in this book. Your instructor has chosen this book not because it makes his or her job teaching your course any easier but because he or she wants you, the student, to see how sociology helps us to understand how the small, private experiences of our everyday lives are connected to this thing we call society. I hope you learn to appreciate this important message, and I hope you enjoy reading this book as much as I enjoyed writing it.

Have fun,

David M. Newman
Department of Sociology and Anthropology
DePauw University
Greencastle, IN 46135
E-mail: dnewman@depauw.edu

• Acknowledgments •

A book project such as this one takes an enormous amount of time to develop. Over the span of 12 editions, I've spent thousands of hours on this book—typing away at my computer, endlessly searching the web, fretting over what I should and shouldn't include, proofreading for mistakes—either holed up in my isolated and very cluttered third-floor office or tucked away in the quiet corner of a library. Yet as solitary as this project was, I could not have done it alone. Over the years, many people have provided invaluable assistance to make this book a reality. Without their generous help and support, it wouldn't have been written, and you'd be reading some other sociologist's list of people to thank. Because I have revised rather than rewritten this book, I remain indebted to those who have helped me at some point during the writing of all 12 editions.

First, I would be remiss if I didn't thank the former publisher and president of Pine Forge Press, Steve Rutter. More than two decades ago, when I was a brand new (and naïve) author, he pushed, prodded, and cajoled me into exceeding my expectations and overachieving. The numerous suggestions he offered on the early editions of this book made it a better one. Likewise, my former editor, Becky Smith, must be thanked for helping me through the maze of details and difficulties that cropped up during the many previous versions of this book. Even though she no longer edits my books, hers is the grammar-correcting, thesaurus-wielding voice in my head whenever I write.

As for this edition, I would like to extend my sincere gratitude to Jeff Lasser, Adeline Wilson, and Nevair Kabakian at SAGE for their insight and guidance in putting together this newest edition. Having already written eleven editions of this book, I was definitely an old dog with absolutely no desire to learn any new tricks when these individuals became involved. To their credit, they let me write as I have always written. For their trust, I am eternally grateful.

I would also like to express my thanks to Jamie Chapman for creating the student study site materials and instructor teaching resources.

As always, I appreciate the many helpful comments offered by the reviewers of the 12 editions of this book:

Sharon Abbott, Fairfield University

Deborah Abowitz, Bucknell University

Stephen Adair, Central Connecticut State University

Rebecca Adams, University of North Carolina, Greensboro

Ron Aminzade, University of Minnesota

Afroza Anwary, Carleton College

George Arquitt, Oklahoma State University

Carol Auster, Franklin and Marshall College

Ellen C. Baird, Arizona State University

Ellen Berg, California State University, Sacramento

Mildred Biaku, University of Alabama at Birmingham

Michael G. Bisciglia, Southeastern Louisiana University

David Bogen, Emerson College

Frances A. Boudreau, Connecticut College

David L. Briscoe, University of Arkansas at Little Rock

Todd Campbell, Loyola University, Chicago

Wanda Clark, South Plains College

Thomas Conroy, St. Peter's College

Norman Conti, Duquesne University

Maia Greenwell Cunningham, Citrus College

Doug Currivan, University of Massachusetts, Boston

Karen Dalke, University of Wisconsin, Green Bay

Jeff Davidson, University of Delaware

Kimberly Davies, Augusta State University

Tricia Davis, North Carolina State University

Michelle Deming, University of South Carolina

James J. Dowd, University of Georgia, Athens

Laura A. Dowd, University of Georgia, Athens

Charlotte A. Dunham, Texas Tech University

Donald Eckard, Temple University

Charles Edgley, Oklahoma State University

Rachel Einhower, Purdue University

June Ellestad, Washington State University

Shalom Endleman, Quinnipiac College

Rebecca Erickson, University of Akron

Kimberly Faust, Winthrop University

Patrick Fontane, St. Louis College of Pharmacy

Michael J. Fraleigh, Bryant University

Volker Frank, University of North Carolina, Asheville

Sarah N. Gaston, Texas A&M University

Farah Gilanshah, University of Minnesota–Morris

Barry Goetz, University of Dayton

Lorie Schabo Grabowski, University of Minnesota

Valerie Gunter, University of New Orleans

Roger Guy, Texas Lutheran University

John R. Hall, University of California, Davis

Charles Harper, Creighton University

Douglas Harper, Duquesne University

Tara Hardinge, California State University, Long Beach

Lori Heald, East Carolina University

Peter Hennen, University of Minnesota

Max Herman, Rutgers University

Cynthia Hewitt, Morehouse College

Christine L. Himes, Syracuse University

Susan Hoerbelt, Hillsborough Community College

Amy Holzgang, Cerritos College

Kate Hovey, Central New Mexico Community College

W. Jay Hughes, Georgia Southern University

Gary Hytreck, Georgia Southern University

Valerie Jenness, University of California, Irvine

Kimberly Johanek, Boise State

Kathryn Johnson, Barat College

Richard Jones, Marquette University

Tom Kando, California State University, Sacramento

Steve Keto, Kent State University

Peter Kivisto, Augustana College

Lisa Konczal, Barry University

Marc LaFountain, State University of West Georgia

Sharon Melissa Latimer, West Virginia University

Joseph Lengermann, University of Maryland, College Park

Linda A. Litteral, Grossmont Community College

Julie L. Locher, University of Alabama at Birmingham

David G. LoConto, Jacksonville State University

David A. Lopez, California State University, Northridge

Fred Maher, Temple University

Kristen Marcussen, University of Iowa

Benjamin Mariante, Stonehill College

Joseph Marolla, Virginia Commonwealth University

Michallene McDaniel, University of Georgia

James R. McIntosh, Lehigh University

Jerome McKibben, Fitchburg State University

Ted P. McNeilsmith, Adams State College

Dan Miller, University of Dayton

Melinda Milligan, Sonoma State University

John R. Mitrano, Central Connecticut State University

Susannne Monahan, Montana State University

Harvest Moon, The University of Texas at Arlington

Kelly Murphy, University of Pittsburgh

Elizabeth Ehrhardt Mustaine, University of Central Florida

Daniel Myers, University of Notre Dame

Anne Nurse, College of Wooster

Marjukka Ollilainen, Weber State University

Toska Olson, Evergreen State College

Liza A. Pellerin, Ball State University

Larry Perkins, Oklahoma State University, Stillwater

Bernice Pescosolido, Indiana University, Bloomington

Mike Plummer, Boston College

Edward Ponczek, William Rainey Harper College

Tanya Poteet, Capital University

Sharon E. Preves, Grand Valley State University

Kennon J. Rice, North Carolina State University

Judith Richlin-Klonsky, University of California, Los Angeles

Robert Robinson, Indiana University, Bloomington

Mary Rogers, University of West Florida

Sally S. Rogers, Montgomery College

Wanda Rushing, University of Memphis

Michael Ryan, University of Louisiana, Lafayette

Scott Schaffer, Millersville University

Aileen Schulte, State University of New York, New Paltz

Dave Schweingruber, Iowa State University

Mark Shibley, Southern Oregon University

Thomas Shriver, Oklahoma State University

Toni Sims, University of Louisiana, Lafayette

Kathleen Slevin, College of William and Mary

Melissa Sloan, Drew University

Lisa White Smith, Christopher Newport University

Eldon E. Snyder, Bowling Green State University

Nicholas Sofios, Providence College

George Spilker, Clarkson College

Melanie Stander, University of Washington

Beverly Stiles, Midwestern State University

Kandi Stinson, Xavier University

Richard Tardanico, Florida International University

Robert Tellander, Sonoma State University

Kathleen Tiemann, University of North Dakota

Steven Vallas, George Mason University

Tom Vander Ven, Indiana University, South Bend

John Walsh, University of Illinois, Chicago

Gregory Weiss, Roanoke College

Marty Wenglinski, Quinnipiac College

Stephan Werba, Catonsville Community College

Cheryl E. Whitley, Marist College

Norma Williams, University of North Texas

Janelle Wilson, University of Minnesota, Duluth

Mark Winton, University of Central Florida

Judith Wittner, Loyola University, Chicago

Cynthia A. Woolever, Hartford Seminary

Don C. Yost, Mountain State University

Ashraf Zahedi, Stanford University

Stephen Zehr, University of Southern Indiana

I also want to express my appreciation to the many colleagues, students, and friends who have offered cherished assistance throughout the production of all 12 editions of this book and have put up with my incessant whining about how hard it all was. Some offered bits of advice on specific topics; others provided general support and encouragement, which helped me retain my sanity. Jodi O'Brien, after close to 30 years of friendship and more than a decade of coediting, continues to graciously remind me that there's more to life than writing a book. And I'd also like to acknowledge the library staffs at my school, DePauw University, and at Bates College in Maine, where I spent many hours over the summers putting the final touches on this book.

I'm pleased to express deep gratitude to my sons, Zach and Seth, my new baby daughter, Hazel, and my students, who, over the years, have kept me curious and prevented me from taking myself too seriously. And finally, my deepest thanks must go to my wife, Rebecca Upton, whose love, eternal optimism, kind support, and unwavering confidence consistently inspire me to push beyond my intellectual limitations, and to C. Mokolodi Underfoot, whose crooked grin and wagging tail never fail to brighten my day.

• About the Author •

David M. Newman earned his BA from San Diego State University in 1981 and his graduate degrees from the University of Washington in Seattle (MA 1984, PhD 1988). After a year at the University of Connecticut, David came to DePauw University in 1989 and has been there ever since. David teaches courses in Contemporary Society, Deviance, Mental Illness, Family, Social Psychology, and Research Methods. He has published numerous articles on teaching and has presented research papers on the intersection of gender and power in intimate relationships. Recently most of his scholarly activity has been devoted to writing and revising several books, including *Sociology: Exploring the Architecture of Everyday Life: Brief Edition* (Sage, 2017); *Identities and Inequalities: Exploring the Intersections of Race, Class, Gender, and Sexuality* (McGraw-Hill, 2017); and *Families: A Sociological Perspective* (McGraw-Hill, 2009). His most recent book, *Redemption or Stigma? The Promise, Practice and Price of Second Chances in American Culture* (Lexington Books), is projected to be published in 2019. It examines the cultural meaning, institutional importance, and social limitations of "second chance" and "permanent stigma" narratives in everyday life.

The Individual and Society

What is the relationship between your private life and the social world around you? Part I introduces you to the guiding theme of this book: Our personal, everyday experiences affect and are affected by the larger society in which we live. In Chapters 1 and 2 I discuss the sociological perspective on human life and the ways in which it differs from the more individualistic approaches of psychology and biology. You will read about what society consists of and get a glimpse into sociologists' attempts to understand the two-way relationship between the individual and society.

As you read on, keep in mind a metaphor that will be used throughout the book to help explain the nature of society: architecture. Like buildings, societies have a design discernible to the alert eye. Both are constructed by bringing together a wide variety of materials in a complex process. Both, through their structure, shape the activities within. At the same time, both change. Sometimes they change subtly and gradually as the inhabitants go about their lives; other times they are deliberately redecorated or remodeled. As you make your way through this book, see if you can discover more ways in which buildings and societies are alike.

Taking a New Look at a Familiar World

- Sociology and the Individual
- The Insights of Sociology
- The Sociological Imagination

André graduated from college in 2017. He had been a model student. When not studying, he found time to help kids read at the local elementary school and actively participated in student government at his own school. He got along well with his professors, his grades were excellent, he made the dean's list all 4 years, and he graduated Phi Beta Kappa. As a computer science major with a minor in economics, André thought his future was set: He would land a job at a top software company or perhaps a stock brokerage firm and work his way up the ladder so that he'd be earning a six-figure income by the time he was 30.

But when André entered the job market and began applying for jobs, things didn't go exactly according to plan. Despite his credentials, nobody seemed willing to hire him full time. He was able to survive by taking temporary freelance programming jobs here and there and working nights at the Gap. Although most of his classmates had similar difficulties finding jobs, André began to question his own abilities: "Do I lack the skills employers are looking for? Am I not trying hard enough? What the heck is wrong with me?" His friends and family were as encouraging as they could be, but some secretly wondered if André wasn't as smart as they'd thought he was.

Michael and Louise were both juniors at a large university. They had been dating each other exclusively for the past 2 years. By all accounts, the relationship seemed to be going quite well. In fact, Michael was beginning to think about marriage, children, and living happily ever after. Then one day out of the blue, Louise dropped a bombshell. She texted Michael that she thought their relationship was going nowhere and perhaps they ought to start seeing other people.

Michael was stunned. "What did I do?" he asked her. "I thought things were going great. Is it something I said? Something I did? Tell me. I can change."

She said no, he hadn't done anything wrong; they had simply grown apart. She told him she just didn't feel as strongly about him as she used to.

Even though he let his friends talk him into immediately changing his relationship status on Facebook, Michael was devastated. They tried to comfort him. "She wasn't any good for you anyway," they said. "We always thought she was a little creepy. She probably couldn't be in a serious relationship with anybody. It wasn't your fault; it was hers."

In both of these stories, notice how people immediately try to explain an unfortunate situation by focusing on the personal characteristics and attributes of the individuals involved. André blames himself for not being able to land a job in his field; others, although supportive, harbor doubts about his intelligence and drive. Michael wonders what he did to sour his relationship with Louise; his friends question Louise's psychological stability. Such reactions are not uncommon. We have a marked tendency to rely on **individualistic explanations**, attributing people's achievements and disappointments to their personal qualities.

So why can't André, our highly intelligent, well-trained, talented college graduate, land a permanent job in his field? It's certainly possible that he has some personal flaw that makes him unemployable: lack of motivation, laziness, negative attitude, bad hygiene, a snooty demeanor, and so on. Or maybe he just doesn't come across as particularly smart during job interviews.

But by focusing exclusively on such individual "deficiencies," we risk overlooking the broader societal factors that may have affected André's job prospects. For instance, the employment situation for college graduates like André was part of a broader economic trend that began with the global financial crisis of 2008 and continued to suppress the job market by the time he got his degree. At the time I was writing this chapter, 4.1% of American adults (about 7 million people) were officially unemployed and about a quarter of them had been unemployed for at least 27 weeks. Incidentally, the official unemployment rate only counts people who have been actively seeking employment for the past month. Thus it doesn't include the 5.3 million people who were employed part time even though they wanted to work full time, the 1.6 million "marginally attached" unemployed people who had looked for a job sometime in the past year (just not in the past month), and the 514,000 so-called "discouraged" workers who had lost hope and given up looking for employment (U.S. Bureau of Labor Statistics, 2017c). So you see, even though the unemployment rate is lower than it was, say 10 years ago, a lot of people remain in André's boat.

But he's got a college education. That should help, right? Well, it turns out that college degrees are not necessarily a guarantee of fruitful employment. Even though the economy has been steadily improving over the past decade, the unemployment rate for recent college graduates has remained fairly stable: 5.6% today compared with 5.5% in 2007 (the year prior to the Great Recession). To put it another way, in 2000, 38% of college graduates between the ages of 22 and 27 were underemployed (that is, working in jobs that didn't require a college degree); by 2016, that figure increased to over 45%. In addition, less than 30% of employed college graduates work in a job that provides retirement or pension benefits. And 1 out of 10 recent college graduates is neither employed nor pursuing more education in graduate or professional school (Kroeger, Cooke, & Gould, 2016).

New graduates do fare better than other young people who don't have college degrees (Pew Charitable Trusts, 2013). For instance, college graduates earn 98% more per hour on average than people without a degree (cited in Leonhardt, 2014). However, the average starting salary for college graduates has stagnated in recent years. In fact, since 2000, the wages of young college graduates has actually dropped by 7.7% (Shierholz, Davis, & Kimball, 2014). To make money matters worse, the average 2016 college graduate has $37,172 in student loan debt, up 6% from the previous year (Student Loan Hero, 2017).

In addition, their future outlook may not be so great. In a survey conducted by the National Association of Colleges and Employers (2016), only about 5% of employers indicate that they intend to hire more college graduates than they did the previous year; a third said they intend to hire *fewer* graduates. Indeed, according to some economists, for the next 10 to 15 years, recent graduates will probably earn less and have more bouts of unemployment than if they had graduated at a time when jobs were more plentiful (Kroeger, Cooke, & Gould, 2016).

So you see, André's employability and his chances of earning a good living were as much a result of the economic forces operating at the time he began looking for a job as of any of his personal qualifications. Had he graduated only 5 years earlier—when the unemployment rate hovered around 10%—his job prospects would have been much worse. But had he graduated 5 years later—when employment opportunities are projected to improve even more for graduates in his field—his prospects would have been much brighter.

And what about Michael and Louise? It seems perfectly reasonable to conclude that something about either of them or the combination of the two caused their breakup. We tend to view dating relationships—not to mention marriages—as successes or failures based solely on the traits or behaviors of the two people involved.

But how would your assessment of the situation change if you found out that Lee—to whom Louise had always been secretly attracted—had just broken up with his longtime girlfriend, Julie, and was now available? Like it or not, relationships are not exclusively private entities; they're always being influenced by forces beyond our control. They take place within a larger network of friends, acquaintances, ex-partners, coworkers, fellow students, and people as yet unknown who may make desirable or, at the very least, acceptable dating partners. On Facebook, people routinely post up-to-the-minute changes in the status of their relationships, thereby instantaneously advertising shifts in their availability.

When people believe they have no better alternative, they tend to stay with their present partners, even if they are not particularly satisfied. When people think that better relationships are available to them, they may become less committed to staying in their present ones. Indeed, people's perceptions of what characterizes a good relationship (such as fairness, compatibility, affection) are less likely to determine when and if it ends than the presence or absence of favorable alternatives (Felmlee, Sprecher, & Bassin, 1990). Research shows that the risk of a relationship ending increases as the supply of potential alternative relationships increases (South & Lloyd, 1995).

In addition, Louise's decision to leave could have been indirectly affected by the sheer number of potentially obtainable partners—a result of shifts in the birthrate 20 years or so earlier. Today, there are roughly 126 U.S. men between 25 and 34 who are single, divorced, or widowed for every 100 women in the same categories (K. Parker, Wang, & Rohal, 2014). For a single, heterosexual woman like Louise, such a surplus of college-age men increases the likelihood that she would eventually find a better alternative to Michael. Fifty years ago, however, when there were 180 single men for every 100 single women, her chances would have been even better. The number of available alternatives can also vary geographically. For instance, Michael's prospects would improve if he were living in Auburn, Maine, where there are 81 unmarried men for every 100 unmarried women, but his chances would sink if he lived in Mansfield, Ohio, where there are 215 unmarried men for every 100 unmarried women (Pew Research Social and Demographic Trends, 2014). In sum, Michael's interpersonal value, and therefore the stability of his relationship with Louise, may have suffered not because of anything he did but because of population forces over which he had little, if any, control.

Let's take this notion beyond Louise and Michael's immediate dating network. For instance, the very characteristics and features that people consider desirable (or undesirable) in the first place reflect the values of the larger culture in which they live. Fashions and tastes are constantly changing, making particular characteristics (e.g., hairstyle, physique, clothing), behaviors (smoking, drinking, sharing feelings), or life choices (educational attainment, occupation, political affiliation) more or less attractive. And broad economic forces can affect intimate choices even further. In China, where there are about 41 million *more* unmarried young men than women (Tsai, 2012a), single women can be especially choosy when it comes to romantic partners, often requiring that suitors be employed and own their own homes before they'll even consider them for a date (Jacobs, 2011).

The moral of these two stories is simple: To understand experiences in our personal lives, we must move past individual traits and examine broader societal characteristics and trends. External features beyond our immediate awareness and control often exert as much influence on the circumstances of our day-to-day lives as our "internal" qualities. We can't begin to explain an individual's employability without examining current and past economic trends that affect the number of jobs available and the number of people who are looking for work. We can't begin to explain why relationships work or don't work without addressing the broader interpersonal network and culture in which they are embedded. By the same token, we can't begin to explain people's ordinary, everyday thoughts and actions without examining the social forces that influence them.

Sociology and the Individual

Herein lies the fundamental theme of **sociology**—the systematic study of human societies—and the theme that will guide us throughout this book: Everyday social life—our thoughts, actions, feelings, decisions, interactions, and so on—is the product of a complex interplay between societal forces and personal characteristics. To explain why people are the way they are, believe the things they believe, or do the things they do, we must understand the interpersonal, historical, cultural, technological, organizational, and global environments they inhabit. To understand either individuals or society, we must understand both (C. W. Mills, 1959).

Of course, seeing the relationship between individuals and social forces is not always so easy. The United States is a society built on the image of the rugged, self-reliant individual. Not surprisingly, it is also a society dominated by individualistic understandings of human behavior that seek to explain problems and processes by focusing exclusively on the character, the psychology, or even the biochemistry of each person. Consequently, most of us simply take for granted that what we choose to do, say, feel, and think are private phenomena. Everyday life seems to be a series of free personal choices. After all, we choose what to major in, what to wear when we go out, what and when to eat, who our mates will be, and so on.

But how free are these decisions? Think about all the times your actions have been dictated or at least influenced by social circumstances over which you had little control. Have you ever felt that because of your age or gender or race, certain opportunities were closed to you? Your ability to legally drive a car, drink alcohol, or vote, for instance, is determined by society's prevailing definition of age. When you're older, you may be forced into retirement despite your skills and desire to continue working. Gender profoundly affects your choices, too. Some occupations, such as bank executive and engineer, are still overwhelmingly male, whereas others, such as registered nurse and preschool teacher, are almost exclusively female. Likewise, the doctrines of your religion may limit your behavioral choices. For a devout Catholic, premarital sex or even divorce is unlikely. Each day during the holy month of Ramadan, a strict Muslim must abstain from food and drink from sunrise to sunset. An Orthodox Jew would never dream of drinking milk and eating meat at the same meal. Even universal bodily needs can be influenced by our social context.

MICRO-MACRO CONNECTION
A SOCIOLOGY OF SLEEP

Everybody sleeps. Indeed, at certain moments in our lives—when we've pulled an all-nighter studying for finals, when we're sick, when we become new parents—sleep may be the most all-encompassing preoccupation we have. Indeed, one of the major ailments of modern life is lack of sleep. According to one poll, nearly two thirds of Americans complain that they don't get enough sleep. In the United States alone, there are over 2,000 sleep clinics to treat people's sleep problems. "Fatigue management" is now a growing therapeutic field (cited in Kolbert, 2013).

Sleep is obviously experienced differently by different individuals. I'm sure you know people who say they can't function on less than 10 hours of sleep a night while others say they're wide-awake and perky on just four.

But sleep preferences are not just a matter of individual adaptation. Children, for example, typically require much more sleep than adults, especially in their first several years of life. Even here, though, individual needs can be overridden by broader social concerns. A major accomplishment of parenting is getting children to fit their sleeping patterns into the parents' schedule. "My baby slept through the night last night!!" is a celebratory exclamation all new parents long to shout. But it's not always easy. What parent hasn't experienced the struggle of trying to get a fussy baby or combative toddler to sleep at night? But parent-child conflict over sleep never completely disappears. Try waking up a surly teenager on a school day morning sometime. Incidentally, the problem of dozy teenagers has become so bad that the American Academy of Pediatrics (2014) recently issued a policy statement recommending a later start of the school day in middle and high school so that teens can get enough sleep at night.

According to sociologist Simon Williams (2011), sleep is "a window onto the social world" (p. 27). How, when, where, how much, and with whom we sleep is always a product of social, cultural, historical, and even economic forces. For homeless people on the streets of Delhi, India, for instance, finding some way and somewhere to sleep is a nightly struggle:

> The bicycle rickshaw pullers . . . fold their bodies into strange angles on the four-foot seats of their vehicles. The day laborers curl their bodies on the frigid sidewalk, sometimes spooned against other men for warmth (E. Barry, 2016, p. A6).

With so many people in such desperate need of sleep, dishonest vendors—what the locals call the "sleep mafia"—sell filthy blankets to those who can scarcely afford food, jacking up their prices when the temperature drops. Essentially, these individuals decide who sleeps where, how well they sleep, and for how long.

All societies must organize the sleep of their members in some way. Think about when and where it's appropriate to sleep. At night? In the privacy of your own home? Of course. American adults are expected to go to sleep somewhere around 11:00 at night and wake up around 7:00 in the morning—what one anthropologist refers to as "consolidated sleeping" (Wolf-Meyer, 2012). Anything else—"sleeping during the day, sleeping in bursts, waking up in the middle of the night"—is considered unsound, even abnormal and perhaps subject to some kind of therapeutic intervention (Kolbert, 2013, p. 25).

At times, going without sleep can be worn as a boastful badge of honor or pride. "If you snooze, you lose," "I'll have time to sleep when I'm dead," and all that. But this clearly can be taken too far. "Drowsiness . . . is increasingly regarded as the new drunkenness: a culpable state, since, we are every bit as dangerous behind the wheel when we're drowsy as when we are drunk" (S. Williams, 2011, pp. 27–28). Indeed, the U.S. Department of Transportation estimates that "driving while drowsy" causes 40,000 injuries and over 1,500 deaths a year on U.S. roads (cited in Kolbert, 2013).

We tend to believe that "lying unconscious for eight hours straight [belongs] to a natural order" (Barron, 2016, p. 27). But the "8 hours of sleep a night" ideal has not always characterized people's lives. Up until the mid-19th century, it was common for people to sleep in segments throughout the day. They may have gone to bed in the later afternoon or early evening, slept for several hours, woken up and engaged in a few hours of activity—what the French referred to as *dorveille*, or "wakesleep"—then gone to bed for a "second sleep." In some societies, periods of daytime sleep are a common part of the culture. The *siesta* in some Mediterranean countries and the midday rest in some Asian societies are held as acceptable, even valued, practices.

However, such a pattern was not (and today is not) conducive to a complex, global world that hinges on employment and profit. For years, the taken-for-granted

(Continued)

(Continued)

9 to 5 workday and Monday through Friday workweek have had a significant impact on how we divide and define time. Most of us can easily make distinctions between workdays and non-workdays (holidays and weekends); between work hours and rest hours. And it's pretty clear in which of these times sleep is considered appropriate.

Yet the boundary between work (wakefulness) and home (sleep) is not always so clear. In certain occupations that involve the operation of heavy machinery—like long-distance truckers, train conductors, and airplane pilots—tired workers pose obvious safety hazards. Hence they have mandatory downtime policies and work hour limitations. But as the pace of life has sped up, even office-based, non-manual occupations are facing the problem of worker fatigue due to lack of sleep. It's estimated that drowsiness costs the U.S. economy hundreds of billions of dollars each year in higher stress and lost productivity (Baxter & Kroll-Smith, 2005). One third of respondents in one poll indicated that they'd fallen asleep at work in the previous month (National Sleep Foundation, 2008).

Some sociologists have argued that recent changes in the workplace—flexible schedules, telecommuting, home-based work—have begun to blur the time-honored boundaries between public and private, work and home, and given rise to shifting conceptions of sleep. In particular, they cite the greater acceptability of the workplace nap as evidence of changing attitudes toward sleep and wakefulness: "Once a taboo act engaged in by those who knew they were violating company rules, workplace napping is emerging, albeit unevenly, in American work culture as a tolerated, if not prescribed, behavior" (Baxter & Kroll-Smith, 2005, p. 34). More and more companies have come to the conclusion that restorative naps are a relatively cheap solution to the problem of excessive drowsiness. Many now provide nap rooms (or serenity rooms) for their employees, where they can find comfortable sofas, soothing lighting, and enforced bans on tablet and smartphone usage.

I don't think we're yet to the point where *all* American employees will have opportunities to take periodic power naps at work. We're not in danger of becoming a *siesta* culture anytime soon. However, I hope you can now see that "the very places, spaces [and] schedules . . . of sleep are themselves deeply social, cultural, historical, and political matters—and potentially subject to contestation and change" (S. Williams, 2011, p. 31). Even in something so natural as sleep, society interacts with the individual to shape the experience.

Then there's the matter of personal style—your choices in hairstyle, dress, music, videos, and the like. Large-scale marketing strategies can actually create a demand for particular products or images. Your tastes, and therefore your choices as a consumer, are often influenced by decisions made in far-off corporate boardrooms. Would Ariana Grande, Ed Sheeran, Taylor Swift, or Zayn have become so popular without a tightly managed and slickly packaged publicity program designed to appeal to adolescents and preadolescents? One California company, called Jukin Media, is the leader in a new industry that determines whether or not your web video will go viral. Once its researchers determine that a video of, say, a baby tasting lemons for the first time or dogs and parakeets becoming friends is good enough, the company contacts the clip's owner and purchases the licensing rights. Then it's just a matter of time before the video is splashed all over the Internet, becoming what millions of us think is the month's hot new meme (Kelles, 2017).

National and international economic trends also affect your everyday life. You may lose your job or, like André, face a tight job market as a result of economic fluctuations brought about by increased global competition or a severe recession. Or, because of the rapid development of certain types of technology, the college degree that may be your ticket to a rewarding career today may not qualify you even for a low-paying, entry-level position 10 years from now. In one poll, 75% of young adults who dropped out of college cited the financial need to work full time as the principal reason why it would be hard for them to go back to school (Lewin, 2009). And if you finish your degree but don't get a good job right out of college, you may have to move back home—like one third of people in their 20s and 30s these days (Fry, 2016a)—and live there for years after you graduate, not because you can't face the idea of living apart from your beloved parents but because you can't earn enough money to support yourself. In fact, by 2014, for the first time in 130 years, more adults in this age group were living with their parents than were living with a spouse or partner in their own household. If you think this is troubling, consider what it's like in Slovakia where 74% of 18- to 34-year-olds live with their parents, regardless of employment or marital status (Lyman, 2015).

Government and politics affect our personal lives, too. A political decision made at the local, regional, national, or even international level may result in the closing of a government agency you depend on, make the goods and services to which you have grown accustomed either more expensive or less available, or reduce the size of your paycheck after taxes are taken out. Workplace family-leave policies or health insurance regulations established by the government may affect your decision whether and when to have a baby or to undergo the elective surgery you've been putting off. If you are gay, lesbian, bisexual, or transgender, the federal and state governments can determine whether or not you can be fired from your job simply because of your sexual orientation. In the United States, decisions made by the U.S. Supreme Court can increase or limit your ability to control your fertility, sue an employer for discrimination, use your property however you please, carry a concealed weapon in public, legally marry, or keep the details of your life a private matter.

People's personal lives can also be touched by events that occur in distant countries:

- In 2011, a massive earthquake and deadly tsunami crippled many Japanese companies that manufacture car parts, resulting in a drop in automobile production in U.S. plants. That same year, violent protests in Arab countries like Libya, Egypt, Syria, and Yemen sparked fears of reduced oil imports and drove U.S. gasoline prices up over $4.00 a gallon.

- In the fall of 2014, an outbreak of the deadly Ebola virus in several West African countries grabbed the world's attention. There were over 20,000 documented cases in Guinea, Liberia, and Sierra Leone and about 8,000 deaths. In the United States, there have been 4 cases and 1 death (Centers for Disease Control, 2015b). But even though the risk of contracting this disease in the United States is exceedingly low, one fifth of Americans worry about getting it (Gallup, 2014). Immediately following the outbreak in West Africa, the Department of Homeland Security implemented travel restrictions to these countries and imposed elevated screening for passengers arriving from them. Anxieties grew. A train station in Dallas was shut down when a passenger was reported to have vomited on the platform. A cruise ship was blocked from docking in Mexico because a passenger worked in the Texas hospital where an Ebola patient died. Schools were shut down when it was suspected that an employee might have been on the same plane as an Ebola patient. Experts feared that the entire international business travel industry could suffer huge financial losses (Sharkey, 2014).

- Similarly, in 2016, fear of the Zika outbreak—a virus that has been linked in several Latin American countries to babies born with microcephaly (a severe reduction in the size of a child's head)—affected some U.S. women's decisions to become pregnant. Some people in Florida, where there had been some reports of Zika cases, were simply too afraid to leave their homes.

- Between 2015 and 2017, ISIS attacks killed several hundred people in Paris, Brussels, Istanbul, London, and other places across Europe. Following each attack, many cities in the United States heightened police security in popular public venues. In fact, terrorist attacks in foreign countries routinely result in travel restrictions and increased safety measures here.

- In June 2016, voters in the United Kingdom voted to withdraw from the European Union. Even though the actual withdrawal (known as "Brexit") will take years, the fallout of the decision was being assessed around the world within hours of the vote. Stock markets worldwide suffered as fear of global economic calamity spread.

These are only some of the ways in which events in the larger world can affect individual lives. Can you think of others?

The Insights of Sociology

Sociologists do not deny that individuals make choices or that they must take personal responsibility for those choices. But they are quick to point out that we cannot fully understand the things happening in our lives, private and personal though they may be, without examining the influence of the people, events, and societal features that surround us. By showing how social processes can shape us, and how individual action can in turn affect those processes, sociology provides unique insight into the taken-for-granted personal events and the large-scale cultural and global processes that make up our everyday existence.

Other disciplines study human life, too. Biologists study how the body works. Neurologists examine what goes on inside the brain. Psychologists study what goes on inside the mind to create human behavior. These disciplines focus almost exclusively on structures and processes that reside *within* the individual. In contrast, sociologists study what goes on *among* people as individuals, groups, or societies. How do social forces affect the way people interact with one another? How do individuals make sense of their private lives and the social worlds they occupy? How does everyday social interaction create "society"?

Personal issues like love, sexuality, poverty, aging, and prejudice are better understood within the appropriate societal context. For instance, U.S. adults tend to believe that they marry purely for love, when in fact society pressures people to marry from the same social class, religion, and race (P. L. Berger, 1963). Sociology, unlike other disciplines, forces us to look outside the tight confines of individual anatomy and personality to understand the phenomena that shape us. Consider, for example, the following situations:

- A 14-year-old girl, fearing she is overweight, begins systematically starving herself in the hope of becoming more attractive.

- A 55-year-old stockbroker, unable to find work since his firm laid him off, sinks into a depression after losing his family and his home. He now lives on the streets.

- A 46-year-old professor kills herself after learning that her position at the university will be terminated the following year due to budget cuts.

- The student body president and valedictorian of the local high school cannot begin or end her day without several shots of whiskey.

What do these people have in common? Your first response might be that they all have terrible personal problems that have made their lives suck. If you saw them only for what they've become—the "anorexic," the "homeless person," the "suicide victim," or the "alcoholic"—you might think they have some kind of personality defect, genetic flaw, or mental problem that renders them incapable of coping with the demands of contemporary life. Maybe they simply lack the willpower to pick themselves up and move on. In short, your immediate tendency may be to focus on the unique, perhaps "abnormal," characteristics of these people to explain their problems.

But we cannot downplay the importance of their *social* worlds. There is no denying that we live in a society that exalts lean bodies, values individual achievement and economic success, and encourages drinking to excess. Some people suffer under these conditions when they don't measure up. This is not to say that all people exposed to the same social messages inevitably fall victim to the same problems. Some overcome their wretched childhoods, others withstand the tragedy of economic failure and begin anew, and some are immune to narrowly defined cultural images of beauty. But to understand fully the nature of human life or of particular social problems, we must acknowledge the broader social context in which these things occur.

The Sociological Imagination

Unfortunately, we often don't see the connections between the personal events in our everyday lives and the larger society in which we live. People in a country such as the United States, which places such a high premium on individual achievement, have difficulty looking beyond their immediate situation. Someone who loses a job, gets divorced, or flunks out of school in such a society has trouble imagining that these experiences are somehow related to massive cultural or historical processes.

The ability to see the impact of these forces on our private lives is what the famous sociologist C. Wright Mills (1959) called the **sociological imagination**. The sociological imagination enables us to understand the larger historical picture and its meaning in our own lives. Mills argued that no matter how personal we think our experiences are, many of them can be seen as products of society-wide forces. The task of sociology is to help us view our lives as the intersection between personal biography and societal history and thereby to provide a means for us to interpret our lives and social circumstances.

Getting fired, for example, is a terrible, even traumatic, private experience. Like our friend André at the beginning of this chapter, feelings of personal failure are inevitable when one loses a job. But would your feelings of failure differ if you lived in Fargo, North Dakota—where the unemployment rate is less than 2%—versus El Centro, California—where the rate is 22% (U.S. Bureau of Labor Statistics, 2016d)? If yes, then we must see unemployment not as a personal malfunction but as a social problem that has its roots in the economic and political structures of society. Listen to how one columnist described his job loss:

Five years ago, when the magazine dismissed me, fewer Americans were unemployed than are now, and I felt like a solitary reject in a nation of comfortable successes. . . . If I were to get the same news now, in an era of mass layoffs and major bankruptcies, I wonder if I would suffer as I did then. . . . Maybe I would just shrug instead and head outside for a relaxing bike ride. (Kirn, 2009, p. 13)

Such an easygoing response to being fired is probably uncommon. Nevertheless, his point is important sociologically: Being unemployed is not a character flaw or personal failure if a significant number of people in one's community are also unemployed. We can't explain a spike in the unemployment rate as a sudden increase in the number of incompetent or unprepared individual workers in the labor force. As long as the economy is arranged so that employees are easily replaced or slumps inevitably occur, the social problem of unemployment cannot be solved at the personal level.

The same can be said for divorce, which people usually experience as an intimate tragedy. But in the United States, it's estimated that 4 out of every 10 marriages that begin this year will eventually end in divorce. And divorce rates are increasing dramatically in many countries around the world. We must therefore view divorce in the context of broader historical changes occurring throughout societies: in family, law, religion, economics, and the culture as a whole. It is impossible to explain significant changes in divorce rates over time by focusing exclusively on the personal characteristics and behaviors of divorcing individuals. Divorce rates don't rise simply because individual spouses have more difficulty getting along with one another than they used to, and they don't fall because more husbands and wives are suddenly being nicer to each other.

Mills did not mean to imply that the sociological imagination should debilitate us—that is, force us to powerlessly perceive our lives as wholly beyond our control. In fact, the opposite is true. An awareness of the impact of social forces or world history on our personal lives is a prerequisite to any efforts we make to change our social circumstances.

Indeed, the sociological imagination allows us to recognize that the solutions to many of our most serious social problems lie not in changing the personal situations and characteristics of individual people but in changing the social institutions and roles available to them (C. W. Mills, 1959). Drug addiction, homelessness, sexual violence, hate crimes, eating disorders, suicide, and other unfortunate situations will not go away simply by treating or punishing a person who is suffering from or engaging in the behavior.

Several years ago, as I was working on an earlier edition of this book, a tragic event occurred at the university where I teach. On a pleasant May night at the beginning of final exam week, a first-year student killed himself. The incident sent shock waves through this small, close-knit campus.

As you would expect in such a situation, the question on everyone's mind was, "Why did he do it?" Although no definitive answer could ever be obtained, most people simply concluded that it was a "typical" suicide. They assumed that he must have been despondent, hopeless, unhappy, and unable to cope with the demands of college life. Some students said they heard he was failing some of his courses. Others said they heard he didn't get into the fraternity he wanted or that he was a bit of a loner. In other words, something was wrong with *him*.

As tragic as this incident was, it was far from unique. Between 1950 and 2010, the U.S. suicide rate more than doubled for people between the ages of 15 and 24 (National Center for Health Statistics, 2014). In fact, the suicide rate for 10- to 14-year-olds has tripled since 2000 (S. C. Curtin, Warner, & Hedegaard, 2016). Suicide is the third leading cause of death among 10- to 14-year-olds—following accidents and homicides—and second leading cause of death among 15- to 34-year-olds. In 2015, 17% of U.S. high school students reported that they had seriously considered attempting suicide during the previous year, and about 8% had actually attempted suicide one or more times during the same period (Centers for Disease Control and Prevention, 2015e).

Focusing on individual feelings such as depression, hopelessness, and frustration doesn't tell us why so many people in this age group commit suicide, nor does it tell us why rates of youth suicide increase—or for that matter decrease—from decade to decade. So, to understand why the student at my university made such a choice, we must look beyond his private mental state and examine the social and historical factors that may have affected him.

Clearly, life in contemporary developed societies is focused on individual achievement—being well dressed, popular, and successful—more strongly than ever before. Young people face almost constant pressure to "measure up" and define their identities, and therefore their self-worth, according to standards set by others (Mannon, 1997). Although most adjust pretty well, others can't. In addition, as competition for scarce financial resources becomes more acute, young people are likely to experience heightened levels of stress and confusion about their own futures. To some, expectations regarding educational success have spun out of control, resulting in a national school-related stress epidemic. As one teacher put it, "We are sitting on a ticking time bomb" (quoted in Abeles, 2016, p. 2). When the quest for success begins earlier and earlier, the costs of not succeeding increase. For instance, the suicide rate among high school students in one affluent school district in Silicon Valley—where performance pressures are particularly acute—is between four and five times the national average (Rosin, 2015).

Growing educational expectations may explain why suicides among young African American men (ages 15–24), once quite rare and still relatively less frequent than suicides among other ethnic groups, tripled from 4.1 deaths per 100,000 people in 1960 to 12.0 deaths in 2015 (see Exhibit 1.1). Some experts have blamed these trends on a growing sense of hopelessness and a long-standing cultural taboo against discussing mental health matters. Others, however, have cited broader social factors, brought about, ironically, by the growing economy of the late 20th century and the more recent recovery from the 2008 recession. As more and more black families move into the middle class, they feel increasing pressure to compete in traditionally white-dominated professions and social environments.

You'll also notice in Exhibit 1.1 that the suicide rates of both black and white young women has consistently been lower than those of young men. Can you think of a sociological reason to account for this fact? Is it less stressful being a teenage girl than a teenage boy?

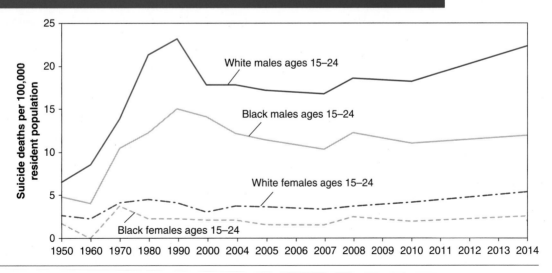

EXHIBIT 1.1 ● What Effect Do Race and Gender Have on Young People's Desire to Commit Suicide?

Source: National Center for Health Statistics, 2015a, Table 30.

In other societies, different types of social changes may account for fluctuations in suicide rates. For instance, Japan has one of the highest suicide rates in the world (23.1 per 100,000 people; World Health Organization, 2016b), 60% greater than that of the United States. In the late 1990s and early 2000s, Japan saw its unemployment and bankruptcy rates rise to record levels as companies grappled with a severe economic recession. According to Japan's National Police Agency, more than 25% of suicides were caused by financial problems such as difficulty paying bills, finding a job, and keeping a business going (cited in J. S. Curtin, 2004). In fact, suicide became such a problem that the East Japan Railway Company installed blue lights above train platforms in its stations in hopes that they would have a soothing effect, thereby reducing the number of people who jump in front of trains to kill themselves ("Japanese Railways," 2009). Although the majority of suicides occur among people in their 60s, rates have increased especially dramatically among elementary school, middle school, and college students. Suicide is now the leading cause of death among Japanese youth (Nippon.com, 2014).

The stress of change due to rapid development has been linked to increased suicide rates in China, too, particularly among rural women, who are most likely to be displaced from their villages (E. Rosenthal, 2002). And in Ireland, which at one point had the fastest-growing rate of suicide in the world, one in four suicides occurs among those ages 15 to 24 (Clarity, 1999). Experts there attribute much of this increase to the weakening of religious prohibition of suicide and the alteration of gender roles, which has left many young men unsure of their place in Irish society.

ÉMILE DURKHEIM
ALL SUICIDES ARE NOT CREATED EQUAL

Sociologists' interest in linking suicide to certain processes going on in society is not new. In one of the classic pieces of social research, the famous sociologist Émile Durkheim (1897/1951) argued that suicide is more likely to occur under particular social circumstances and in particular communities. He was the first to see suicide as a manifestation of changes in society rather than of psychological shortcomings.

How does one go about determining whether rates of suicide are influenced by the structure of society? Durkheim decided to test his theory by comparing existing official statistics and historical records across groups, a research strategy sometimes referred to as the **comparative method**. Many sociologists continue to follow this methodology, analyzing statistics compiled by governmental agencies such as the U.S. Bureau of the Census, the Federal Bureau of Investigation, and the National Center for Health Statistics to draw comparisons of suicide rates among groups.

For about 7 years, Durkheim carefully examined the available data on suicide rates among various social groups in Europe—from different regions of

countries, certain religious or ethnic groups, and so on—looking for important social patterns. If suicides were purely acts of individual desperation, he reasoned, one would not expect to find any noticeable changes in the rates from year to year or from society to society. That is, the distribution of desperate, unstable, unhappy individuals should be roughly equal across time and culture. If, however, certain groups or societies had a consistently higher rate of suicide than others, something more than individual disposition would seem to be at work.

After compiling his figures, Durkheim concluded that there are actually several different types of suicide. Sometimes, he found, people take their own lives when they see no possible way to improve their oppressive circumstances. They come to the conclusion that suicide is preferable to a harsh life that will never improve. Think of prisoners serving life sentences or slaves who take their own lives to escape their miserable confinement and lack of freedom. Durkheim called this type of suicide **fatalistic suicide.**

Other suicides, what he called **anomic suicide**, occur when people's lives are suddenly disrupted by major social events, such as economic depressions, wars, and famines. At these times, he argued, the conditions around which people have organized their lives are dramatically altered, leaving them with a sense of hopelessness and despair as they come to realize they can no longer live the life to which they were accustomed. A study of suicide trends over the past 80 years found that overall rates tend to rise during economic recessions and fall during economic expansions (Luo, Florence, Quispe-Agnoli, Ouyang, & Crosby, 2011). Many experts attribute the 28% increase in suicides among U.S. adults between 35 and 64 in the early 2010s to the economic recession of 2008 (Centers for Disease Control and Prevention, 2013). Similarly, the financial crisis that gripped Europe recently led to a spike in suicide rates in the hardest-hit countries such as Greece, Ireland, and Italy. The problem became so pronounced that European psychiatrists started calling it "suicide by economic crisis" (Reeves, McKee, & Stuckler, 2014).

Conversely, Durkheim argued that people who live in poor countries are, in a sense, "immune" to this type of suicide. He said, "[P]overty protects against anomic suicide because it is a restraint in itself" (Durkheim, 1897/1951, p. 254). Indeed, there is some evidence that people who live in poor countries have a significantly lower risk of depression than those who live in industrialized countries (cited in A. Weil, 2011). What Durkheim couldn't have predicted, however, was the role that communication technology plays in instantly exposing people to the lifestyles of others half a world away. In Durkheim's time, poor people in isolated rural areas had little, if any, knowledge of how wealthier people lived. So they had no way of comparing their lot in life to others who were better off. Today the Internet is available in some of the remotest regions of the world, providing people with instant information about (and instant comparisons to) the comforts and privileges of the more affluent. So do you think that poverty protects people from committing suicide?

Durkheim also discovered that suicide rates in all the countries he examined tended to be consistently higher among widowed, single, and divorced people than among married people; higher among people without children than among parents; and higher among Protestants than among Catholics. Did this mean that unmarried people, childless people, and Protestants were more unhappy, depressed, or psychologically dysfunctional than other people?

Durkheim didn't think so. Instead, he felt that something about the nature of social life among people in these groups increased the likelihood of what he called **egoistic suicide.**

Durkheim reasoned that when group, family, or community ties are weak or de-emphasized, people feel disconnected and alone. He pointed out, for instance, that the Catholic Church emphasizes salvation through community and binds its members to the church through elaborate doctrine and ritual; Protestantism, in contrast, emphasizes individual salvation and responsibility. This religious individualism, he believed, explained the differences he noticed in suicide rates between Catholics and Protestants. Self-reliance and independence may glorify one in God's eyes, but they become liabilities if one is in the throes of personal tragedy.

Durkheim feared that life in modern society tends to be individualistic and dangerously alienating. Over a century later, contemporary sociologists have found evidence supporting Durkheim's insight (e.g., Bellah, Madsen, Sullivan, Swidler, & Tipton, 1985; Riesman, 1950). Many people in the United States today don't know and have no desire to know their neighbors. Strangers are treated with suspicion. In the pursuit of economic opportunities, we have become more willing to relocate, sometimes to regions far from family and existing friends and colleagues—the very people who could and would offer support in times of need.

The structure of our communities discourages the formation of bonds with others, and, not surprisingly, the likelihood of suicide increases at the same time. In the United States today, the highest suicide rates can be found in sparsely populated states like Alaska, New Mexico, Montana, Nevada, and Wyoming (Centers for Disease Control and Prevention, 2015a). Exhibits 1.2a and 1.2b show this pattern. These states tend to have a larger proportion of new residents who are not part of an established community. People tend to be more isolated, less likely to seek help or comfort from others in times of trouble, and therefore more susceptible to suicide than people who live in more populous states. It's worth noting that sparsely populated rural areas also have higher rates of gun ownership than other areas of the United States. More than half of the rural youths who kill themselves do so with a firearm. Indeed, gun suicides in general are three times more common in rural areas than in urban areas (Beck, 2015b).

Durkheim also felt, however, that another type of suicide (what he called **altruistic suicide**) is more likely when the ties to one's community are too strong

(Continued)

(Continued)

instead of too weak. He suggested that in certain societies, individuality is completely overshadowed by one's group membership; the individual literally lives for the group, and personality is merely a reflection of the collective identity of the community. In some cases, commitment to a particular political cause can be powerful enough to lead some people to take their own lives. In India, the number of politically motivated suicides doubled between 2006 and 2008. For example, a few years ago 200 people took their own lives in support of efforts to establish a separate state, Telangana, in southern India (Polgreen, 2010). Spiritual loyalty can also lead to altruistic suicide. Some religious sects require their members to reject their ties to outside people and groups and to live by the values and customs of their new community. When members feel that they can no longer contribute to the group and sustain their value within it, they may take their own lives out of loyalty to cultural expectations.

A terrible example of the deadly effects of overly strong ties occurred in 1989, when four young Korean sisters, ranging in age from 6 to 13, attempted to kill themselves by ingesting rat poison. The three older sisters survived; the youngest died. The eldest provided startling

sociological insight into this seemingly senseless act: Their family was poor; the father supported everyone on a salary of about $362 a month. The girl told the authorities that the sisters had made a suicide pact to ease their parents' financial burden and leave enough money for the education of their 3-year-old brother. Within the traditional Korean culture, female children are much less important to the family than male children. These sisters attempted to take their lives not because they were depressed or unable to cope but because they felt obligated to sacrifice their personal well-being for the success of their family's male heir ("Korean Girls," 1989).

Just as the suicide pact of these young girls was tied to the social system of which they were a part, so, too, was the suicide of the young college student at my university. His choices and life circumstances were also a function of the values and conditions of his particular society. No doubt he had serious emotional problems, but these problems may have been part and parcel of his social circumstances. Had he lived in a society that didn't place as much pressure on young people or glorify individual achievement, he might not have chosen suicide. That's what the sociological imagination helps us understand.

EXHIBIT 1.2A ● The More Crowded the State, the Lower the Suicide Rate					
State	Suicide Rate per 100,000 Resident Population	Persons per Square Mile	State	Suicide Rate per 100,000 Resident Population	Persons per Square Mile
United States	**13.4**	**91.0**	Idaho	19.6	20.0
Alabama	14.7	95.9	Illinois	10.9	231.6
Alaska	22.7	1.3	Indiana	14.4	184.4
Arizona	18.5	60.1	Iowa	13.1	55.9
Arkansas	17.4	57.2	Kansas	15.7	35.6
California	10.9	251.3	Kentucky	16.5	112.1
Colorado	20.2	52.6	Louisiana	14.6	108.1
Connecticut	10.5	741.6	Maine	16.5	43.1
Delaware	13.5	485.5	Maryland	10.1	618.8
District of Columbia	7.9	11,011.1	Massachusetts	8.8	871.1
Florida	15.3	378.0	Michigan	13.7	175.5
Georgia	12.8	177.6	Minnesota	12.6	68.9
Hawaii	14.4	222.9	Mississippi	12.7	63.8

(Continued)

State	Suicide Rate per 100,000 Resident Population	Persons per Square Mile	State	Suicide Rate per 100,000 Resident Population	Persons per Square Mile
Missouri	16.8	88.5	Pennsylvania	14.2	286.1
Montana	24.5	7.1	Rhode Island	10.7	1,021.8
Nebraska	13.3	24.7	South Carolina	15.6	162.9
Nevada	20.2	26.3	South Dakota	16.5	11.3
New Hampshire	18.6	148.6	Tennessee	14.5	160.1
New Jersey	8.8	1,218.1	Texas	12.1	105.2
New Mexico	21.5	17.2	Utah	19.0	36.5
New York	8.6	420.1	Vermont	19.8	67.9
North Carolina	13.6	206.6	Virginia	13.5	212.3
North Dakota	18.5	11.0	Washington	15.8	107.9
Ohio	12.9	284.2	West Virginia	19.4	76.7
Oklahoma	19.0	57.0	Wisconsin	13.4	106.6
Oregon	19.7	42.0	Wyoming	20.5	6.0

Sources: Centers for Disease Control and Prevention, 2015a, Table LCWK9; ProQuest Statistical Abstract, 2017, Table 15.

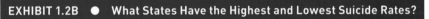

EXHIBIT 1.2B   ●   What States Have the Highest and Lowest Suicide Rates?

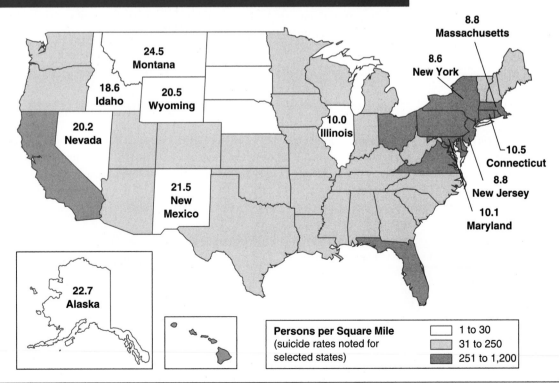

Sources: Centers for Disease Control and Prevention, 2015a, Table LCWK9; ProQuest Statistical Abstract, 2017, Table 15.

Conclusion

In the 21st century, understanding our place within cultural, historical, and global contexts is more important than ever. The world is shrinking. Communication technology binds us to people on the other side of the planet. Increasing ecological awareness opens our eyes to the far-reaching effects of environmental degradations. The changes associated with colossal events in one country (political revolutions, terrorist attacks, natural disasters, economic crises, school shootings, cultural upheavals) often quickly reverberate around the world. The local and global consequences of such events often continue to be felt for years.

When we look at how people's lives are altered by such phenomena—as they sink into poverty or ascend to prosperity; stand in bread lines or enter a career previously unavailable; or find their sense of ethnic identity, personal safety, or self-worth altered—we can begin to understand the everyday importance of large-scale social change.

However, we must remember that individuals are not just helpless pawns of societal forces. They simultaneously influence and are influenced by society. We live in a world in which our everyday lives are largely a product of structural, or **macrolevel**, societal and historical processes. Society is an objective fact that coerces, even creates us (P. L. Berger, 1963). At the same time, we constantly create, maintain, reaffirm, and transform society. Hence, society is part and parcel of individual-level human interaction, what sociologists call **microlevel** everyday phenomena (R. Collins, 1981). But although we create society, we then collectively "forget" we've done so, believe it exists independently of us, and live our lives under its influence. The Micro-Macro Connections found throughout the book will help you see this interrelationship between macrolevel societal forces and many of the microlevel experiences we have as individuals.

The next chapter provides a more detailed treatment of this theme. Then, in Part II, I examine how society and our social lives are constructed and ordered. I focus on the interplay between individuals and the people, groups, organizations, institutions, and culture that collectively make up our society. Part III focuses on the structure of society, with particular attention to the various forms of social inequality.

Your Turn

The sociological imagination serves as the driving theme throughout this book. It's not a particularly difficult concept to grasp in the abstract: Things that are largely outside our control affect our everyday lives in ways that are sometimes not immediately apparent; our personal biographies are a function, at least in part, of broader historical circumstances. Yet what does this actually mean? How can you see the impact of larger social and historical events on your own life? One way is to find out what events were going on at the time of your birth. Go to the library and find a newspaper and a popular magazine that were published on the day you were born. It would be especially useful to find a newspaper from the town or city in which you were born. What major news events took place that day? What were the dominant social and political concerns at the time? What was the state of the economy? What was considered fashionable in clothing, music, movies, and so forth? Ask your parents or other adults about their reactions to these events and conditions.

How do you think those reactions affected the way you were raised and the values of your family? What have been the lasting effects, if any, of these historical circumstances on the person you are today? In addition, you might want to check newspapers and magazines and the Internet to determine the political, economic, global, and cultural trends that were prominent 15 or so years later when you entered high school. The emergence from adolescence into young adulthood is a significant developmental stage in the lives of most people. It often marks the first time that others—including parents and other adults—take us seriously. And it is arguably the most self-conscious time of our lives. Try to determine how these dominant social phenomena will continue to influence your life after college. Imagine how different your life might have been had these social conditions been different—for instance, a different political atmosphere, a stronger or weaker economy, a more tolerant or more restrictive way of life, and so on.

Chapter Highlights

- The primary theme of sociology is that our everyday thoughts and actions are the product of a complex interplay between massive social forces and personal characteristics. We can't understand the relationship between individuals and societies without understanding both.

- The sociological imagination is the ability to see the impact of social forces on our private lives—an awareness that our lives lie at the intersection of personal biography and societal history.

- Rather than studying what goes on within people, sociologists study what goes on between people, whether as individuals, groups, organizations, or entire societies. Sociology forces us to look outside the tight confines of our individual personalities to understand the phenomena that shape us.

Key Terms

altruistic suicide: Type of suicide that occurs where ties to the group or community are considered more important than individual identity

anomic suicide: Type of suicide that occurs when the structure of society is weakened or disrupted and people feel hopeless and disillusioned

comparative method: Research technique that compares existing official statistics and historical records across groups to test a theory about some social phenomenon

egoistic suicide: Type of suicide that occurs in settings where the individual is emphasized over group or community connections

fatalistic suicide: Type of suicide that occurs when people see no possible way to improve their oppressive circumstances

individualistic explanation: Tendency to attribute people's achievements and failures to their personal qualities

macrolevel: Way of examining human life that focuses on the broad social forces and structural features of society that exist above the level of individual people

microlevel: Way of examining human life that focuses on the immediate, everyday experiences of individuals

sociological imagination: Ability to see the impact of social forces on our private lives

sociology: Systematic study of human societies

SAGE edge™ edge.sagepub.com/newman12e

SAGE edge offers a robust online environment featuring an impressive array of free tools and resources for review, study, and further exploration, keeping both instructors and students on the cutting edge of teaching and learning.

Seeing and Thinking Sociologically

- How Individuals Structure Society
- Social Influence: The Impact of Other People in Our Everyday Lives
- Societal Influence: The Effect of Social Structure on Our Everyday Lives
- Three Perspectives on Social Order

Over two decades ago, ethnic violence erupted in the small African nation of Rwanda. The Hutu majority had begun a systematic program to exterminate the Tutsi minority. Soon, gruesome pictures of the tortured and dismembered bodies of Tutsi men, women, and children began to appear on television screens around the world. When it was over, more than 800,000 Tutsis had been slaughtered—half of whom died between April and July 1994. Surely, we thought, such horror must have been perpetrated by bands of vicious, crazed thugs who derived some sort of twisted pleasure from committing acts of unspeakable cruelty. Or maybe these were the extreme acts of angry soldiers, trained killers who were committed to destroying the enemy as completely as possible.

Actually, much of the responsibility for these atrocities lay elsewhere, in a most unlikely place: among the ordinary, previously law-abiding Rwandan citizens. Many of the participants in the genocide were the least likely brutes you could imagine. For instance, here's how one woman described her husband, a man responsible for many Tutsi deaths:

> He came home often. He never carried a weapon, not even his machete. I knew he was a leader. I knew the Hutus were out there cutting Tutsis. With me, he behaved nicely. He made sure we had everything we needed. . . . He was gentle with the children. . . . To me, he was the nice man I married. (quoted in Rwandan Stories, 2011, p. 1)

Pauline Nyiramasuhuko, a former social worker and the country's minister of family and women's affairs, promised the Tutsis in one village that they would be safe in a local stadium. When they arrived there, armed militia were waiting to kill them. She instructed one group of soldiers to burn alive a group of 70 women and girls, adding, "Before you kill the women, you need to rape them" (quoted in Zimbardo, 2007, p. 13). In 2011, a United Nations tribunal found that she had used her political position to help abduct and kill uncounted Tutsi men, women, and children and sentenced her to life in prison (Simons, 2011).

Some of the most gruesome attacks occurred in churches and missions (Lacey, 2006). Two Benedictine nuns and a National University of Rwanda physics professor stood trial for their role in the killings. The nuns were accused of informing the military that Tutsi refugees had sought sanctuary in the church and of standing by as the soldiers massacred them. One nun allegedly provided the death squads with cans of gasoline, which were used to set fire to a building where 500 Tutsis were hiding. The professor was accused of drawing up a list for the killers of Tutsi employees and students at the university and then killing at least seven Tutsis himself (Simons, 2001). A Catholic priest was sentenced to 15 years in prison for ordering his church to be demolished by bulldozers while 2,000 ethnic Tutsis sought refuge there. Indeed, some have argued that Rwandan churches themselves were complicit in the genocide from the beginning (T. Longman, 2009; Rittner, 2004).

A report by the civil rights organization African Rights provides evidence that members of the medical profession were deeply involved, too (M. C. Harris, 1996). The report details how doctors joined with militiamen to hunt down Tutsis, turning hospitals into slaughterhouses. Some helped soldiers drag sick and wounded refugees out of their beds to be killed. Others took advantage of their position of authority to organize roadblocks, distribute ammunition, and compile lists of Tutsi colleagues, patients, and neighbors to be sought out and slaughtered. Many doctors who didn't participate in the actual killing refused to treat wounded Tutsis and withheld food and water from refugees who sought sanctuary in hospitals. In fact, the president of Rwanda and the minister of health were both physicians who were eventually tried as war criminals.

Average, well-balanced people—teachers, social workers, priests and nuns devoted to the ideals of charity and mercy, and physicians trained to heal and save lives—had changed, almost overnight, into cold-hearted killers. How could something like this have happened? The answer to this question lies in the sociological claim that individual behavior is largely shaped by social forces and situational contingencies. The circumstances of large-scale ethnic hatred and war have the power to transform well-educated, "nice" people with no previous history of violence into cruel butchers. Tragically, such forces were at work in many of the 20th and 21st centuries' most infamous examples of human brutality, such as the Nazi Holocaust during World War II and, more recently, large-scale ethnic massacres in Cambodia, Iraq, Bosnia, Burma, Kosovo, the Democratic Republic of the Congo, the Darfur region of Sudan, and Syria, as well as Rwanda.

But social circumstances don't just create opportunities for brutality; they can also motivate ordinary people to engage in astounding and unexpected acts of heroism. The 2004 film *Hotel Rwanda* depicts the true story of Paul Rusesabagina, a hotel manager in the Rwandan capital, Kigali, who risked his own life to shelter over a thousand Tutsi refugees from certain death. Rusesabagina was a middle-class Hutu married to a Tutsi and the father of four children. He was a businessman with an eye toward turning a profit and a taste for the finer things in life. But when the genocide began, he used his guile, international contacts, and even water from the swimming pool to keep the refugees alive.

In this chapter, I examine the process by which individuals construct society and the way people's lives are linked to the social environment in which they live. The relationship between the individual and society is a powerful one—each continually affects the other.

How Individuals Structure Society

Up to this point, I have used the word *society* rather loosely. Formally, sociologists define **society** as a population living in the same geographic area who share a culture and a common identity and whose members are subject to the same political authority. Societies may consist of people with the same ethnic heritage or of hundreds of different groups who speak a multitude of languages. Some societies are highly industrialized and complex; others are primarily agricultural and relatively simple in structure. Some are very religious; others are distinctly secular.

According to the 19th-century French philosopher Auguste Comte, all societies, whatever their form, contain both forces for stability, which he called "social statics," and forces for change, which he called "social dynamics." Sometimes, however, people use the term *society* only to mean a "static" entity—a natural, permanent, and historical structure. They frequently talk about society "planning" or "shaping" our lives and describe it as a relatively unchanging set of organizations, institutions, systems, and cultural patterns into which successive generations of people are born and socialized.

As a result, sociology students often start out believing not only that society is powerfully influential (which, of course, it is) but also that it is something that exists "out there," completely separate and distinct from us (which it isn't). It is tempting to view society simply as a "top down" initiator of human activity, a massive entity that methodically shapes the lives of all individuals within it like some gigantic puppeteer manipulating a bunch of marionettes. This characterization is weird but not entirely inaccurate. Society does exert influence on its members through certain identifiable structural features and historical circumstances. The concept of the sociological imagination discussed in Chapter 1 implies that structural forces beyond our direct control do shape our personal lives.

But this view is only one side of the sociological coin. The sociological imagination also encourages us to see that each individual has a role in forming a society and influencing the course of its history. As we navigate our social environments, we respond in ways that may modify the effects and even the nature of that environment (House, 1981). As one sociologist has written,

> No [society], however massive it may appear in the present, existed in this massivity from the dawn of time. Somewhere along the line each one of its salient features was concocted by human beings. . . . Since all social systems were created by [people], it follows that [people] can also change them. (P. L. Berger, 1963, p. 128)

To fully understand society, then, we must see it as a human creation made up of people interacting with one another. Communication plays an important role in the construction of society. If we couldn't communicate with one another to reach an understanding about society's expectations, we couldn't live together. Through day-to-day conversation, we construct, reaffirm, experience, and alter the reality of our society. By responding to other people's messages, comments, and gestures in the expected manner and by talking about social abstractions as real things, we help shape society (Shibutani, 1961).

Imagine two people sitting on a park bench in 2017 discussing the global threat of ISIS, the deadly terrorist organization known for its numerous massacres of civilians, video recordings of the beheadings of Western hostages, and oppressive control of large areas of Iraq and Syria. It's estimated that between 2002 and 2015, ISIS killed over 33,000 people and injured more than 41,000 others in nearly 5,000 separate terrorist attacks (National Consortium for the Study of Terrorism and Responses to Terrorism, 2016). Because of ISIS brutality and the ongoing civil war in Syria, half of that country's pre-war population—more than 11 million people—have been killed or forced to flee their homes. The plight of Syrian refugees has been called the worst humanitarian crisis of our time (Mercy Corps, 2017). Person A believes that the United States should intervene with the full force of its military—land, sea, and air. Person B believes that the United States should stay out of it, expressing fear that we could be drawn into another costly military action where we have no clear allies, no chance of victory, and no clear exit strategy. The debate becomes heated: One person thinks that we have an ethical obligation to come to the aid of people being massacred; furthermore, if we don't get involved, we will be seen as weak, thereby placing our own citizens at risk of attack both here and abroad. The other person thinks we have more pressing problems to attend to at home and supports a strategy of limited involvement: intelligence sharing, economic sanctions, and the training of local forces to fight their own battle. These two people obviously don't agree on the role that the United States should play in international humanitarian crises. But merely by discussing the threat of ISIS and the Syrian refugee crisis, they are acknowledging that these things exist. In talking about such matters, people give shape and substance to society's ideals and values (Hewitt, 1988).

Even something as apparently unchangeable as our society's past can be shaped and modified by individuals. We usually think of history as a fixed, unalterable collection of social events that occurred long ago; only in science fiction novels or those old *Back to the Future* movies can one "go back" and change the past. No one would question that the Declaration of Independence was signed in 1776; that John F. Kennedy was assassinated on November 22, 1963; that hijackers flew passenger jets into the Pentagon and the World Trade Center on September 11, 2001; that two brothers set off bombs at the Boston Marathon on April 15, 2013, killing 3 and injuring 264; that the U.S. Supreme Court legalized same-sex marriage on June 26, 2015; or that Donald Trump was elected the 45th president of the United States on November 8, 2016.

Although such historical events themselves don't change, their meaning and relevance can. Consider the celebration in 1992 of the 500th anniversary of Columbus's voyage to the Americas. For generations, American schoolchildren have been taught that Columbus's 1492 "discovery" represented a triumphant step forward for Western civilization. We even have a holiday in his honor. However, increasing sensitivity to the past persecution of Native Americans has forced many people to reconsider the historical meaning of Columbus's journey. In fact, some historians now consider this journey and what followed it to be one of history's most dismal examples of reckless and deadly prejudice. So, you see, history might best be regarded as a work in progress.

When we view society this way, we can begin to understand the role each of us has in maintaining or altering it. Sometimes the actions of ordinary individuals mobilize larger groups of people to collectively alter some aspect of society.

Consider the story of a Pakistani girl named Malala Yousafzai. In 2009, when she was 11, Malala began writing a blog for the BBC detailing her life under the Taliban who, at the time, were seeking to control the Swat Valley region of Pakistan where she lived. She wrote about the importance of education for young girls, something the Taliban were trying to ban.

As her blog gained a greater international following, she became more prominent, giving interviews in newspapers and on television. But her increased visibility also meant that she was becoming a greater threat to the Taliban. So in October, 2012, a gunman boarded Malala's school bus, walked directly up to her, and shot her in the face. She remained unconscious for days and was flown to a hospital in England. Not only did she survive the shooting, but she redoubled her efforts to advocate on behalf of girls' education all around the world. The assassination attempt received worldwide coverage and provoked an outpouring of international sympathy. The United Nations drafted a petition in her name calling on Pakistan—and other countries—to end educational discrimination against girls. Since then, she has spoken before the United Nations, met with world leaders like Queen Elizabeth and President Obama, and, in 2014—at the ripe old age of 17—was awarded the Nobel Peace Prize. Although she has not been able to return to her home country since she was shot, her work and perseverance have spawned a global movement to ensure educational access for all girls. The Malala Fund has raised millions of dollars for local education projects in places like Kenya, Sierra Leone, Nigeria, Pakistan, and Syria to secure girls' rights to a minimum of 12 years of quality education (Malala Fund, 2016). In 2015, world leaders, meeting at the United Nations, followed Malala's lead and committed to delivering free, quality primary and secondary education for every child by 2030.

Social Influence: The Impact of Other People in Our Everyday Lives

We live in a world with other people. Not the most stunningly insightful sentence you've ever read, I'm guessing. But it is key to understanding the sociology of human behavior. Our everyday lives are a collection of brief encounters, extended conversations, intimate interactions, and chance collisions with other people. In our early years, we may have our parents, siblings, uncles, aunts, and grandparents to contend with. Soon, we begin to form friendships with others outside our families. Over time, our lives also become filled with connections to other people—classmates, teachers, coworkers, bosses, spiritual leaders, therapists—who are neither family nor friends but who have an enormous impact on us. And, of course, we have frequent experiences with total strangers: the person at the local coffee shop who serves us our daily latte, the traveler who sits next to us on an airplane, the tech support specialist who helps us when our documents won't print or our iPads freeze.

If you think about it, understanding what it means to be alone requires that we know what it's like to be with other people. As I will discuss in Chapters 5 and 6, much of our private identity—what we think of ourselves, the type of people we become, and the images of ourselves we project in public—comes from our contact with others.

Sociologists tell us that these encounters have a great deal of *social influence* over our lives. Whether we're aware of their doing so or not, other people affect our thoughts, likes, and dislikes. Consider why certain songs, books, or films become blockbuster hits. We usually think their popularity is a consequence of a large number of people making their own independent decisions about what appeals to them. But research shows that popularity is a consequence of social influence (Salganik, Dodds, & Watts, 2006). If one object happens to be slightly more popular than others—such as a particular song that gets downloaded a lot from iTunes—it tends to become more popular as more people are drawn to it. As one sociologist put it, "People tend to like what other people like" (D. J. Watts, 2007, p. 22). Similarly, the making of art is not just a function of the vision that exists in the minds of solitary artists, it is an enterprise in which many people—suppliers, dealers, critics, consumers, as well as creators—play a role in producing a piece that the community decides is "art." In this sense, even individual creativity cannot be understood outside its social and cultural context (Becker, 2008).

In a more direct sense, we often take other people's desires and concerns into account before we act. Perhaps you've decided to date someone, only to reconsider when you asked yourself, "Would my mother like this person?" Those who influence us may be in our immediate presence or hover in our memories. They may be real or imagined, loved or despised. And their effects on us may be deliberate or accidental.

Imagine for a moment what your life would be like if you had never had contact with other people (assuming you could have survived this long!). You wouldn't know what love is, or hate or jealousy or compassion or gratitude. You wouldn't know if you were attractive or unattractive, bright or dumb, witty or boring. You'd lack some basic information, too. You wouldn't know what day it was, how much a pound weighs, where Switzerland is, or how to read. Furthermore, you'd have no language, and because we use language to think, imagine, predict, plan, wonder, fantasize, and reminisce, you'd lack these abilities as well. In short, you'd lack the key experiences that make you a functioning human being.

Contact with people is essential to a person's social development. But there is much more to social life than simply bumping into others from time to time. We act and react to things and people in our environment as a result of the meaning we attach to them. At the sight of Mokolodi, my big goofy Labrador retriever, playfully barreling toward it, a squirrel instinctively runs away. A human, however, does not have such an automatic reaction. We've all learned from past experiences that some animals are approachable and others aren't. So we can think, "Do I know this dog? Is it friendly or mean? Does it want to lick my face or tear me limb from limb?" and respond accordingly. In short, we usually interpret events in our environment before we react.

The presence of other people may motivate you to improve your performance—for example, when the high quality of your tennis opponent makes you play the best match of your life. But their presence may at other times inhibit you—as when you forget your lines in the school play because your ex-boyfriend's in the audience glowering at you. Other people's presence is also essential for the expression of certain feelings or bodily functions. We've all experienced the unstoppable urge to yawn after watching someone else yawn. But have you ever noticed the contagion of coughing that often breaks out in class during a lecture or exam? Research has shown that coughing tends to trigger coughing in those who hear it (cited in R. Provine, 2012). And think about the fact that you can't tickle yourself. Being tickled is the product of a *social* interaction. Indeed, according to one study of laughter, people are about 30 times more likely to laugh when they're around other people than when they're alone (Provine, 2000).

And our personal contentment and generosity can be linked to others as well. One recent study found that just knowing someone who is happy—whether she or he is a relative, friend, or acquaintance—significantly increases your own chances of happiness (Fowler & Christakis, 2008). Another found that shoppers are significantly happier when shopping with other people, no matter what they buy (Goldsmith, 2016). Such influence can be found in the online world, too. Twitter users prefer to follow other Twitter users who exhibit comparable moods. That is, happy users tend to retweet or reply to other happy users (Bollen, Gonçalves, Ruan, & Mao, 2012). Research also suggests that the presence of female family members (wives, sisters, daughters, mothers) can make men more generous, compassionate, and empathetic. The founder of Microsoft, Bill Gates, has consistently cited the inspiration provided by his wife and mother in setting up his charitable foundation, which has given away tens of billions of dollars.

The influence of others goes beyond emotions, behaviors, and performances. Even our physical well-being is affected by those around us. According to researchers in Japan, the risk of heart attack is three times higher among women who live with their husbands and their husbands' parents than among women who just live with their husbands (cited in Rabin, 2008). Similarly, a recent study of 2,000 American married couples found that people with happy spouses have fewer physical impairments, engage in more exercise, and rate their overall health as better than people with unhappy spouses (Chopik & O'Brien, 2016). In fact, three decades of research have shown that having a large network of friends can even increase life expectancy (Holt-Lunstad, Smith, & Layton, 2010).

Consider also the way people eat. Most of us assume that we eat when we're hungry and stop when we're full. But our eating tendencies reflect the social influences that surround us. For instance, when we eat with other people, we adjust our pace to their pace. We also tend to eat longer—and therefore more—when in groups than when we're by ourselves. One researcher found that people, on average, eat 35% more food when they're with one other person than when they're alone. That figure goes up to 75% more when eating with three other people (DeCastro, 1994, 2000). This may explain why a person's chances of becoming obese increase significantly when he or she has a close friend who is obese (Christakis & Fowler, 2007). As one researcher put it, "Weight can be inherited, but it can also be contagious" (Wansink, 2006, p. 99).

And, of course, other people can sometimes purposely sway our actions. I'm sure you've been in situations in which people have tried to persuade you to do things against your will or better judgment. Perhaps someone convinced you to steal a candy bar, skip your sociology class, or disregard the speed limit. On occasion, such social influence can be quite harmful.

STANLEY MILGRAM

ORDINARY PEOPLE AND CRUEL ACTS

If a being from another planet were to learn the history of human civilization, it would probably conclude that we are tremendously cruel, vicious, and evil creatures. From ethnic genocides to backwater lynchings to war crimes to school bullying, humans have always shown a powerful tendency to viciously turn on their fellow humans.

The curious thing is that people involved in such acts often show a profound capacity to deny responsibility for their behavior by pointing to the influence of others: "My friend made me do it" or "I was only following orders." That leaves us with a very disturbing question: Can an ordinary, decent person be pressured by another to commit an act of extreme cruelty? Or, conversely, do cruel actions require inherently cruel people?

In a classic piece of social research, social psychologist Stanley Milgram (1974) set out to answer

these questions. He wanted to know how far people would go in obeying the commands of an authority. He set up an experimental situation in which a subject, on orders from an authoritative figure, flips a switch, apparently sending a 450-volt shock to an innocent victim.

The subjects responded to an advertisement seeking participants in a study on memory and learning. On a specified day, each subject arrived at the laboratory and was introduced to a stern-looking experimenter (Milgram) wearing a white lab coat. The subject was also introduced to another person who, unknown to the subject, was actually an accomplice of the experimenter.

Each subject was told he or she would play the role of "teacher" in an experiment examining the effects of punishment on learning; the other person would play the role of the "learner." The teacher was taken to a separate room that held an ominous-looking machine the researcher called a "shock generator." The learner was seated in another room out of the sight of the teacher and was supposedly strapped to an electrode from the shock generator.

The teacher read a series of word pairs (e.g., blue–sky, nice–day, wild–duck) to the learner. After reading the entire list, the teacher read the first word of a pair (e.g., blue) and four alternatives for the second word (e.g., sky, ink, box, lamp). The learner had to select the correct alternative. Following directions from the experimenter, who was present in the room, the teacher flipped a switch and shocked the learner whenever he or she gave an incorrect answer. The shocks began at the lowest level, 15 volts, and increased with each subsequent incorrect answer all the way up to the 450-volt maximum.

As instructed, all the subjects shocked the learner for each incorrect response. (Remember, the learner was an accomplice of the experimenter and was not actually being shocked.) As the experiment proceeded and the shocks became stronger, the teacher could hear cries from the learner. Most of the teachers, believing they were inflicting serious injury, became visibly upset and wanted to stop. The experimenter, however, ordered them to continue—and many did. Despite the tortured reactions of the victim, 65% of the subjects complied with the experimenter's demands and proceeded to the maximum, 450 volts.

Milgram repeated the study with a variety of subjects and even conducted it in different countries, including Germany and Australia. In each case, about two thirds of the subjects were willing, under orders from the experimenter, to shock to the limit. Milgram didn't just show that people defer to authority from time to time. He showed just how powerful that tendency is (Blass, 2004). As we saw with the Rwandan genocide, given the "right" circumstances, ordinarily nice people can be compelled to do terrible things they wouldn't have done otherwise.

Milgram's research raises questions not only about why people would obey an unreasonable authority but also about what the rest of us think of those who do. A study of destructive obedience in the workplace—investigating actions such as dumping toxic waste in a river and manufacturing a defective automobile—found that the public is more likely to forgive those who are responsible when they are believed to be conforming to company policy or obeying the orders of a supervisor than when they are thought to be acting on their own (V. L. Hamilton & Sanders, 1995).

Milgram's study has generated a tremendous amount of controversy. For over four decades, this pivotal piece of research has been replicated, discussed, and debated by social scientists (Burger, 2009). It has made its way into popular culture, turning up in novels, plays, films, and songs (Blass, 2004). Since the original study, other researchers have found that in small groups, people sometimes collectively rebel against what they perceive to be unjust authority (Gamson, Fireman, & Rytina, 1982). Nevertheless, Milgram's findings are discomforting. It would be much easier to conclude that the acts of inhumanity we read about in our daily newspapers (such as soldiers raping civilians or killing unarmed noncombatants) are the products of defective or inherently evil individuals— a few "bad apples." All society would have to do then is identify, capture, and separate these psychopaths from the rest of us. But if Milgram is right—if most of us could become evil given the "right" combination of situational circumstances—then the only thing that distinguishes us from evildoers is our good fortune and our social environment.

Societal Influence: The Effect of Social Structure on Our Everyday Lives

If you stopped reading this chapter here, you'd be inclined to think that societies are made up of a bunch of people exerting all kinds of influence on one another. But social life is much more than that. Society is not just a sum of its human parts; it's also the way those parts are put together, related to each other, and organized (Coulson & Riddell, 1980). Statuses, roles, groups, organizations, and institutions are the structural building blocks of society. Culture is the mortar that holds these blocks together. Although society is dynamic and constantly evolving, it has an underlying macrolevel structure that persists.

Statuses and Roles

One key element of any society is its collection of **statuses**—the positions that individuals within the society occupy. When most of us hear the word *status*, we tend to associate it with rank or prestige. But here we're talking about a status as any socially defined position a person can occupy: cook, daughter, anthropologist, husband, regular blogger, electrician, Facebook friend, shoplifter, and so on. Some statuses may, in fact, be quite prestigious, such as prime minister or president. But others carry very little prestige, such as gas station attendant or Pepsi drinker. Some statuses require a tremendous amount of training, such as physician; others, such as ice cream lover, require little effort or none at all.

We all occupy many statuses at the same time. I am a college professor, but I am also a son, uncle, father, brother, husband, friend, sushi lover, dog owner, occasional poker player, mediocre runner with a bad back, homeowner, Cubs' fan, and author. My behavior at any given moment is dictated to a large degree by the status that's most important at that particular time. When I am training for a half marathon, my status as professor isn't particularly relevant. But if I decide to run in a race instead of showing up to proctor the final exam in my sociology course, I will be in big trouble!

Sociologists often distinguish between ascribed and achieved statuses. An **ascribed status** is a social position we acquire at birth or enter involuntarily later in life. Our race, sex, ethnicity, and identity as someone's child or grandchild are all ascribed statuses. As we get older, we enter the ascribed status of teenager and, eventually, old person. These aren't positions we choose to occupy. An **achieved status**, in contrast, is a social position we take on voluntarily or acquire through our own efforts or accomplishments, such as being a student or a spouse or an engineer.

Of course, the distinction between ascribed and achieved status is not always so clear. Some people become college students not because of their own efforts but because of parental pressure. Chances are the religion with which you identify is the one you inherited from your parents. However, many people decide to change their religious membership later in life. Moreover, as we'll see later in this book, certain ascribed statuses (sex, race, ethnicity, and age) directly influence our access to lucrative achieved statuses.

Whether ascribed or achieved, statuses are important sociologically because they all come with a set of rights, obligations, behaviors, and duties that people occupying a certain position are expected or encouraged to perform. These expectations are referred to as **roles**. For instance, the role expectations associated with the status "professor" include teaching students, answering their questions, grading them impartially, and dressing appropriately. Any out-of-role behavior may be met with shock or suspicion. If I consistently showed up for class in a thong and tank top, that would certainly violate my "scholarly" image and call into question my ability to teach (not to mention my sanity).

Each person, as a result of her or his own skills, interests, and life experiences, defines roles differently. Students enter a class with the general expectation that their professor is knowledgeable about the subject and that he or she is going to teach them something. Each professor, however, may have a different method of meeting that expectation. Some professors are very animated; others remain stationary behind a podium. Some do not allow questions until after the lecture; others constantly encourage probing questions from students. Some are meticulous and organized; others disheveled and absent-minded.

People engage in typical patterns of interaction based on the relationship between their roles and the roles of others. Employers are expected to interact with employees in a certain way, as are doctors with patients and salespeople with customers. In each case, actions are constrained by the role responsibilities and obligations associated with those particular statuses. We know, for instance, that lovers and spouses are supposed to interact with each other differently from the way acquaintances or friends are supposed to interact. In a parent–child relationship, both members are linked by certain rights, privileges, and obligations. Parents are responsible for providing their children with the basic necessities of life—food, clothing, shelter, and so forth. These expectations are so powerful that not meeting them may make the parents vulnerable to charges of negligence or abuse. Children, in turn, are expected to abide by their parents' wishes. Thus, interactions within a relationship are functions not only of the individual personalities of the people involved but also of the role requirements associated with the statuses they occupy.

We feel the power of role expectations most clearly when we have difficulty meeting them or when we occupy two conflicting statuses simultaneously. Sociologists use the term **role strain** to refer to situations in which people lack the necessary resources to fulfill the demands of a particular role, such as when parents can't afford to provide their children with adequate food, clothing, or shelter. Sometimes this strain can be deadly. For instance, physicians are more than twice as likely to commit suicide as non-physicians and almost 10% of fourth-year medical students and first-year residents have had suicidal thoughts (cited in Sinha, 2014). Why? Young doctors feel significant pressure to project intellectual and emotional confidence in the face of life-or-death situations. As one first-year resident put it, "[W]e masquerade as strong and untroubled professionals even in our darkest and most self-doubting moments" (Sinha, 2014, p. A23). A doctor in her or his last year of medical school is usually expected to care for four patients at a time. But within a few months of graduation, he or she will be required to oversee the treatment of perhaps 10 patients on any given day. This drastic increase in responsibility can lead to overwhelming role strain.

Role conflict describes situations in which people encounter tension in trying to cope with the demands of incompatible roles. People may feel frustrated in their efforts to do what they feel they're supposed to do when the role expectations of one status clash with the role expectations of another. For instance, a mother (who also happens to be a prominent sociologist) may have an important out-of-town conference to attend (status of sociologist) on the same day her 10-year-old son is appearing as a talking pig in the school play (status of parent). Or a teenager who works hard at his job at the local ice cream shop (status of employee) may be frustrated when his buddies arrive and expect him to sit and chat or to give them free ice cream (status of friend).

Role conflict can sometimes raise serious ethical or legal concerns. For instance, in states that use lethal injection as a means of execution, it is necessary to have a licensed anesthesiologist present to ensure that the prisoner is unconscious when paralyzing and heart-stopping drugs are administered. Ordinarily, the role expectations of doctors emphasize ensuring the health and well-being of the people they treat. But when doctors are part of an execution team, they are expected to use their medical skills and judgment to make killing more humane and less painful. The American Medical Association condemns physicians' involvement in executions as unethical and unprofessional, stating that selecting injection sites, starting intravenous lines, and supervising the administration of lethal drugs violates a doctor's oath to heal or at least "do no harm." In fact, doctors who violate these guidelines face censure and perhaps even the loss of their license (Jauhar, 2017).

Groups

Societies are not simply composed of people occupying statuses and living in accordance with roles. Sometimes individuals form well-defined units called groups. A **group** is a set of people who interact more or less regularly with one another and who are conscious of their identity as a group. Your family, your colleagues at work, and any clubs or sports teams to which you belong are all social groups.

Groups are not just collections of people who randomly come together for some purpose. Their structure defines the relationships among members. When groups are large, enduring, and complex, each individual within the group is likely to occupy some named position or status—mother, president, supervisor, linebacker, and so forth.

Group membership can also be a powerful force behind one's future actions and thoughts. Sociologists distinguish between **in-groups**—the groups to which we belong and toward which we feel a sense of loyalty—and **out-groups**—the groups to which we don't belong and toward which we feel a certain amount of antagonism. For instance, a girl who is not a member of the popular clique at school, but wants to be, is likely to structure many of her daily activities around gaining entry into that group.

In addition, like statuses and roles, groups come with a set of general expectations. A person's actions within a group are judged according to a conventional set of ideas about how things ought to be. For example, a coworker who always arrives late for meetings or never takes his or her turn working an undesirable shift is violating the group's expectations and will be pressured to conform.

The smallest group, of course, is one that consists of two people, or a **dyad**. According to the renowned German sociologist Georg Simmel (1902/1950), dyads (marriages, close friendships, etc.) are among the most meaningful and intense connections we have. The problem, though, is that dyads are by nature unstable. If one person decides to leave, the group completely collapses. Hence, it's not surprising that for society's most important dyads (i.e., marriages), a variety of legal, religious, and cultural restrictions are in place that make it difficult for people to dissolve them.

The addition of one person to a dyad—forming what Simmel called a **triad**—fundamentally changes the nature of the group. Although triads might appear more stable than dyads because the withdrawal of one person needn't destroy the group, they develop other problems. If you're one of three children in your family, you already know that triads always contain the potential for **coalitions**—where two individuals pair up and perhaps conspire against the third.

Groups can also be classified by their influence on our everyday lives. A **primary group** consists of a small number of members who have direct contact with each other over a relatively long period of time. Emotional attachment is high in such groups, and members have intimate knowledge of each other's lives. Families and networks of close friends are primary groups. A **secondary group**, in contrast, is much more formal and impersonal. The group is established for a specific task, such as the production or sale of consumer goods, and members are less emotionally committed to one another. Their roles tend to be highly structured. Primary groups may form within secondary groups, as when close friendships form among coworkers, but in general, secondary groups require less emotional investment than primary groups.

Like societies, groups have a reality that is more than just the sum of their members; a change in a group's membership doesn't necessarily alter its basic structure. Secondary groups can endure changing membership relatively easily if some, or even all, individuals leave and new ones enter—as, for example, when the senior class in a high school graduates and is replaced the following year by a new group of students. However, change in primary groups—perhaps through divorce or death—produces dramatic effects on the structure and identity of the group, even though the group itself still exists.

VISUAL ESSAY—I GOTTA BE ME (OR US)

REUTERS/Ali Al-Saadi/Pool

REUTERS/Sergei Karpukhin

David L. Ryan/The Boston Globe via Getty Images

VCG/VCG/Getty Images

Living in a modern society always requires striking a balance between the things that make you feel like a unique individual and the things that make you feel like you're a part of something bigger. From your own personal perspective, it's easy to see what makes you different from everybody else. After all, only you have direct knowledge of your thoughts, feelings, internal physical state, and so on. But when you take a step back and look at the things that connect you to others, a very different picture emerges. And that picture can change as the social circumstances in which you find yourself change. When you're at your grandfather's 70th birthday party, you'll likely see yourself one way; but when you're lined up at commencement with all your fellow graduates you may see yourself completely differently.

In these photos, you can see various structural situations in which individual uniqueness seems almost nonexistent and uniformity rules the day: the military, a monastery, a college sorority. Why do you suppose it's so important that people in these photos look, dress, and act alike? Why is it important for their individuality to be minimized or even destroyed in these environments? Can you think of times in your own life when your group membership totally overshadowed your individual identity? What about the opposite? When do you find yourself emphasizing your individuality over your group identity? How might a sociologist explain these two different experiences?

Although people of the same race, gender, ethnicity, or religion are not social groups in the strictest sense of the term, they function like groups in that members share certain characteristics and interests. They become an important source of a person's identity. For instance, members of a particular racial or ethnic group may organize into a well-defined unit to fight for a political cause. The feelings of "we-ness" or "they-ness" generated by such group membership can be constructive or dangerous, encouraging pride and unity in some cases and anger, bitterness, and hatred toward outsiders in others.

Organizations

At an even higher level of complexity are social units called **organizations**, networks of statuses and groups created for a specific purpose. The International Brotherhood of Teamsters, Harvard University, Google, the Transportation Security Administration, the National Organization for Women, and the Methodist Church are all examples of organizations. Organizations contain groups as well as individuals occupying clearly defined statuses and taking on clearly defined roles.

Some of the groups within organizations are transitory; some are more permanent. For instance, a university consists of individual classes that form at the beginning of a semester and disband at its end, as well as more permanent groups such as the faculty, administration, secretarial staff, maintenance staff, and alumni.

Large, formal organizations are often characterized by a *hierarchical division of labor*. Each person in an organization occupies a position that has a specific set of duties and responsibilities, and those positions can be "ranked" according to their relative power and importance. At Honda, for instance, assembly-line workers typically don't make hiring decisions or set budgetary policies, and the vice president in charge of marketing doesn't spray paint the underbodies of newly assembled Accords. In general, people occupy certain positions in an organization because they have the skills to do the job required of them. When a person can no longer meet the requirements of the job, she or he can be replaced without seriously affecting the functioning of the organization.

Organizations are a profoundly common and visible feature of everyday social life, as you'll see in Chapter 9. Most of us cannot acquire food, get an education, pray, undergo lifesaving surgery, or earn a salary without coming into contact with or becoming a member of some organization. To be a full-fledged member of modern society is to be deeply involved in some form of organizational life.

Social Institutions

When stable sets of statuses, roles, groups, and organizations form, they provide the foundation for addressing fundamental societal needs. These enduring patterns of social life are called **social institutions**. Sociologists usually think of institutions as the building blocks that organize society. They are the patterned ways of solving the problems and meeting the requirements of a particular society. Although there may be conflict over what society "needs" and how best to fulfill those needs, all societies must have some systematic way of organizing the various aspects of everyday life.

Key social institutions in modern society include the family, education, economics, politics and law, and religion. Some sociologists add medicine and health care, the military, and the mass media to the list. I'll be talking about these social institutions throughout the book. But for now, here are some short descriptions:

Family. All societies must have a way of replacing their members, and reproduction is essential to the survival of human society as a whole. Within the institution of family, sexual relations among adults are regulated; people are cared for; children are born, protected, and socialized; and newcomers are provided an identity—a "lineage"—that gives them a sense of belonging. Just how these activities are carried out varies from society to society. Indeed, different societies have different ideas about which relationships qualify for designation as family. But the institution of family, whatever its form, remains the hub of social life in virtually all societies (J. H. Turner, 1972).

Education. Young people need to be taught what it means to be a member of the society in which they live and how to survive in it. In small, simple societies, the family is the primary institution responsible for socializing new members into the culture. However, as societies become more complex, it becomes exceedingly difficult for a family to teach its members all they need to know to function and survive. Hence, most modern, complex societies have an elaborate system of schools—preschool, primary, secondary, post-secondary, professional—that not only create and disseminate knowledge and information but also train individuals for future careers and teach them their "place" in society.

Economy. From the beginning, human societies have faced the problems of securing enough food and protecting people from the environment (J. H. Turner, 1972). Today, modern societies have systematic ways of gathering resources, converting them into goods and commodities, and distributing them to members. In addition, societies provide ways of coordinating and facilitating the operation of this massive process. For instance, banks, accounting firms, insurance companies, stock brokerages, transportation agencies, and computer networks don't produce goods themselves but provide services that make the gathering, producing, and distributing of goods possible. To facilitate the distribution of both goods and services, economic institutions adopt a system of common currency and an identifiable mode of exchange. In some societies, the economy is driven by the value of efficient production and the need to maximize profits; in others, the collective well-being of the population is the primary focus.

Politics and Law. All societies face the problem of how to preserve order, avoid chaos, and make important social decisions. The legal system provides explicit laws or rules of conduct and mechanisms for enforcing those laws, settling disputes, and changing outdated laws or creating new ones (J. H. Turner, 1972). These activities take place within a larger system of governance that allocates and acknowledges power, authority, and leadership. In a democracy, the governance process includes the citizens, who have a say in who leads them; in a monarchy, kings or queens can claim that their birthright entitles them to positions of leadership. In some societies, the transfer of power is efficient and mannerly; in others, it is violent.

Religion. In the process of meeting the familial, educational, economic, and political needs of society, some individuals thrive, whereas others suffer. Hence, all societies also face the problem of providing their less successful members with a sense of purpose and meaning in their lives. Religion gives individuals a belief system for understanding their existence as well as a network of personal support in times of need. Although many members of a given society may actively reject religion, it remains one of the most enduring and powerful social institutions. Although religion provides enormous comfort to some people, it can also be a source of hatred and irreparable divisions.

Medicine and Health Care. One of the profoundly universal facts of human life is that people get sick and die. In some societies, healing the sick and managing the transition to death involves spiritual or supernatural intervention; other societies rely on science and modern technology. Most modern societies have established a complex system of health care to disseminate medical treatments. Doctors, nurses, hospitals, pharmacies, drug and medical equipment manufacturers, and patients all play an active role in the health care system.

Military. To deal with the possibility of attack from outside and the protection of national interests, many societies maintain an active military defense. However, militaries are used not only to defend societies but also, at times, to attack other countries in order to acquire land, resources, or power. In other cases, the military is used for political change, as when U.S. armed forces were mobilized to overthrow the government of Saddam Hussein in Iraq in 2003.

Mass Media. In very small, relatively close-knit societies, information can be shared through word of mouth. However, as societies become more complex, the dissemination of information requires a massive coordinated system. The modern mass media—radio, newspapers, television, and the Internet—provide coverage of important societal events so individuals can make informed decisions about their own lives. But the media do more than report events of local, national, and international significance. They also actively mold public opinion and project and reinforce a society's values.

You can see that the social institutions within a society are highly interrelated. Take, for instance, the connections between medical research and economics. A constant stream of recent studies has affirmed the presence of a dangerous "epidemic" in competitive football: traumatic head injuries. It's not uncommon for players—from high school to the pros—to sustain hits to the head equivalent to the impact of a 25-mph car crash. Some studies suggest that as many as 15% of players suffer some type of brain damage each season (cited in Lehrer, 2012). In 2014, the National Football League conceded that brain trauma will affect one in three professional players after their careers end (Belson, 2014). In the past, players who "got their bell rung" were quickly resuscitated after such hits so they could be sent back into the game as quickly as possible. But it's clear now that the brain damage these hits cause can have lasting consequences including long-term memory loss, depression, mood disorders, and suicidal tendencies—a condition known as chronic traumatic encephalopathy (CTE). Eight in ten of these cases go unrecognized until it is too late (Congeni, 2009). According to one study, the risk of fatal degenerative brain disease among former NFL players is three times higher than same-age, non-football players in the general public; the risk of Alzheimer's disease is four times higher (Lehman, Hein, Baron, & Gersic, 2012). In 2017, researchers at Boston University found evidence of CTE in the brains of 110 out of 111 deceased NFL football players (Mez, Daneshvar, & Kiernan, 2017). But football is a big business with far-reaching economic ties. The 32 NFL teams have a combined value of $75 billion, more than all Major League Baseball and National Basketball Association teams *combined* (Gaines, 2016). At the college level, football is the number one revenue-generating activity for most large universities. Hence it's not surprising that with such deep economic investments, the football industry has been slow to heed medical research and take any sort of significant step to reduce the game's violence, and hence the likelihood of deadly brain injuries.

To individual members of society, social institutions appear natural, permanent, and inevitable. Most of us couldn't imagine life without a family. Nor could most of us fathom what society would be like without a stable system of government, a common currency, schools to educate our children, or an effective health care system. It is very easy, then, to think that institutions exist independently of people.

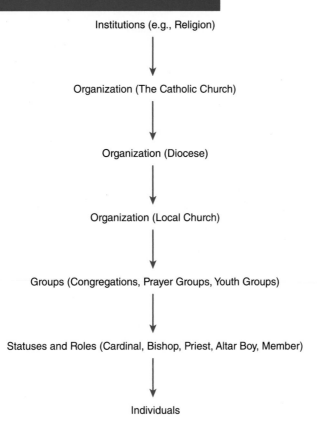

EXHIBIT 2.1 ● Social Structure and the Individual

Institutions (e.g., Religion)

↓

Organization (The Catholic Church)

↓

Organization (Diocese)

↓

Organization (Local Church)

↓

Groups (Congregations, Prayer Groups, Youth Groups)

↓

Statuses and Roles (Cardinal, Bishop, Priest, Altar Boy, Member)

↓

Individuals

But one of the important themes that will be revisited throughout this book is that we each have a role to play in maintaining or changing social institutions, as when citizens alter the political shape of a country by voting out of office an administration with which they've grown displeased. Although the effects of changes can be felt at the organizational and institutional levels, they are ultimately initiated, implemented, or rejected, and, most important, experienced by individual people. The interrelationships between individuals and the various components of social structure can be seen in Exhibit 2.1.

MARION NESTLE

YOU ARE WHAT YOU EAT: THE ECONOMICS AND POLITICS OF FOOD

Institutional influence is sometimes not so obvious. For instance, we usually think of nutrition as an inherent property of the foods we eat. Either something is good for us or it's not good for us, right? And we trust that the nutritional value of certain foods emerges from scientific discovery. We rarely consider the economic and political role that food companies play in shaping our tastes and our dietary standards (Pollan, 2007).

(Continued)

(Continued)

Marion Nestle (2002), a professor of nutrition and food studies, wanted to examine the institutional underpinnings of our ideas about health and nutrition. She faced an interesting data-gathering dilemma, however. No one involved in the food industry was willing to talk to her "on the record." So she compiled information from government reports, newspapers, magazines, speeches, advocacy materials, conference exhibits, and supermarkets. She also used information that she'd previously received from lobbying groups and trade associations representing diverse interests such as the salt, sugar, vitamin, wheat, soybean, flaxseed, and blueberry industries.

Despite alarming levels of food hunger among the world's population (see Chapter 10), the United States has so much food that we could feed all our citizens twice over. Many Americans regularly buy or prepare more food than they actually need (hence, the popularity of "doggie bags" and leftovers). The food industry is therefore highly competitive. But like all major industries, companies are beholden to their stockholders rather than to the consuming public. Marketing foods that are healthy and nutritious is a company's goal only if it can increase sales.

Food marketers have long identified children as their most attractive targets. According to Nestle, the attention paid to children has escalated in recent years because of their increasing responsibility for purchasing decisions. Children between 6 and 19 are estimated to influence upward of $500 billion in food purchases each year (cited in Nestle, 2002). By age 7, most children can shop independently, ask for information about what they want, and show off their purchases to other children.

Soft drink companies have become especially adept at targeting young people with diverse marketing strategies. Soft drinks have replaced milk as the primary beverage in the diets of American children as well as adults (Nestle, 2002). Vending machines, which tend to be stocked with high-calorie soft drinks and sports drinks as well as other "junk" foods, exist in 17% of elementary schools, 82% of middle schools, and 97% of high schools (cited in Kalb, 2010). Nearly three quarters of students who use campus vending machines buy sugar-sweetened beverages (Wiecha, Finkelstein, Troped, Fragala, & Peterson, 2006). The typical American teenage boy gets about 9% of his daily caloric intake from soft drinks, and about 20% of 1- and 2-year-olds regularly drink soda (Schlosser, 2001).

One of the most controversial marketing strategies in the soft drink industry is the "pouring rights" agreement, in which a company buys the exclusive right to sell its products in all schools in a particular district. For instance, Coca-Cola paid the Rockford, Illinois, school district $4 million up front and an additional $350,000 a year for the next 10 years to sell its beverages in the schools (cited in Philpott, 2012). In financially strapped districts, a pouring rights contract often supplies a significant part of the district's annual funding. It may be the only thing that allows a school system to buy much-needed resources like computers and textbooks. It's estimated that about 80% of American public schools have pouring rights contracts with either Coca-Cola or Pepsi (Philpott, 2012). And it's not just in schools. Coca-Cola and Pepsi continue to compete against each other for multimillion-dollar pouring rights contracts at youth sport complexes . . . and even at the Little League World Series (Cook, 2013).

Besides the lump sum agreed to in the contract, companies frequently offer school districts cash bonuses if they exceed certain sales targets. Hence, it is in the district's financial interest to encourage students to consume more soft drinks. In light of such incentives, ethical implications and health concerns become secondary. Indeed, many school districts justify these agreements by saying that soft drinks pervade the culture and students will drink them anyway, so why not get some benefit?

In addition to the long-term health effects of heavy soft drink consumption, however, Nestle points out that students learn a somewhat cynical lesson: that school officials are sometimes willing to compromise nutritional principles (and the students' physical well-being) for financial gain. Pouring rights contracts can also have a serious impact on long-term school funding. While they may solve short-term financial needs, they may also hamper efforts to secure adequate federal, state, and local funding for public education. Taxpayers may come to the conclusion that raising taxes to support public schools is unnecessary if the bulk of a district's operating budget comes from these commercial contracts.

In 2014, the U.S. Department of Agriculture released nutritional guidelines for snack foods sold in schools. The guidelines set minimum requirements for calories and fats allowed, encourage schools to offer low-fat and whole-grain snack foods, and limit the availability of sugary drinks. They don't, however, apply to after-school sporting events or fund-raisers, where candy and soft drinks can still be sold (Nixon, 2013). In 2015, the Food and Drug Administration began taking steps to remove artificial trans fat from processed foods and General Mills removed artificial colors and flavors from its breakfast cereals.

No matter what the outcome of these actions, soft drink and food companies will continue to play a significant role in school district budgets. In this role, we can see how a child's food choices in school are linked deeply and profoundly to broader educational, political, and economic needs—often with less attention paid to nutritional considerations and individual health.

Culture

The most pervasive element of society is **culture**, which consists of the language, values, beliefs, rules, behaviors, and physical artifacts of a society. Think of it as a society's "personality." Culture gives us codes of conduct—proper, acceptable ways of doing things. We usually don't think twice about it, yet it colors everything we experience.

Human societies would be chaotic and unlivable if they didn't have cultures that allow people to live together under the same set of general rules. But culture can also sometimes lead to tragedy. In 2012, an independent commission in Japan released the findings of its investigation of the nuclear disaster at the Fukushima power plant following the deadly 2011 earthquake and tsunami. The commission concluded that the disaster was human made and preventable, citing, among other things, certain elements of Japanese culture that suppress dissent and outside opinion. The chair of the commission put it this way:

> What must be admitted, very painfully, is that this was a disaster "Made in Japan." Its fundamental causes are to be found in the ingrained conventions of Japanese culture: our reflexive obedience; our reluctance to question authority; our devotion to "sticking with the program"; our groupism; and our . . . [narrow-mindedness]. (quoted in Tabuchi, 2012, p. 7)

Culture is particularly apparent when someone questions or violates it. Those who do not believe what the majority believes, see what the majority sees, or obey the same rules the majority obeys are likely to experience punishment, psychiatric attention, or social ostracism. I will discuss the power of culture in more detail in Chapter 4, but here we should look at two key aspects of culture that are thoroughly implicated in the workings of social structure and social influence: values and norms.

Values

Perhaps no word in the English language carries more baggage than *values*. People throw around terms such as *moral values*, *traditional values*, *family values*, and *American values* with little thought as to what they actually mean. Sociologically speaking, a **value** is a standard of judgment by which people decide on desirable goals and outcomes (Hewitt & Hewitt, 1986). Values represent the general criteria on which our lives and the lives of others can be judged. They justify the social rules that determine how we ought to behave. For instance, laws against theft clearly reflect the value we place on personal property.

Different societies emphasize different values. Success, independence, and individual achievement are seen as important values in U.S. society. In other societies, such as Vietnam, people are more likely to value group obligation and loyalty to family.

Some of the things we profess to value in the abstract may not, in fact, characterize our actual everyday experiences. For instance, we say that "honesty" and "open communication" are the foundational values of any strong relationship. But think of how many times you've lied to a potential romantic partner ("You're the most beautiful person in the room" or "No, that dress does *not* make you look fat") in order to make them feel better about themselves. Likewise, every parent knows that lying to their kids about everything from the arrival of Santa Claus to the horrible things that will happen if they don't eat their peas is a key component of raising a child. As one author put it, "If you want to have love in your life, you'd better be prepared to tell some lies and to believe some lies" (C.Martin, 2015, p. 4).

Values within a society sometimes come into conflict. The value of privacy ("stay out of other people's business") and the value of kindness ("help others in need") may clash when we are trying to decide whether to help a stranger who seems to require assistance. Similarly, although the value of cooperation is held in high esteem in contemporary U.S. society, when someone is taking a final exam in a sociology class, cooperation is likely to be defined as cheating. When the key values that characterize a particular social institution come into conflict, the result may be widespread legal and moral uncertainty among individuals.

MICRO-MACRO CONNECTION
FAMILY PRIVACY CAN BE HAZARDOUS TO A CHILD'S HEALTH

One such conflict between values in a society involves the cultural value of family privacy. Contemporary U.S. life is built on the assumption that what a family does in the privacy of its home is, or at least should be, its own business. Family life, many people believe, is best left to family members, not to neighbors, the government, the courts, or other public agencies. Consequently, American families are endowed with significant autonomy—the right to make decisions about their future or about treatment of their members (see Chapter 7).

Privacy has not always characterized American families. Before the 19th century, people felt free to enter others' homes and tell them what to wear and how to treat their children. The development of the value of family privacy and autonomy emerged with the separation of home and work and the growth of cities during the late 19th century (Parsons, 1971). Innovations in the amenities available within the home—indoor plumbing, refrigerators, telephones, radios, televisions, central air conditioning, and computers, for example—have all increased the privacy and isolation of American households. Our need to leave home for entertainment, goods, or services has been considerably reduced. Air conditioners, for instance, allow us to spend hot, stuffy summer evenings inside our own homes instead of on the front porch or at the local ice cream parlor. With the Internet, text messaging, Facebook, Twitter, and home shopping cable networks, family members can survive without ever leaving the privacy of their home. The institution of family has become increasingly self-contained and private.

But the ability to maintain family privacy has always varied along social class lines. In poor households, dwellings are smaller and more crowded than more affluent homes, making privacy more difficult to obtain. Thin walls separating cramped apartments hide few secrets. Mandatory inspections by welfare caseworkers and housing authorities further diminish privacy. And poor families must often use public facilities (health clinics, Laundromats, public transportation, etc.) to carry out day-to-day tasks that wealthier families can carry out privately.

Moreover, the value we place on the well-being of children can come into direct conflict at times with the value of family privacy. At what point should a state agency intervene and violate the privacy of the family to protect the welfare of a child? Does it better serve society's interests to protect family privacy or to protect children from harm?

Parents have never had complete freedom to do as they wish with their children. We're horrified at the thought of a parent beating his or her child to the point of injury or death. But we're equally horrified, it seems, at the thought of the state intruding on parents' right to raise their children as they see fit. In the United States, parents have the legal right to direct the upbringing of their children, to determine the care they receive, and to use physical means to control their children's behavior. From a sociological perspective, injuring children can sometimes be the extreme outcome of the widely practiced and accepted belief that parents have the right to use physical punishment to discipline their own kids.

Concern with parents' privacy rights is often framed as a freedom-of-religion issue. Forty-seven states allow parents to refuse certain medical procedures for their children on religious grounds, such as immunizations, screenings for lead poisoning, and physical examinations. Six states even have statutes that excuse students with religious objections from simply studying about diseases in school (CHILD, 2016).

But it's unclear what ought to be done when parents' religious beliefs result in the injury or death of a child. Two members of the Word of Life Christian Church in upstate New York—a church whose teachings encouraged parents to use all manner of physical punishment to discipline their children—pled guilty to assault charges in the death of their teenage son. He was savagely beaten by six people, including the parents and an older sister, for 14 hours in what church members called a "counseling session" designed to get him to confess his sins and ask for forgiveness (McKinley & Mueller, 2015). Over the past three decades, more than 300 children have died after their parents decided to withhold medical care because of their religious beliefs (cited in D. Johnson, 2009). Thirty-eight states and the District of Columbia allow religion as a defense in cases of child abuse or neglect. Idaho, Iowa, and Ohio allow religious defenses for manslaughter charges, and Delaware, West Virginia, and Arkansas permit religious defenses in cases of murder (CHILD, 2016).

Nevertheless, the government does sometimes violate the privacy of a family when that family's religious or cultural beliefs lead to the death or injury of a member. For instance, in 2012, an Oregon couple pleaded guilty to negligent homicide in the death of their 16-year-old son, who had died from an infection associated with a burst appendix. Instead of seeking medical attention when he became feverish, the parents—members of a church that eschews medicine called the General Assembly and Church of the First Born—prayed for him. He died 5 days later (Newcomb, 2012). In 2014, a Canadian couple was charged with

criminal negligence after their 14-month-old son died from a treatable infection. Prosecutors said that the child's death was preventable and that his body had been severely weakened by the family's strict, vegan diet. The couple shunned traditional medical interventions in favor of prayer (R. White, 2014).

Concern over increases in juvenile violence has led some cities and states to enact laws that punish parents for not properly *supervising* their children. Most states have parental liability laws that can hold parents responsible for their children's vandalism, theft, truancy, curfew violations, or illegal downloads (FindLaw.com, 2016). In 2005, a jury in Ohio determined that the parents of a 17-year-old boy who assaulted a young girl didn't do enough to stop him and were therefore responsible for paying the victim 70% of the damages she was awarded ($7 million; Coolidge, 2005). In 2007, a Virginia couple was sentenced to 27 months in jail for hosting an underage drinking party for their child, even though no one was hurt at the party and no one drove (Deane, 2007). Such cases illustrate the profound effects of cultural and political values on the everyday lives of individuals. Situations such as these pit the privacy and autonomy of families against society's institutional responsibility to protect children and create new citizens.

Norms

Norms are culturally defined rules of conduct. They specify what people should do and how they should pursue values. They tell us what is proper or necessary behavior within particular roles, groups, organizations, and institutions. Thousands of norms guide the minor and the grand details of our lives, from the bedroom to the classroom to the boardroom. You can see, then, that norms serve as the fundamental building blocks of social order.

Norms make our interactions with others reasonably predictable. Americans expect that when they extend a hand to another person, that person will grasp it and a brief handshake will follow. They would be shocked if they held out their hand and the other person spit on it or grabbed it and wouldn't let go. In contrast, people in some societies commonly embrace or kiss each other's cheek as a form of greeting, even when involved in a formal business relationship. A hearty handshake in those societies may be interpreted as an insult. In Thailand, people greet each other by placing the palms of their hands together in front of their bodies and slightly bowing their heads. This greeting is governed by strict norms. Slight differences in the placement of one's hands reflect the social position of the other person—the higher the hands, the higher the position of the person being greeted. Norms like these make it easier to "live with others" in a relatively harmonious way (see Chapter 4).

Social Structure in a Global Context

A discussion of social structure would not be complete without acknowledging the fact that statuses, roles, groups, organizations, social institutions, and culture are sometimes influenced by broad societal and historical forces at work in the world. One such force with deep implications for contemporary society is **globalization**, the process through which people's lives all around the world become increasingly interconnected—economically, politically, environmentally, and culturally (see Chapter 9 for more detail). For instance, when representatives of 170 countries recently signed a global deal that would phase out the use of hydrofluorocarbons—a substance used in cheap air conditioners that is linked to global warming—millions of poor people in India—one of the planet's hottest countries—were denied the one affordable appliance they could buy to ease their heat-related suffering (E. Barry & Davenport, 2016).

International financial institutions and foreign governments often provide money to support the building of hydroelectric dams in poor countries. According to the World Commission on Dams, 1,600 such dams in 40 countries were under construction in 2000 (Bald, 2000). These projects were meant to strengthen societies by providing additional energy sources in areas where power was dangerously deficient. However, they frequently transformed individual lives, social institutions, and indigenous cultures in a negative way. A dam built along the Moon River in Thailand destroyed forests that for centuries were villagers' free source of food, firewood, and medicinal herbs. With the flooding created behind the dam, local farmers lost not only their farmland but also the value of their knowledge of farming methods developed over centuries to adapt to the ebb and flow of the river. A multidam project along the Narmada River in India displaced over 200,000 people and led to violent protests there. The Manantali Dam in Mali destroyed the livelihood of downstream farmers and has resulted in the spread of waterborne diseases (Fountain, 2005). None of these dams would have been built without the funding and political clout of global financial organizations and foreign corporations.

Cultures have rarely been completely isolated from outside influence, because throughout human history people have been moving from one place to another, spreading goods and ideas. What is different today, though, is the speed and scope of these interactions. Several decades ago, overnight mail service and direct long-distance telephone calls increased the velocity of cross-national communication. Advances in transportation technology have made international trade more cost effective and international travel more accessible to ordinary citizens. And today, the Internet has given people around the world instantaneous access to the cultural artifacts and ideals of other societies, no matter where they're located. Through social media and search engines like Google, Yahoo, and Bing, children in Beirut, Baltimore, or Beijing can easily and immediately mine unlimited amounts of the same information on every conceivable topic.

Clearly, societies are more interdependent than ever, and that interdependence matters for individuals around the world. Sometimes the effects are positive. Pharmaceutical breakthroughs in the United States or Europe, for instance, can save lives around the world. Globalization gives us a chance to learn about other societies and learn from them. Other times, however, global influence can have disastrous consequences. Many of today's most pressing societal problems—widespread environmental devastation, large- and small-scale wars, economic crises, viral epidemics, and so on—are a function of globalization to some degree. Closer to home, the establishment of a toy factory in Southeast Asia or a clothing factory in Mexico may mean the loss of hundreds of manufacturing jobs in Kentucky or California.

In short, it is becoming increasingly difficult, if not impossible, to consider ourselves members of a single society unaffected by other societies. All of us are simultaneously members of our own society and citizens of a world community.

Three Perspectives on Social Order

The question of what holds all these elements of society together and how they combine to create social order has concerned sociologists for decades. Sociologists identify three broad intellectual orientations they often use to address this question: the structural-functionalist perspective, the conflict perspective, and symbolic interactionism (see Exhibit 2.2). Each of these perspectives has its advantages and shortcomings. Each is helpful in answering particular types of questions. For instance, structural functionalism is useful in showing us how and why large, macrolevel structures, such as organizations and institutions, develop and persist. The conflict perspective sheds light on the various sources of social inequality that exist in our own and other societies. And symbolic interactionism is helpful in explaining how individuals construct meaning to make sense of their social surroundings. At times, the perspectives complement one another; at other times, they contradict one another.

Throughout the remaining chapters of this book, I will periodically return to these three perspectives—as well as several other perspectives—to apply them to specific social phenomena, experiences, and events.

The Structural-Functionalist Perspective

According to sociologists Talcott Parsons and Neil Smelser (1956), two theorists typically associated with the **structural-functionalist perspective**, a society is a complex system composed of various parts, much like a living organism. Just as the heart, lungs, and liver work together to keep an animal alive, so too do all the elements of a society's structure work together to keep society alive.

EXHIBIT 2.2 ● Sociological Perspectives at a Glance		
Sociological Perspective	**Key Concepts**	**Main Assumption**
Structural-functionalist perspective	Manifest and latent functions Dysfunctions Social stability	Social institutions are structured to maintain stability and order in society
Conflict perspective	Power Inequality Conflict Dominance	The various institutions in society promote inequality and conflict among groups of people
Symbolic interactionist perspective	Symbolic communication Social interaction Subjective meaning	Society is structured and maintained through everyday interactions and people's subjective definitions of their worlds

Social institutions play a key role in keeping a society stable. All societies require certain things to survive. They must ensure that the goods and services people need are produced and distributed; they must provide ways of dealing with conflicts between individuals, groups, and organizations; and they must provide ways to ensure that individuals are made a part of the existing culture.

As we saw earlier in this chapter, institutions allow societies to attain their goals, adapt to a changing environment, reduce tension, and recruit individuals into statuses and roles. Economic institutions, for instance, allow adaptation to dwindling supplies of natural resources or to competition from other societies. Educational institutions train people for the future statuses they will need to fill to keep society going. Religions help maintain the existence of society by reaffirming people's values and preserving social ties among individuals (Durkheim, 1915/1954).

Sociologist Robert Merton (1957) distinguishes between manifest and latent functions of social institutions. **Manifest functions** are the intended, obvious consequences of activities designed to help some part of the social system. For instance, the manifest function of going to college is to get an education and acquire the credentials necessary to establish a career. **Latent functions** are the *unintended*, sometimes unrecognized, consequences of actions that coincidentally help the system. The latent function of going to college is to meet people and establish close, enduring friendships. In addition, college informally teaches students how to live on their own, away from their parents. It also provides important lessons in negotiating the intricacies of large bureaucracies—registering for classes, filling out forms, learning important school policies—so that students figure out how to "get things done" in an organization. These latent lessons will certainly help students who enter the equally large and bureaucratic world of work after they graduate (Galles, 1989).

From the structural-functionalist perspective, if an aspect of social life does not contribute to society's survival—that is, if it is *dys*functional—it will eventually disappear. Things that persist, even if they seem to be disruptive, must persist because they contribute somehow to the survival of society (Durkheim, 1915/1954). Take prostitution, for example. A practice so widely condemned and punished would appear to be dysfunctional for society. But prostitution has existed since human civilization began. Some structural functionalists suggest that prostitution satisfies sexual needs that may not be met through more socially acceptable means, such as marriage. Customers can have their physical desires satisfied without having to establish the sort of emotional attachment to another person that would destroy a preexisting marriage, harm the institution of family, and ultimately threaten the entire society (K. Davis, 1937).

Structural functionalism was the dominant theoretical tradition in sociology for most of the 20th century, and it still shapes sociological thinking to a certain degree today. But it has been criticized for accepting existing social arrangements without examining how they might exploit or otherwise disadvantage certain groups or individuals within the society.

The Conflict Perspective

The **conflict perspective** addresses the deficiencies of structural functionalism by viewing the structure of society as a source of inequality that benefits some groups at the expense of other groups. Conflict sociologists are likely to see society not in terms of stability and acceptance but in terms of conflict and struggle. They focus not on how all the elements of society contribute to its smooth operation and continued existence but on how these elements promote divisions and inequalities. Social order arises not from the societal pursuit of harmony but from dominance and coercion. The family, government, religion, and other institutions foster and legitimate the power and privilege of some individuals or groups at the expense of others.

Karl Marx, perhaps the most famous scholar associated with the conflict perspective, focused exclusively on economic arrangements. He argued that all human societies are structured around the production of goods that people need to survive. The individuals or groups who control the means of production—land in an agricultural society, factories in an industrial society, computer networks and information in a postindustrial society—have the power to create and maintain social institutions that serve their interests. Hence, economic, political, and educational systems in a modern society support the interests of those who control the wealth (see Chapter 10).

Marx believed that when resources are limited or scarce, conflict between the "haves" and the "have-nots" is inevitable and creates a situation in which those in power must enforce social order. He said this conflict is not caused by greedy, exploitative individuals; rather, it is a by-product of a system in which those who benefit from inequality are motivated to act in ways that maintain it.

Contemporary conflict sociologists are interested in various sources of conflict and inequality. One version of the conflict perspective that has become particularly popular among sociologists in the past few decades is the **feminist perspective**. Feminist sociologists focus on gender as the most important source of conflict and inequality in social life. Compared with men, women in nearly every contemporary society have less power, influence, and opportunity. In families, especially in industrialized societies, women have traditionally been encouraged to perform unpaid household labor and childcare duties, whereas men have been free to devote their energy and attention to earning money and power in the economic marketplace. Women's lower wages when they do work outside the home are often justified by the assumption that their paid labor is secondary to that of their husbands'. But as women in many societies seek equality in education, politics, career, marriage, and other areas of social life, their activities inevitably affect social institutions (see Chapter 12 for more details). The feminist perspective helps us understand the difficulties men and women face in their everyday lives as they experience the changes taking place in society.

Because this perspective focuses so much on struggle and competing interests, it tends to downplay or overlook the elements of society that different groups and individuals share. In addition, its emphasis on inequality has led some critics to argue that it is a perspective motivated by a particular political agenda and not the objective pursuit of knowledge.

Symbolic Interactionism

The structural-functionalist and the conflict perspectives differ in their assumptions about the nature of society, yet both analyze society mostly at the macro or structural level, focusing on societal patterns and the consequences they produce. In contrast, **symbolic interactionism** attempts to understand society and social structure through an examination of the microlevel interactions of people as individuals, pairs, or groups.

These forms of interaction take place within a world of symbolic communication. A **symbol** is something used to represent or stand for something else (Charon, 1998). It can be a physical object (like an engagement ring, standing for betrothal), a characteristic or property of objects (like the pink color of an equal sign, standing for same-sex marriage rights), a gesture (like a thumb pointed up, standing for "everything's OK"), or a word (like the letters d-o-g, standing for a particular type of household pet, or M-o-k-o-l-o-d-i, standing for *my* particular pet).

Symbols are created, modified, and used by people through their interactions with others. We concoct them and come to agree on what they should stand for. Our lives depend on such agreement. For instance, imagine how chaotic—not to mention dangerous—automobile travel would be if we didn't all agree that green stands for go and red stands for stop.

Symbols don't bear any necessary connection to nature. Rather, they're arbitrary human creations. There's nothing in the natural properties of "greenness" that automatically determines that green should stand for "go." We could have decided long ago that purple meant go. It wouldn't have mattered as long as we all learned and understood this symbol.

Most human behavior is determined not by the objective details of a given situation but by the symbolic meanings people attach to them (Weber, 1947). When we interact with others, we constantly attempt to interpret what they mean and what they're up to. A gentle pat on the shoulder symbolizes one thing if it comes from someone with whom you are romantically involved but something quite different if it comes from your mother or your boss.

Society, therefore, is not a structure that exists independent of human action. It is "socially constructed," emerging from the countless symbolic interactions that occur each day between individuals. Each time I refer to "U.S. society," "the school system," "the global economy," "the threat of terrorism," "the alt-right movement," or "the Upton family" in my casual conversations with others, I am doing my part to reinforce the notion that these are real things. By examining how and why we interact with others, symbolic interactionism reveals how the everyday experiences of people help to construct and maintain social institutions and, ultimately, society itself.

This perspective reminds us that for all its structural elements, society is, in the end, people interacting with one another. But by highlighting these microlevel experiences, symbolic interactionism runs the risk of ignoring the larger social patterns and structures that create the influential historical, institutional, and cultural settings for people's everyday interactions.

Conclusion

Living with others, within a social structure, influences many aspects of our everyday lives. But we must be cautious not to overstate the case. Although the fundamental elements of society are not merely the direct expressions of the personalities of individuals, we must also remember that people are more than "robots programmed by social structure" (G. Swanson, 1992, p. 94).

The lesson I hope you take from this chapter—and, in fact, from the entire book—is that the relationship between the individual and society is reciprocal. One cannot be understood without accounting for the other. Yes, this thing we call "society" touches our lives in intimate, important, and sometimes not altogether obvious ways. And yes, this influence is often beyond our immediate control. But society is not simply a "forbidding prison" that mechanically determines who we are and what we do (P. L. Berger, 1963). We as individuals can affect the very social structure that affects us. We can modify role expectations, change norms, create or destroy organizations, revolutionize institutions, and even alter the path of world history.

Your Turn

Alcohol occupies an important but problematic place in many societies. We decry its evils while simultaneously encouraging its use in times of leisure, celebration, despair, disappointment, anger, and worry.

The physical effects of being "under the influence"—vomiting, hangovers, liver damage—are a biological consequence of the presence of alcohol in the body. When a person's blood alcohol level reaches a certain point, that person will have trouble walking and talking; at a higher level, she or he will pass out and perhaps even die.

But is the social behavior we see in drunken people reducible to a chemical reaction in the body? The traditional explanation for drunken behavior is that the chemical properties of alcohol do something to the brain that reduces inhibitions. If this were true, though, drunken behavior would look the same everywhere. The fact is, social behavior under the influence of alcohol can vary from culture to culture. The way people handle themselves when drunk "is determined not by alcohol's toxic assault on the seat of moral judgment, conscience, or the like but by what their society makes of and imparts to them concerning the state of drunkenness" (MacAndrew & Edgerton, 1969, p. 165).

Ask people who grew up in a culture different from yours (e.g., students who grew up in a different country or in a different socioeconomic class or geographic region) how people behave when drunk. Do these behaviors differ from those you've observed? Have them describe their first drunken experience. Are there similarities or differences in how people are introduced to alcohol?

Also ask the same questions of people from different sexes, races, ethnic groups, and age groups. Are there variations in the "drunken experience" within a society? What do these differences illustrate about the norms and values of these different groups? You might also ask some young children to describe how drunk people act. Are there any similarities in the images they have of drunkenness? Do you consider their ideas about drunkenness accurate? Where do you think their ideas about alcohol come from?

Use the results of these interviews to explain the role of social and societal influence on people's personal lives. Do you think your conclusions can be expanded to other private phenomena, such as sexual activity or religious experiences? Why or why not?

Note: All colleges and universities require that any student research project involving human subjects—even if it just entails asking people questions—be approved by a campus or departmental review committee. For instance, you will probably be required to show that your interviewees have consented to participate and that you've guaranteed that their identities will not be divulged. Make sure you talk to your instructor before proceeding with this exercise to see what steps you have to take in order to have it approved by the appropriate campus committee.

Chapter Highlights

- Although society exists as an objective fact, it is also created, reaffirmed, and altered through the day-to-day interactions of the very people it influences and controls.

- Humans are social beings. We look to others to help define and interpret particular situations. Other people can influence what we see, feel, think, and do.

- Society consists of socially recognizable combinations of individuals—relationships, groups, and organizations—as well as the products of human action—statuses, roles, culture, institutions, and broad societal forces such as globalization.

- There are three major sociological perspectives. The structural-functionalist perspective focuses on the way various parts of society are structured and interrelated to maintain stability and order. The conflict perspective emphasizes how the various elements of society promote inequality and conflict among groups of people. Symbolic interactionism seeks to understand society and social structure through the interactions of people and the ways in which they subjectively define their worlds.

Key Terms

achieved status: Social position acquired through our own efforts or accomplishments or taken on voluntarily

ascribed status: Social position acquired at birth or taken on involuntarily later in life

coalition: Subgroup of a triad, formed when two members unite against the third member

conflict perspective: Theoretical perspective that views the structure of society as a source of inequality that always benefits some groups at the expense of other groups

culture: Language, values, beliefs, rules, behaviors, and artifacts that characterize a society

dyad: Group consisting of two people

feminist perspective: Theoretical perspective that focuses on gender as the most important source of conflict and inequality in social life

globalization: Process through which people's lives all around the world become economically, politically, environmentally, and culturally interconnected

group: Set of people who interact more or less regularly and who are conscious of their identity as a unit

in-groups: The groups to which we belong and toward which we feel a sense of loyalty

latent function: Unintended, unrecognized consequences of activities that help some part of the social system

manifest functions: Intended, obvious consequences of activities designed to help some part of the social system

norm: Culturally defined standard or rule of conduct

organization: Large, complex network of positions created for a specific purpose and characterized by a hierarchical division of labor

out-groups: The groups to which we don't belong and toward which we feel a certain amount of antagonism

primary group: Collection of individuals who are together for a relatively long period, whose members have direct contact with and feel emotional attachment to one another

role: Set of expectations—rights, obligations, behaviors, duties—associated with a particular status

role conflict: Frustration people feel when the demands of one role they are expected to fulfill clash with the demands of another role

role strain: Situations in which people lack the necessary resources to fulfill the demands of a particular role

secondary group: Relatively impersonal collection of individuals that is established to perform a specific task

social institution: Stable set of roles, statuses, groups, and organizations—such as the institutions of education, family, politics, religion, health care, or the economy—that provides a foundation for behavior in some major area of social life

society: A population of people living in the same geographic area who share a culture and a common identity and whose members are subject to the same political authority

status: Any named social position that people can occupy

structural-functionalist perspective: Theoretical perspective that posits that social institutions are structured to maintain stability and order in society

symbol: Something used to represent or stand for something else

symbolic interactionism: Theoretical perspective that explains society and social structure through an examination of the microlevel, personal, day-to-day exchanges of people as individuals, pairs, or groups

triad: Group consisting of three people

value: Standard of judgment by which people decide on desirable goals and outcomes

SAGE edge™ edge.sagepub.com/newman12e

SAGE edge offers a robust online environment featuring an impressive array of free tools and resources for review, study, and further exploration, keeping both instructors and students on the cutting edge of teaching and learning.

The Construction of Self and Society

Part II examines the basic architecture of individual identities and of society: how reality and truth are constructed; how social order is created and maintained; how culture and history influence our personal experiences; how societal values, ideals, and norms are instilled; and how we acquire our sense of self. The tactical and strategic ways in which we present images of ourselves to others are also addressed. You will see how we form relationships and interact within small, intimate groups. The section closes with a look at how we define "acceptable" behavior and how we respond to those who "break the rules."

3

Building Reality

The Social Construction of Knowledge

- Understanding the Social Construction of Reality
- Laying the Foundation: The Bases of Reality
- Building the Walls: Conflict, Power, and Social Institutions
- Appreciating the Contributions of Sociological Research

The year was 1897. Eight-year-old Virginia O'Hanlon became upset when her friends told her there was no Santa Claus. Her father encouraged her to write a letter to the *New York Sun* to find out the truth. The editor's reply—which included the now famous phrase, "Yes, Virginia, there is a Santa Claus!"—has become a classic piece of American folklore. "Nobody sees Santa Claus," the editor wrote, "but that is no sign that there is no Santa Claus. The most real things in the world are those that neither children nor men [*sic*] can see" ("Is There a Santa Claus?" 1897).

Drug experts have been concerned for years about the illicit use of stimulants commonly prescribed for attention deficit hyperactivity disorder (such as Adderall and Ritalin) among college students who want to enhance their concentration and test performance. But recently, researchers have started to worry about the use of these drugs among workers in high-stress professions who want to increase their productivity. Unfortunately, reliable research on the prevalence of ADHD drugs in the workplace does not yet exist. Nonetheless, one neurologist believes that "even without conclusive data, misuse [is] *undoubtedly* rising" [emphasis added] (quoted in Schwarz, 2015a, p. 1).

In December 2016, a 28-year old North Carolina man named Edgar Welch loaded his car with weapons and drove to a pizzeria in Washington, DC, where he believed children were being held hostage in the basement. He entered the restaurant and fired several shots. Fortunately no one was struck and he was quickly arrested. Edgar said he took these actions because he believed that Hillary Clinton and her campaign chair, John Podesta, ran a secret child sex trafficking ring in the back of the restaurant. Though the baseless conspiracy theories he got through social media were completely debunked, Welch was convinced they were true and decided to "self investigate" (Mahler, 2017, p. 9).

What do these three very different examples have in common? They all reflect the fickle nature of "truth" and "reality." Young Virginia was encouraged to believe in the reality of something she could and would never perceive with her senses. She no doubt learned a different sort of truth about Santa Claus when she got older, but the editor urged her to take on faith that Santa Claus, or at least the idea of Santa Claus, exists despite the lack of objective proof. That sort of advice persists. A survey of 200 child psychologists around the United States found that 91% of them advised parents not to tell the truth when their young children asked about the existence of Santa Claus (cited in Stryker, 1997).

Likewise, the drug researcher urges people to believe in something that has not been demonstrated scientifically. What's important is that the conclusion feels right even if it is not based on hard evidence. And Edgar Welch rejected the facts of the "reality-based community" as dishonest and corrupt, opting instead for a "do-it-yourself" approach to truth (Mahler, 2017).

Alternative versions of facts can sometimes have dangerous consequences. Consider the case of Jenny McCarthy, the former *Playboy* model and MTV star who has written several best-selling books in which she claims that the measles, mumps, and rubella vaccine—something most infants in this country routinely receive—had *probably* given her son autism. Instead of providing supportive research evidence (principally because there really is none), McCarthy based her conclusion on her own intuition—what she called "mommy instinct"—and information she'd picked up on the Internet (she once proudly proclaimed, "The University of Google is where I got my degree from"; quoted in Achenbach, 2015, p. 5). Many well-known people, including President Donald Trump, support McCarthy's anti-vaccine movement. Early in his presidency, Trump talked of creating a presidential commission on "vaccine safety."

The Centers for Disease Control and Prevention, the Institute of Medicine, the Autism Science Foundation, and the National Academy of Sciences, however, have all concluded there is no link between vaccines and autism. Nevertheless, the contention that vaccines could harm children struck an emotional chord with many fretful parents. Consequently in some states the percentage of children who get this vaccine as well as other vaccines consistently dropped within the span of a few years. Perhaps not coincidentally, measles cases rose. In 2010, there were only 63 confirmed cases of measles in the United States. In 2014, there were 667 (Centers for Disease Control and Prevention, 2016d). The vast majority of these cases were in persons who had not been vaccinated. As a result, in 2015, California became the first state to require parents to vaccinate their children, regardless of personal or religious opposition. That same year, Google changed its search algorithm so that entering the term "vaccination" brought actual medical information to the top of the results list rather than discredited claims (G. Johnson, 2015). By the way, as the popularity of McCarthy's anti-vaccine movement dropped, so too did the number of measles cases—there were 188 cases in 2015 and 62 in 2016 (Centers for Disease Control and Prevention, 2016d).

Such precarious uses of truth may appear foolish or even deceitful. Yet much of our everyday knowledge is based on accepting as real the existence of things that can't be seen, touched, or proved—"the world taken-for-granted" (P. L. Berger, 1963, p. 147). Like Virginia, we learn to accept the existence of things such as electrons, the ozone layer, black holes in the universe, love, and God, even though we cannot see them. And like Jenny McCarthy or Edgar Welch, many people come to accept unsubstantiated conclusions in the face of contradictory evidence as long as they support their interests or preconceived beliefs. As former president Barack Obama put it after leaving office, "Increasingly we become so secure in our bubbles that we start accepting only information, whether it's true or not, that fits our opinions, instead of basing our opinions on the evidence that is out there" (quoted in Shane, 2017, p. A17). In fact, "science denial" has become a hallmark of government policy. Shortly after replacing Obama in 2017, President Trump ordered all mentions of climate change purged from the official White House website and the Environmental Protection Agency was told to take down its climate change webpage. Indeed, to some observers, such disavowal of established facts coupled with purposeful distortion has made reality more vulnerable than anyone ever thought possible (Gladstone, 2017). Some news organizations have become so frustrated that they've abandoned the hallmark journalistic value of objectivity and now use terms like "wrongly," "falsely," "with no evidence," "debunked claim," and even "lie" to characterize statements issued by the White House (D. Barry, 2017).

So, how do we come to know what we know? How do we learn what is real and what isn't? In this chapter, I examine how sociologists discover truths about human life. But to provide the appropriate context, I must first present a sociological perspective on the nature of reality. How do individuals construct their realities? How do societal forces influence the process?

Understanding the Social Construction of Reality

In Chapter 2, I noted that the elements of society are human creations that provide structure to our everyday lives. They also give us a distinctive lens through which we perceive the world. For example, because of their different statuses and their respective occupational training, an architect, a real estate agent, a police officer, and a firefighter can each look at the same building and see very different things: "a beautiful example of early Victorian architecture," "a moderately priced fixer-upper," "an easy target for a thief," or "a dangerous fire hazard." Mark Twain often wrote about how the Mississippi River—a waterway he saw every day as a child—looked different after he became a riverboat pilot. What he once saw as a place for fun and relaxation, he later saw for its treacherous currents, eddies, and other potential perils.

What we know to be true or real is always a product of the culture and historical period in which we exist. It takes an exercise of the sociological imagination, however, to see that what we ourselves "know" to be true today—the laws of nature, the causes and treatments of certain diseases, and so forth—may not be true for everyone everywhere or may be replaced by different truths tomorrow (Babbie, 1986). For example, in some cultures, the existence of spirits, witches, and demons is a taken-for-granted part of everyday reality that others might easily dismiss as fanciful. On the other side of the coin, the Western faith in the curative powers of little pills—without the intervention of spiritual forces—might seem far-fetched and naïve to people living in cultures where illness and health are assumed to have supernatural causes.

Beliefs about what is true change over time too. In 1900, a doctor might have told a patient with asthma to go to the local tobacconist for cigarettes; people with colds may have been told to inhale formaldehyde (Zuger, 1999). Many pieces of taken-for-granted 20th-century child development advice—such as infants need to be bathed every day; picking up babies when they're crying spoils them; infants need to be on a strict feeding schedule; and the safest way to put babies to sleep is on their stomachs—have been called into question by contemporary pediatricians (First, 2011). Sixty years ago, obstetricians encouraged pregnant women to have a martini or a glass of wine each night to calm their nerves. Doctors also believed that alcohol prevented premature labor. Hence, women arriving at the hospital in early labor were often handed vodka or even given alcohol intravenously (Hoffman, 2005). You sure don't see that anymore. In recent years, we've seen the medical field reverse its stand on the criteria used to define autism (Carey, 2012), the utility of vitamin D and calcium supplements (Begley, 2011), routine mammograms for healthy women over 40 (Bleyer & Welch, 2012), acceptable blood pressure levels in people over 60 (Kolata, 2013), and the necessity of regular blood tests for prostate cancer in healthy men (G. Harris, 2011c).

According to one researcher, about a third of major medical studies are eventually contradicted by further research (Ioannidis, 2005). The frequency with which medical "truths" emerge only to be reversed or debunked later on led one columnist to write, with a fair amount of exasperation, "Sometimes you really do want to tell the medical profession to just make up its mind" (G. Collins, 2011, p. A23). Quite possibly, people 100 years from now will look back at the early 21st century and regard some of our taken-for-granted truths as mistaken, misguided, or downright laughable.

The process through which facts, knowledge, truth, and so on are discovered, made known, reaffirmed, and altered by the members of a society is called the **social construction of reality** (P. L. Berger & Luckmann, 1966). This concept is based on the simple assumption that knowledge is a human creation. Ironically, most of us live our lives assuming that an objective reality exists, independent of us and accessible through our senses. Sayings like "Seeing is believing" and "Pics or it didn't happen" reinforce the assumption that our eyes can tell us what is real. We are quite sure trees and tables and trucks don't exist simply in our imaginations. We assume this reality is shared by others and can be taken for granted as reality (Lindesmith, Strauss, & Denzin, 1991).

At times, however, what we define as real seems to have nothing to do with what our senses tell us is real. Picture a 5-year-old child who wakes up in the middle of the night screaming that monsters are under her bed. Her parents comfort her by saying, "There aren't any monsters. You had a nightmare. It's just your imagination." The next day, the child comes down with the flu and wants to know why she is sick. The parents respond by saying,

> You've caught a virus, a bug.
>
> A bug? You mean like an ant or a beetle?
>
> No. It's the sort of bug you can't see, but it's there.

Granted, viruses can be seen and verified with the proper magnification equipment, but without access to such devices, the child has to take her parents' word for it that viruses are real. In fact, most of us accept the scientific reality of viruses without ever having seen them for ourselves. The child learns to accept the authoritative claims of her parents that something that was "seen" (the nightmare monster) is not real, although something that was not seen (the virus) is real. Hence, reality often turns out to be more a matter of collective agreement than something inherent in the natural world.

Sociologists, particularly those working from the conflict perspective and symbolic interactionism, strive to explain the social construction of reality in terms of both its causes and its consequences. Their insights help explain many of the phenomena that influence our daily lives.

Laying the Foundation: The Bases of Reality

Think of society as a building constructed by the people who live and work in it. The building's foundation, its underlying reality, determines its basic shape and dimensions. And the foundation is what makes that building solid and helps it stand up through time and the elements. For students of architecture as well as sociology, the first thing to understand is the way the foundation is prepared.

Symbolic interactionism encourages us to see that people's actions toward one another and interpretations of situations are based on their definitions of reality, which are in turn learned from interactions with those around them. What we know to be real and true, we share with others:

> My wife might tell me that her phone says it's going to rain, so I should take my umbrella, and every step of that transaction would be meaningless without the fundamental assumption of [a commonly held] truth. (Child, 2016, p. 67)

Imagine how difficult it would be to believe in something no one else around you thought existed. Psychiatrists use terms such as *hallucination* and *delusion* to describe things experienced by people who see, hear, or believe things that others don't.

The social construction of reality is a process by which human-created ideas become so firmly accepted that to deny them is to deny common sense. Of course, some features of reality are grounded in physical evidence—fire is hot, sharp things hurt. But other features of reality are often based not on sensory experiences but on forces such as culture and language, self-fulfilling prophecies, and faith.

Culture and Language

As I mentioned in Chapter 2, we live in a symbolic world and interact chiefly through symbolic communication—that is, through language. Language gives meaning to the people, objects, events, and ideas of our lives. In fact, language reflects and often determines our reality (Sapir, 1949; Whorf, 1956). Thus, language is a key tool in the construction of society.

Within a culture, words evolve to reflect the things that have practical significance. Solomon Islanders have nine distinct words for *coconut*, each specifying an important stage of its growth, but they have only one word for all the meals of the day (M. M. Lewis, 1948). The Hanunóo people of the Philippines have different names for 92 varieties of rice, allowing them to make distinctions all but invisible to English-speaking people, who lump all such grains under a single word: *rice* (Thomson, 2000). Yet a traditional Hanunóo coming to this country would be hard pressed to see the difference between the vehicles we call *sedans, SUVs, hybrids, minivans, hatchbacks,* and *station wagons.*

Language also reflects prevailing cultural values. Consider, for instance, the words we use to describe spatial positioning. In most Western languages, English included, if you wanted to give someone directions to your house, you'd say something like, "After the stop sign, take the first left, then the second right. You'll see a brown duplex in front of you. Ours is the door on the right." You wouldn't say, "After the stop sign, drive north, then on the second street drive east and you'll see a brown duplex directly to the east. Ours is the southern door." The two sets of directions may identify the same route, but the first uses *egocentric* coordinates, which rely on the location of our own bodies relative to the destination in question. The second set of directions—which would be common in some areas of the world like Polynesia, northern Australia, Namibia, and Bali—uses fixed *geographic* coordinates, which stay the same no matter which way we're facing (Deutscher, 2010). Speakers of Guugu Yimithirr, an Australian Aboriginal language, orient their lives exclusively around geographic coordinates. If they wanted to warn a walking companion of impending danger on the path, they'd say, "There's a hole in the ground north of your western foot" rather than, "There's a hole in front of your left foot." Indeed, the Guugu Yimithirr have no idea what *left, right, in front of you,* or *behind you* mean. Notice how these two linguistic approaches reflect very different cultural beliefs about the importance of the individual:

> If you saw a Guugu Yimithirr speaker pointing at himself, you would naturally assume he meant to draw attention to himself. In fact, he is pointing at a [geographic] direction that happens to be behind his back. While we [English speakers] are always at the center of the world, and it would never occur to us that pointing in the direction of our chest could mean anything other than to draw attention to ourselves, a Guugu Yimithirr speaker points through himself, as if he were thin air and his own existence were irrelevant. (Deutscher, 2010, p. 47)

In addition to affecting perceptions of reality, language reinforces prevailing ideas and suppresses conflicting ideas about the world (Sapir, 1929). In a highly specialized market economy such as the United States, for example, the ability to distinguish linguistically between "real" work, "house" work, and "volunteer" work allows us to telegraph our attitudes about a person's worth to society. In small agricultural societies, where all people typically perform tasks to provide the basic necessities and to ensure the survival of their tight-knit community, work is work no matter where it takes place or whether or not you're paid to do it.

Language can also pack an enormous emotional wallop. Words can make us happy, sad, disgusted, angry, violent, afraid, or upset. Many college campuses around the country now require course syllabi to include "trigger warnings," cautionary notices that topics covered in class (and the language used to discuss them) could contain potentially traumatic subject matter that might upset some students.

Racial, ethnic, sexual, or religious slurs can be particularly volatile. Among heterosexual adolescents, for example, homophobic name-calling (*queer, fag, dyke*) is one of the most common modes of bullying and coercion in high school (Pascoe, 2010). In 2013, the actor Alec Baldwin was caught on camera outside his Manhattan apartment calling a photographer a *cocksucking fag.* Baldwin wasn't disparaging the man's sexual orientation. I doubt he even knew what it was. Instead, he was enraged by the intrusion of paparazzi into his private life and no doubt thought using this term would be the most effective means of communicating his utter contempt for the practice. In 2014, the pop singer Justin Bieber faced a backlash from both fans and critics when a 5-year old video surfaced of him singing a parody of his song "One Less Lonely Girl," in which he substitutes the word *nigger* for *girl.* A separate video released that same year showed him using the word *nigger* as he told a racist joke.

It's important to remember that languages are fluid. Hence they can expand, contract, and shift over time. For instance, every December, newspapers and websites list the words or phrases that became popular that year and entered the cultural lexicon. In 2014, terms such as *emoji, copypasta, ice bucket challenge, polar vortex, rekt,* and *turnt* appeared. According to various online sources, 2016 saw the entry of words like *woke, bigly, Brexit, wetbrooming, high key, non-binary, suh, sus,* and *hundo-p* into everyday conversations and texts. No doubt future versions will contain a whole host of common terms no one's heard of yet.

The emotional effect of words can have health implications, too. Researchers estimate that an antibiotic-resistant intestinal bacterium called *Clostridium difficile* infects about a million people and kills 14,000 in the United States each year (Grady, 2013; Pollan, 2013). Symptoms include profuse diarrhea, uncontrollable vomiting, high fever, and significant weight loss. The most effective treatment for this condition, by far, is a procedure called a "fecal transplant" in which feces taken from healthy donors is infused into patients infected with *Clostridium difficile* (van Nood, 2013). The healthy feces, which contain thousands of strains of "good" bacteria, is diluted with salt water, sanitized, and deodorized before being pumped into patients usually via a tube inserted through the nose. In 2015, a company called OpenBiome opened the first stool bank, distributing feces in frozen and freeze-dried pill forms to patients suffering from *Clostridium difficile* (P. A. Smith, 2015). Neither the fecal fluid nor the fecal pill bear any resemblance, either by sight or smell, to their original form. Yet despite its demonstrable success—as one author put it, "Rarely does medical science come up with a treatment so effective, inexpensive, and free of side effects" (Roach, 2013, pp. 320–321)—many patients who could be helped refuse to consider the treatment. And even though the first fecal transplant was performed over half a century ago, no U.S. insurance company formally recognizes (and will pay for) the procedure (Roach, 2013). Why? Because people can't get past the disgust—what some refer to as the "ick factor"—associated with the term *fecal transplant* (Belluck, 2014).

The broader demands of everyday life also influence the way language is used. For instance, as societies become more developed, the pace of life quickens, and we become impatient. This phenomenon is reflected in the compression (and subsequent speedup) of language over the years. Contractions (like *we're* and *isn't*) shorten words. Portmanteaus combine two existing words into one, like *brunch* for "breakfast and lunch," *docudrama* for "documentary and drama," and *webinar* for "web seminar" (Garner, 2010). Technology contracts language even further. If you do a lot of tweeting or texting, you have no doubt made use of "shortspeak"—the reduction of words and sentences through the use of abbreviations, acronyms, and emojis. We don't even have to finish typing our words anymore. As I'm sure you know, online search engines routinely use autofill to complete entries even before you're done typing them. A few years ago, Google engineers discovered that a delay of 400 *milliseconds* between a keyboard click and a computer response—roughly the time it takes to blink an eye—is too long for some people and may actually cause them to use the search engine less. As one engineer put it, "Subconsciously, you don't like to wait. Every millisecond matters" (quoted in Lohr, 2012, p. A1).

Within a culture, certain groups sometimes develop a distinctive language, known as *jargon*, which allows members to communicate with one another clearly and quickly. Surfers, snowboarders, and gamers each have a specialized vocabulary (not understandable to most outsiders) through which they can efficiently convey to others information about wave quality, snow conditions, or changes in the latest version of *Call of Duty*. Teenagers must keep up with a constantly evolving vocabulary to avoid falling out of favor with their peers. At the same time, jargon can sometimes create boundaries and therefore mystify and conceal meaning from outsiders (Farb, 1983). For instance, first-year medical students spend countless hours memorizing a new vocabulary as if they were learning a foreign language (Hartzband & Groopman, 2011). By using esoteric medical terminology when discussing a case in front of a patient, health care professionals define who is and who isn't a member of their group, reinforce their image as highly trained experts, and keep the patient from interfering too much in their decision making. Often medical information has to be conveyed quickly, making it even more incomprehensible to outsiders. See if you can figure out the patient's condition from how this intensive care nurse described it to an attending physician:

IL-2 patient, hypotensive, B.P. hovering between 70 over 40 to 60 over 30, occasionally tachy, bolused once this morning for a pressure of 80 over 50, getting another bolus right now, already fluid overloaded, crackles at the bases. (T. Brown, 2010, p. 5)

This sort of communication roadblock has become a cause for concern in the field of medicine. Research indicates that two thirds of patients are discharged from hospitals without even knowing what their diagnosis is and 60% of patients misunderstand the directions they receive from visits to their doctor's office (cited in Joshi, 2015). Consequently, many books and websites now help patients overcome their position of powerlessness by instructing them on how and when to ask physicians the right questions so they can make informed decisions about a course of treatment. For their part, some medical schools require their students to be trained in how to avoid jargon (at the same time they're learning it) and how to listen to their patients (D. Franklin, 2006). And there is some evidence that doctor–patient interactions have become a bit more patient-centered and collaborative in recent years (Peck & Conner, 2011).

Language is sometimes used to purposely conceal as well. A *euphemism* is an innocuous expression substituted for one that might be offensive. On the surface, people use such terms in the interests of politeness and good taste, such as saying "perspiration" instead of "sweat," "bathroom tissue" instead of "toilet paper," or "no longer with us" instead of "dead." However, euphemisms also shape perceptions and emotions. Does it matter, for instance, whether an economic crisis is called a *downturn*, *slump*, *recession*, *crash*, *depression*, or *meltdown*? Political regimes routinely use euphemisms to cover up, distort, or frame their actions in a more positive light. Here are a few examples of euphemisms, followed by their real meanings. Can you think of others?

- Pre-owned—used

- Seasoned—old

- Misinformation—lies

- Economically nonaffluent—poor

- Big boned; full-figured—overweight

- Correctional facility—prison

- Adult entertainment—pornography

- Sleeping with; doing it; going all the way—having sex

- Postconsumer waste material—garbage

- Between jobs—unemployed

- Deselected, involuntarily separated, downsized, nonretained, given a career change opportunity, vocationally relocated, streamlined, or dehired—fired

In sum, words help frame or structure social reality and give it meaning. Language also provides people with a cultural and group identity. If you've ever spent a significant amount of time in a foreign country or even moved to a new school, you know you cannot be a fully participating member of a group or a culture until you share its language.

MICRO-MACRO CONNECTION
THE WORDS OF WAR

The governmental or political use of language illustrates how words can determine the course of people's everyday lives both at home and abroad. We all know what the word *war* means: It's when two opposing forces wage battle against one another, either until one side surrenders or until both agree to a truce. The vocabulary of war is vast, containing words such as *troops, battle, regiments, ammunition, artillery, allies, enemies, heroes, casualties,* and so forth.

In wartime, there is good and evil, us and them, victory and defeat. The language of war contains euphemisms, too, designed to minimize the public's discomfort and increase its support: *collateral damage* (civilian deaths during military combat), *surgical strikes* (attacks intended to destroy a specific target and minimize *collateral damage*), *friendly fire* (accidental shooting at fellow soldiers), *pullback* (retreat), *sectarian violence* (civil war), *enhanced interrogation* (torture), *boots on the ground* (soldiers deployed in long-term combat operations).

Once a conflict is defined as a war, people's lives are subjected to a different set of rules and expectations. War rallies people around their collective national identity and a common objective, creating mandatory expressions of patriotism and a willingness to fight and make sacrifices (Redstone, 2003). The interpretation of people's behavior dramatically changes as well. For example, some characterized the atrocities that occurred during the conflict in Bosnia-Herzegovina in the 1990s as the normal consequences of war. However,

> [i]s wide-scale sexual violence, including the rape of women and the forced oral castration of men, neighbors burning down their neighbors' homes, the murder and targeting for murder of civilians—men and women, children, the elderly, and infirm—"normal" simply because it takes place within the context of something we call "war"? (Wilmer, 2002, p. 60)

Immediately after the attacks of September 11, 2001, then-president Bush unofficially declared a war on terrorism, which continues to this day. But the administration later opted for the term *War on Terror* and then *Global War on Terror* rather than *War on Terrorism*, evoking both the violent actions of terrorists and the fear they're trying to create. In 2005, the administration shifted its language and began testing a new slogan, *A Global Struggle Against Violent Extremism*, in an attempt to convey the impression that the war was as much an ideological battle as it was a military mission (Schmitt & Shanker, 2005). The Obama administration continued to use equally ambiguous terms like *Overseas Contingency Operation* and *Systematic Effort to Dismantle Terrorist Organizations,* thereby avoiding reference to "war" and "violence" altogether. Whether the enemy is an identifiable organization like al-Qaeda, ISIS, and the Taliban or a hazier foe like *terror, terrorism, terrorist networks, violent extremism,* or *Islamic extremism*, invoking the vocabulary of war has some strategic advantages—among them, justifying actions that would not be acceptable in any other context. As one columnist put it, "In wartime, words are weapons" (Safire, 2006, p. 16). By continually using the language of war, an administration can frame the expansion of government powers and the limitation of civil liberties as the steps we need to take to protect freedom, bring "enemies" and "evildoers" to justice, and avoid another catastrophe.

In a wartime mode, even though concerns about national security are warranted and fears of attack are very real, the system, according to one prominent law professor, "by definition sweeps very broadly and ends up harming hundreds if not thousands of people" (quoted in Liptak, 2003, p. A1). Actions that in other contexts would be unacceptable occur largely without debate or opposition, reflecting the power of language in shaping the social reality of everyday life.

Even in the absence of a foreign enemy, militarized vocabularies and tactics can shape perceptions. In the past few years, we've witnessed more and more police departments around the country resorting to a military model—camouflage gear, military-grade vehicles, weapons, and ammunition—to frame their interactions with the public (Kraska, 2007). For instance, in the immediate aftermath of the 2013 Boston Marathon bombing, "the police sent armored cars into the streets and deployed officers dressed like Storm Troopers, who carried assault rifles and fanned out across neighborhoods as though they were in an infantry division in Afghanistan" (Filkins, 2016, p. 1).

Through its "1033 Program," the Department of Defense provides local police departments with military weapons, munitions, high-tech surveillance equipment, armored personnel carriers, mine-resistant ambush-protected tanks, even helicopters free of charge. Since the

(Continued)

(Continued)

program was created in the 1990s, the Defense Department has donated over $5.1 billion worth of non-lethal military equipment to local police departments (Dansky, 2014). In addition, local governments have received approximately $34 billion in grants from the Department of Homeland Security to buy their own military equipment from private suppliers (Filkins, 2016). And it's not just equipment. Contemporary police training programs routinely teach members of SWAT teams to think and act like soldiers (American Civil Liberties Union, 2014). Such militarization encourages officers to adopt a "warrior" mentality and think of the citizens they're supposed to safeguard as enemies (American Civil Liberties Union, 2014). As one former Marine asked, "When did 'protect and serve' turn into 'us versus them'?" (Szoldra, 2014, p. 1).

Self-Fulfilling Prophecies

As you will recall from Chapter 2, we do not respond directly and automatically to objects and situations; instead, as the symbolic interactionist perspective points out, we use language to define and interpret them, and then we act according to those interpretations. By acting on the basis of our definitions of reality, we often create the very conditions we believe exist. A **self-fulfilling prophecy** is an assumption or prediction that, purely as a result of having been made, causes the expected event to occur and thus confirms the prophecy's own "accuracy" (Merton, 1948; Watzlawick, 1984). Every holiday season, we witness the stunning effects of self-fulfilling prophecies on a national scale. Each September, the toy industry releases the results of its annual survey of retailers, predicting which toys will be the top sellers at Christmas. Usually, one toy in particular emerges as the most popular, hard-to-get gift of the year. In the 1980s, it was Cabbage Patch Kids. In the early 1990s, it was Mighty Morphin Power Rangers and Ninja Turtles. More recently, items such as Beanie Babies, SpongeBob SquarePants toys, Razor scooters, ripsticks, American Girl dolls, toy digital cameras, Legos, figurines from *Frozen* or *Star Wars,* and hatchimals have taken their turn as the "must have" toy of the year. By around November, we begin to hear the hype about unprecedented demand for the toy and the likelihood of a shortage. Powerful retail store chains, such as Toys"R"Us and Walmart, may announce the possibility of rationing: one toy per family. Fueled by the dreaded image of a disappointed child's face at Christmas, thousands of panicked parents and grandparents rush to stores to make sure they're not left without. Some hoard extras for other parents they know. As a result, supplies of the toy—which may not have been perilously low in the first place—become severely depleted, thereby bringing about the predicted shortage. The mere belief in some version of the reality creates expectations that can actually make it happen.

Self-fulfilling prophecies are particularly powerful when they become an element of social institutions. In schools, teachers can subtly and unconsciously encourage the performance they expect to see in their students. For instance, if they believe their students are especially intelligent, they may spend more time with them or unintentionally show more enthusiasm when working with them. As a result, these students may come to feel more capable and intelligent and actually perform better (R. Rosenthal & Jacobson, 1968).

Self-fulfilling prophecies can often affect people's physical health, too. For years, doctors have recognized the power of the "placebo" effect—the tendency for patients to improve because they have been led to believe they are receiving some sort of treatment even though they're not. For instance, in one study, 42% of balding men taking a placebo drug either maintained or increased the amount of hair on their heads (cited in Blakeslee, 1998). Researchers estimate that in studies of new drugs, between 35% and 75% of patients benefit from taking dummy pills. In 1999, a major pharmaceutical company halted development of a new antidepressant drug it had been promoting because studies showed that placebo pills were just as effective in treating depression (Talbot, 2000). Even when patients know they're taking placebos, the effects can be significantly better than if they underwent no treatment at all (Kaptchuk et al., 2010). Placebos are especially effective when it comes to pain relief. So given the troubling epidemic of prescription opioid painkiller addiction (Vicadin, Oxycontin, Fentanyl, Percocet, etc.) we've seen in recent years, perhaps it's not so surprising that some scholars have advocated the "deceptive" use of placebos in place of active opioid drugs (Marchant, 2016).

The inverse of the placebo effect is the creation of expectations that make people worse, sometimes referred to as the "nocebo" effect. Anthropologists have documented numerous mysterious and scientifically difficult-to-explain deaths that follow the pronouncement of curses or evil spells (Watzlawick, 1984). In one study, a team of gastroenterologists asked experimental subjects (some who suffered from lactose intolerance and some who didn't) to ingest lactose. The researchers told them they were examining its effects on bowel symptoms. In reality, all the subjects received sugar water. Yet 44% of those with known lactose intolerance—as well as 26% of those without it—complained of gastrointestinal symptoms (Enck & Häuser, 2012). In another study, patients with asthma were given a bronchodilator (a drug that widens air passages, making breathing easier) but were told it was a bronchoconstrictor (a drug that narrows air passages, making breathing more difficult). Half of them experienced difficulty breathing after the treatment (cited in "The Nocebo Response," 2005). It's estimated that somewhere between 4% and 26% of people in medical trials who receive fake drugs eventually withdraw from the study because of the "drug's" side effects, like nausea or dizziness. In other words, in many cases where people expect to get worse, they do. As one doctor put it, "[W]ords are the most powerful tool a doctor possesses, but words, like two-edged swords, can maim as well as heal" (quoted in Enck & Häuser, 2012, p. 4). Once again, we see how human beings shape reality as much as reality shapes them.

Faith and Incorrigible Propositions

David Blaine is a famous performer and illusionist who combines sophisticated magic tricks with a hint of comedy. In one of his classic stunts, he approaches people on the street and, after a few moments, appears to rise up and float several inches off the ground for a few seconds. Suppose you saw him perform such a feat in person. He looks as if he is levitating, but you "know better." Even though your eyes tell you he is floating in midair, you have learned that it's just not possible. Rather than use this experience to entirely abandon your belief that people can't float in midair, you'll probably come up with a series of "reasonable" explanations: "Maybe it's an optical illusion, and it just looks like he's floating." "I'm sure there are wires holding him up." To acknowledge the possibility that he is literally floating is to challenge the fundamental reality on which your everyday life is based. It is an article of faith that people aren't capable of levitating.

Such an unquestionable assumption, called an **incorrigible proposition**, is a belief that cannot be proved wrong and has become so much a part of common sense that one continues to believe it even in the face of vast contrary evidence. By explaining away contradictions with "reasonable" explanations, we strengthen the correctness of the initial premise (Watzlawick, 1976). In the process, we participate in constructing a particular version of reality. For instance, if an incorrigible proposition for you is that women are inherently less aggressive than men, seeing an especially violent woman might lead you toward explanations that focus on the peculiar characteristics of *this particular* woman. Maybe *she's* responding to terrible circumstances in her life; maybe *she* has some kind of chemical imbalance or neurological disorder. By concluding that she is an exception to the rule, the rule is maintained.

In 2011, some evangelical Christians claimed that on May 21 of that year, God would send devastating earthquakes and begin a process that in 5 months would destroy the world. Believers would be spared and raised to heaven in "the rapture." When dooms-day didn't materialize and the world still existed on May 22, those who believed in the prophecy provided a variety of rationalizations that allowed them to maintain the original belief. For instance, some pointed to human fallibility: "I don't know where we went wrong other than that we obviously don't understand Scriptures in the way that we should" (quoted in Hagerty, 2011, p. 1). Others argued that May 21 only marked the beginning of a 5-month countdown to the end of the world and that the *real* day to worry about was *October* 21. When that didn't happen either, some claimed that the prayers of the believers actually worked and that God delayed judgment so that more people could be saved.

HUGH MEHAN AND HOUSTON WOOD

THE INFALLIBLE ORACLE

Sociologists Hugh Mehan and Houston Wood (1975) fur-thered our understanding of incorrigible propositions by examining the research of the anthropologist E. E. Evans-Pritchard (1937). Evans-Pritchard described an elaborate ritual practiced by the Azande, a small African society located in southwestern Sudan. When faced with important decisions—where to build a house, whom to marry, and so on—the Azande consulted an oracle, or a powerful spirit. They prepared for the consultation by following a strictly prescribed ceremony. A substance was extracted from the bark of a certain type of tree and prepared in a special way during a séance-like ritual. The Azande believed that a powerful spirit would enter the potion during this ceremony. They then posed a ques-tion to the spirit in such a way that it could be answered either yes or no and fed the substance to a chicken. If the chicken lived, they would interpret the answer from the spirit as yes; if the chicken died, the answer was no.

Our Western belief system tells us the tree bark obviously contains some poisonous chemical. Certain chickens are physically able to survive it, others aren't. But the Azande had no knowledge of the bark's poisonous qualities or of chicken physiology. In fact, they didn't believe the tree or the chicken played a part in the ceremony at all. The ritual of gathering bark and feeding it to a chicken transformed the tree into the spirit power (not unlike how consecrated bread and wine become the body and blood of Christ in the Roman Catholic Eucharist). The chicken lived or died not because of a physical reaction to a chemical but because the oracle "hears like a person and settles cases like a king" (Evans-Pritchard, 1937, p. 321).

But what if the oracle was wrong? What if an Azande was told by the oracle to build a house by the river and the river overflowed its banks, washing away the house? How could they reconcile these sorts of incon-sistencies with a belief in the infallibility of the oracle?

To us, the answer is obvious: There was no spirit, no magic, just the strength of the poison and the fitness of the chickens it was fed to. We see these bad decisions as contradictions, because we view them from the reality of Western science. We observe this ritual to determine if in fact there is an oracle, and of course we're predisposed to believe there isn't. We are looking for proof of the exis-tence of something of which we are highly skeptical.

For the Azande, though, the contradictions were not contradictions at all. They knew the oracle existed. This was their fundamental premise, their incorrigible proposition. It was an article of faith that could not be questioned. All that followed for the Azande was experienced from this initial assumption, and they had ways of explaining contradictions to their truths, just as we do. When the oracle failed to give them proper advice, they would say things like, "A taboo must have been breached" or "Sorcerers must have intervened" or "The ceremony wasn't carried out correctly."

Protecting incorrigible propositions is essential for the maintenance of reality systems. By explaining away contradictions, we are able to support our basic assumptions and live in a coherent and orderly world.

Building the Walls: Conflict, Power, and Social Institutions

We, as individuals, play an important role in coordinating, reproducing, and giving meaning to society in our daily interactions. But we are certainly not completely free to create whatever version of social reality we want to create. We are, after all, born into a preexisting society with its norms, values, roles, relationships, groups, organizations, and institutions. Just as the walls of a building constrain the ability of the inhabitants to move about, directing them through certain predetermined doorways and corridors, these features of society influence our thoughts and deeds and consequently constrain our ability to freely construct our social world (Giddens, 1984). As Karl Marx (1869/1963) wrote, "[People] make their own history, but they do not make it just as they please; they do not make it under circumstances chosen by themselves, but under circumstances directly encountered, given and transmitted from the past" (p. 15).

As the conflict perspective points out, certain people or groups of people can be more influential in defining reality than others. In any modern society, where socioeconomic classes, ethnic and religious groups, age groups, and political interests struggle for control over resources, there is also a struggle for the power to determine or influence that society's conception of reality (Gans, 1971). Those who emerge successful gain control over information, define values, create myths, manipulate events, and influence what the rest of us take for granted. Conflict theorists therefore argue that people with more power, prestige, status, wealth, and access to high-level policymakers can turn their perceptions of the world into the entire culture's perception. In other words, "He who has the bigger stick has the better chance of imposing his definitions of reality" (P. L. Berger & Luckmann, 1966, p. 109). That "bigger stick" can be wielded in several ways. Powerful social institutions and the people who control them play a significant role in shaping and sustaining perceptions of reality for everybody else. But if you wish to develop the sociological imagination, you need to understand the role of not only these larger forces in shaping private lives but also private individuals who struggle to shape public reality.

The Economics of Reality

Definitions of reality frequently reflect underlying economic interests. Consider, for instance, the story of a once-successful painter named Marla Olmstead. In the mid-2000s, art critics began to compare Marla's paintings—in both style and spirit—with the work of master artists like Jackson Pollock, Pablo Picasso, and Claude Monet. They sold for thousands of dollars apiece and appeared in some of New York's finest art galleries. One gallery owner thought that each of her paintings could easily have sold for $50,000 (Marla Olmstead, 2004). Many art critics described her pieces as rhythmic, beautiful, and magical. She was featured on *Today* and *60 Minutes* as well as in the *New York Times* and *Time* magazine. Marla garnered all this attention not because of the quality of her work alone but because of who she was at the time. When she first burst onto the artistic scene a decade ago, Marla was 4 years old—and she'd already been "painting" for 2 years.

At that young age, Marla used bright acrylic paints, which she splattered and scraped on large 36-square-foot canvases. She sometimes worked on one piece for days at a time, and her parents never knew exactly when she was done. When she decided she'd finished, she gave her paintings titles, printed her name at the bottom, and went on to a more typical interest for a young girl: a TV show, a doll, a swim in the pool.

While some critics doubted whether she was solely responsible for her work (in 2007, she was the subject of a skeptical documentary called *My Kid Could Paint That*), there's no doubt that she was a force in the art world. But was Marla's early work the expression of a creative, visionary prodigy, or was it the result of a child playing around with paint? Such a question is not trivial. It reflects a deeper issue regarding the role of economics in shaping the way social reality is defined.

The key concerns from the conflict perspective are who benefits economically and who loses from dominant versions of reality. Take mental illness, for example. The number of problems officially defined by the American Psychiatric Association (APA) as mental disorders and defects has now reached nearly 400 (Horwitz, 2002). In defining what constitutes a mental disorder, the APA unwittingly reflects the economic organization of U.S. society. In the United States, individuals seldom pay the total costs of health care services out of their own pockets. Most of the money for medical treatment comes from the federal and state governments or from private insurance companies. Only if problems such as gambling, depression, anorexia, and cocaine addiction are formally defined as illnesses is their treatment eligible for medical insurance coverage. In 2010, the U.S. Department of Veterans Affairs changed its definition of posttraumatic stress disorder, making it substantially easier for hundreds of thousands of veterans to receive compensatory benefits. Posttraumatic stress disorder is a condition characterized by emotional numbness, irritability, and flashbacks following the experience or observation of some traumatic event. In the past, only soldiers who had been in combat and who could document specific firefights, bomb blasts, or mortar attacks qualified for benefits. Under the new rule, veterans only have to prove they served in a war zone and in a job consistent with the events they say caused their condition. The rule also allows compensation for service members who have a good reason to fear traumatic events even if they didn't experience them firsthand. It's estimated that this new rule has cost the government in the range of $5 billion in treatment costs (Dao, 2010b).

Another example of how economics affects the social construction of reality is our society's history of attempts to protect people with disabilities. Over 39.6 million adults and children in the United States have some type of disability (ProQuest Statistical Abstract, 2017). The 1990 Americans with Disabilities Act (ADA) defines disability as a physical or mental impairment that substantially limits one or more of the major life activities of such individuals (U.S. Department of Justice, 2010). Under this law, employers are required to accommodate employees who have a documented disability and are forbidden to fire them simply because of their disability. For instance, a company that has wheelchair-bound employees must have ramps or elevators that give these workers access to all areas of the building. Ironically, the added cost of employing disabled workers may actually work to their disadvantage by making them less attractive to potential hirers in the first place. One study found an 11% drop in the employment rate of people with disabilities after the ADA was enacted (DeLeire, 2000). Moreover, highly publicized stories of employees with questionable disabilities seeking accommodations—for example, an office worker allergic to perfume demanding that his employer install an expensive new air filtration system—give the impression that the ADA is placing an excessive economic burden on companies. Although powerful businesses and industries were not able to prevent this act from being passed in the first place, they have been able to create a reality that still works in their interest.

The Politics of Reality

The institution of politics is also linked to societal definitions of reality. To a great extent, politics is about controlling public perceptions so people will do things or think about issues in ways that political leaders want them to. During important political campaigns, we can see such attempts to influence public perception. Mudslinging, euphemistically called "negative campaigning," has become as common an element of the U.S. electoral process as speeches, debates, baby kissing, and patriotic songs.

VISUAL ESSAY—WHAT IS ART?

Jean-Louis Atlan/Paris Match via Getty Images

Jean-Louis Atlan/Paris Match via Getty Images

AP Photo/Kevin Rivoli

© Everett Collection/Alamy

In this chapter, we've been exploring how people collectively construct reality. Most of the time, we agree with others about what's real and what isn't; other times, though, these definitions conflict. That's important to know because how we ultimately define things can have enormously important consequences—personally, socially, politically . . . and even financially. On this page, you can see some images of Marla Olmstead, back when she was the 4-year-old little girl who took the art world by storm with her vivid paintings.

To some people, these works are just the random doodles of a 4-year-old; to others, they are masterpieces of an artistic genius. What do you think? What or who should determine what counts as art and who gets to be called an artist? Several years ago, a New York performance artist gave birth to her son during a live public exhibition and invited the audience to witness the labor. Was this art?

The investors and collectors who paid thousands of dollars for each of Marla's paintings clearly have a continuing stake in the pieces being defined as art. But what if she had never come to their attention and never sold a single painting? For something to be considered art, does it have to have some economic exchange value? Think of all the thousands of struggling artists who never sell anything their entire lives. How do you think they felt about Marla's instant and apparently effortless success? Would they have been less inclined to define her as an "artist" than the investors who bought her work? Marla is now an ordinary high school student, with interests in science, music, and sports. She has no desire to become a professional painter. In fact, she hasn't had a major showing of her work since 2013 (Basler, 2015). Does that change the value of the paintings she produced at age 4? In other words, does someone have to be a "career artist" for her or his work to retain its market value?

Most politicians know that if you say something untrue or unsubstantiated about an issue or opponent often enough, people will believe it. The actual validity of claims becomes irrelevant as accusations are transformed into "fact" and become solidified in the minds of the voting public. The problem has become so acute that most news organizations employ full-time "fact checkers" to monitor the accuracy of what major U.S. politicians say in advertisements, debates, speeches, interviews, and news releases. In fact, while companies that sell consumer products must meet some standard of accuracy in their advertising, there are no federal truth-in-advertising laws for political campaign ads. To put it bluntly, candidates have the legal right to lie ("Bunk Busters," 2007).

Ironically, constant public denials of bogus charges often reinforce their reality and keep them in the news. In 2011, President Obama was forced to hold a news conference and present his birth certificate because the false claims that he isn't a U.S. citizen—which first arose during the 2008 election campaign—wouldn't go away. Even when Donald Trump—the highest profile advocate of the claim that Obama was not an American citizen—"admitted" in a 2016 news conference that Obama was born in this country, over 40% of Republicans continued to believe that he wasn't (Durkin, 2016).

When the lives of thousands of citizens are at stake and public opinion is crucial, information control becomes particularly tight. Between September 2001 and the invasion of Iraq in March 2003, the Bush administration worked diligently to foster a belief that Iraq and its then dictator, Saddam Hussein, played a direct role in the September 11 attacks and had stockpiles of weapons of mass destruction. They were quite successful. Immediately after the attacks, national opinion polls showed that only 3% of Americans mentioned Iraq or Saddam Hussein when asked who was responsible. But by January 2003, 44% of Americans reported that either "most" or "some" of the hijackers were Iraqi citizens. In fact, none were (Feldmann, Marlantes, & Bowers, 2003). Two years after the attacks, 69% of Americans said in a *Washington Post* poll that they thought it at least likely that Hussein was involved in the attacks, even though the link between Iraq and al-Qaeda was never established (Milbank & Deane, 2003). Nevertheless, these beliefs provided the kind of public support necessary to justify the military invasion and occupation of Iraq. In 2008, the Center for Public Integrity (2008) concluded that the administration had made close to 1,000 false public statements on either the existence of weapons of mass destruction or the link between al-Qaeda and Iraq. Such a molding of public perception is accomplished most notably through the media.

The Medium Is the Message

Communication media are the primary means by which we are entertained and informed about the world around us (see Chapter 5). But the messages we receive from the media also reflect dominant cultural values (Gitlin, 1979). In television shows and other works of fiction, the way characters are portrayed, the topics addressed, and the solutions imposed on problems all link entertainment to the economic system and prevailing societal tastes in consumption.

The media are also our primary source of information about local, national, and international events and people. News broadcasts, newspapers, and online news outlets tell us about things we cannot experience directly, making the most remote events meaningful (Molotch & Lester, 1974). The way we look at the world and define our lives within it is therefore shaped and influenced by what we see on Internet news sites, watch on TV news shows, hear on the radio, or read in our daily papers.

Because the news is the means by which political realities are disseminated to the public, it is an essential tool in maintaining social order (Hallin, 1986; Parenti, 1986). In many societies, news sources don't even try to hide the fact that they are mouthpieces of one faction or another. In repressive societies, the only news sources allowed to operate are those representing the government. In North Korea, for instance, the flow of news information is clearly controlled by the government. People who live in societies with a cultural tradition of press independence, in contrast, assume that news stories are purely factual—an accurate, objective reflection of the "world out there" (Molotch & Lester, 1975). However, one only needs to compare the coverage of political events on right-leaning networks like Fox News to left-leaning networks like MSNBC to conclude that, like everything else, news is a constructed reality.

Hundreds, perhaps thousands, of potentially newsworthy events occur every day. Yet we'll see maybe 10 of them on our favorite evening broadcast or the home page of our favorite online news service. These events exist as news not because of their inherent importance but because of the practical, political, or economic purposes they serve. The old newsroom adage "If it bleeds, it leads" attests to the fact that events with shocking details—which appeal to the public's fondness for the sensational—are those most likely to be chosen. At its most independent, the news is still the product of decisions made by reporters, editors, network executives, and corporation owners, all of whom have their own interests, biases, and values (Molotch & Lester, 1974).

The manipulation of events for political gain is such an ordinary part of the cultural landscape that it's become institutionalized with its own term: *spin*. To put a spin on an event is to give it a particular interpretation, often one that is to the speaker's advantage. Spin is a valuable political resource. Every U.S. president, whether Republican or Democrat, has staff members who spin the facts to put his policies in the best possible light, often by withholding information from the public, fudging statistics, issuing nondenial denials, or exaggerating the progress or benefits of particular actions and policies (Stolberg, 2004). Spin has become a profession in its own right. Immediately following a televised presidential debate, for instance, a gaggle of trained supporters (the "spin doctors") for the candidates situate themselves in a specified area—called "spin alley"— where they creatively provide television viewers with a version of the outcome that benefits their candidate. Top aides and party officials are dispatched to various blogs, cable news programs, and local news studios to sing their candidate's praises and accuse the opponent of lies and misstatements. Sometimes it's clear that the spin has little connection to reality. During the 2016 campaign, the Republican National Committee released blogs declaring that Mike Pence had "clearly won" the vice presidential debate against Tim Kaine. Now that's not surprising. What was surprising was that this statement was released hours *before* the debate actually took place.

Although "freedom of expression" and "freedom of the press" are core American values, media manipulation of information has been not only tolerated but encouraged in some situations. Take the coverage of the military actions in Iraq and Afghanistan following the attacks of September 11, 2001. During the initial stages of the war, press coverage seemed to be relatively open. The Pentagon allowed hundreds of "embedded" reporters to accompany fighting forces and transmit their stories from the front battle lines. According to one study, 61% of their reports during the first 3 days of the war were live and unedited (Project for Excellence in Journalism, 2005). By granting such unprecedented access, Pentagon officials hoped that these reporters would convey the "heroism and hard work" of American soldiers to a worldwide audience and in the process discredit Iraqi propaganda (Getlin & Wilkinson, 2003).

But even then, some media critics were concerned that the reporters were tools of the military, especially given their often close attachment to the soldiers with whom they were traveling. The Pentagon required embedded journalists to sign a contract giving the military control over the content of their stories (Jamail, 2007). According to one study, 80% of embedded reports included no commentary at all from soldiers (Project for Excellence in Journalism, 2005).

For everyday news stories, even in societies that restrict the press, official censorship is usually unnecessary. Because of the economic pressures to attract audiences and keep their attention, TV networks and newspapers usually censor themselves (Bagdikian, 1991). Reporters pursue stories that are relatively easy to research and that have immediate interest for audiences. Less exciting, more complicated stories don't get enough journalistic resources or are cut in the editing process. We usually have no way of knowing which events have *not* been selected for inclusion in the day's news or which plausible alternatives are kept out of the public eye.

The economic and political motivation for such selectivity becomes apparent when we consider who owns the media. In 1983, 50 companies controlled 90% of all U.S. media outlets. Today, just six companies—Comcast, Disney, News Corp, Time Warner, Viacom, and CBS—own 90% of all national TV, radio, cable, print, and Internet outlets, concentrating control over what we see, hear, and read (Lutz, 2012). At the local level, four companies—Sinclair, Nexstar, Tribune, and Gannett—own 341 TV stations in 93% of all U.S. media markets (Free Press, 2016).

Many media observers fear that the concentration of corporate-owned news outlets twists certain stories to promote particular economic or political interests. In recent years, media owners have refused to run advertisements, stories, or commentaries that supported single-payer health insurance, criticized U.S. military intervention, or opposed certain international trade agreements. Television and print journalists have been fired, forced to resign, or reassigned for presenting stories critical of subsidiaries owned by the parent company (Parenti, 2006).

As the viewing and listening public, our recourse is difficult. To criticize faulty government policies and consider solutions to difficult social problems, we need solid information, which is frequently unavailable or difficult to obtain. The growth in popularity of podcasting, blogs, Internet Protocol television, live stream radio stations, and subscription satellite networks may be a sign that some citizens have grown weary of the filtered and sometimes partisan information they receive from traditional news sources. Indeed, trust of the news media has reached an all-time low (Swift, 2016), which may explain why so many people now turn to deliberately fake news/comedy shows like *The Daily Show, Full Frontal, The Onion,* and *Last Week Tonight* to keep abreast of national and world events.

So the challenge we face in our own private lives is to recognize the processes at work in the social construction of reality and to take them into account as we "consume" the news. A critical dimension of the sociological imagination is the ability to "read silences"—to be attentive to what the mass media *don't* say. Fortunately, one of the purposes of sociology is to scientifically amass a body of knowledge that we can use to assess how our society really works.

Moral Entrepreneurs

Individual efforts to control the construction of reality are difficult. But we are not consigned to meekly accept the reality presented to us by powerful organizations and institutions. Individuals banding together in interest groups have managed time and again to contribute to the construction of social reality. For instance, they have created new understandings of the rights of ethnoracial minorities, brought environmental degradation to the public's attention, and changed our attitudes toward particular social problems.

Although economic and political power have been the motivating concerns of many of these groups, certain people have had moral concerns they passionately want translated into law. Groups that seek to outlaw or increase the punishment for such things as pornography, drunk driving, abortion, and gambling, as well as groups that promote gun control, literacy, awareness of domestic violence, and support for AIDS research, are crusading for the creation of a new public conception of morality. These **moral entrepreneurs** (Becker, 1963) need not be wealthy or influential individuals. Instead, by virtue of their initiative, access to decision makers, skillful use of publicity and public relations, and success in neutralizing any opposing viewpoints, they are able to turn their interests into public policy (Hills, 1980). For instance, in 2015, a Maine woman embarked on a nationwide, 60-day road trip to call attention to the public safety problem caused by elderly people driving. She met with legislators, volunteer organizations, doctors, and even groups of elderly people to share the story of her son, who was run over by an 84-year-old driver (Washuk, 2015).

Sometimes groups seek to convince the public that a phenomenon that is currently a crime ought not be. For instance, people trying to convince legislators to legalize the use of marijuana for medicinal purposes have shown moderate success by emphasizing the medical properties of marijuana (pain or nausea relief) and disregarding the psychoactive effects associated with its recreational use (getting "high"). Indeed, many avoid the term *marijuana* entirely, opting instead for the more scientific-sounding *cannabis* (Chapkis, 2010).

Appreciating the Contributions of Sociological Research

Up to this point, I've been describing how individuals, groups, organizations, and various social institutions go about constructing reality. We've seen that these realities sometimes shift with time, place, and individual perception. Faced with this type of fluctuation, sociologists, as well as scholars in other disciplines, seek to identify a more "real" reality through systematic, controlled research. The rules sociologists abide by when conducting research give them confidence that they are identifying more than just a personal version of reality. They hope to determine a reality as it exists for a community of people at a particular point in time.

Moving beyond the level of individual conclusions about the nature of social reality is crucial if we are to escape the distortions of personal interests and biases. A danger of relying solely on individual perceptions is that we are likely to conclude that what we experience is what everyone experiences. For example, the famous psychiatrist Sigmund Freud used his own childhood as the ultimate "proof" of the controversial concept called the Oedipus complex (the belief that sons are secretly in love with their mothers and jealous of their fathers). He wrote to a friend in 1897, "I have found, in my own case too, being in love with the mother and jealous of the father, and I now consider it a universal event of early childhood" (quoted in Astbury, 1996, p. 73).

To avoid the risk of such overgeneralizations, sociologists try to determine what most people believe or how most people behave. But in doing so, they sometimes run the risk of simply restating what people already know. Indeed, a criticism of sociology you hear from time to time is that it is just a fancy version of common sense. A lot of the things that we think are obvious based on our personal observations, however, turn out not to be so straightforward under the closer scrutiny of social research. Consider the following "commonsense facts":

- Violent crimes like rape, assault, and murder occur most often between total strangers.

- Because of the high divorce rate in the United States, people are reluctant to get married.

- American children today are more likely to live in a single-parent household than they were 100 years ago.

Most of us probably assume these statements are true. Chances are, given what you've seen online or on television, they make a lot of sense. But how accurate are they?

According to the U.S. Bureau of Justice Statistics (Truman & Morgan, 2016), only 36% of all nonlethal violent crimes in the United States are perpetrated by strangers. The FBI (2011) reports that of homicides where the relationships of victims and offenders are known, just 21% occur between strangers. And in 20% of rapes and sexual assaults that involve college-age female victims, the attacker is unknown to the victim (Sinozich & Langton, 2014).

According to the U.S. Bureau of the Census (ProQuest Statistical Abstract, 2017), only 11% of men and 9.5% of women between the ages of 55 and 64 have never been married. In fact, about 40% of marriages in 2013 included at least one person who had been previously married. Forty-two million Americans have been married more than once (Livingston, 2014). Although we are quite willing to end a bad marriage, we still tend to place a high value on the institution of marriage itself.

The percentage of children who don't live with both their parents—about 31% of all children (ProQuest Statistical Abstract, 2017)—is roughly the same as it was a century ago. At that time, life expectancy was much lower than it is today, so it was highly likely that before reaching adulthood a child would lose at least one parent to death (Kain, 1990).

As you can see, sometimes commonsense "facts" don't hold up under the weight of evidence provided by social research.

The Empirical Nature of Sociological Research

Research is all around us. Throughout our lives, we are flooded with statistics that are supposedly the result of scientific studies—which detergents make clothes brighter, which conditioners repair hair better, which dog food tastes best, which wireless providers have the widest 4G coverage, which chewing gum dentists recommend for their gum-chewing patients. Many of the important decisions we make, from purchasing a car to opting for a particular surgical procedure, are supported by some sort of research.

In addition, a significant proportion of our own lives is spent *doing* research. Every time we seek out the opinions of others, gauge the attitude of a group, or draw conclusions about an observed event, we engage in a form of research. Say, for example, you thought your exam scores would improve if you studied with others, so you formed a study group. After the exam, you compared your grade with the grade you received on the previous exam (when you just studied on your own) to see if there was any significant improvement. If there was, you would likely attribute your better performance to the study group. This is the essence of research: You had an idea about some social process, and you went out and tested it to see if you were correct.

Although useful and common, such casual research is fraught with problems. We may make inaccurate or selective observations, overgeneralize on the basis of a limited number of observations, or draw conclusions that protect our own interests (Babbie, 1992). Maybe your exam score would have improved even without the study group because you had a better understanding of the material this time and had a better sense of what the instructor expected.

Sociological research, which is a much more sophisticated and structured form of the sort of individual inquiry we use every day, can avoid some of these pitfalls. Of course, sociological researchers are human beings, and they too make errors in observation, generalization, and analysis. But they have a greater chance of avoiding these errors because, first and foremost, sociological research is an empirical endeavor. **Empirical research** operates on the assumption that answers to questions about human behavior can be ascertained through controlled, systematic observations in the real world. Individuals can reach naïve conclusions based on their personal impressions of what happens in society. Great scholars can spend years thinking about human life and developing logical explanations about particular social phenomena. But for most sociologists, the strength of an explanation depends on how much empirical support it has.

Another characteristic of sociological research that makes it a better reflection of social reality than individual inquiry is that it is **probabilistic**. Instead of making absolute predictions, most sociologists prefer to state that under certain conditions, particular phenomena are likely to occur. In other words, human behavior operates within the laws of probability. Whenever sociologists set out to find the reasons, say, for why people hold prejudiced beliefs or why some countries have a higher birth rate than others, they are searching for the factors that would explain these phenomena most but not all of the time. For instance, adults with less than a high school education are more likely than adults with college degrees to be prejudiced against members of other ethnoracial groups. But that doesn't mean that every single high school dropout is a bigot or that every person with a PhD embraces those who are ethnically or racially different. By focusing on the probability of some phenomenon occurring while at the same time allowing for exceptions and variations, sociologists provide a view of reality that simultaneously reflects the way things are and the way they can be.

Qualitative and Quantitative Research

In contrast to the casual way we carry out our personal research, sociologists seek to define reality through a careful process of collecting information and answering questions. Some sociologists collect nonnumeric information (text, written words, phrases, symbols, observations) that describes people, actions, or events in social life (called **qualitative research**; Neuman, 1994). Others collect numeric data and rely on precise statistical analysis (called **quantitative research**). And some use a combination of both.

Qualitative researchers often go out and observe people and events as they happen in society. For instance, qualitative researchers interested in how additional children affect parents' ability to balance the demands of work and home may spend an entire day with a family, listening, observing, and asking questions. Once they've collected enough information, they go about interpreting their observations, looking for identifiable patterns in people's everyday lives.

Quantitative sociological researchers methodically record observations across a variety of situations; they design and choose questions in advance and ask them in a consistent way of a large number of people; they use sophisticated techniques to ensure that the characteristics of the people in a study are similar to those of the population at large; and they use computers to generate statistics from which confident conclusions can be drawn.

Both kinds of sociological research are subjected to the scrutiny of peers, who will point out any mistakes and shortcomings. Researchers are obligated to report not only their results but also the methods they used to record observations or collect data and the conditions surrounding the study. Such detailed explanations allow other researchers to *replicate* a study—that is, to perform it themselves to see if the same results are obtained. The more a particular research result is replicated, the greater its acceptance as fact in the academic community. For instance, in 2013, a study in the journal *Science* reported that the more literary fiction people read, the greater their ability to interpret the facial expressions and emotional states of others (Kidd & Castano, 2013). However, subsequent studies failed to replicate these results, thereby casting doubt on the original researchers' contention that the world would be a better place if we simply read more fiction (J. Frankel, 2016).

Theories, Variables, and Hypotheses

Whether qualitative or quantitative, social research is purposeful. Unlike personal research, which may be motivated by a hunch, whim, or immediate need, most social research is guided by a particular theory. A **theory** is a set of statements or propositions that seeks to explain or predict a particular aspect of social life (Chafetz, 1978). Theory does not, as is popularly thought, mean conjecture or speculation. Ideally, theories explain the way things are, not the way they ought to be.

Research and theory closely depend on each other. Research without any underlying theoretical reasoning is simply a string of meaningless bits of information (C. W. Mills, 1959); theory without research is abstract and speculative.

Some theories—such as structural functionalism, the conflict perspective, and symbolic interactionism—are quite broad, seeking to explain why social order exists or how societies work overall. Other theories are more modest, seeking to explain more narrowly certain behaviors among specific groups of people. For example, Travis Hirschi (1969) developed a theory of juvenile delinquency called "social control theory," in which he argued that delinquent acts occur when an individual's bond to society is weak or broken. These bonds are derived from a person's attachments to others who obey the law, the rewards a person gains by acting nondelinquently (commitments), the amount of time a person engages in nondelinquent activity (involvements), and the degree to which a person is tied to society's conventional belief system.

To test theories, sociologists must translate abstract propositions into testable hypotheses. A **hypothesis** is a researchable prediction that specifies the relationship between two or more **variables**. A variable is any characteristic, attitude, behavior, or event that can take on two or more values or attributes. For example, the variable "marital status" has several categories: never married, cohabiting, married, separated, divorced, widowed. The variable "attitudes toward capital punishment" has categories ranging from "strongly in favor" to "strongly oppose."

Hirschi was interested in why juveniles engage in delinquent behavior. Such a question is far too general to study empirically, so he developed a clear, specific, empirically testable prediction, or hypothesis, specifying a relationship between two variables: Strong "social bonds" will be associated with low levels of "delinquency."

In developing their hypotheses, sociologists distinguish between independent and dependent variables. The **independent variable** is the factor presumed to influence or create changes in another variable. The **dependent variable** is the one assumed to depend on, be influenced by, or change as a result of the change in the independent variable. If we believe that gender affects people's attitudes toward capital punishment, then "gender" would be the independent variable influencing "attitudes toward capital punishment," the dependent variable. For Hirschi's theory of juvenile delinquency, the strength of the social bond was the independent variable, and level of delinquency was the dependent variable.

The assumption behind most research that tests a hypothesis is that the independent variable *causes* changes to occur in the dependent variable—for instance, that a weak social bond *causes* a young person to become delinquent. But just because two variables seem to be related doesn't necessarily mean a causal relationship exists.

In fact, the two variables may not be related at all but merely seem to be associated with each other due to the effect of some third variable. Sociologists call such misleading relationships spurious. A classic example of a **spurious relationship** is the apparent association between children's shoe size and reading ability. It seems that as shoe size increases, reading ability improves (Babbie, 2007). Does this mean that the size of one's feet (independent variable) *causes* an improvement in reading skills (dependent variable)? Certainly not. This illusory relationship is caused by a third factor, age, that is related to shoe size (older kids have bigger feet) as well as reading ability (older kids can read better than younger kids). Hence, when researchers attempt to make causal claims about the relationship between an independent and a dependent variable, they must control for—or rule out—other variables that may be creating a spurious relationship. Can you think of a third variable that might strengthen or weaken a person's social bond *and* influence his or her tendency toward delinquent behavior?

Aside from concern with spuriousness, quantitative social researchers, like Hirschi, face the problem that many of the concepts that form the basis of theories are abstract and not easy to observe or measure empirically. We can't directly see concepts such as "attachments" or "commitments." So they must be translated into **indicators**: events, characteristics, or behaviors that can be observed or quantified.

In his survey of 1,200 boys in Grades 6 through 12, Hirschi derived a set of indicators for his independent variable, the strength of the social bond. To determine young people's attachments to law-abiding others, Hirschi measured their attraction to parents, peers, and school officials. To determine the degree to which they derived rewards from acting nondelinquently (commitment), he asked them to assess the importance of things such as getting good grades. To determine the proportion of their lives spent in conventional activities (involvement), he asked them how much time they spent in school-oriented activities. Finally, to determine their ties to a conventional belief system, he asked them questions about their respect for the law and the police.

Hirschi measured the dependent variable, delinquent activity, by asking the boys if they'd ever stolen things, taken cars for rides without the owner's permission, banged up something on purpose that belonged to somebody else, or beaten up or hurt someone on purpose. In addition, he used school records and police records to measure delinquent acts that had come to the attention of authorities.

The empirical data he collected supported his hypothesis. The boys who indicated close attachments to their parents and peers, who got good grades, who were involved in lots of school-related activities, and who had high levels of respect for the law were the boys who didn't get into trouble. Hirschi was therefore able to use these results to strengthen the power of his original theory.

Modes of Research

Although the answers to important sociological questions are not always simple or clear, the techniques sociologists use to collect and examine data allow them to draw informed and reliable conclusions about human behavior and social life. The most common techniques are experiments, field research, surveys, and unobtrusive research.

Experiments

An **experiment** is typically a research technique designed to elicit some sort of behavior under closely controlled laboratory circumstances. In its ideal form, the experimenter randomly places participants into two groups, then deliberately manipulates or introduces changes into the environment of one group of participants (called the experimental group) and not the other (called the control group). Care is taken to ensure that the groups are relatively alike except for the variable that the experimenter manipulates. Any observed or measured differences between the groups can then be attributed to the effects of the experimental manipulation.

Experiments have a significant advantage over other types of research because the researcher can directly control all the relevant variables. Thus, conclusions about the independent variable causing changes in the dependent variable can be made more convincingly. The artificial nature of most laboratory experiments, however, may make subjects behave differently than the way they would in their natural settings, leading some people to argue that laboratory experimentation in sociology is practically impossible (Silverman, 1982).

To overcome this difficulty, some sociologists have created experimental situations outside the laboratory. Arthur Beaman and his colleagues (Beaman, Klentz, Diener, & Svanum, 1979) conducted an experiment to see whether self-awareness decreases the likelihood of engaging in socially undesirable behavior—in this case, stealing. The researchers set up situations in which children arriving at several homes on Halloween night were sent into the living room alone to take candy from a bowl. The children were first asked their names and ages and then told, "You may take only one of the candies." For the experimental group, a large mirror was placed right next to the candy bowl so that the children couldn't help but see themselves. For the control group, there was no mirror. In the control group, 37% of the children took more than one candy, but only 4% of the children in the experimental group took more than one candy. The researchers concluded from this experiment that self-awareness—brought about by seeing one's reflection in a mirror—can significantly reduce dishonesty.

Experimental research outside the laboratory can also be used to inform public policy. In 2010, the City of New York embarked on a multi-year experimental test of the effectiveness of its 6-year-old homelessness prevention program, a $23 million endeavor called Homebase. Half of the test subjects—people who are unable to pay their rent and therefore risk eviction—are being denied assistance from the program as researchers observe them to see if they become homeless. The other half receive the program's regular assistance services, including tenant–landlord mediation, emergency rental assistance, and job training (Buckley, 2010). The city hopes to determine if the program's intervention actually makes a difference in reducing the number of homeless. But some public officials have denounced the experiment as unnecessarily cruel.

Field Research

In **field research**, qualitative sociologists observe events as they actually occur, without selecting experimental and control groups or purposely introducing any changes into the subjects' environment. Field research can take several forms. In **nonparticipant observation**, the researcher observes people without directly interacting with them and without their knowing that they are being observed. Sociologist Lyn Lofland (1973), for example, studied how strangers relate to one another in public places by going to bus depots, airports, stores, restaurants, and parks and secretly recording everything she saw.

Participant observation requires that the researcher interact with subjects. In some cases, the researcher openly identifies herself or himself. For instance, to gain insight into how people balance work and family, sociologist Arlie Russell Hochschild (1997) observed employees over a period of 3 years at a large public relations company she called Amerco. She was particularly interested in why employees tend not to take advantage of available family leave policies. At Amerco, only 53 of 21,000 employees—all of them women—chose to switch to part-time work in response to the arrival of a new baby. Less than 1% of the employees shared a job or worked at home, even though the company permits it. Most of the workers worked a lot of overtime, coming in early and staying late. So why were these workers so unwilling to change their work lives to spend more time with their families even when the company would have supported them in doing so? Through her long-term observations of Amerco, Hochschild came to the conclusion that work has become a form of "home" and home has become "work." For many people at Amerco, home had become a place of frenzied activity and busy schedules, whereas work had become a sort of nurturing refuge where they could relax and share stories with friends. So they actually preferred spending more time at work.

This type of qualitative field research can be quite time consuming. Researchers can conduct only a limited number of interviews and can observe only a limited number of people and events. Hochschild collected rich information about people's work–family trade-offs, but she could study only one corporation. It's risky to generalize from the experiences of a small group of workers in one company in one society to all workers in all sorts of work environments.

In more delicate situations where the people being studied don't want their actions made public, the researcher may have to conceal his or her identity in order to gather accurate information. For instance, researchers have gone "undercover" to study everything from doomsday cults (Festinger, Riecken, & Schacter, 1956) to college sororities (Robbins, 2004). Sociologist Julia O'Connell Davidson (2002) wanted to examine the issue of power and control in the relationships between prostitutes and their clients. To study this topic, she posed as a "receptionist" for a prostitute she called "Desiree," fielding phone calls and supervising the "waiting room" for the clients who had arrived to see Desiree. While Desiree knew O'Connell Davidson was a sociologist, the clients did not. If these men knew they were being studied, they might have altered their conversations and behaviors to cover up potentially damaging information.

Surveys

When it is impossible or impractical to carry out field observations or to set up a controlled experimental situation, social researchers use the survey method. **Surveys** require that the researcher pose a series of questions to respondents orally, electronically, or on paper. The questions should be sufficiently clear so they are understood by the respondent the way the researcher wants them to be understood and measure what the researcher wants them to measure. In addition, the respondent is expected to answer the questions honestly and thoughtfully. The answers are often recorded in numerical form so they can be statistically analyzed.

All of us have experienced surveys of one form or another. Every 10 years, people who live in the United States are required to fill out questionnaires for the U.S. Census Bureau. You've probably filled out an evaluation form at the end of a college course. Or perhaps you've been interviewed in a shopping mall or have received an e-mail or text asking you to respond to a "brief survey" about a particular product or service.

Surveys typically use standardized formats. All subjects are asked the same questions in the same way, and large samples of people are used as subjects. One survey that has provided the basis for much sociological research on families is the National Survey of Families and Households. First conducted in the late 1980s, it includes information derived from interviews with over 13,000 respondents. A second wave of the survey, conducted between 1992 and 1994, and a third wave between 2001 and 2003 included interviews with surviving members of the original sample. The sample covers a diverse array of households, including single-parent families, families with stepchildren, cohabiting couples, and recently married persons. A great deal of family information was collected from each respondent, including family arrangements in childhood, dating experiences, experiences of leaving home, marital and cohabitation experiences, details of contact with kin, and data on economic well-being, as well as education, childbearing, and employment histories. Some of the research discussed in this book is based on analyses of data collected from this survey.

When sociologists Philip Blumstein and Pepper Schwartz (1983) undertook a massive study of intimate couples in the United States, they sent questionnaires to people from every income level, age group, religion, political ideology, and educational background. Some of their respondents were cohabiting; others were married. Some had children; others were childless. Some were heterosexual, others homosexual. All couples filled out a 38-page questionnaire that asked questions about their leisure activities, emotional support, housework, finances, sexual relations, satisfaction, relations with children, and so forth. More than 6,000 couples participated. From these surveys, Blumstein and Schwartz were able to draw conclusions about the importance of money, work, sexuality, power, and gender in couples' lives.

Unobtrusive Research

All the methods I've discussed so far—whether quantitative or qualitative—require the researcher to have some contact with the people being studied: giving them tasks to do in an experiment, watching them (with or without their knowing that they are participating in social research), or asking them questions. But the very act of intruding into people's lives may influence the phenomena being studied. This problem, known as **reactivity**, calls into question the accuracy of the data that are collected, thereby threatening the credibility of the research.

In the late 1920s, an engineer and a time study analyst (Roethlisberger & Dickson, 1939) were hired to study working conditions and worker productivity at an electric company in Hawthorne, Illinois. They were interested in finding out whether changing certain physical conditions in the plant could improve workers' productivity and satisfaction. They quickly discovered that increasing the lighting in the workroom was linked with workers' producing more. Increasing the brightness of the lights again the next day increased productivity even further. To bolster their conclusion, they decided to dim the lights to see if productivity dropped. Much to their dismay, productivity increased again when they darkened the room. They soon realized that the workers were responding more to the attention they were receiving from the researchers than to changes in their working conditions. This phenomenon is known as the "Hawthorne effect."

To avoid such influence, sociologists sometimes use another research technique, unobtrusive research, which requires no contact with people at all. **Unobtrusive research** is an examination of the evidence of social behavior that people create or leave behind. There are several types of unobtrusive research.

Analysis of existing data (also known as secondary data) relies on data gathered earlier by someone else for some other purpose. Émile Durkheim used this technique when he examined different suicide rates for different groups to gain insight into the underlying causes of suicide (see Chapter 1). Analysis of existing data is still used extensively by sociologists today. One of the most popular and convenient sources of data is the U.S. Census. Studies that examine broad, nationwide trends (e.g., marriage, divorce, or premarital childbearing rates) typically use existing census data.

Content analysis is the study of documented communications—books, speeches, poems, song lyrics, television commercials, websites, and so forth. This method is particularly useful for documenting cultural shifts over time. For example, sociologists Bernice

Pescosolido, Elizabeth Grauerholz, and Melissa Milkie (1997) analyzed close to 2,000 children's picture books published from 1937 to 1993 to see if there were any changes in the way African Americans were portrayed. They believed that these depictions could tell a lot about the shifting nature of race relations in the larger society. The researchers looked not only at the number of black characters in these books but also at whether they were portrayed positively or negatively. They found, among other things, that in times of high uncertainty in race relations and substantial protest and conflict over existing societal norms, Blacks virtually disappeared from picture books. Furthermore, depictions of intimate, equal interracial interactions and portrayals of Blacks as primary characters remained rare.

Psychologists Jean Twenge, Keith Campbell, and Brittany Gentile (2012) analyzed the content of American books published between 1960 and 2008 using the Google Books Ngram database. This search engine allows you to assess how often a particular word or phrase appears in the millions of digitized books found in the database. The researchers found that over the span of 48 years, individualistic words and phrases like "personalized," "self," "unique," "I come first," and "I can do it myself" became more common, while words that reflected a more communal orientation, such as "community," "collective," "share," "united," and "common good" became less common. From these data they were able to argue that we are experiencing a shift in language usage reflective of a larger cultural ethos that has been increasingly characterized by a focus on the self and a reduced sense of group identity and responsibility.

Historical analysis relies on existing historical documents as a source of research information. Sociologist Kai Erikson (1966) was interested in how communities construct definitions of acceptable and unacceptable behavior. For his book *Wayward Puritans*, he studied several "crime waves" among the Puritans of the Massachusetts Bay Colony in the late 17th century. Erikson examined court cases, diaries, birth and death records, letters, and other written documents of the period. Piecing together fragments of information 300 years old was not easy, but Erikson was able to draw some conclusions. He found that each time the colony was threatened in some way—by opposing religious groups, betrayals by community leaders, or the king of England's revocation of its charter—the number of convicted criminals and the severity of punishments significantly increased. Erikson believed that these fluctuations occurred because the community needed to restate its moral boundaries and reaffirm its authority.

Visual sociology is a method of studying society through photographs, video recordings, and film. Some visual sociologists use these media to gather sociological data—much as documentary photographers and filmmakers do. The visual images they create are meant to tell a sociological story. Other visual sociologists analyze the meaning and purpose of existing visual texts, such as sports photographs, TV advertisements, and the photographic archives of corporations. The visual essays that appear throughout this book use this methodology to examine important issues of sociological interest.

All these methods allow sociological researchers to collect information without intruding on and possibly changing the behavior of the people and groups they're studying.

The Trustworthiness of Social Research

Most sociologists see research as not only personally valuable but central to improving human knowledge and understanding. However, as consumers of this research, we must always ask, "How accurate is this information?" Sometimes it's difficult to interpret the evidence we come across in scholarly research articles (see Exhibit 3.1). Moreover, because we have a tendency to believe what we read in print or see reported on television or posted on websites, much of what we see may be either inaccurate or misleading. To evaluate the results of social research, we must examine the researcher's samples, the indicators used to measure important variables, and the researcher's personal qualities—namely, values, interests, and ethics.

Samples

Frequently, sociological researchers are interested in the attitudes, behaviors, or characteristics of large groups—college students, women, Instagram subscribers, single parents, and so on. It would be impossible to interview, survey, observe, or experiment on all these people directly. Hence, researchers must select a smaller **sample** of respondents from the larger population. The characteristics of this subgroup are supposed to approximate the characteristics of the entire population of interest. A sample is said to be **representative** if the small group being studied is in fact typical of the population as a whole. For instance, a sample of 100 students from your university should include roughly the same proportion of first-year students, sophomores, juniors, and seniors that characterizes the entire school population. Sampling techniques have become highly sophisticated, as illustrated by the relative accuracy of polls conducted to predict election results.

In the physical sciences, sampling is not such an issue. Certain physical or chemical elements are assumed to be identical. One need only study a small number of vials of liquid nitrogen, because one vial of nitrogen should be the same as any other. Human beings, however, vary widely on every imaginable characteristic. You couldn't make a general statement about all Americans on the basis of an interview with one person. For that matter, you couldn't draw conclusions about all people from observing a sample consisting only of Americans, men, or teenagers. Samples that are not representative can lead to inaccurate and misleading conclusions.

EXHIBIT 3.1 ● Questions to Ask When You Read a Research Article

As you read a piece of published sociological research, you may be more able to assess the value of the research and the results if you ask yourself some questions about the article:

- What is the basic research problem the researcher is investigating?

- Is the research question derived from a particular sociological theory?

- Were any hypotheses stated? How were these hypotheses different from those tested in previous research?

- What type of research was used? Experiment? Survey? Use of existing statistics? Field research? Unobtrusive research?

- What were the independent and dependent variables? Did the author explain how the variables were measured?

- Who were the subjects in the study? How were they selected? Did the author think the sample was representative of the general population?

- What did the research find? How clearly were the statistical results discussed?

- Is there anything else you'd want to know about how the research was carried out that wasn't discussed by the author?

Source: Adapted from Schutt, 2015, Appendix A.

Note the sampling problems revealed in the following letter to the editor of a small-town newspaper in the rural Midwest:

> I went to a restaurant yesterday for lunch. I began to feel guilty, when I reached into my pocket for a cigarette. . . . I was thinking of the government figures which estimated cigarette smokers at 26% of the population of the United States. But everywhere I looked inside that room, people were smoking. I decided to count them. There were 22 people in the room. . . . I was surprised to discover that the government's figures were an outright fabrication. . . . Seventeen people out of the 22 were cigarette smokers. . . . [T]hat accounts for over 77% of the people in that restaurant. . . . The government's figures are understated by 51% and just plain wrong! (*Greencastle Banner Graphic*, 1992)

This letter writer assumed that the 22 people who frequented a small restaurant in a small, relatively poor rural town on a single day were an accurate representation of the entire U.S. population. Such a conclusion overlooks some important factors. Government studies show that the lower a person's income, the greater the likelihood that person will be a smoker. Furthermore, people in blue-collar or service jobs are more likely to smoke than people in white-collar jobs. Finally, the prevalence of smoking tends to be higher in rural areas of the Midwest and South than in other parts of the country (U.S. Department of Health and Human Services, 2006).

MICRO-MACRO CONNECTION
THE WEIRDEST PEOPLE IN THE WORLD

Biased samples can be especially misleading when researchers attempt to make broad statements about human nature. For instance, American undergraduate students make up about two thirds of subjects in all U.S. psychological studies, the topics of which range from visual perceptions to beliefs about fairness and cooperation. However, according to one recent review of such experiments, these subjects are totally unrepresentative of people worldwide. They may be similar to other subjects from societies that are Western, educated, industrialized, rich, and democratic (WEIRD), but not representative of humans at large:

> Sampling from a thin slice of humanity would be less problematic if researchers confined their interpretations to the populations from which they sampled. However, despite their narrow samples, behavioral scientists often are interested in drawing inferences about the *human* mind and *human* behaviour. . . . Leading scientific journals and university textbooks routinely publish research findings claiming to generalize to "humans" or "people" based on research done entirely with WEIRD undergraduates. (Henrich, Heine, & Norenzayan, 2010, p. 63)

In one common experiment on fairness and cooperation in decision making, one subject (the "proposer") in a pair is given a sum of money and told that she or he can offer any portion of it to a second subject (the "responder"), who then decides whether to accept or reject the offer. If the responder accepts the offer, both subjects receive the proposed amount; if the responder rejects the offer, both subjects get nothing. Among WEIRD undergraduate subjects, proposers typically offer about 50% of the original amount and responders tend to reject offers below 30%. From these findings researchers have concluded that humans have a highly evolved sense of justice, leading us to make fair offers and to punish unfair ones, even if it comes at our own expense.

But when this experiment was conducted with subjects drawn from 23 small-scale societies in Africa, the Amazon rain forest, Oceania, Siberia, and Papua New Guinea, proposers made much smaller offers—in some cases, around 25%—and responders usually didn't reject them. In fact, in half of these societies, responders tended to reject offers only when they were *too high* (Henrich et al., 2010). Hence, experiments that utilize samples of WEIRD subjects may be measuring a specific set of social norms that emerge in societies where people regularly deal with money, markets, and strangers and not some universal component of human nature.

Indicators

As you recall, one problem sociologists face when doing research is that the variables they are interested in studying are often difficult to see. What does powerlessness look like? How can you identify marital satisfaction? How would you recognize alienation or social class? Sociologists thus resign themselves to measuring indicators of things that cannot be measured directly. Researchers measure events and behaviors commonly thought to accompany a particular variable, hoping that what they are measuring is a valid indicator of the concept they are interested in.

Suppose you believe that people's attitudes toward abortion are influenced by the strength of their religious beliefs, or "religiosity." You might hypothesize that the stronger a person's religious beliefs, the less accepting he or she will be of abortion rights. To test this hypothesis, you must first figure out what you mean by "religious." What might be an indicator of the strength of someone's religious beliefs? You could determine whether the subjects of your study identify themselves as members of some organized religion. But this indicator might not tell you how religious your subjects are because many people identify themselves as, say, Catholic or Jewish but are not religious at all. Likewise, some people who consider themselves quite religious don't identify with any organized religion. So this measure would focus on group differences but would fail to capture the intensity of a person's beliefs or the degree of religious interest.

Perhaps a better indicator would be some quantifiable behavior, such as the frequency of attendance at formal religious services (Babbie, 1986). Arguably, the more someone attends church, synagogue, or mosque, the more religious that person is. But here, too, we run into problems. Church attendance, for instance, may reflect family pressure, habit, or the desire to visit with others rather than religious commitment. Furthermore, many very religious people are unable to attend services because they are sick or disabled. As you can see, indicators seldom perfectly reflect the concepts they are intended to measure.

Surveys are particularly susceptible to inaccurate indicators. A loaded phrase or an unfamiliar word in a survey question can dramatically affect people's responses in ways unintended by the researcher. For instance, when asked if state civil rights laws should be expanded to include sexual orientation and gender identity, 50% of Indiana respondents said they were in favor. However, when the term *civil rights* was taken out and respondents were instead asked about protecting LGBT people from housing, employment, commercial, and public service discrimination, support jumped to 70% (Wang, 2015). During the campaign leading up to the 2016 presidential election, Donald Trump famously announced his desire to ban Muslim noncitizens from entering the United States. Several polling organizations quickly set about measuring the public's opinion on the matter. Their findings—and therefore any assessment of the voting public's position on this issue—varied greatly, depending on how they asked the question (J. Barro, 2015):

- *NBC News/Wall St. Journal:* "Recently Donald Trump has called for a total and complete shutdown for any Muslim being allowed to enter the United States. Do you favor or oppose this proposal?" Twenty-five percent were in favor; 57% opposed.

- *Rasmussen Reports:* "Do you favor or oppose a temporary ban on all Muslims entering the United States until the federal government improves its ability to screen out potential terrorists from coming here?" Forty-six percent were in favor; 40% opposed.

Why do you think the different wording of these two questions led to the starkly different responses? The first poll was conducted over the phone, while the second one was done online. How do you suppose that might have influenced people's answers?

Values, Interests, and Ethics in Sociological Research

Along with samples and indicators, the researcher's own qualities can influence social research. Ideally, research is objective and nonbiased and measures what is and not what should be. However, the questions researchers ask and the way they interpret observations always take place in a particular cultural, political, and ideological context (Ballard, 1987; Denzin, 1989).

Consider the impact of values and interests. If prevailing social values identify an intact nuclear family as the best environment for children, then most researchers will be prone to notice the disadvantages and perhaps ignore the advantages of other family arrangements. Furthermore, research is sometimes linked to narrowly defined political interest, as when environmental groups fund research showing the damaging effects of global warming. For more than two decades, the National Rifle Association has conducted a successful campaign to prevent federal funding of research on gun violence (Dean, 2017). Other times research reflects powerful economic interests, as when tobacco companies fund research that downplays the relationship between cigarette smoking and cancer. A few years ago, a legal investigation found that between 1998 and 2005, 26 scientific journal articles on the use of the hormone replacement drugs Premarin and Prempro for menopausal women were written by ghostwriters who were on the payroll of Wyeth, the pharmaceutical company that manufactured Premarin (Singer, 2009). That same year, an investigation by the Department of Health and Human Services found that the Food and Drug Administration does almost nothing to monitor financial conflicts of interest of doctors who conduct clinical trials of drugs and medical devices (cited in G. Harris, 2009).

But it's not just a problem of unscrupulous researchers or financial benefactors. Academic journals are notoriously reluctant to publish studies that show no support for the hypothesized relationship between one variable and another. A reexamination of clinical trial studies of antidepressants conducted between 1987 and 2004 found that medical journals had a significant bias toward publishing studies with positive results (E. H. Turner, Matthews, Linardatos, Tell, & Rosenthal, 2008). This problem has become so bad that an organization of 12 major medical journals proposed that pharmaceutical companies be required to register clinical trials at *the beginning* of drug studies so that negative and not just positive results would be publicly available (Meier, 2004).

We must remember that sociologists are people just like the rest of us, with their own biases, preconceptions, and expectations. Sociologists' values determine the kinds of information they gather about a particular social phenomenon. If you were conducting research on whether the criminal justice system is fair, would you study criminals, politicians, law enforcement personnel, judges, or victims? Each group would likely provide a different perception of the system. The most accurate picture of reality is likely to be based on the views of all subgroups involved.

In fact, values can influence the questions that researchers find important enough to address in the first place (Reinharz, 1992). For instance, research on families has historically reflected the interests of men. The term *labor force* has traditionally referred to those working for pay and has excluded those doing unpaid work, such as housework and volunteer jobs—areas that have always been predominantly female. Thus, findings on labor force participation are more likely to reflect the significant elements of men's lives than of women's lives. You can see that a lack of data does not necessarily indicate that a phenomenon or a problem doesn't exist. Perhaps all it indicates is that no researcher has yet undertaken a systematic study of it.

Ethics is another personal quality that affects the trustworthiness of social research. Research, as I mentioned earlier, often represents an intrusion into people's lives; it may disrupt their ordinary activities, and it often requires them to reveal personal information about themselves. Ethical researchers agree, therefore, that they should protect the rights of subjects and minimize the amount of harm or disruption subjects might experience as a result of being part of a study. Ethical researchers agree that no one should be forced to participate in research, that those who do participate ought to be fully informed of the possible risks involved, and that every precaution ought to be taken to protect the confidentiality and anonymity of participants. Sociologists almost always conduct their research under the scrutiny of university review committees for the protection of human participants.

At the same time, however, researchers must attempt to secure the most accurate—and perhaps most useful—information possible. Sometimes, this requirement conflicts with ethical considerations. In 2007, the federal government began a 5-year, $50 million project designed to improve the way hospital patients are treated after car accidents, shootings, heart attacks, and other emergencies. Because such patients are often unconscious when they arrive at the hospital, researchers were allowed to conduct medical experiments on them without their consent, something that goes against usual ethical research protocol (Stein, 2007).

And what about research that requires information about people who may be involved in dangerous or criminal behavior or who do not want or cannot have their identities revealed? Sociologist Patricia Adler (1985) was interested in studying the worlds of drug dealers and smugglers. The illegal nature of their work makes them, by necessity, secretive, deceitful, and mistrustful—not the sort of individuals who make ideal surveyor interview respondents. So Adler had to establish a significant level of rapport and trust. Although she never became actively involved in drug trafficking, she did become a part of the dealers' and smugglers' social world and participated in their daily activities. Only by studying these criminals in their natural setting was she able to see the full complexity of the world of drug smuggling. Her research, however, raises important questions related to trustworthiness and ethics: Did her closeness to her subjects make it impossible to study them objectively? Did she have an obligation to report illegal activity to law enforcement officials?

LAUD HUMPHREYS

SHOULD SOCIOLOGISTS STUDY ANONYMOUS SEXUAL ENCOUNTERS IN PUBLIC BATHROOMS?

Most sociologists agree that the need to understand the depth and complexity of the drug world outweighed the ethical issues raised by Adler's research strategy. There is less agreement and more controversy, however, over situations in which researchers misrepresent their identities in order to gather information. Consider the 1970 study called *The Tearoom Trade* by Laud Humphreys, a study many sociologists find ethically indefensible. Humphreys was interested in studying anonymous and casual homosexual encounters among strangers. He decided to focus on interactions in "tearooms," which are places, such as public restrooms, where male homosexuals go for anonymous sex. (This study was done well before the HIV/AIDS epidemic significantly curtailed such activity.)

Because of the potentially stigmatizing nature of this phenomenon, Humphreys couldn't just come right out and ask people about their actions. So he decided to engage in a secretive form of participant observation. He posed as a lookout, called a "watchqueen," whose job was to warn of intruders as the people he was studying engaged in sexual acts with one another in public restrooms. In this way, he was able to conduct very detailed observations of these encounters.

Humphreys also wanted to know about the regular lives of these men. Whenever possible, he wrote down the license numbers of the participants' cars and tracked down their names and addresses with the help of a friend in the local police department.

About a year later, he arranged for these individuals to be part of a simple medical survey being conducted by some of his colleagues. He then disguised himself and visited their homes, supposedly to conduct interviews for the medical survey. He found that most of the men were heterosexual, had families, and were respected members of their communities. In short, they led altogether conventional lives.

Although this information shed a great deal of light on the nature of anonymous homosexual acts, some critics argued that Humphreys had violated the ethics of research by deceiving his unsuspecting subjects and violating their privacy rights. Some critics also noted that Humphreys might have been sued for invasion of privacy if he had not been studying a group of people rendered powerless by their potential embarrassment. Others, however, supported Humphreys, arguing that he couldn't have studied this topic any other way. In fact, his book won a prestigious award. But over 40 years later, the ethical controversy surrounding this study remains.

Conclusion

In this chapter, I have described some of the processes by which reality is constructed, communicated, manipulated, and accepted. Reality, whether in the form of casual observations or formal research, is ultimately a human creation. Different people can create different conceptions of reality.

This issue can be raised from a personal level to a global one. People in every culture believe that their reality is the paramount one. Who is right? Can we truly believe that a reality in direct conflict with ours is equally valid? If we profess that everyone should have the right to believe what she or he wants, are we acknowledging the socially constructed nature of reality or merely being tolerant of those who are not "smart enough" to think as we do? Do we have the right to tell other people or other cultures that what they do or believe is wrong only because it conflicts with our definition of reality? Exasperating and complex, these questions lie at the core of international relations, global commerce, and everyday life.

Your Turn

The reality we take for granted is a social construction. This is particularly apparent when we look at the information presented to us as fact through published academic research, word of mouth, or the media. Reality is influenced by the individuals and organizations responsible for creating, assembling, and disseminating this information.

Choose an event that is currently making national headlines. It could be a story about the president or Congress, a major tragedy or natural disaster, a celebrity scandal, or a highly publicized criminal trial. Over the course of a week, analyze how this story is being covered by the following:

(Continued)

(Continued)

- Your local newspaper

- The major national newspapers (*USA Today, The New York Times, The Washington Post, The Wall Street Journal*)

- Mainstream news magazines (*Time, Newsweek, U.S. News & World Report*)

- Alternative magazines (*Utne Reader, Mother Jones, In These Times*, etc.)

- A local TV station

- A major TV network (NBC, CBS, ABC, Fox, CNN)

- Online news service (such as Newslink, Google News, Yahoo News)

- Late-night talk shows featuring topical comedy (such as *The Daily Show, Last Week Tonight, The Late Show, Conan, Late Night,* or *The Tonight Show*)

Pay particular attention to the following:

- The amount of time or space devoted to the story

- The "tone" of the coverage (Supportive or critical? Purely factual or reflective of certain political opinions? Specific, objective language or biased, inflammatory language?)

Summarize your findings. What were the differences in how the story was covered by the different media outlets? What were the similarities?

Interpret your findings. What do these differences and similarities suggest about the people who run these organizations? Whose political or economic interests are being served or undermined by the manner in which the story is being presented to the public? Which medium do you think is providing the most accurate, objective coverage? Why?

Chapter Highlights

- The social construction of reality (truth, knowledge, etc.) is the process by which reality is discovered, made known, reinforced, and changed by members of society.

- Language is the medium through which reality construction takes place. It enables us to think, interpret, and define. Linguistic categories reflect aspects of a culture that are relevant and meaningful to people's lives.

- Not all of us possess the same ability to define reality. Individuals and groups in positions of

power have the ability to control information, define values, create myths, manipulate events, and ultimately influence what others take for granted.

- The purpose of a discipline such as sociology is to amass a body of knowledge that provides the public with useful information about how society works. This is done, quantitatively and qualitatively, through systematic social research—field research, surveys, and unobtrusive research. It is important to keep in mind, however, that this form of reality is also a social construction, shaped by the people who fund, conduct, and report on social research.

Key Terms

analysis of existing data: Type of unobtrusive research that relies on data gathered earlier by someone else for some other purpose

content analysis: Form of unobtrusive research that studies the content of recorded messages, such as books, speeches, poems,

songs, television shows, websites, and advertisements

dependent variable: Variable that is assumed to be caused by, or to change as a result of, the independent variable

empirical research: Research that operates from the ideological position that questions about human behavior can be answered only through controlled, systematic observations in the real world

experiment: Research method designed to elicit some sort of behavior, typically conducted under closely controlled laboratory circumstances

field research: Type of social research in which the researcher observes events as they actually occur

historical analysis: Form of social research that relies on existing historical documents as a source of data

hypothesis: Researchable prediction that specifies the relationship between two or more variables

incorrigible proposition: Unquestioned cultural belief that cannot be proved wrong no matter what happens to dispute it

independent variable: Variable presumed to cause or influence the dependent variable

indicator: Measurable event, characteristic, or behavior commonly thought to reflect a particular concept

moral entrepreneurs: Groups that work to have their moral concerns translated into law

nonparticipant observation: Form of field research in which the researcher observes people without directly interacting with them and without letting them know that they are being observed

participant observation: Form of field research in which the researcher interacts with subjects, sometimes hiding his or her identity

probabilistic: Capable only of identifying those forces that have a high likelihood, but not a certainty, of influencing human action

qualitative research: Sociological research based on nonnumeric information (text, written words, phrases, symbols, observations) that describes people, actions, or events in social life

quantitative research: Sociological research based on the collection of numeric data that uses precise statistical analysis

reactivity: A problem associated with certain forms of research in which the very act of intruding into people's lives may influence the phenomenon being studied

representative: Typical of the whole population being studied

sample: Subgroup chosen for a study because its characteristics approximate those of the entire population

self-fulfilling prophecy: Assumption or prediction that in itself causes the expected event to occur, thus seeming to confirm the prophecy's accuracy

social construction of reality: Process through which the members of a society discover, make known, reaffirm, and alter a collective version of facts, knowledge, and "truth"

spurious relationship: A false association between two variables that is actually due to the effect of some third variable

survey: Form of social research in which the researcher asks subjects a series of questions verbally, online, or on paper

theory: Set of statements or propositions that seeks to explain or predict a particular aspect of social life

unobtrusive research: Research technique in which the researcher, without direct contact with the subjects, examines the evidence of social behavior that people create or leave behind

variable: Any characteristic, attitude, behavior, or event that can take on two or more values or attributes

visual sociology: Method of studying society that uses photographs, video recordings, and film either as means of gathering data or as sources of data about social life

SAGE edge™ edge.sagepub.com/newman12e

SAGE edge offers a robust online environment featuring an impressive array of free tools and resources for review, study, and further exploration, keeping both instructors and students on the cutting edge of teaching and learning.

Building Order

Culture and History

- Dimensions of Culture
- Cultural Expectations and Social Order
- Cultural Variation and Everyday Experience

In Madagascar, the harvest months of August and September mark the *famadihana*—the "turning of the bones." Families receive messages from *razana*—their dead loved ones—who may say they are uncomfortable or need new clothes. In an elaborate ceremony that can last for days, families feast, sing, and dig up the graves of the deceased. The bodies are wrapped in shrouds and seated at the dinner table. Loved ones run their fingers over the skeletons through the shroud. Family news is whispered to them, and toasts are drunk. Widows and widowers can often be seen dancing with the bones of their dead spouses. The exhumed bones are then oiled and perfumed and laid back onto their "beds" inside the family tomb (Bearak, 2010; Perlez, 1991).

In the late 19th and early 20th centuries, dating and courtship in North America were based on a ritualized system known as "calling." Although the process varied by region and social class, the following general guidelines were involved:

> When a girl reached the proper age or had her first "season" (depending on her family's social level), she became eligible to receive male callers. At first her mother or guardian invited young men to call; in subsequent seasons the young lady . . . could bestow an invitation to call upon any unmarried man to whom she had been properly introduced at a private dance, dinner, or other "entertainment.". . . Young men . . . could be brought to call by friends or relatives of the girl's family, subject to her prior permission. . . . The call itself was a complicated event. A myriad of rules governed everything: the proper amount of time between invitation and visit (two weeks or less); whether or not refreshments should be served . . . ; chaperonage (the first call must be made on mother and daughter . . .); appropriate topics of conversation (the man's

interests, but never too personal); how leave should be taken (on no account should the woman accompany [her caller] to the door nor stand talking while he struggles with his coat). (B. L. Bailey, 1988, pp. 15–16)

How could anybody dig up a relative's corpse? Why would young men and young women follow such elaborate rules just so they could go on a date? These practices may seem peculiar, silly, or backward to most of us, but to the people involved, they are or were simply the taken-for-granted, "right" ways of doing things.

Some of the things you do may seem equally incomprehensible to an outside observer:

- You may not think twice about eating a bloody T-bone steak, but someone from a culture that views cows as sacred would be disgusted at the thought.

- You may think a Spaniard's fondness for bullfighting is "absurd" or "cruel," yet millions of people in the United States shell out a lot of money each year to watch large men in brightly colored shirts and helmets knock each other down—sometimes to the point of unconsciousness—while they chase, throw, carry, and kick an inflated object made out of the hide of a dead animal.

- You may pity the turn-of-the-century woman who squeezed her body into an ultra tight corset to achieve the wasp-waisted figure men considered attractive, yet many women today (and some men) routinely use harsh chemicals to change the color of their hair, pay to have someone cut into their faces to decrease the size of their noses or tighten the skin around their chins, or reduce their food intake to the point of starvation in order to look slender.

- You would likely be horrified by a particular practice of the Parsi in Mumbai, India: leaving the bodies of their dead relatives on the rooftops of some buildings so they can be eaten by vultures (G. Harris, 2012). Similarly, you might be dumbfounded by the survivors of serious accidents or illnesses in a small Spanish village who ritually stage their own funerals (to the point of being paraded around town in coffins) as a way of expressing gratitude for their survival (Minder, 2017). Yet some Americans pay hundreds of dollars to have the cremated remains of their loved ones turned into fashionable pendants to wear around their necks or stuffed into shotgun shells and ceremoniously fired into the air.

Clearly, the legitimacy of certain practices and ideas can be understood only within the unique context of the group or society in which they occur. What is considered abnormal in one case may be perfectly normal, even necessary, in another. It takes a sociological imagination to see that time and place have a great influence on what people consider normal.

Ancestor worship in Madagascar is a custom that has been around for centuries, impervious to the arrival of Christian churches and Western ideals. To the people who practice it, the ritual of burial, disinterment, and reburial is more important than marriage. The physical body may die, but the *fanahy*, or soul, lives on. The Malagasy believe that spirits stay with the bones and have needs for earthly goods like food and clothing. It's up to the living to provide these things. In exchange, the dead take care of living relatives by determining their health, wealth, and fertility and by helping them communicate with God. As one man said after tending to the remains of his dead grandfather, "It is good to thank the ancestors in person because we owe them everything. . . . I am asking them for good health, and of course if they would help me to accumulate wealth, this is also a good idea" (quoted in Bearak, 2010, p. A7). In short, the custom is quite rational and beneficial: The individual's own earthly well-being and spiritual salvation depend on it.

Likewise, the practice of calling was an integral part of late-19th-century U.S. culture. It maintained the social class structure by serving as a test of suitability, breeding, and background (B. L. Bailey, 1988). Calling enabled the middle and upper classes to protect themselves from what many at the time considered the "intrusions" of urban life and to screen out the disruptive effects of social and geographic mobility, which reached unprecedented levels at the turn of the century. It also allowed parents to control the relationships of their children, thereby increasing the likelihood that their pedigree would remain intact.

These phenomena illustrate the important role played by culture and history in creating social order. Whether we're talking about our own ordinary rituals or those practiced by some distant society, the normative patterns that mark the millions of seemingly trivial actions and social encounters of our everyday lives are what make society possible. They tell us what to expect from others and what others should expect from us. In this chapter, by looking at the various taken-for-granted aspects of culture that lend structure to our daily lives, I examine how order is created and maintained in society. In the process, I compare specific aspects of our culture with others, past and present.

Dimensions of Culture

In Chapter 2, you saw that culture is one of the key elements that shape the structure of a society. It consists of the shared, taken-for-granted values, beliefs, objects, and rules that guide people's lives. In everyday conversation, however, the term *culture* is often used only when discussing something "foreign." We rarely feel the need to question why we do certain things in the course of our daily lives—we just do them. It's other people in other lands whose rituals and beliefs need explaining. What we often fail to realize is that culture is "doing its job" most effectively when it is unnoticed. Only in times of dramatic social change and moral uncertainty or when circumstances force us to compare our society with another—like when you travel abroad—do we become aware that a distinct set of cultural rules and values influences us, too.

To a large degree, we are products of the culture and historical epoch in which we live. From a very young age we learn, with a startling amount of accuracy, that certain dwellings, food, tools, clothing, modes of transportation, music, vocabulary, sports, and art characterize our culture and make it different from others. Without much conscious effort, we also learn what to believe, what to value, and which actions are proper or improper both in public and in private.

Material and Nonmaterial Culture

Culture consists of all the products of a society that are created over time and shared by members of that society. These products may be tangible or intangible. The term **nonmaterial culture** refers to all the nonphysical products of society that are created over time and shared: knowledge, beliefs, customs, values, morals, and so on. Nonmaterial culture also includes common patterns of behavior and the forms of interaction appropriate in a particular society. It is a "design for living" that distinguishes one society from another. Like an owner's manual for social life, nonmaterial culture tells us how our society works, what is possible, what to value, how to conduct our everyday lives, and what to do if something breaks down. Without an understanding of a society's nonmaterial culture, people's behaviors—not to mention the symbolic significance of their material world—would be thoroughly incomprehensible.

The values that reside in nonmaterial culture often support a given society's economic and political systems. For example, in most Western industrialized countries, individual success is typically measured in financial terms, like a high-paying job and substantial accumulated wealth. In fact, in the United States, the well-being of the entire population is gauged by a measure called the gross national product—the total dollar value of all goods and services produced for consumption during a particular time period. However, in Bhutan—a tiny Buddhist kingdom in the Himalaya Mountains—the country's well-being is judged not by its economic output but by how happy its people are. Bhutanese officials have even developed something called the Index of Gross National Happiness, which determines the country's level of happiness by measuring things such as psychological well-being, physical fitness, environmental health, educational attainment, cultural diversity and resilience, living standards, time use, good governance, and community vitality (Gross National Happiness, 2015). In fact, Bhutan's constitution directs the country's leaders to consult the Index of Gross National Happiness when considering new legislation (Schultz, 2017).

Material culture includes the physical artifacts and objects that shape or reflect the lives of members of a particular society: distinctive clothing and architecture, inventions, food, artwork, music, and so on. Elements of material culture occasionally take on powerful emotional value. Some of the most important elements of material culture are technological achievements, which are the ways in which members of a society apply knowledge to adapt to changing social, economic, or environmental conditions. For instance, plastic products have provided people with cheaper and more convenient packaging of needed goods—and in the process have forever altered shopping and consumption patterns.

Similarly, the advent of the automobile in the early 20th century gave people greater mobility to take advantage of economic or residential opportunities elsewhere and thereby dramatically changed how and where they lived. It's impossible to imagine society without cars. Today, the average number of cars per household (2.1) almost matches the average number of people per household (2.54; Bureau of Transportation Statistics, 2012; ProQuest Statistical Abstract, 2017). Since the interstate highway system was developed in 1956, the distance Americans drive annually has increased from 628 million miles to 2.71 trillion (Federal Highway Administration, 2016; R. Sullivan, 2006), although in the past few years factors like higher gas prices, new licensing laws, and improvements in technology that support alternative transportation have actually reduced the number of miles young people drive (U.S. PIRG Education Fund, 2012). The highway system made cross-country travel and the growth of suburbs possible. Moreover, our national economy would crumble without the ubiquitous long-haul trucks that transport needed goods to every corner of the country. The influence of the automobile is especially noticeable today in places such as Nepal and rural China, where it is beginning to have a similar dramatic impact on people's lives.

Changes in material culture often transform the physical environment, creating the need for additional alterations in material and nonmaterial culture. The enormous amount of nonbiodegradable plastic piling up in overflowing landfills, for example, has spawned a vast array of advances in recycling and other ecofriendly technologies. Likewise, a heavy reliance on automobiles has created several serious problems throughout the world: air pollution, depletion of fossil fuel reserves, suburban sprawl, and constant traffic. These problems in turn have created the need for changes in travel patterns and arrangements as well as further material developments, such as an entire "green" industry that includes sustainable home products, pollution-reducing devices, hybrid automobiles, smart home thermostats, and alternative-fuel sources (for more, see Chapter 14).

Global Culture

Although culture gives each society its distinctive character, cultural "purity" is all but obsolete (Griswold, 1994). Transnational media, global communication and transportation systems, and centuries of international migration have contributed to a worldwide swapping of cultural elements. For instance, China has a long cultural tradition of distaste for physical embraces between strangers. As one person put it, "If we're hugging all the time, hugging people who shouldn't be hugged, then the thrill will evaporate, and that's just a waste" (quoted in Tatlow, 2014, p. A6). However, exposure to the West—through media depictions of affection and personal experiences living overseas—are making Chinese people more comfortable with casual hugging. In fact, concern that the traditional aversion to physical contact could hold young people back in international relations has led some elementary schools to begin offering classes in "emotional intelligence" so that children will become comfortable touching (and being touched by) strangers (Tatlow, 2014).

But in many societies, people see the imported elements of culture as dangerous encroachments on long-held traditions and national unity. Of special concern is the increasing influence of U.S. culture on other countries. For instance, even in bad economic times, U.S. retailers are a common fixture around the globe. Each year more than 260 million customers visit nearly 11,500 Wal-Mart stores in 28 countries (Wal-Mart, 2016). Starbucks has nearly 23,000 coffeehouses in 67 countries (Starbucks, 2016). American pizza, too, which originally came to us from Naples, Italy, has migrated to every corner of the globe. Domino's Pizza now has 12,900 stores in more than 80 countries around the world (Domino's, 2016). And Amazon.com reported $33.5 billion in net sales from *orders outside* the United States in 2015 (Statista, 2016a).

MICRO-MACRO CONNECTION
THE CHAIR

Even the simplest and most taken-for-granted material objects of our everyday lives carry enormous cultural weight. Take, for example, the common chair. We spend a huge chunk of our lives sitting in chairs—in dining rooms, living rooms, classrooms, offices, cars, movie theaters, restaurants, and so on. You're probably sitting in one at this very moment.

Chairs supposedly make our lives comfortable. To be able to relax, kick off your shoes, and plop down on the old La-Z-Boy after a hard day's work is one of life's great pleasures. But such comfort has a steep cost. Ironically, lower back pain, often caused by bad sitting posture or poorly designed chairs, is second only to the common cold as the leading cause of absenteeism from work (Cranz, 1998). Our sedentary lifestyle has created a nation of people who are woefully out of shape.

Like all pieces of material culture, chairs are human creations. But once they're built, they start to shape us. The type of chair you use when you're in your sociology class immediately places you in the role of student. And whether these chairs are arranged in rows or in a circle determines the degree of interaction expected of you in class. Children's first institutional lessons in controlling their bodies typically involve the chairs they are told to "sit still" in. Sitting quietly in rows of hard, straight chairs is not a natural state of being for young children. As one design expert put it, "The chair . . . originated in the industrial ordering of education. It is maintained by . . . unimaginative administrators who see no other possible arrangement of the body, or bodies, or any possible downside to the lower back from six hours of enforced sitting" (quoted in A. Baker, 2013, pp. A1, A3).

But it certainly helps teachers maintain authority and contain disruptive behaviors.

Chairs often take on important cultural significance beyond their functionality. For instance, the chair a person sits in may define that person's social status. In antiquity, only the most powerful and prestigious members of a society had access to chairs; the throne is one of the most enduring symbols of royalty worldwide. When the Pope issues an authoritative decree to Catholics around the world, he is said to be speaking *ex cathedra*, which literally means "from the chair." In some families, children know the consequences of sitting in or otherwise sullying "Dad's chair." The "chair" of an academic department can wield a great deal of power. On the other end of the spectrum, the "electric chair" is reserved for the lowest and most despicable of citizens, whose heinous crimes have led society to pronounce them unfit to live.

The right-angled posture required to sit in a chair, which we assume to be the universally proper way to sit, is used by only a third to half of people worldwide (Cranz, 1998). In many parts of the world, people sit on floors, mats, carpets, or platforms. A Chinese man will likely squat when waiting for a bus, a Japanese woman kneels when eating, and an Arab might sit cross-legged on the floor when reading.

Regardless of whether we use a chair or what sort of chair we use, one thing is clear: This habit was created, modified, nurtured, and reformed in response to cultural—and not anatomical—forces. Our subjective experiences of comfort are socially constructed, and our bodies respond accordingly. For the American, it *really is* more comfortable to sit in a chair, and for the rural Arab it *really is* more comfortable to sit on the floor. That these choices are experienced subjectively as personally pleasant shows that culture is at work here.

In general, people in other countries tend to admire the United States for its wealth, technology, science, and popular culture (music, movies, television and so on; Pew Global Attitudes Project, 2012). Consider, for instance, *Qingming,* an annual festival in Cambodia when families honor their dead relatives. During this celebration people burn offerings to provide for their ancestors in the spirit world. They will burn "gifts" like cardboard automobiles, cell phones, jewelry, and other supplies their departed ancestors might need in the hereafter. They also burn fake money. But many families refuse to use Cambodia's currency, the riel. Instead, they burn paper replicas of American dollars, which they believe provide the spirits of their ancestors with more luxurious otherworldly purchasing power (Wallace, 2016).

But not all countries welcome the United States' cultural influence. Two decades ago, culture ministers from 20 different countries on four continents met to discuss how best to maintain their own cultures in a global environment dominated by U.S. media (Croteau & Hoynes, 2000). They were responding to examples like these:

- Approximately two thirds of French respondents to a survey feel that the United States exerts too much cultural influence on Europe (Daley, 2000). France is now the most successful market for McDonald's in Europe (Sexton, 2009); hence the fast-food restaurant has become a symbol of what many French consider to be the despicable intrusion of U.S. food culture. Several years ago, a French sheep farmer named José Bové became something of a national hero for vandalizing McDonald's restaurants. Some called him "the French Gandhi." Bové is now a spokesperson for *Via Campesina*, an organization that promotes "food sovereignty," the right of countries to define their own food systems.

- In Austria, an organization called the Pro-Christkind Association launched a campaign against Santa Claus several years ago, claiming that he is nothing more than an advertising symbol of American culture and consumption habits (Landler, 2002). The group now has an anti-Santa Facebook page.

- Okinawa, Japan, has historically had the highest proportion of people over the age of 100 in the world and the greatest life expectancy of any region in Japan. But due to the U.S. military presence there, Okinawans are now living and eating like Americans. They walk less, eat fewer vegetables, and eat more hamburgers than they used to. Okinawa has the most American-style fast-food restaurants of any city in Japan. As a result, average weight and rates of heart disease, cerebral hemorrhage, and lung cancer have all increased. Okinawans now rank 26th in life expectancy among the Japanese administrative regions (Onishi, 2004; Takayama, 2003).

Emotions can run especially high when the integrity of a culture's language is at stake. About 60% of all existing human languages have fewer than 10,000 speakers (R. G. Gordon, 2005). These languages are highly vulnerable to disappearance in a global culture. Indeed, linguists predict that half of the 7,000 or so languages spoken worldwide today will disappear by the middle of this century (Austin, 2008). Taking their place will be a handful of dominant languages that, in a technologically connected world, are seen as "linguistic passports" to education and a successful economic future (P. H. Lewis, 1998).

Foremost among these major languages, of course, is English, which today shapes communication all over the world. People in Japan go to see their favorite teams play *beisuboru* and then order bottles of *bi-ru* (pronounced beer-oo) at their local pubs. In concerts, Chinese entertainers sing into their *maikefengs* (pronounced my-kuh-fung). In many Spanish-speaking countries, people type e-mails on a *computadora* and text on a *telefono móvil*. Germans seeking to avoid unwanted pregnancies might seek a prescription for an *antibabypille*. The French commonly use terms like *le weekend,* and *les jeans.* Hausa speakers in western Africa refer to their local priest as *faadaa* (Harbeck, 2013). In Botswana, Setswana speakers getting some exercise at their local fitness center are *go-gymming.*

People recognize that in a world of collapsing borders, a common language is useful. And because of pervasive U.S. cultural influences and technologies, English is an understandable choice. For instance, even though less than 30% of Internet users are native English speakers (Internet World Stats, 2014), most of the world's electronically stored information is in English (Crystal, 2003). It is estimated that over 900 million people now speak English as either a first or a second language ("How Many People," 2013). In Europe, nearly all children learn English (see Exhibit 4.1). In fact, there are more people who speak English as their second language than there are people who speak it as their first (Mydans, 2007).

But not everyone is happy about such developments. In French-speaking Quebec, Canada, large American retailers like Costco, Walmart, Toys"R"Us, and Best Buy are required by law to serve their customers in French and post signs in French along the aisles (I. Austen, 2012). In 2013, French legislators proposed a law that would require universities to teach more of their courses in English. Supporters argued that the lack of English was a major factor in France's declining economic competitiveness around the world. Opponents, however, took to the streets in loud and fierce protest. One scholar called the proposal a "suicidal project" and a "sacrifice to Americanization"; another called it a "drive toward self destruction" (quoted in de la Baume, 2013, p. A10).

In the United States, many people are concerned with the encroaching influence not of English but of Spanish. Today, over 39 million U.S. residents speak Spanish as their first language; in Los Angeles, 43% of residents over the age of 5 speak Spanish at home; less than 40% of residents speak only English at home (ProQuest Statistical Abstract, 2017). Immigrants are actually making the transition to speaking English more quickly than in the past, and over 90% of residents with a foreign-born parent prefer to speak only English at home (Kent & Lalasz, 2006). Indeed, 80% of the children who speak Spanish as their

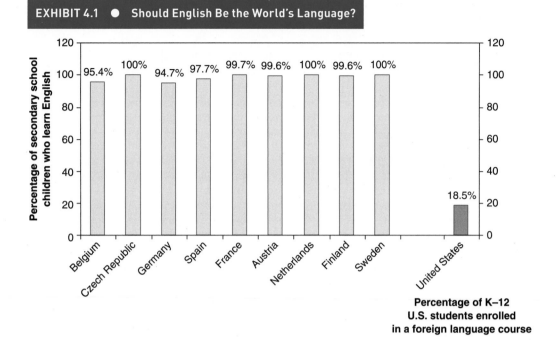

EXHIBIT 4.1   ●   Should English Be the World's Language?

Sources: American Council on the Teaching of Foreign Languages, 2016; Eurostat, 2016b)

first language speak English "very well" (ProQuest Statistical Abstract, 2017). Nevertheless, many U.S. citizens fret that English is losing its primacy when they see street signs, billboards, election ballots, and automated teller machines in Spanish. Up until a few years ago, the state of Arizona sent government monitors into classrooms to make sure that teachers didn't have heavy Spanish accents. Those who did were cited for violations and required, with the help of their school districts, to improve their English (Lacey, 2011). Indeed, 32 states have declared English as their official language (U.S. English, 2016).

Subcultures

Sociologists and anthropologists usually speak of culture as a characteristic of an entire society. But culture can also exist in smaller, more narrowly defined units. A **subculture** consists of the values, behaviors, and physical artifacts of a group that distinguish it from the larger culture. Think of it as a culture within a culture. Certain racial and ethnic groups, religions, age groups, and even geographic areas can all constitute subcultures.

To see a common subculture, you don't have to look any further than your own school. You're probably well aware of the material and nonmaterial subculture that is unique to your campus. Perhaps some landmark—a bell tower or ornate archway—is the defining symbol of the university, or maybe a boulder or tree or fountain occupies a hallowed place in campus lore. I'm sure you know your school mascot and the school colors. In addition, when you first arrived at school, you probably had to learn a tremendous amount of new information about the nonmaterial subculture just to survive—how to register for courses; how to address a professor; where to eat and study; what administrators, faculty, and fellow students expect of you; and so on. At my university, the student newspaper publishes a glossary of common words, phrases, acronyms, and nicknames at the beginning of each academic year to aid first-year students in their adjustment to life on campus. Just as you have to learn how to be a member of your society, you have to learn how to be a member of your university subculture.

SUSAN BLUM

IT'S OK, EVERYONE'S DOING IT: PLAGIARISM AND THE COLLEGE SUBCULTURE

If people based their understanding of the state of American higher education on stories they see in popular media, it would appear as if we're experiencing an epidemic of cheating in college classrooms nationwide. According to the International Center for Academic Integrity (2015), 68% of undergraduate and 43% of graduate students admit to having cheated on tests or written assignments. Even at Harvard, our most venerated university, 125 students were accused of collaborating on a take-home exam in an introductory government class (Pérez-Peña, 2012b). Honor codes have been implemented nationwide (Blum, 2009). At my university, incoming first-year students receive a "gift" upon their arrival on campus: a book called *Doing Honest Work in College* (Lipson, 2004). It's easy to conclude from all this that a "cheating subculture" populated by unethical and dishonest ne'er-do-wells more interested in *having* a degree than in *earning* one is thriving on college campuses from Maine to California.

Anthropologist Susan Blum—a college professor herself for over 20 years—spent 3 years studying college plagiarism and talking to students at an elite private university to determine if such a "cheating subculture" actually exists. What she found, much to her surprise, was something far more complicated than the notion that colleges have become a cesspool of student immorality:

> The topic of plagiarism in college sits like a big spider in a web of other factors having to do with the nature of higher education . . . the nature of texts and authorship, and the nature and motives of the person doing the work turned in for credit. The Internet is part of the story, but not in the way people usually think about it. Morality is also part of the problem, but not because most students are immoral. . . . If more than half of all students plagiarize, then there is clearly some cultural influence urging them to do so. (Blum, 2009, p. 3, 6)

For one thing, life for college students today is high stakes and high pressure. Although she herself warns against drawing broad conclusions and acknowledges that there are different types of plagiarism that range from innocuous to severe, Blum argues that most students today live in an environment of busyness. They spend an inordinate amount of their time trying to juggle numerous academic, social, financial, and familial demands. The pressures can be overwhelming. They are expected to be sociable, to work together,

and to be "outgoing" while staying digitally connected 24/7. And with the high cost of tuition, many students—particularly those who attend elite colleges—often feel that parents monitor their every action and achievement to see if they're "getting their money's worth."

So it seems obvious that some students would resort to "cutting corners." But ultimately what's most important, according to Blum, is the disconnect between students' academic expectations and those of their (older) professors. It's not that there's a rampant "cheating subculture." The problem is that two distinct and age-specific subcultures exist uncomfortably side-by-side in the same classroom.

Professors come from a generation with a clear sense of intellectual ownership. They simply take for granted that authors' published ideas belong to them. Hence using those ideas in a research paper requires an attributed citation:

> If plagiarism involves *improperly* taking another person's words and claiming them as one's own, it follows that (1) there are proper ways to take others' words, (2) people can "own" words, and (3) others' words (ideas as well as texts) can be distinguished from one's own. (Blum, 2009, p. 29)

Today's students, however, have come of age in a Facebook/Twitter/Wikipedia digital environment where ideas are often created communally; their ties to a particular individual are either unknown or irrelevant. To today's students, words no longer belong to people. For example, TV shows borrow plot lines from other shows; rappers sample from the songs of their predecessors. Where older generations would be inclined to see these activities as a form of theft, today's students may see them as an indicator of reverence.

To Blum it's not at all surprising, then, that students feel quite comfortable using the Internet collaboratively and patching together papers the way they create playlists for their iPods. In short, written ideas—like everything else college students routinely download—aren't considered private property. Therefore, using someone else's words is not considered stealing.

Consequently, since the idea of individually created "text" is changing, the concept of plagiarism itself—inappropriately taking and using someone else's ideas—may also be changing. The effect this shift will have on the writing enterprise—indeed on higher education writ large—remains to be seen.

History: The "Archives" for Everyday Living

Like culture, history is simultaneously everywhere and invisible. We rarely see the connection between our personal lives and the larger historical context in which we live. Just as culture tends to be equated with the foreign, history tends to be equated with the past. Yet it too has a pervasive influence on today's society.

It is all too easy to use contemporary criteria to judge the thoughts and actions of people who lived long ago. Abraham Lincoln, known as one of history's most influential proponents of liberty and equality, once said, "There is a physical difference between the white and black races which I believe will forever forbid the two races living together on terms of social and political equality" (quoted in S. J. Gould, 1981, p. 35). Similar views of racial separation were voiced by important historical figures such as Benjamin Franklin, Thomas Jefferson, and Charles Darwin. Such comments, if uttered today, would be taken as indications of a deeply held prejudice.

However, we must understand such beliefs and behaviors not merely as signs of personal bigotry but as reflections of the dominant cultural belief system of the times. In other words, they are social constructions. As repugnant as we might find these attitudes, they were taken as undeniable truths by the scientific communities of their era. Innate "racial inferiority" was as much an established "scientific fact" as the germ theory of disease is today. (See Chapter 11 for more detail on the belief in innate racial inferiority.) The norms and values that govern everyday life in a given society are also likely to change over time. Some cultural practices that were wholly unacceptable in the past have now become commonplace. Premarital sex and househusbands no longer incite the sort of moral outrage or suspicion that they once did.

Other acts have become less acceptable, even criminal. In the United States, there was a time when people could smoke cigarettes anywhere and anytime they pleased—in supermarkets, airplanes, movie theaters, even hospitals. Now, with the increase in health awareness, smoking in public buildings (and even outdoor public facilities) has been severely restricted or outlawed in many locales. Some 36 states now have laws in effect that require workplaces, bars, or state-run gambling establishments to be 100% smoke free. Nearly 600 cities and counties restrict e-cigarette use in smoke-free locations (American Nonsmokers' Rights Foundation, 2016). Hospitals in some states now have hiring policies that make smoking a reason to turn down job applicants. They argue that they want to increase worker productivity, cut health care costs, and encourage healthier living. Application forms warn of "tobacco-free hiring," and job seekers must submit to urine tests for nicotine as part of the application process (Sulzberger, 2011).

Historical shifts in the cultural acceptance of certain behaviors involve more than just a societal realization of the danger of such behaviors. Actually, as the conflict perspective would point out, such designations are greatly influenced by social and economic concerns. Take, for instance, the criminalization of opium—the substance from which heroin is derived. During the 19th century, the use of opium was legal in many parts of the world; it was commonly used for therapeutic purposes as a pain reliever, a cold medicine, and a cough suppressant (Inciardi, 1992). The typical "heroin addict" at that time in the United States was a white middle-class housewife.

By the early 20th century, however, things had changed considerably. In the United States, there was a growing fear, particularly on the West Coast, of economic competition from Chinese laborers who had been "imported" to work on the railroads. Workers began to see Chinese immigrants as a direct threat to their material interests. At the same time, these immigrants became equated with opium use (Hagan, 1985). A moral consensus soon emerged that focused on the presumed link between the Chinese and narcotics (Bonnie & Whitebread, 1974). It wasn't long before opium use became the dreaded "Oriental dope problem." By 1914, tight legislative controls restricted U.S. distribution of opium to authorized medical prescriptions only. By 1925, opium was completely outlawed (Becker, 1963).

Cultural Expectations and Social Order

Despite periodic shifts in the acceptability of certain acts, culture and history provide people with a common bond—a sense of shared personal experiences. That we can live together at all depends on the fact that we share a tremendous amount of cultural and historical knowledge. This knowledge allows us to predict, with a fair amount of certainty, what most people will do in a given situation. For instance, I can assume that when I say, "Hi, how are you?" you will reply "Fine." You probably won't launch into some long-winded explanation of your mental, physical, and emotional condition at that precise moment, because doing so would violate the cultural rules governing such casual greetings.

The actions of individuals are not simply functions of personality types or psychological predispositions; rather, they are also a reflection of shared cultural expectations. Culture provides us with information about which of these actions are preferred, accepted, or disapproved of at a given time (McCall & Simmons, 1978). Take, for example, sexuality. Despite the unprecedented visibility and social acceptance of gay, lesbian, bisexual, and transgender people, U.S. society can still be characterized as being a **heteronormative culture**—that is, a culture where heterosexuality is the normal, taken-for-granted mode of sexual expression. Social institutions and policies reinforce the belief that sexual relationships between males and females are expected and unremarkable. Cultural representations of just about every aspect of intimate and family life—dating, sex, marriage, childbearing, erectile dysfunction, and so on—presume a world in which men are sexually and affectionately attracted to women and women to men (Macgillivray, 2000). Think of the flurry of magazine and TV advertisements we're subjected to in the weeks prior to Valentine's Day that depict men and women embracing, gazing longingly into each other's eyes, and buying each other expensive jewelry. Adolescent girls seeing a gynecologist for the first time can expect to be given information on birth control, highlighting the assumption that they will have sex with men—it's just a matter of when. Even some sports reflect a heteronormative culture. In competitive figure skating, the "pairs" competition always consists of women partnered with men (Wildman & Davis, 2002). The 2007 film *Blades of Glory* humorously satirized this basic assumption by depicting two men skating with one another in the pairs event.

In heteronormative cultures, heterosexuals are socially privileged because their relationships and lifestyles are affirmed in every facet of society. Such privilege includes having positive media images of people with the same sexual orientation; not having to lie about who you are, what you do, and where you seek entertainment; not having to worry about losing a job because of your sexual orientation; receiving validation from your religious community; and being able to donate blood without having to disclose your sexual history.

Recall from Chapter 2 that norms are the rules that govern the routine social encounters in which we all participate. Although many everyday norms are sometimes difficult to identify and describe, they reflect commonly held assumptions about conventional behavior. For instance, people who live in large cities like New York or Chicago quickly learn a large array of rules for walking along busy sidewalks: avoid bumping into others (while staying comfortably close), follow whoever is in front of you, and keep up with those next to you. These rules are so well learned that most residents automatically adjust their walking behavior to those around them:

While striding forward, we turn ever so slightly to the side, pulling in our bellies and leading with the shoulder instead of the nose. This lets us barely brush against passing pedestrians, our hands to our torsos and faces turned away politely. (Horowitz, 2012, p. 5)

Norms can be generalized to similar situations within a culture. That is, we can be reasonably certain that grocery store or doctor's office or restaurant behavior that is appropriate in Baton Rouge will be appropriate in Bakersfield or Butte as well. Our experiences in these places would be chaotic if there weren't a certain degree of agreement over how we should act. Without such unspoken rules and expectations, every situation would have to be interpreted, analyzed, and responded to as if it were an entirely new occasion. Social life would be utterly unmanageable.

Cultural norms are not static rules, however. They often change as the culture itself changes. A compelling reason for norms to change is to accommodate new technologies.

MICRO-MACRO CONNECTION
CAN YOU HEAR ME NOW?

No doubt the most popular technological device in the world today is the cell phone. Cell phones were first marketed to the public in 1984. Initially, only wealthy busines people or celebrities could afford them or make the case that they needed them. Ten years later there were 24 million U.S. cell phone subscribers. Today, that figure is around 378 million—more than the number of people living in the United States (see Exhibit 4.2). Forty-eight percent of American households have no landline telephone service, only wireless. In 2015, people talked for 2.88 trillion minutes and sent 1.89 trillion text messages on their cell phones (CTIA-The Wireless Association, 2016). What was once the sole province of the well-to-do is now a mass-market item that virtually everyone can obtain. And the United States isn't even near the top worldwide when it comes to cell phone usage. According to the World Economic Forum, Americans rank below 71 other countries in the degree to which cell phones have come to dominate contemporary communication (cited in Giridharadas, 2010). Many developing countries in Africa and Asia have gone from very low percentages of traditional telephone ownership a decade ago to very high percentages of cell phone ownership today, completely leapfrogging past the landline technology stage of growth.

Moreover, phones aren't simply phones anymore. In fact, the amount of time people spend actually talking on their phones hasn't increased much over the past several years, even though cell phone ownership has grown (see Exhibit 4.2). American youth send and receive an average of about 109 text messages a day, compared to 17 phone calls (A. Smith, 2011). Indeed, "talking" on a phone has almost become passé. As one iPhone user put it, "I probably only talk to someone verbally on it once a week" (quoted in Wortham, 2010, p. A1).

Instead, people spend the bulk of their time using all the extras on today's smartphones: turn-by-turn GPS navigation systems; web browsers; video cameras; e-mail; social media like Facebook, Instagram, Tumblr, Pinterest, Twitter, and Snapchat; transportation systems like Uber and Lyft, wireless payment systems, and text messaging. Two thirds of Americans now own smartphones (A. Smith, 2015). Clearly smartphones have completely revolutionized our lives: the way we communicate, work, find stores and restaurants, get rides, monitor our exercise, listen to music, play games, travel, control the temperature in our homes, and form relationships.

In the pre–cell phone days, people took great pains to keep conversations private. And they were by necessity stationary: Phones were either in people's own homes or their workplaces, tethered to a wall or desk. When people had to use a phone away from home or work, they turned to public telephone booths—relics of material culture that have gone the way of the dinosaur. In these enclosed boxes, people could deposit a dime or a quarter and shut out the rest of the world while talking privately on the phone.

(Continued)

(Continued)

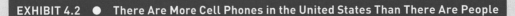

EXHIBIT 4.2   ●   There Are More Cell Phones in the United States Than There Are People

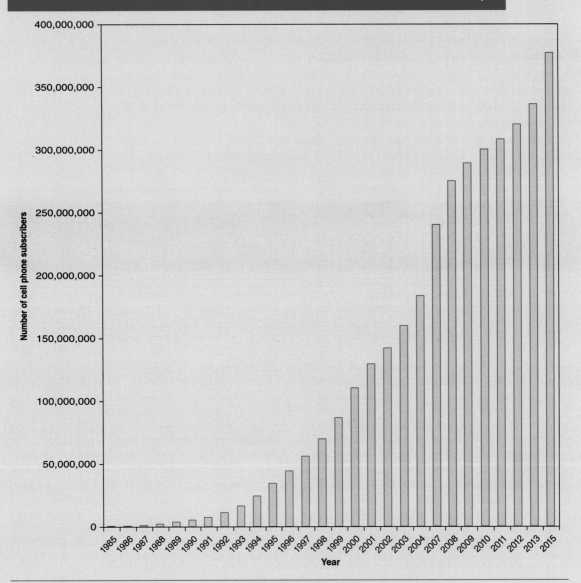

Source: Figure of the Year-End 2016 Annual Wireless Industry Survey Results, from CTIA–The Wireless Association's Annual wireless industry survey. Used with the permission of CTIA–The Wireless Association®.

Cell phones changed all that. For one thing, these devices completely altered our sense of place. When phones were anchored in a particular location, you knew when you called someone where that person was. Today you never know. Even area codes, which once at least designated where a person was calling from, are pretty much useless as markers of location. Hence the first question people typically ask when calling someone's cell phone is not "How are you?" but "Where are you?" The other day I called a friend's cell phone. There was no answer, and the voicemail greeting started out with the common "I'm not here right now." I had to laugh. What does "here" actually mean when someone's phone is, by design, not here (or anywhere in particular, for that matter)?

It's important to realize that cellular technology did not develop in response to millions of people clamoring for constant access. It was the other way around. People's "need" to constantly talk to (or text) others as they go about their daily lives grew *as a result of* access to wireless technology that makes communication possible anywhere and anytime. My students know to turn off their ringers before coming to class. But it's rare these days to get through a class period without hearing the telltale buzzing sound of a phone on "vibrate." And it's common on campuses all across the country to see scores of students spilling from rooms into the hallway at the end of class already texting on their phones (and I doubt it's to share the scintillating sociological insight they've just attained!). People talking or texting while riding stationary bikes in fitness centers, using toilets in public restrooms, or, of course, driving has become ubiquitous.

This last tendency has become, in many states, a major focus of legislative action designed to outlaw drivers' use of cell phones. Road fatalities due to distracted driving rose by 8% between 2014 and 2015 (Richtel, 2016). Currently, 14 states and the District of Columbia ban the use of handheld cell phones by all drivers, 38 states ban all cell phone use (including hands-free phones) among drivers under 18, and 46 states ban texting while driving (Governors Highway Safety Association, 2016). The city of Seattle passed a law in 2017 designating "driving under the influence of electronics" as a punishable crime. The National Transportation Safety Board has called for a ban on *all* cell phone use by *all* drivers, saying the recommendation is based on a decade of research into distraction-related accidents (Richtel, 2011).

Wary of people's willingness to voluntarily give up texting and driving, some states are considering the use of a device, called a textalyzer, whereby an officer arriving at the scene of an accident could ask for the phones of the drivers involved, connect them to his or her laptop, and check for touchscreen use or typing at the time of the crash. To avoid any privacy concerns, the device would not give the officer access to the *content* of any e-mails or texts (Richtel, 2016).

Some airlines now allow passengers to use their phones until the plane pushes back from the gate and again the instant the plane touches down. But that's not good enough for some people, and so the Federal Aviation Administration in 2013 announced a new federal policy that allows "gate-to-gate" use of portable electronic devices, though for now it still prohibits airborne calls using cell phones. The European Union approved a policy allowing cell phone use in flights over European airspace some years ago. Such conversational urgency was unknown a mere 10 years ago.

In public places, huffs of disgust and resentful rolled eyes continue to await the person whose "Shake It Off" ringtone goes off while in line at the supermarket. The sound of someone chatting loudly on a cell phone is clearly part of "the soundtrack of daily life" (Wingfield, 2011, p. B1). And people quickly lose patience with those who decide to take a call in the middle of a face-to-face conversation:

> I'm fine with people stepping aside to check something, but when I'm standing in front of someone and in the middle of my conversation they whip out their phone, I'll just stop talking to them and walk away. If they're going to be rude, I'll be rude right back. (quoted in Carr, 2011, p. 12)

The rapid diffusion of such a visible technology initially caught us by surprise. As one author put it over a decade ago, "We should recognize that we're on a technological roller coaster and things are changing fast and there are levels of rudeness that we are just discovering" (quoted in Belson, 2004, p. 14). In fact, we've become so obsessed with staring at our smartphones that a new industry of distraction-reducing products has developed to help us disengage from them. Some apps will silence e-mail, text, or Facebook notifications while allowing crucial alerts to get through. Another limits owners' access to apps they overuse. And one company concluded a Kickstarter campaign a few years ago for a "revolutionary" product called "Light Phone," a credit-card-sized phone that does nothing but place and receive phone calls! (Dougherty, 2015).

As with other forms of technology, people will eventually come to some normative agreement about proper smartphone etiquette in different social situations. Until then, we'll simply have to find ways to cope with this ubiquitous technological distraction.

Social Institutions and Cultural Norms

Large social institutions are closely tied to culture. For one thing, some institutions reflect deeply held cultural values. A free-market economy, for instance, reflects the cultural values of achievement, competition, material acquisition, and so on. A democratic government reflects the values of individual freedom and citizen participation.

As we'll see in the following chapter, other institutions—such as education, religion, and family—provide the mechanisms through which culture and subculture are transmitted across generations.

Institutions are also strongly supported by cultural norms. When a pattern of behavior becomes widely accepted within a particular social institution and is taken for granted in society, sociologists say it has become an **institutionalized norm** (DiMaggio & Powell, 1991). For instance, the institutionalized (that is, culturally acceptable) way of becoming financially successful in most developed societies is to earn a college degree, get a job in an entry-level position somewhere, and eventually work your way to the top. Even things that most of us would condemn have, at times, been institutionalized and encouraged by society. Slavery, for example, was for several hundred years a culturally, legally, and economically acceptable practice in the United States. The buying and selling of slaves was strongly approved by the nation's most powerful forces as well as by many ordinary people (Birenbaum & Sagarin, 1976).

Institutionalized norms constrain people's behavior by making some lines of action unthinkable. But they don't just limit options; they also establish the setting in which people discover their preferences and begin to see the world in a particular way (DiMaggio & Powell, 1991). The military ritualizes the process of becoming a full-fledged member through training, oaths of allegiance, and public recognition of the passage from one rank to another. In doing so, it ensures conformity to military norms and an understanding of the "rules of engagement," the specific norms that govern fighting on the battlefield. Religious congregations reinforce "appropriate" lifestyles and downplay inappropriate ones through collective worship services.

Shifts in one institution are often linked to shifts in another. The abolition of slavery in the United States, for instance, meant that the entire economic system of the South had to be restructured, from an agrarian plantation economy to one characterized by smaller landholdings and increased industrial production. In Russia, the collapse of communism nearly three decades ago strengthened the role of religious organizations in providing people with normative guidelines. In the United States today, the fact that women are no longer expected to be the sole caretakers of children has meant an increase in the number of mothers who enter the paid labor force, which in turn has created a higher demand for organized day care as well as increased pressure on legislatures to enact laws protecting the interests of working parents (see Chapter 7).

Norms and Sanctions

Most norms provide only a general framework of expectations; rarely do they tell us precisely how to act, and rarely do all people follow them at all times. Furthermore, norms may be ambiguous or contradictory. It is no surprise, then, that actual behavior sometimes departs markedly from normative expectations. When it does, negative **sanctions** may be applied. A sanction is a direct social response to some behavior; a negative sanction is one that punishes or otherwise discourages violations of social norms and symbolically reinforces the culture's values and morals.

Different norms evoke different sanctions when violated. **Mores** (pronounced MORE-ayz) are norms, sometimes codified into laws, which are taken very seriously by society. Violation of some mores can elicit severe, state-sponsored sanctions, such as serving time in prison for armed robbery. Other mores may be equally serious but much less formally stated. Sanctions for violating these norms may take the form of public ostracism or exclusion from the group, as when one is excommunicated for going against the moral doctrine of one's church.

The vast majority of everyday norms are relatively minor, however; violations of these norms, called **folkways**, carry much less serious punishment. For instance, if I chew with my mouth open and food dribbles down my chin, others will show outward signs of disapproval and consider me a "disgusting pig." I may receive fewer dinner invitations as a result, but I won't be arrested or banished from my community.

The difference between mores and folkways is not always clear. A few years ago, the Spanish village of La Toba passed an ordinance outlawing dozens of "rude" public behaviors including burping, slurping soup, picking one's nose, coughing without covering one's mouth, and adjusting underwear (C. Wilson, 2012). Some economists have even advocated taxing behaviors that, although not illegal, might be damaging or annoying to others, such as playing music too loudly or driving in congested city areas at peak traffic times. In London, drivers have to pay what amounts to about $16 to enter the central part of the city during rush hours (Davidson, 2013).

According to the structural-functionalist perspective, each time a community moves to sanction an act, it strengthens the boundaries between normative and nonnormative behavior (Erikson, 1966). In the process, the rest of us are warned of what is in store if we, too, violate the norms. In the 17th century, for example, criminals and religious heretics were executed at high noon in the public square for all to see. The spectacle was meant to be a vivid and symbolic reaffirmation of the community's norms. Today, such harsh sanctions are likely to be hidden from the public eye. However, the publicity surrounding executions, as well as the visibility of less severe sanctions, serves the same purpose—to declare to the community where the line between acceptable and unacceptable behavior lies. By sanctioning the person who violates a norm, society informs its members what type of person cannot live "normally" within its boundaries (Pfohl, 1994).

MICRO-MACRO CONNECTION
CAN CULTURE TELL YOU WHAT TO FEEL?

We all experience emotions as physical, sometimes instantaneous responses to life events. Thus, we're inclined to see emotions as natural and universal. Yet emotional display comes under the strict control of cultural norms. In rural areas of Greece, widows traditionally are expected to mourn over the loss of their husbands—most notably by wearing black—for the rest of their lives. That would be seen as excessive in the United States, where more than 2 straight months of grieving might be considered an indicator of major depression (American Psychiatric Association, 2013).

Every society has unwritten rules about which emotions are appropriate to feel, which are appropriate to display, and how intense the emotional display should be under specific circumstances. For instance, in our culture, we're supposed to be sad at funerals, happy at weddings, and angry when we are insulted. We're supposed to feel joy when we receive

good news but not show too much of it if our good fortune is at someone else's expense. In extreme cases, the violation of emotional display norms can lead to grave sanctions, such as a diagnosis of mental illness (Pugliesi, 1987; Thoits, 1985).

When people hide or alter their emotions to fit the situation, they are playing a significant role in maintaining social order within broader social institutions. Take the popular TV show *American Idol*, for example. In the season finale, when the field is finally reduced to the last two contestants, the camera zooms in on both of them. They stand on stage holding hands in shaky anticipation of the final verdict. The lights are dimmed. When the winner is announced, the runner-up is the picture of grace and charm, all smiles and congratulations. But we know better. This person has just lost the contest of her or his life on national television and has got to be sad, angry, or at the very least disappointed. To add insult to

(Continued)

(Continued)

injury, she or he is then gently escorted offstage so the winner can have the spotlight. Why does the runner-up suppress the urge to show true emotions? Part of the reason is that he or she understands that there's more at stake than personal feelings. Imagine what would happen to the *American Idol* phenomenon if the runners-up started displaying their bitterness onstage—screaming at the host, threatening the judges, shunning the winners, or demanding a recount.

Norms about expressing emotions are often linked to institutional concerns and needs. In her book *The Managed Heart*, Arlie Russell Hochschild (1983) describes the feeling rules required by occupations in which employees have a great deal of contact with the public. Flight attendants, for example, must constantly be good-natured and calm under dangerous conditions. They must make their work appear effortless and handle other people's feelings as deftly as their own. This ability is not just a matter of living up to social expectations—it is part of their job description. A "smile" becomes an economic asset and a public relations tool.

Likewise, doctors and nurses are trained to show compassionate concern for their patients, not disgust or alarm. Furthermore, they cannot become too emotionally involved with suffering patients, because they see pain and death every day. It is difficult not to become attached to patients, but such emotional outlay would inevitably lead to burnout, making effective job performance impossible. We want our health care providers to show that they like us, but doctors and nurses are most successful in their jobs when they can keep their emotions under control.

Some companies include explicit instructions on emotional control and display as part of their training programs for new employees. This is especially true in service-sector jobs where contact with customers occurs over the phone. The telephone performance guidelines for one insurance company included the following directives:

> Remember, smiling can be heard as well as seen. . . . Have a smile in your voice and avoid sounding abrupt. . . . Try to make the caller feel you are there for them . . . [and avoid] a disinterested, monotonous tone to voice. . . . Use language which conveys understanding of and empathy for the caller's individual situation, e.g., "are you OK?" "was anyone hurt?" "that must have been very distressing for you." (Cameron, 2000, pp. 334–335)

The ability to enact convincing performances has become even more important given the rise of management techniques that use customer or client input as a means of assessing employees. Many service sector companies survey customers, monitor phone calls, and use undercover "secret shoppers" or other forms of surveillance to gather information on workers, making appropriate emotional display even more important. A. R. Hochschild (1983) warns that this kind of "emotional labor" eventually takes a heavy psychological toll on the workers, who are required to adopt a display of emotions that reflects corporate needs and not their own. These people become increasingly estranged from their true feelings.

Although it is not surprising that organizations would have an interest in emotional displays by members, it is perhaps less obvious that particular emotions are linked to larger societal concerns such as politics and economics, often as a method of social control (Kearl & Gordon, 1992). For instance, the conflict perspective points out that some regimes may use fear to quell dissent and enforce obedience. In the early 20th century, in response to the increasing political and economic strength of African Americans, many white Southerners used fear to control Blacks through the threat of lynching and other forms of violence. Similarly, religious leaders often use the fear of eternal damnation to make sure their followers cooperate.

The effectiveness of invoking emotions such as guilt, anxiety, and shame waxes and wanes as social climates change. In the past, when communities were smaller and more interdependent, social behavior could be easily regulated by the threat of shame. If people broke a law or violated some norm of morality, they would bring humiliation on themselves, their families, and the community at large. But as societies became more complex, such close ties began to disappear. Today, the political control of behavior through emotion is more likely to be directed inward, in the form of guilt and anxiety. For instance, if working mothers are implicated by politicians as contributing to the "breakdown" of the traditional family by leaving the raising of their children to others, more and more mothers will experience guilt when they seek employment outside the home (Berg, 1992).

Norms governing the expression of emotions give us a way to communicate and maintain social order. They perpetuate institutions by creating powerful cultural expectations that are difficult to violate.

Cultural Relativism and Ethnocentrism

When it comes to examining the cultures of different societies, sociologists are inclined to adopt a position of **cultural relativism**, the principle that people's beliefs and activities should be interpreted in terms of their own culture. In other words, practices that might conflict with our cultural values are still considered valid because they reflect the values of that culture. Maintaining a culturally relativist position becomes especially difficult when the practice in question is considered brutal or oppressive. Take, for instance, the practice of female genital mutilation/cutting (FGM/C), a procedure that entails the removal of a young girl's clitoris and/or the destruction of the labia and vulva. In the countries where FGM/C is practiced, women are expected to be virgins when they marry. The ritual therefore serves to simultaneously control young women's sexuality and ensure their "marriageability." But to some international health organizations and to people in societies that acknowledge or even celebrate female sexuality, such a practice is abhorrent and a violation of the human rights of girls and women (World Health Organization, 2016a). A decades-long worldwide campaign to end FGM/C has led many countries to ban the practice. In 2012, the United Nations General Assembly passed a resolution urging countries to condemn all practices that harm women and girls, in particular FGM/C.

However, it persists as a local custom in 30 countries in Africa, the Middle East, and Asia. Where the practice exists, prevalence rates vary widely across countries—from over 90% of all girls in Somalia and Guinea to less than 2% in Uganda and Togo—and between communities and regions within a particular country (Population Reference Bureau, 2012, 2013). Because of international migration, it's estimated that over 500,000 women and girls in the United States today have either undergone or are at risk of the procedure, more than twice the number in 2000. This increase reflects an increase in immigration rather than an increase in the share of women and girls being cut (Mather & Feldman-Jacobs, 2015). The World Health Organization (2016a) estimates that more than 200 million girls and women today are living with the consequences of this procedure, which is usually carried out sometime between infancy and age 15.

Cultural relativism is not part of the way most of us are raised. Instead, people are inclined to evaluate other cultures in comparison to their own. This tendency is called **ethnocentrism**. As children, most people are taught that they live in the greatest country on earth. Many also learn to take pride in their religious, racial, or ethnic group. But the belief that one group or country is the "best" means that others are "not the best." Forty-nine percent of Americans believe that their culture is superior to others (Wike, 2012). The figure rises to 90% in South Korea and Indonesia (cited in Rieff, 2006).

Ethnocentrism results from the nature of human interaction itself. Much of our everyday lives is spent in groups and organizations. By their very character, these collectivities consist of individuals with some, though not necessarily all, shared interests. The same is true for larger cultures. To the extent that we spend a majority of our time with others "like us," our interactions with others "not like us" will be limited, and they will remain "foreign" or "mysterious." Similarity breeds comfort; difference breeds discomfort. For example, despite laws against the practice, many Japanese shopkeepers are so uncomfortable dealing with foreigners that they refuse to serve them (French, 1999). In fact, when Japanese citizens who have lived abroad for a long time return to Japan, they find that they are no longer regarded as fully Japanese and are treated with the sort of cold disdain foreigners there often experience (French, 2000).

ABHIJIT BANERJEE AND ESTHER DUFLO

WHY WOULD YOU BUY THAT? HOW CULTURE AFFECTS THE PURCHASING DECISIONS OF POOR PEOPLE

Ethnocentrism often reveals itself in harsh judgments of lifestyles that seem to challenge one's own cultural values. People often look incredulously at others who make decisions that contradict what they would do under similar circumstances. When such decisions lead to additional—or, from the observer's perspective, avoidable—suffering, sympathy wanes.

Take, for instance, the way poor families with very little money prioritize their purchases. Two MIT economists, Abhijit Banerjee and Esther Duflo (2006), studied spending patterns among poor households in 13 countries in Africa, Asia, and Latin America. They examined both "poor" households—where people live on less than $2 a day per capita—and "extremely poor" households—where they live on less than $1 a day.

The researchers started with a basic—and perhaps ethnocentric—assumption: that when people have very little money, they should spend what they do have on basic necessities such as food, clothing, and education for their children. Instead, much to their chagrin, they found that families in some of the poorest areas in the world spend a relatively high proportion of their meager money on "frivolous" things like alcohol and cigarettes. In rural Mexico, for example, families spend less than half their budget on food, even though hunger and malnutrition are common. Especially surprising to the researchers was the tendency for spending on celebratory festivals to be an important part of the budget of many extremely poor households. In South Africa, 90% of households living on less than $1 a day spent some of their money on festivals. In one Indian state, Udaipur, more than 99% of extremely poor households had spent money the previous year on weddings, funerals, or religious celebrations. As the authors put it:

> It is hard to escape the conclusion that the poor do see themselves as having a significant amount of choice, and choose not to exercise it in the direction of spending more on food—the typical poor household in Udaipur could spend up to 30 percent more on food than it actually does, just based on what it spends on alcohol, tobacco, and festivals. (A. V. Banerjee & Duflo, 2006, p. 6)

An American newspaper columnist responding to this study was even less forgiving:

> If the poorest families spent as much money educating their children as they do on wine, cigarettes, and prostitutes, their children's prospects would be transformed. Much suffering is caused not only by low incomes, but also by shortsighted private spending decisions by heads of households. . . . I've seen too many children dying of malaria for want of a bed net that the father tells me is unaffordable, even as he spends larger sums on liquor. If we want . . . children to get an education and sleep under a bed net, . . . the simplest option is for their dad to spend fewer evenings in the bar. (Kristof, 2010, p. 9)

Not everyone agrees that poor people can't be trusted to spend their money appropriately. One international charity organization, called GiveDirectly, gives money to poor people around the world without any conditions on how they spend it. One study found positive and sustainable effects of these unconditional cash transfers on a wide range of outcomes including assets, earnings (from sources other than the payments), food security, mental health, and domestic violence. And contrary to popular stereotypes, the study found no evidence that recipients were blowing the money on alcohol or tobacco (Haushofer & Shapiro, 2016). Other assessments of this program have found that children from families that receive these payments are more likely to stay in school and less likely to get sick (GiveDirectly, 2016; Goldstein, 2013).

Furthermore, Banerjee and Duflo based their assessment on existing surveys of people's consumption patterns. They had no information on the reasons people bought what they did or the cultural belief systems under which they live their lives. In some cultures, for instance, festivals celebrating gods or goddesses are the expressions of devotion that can lead to a better eternal life. In other cultures, buying something beyond one's means or something that appears frivolous, like a bottle of wine, might be the only way a family can establish its social status in the community; and these social needs may outweigh the more immediate needs of individual family members. Some indigenous peoples of the Pacific Northwest practice a ritual called *potlatch*, where people with very few economic resources give away or destroy much of what they have. In these cultures, the status of any given family is determined not by who has the most but by who gives away the most. In short, all cultures may not abide by the same definition of "basic needs." Hence, to an outsider focused on survival issues who doesn't understand the broader cultural context in which people make their choices, the kinds of consumption patterns these researchers identified do indeed look ill-considered and irrational.

Another reason for the existence of ethnocentrism is the loyalty we develop to our particular culture or subculture (Charon, 1992). Different values, beliefs, and behaviors come to be seen not merely as different ways of thinking and acting but as threats to our own beliefs and values. Such perceptions, for instance, underlie much of the resentment of and hostility toward recently arrived immigrants. Even groups whose position in society is strong and secure can find the encroachment of other ways of life threatening:

- A Honolulu restaurant made headlines several years ago for its policy of adding a 15% gratuity to the checks of all non–English-speaking patrons. The owner claimed he put the policy into place because Asian guests routinely fail to tip. "It's not a part of their culture," he said. "They spend a lot of money, but they don't tip" (quoted in McKinley, 2011, p. A16).

- In 2011, a bill introduced in the California legislature sought to ban the sale and possession of shark fins because of the brutal way the fins are hacked off live sharks. Similar bills have been presented in Oregon and Washington. But shark fins are a centuries-old delicacy among Chinese residents, who perceive the proposed law as an assault on their cultural traditions (P. L. Brown, 2011).

- Every December, religiously conservative bloggers and media personalities begin complaining about how the use of "Happy Holidays" and "Seasons Greetings" instead of "Merry Christmas" is an attack on Christianity, even though 9 out of 10 Americans observe the holiday. In 2017, President Trump, in a speech about religious liberty, promised his audience that "we're going to start saying 'Merry Christmas' again" (quoted in Wang, 2017b, p. 1). Two years earlier, then-candidate Trump threatened to launch a boycott of Starbucks after the coffee company abandoned its original Christmas-themed holiday cup design—which was never all that Christmas-y in the first place—for a plain red one (McGill, 2016).

Ethnocentrism is also encouraged by institutional ritual and symbolism. In this country, saying the Pledge of Allegiance at the beginning of the school day, playing the "Star-Spangled Banner" and "God Bless America" at sports events, and observing holidays such as Memorial Day, the Fourth of July, and Veterans Day all reinforce loyalty to U.S. culture. The American flag is considered such an important national symbol that an entire code of etiquette with specific instructions on how to display it exists to ensure that it is treated with reverence. You will recall the recent fury directed toward NFL players who knelt during the presentation of the flag and the playing of the national anthem in protest of the unequal treatment of African Americans. Many people were outraged because they considered such a gesture a treasonous form of disrespect. These are the "sacred objects" of U.S.

culture (Durkheim, 1915/1954). The importance of these objects is especially pronounced when people in society feel threatened. After the September 11, 2001, attacks and during the wars in Iraq and Afghanistan, an enormous number of American flags, patriotic songs, pins, T-shirts, and magnetic ribbons on cars exploded onto the cultural landscape.

Religious artifacts, heritage symbols, and distinctive ethnic clothing all foster a sense of pride and identity and hold a community of similar people together, often to the exclusion of others. We saw the power of certain symbols to simultaneously create pride and disgust in 2015 when a white supremacist in Charleston, South Carolina, murdered nine black worshipers during a church Bible study. Online photos of the killer prior to the massacre showed him holding the Confederate battle flag, a symbol of Southern history and tradition to some but a symbol of slavery, racial hatred, and treason to others. In the days after the slaughter, support for the removal of the flag from public places throughout the South grew stronger, indicating a shift in its symbolism. EBay, Walmart, Amazon, and Sears all announced they would no longer sell the flag. Politicians in Alabama, Mississippi, and South Carolina called for its swift removal from state government property.

Sometimes respect for these cultural objects must be enforced under threat of punishment. For years, some members of the U.S. Congress have been trying to ensure loyalty to the American flag by proposing a constitutional amendment banning its desecration. In 2012, eight teachers in Osaka, Japan, were punished for not standing and singing the *Kimigayo,* the Japanese national anthem, at the beginning of the school day. They faced reprimands, pay cuts, and suspensions for their actions ("8 Osaka Teachers," 2012). India has a law, the Prevention of Insults to National Honour Act, that prohibits the desecration of the country's national symbols, including the national flag, the constitution, and the national anthem.

Cultural Variation and Everyday Experience

As populations grow more ethnically and racially diverse and as the people of the world become linked more closely by commerce, transportation, and communication, the likelihood of individuals from different cultures and subcultures living together increases. An awareness of cultural differences helps ease everyday interactions in a multicultural society and can be crucial in international relations:

- In Iran, people are expected to give false praise and make insincere promises. They are expected to tell others what they want to hear in order to avoid conflict or offer hope when, clearly, there is none. This practice, known as *taarof*, is considered polite, not offensive. Children learn from an early age to pick up on nuances in others' comments. The practice has its historical roots in centuries of occupation by foreign powers, which taught Iranians the value of hiding their true feelings. As one Iranian psychologist put it, "When you tell lies, it can save your life" (quoted in Slackman, 2006, p. 5).

- In Afghanistan, the thumbs-up gesture—a sign of approval in the United States—is the equivalent of giving someone "the finger." To reduce potentially dangerous cultural clashes during the war in Afghanistan, the U.S. Marine Corps distributed "Culture Smart Cards" to U.S. military personnel upon their arrival. The cards contained instructions on matters such as how to shake hands, what gestures are appropriate, and how to act when in Afghan homes (Edidin, 2005).

- In some parts of the world, a practice known as "avoidance speech" imposes strict rules on how a person talks to the parents of his or her spouse. For instance, Kambaata-speaking women in Ethiopia follow a rule, called *ballishsha,* which forbids them from using words that begin with the same syllable as the name of their mother- or father-in-law. In parts of India, a daughter-in-law cannot use words that begin with the same letters as her in-laws' names. And among some aboriginal cultures in Australia, men and their mothers-in-law are not allowed to directly talk to one another (Rousseau, 2017).

In all these cases, you can see how important it is to know of such tendencies. Without such knowledge, the risk of misunderstandings and perhaps even conflict increases.

Cultural variation reflects more than just differences in people's habits and customs. It indicates that even the most taken-for-granted truths in our lives, the things we assume are universal and unambiguous, are subject to different interpretations and definitions worldwide. Two important examples of such variation are beliefs about health and illness and definitions of the sexes.

Health and Illness

A prominent doctor once said, "A disease does not exist until we name it" (quoted in Kolata, 2011, p. 3). In other words, we can't claim to have a disease that is not recognized as real in our culture. In Malaysia, a man may be diagnosed with *koro,* a sudden, intense anxiety that his sexual organs will recede into his body, causing death. In some Latin American countries, a person can suffer from *susto,* an illness tied to a frightening event that makes the soul leave the body, causing unhappiness and sickness (American Psychiatric Association, 2013). Experts estimate that as many as one million Japanese youth (or about 1% of the population) suffer from *hikikomori,* a phenomenon whereby alienated adolescents (mostly boys) withdraw from social life and sequester themselves in their rooms for months or even years (Stainbrook, 2014). None of these conditions exists as a medical diagnosis elsewhere in the world. But they are not simply anthropological curiosities. They show that culture shapes everyday notions of health and illness.

Even more compelling, though, are the dramatic cultural differences in medical treatment among societies that share many other values, beliefs, norms, and structural elements. In the United States, medical treatment tends to originate from an aggressive "can do" cultural spirit. Diseases are enemies that need to be conquered. Words like "fight" and "battle" are frequently invoked to describe the struggles of people receiving cancer treatment. Their stoicism in facing the disease, undergoing surgery, or enduring the powerful side effects of chemotherapy are often considered signs of "bravery." If they recover, they've "beaten" or "defeated" the cancer; if they succumb, they've "lost the good fight" (Jennings, 2010).

Consequently, doctors in the United States are much more likely than European doctors to prescribe drugs and resort to surgery (Payer, 1988). Women in the United States are more likely than their European counterparts to undergo radical mastectomies, deliver their babies by cesarean section, and undergo routine hysterectomies while still in their 40s. Americans tend to see their bodies as machines that require routine maintenance. Hence they remain devoted to the "annual physical exam," even though decades of scientific research has shown that such check-ups—and the routine screenings they often involve—make little difference in people's overall health. Indeed, for healthy adults with no symptoms, annual physicals are more likely to find false positives than real disease (E. Rosenthal, 2012a).

VISUAL ESSAY—GREETINGS AND SALUTATIONS

GORDON WILTSIE/National Geographic Creative

John Eastcott & Yva Momatiuk/National Geographic/Getty Images

XPACIFICA/National Geographic Creative

Shaukat Ahmed/LightRocket/Getty Images

Whitney Curtis/Invision for Kingsford/AP Images

Culture is a guide for everyday living. What makes culture especially important is how it dictates the thousands of microlevel experiences in people's day-to-day lives—the things we rarely stop and think about. Take, for instance, the way people greet one another. In New Zealand, people touch noses; in Japan, they bow; in France, they kiss each other on the cheek; in Nepal, they put their hands together as if in prayer; in India, a visitor might receive a *bindi*, a colorful dot placed on the forehead, as a form of welcome; in the United States, a firm handshake will do.

Consider the various ways *you* greet the people in your life. A handshake? A kiss? An affectionate embrace? A fist bump? A nonchalant nod? A bro hug? How does the relationship you have with someone influence the way you greet him or her? Does it matter if that person is older or younger? A friend or a stranger? Someone of your sex or a different sex? Someone of your race or a different race? What about the location? Do you greet people differently when they arrive at your house than when you see them, say, in between classes on campus? Think of the broader implications of these different cultural expectations. Use your sociological imagination to examine why it's so important to know that people from different cultures greet (or for that matter, converse with, touch, or say goodbye to) each other differently.

In contrast, British medicine is much more subdued. British physicians don't recommend routine examinations, seldom prescribe drugs, and order about half as many X-ray studies as U.S. doctors do. British patients are also much less likely to have surgery. These attitudes also influence perceptions of patients. People who are quiet and withdrawn—something U.S. doctors might consider as symptoms of clinical depression—tend to be seen by British psychiatrists as perfectly normal.

Ironically, despite their more aggressive approach, Americans are actually much sicker than their British counterparts, even though the United States spends nearly three times as much on health care per person than Great Britain (The Commonwealth Fund, 2015). They suffer higher rates of conditions like diabetes, heart disease, and obesity and have a lower life expectancy. These differences exist even when controlling for social class. According to one study, the richest one third of U.S. citizens are in worse health than the poorest one third of Britons (Banks, Marmot, Oldfield, & Smith, 2006). In fact, when compared to other wealthy, industrialized countries—not just Great Britain—Americans fare worse in such major health indicators as infant mortality, HIV/AIDS, drug-related deaths, obesity, diabetes, heart disease, and several types of cancer. The United States also has higher incidences of medical mistakes and malpractice (GBD 2015 Healthcare Access and Quality Collaborators, 2017; Institute of Medicine, 2013). Indeed, of 34 high-income, industrialized nations, the United States ranks 29th in terms of life expectancy for newborn girls (Woolf & Aron, 2013). A French baby born today can expect to live 3½ years longer than an American baby (Porter, 2016).

In addition to determining the nature of illness, cultural attitudes determine what it means to be sick and how individuals experience sickness. Each society has a **sick role**, a widely understood set of rules about how people are supposed to behave when sick (Parsons, 1951). The sick role entails certain obligations (things sick people are expected to do) as well as certain privileges (things sick people are entitled to). Here are some common elements of the sick role in U.S. society:

- Because we tend to think of most illnesses as things that happen to people, individuals may be exempted from responsibility for the condition itself. At the same time, though, they're expected to recognize the condition as undesirable and something that should be overcome as soon as possible.

- Individuals who are allowed to occupy the sick role are excused from ordinary daily duties and expectations. This privilege varies with the severity of the illness. Compare someone with cancer to someone with a cold, for instance. National legislation—in the form of the Family and Medical Leave Act—and private workplace sick leave policies are the institutional manifestations of these expectations.

- Depending on the magnitude of the malady, sick people may be given relief from the ordinary norms of etiquette and propriety. Think of the nasty moods, actions, or insults you're able to "get away with" when you're sick that people wouldn't tolerate from you if you were well.

- Sick people are entitled to ask for and receive care and sympathy from others. But sympathy requests operate under their own set of cultural regulations. For instance, one should not claim too much sympathy, for too long, or for too many problems. In other words, sick people are expected to downplay their problems to avoid the appearance of self-pity. At the same time, though, they are expected to graciously accept some expressions of sympathy so as not to appear ungrateful (C. Clark, 1997).

- People occupying the sick role are required to take the culturally prescribed actions that will aid in their recovery, including, if the condition is serious enough, seeking help from a culturally appropriate health care professional (Parsons, 1951). Sometimes, to obtain the privilege of exemption from normal social obligations, people must be documented as officially ill from a culturally acceptable source. In the United States, that means a "doctor's note" (Lorber, 2000). Without such validation, your boss might not give you the day off, or your instructor might not allow you to miss an exam and reschedule it for a later date.

- Sick people are obligated to think of others as well as themselves. Hence, they are required to take precautions to avoid infecting those around them. In some cultures, sick people are expected to wear surgical masks in public to prevent contamination.

Failure on the part of sick people either to exercise their rights or to fulfill the obligations of the sick role—as when a person shows up at work with a persistent cough and a 102-degree fever—may elicit sanctions from the group (Crary, 2007). Moreover, those who do not appear to want to recover or who seem to enjoy being sick quickly lose sympathy. A person may also give up legal rights by not seeking or following expert advice. Parents who, because of their religious beliefs, prevent culturally approved medical intervention for their sick children have been arrested and charged with child endangerment or worse. If you are hospitalized and your attending physician doesn't think you ought to be discharged, but you leave anyway, your records will indicate that you have left "AMA"—against medical advice. This designation protects the doctor and the hospital from any liability should your condition worsen.

Like illness itself, sick role expectations are culturally influenced. For instance, when recent Latin American immigrants to the United States fall ill, they are likely to make a visit to the local *botanica* rather than a doctor. *Botanicas* are stores that sell all manner of folk remedies, religious objects, amulets, oils, perfumes, and other products purported to have curative powers. These practices, which combine alternative medicine with Roman Catholicism and other spiritual practices, are used to treat everything from arthritis to financial problems (Trotter & Chavira, 1997).

While different cultures define the sick role differently, it can also vary considerably along social class lines within the same culture (Freund & McGuire, 1991). Someone might have a debilitating disease, but without health insurance she or he may not have the wherewithal to seek the care of health professionals (and receive an official diagnosis) or may not be able to take time off from work for fear of losing her or his job. In short, socioeconomic factors may preclude such people from claiming sick role status.

The Sexes

The culture we grow up in shapes our most fundamental beliefs, even about what most people would consider the basic, universal facts of life. For instance, we take for granted that humans can be divided into two clearly identifiable sexes that are genetically determined at the moment of conception. If you asked someone how to distinguish between males and females, the response would probably focus on observable physical characteristics—body shape, hair, voice, facial features, and so on. When biologists distinguish between the sexes, they too refer to biological traits—for example, chromosomes (XX for female, XY for male), sex glands (ovaries or testes), hormones (estrogen or testosterone), genitalia (vagina or penis), reproductive capacities (pregnancy or impregnation), germ cells produced (ova or sperm), and secondary sex characteristics (hips and breasts or facial hair and deep voice).

These characteristics, and hence the two sex categories, male and female, are usually assumed to be biologically determined, permanent, universal (males are males and females are females no matter what country or what era you live in), exhaustive (everyone can be placed into one or the other category), and mutually exclusive (you can only be one or the other sex; you can't be both). This set of beliefs is called the **sexual dichotomy**.

If you think about it, our entire culture is built around the sexual dichotomy. We have separate clothing sections for men and women, separate hygienic products, separate sections in shoe stores, separate public restrooms (though this is changing), separate sports leagues, and so on. The sexual dichotomy is so obvious that we simply assume it to be in the nature of things. Our casual references to the "opposite" sex reinforce how much we take the sexual dichotomy for granted; when two things are opposite, it implies there's nothing in between.

But on closer inspection, the natural reality of the sexual dichotomy begins to break down. Throughout human history and across all societies, certain people have transcended the categories of male and female. They may be born with anatomical and/or genital configurations that don't fit neatly into one or the other category. Or they may identify as **transgender** and simply choose to live their lives in ways that don't conform to existing gender expectations associated with their assigned sex (see Chapter 5 for more information about the distinction between sex and gender).

Transsexuals—people who identify with a different sex and sometimes undergo hormone treatment and surgery to change their sex—challenge the idea that male and female are permanent biological characteristics. It's estimated that 1 in 30,000 men and 1 in 100,000 women in the United States undergo sex reassignment surgery each year, although many advocates consider this figure an underestimate (Conway, 2013). In 2008, a female-to-male transsexual named Thomas Beatie made international headlines when he gave birth to a baby girl. Although Thomas had his breasts removed, was taking testosterone (which deepened his voice and gave him facial hair), and was legally a man, he had kept his female reproductive organs.

The growing number and visibility of transgender and transsexual individuals has placed new pressures on a variety of social institutions like schools and public recreational facilities to serve their needs or risk charges of discrimination. For instance, cities around the country continue to grapple with how to accommodate transgender individuals' use of sex-segregated restrooms in schools and public pools. As you may recall, a firestorm erupted in 2016 when North Carolina passed a so-called "bathroom law," which required transgender people to use the public restroom that coincided with sex on their birth certificate and not with the sex with which they identify. Legislators in Texas began debating a similar bill in 2017.

The problem is especially acute for single-sex colleges that must find ways to house and meet the needs of their students who enter the school as one sex but who present as or transition to a different sex after their arrival on campus. Hollins University, a women's college in Virginia, has a policy whereby it confers diplomas only to women. Hence it encourages students who are in transition to transfer to other schools. But Mount Holyoke and Mills College will admit those who identify on their applications as trans men. Wellesley College only considers female applicants for admission, but once admitted and enrolled, a trans student is allowed to remain (Padawer, 2014).

In addition, as it becomes more common (and acceptable) for children and adolescents to openly question their sexual identity, more are opting for physical sex reassignment at younger ages. No law prohibits minors from receiving hormone treatment or even surgical reconstruction, but both private and public insurers generally refuse to cover these procedures for people under 18. Some advocacy groups have begun fighting for coverage for procedures at younger ages, perhaps as early as puberty (Hartocollis, 2015).

The impermanence of sex has, from time to time, received official institutional recognition of sorts. In 2015, the Pentagon unveiled a plan that would allow transgender people to openly serve in the military (though at the time of this writing, President Trump had publicly voiced a desire to rescind the policy). Several years earlier, the Ladies Professional Golf Association voted to eliminate the tour's requirement that players be "female at birth" and to allow transgender athletes to compete (Thomas, 2010). Fifteen years ago, the International Olympic Committee, which sets guidelines for athletes' participation in the Olympic Games, adopted a policy that allowed transsexuals to compete in the 2004 Athens Olympic Games as long as they had undergone sex reassignment surgery and had begun hormone treatment at least 2 years prior to competition. In 2016, it amended this policy so that surgery is no longer required. Now female-to-male transgender athletes are eligible to take part in men's competitions "without restriction." However, male-to-female transgender athletes need to demonstrate that their testosterone level has been below a certain cutoff point for at least 1 year before their first competition (*The Guardian*, 2016).

Although transgender and transsexual individuals can challenge the assumption of sexual permanence when they transition, they don't necessarily challenge the belief that there are only two sex categories. But that assumption is contested in some cultures.

In Navajo culture, for instance, one could be identified as male, female, or *nadle*—a third sex assigned to those whose sex-typed anatomical characteristics were ambiguous at birth (Lang, 1998). Physically normal individuals also had the opportunity to choose to become *nadle* if they so desired. The gender status of *nadle* is simultaneously masculine and feminine. They are allowed to perform the tasks and take up the occupations of both men and women. In Samoa, *fa'afafines* are biological men who embody female traits and live their lives as women. The *hijras* of India are born as men, but by choice they have their genitals surgically removed (Reddy, 2005). This operation transforms them not into women but into *hijras*, who appear feminine—dressing, standing, walking, and sitting as women. Many figures in Hindu mythology are neither male nor female. Hence, Indian culture not only accommodates the *hijras* but views them as meaningful, even powerful beings. Though they have been a part of Indian culture since ancient times, it wasn't until 2014 that the Indian Supreme Court officially recognized the 5 to 6 million *hijras* living in India as an official—and legal—third gender category (Keck, 2014). Similarly, other countries have recently taken steps to legally recognize sex categories other than male and female. Australians and Canadians can choose to list their sex as indeterminate (symbolized as "X") on their passports. In Germany, parents can choose "no gender" on their babies' birth certificates.

Cross-cultural examples like these illustrate that our taken-for-granted beliefs about sex and gender are not held worldwide. In other cultures, sex needn't be dichotomous, exhaustive, or permanent.

The sexual dichotomy is not challenge-free in the United States either. Consider the standard of mutual exclusivity, for example. **Intersexuals** (or "people with disorders of sexual development" as they are now known) are individuals in whom sexual differentiation is either incomplete or indistinct. They may have the chromosomal pattern of a female but the external genitals of a male, or they may have both ovaries and testicles. Experts estimate that about 1% of all babies born have some form of intersexuality, meaning that they are born with sexual organs that don't completely fit into the standard sex categories (Intersex Society of North America, 2008).

It is interesting to note that the medical response to intersexuals generally supports the cultural and historical belief that there are two and only two sexes. Intersexuality is typically defined by doctors and medical researchers as a defective combination of the two existing categories and not as a third, fourth, or fifth category unto itself. Traditionally, on diagnosis of intersexuality, a decision was always made to define the individual as either male or female. In societies with advanced medical technology, surgical and chemical means may be used to establish consistency between visible anatomy and the social label. About 2 babies in 1,000 receive surgery to "normalize" their appearance (Intersex Society of North America, 2008). About 90% are designated female because creating a vagina is considered surgically easier than creating a penis (Angier, 1997).

The medical profession continues to have difficulty postponing or avoiding surgery in these cases because to do so would undermine our cultural understanding of sex. Drastic intervention is considered appropriate not because the infant's life is threatened but because an entire social structure organized around having two and only two sexes is being threatened (Lorber, 1989). The male-female dichotomy in our culture is so essential to our way of life that those whose bodies challenge it are often considered disloyal to the most fundamental of biological "facts." To suggest that the labels "male" and "female" are not sufficient to categorize everyone is to threaten a basic organizing principle of social life. So pervasive is this thinking that one doctor estimated her chances of persuading the parents of an intersexual child *not* to choose surgery at zero (E. Weil, 2006).

However, an increasingly vocal group of people with disorders of sexual development protest this approach. They argue that many of the surgical techniques used to "correct" the problem of visually ambiguous genitals are mutilating and potentially harmful. They cite cases of people being robbed of any sexual sensation in the attempt to surgically "normalize" them—that is, give them the physical appearance of either a male or a female. In 2013, the United Nations released a statement condemning the medical profession's practice of performing irreversible surgeries on babies and young children to "normalize" their genital appearance (G. Davis, 2013). An organization called Accord Alliance (2014) now recommends that surgical intervention, if done at all, should not occur until puberty, when the individual involved can be fully informed and included in all the decision-making. Even the American Medical Association's Board of Trustees has proposed a new policy that would ban such surgery on infants and young children unless the condition was life-threatening (Crary, 2017).

Conclusion

Over the span of a year or two, most cultures seem to have a stable set of norms about the acceptability of certain behaviors. This stability is illusory, however. From the perspective of a generation or even a decade later, that sense of order would give way to a sense of change (McCall & Simmons, 1978). Behaviors, values, beliefs, and morals fluctuate with startling frequency. Thus, comparisons across eras, in addition to comparisons across cultures, can provide rich insight into shifting definitions of acceptability, the nature of everyday life, and ultimately large-scale social change and stability.

The cultural and historical underpinnings of our private lives help us see the relationship between the individual, society, and social order. Cultural practices add continuity and order to social life.

To an individual, culture appears massive and unrelenting; but at the same time, it cannot exist without people. Norms govern our lives, whether we live by them or rebel against them. But to fully understand the relationship between the individual and society, we must look beyond the fact that culture and history shape our lives; we must see them as human constructions as well.

Your Turn

Although everyday cultural norms underlie all we do, they remain largely unnoticed and unquestioned. The best proof of the existence of these norms lies in our reactions when they are violated. This exercise entails a small breach of a common cultural norm. The following suggestions are based on an exercise used by sociologist Jodi O'Brien at Seattle University:

- Make a purchase in a department store and offer to pay more than the listed price. Try to convince the clerk that you think the merchandise is worth the price you are offering.

- Send a close family member a birthday card months away from his or her actual birthday.

- Quietly talk to yourself in a public place.

- Stand or sit close to a stranger or, conversely, stand far away from a good friend or lover during the course of an ordinary conversation.

- Select an occasion—going to class, going on a date, going to the library—and dress differently from the expected "uniform." Treat your attire as absolutely appropriate to the circumstances.

- Whenever someone says to you, "See you later," ask her or him probing questions: "When?" "Do you have some plans to get together later?" "What do you mean by 'see'?" and so on. Or when someone says, "How's it going?" ask, "What do you mean by 'it'?" or "What do you mean by 'going'?"

- In a restaurant, offer to pay for your meal before you order it, or order dessert first, then the main course, then appetizers, and then drinks.

If you like, you can choose a different unspoken norm as long as it is one that lends order and predictability to daily social interactions. Be creative!

It is particularly important that this behavior be neither flagrantly bizarre—such as going to class dressed as a chicken—nor a violation of the law. Such acts do not address the power of the subtle, unspoken norms that, symbolic interactionism argues, make social life orderly. Also, do not do anything that might seriously inconvenience or humiliate someone else or put you in danger. Finally, make sure the norm has something to do with keeping order in face-to-face interactions. For instance, coming to class 10 minutes late violates a cultural norm, but it doesn't disrupt interactional order. Above all, remember to treat your violation as perfectly normal. You must give the impression that what you are doing is perfectly acceptable and ordinary.

As you conduct your exercises, record your own feelings and reactions as well as those of the people around you. What were people's initial responses to you? What did they do to try to "normalize" your behavior? How did you feel breaching this norm? Were you nervous? Was it uncomfortable? If so, why?

If possible, try also to debrief your subjects afterward: Tell them what you were really doing, and then interview them regarding their interpretations of the experience. You are likely to collect additional information on how people attempt to "explain away" unusual and strange circumstances and how they attempt to restore order to the situation. What are the implications of these sorts of "experiments" for understanding human behavior and the nature of social order in this society?

Chapter Highlights

- Culture provides members of a society with a common bond, a sense that we see certain facets of society in similar ways. That we can live together at all depends on the fact that members of a society share a certain amount of cultural knowledge.

- Norms—the rules and standards that govern all social encounters—provide order in our lives. They reflect commonly held assumptions about conventional behavior. Norm violations mark the boundaries of acceptable behavior and symbolically reaffirm what society defines as right and wrong.

- The more ethnically and culturally diverse a society, the greater the likelihood of normative clashes between groups.

- Over the span of a few years, most cultures present an image of stability and agreement regarding normative boundaries. This agreement is illusory, however. Over a generation or even a decade, that sense of order is replaced by a sense of change.

Key Terms

cultural relativism: Principle that people's beliefs and activities should be interpreted in terms of their own culture

ethnocentrism: Tendency to judge other cultures using one's own as a standard

folkway: Informal norm that is mildly punished when violated

heteronormative culture: Culture in which heterosexuality is accepted as the normal, taken-for-granted mode of sexual expression

institutionalized norm: Pattern of behavior within existing social institutions that is widely accepted in a society

intersexuals: Individuals in whom sexual differentiation is either incomplete or ambiguous (also known as people with disorders of sexual development)

material culture: Artifacts of a society that represent adaptations to the social and physical environment

mores: Highly codified, formal, systematized norms that bring severe punishment when violated

nonmaterial culture: Knowledge, beliefs, customs, values, morals, and symbols that are shared by members of a society and that distinguish the society from others

sanction: Social response that punishes or otherwise discourages violations of a social norm

sexual dichotomy: Belief that two biological sex categories, male and female, are permanent, universal, exhaustive, and mutually exclusive

sick role: Set of norms governing how one is supposed to behave and what one is entitled to when sick

subculture: Values, behaviors, and artifacts of a group that distinguish its members from the larger culture

transgender: State in which one's gender expression or identity does not conform to her or his assigned sex

transsexuals: People who identify with a different sex and sometimes undergo hormone treatment and surgery to change their sex

SAGE edge™ edge.sagepub.com/newman12e

SAGE edge offers a robust online environment featuring an impressive array of free tools and resources for review, study, and further exploration, keeping both instructors and students on the cutting edge of teaching and learning.

5

Building Identity
Socialization

- Genes, Social Structure, and the Construction of Human Beings
- Socialization: Becoming You
- Socialization and Stratification: Growing Up With Inequality
- Institutions and Socialization

When I was young, my family lived just outside of New York City. One day, shortly after my ninth birthday, my parents sat me down along with my two older siblings and told us that we were going to be moving. They had narrowed down our ultimate destination to two possibilities: Laredo, Texas, or Burbank, California, a Los Angeles suburb. After some rather intense discussion, they chose Burbank. And so we headed "out West," where from age 9 to age 18, I lived in the shadow of the entertainment industry and all its glamour, glitz, and movie stars. It wasn't long before I became a typical sun-worshipping Southern California kid.

I often wonder how differently I would have turned out if my parents had chosen Laredo and I had spent my formative years along the Texas-Mexico border instead of the show business capital of the world. Would I have a fondness for cowboy hats and snakeskin boots instead of flip-flops and shorts? Would I have grown up loving country music instead of the Beach Boys? Would my goals, beliefs, or sense of morality be different? In short, would I be a different person?

Try to imagine what your life would be like if you had grown up under different circumstances. What if your father had been a harpsichord enthusiast instead of an avid baseball aficionado? What if your family was Muslim instead of Episcopalian? What if you had an older brother instead of a younger sister? What if you had lived on a farm instead of in a big city? What if you had been born in the 1960s instead of the 1990s? Would your tastes, preferences, and hobbies be different? How about your values, ambitions, and aspirations? More profoundly, would your self-concept, self-esteem, personality—the very essence of who you are—be changed too?

Consider the broader social and historical circumstances of your life. What kind of impact might they have on the type of person you are? Talk to very old people who were children back in the 1930s, and they will speak of the permanent impact that the Great Depression had on them (Elder & Liker, 1982). Imagine spending your childhood as a Jew in Nazi Germany. That couldn't help but shape your outlook on life. The same can be said for growing up poor and black in Mississippi in the segregated 1950s or wealthy and white in Utah during the George W. Bush presidency.

Becoming the person you are cannot be separated from the people, historical events, and social circumstances that surround you. In this chapter, I examine the process of socialization—how we learn what's expected of us in our families, our communities, and our culture and how we learn to behave according to those expectations. The primary focus will be on the development of identity. **Identity** is our most essential and personal characteristic. It consists of our membership in various social groups (race, ethnicity, religion, gender, etc.), the traits we show to others, and the traits they ascribe to us. Our identity locates us in the social world, thoroughly affecting everything we do, feel, say, and think in our lives. Most people tend to believe that our self-concept, our sense of "maleness" or "femaleness," and our racial and ethnic identities are biologically or psychologically determined and therefore permanent and unchangeable. But as you will discover, these characteristics are social constructions: as much a product of our social setting and the significant people in our lives as a product of our physical traits and innate predispositions.

Genes, Social Structure, and the Construction of Human Beings

The question of how we become who we are has for centuries occupied the attention of biologists, psychologists, anthropologists, sociologists, philosophers, poets, and novelists. The issue is often framed as a debate between *nature* (we are who we are because we were born that way) and *nurture* (we are who we are because of the way we were treated while growing up). Are we simply the predetermined product of our genes and biochemistry, or are we "created" from scratch by the individuals and social institutions that surround us?

The answer to this question swings back and forth depending on the dominant cultural mood. In the late 19th and early 20th centuries, genetic inheritance was a popular explanation for human behavior, including a host of social problems ranging from poverty and crime to alcoholism and mental deficiency. Scientists, borrowing from the selective breeding practices used with thoroughbred racehorses and livestock, advocated programs of **eugenics**, or controlled mating, to produce "better" citizens and to ensure that the "defective" genes of troublesome individuals would not be passed on to future generations. These ideas were put into practice largely through programs of forced sterilization. Similar theories of genetic superiority and inferiority became the cornerstone of Adolf Hitler's horrors in Nazi Germany during World War II. After the war, most people wanted to get as far away from such "nature" arguments as possible. So in the 1950s and 1960s, scholars heavily emphasized environmental influences on behavior, especially the role of early family experiences in shaping children's future personalities (S. J. Gould, 1997).

Today, because of the high regard for scientific technology, genetic explanations of human behavior have again become fashionable. In recent years, researchers have claimed that such diverse social phenomena as shyness, impulsiveness, intelligence, aggression, obesity, alcoholism, hoarding, and addiction to gambling are at least partly due to heredity. An economist raised eyebrows a few years back when he argued that because of the power of genetic inheritance, parenting hardly matters. Children's destiny is pretty much genetically predetermined. Healthy, smart, happy, virtuous parents tend to have matching offspring no matter what they do to, with, and for their children. So, he wrote, they should just relax and let their children do, essentially, what they want (B. Caplan, 2011). Similarly, the authors of the best-selling book *Freakonomics* wrote, "It isn't so much a matter of what you *do* as a parent; it's who you are (Levitt & Dubner, 2009, p. 175). Advances in genetic testing technology, like the Human Genome Project—an undertaking, completed in 2003, that mapped all the 20,000 to 25,000 genes in human DNA—and a recently developed technique that uses only a blood sample from a pregnant mother and saliva from the father to map the entire genetic configuration of a fetus (and thereby detect thousands of diseases prenatally; Pollack, 2012), will no doubt add fuel to "nature" arguments in the years to come.

Yet apparently we're not quite ready to say that nurture plays no role. In 2011, a prominent Yale law professor struck a blow for the environmental influence on kids' development when she argued in a popular book that the educational success of Asian children is due largely to the heavy-handed role of mothers, whom she refers to as "Tiger Mothers." She recommended—to all parents, no matter what their ethnic backgrounds—that the prescription for a successful child consists of stressing academic performance, never accepting a mediocre grade, insisting on drilling and practice, and instilling unwavering respect for authority (Chua, 2011). Some affluent parents have even gone so far as to move to another country for a year so their children can be immersed in another culture and become cultivated, global citizens (L. Miller, 2011).

Indeed, when it comes to certain traits, heredity is meaningful only in the context of social experiences. Take intelligence. Many geneticists argue that heredity determines the limits of intelligence (Kirp, 2006). They base this claim on studies that have found that differences in IQ scores between identical twins (who share all their genes) are smaller than differences between fraternal twins (who share only half their genes). But it's impossible to understand intelligence without examining how our genetic makeup interacts with our social experiences. As one author put it,

> You've got genes that are going to give you a certain range of height, or a
> certain range in the color of your eyes, and a certain range of your intelligence.
> But we can't say that there's this separate nature that just does its thing
> separately from nurture. The genes literally do come first, but the way the genes
> act, their influence, actually doesn't take place before they interact with their
> environment. Everything is dependent on this interaction. (Shenk, 2010, p. 44)

Other researchers have found that children's socioeconomic environment can make an enormous difference in their intellectual development. One study of 7-year-olds found that while genes account for most of the variation in IQ scores among twins with wealthy parents, the opposite is the case for twins from impoverished families. In these families, the IQs of identical twins vary just as much as the IQs of fraternal twins (Turkheimer, Haley, Waldron, D'Onofrio, & Gottesman, 2003). The researchers conclude that home life is critical. In a poor and unstable home environment, children's genetic potential cannot be reached. Conversely, affluent families are better equipped to provide the cognitive stimulation needed for neurological development.

As you might suspect, most sociologists would argue that human beings are much more than a collection of genetic predispositions and biological traits. But that doesn't mean that nature is completely irrelevant. Certainly, our outward appearance, our physical strength, and our inherited susceptibility to sickness have some effect on our personal development. Furthermore, our every thought and action is the result of a complex series of neurological and electrochemical events in our brains and bodies. When we feel the need to eat, we are reacting to a physiological sensation—stomach contractions—brought about by a lowering of blood sugar. Satisfying hunger is clearly a biological process. But the way we react to this sensation cannot be predicted by physiology alone. What, when, how, and how often we eat are all matters of cultural forces that we learn over time. When you say something like, "I'm exhausted, but it's too early to go to bed," you're signaling the power of cultural training in overriding physical demands.

Likewise, society can magnify genetic and physical differences or cover them up. We've collectively decided that some differences are socially irrelevant (e.g., eye color) and that some are important enough to be embedded in our most important social institutions (e.g., sex and skin color), giving rise to different rights, duties, expectations, and access to educational, economic, and political opportunities.

The relatively new field of *epigenetics* focuses on how genes are not passive blueprints. Instead, their expression or suppression is dictated by environmental influences, which helps explain why identical twins can look different and have different health-related experiences (Mukherjee, 2016). The life we lead and the world we live in can therefore be just as powerful as our genetic code in the development of temperament, body shape, and predisposition to disease (Shulevitz, 2012). So while our genes may have a role to play in who we become, the behaviors and attitudes of significant people in our lives and the cultural and institutional forces that structure our lives are just as, if not more, important (Eliot, 2010). As these things change, so do we. This proposition is not altogether comforting. It implies that who we are may in some ways be "random," the result of a series of social coincidences, accidental injuries, chance encounters, decisions made by others, and political, economic, and historical events that are in large measure beyond our control—like growing up in California rather than Texas.

Socialization: Becoming You

The structural-functionalist perspective reminds us that the fundamental task of any society is to reproduce itself—to create members whose behaviors, desires, and goals correspond to those that the particular society deems appropriate and desirable. Through the powerful and ubiquitous process of **socialization**, the needs of the society become the needs of the individual.

Socialization is a process of learning. To be socialized is to be trained to think and behave appropriately. It is the means by which people acquire a vast array of important social skills, such as driving a car, converting fractions into decimals, speaking the language correctly, or using a fork instead of a knife to eat peas. But socialization is also the way we learn how to perceive our world; how to interact with others; what it means to be male or female; how, when, why, and with whom to be sexual; what we should and shouldn't do to and for others under certain circumstances; what our society defines as moral and immoral; and so on. In short, it is the process by which we internalize all the cultural information I discussed in Chapter 4.

This learning process is carried out by the various individuals, groups, organizations, and institutions a person comes into contact with during the course of his or her life. These entities—whom sociologists refer to as **agents of socialization**—can be family, friends, peers, teammates, teachers, schools, religious institutions, and the media. They can influence our self-concepts, attitudes, tastes, values, emotions, and behavior.

Although socialization occurs throughout our lives, the basic, formative instruction of life begins early on. Young children must be taught the fundamental values, knowledge, and beliefs of their culture. Some of the socialization that occurs during childhood—often called **anticipatory socialization**—is the primary means by which young individuals acquire the values and orientations found in the statuses they will likely enter in the future (Merton, 1957). Household chores, a childhood job, organized sports, dance lessons, dating, and many other types of experiences give youngsters an opportunity to rehearse for the kinds of roles that await them in adulthood.

The Acquisition of Self

The most important outcome of the socialization process is the development of a sense of self. The term **self** refers to the unique traits, behaviors, and attitudes that distinguish one person from the next. The self is both the active source of behavior and its passive object (Mead, 1934).

As an active source, the self can initiate action, which is frequently directed toward others. Imagine, for example, that Donna and Robert are having dinner in a restaurant. Donna has a self that can perceive Robert, talk to him, evaluate him, tell him what to order, and maybe even try to persuade him to act in a way that is consistent with her interests. At the same time, Donna has a self that is a potential object of others' behavior: She can be perceived, talked to, evaluated, directed, or persuaded by Robert.

Donna can also direct these activities toward herself. She can perceive, evaluate, motivate, and even talk to herself. This is called **reflexive behavior**. To have a self is to have the ability to plan, observe, guide, and respond to one's own actions (Mead, 1934). Think of all the times you have tried to motivate yourself to act by saying something such as, "All right, if I read 20 more pages of my boring sociology book, I'll make myself a hot fudge sundae" or "I won't post a photo of the latest disgusting meal in the campus cafeteria on Instagram until I write five more pages of this chemistry paper." To engage in such activities, you must simultaneously be the motivator and the one being motivated—the seer and the seen.

At this very moment, you are initiating an action: reading this remarkably nonboring sociology book. But you also have the ability (now that I've mentioned it!) to be aware of your reading behavior, to reflexively observe yourself reading, and even to evaluate how well you are doing. This may sound like some sort of mystical out-of-body experience, but it isn't. Nothing is more fundamental to human thought and action than this capacity for reflexive self-awareness. It allows us to control our own behavior and interact smoothly with other self-aware individuals.

At birth, human babies have no sense of self. This is not to say that infants don't act on their own. Anyone who has been around babies knows that they have a tremendous ability to initiate action, ranging all the way from Instagram-worthy cute to downright repulsive. They cry, eat, sleep, play with squeaky rubber toys, and eliminate waste, all with exquisite flair and regularity. From the very first days of life, they respond to the sounds, sights, smells, and touches of others.

But this behavior is not characterized by the sort of reflexive self-awareness that characterizes later behavior. Babies don't say to themselves, "I wonder if Mom will feed me if I increase the volume of my crying to 'demonic scream' level" or "I can't *believe* how funny my babbling and gurgling sound right now." As children grow older, though, they begin to exert greater control over their actions. Part of this transformation is biological. As they mature, they become more adept at muscle control. But physical development is only part of the picture. Humans must acquire certain cognitive capacities through interactions with others, including the abilities to differentiate between self and others, to understand and use symbolic language, and to take the roles of others.

The Differentiation of Self

To distinguish between yourself and others, you must at minimum be able to recognize yourself as a distinct being (Mead, 1934). The first step in the acquisition of self, then, is learning to distinguish our own faces and bodies from the rest of the physical environment. Surprisingly, we don't have this ability at birth. Not only are newborns incapable of recognizing themselves, but they also cannot discriminate the boundaries between their bodies and the bodies of others. Infants will pull their own hair to the point of excruciating pain but aren't yet able to realize that the hair they're pulling with their hands and the hair that they feel being pulled out of their heads is the same hair.

With cognitive growth and social experience, infants gradually recognize themselves as unique physical objects. Most studies in this area indicate that children usually develop this ability at about 18 months (Bertenthal & Fischer, 1978). There's a quick way to tell if a child has reached this stage: the mirror test. Make a large mark on a baby's forehead with a washable marker and hold the youngster up to a mirror. If the child reaches up to wipe away the smudge, you can be reasonably sure she or he recognizes that the image in the mirror is her or his own.

Language Acquisition and the Looking-Glass Self

The next important step in the acquisition of self is the development of speech (Hewitt, 1988). Symbolic interactionism points out that mastery of language is crucial in children's efforts to differentiate themselves as distinct social as well as physical objects (Denzin, 1977). Certainly, language acquisition relies on neurological development. But the ability to grasp the nuances of one's own language requires input from others. Most parents talk to their children from the start. Gradually, children learn to make sounds, imitate sounds, and use sounds as symbols for particular physical sensations or objects. Children learn that the sounds "Mama" and "Dada" are associated with two important objects in their life. Soon children learn that other objects—toys, animals, foods, Aunt Anita, Uncle Marc—have unique sounds associated with them as well.

This learning process gives the child access to the preexisting linguistic world in which his or her parents and others live (Hewitt, 1988). The objects named are not only those recognized within the larger culture but also those recognized within the child's family and social groups. The child learns the names of concrete objects (balls, buildings, furniture) as well as abstractions that cannot be directly perceived (God, happiness, peace, idea).

By learning that people and other objects have names, the child also begins to learn that these objects can be related to one another in a variety of ways. Depending on who is talking to whom, the same person can be called several different names. The object "Dad" is called "David," "Dave," "Dov," "Dr. Newman," "Professor Newman," "Prof," "Mr. Newman," and "Noooo-man" by various other people. Furthermore, the child learns that different people can be referred to by the same name. All those other toddlers playing in the park have someone they also call "Mama."

Amid these monumental discoveries, young children learn that they too are objects that have names. A child who learns that others are referring to her when they make the sound "Hazel" and that she too can use "Hazel" to refer to herself has taken a significant leap forward in the acquisition of self. The child now can visualize herself as a part of the named world and the named relationships to which she belongs.

The self that initially emerges from this process is a rather simple one. "Emma" is just a name associated with a body. A more sophisticated sense of self is derived from the child's ability to learn the meaning of this named object.

Children learn not only the names of objects but their meaning in social life by observing the way other people act toward those objects. By witnessing people sitting on a chair, a child learns what *chair* means. Parental warnings allow them to learn that a *hot stove* is something to be avoided. Similarly, by observing how people act toward them, they learn the meaning of themselves. People treat children in a variety of ways: care for them, punish them, love them, neglect them, teach them. If parents, relatives, and other agents of socialization perceive a child as smart, they will act toward her or him that way. Thus, the child eventually comes to define herself or himself as a smart person. One of the earliest symbolic interactionists, Charles Horton Cooley (1902), referred to this process as the acquisition of the **looking-glass self**. He argued that we use the reaction of others toward us as looking glasses (that is, mirrors) in which we see ourselves and determine our self-worth. Through this process, we imagine how we might look to other people, we interpret their responses to us, and we form a self-concept. If we think people perceive us favorably, we're likely to develop a positive self-concept. Conversely, if we detect unfavorable reactions, our self-concept will likely be negative. Hence, self-evaluative feelings like pride or shame are always the product of the reflected appraisals of others. In short, we need others to see us.

But the development of a self-concept is not just a function of our traits and experiences as others reflect them back to us. How others define the child-as-named-object is also linked to larger societal considerations. Every culture has its own way of defining and valuing individuals at various stages of the life cycle. Children are not always defined, and have not always been defined, as a special subpopulation whose innocence requires nurturing and protection (Ariès, 1962). In some societies, they are expected to behave like adults and are held accountable for their actions just as adults would be. Under such cultural circumstances, a 5-year-old's self-concept may be derived from how well he or she contributes economically to the family, not from how cute or playful he or she is. Moreover, every society has its own standards of beauty and success. If thinness is a culturally desirable characteristic, a thin child is more likely to garner positive responses and develop a positive self-image than a child who violates this norm (i.e., an obese child).

The Development of Role Taking

The socialization process would be pretty simple if everyone in our lives saw us in exactly the same way. But different people expect or desire different things from us. Children eventually learn to modify their behavior to suit a variety of others. Four-year-old Ahmed learns, for instance, that his 3-year-old sister loves it when he sticks his thumb up his nose, but he also knows that his father doesn't find this behavior at all amusing. So Ahmed will avoid such conduct when his father is around but proceed to amuse his sister with this trick when Papa is gone. The ability to use other people's perspectives and expectations in formulating one's own behavior is called **role taking** (Mead, 1934).

Role-taking ability develops gradually, paralleling the increasing maturation of linguistic abilities. Operating from the symbolic interactionist perspective, George Herbert Mead (1934) identified two major stages in the development of role-taking ability and, ultimately, in the socialization of the self: the play stage and the game stage. The **play stage** occurs when children are just beginning to hone their language skills. Role taking at the play stage is quite simple in form, limited to taking the perspective of one other person at a time. Very young children cannot yet see themselves from different perspectives simultaneously.

They cannot yet generalize. Hence they have no idea that certain behaviors may be unacceptable to a variety of people across a range of situations. They know only that this particular person who is in their immediate presence will approve or disapprove of this particular act. Children cannot see that their father's displeasure with public nose picking reflects the attitudes of a larger group and is always unacceptable no matter where or when it takes place. This more sophisticated form of self-control develops at the next stage of the socialization process: the game stage.

The **game stage** occurs about the time when children first begin to participate in organized activities such as school events and team sports. The difference between role taking at the play and game stages parallels the difference between childhood play and game behavior. "Play" is not guided by a specific set of rules. It has no ultimate object, no clearly organized competition, and no winners and losers. Children playing baseball at the play stage have no sense of strategy and may not even be aware of the rules and object of the game. They may be able to hit, catch, and throw the ball but have no idea how their behavior is linked to that of their teammates. If a little girl is playing shortstop and a ground ball is hit to her, she may turn around and throw the ball to the left fielder, not because it will help her team win the game but because that's where her best friend happens to be.

Game behavior, in contrast, requires that children understand the object of the game. They realize that each player on the team is part of an organized network of roles determined by the rules of the game. Children know they must continually adapt their behavior to the team's needs in order to achieve a goal. To do so, they must imagine the group's perspective and anticipate how both their teammates and their opponents will act under certain circumstances. Now our little shortstop will throw the ball to first base to get the batter out, but only after assessing how many outs there are and checking to make sure the opposing runner on second base is not trying to advance to third. It doesn't matter whether she likes or hates the first base player; her team's success depends on her making this play.

With regard to role taking at the game stage, not only does the child learn to respond to the demands of several people, but she or he can also respond to the demands of the community or even society as a whole. Sociologists call the perspective of society and its constituent values and attitudes the **generalized other**. The generalized other becomes larger as a child matures, growing to include family, peer group, school, and finally the larger social community. "Dad doesn't like it when I take off my pants in a restaurant" (play stage) eventually becomes "It's never acceptable to take off one's pants in public" (game stage). Notice how such an understanding requires an ability to generalize behavior across a variety of situations and audiences. The child realizes that "public" consists of restaurants, shopping malls, school classrooms, parks, neighbors' living rooms, and so forth.

This ability is crucial because it enables the individual to resist the influence of specific people who happen to be in his or her immediate presence. The boy who defies his peers by not joining them in an act of petty shoplifting is showing the power of the generalized other ("Stealing, no matter where or with whom, is wrong"). During the game stage, the attitudes and expectations of the generalized other are incorporated into one's values and self-concept.

Real life is not always that simple, though. Sometimes people succumb to the pressures of particular others and engage in behaviors they know are socially unacceptable. Furthermore, individuals from markedly different backgrounds are likely to internalize different sets of group attitudes and values. A devout Catholic contemplating divorce, for instance, is taking the role of a different generalized other than an atheist contemplating divorce. Likewise, the social worlds and social standards of men and women are different, as are those of children and adults, parents and nonparents, middle-class and working-class people, and people who grew up in different cultures.

Nor is role-taking ability static. It changes in response to interactions with others. When people feel that they can understand another person's perspective—say, that of an intimate partner—they are likely to become concerned about or at least aware of how their behavior will affect that other person (Cast, 2004). Furthermore, as we move from one institutional setting to another, we adopt the perspective of the appropriate group and can become, for all intents and purposes, a different person. At school we behave one way, at church another, and at Grandma's house still another. We are as many different people as there are groups and organizations to which we belong.

Common sense suggests that people who have the most knowledge and experience should be the best role takers. For example, parents should be more sensitive to their children's views than vice versa, because they are older and wiser and were children once themselves. However, people in superior positions sometimes pay very little attention to those who are less powerful. They actually tend to be less sensitive and less adept at seeing things from others' point of view—because they don't have to be (Useem, 2017). As a result, they feel no need to conform their behavior to the wishes and desires of their subordinates (Goleman, 2013; Tsushima & Gecas, 2001). One recent study found that members of the lower classes are more adept at identifying the emotions of others than those in the upper class (Kraus, Côte, & Keltner, 2010).

You can see this phenomenon in many other areas of social life. Younger siblings, for instance, are typically more aware of the actions and interests of their older siblings than vice versa. Low-level employees must be sensitive to the behaviors and preferences of those above them if they want to achieve occupational success and mobility. On a broader scale, less powerful nations must have heightened sensitivity to the activities of their more powerful neighbors. I have heard some Canadians complain that they are expected to know virtually everything about the United States—its culture, its geography, its economic system, its laws, and its major politicians—whereas most people in the United States tend to be rather oblivious to even the most accessible elements of Canadian politics and culture, like the name of the prime minister or the provincial capital of Nova Scotia.

In sum, the ability to imagine another person's attitudes and intentions and thereby to anticipate that person's behavior is essential for everyday social interaction. Through role taking, we can envision how others perceive us and imagine what their response may be to some action we're contemplating. Hence, we can select behaviors that are likely to meet with the approval of the person or persons with whom we are interacting and can avoid behaviors that might meet with their disapproval. Role taking is thus a crucial component of self-control and social order. It transforms a biological being into a social being who is capable of conforming her or his behavior to societal expectations. It is the means by which culture is incorporated into the self and makes group life possible (Cast, 2004).

Resocialization

Socialization does not end when childhood ends; it continues throughout our lives. Adults must be **resocialized** into a new set of norms, values, and expectations each time they leave behind old social contexts or roles and enter new ones (Ebaugh, 1988; Pescosolido, 1986; Simpson, 1979). For instance, we have to learn how to think and act like a spouse when we marry (P. L. Berger & Kellner, 1964), like a parent when we have kids (A. Rossi, 1968), like a divorced person when a marriage ends (Vaughan, 1986), and like someone with a different gender when transitioning from one sex to another (Saint Louis, 2017). Every new group or organization we enter, every new friendship we form, every new life-changing experience we have requires the formation of new identities and socialization into new sets of norms and beliefs.

Certain occupations require the formal resocialization of new entrants. Often, the purpose is simply to make sure people who work in the organization share the same professional values, methods, and vocabulary. Many large companies, for example, have orientation programs for new employees to teach them what will be expected of them as they begin their new jobs. Sometimes the purpose is to make new entrants abandon their original expectations and adopt a more realistic view of the occupation. Police recruits who believe their job is to protect people must learn that deadly force is appropriate and sometimes necessary in the line of duty (Hunt, 1985). Medical students may become less idealistic and more realistic as they learn about the exhausting demands of their profession (Becker & Geer, 1958; Hafferty, 1991). Such resocialization is especially important in occupations that deal with highly emotional matters, like death.

SPENCER CAHILL

THE MAKING OF A MORTICIAN: PROFESSIONAL RESOCIALIZATION OF FUNERAL DIRECTORS

Funeral directors routinely deal with death and corpses. They are exposed to sights, smells, and sounds that most people have learned to find frightening or repulsive. And they must discuss cold, practical matters, such as prices and methods of payment, with grief-stricken clients without appearing callous. Thus, the occupational resocialization of funeral directors is as important as that in any other profession that deals with human tragedy (clergy, doctors, nurses, police detectives, etc.). But unlike these other professionals, for whom death is merely one aspect of the job, funeral directors exist solely for the purpose of dealing with death.

To study the process of becoming a funeral director, sociologist Spencer Cahill (1999) spent 5 months as a participant observer in a mortuary science program at a community college. In most states, funeral directors must complete an accredited program in mortuary science before getting their license to practice. Cahill regularly attended classes on topics such as health and sanitation science, psychology of grief, and embalming. He also talked informally with the other students and interviewed eight of them formally. What was especially unique about his research approach was that instead of taking the stance of the detached, objective researcher, Cahill incorporated his own feelings and emotional reactions into his analysis.

He found that the entire mortuary science education program serves to normalize the work, so that students become comfortable with death. Reminders of death are a constant presence. Nothing is hidden. For instance, all the classrooms contain some artifacts of death, such as refrigerated compartments that hold corpses, stainless steel embalming tables, and caskets. All the instructors Cahill observed spread their lecture notes on a body gurney, forgoing the traditional lectern and table. It was also common practice for instructors to leave the door open between the classroom and the embalming laboratory, allowing the lingering smell of decomposing bodies to drift into the classroom.

Because other students on campus tend to shun them, the mortuary science students often stick together, providing an almost constant network of support. From these casual interactions (as well as conversations with their instructors), these students learn an occupational language that communicates professional authority and calm composure toward things most of the public would find upsetting. For example, the students learn to see the corpse not as an individual person with a history and a family but as a series of technical puzzles and problems posed by the cause of death (e.g., ingested substances, chemical changes, injuries sustained before death).

However, Cahill points out that professional socialization is not enough to create funeral directors. He notes that students for whom death has always been a mystery or students who are predisposed to becoming queasy don't last very long in the program. In contrast, those who are familiar with death or who

(Continued)

(Continued)

have somehow worked with the dead before (such as the sons or daughters of funeral directors) are the most likely to succeed.

Eventually, the mortuary science students who complete the program adopt the identity of funeral director. They learn to normalize death and acquire the perceptions, judgments, and emotional management skills required of this occupation.

As one well-socialized student put it, "What we do is far less depressing than what nurses and doctors do. We only get the body after the death and do not have to watch all the suffering" (quoted in Cahill, 1999, p. 109).

Sometimes resocialization is forceful and intense. According to sociologist Erving Goffman, this type of resocialization often occurs in **total institutions** (E. Goffman, 1961). Total institutions are physical settings in which groups of individuals are separated from the broader society and forced to lead an enclosed, formally administered life. Prisons, mental hospitals, monasteries, and military training camps are examples of total institutions. In these locations, previous socialization experiences are systematically destroyed and new ones developed to serve the interests of the larger group. Take military boot camp, for example. The Army alone spends several billion dollars a year and employs thousands of people to turn civilians into battle-ready warriors who look, act, and think like soldiers and learn to see the world from the soldier's perspective (Tietz, 2006). The process is called "total control." To aid in this transformation, recruits are stripped of old civilian identity markers (clothes, personal possessions, hairstyle) and forced to take on new ones that nullify individuality and also identify the newcomers' subordinate status (uniforms, identification numbers, similar haircuts). The newcomer is also subjected to constant scrutiny. Conformity is mandatory. Any misstep is met with punishment or humiliation. Eventually, the individual learns to identify with the ideology of the total institution.

In the boot camp, the uniformity of values and appearance is intended to create a sense of solidarity among the soldiers and thereby make the military more effective in carrying out its tasks. Part of the reason for all the controversy over diversity in the military—first with the inclusion of African Americans, then with women, and now with gay men, lesbians, and transgender individuals—is that it introduces dissimilar beliefs, values, appearances, and lifestyles into a context where, from an institutional perspective, similarity is essential.

The Self in a Cultural Context

When we imagine how others will respond to our actions, we choose from a limited set of lines of conduct that are part of the wider culture. In the United States, the self is likely to incorporate key cultural virtues such as self-reliance and individualism. Hence, personal goals tend to be favored over group goals (Bellah, Madsen, Sullivan, Swidler, & Tipton, 1985). In the United States, people will readily change their group membership as it suits them—leaving one career for another, moving from neighborhood to neighborhood, switching political allegiances or even religions.

The United States is said to be an **individualist culture**, where personal traits and accomplishments are a key part of one's self-concept. We've always admired independent people whose success—usually measured in financial terms—is based on their own achievements and self-reliance (Bellah et al., 1985). Hence, the amount of respect people deserve is determined in large part by their level of individual expertise. For example, before a public speech, a guest lecturer in the United States will likely be introduced to her audience as "a distinguished scholar, a leader in her field" along with a list of academic credentials and scholarly achievements.

In many non–Western cultures, however, people are more likely to subordinate their individual goals to the goals of the larger group and to value obligations to others over personal achievements. In such a setting, known as a **collectivist culture**, personal identity is less important than group identity (Gergen, 1991). In India, for instance, feelings of self-esteem and prestige originate more from the reputation and honor of one's family than from any individual attainments (Roland, 1988). In a collectivist setting, high value is placed on preserving one's public image so as not to bring shame on one's family, tribe, or community (Triandis, McCusker, & Hui, 1990). Overcoming personal interests and temptations to show loyalty to one's group and other authorities is celebrated. Guest lecturers in a collectivist culture would be considered self-centered and egotistical if they mentioned their personal accomplishments and credentials. Japanese public speakers, for instance, commonly begin their lectures by telling the audience how *little* they know about the topic at hand (Goleman, 1990).

But even in an individualist society such as the United States, our personal identities are inseparable from the various groups and organizations to which we belong. Thus, to fully understand how we become who we are, we must know the norms and values of our culture, family, peers, coworkers, and all the other agents of socialization who are a part of our lives.

Socialization and Stratification: Growing Up With Inequality

Socialization does not take place in a vacuum. Your social class, your race and ethnicity, and your sex and gender all become significant features of your social identity. Were you born into a poor or a well-to-do family? Are you a member of a racial minority or a member of the dominant group? Do you identify as male or female? These elements of identity shape your experiences with other people and the larger society and will direct you along a certain life path. In most societies, social class, race and ethnicity, and gender are the key determinants of people's opportunities throughout their lives.

Social Class

Social classes consist of people who occupy similar positions of power, privilege, and prestige. People's positions in the class system affect virtually every aspect of their lives, including political preferences, sexual behavior, religious affiliation, diet, and life expectancy. The conflict perspective points out that even in a relatively open society such as the United States, parents' social class determines children's access to certain educational, occupational, and residential opportunities. Affluent children grow up in more abundant surroundings than less affluent children and therefore have access to more material comforts and enriching opportunities such as good schools, chances to travel to far-off places, private music lessons, and so on. A recent national survey found that 78% of parents whose annual income is above $75,000 say their neighborhood is an excellent place to raise children, but only 42% of parents who earn below $30,000 feel this way. Poorer parents are also more likely to worry about their children getting shot, being kidnapped, and getting in trouble with the law (Pew Research Center, 2015g). Furthermore, lower income increases a child's risk of living in a single-parent household, having unemployed parents, having more than one disability, and dropping out of school (Mather & Adams, 2006).

But the relationship between class and socialization is not simply about parents' providing (or not providing) their children with the trappings of a comfortable childhood. Parents' class standing also influences the values and orientations children learn and the identities they develop.

In Chapter 10, you will learn much more about how social class affects attitudes, behaviors, and opportunities. The important point here is that social class and socialization are closely linked. Sociologist Melvin L. Kohn (1979) interviewed 200 working-class and 200 middle-class American couples who had at least one child of fifth-grade age. He found that the middle-class parents were more likely to promote values such as self-direction, independence, and curiosity than were the working-class parents. More recent studies have found that middle-class parents spend more time than working-class parents cultivating their children's language development (Hart & Risley, 1995). They're also more likely to foster their children's talents through organized leisure activities and logical reasoning (Lareau, 2003).

Conversely, working-class parents are more likely than middle-class parents to emphasize conformity to external authority, a common characteristic of the blue-collar jobs they're likely to have later on (M. L. Kohn, 1979). Principally, they want their children to be neat and clean and to follow the rules.

Of course, not all middle-class parents, or working-class parents, raise their children in these ways, and many factors other than social class influence parental values (J. D. Wright & Wright, 1976). Nevertheless, Kohn found that these general tendencies were consistent regardless of the sex of the child or the size and composition of the family. In a study of African American women, those from middle-class backgrounds reported that their parents had higher expectations of them and were more involved in their education than African American women from working-class backgrounds reported (N. E. Hill, 1997). Moreover, others have found that despite cultural differences, social class standing influences child socialization in societies in Europe (Poland, Germany) and Asia (Japan, Taiwan; Schooler, 1996; Williamson, 1984; Yi, Chang, & Chang, 2004).

Sudden shifts in social class standing—due, for instance, to an unexpected job loss—can also affect the way parents socialize their children. Parents who lose their jobs can become irritable, tense, and moody and their disciplinary style more arbitrary. They may come to rely less on reasoning and more on hostile comments and physical punishment. As a result, children's sense of self, their aspirations, and their school performance suffer (cited in Rothstein, 2001).

Class differences in socialization are also directly related to future goals. Working-class parents tend to believe that eventual occupational success and survival depend on their children's ability to conform to and obey authority (M. L. Kohn, 1979). Middle-class parents are likely to believe that their children's future success will result from assertiveness and initiative. Hence, middle-class children's feelings of control over their own destiny are likely to be much stronger than those of working-class children.

Race and Ethnicity

In 2017, as national attention focused on several high-profile incidents of young, unarmed black men being killed by white police officers, some of my students became embroiled in a heated discussion of the incidents. One student, who was white, expressed concern that because of the terrible actions of these individual officers, all police officers are going to be seen as "racist" bad guys. Young children of all races would now grow up mistrusting or even hating the police. She talked about how, as a child, she had been taught that if she were ever in trouble or lost, she could approach an officer for help. She never questioned whether the police could be trusted.

Several of the African American and Latino/a students in class quickly pointed out that their socialization experiences had been quite different. Parents and others in their neighborhoods had taught them not to trust the police, because officers were just as likely to harass them as to help them. They were taught to seek out neighbors and relatives, not the police, if they ever needed assistance. To them, the police were not knights in shining armor but bullies with badges. The problem has gotten so bad that many parents and civic leaders these days feel it is essential to teach black and Latino/a children how to respond safely when approached by the police. The NAACP (National Association for the Advancement of Colored People, 2016) publishes a guide to interacting with law enforcement called *The 411 on the Five-0*. Among its recommendations are to carry identification at all times, speak when asked to speak, stop when ordered to stop, never make any sudden movements, never touch a police officer, and always display open hands to show there are no weapons. Former attorney general Eric Holder (who is black), talked publicly of a conversation he had with his teenage son about how he should interact with the police, what to say, and how to conduct himself if he was ever stopped or confronted in a way he thought was unwarranted (Franke-Ruta, 2013). Some black and Latino/a parents tell their children not to wear hoodies or baggy pants, fearing the lethal assumptions police might make (Eligon, 2013).

Although the two perspectives of my students are not representative of every white or every person of color in the United States, the interchange illustrates the impact race and ethnicity can have on socialization. For white children, learning about their racial identity is less about defining their race than it is about learning how to handle the privileges and behaviors associated with being white in a predominantly white society (Van Ausdale & Feagin, 2001). Chances are good that schools and religious organizations will reinforce the socialization messages expressed to white children in their families—for example, that "you can be anything you want as long as you work hard."

For children who are members of devalued and sometimes despised ethnoracial minorities, however, learning about their racial or ethnic group takes place in a different and much more complex social environment (Hughes & Chen, 1997). These children must live simultaneously in two different worlds: their family and ethnoracial community, which value them; and the "mainstream" (that is, white) society, which may not (Lesane-Brown, 2006). Hence, they're likely to be exposed to several different types of socialization experiences while growing up: those that include information about the mainstream culture, those that focus on their minority or disadvantaged status in society, and those that focus on the history and cultural heritage of their ethnoracial group (L. D. Scott, 2003; Thornton, 1997). Given the prevalence of anti-Islam rhetoric in society today, Muslim parents often have to address the inevitability of their children hearing hateful things about their religion or being verbally or physically attacked. One parent tells her children they must "work 100 times harder and be 100 times kinder" in order to be accepted (Ingber, 2015). The parent of a 7-year-old daughter said:

> I have had to help her learn how to dial 911 if needed and what she should say. I have made her build a list of trusted adults she can talk to, whether at school or in our neighborhood, and whom she can go to for help. I am scared for [her] safety, and I want to balance keeping her informed and empowered vs. scaring her (quoted in Ingber, 2015, p. A6).

In ethnoracial groups that have been able to overcome discrimination and achieve at high levels—such as some Asian American groups—ethnic socialization can focus simply on the values of their culture of origin. But among groups that by and large remain disadvantaged, such as African Americans, Native Americans, and Latino/as, parents' discussion of race is more likely to focus on preparing their children for prejudice, ethnic hatred, and mistreatment in a society set up to ignore or actively exclude them (McLoyd, Cauce, Takeuchi, & Wilson, 2000). For instance, these children may be taught that "hard work" alone may not be enough to get ahead in this society. Even African American children from affluent homes in racially integrated neighborhoods need reassurances about the racial conflicts they will inevitably encounter. These are lessons that children in the dominant racial group seldom require, for reasons explored in greater depth in Chapter 11.

Gender

As you recall from Chapter 4, the sexual dichotomy—the assumption that there are two and only two sexes—is not universal and is more likely to be challenged than ever before. Cultures are even more likely to differ in what is expected of people based on their sex and in how male and female children are to be socialized.

Before discussing this aspect of socialization, it's necessary to distinguish between two concepts: sex and gender. **Sex** is typically used to refer to a person's biological maleness or femaleness. **Gender** designates masculinity and femininity: the psychological, social, and cultural aspects of maleness and femaleness (Kessler & McKenna, 1978). This distinction is important because it reminds us that male-female differences in behaviors or experiences do not spring naturally from biological differences between the sexes (Lips, 1993).

The gender socialization process begins the moment a child is born. A physician, nurse, or midwife immediately starts that infant on a career as a male or female by authoritatively declaring whether it is a boy or a girl. In most U.S. hospitals, the infant boy is swaddled in a blue blanket, the infant girl in a pink one. From that point on, the developmental paths of U.S. males and females diverge. The subsequent messages that individuals receive from families, books, television, and schools not only teach and reinforce gender-typed expectations but also influence the formation of their self-concepts.

If you were to ask soon-to-be parents whether they preferred sons or daughters or whether they intended to treat their babies differently depending on whether they are boys or girls, most would probably say no. Yet there is considerable evidence that what parents do and what they say they do are two different things (H. Lytton & Romney, 1991; McHale, Crouter, & Whiteman, 2003). This is especially true for fathers (see Exhibit 5.1). One study of pregnant women found that when they knew the sex of their fetus, they described the prenatal movements of their sons and daughters quite differently. Sons' movements were described with words like "vigorous" and "strong" while daughters' movements were described with terms like "not excessively energetic" or "not terribly active" (B. K. Rothman, 1988).

In another study, 30 first-time parents were asked to describe their infants at less than 24 hours old. They frequently resorted to common gender stereotypes. Those with daughters described them as "tiny," "soft," "fine featured," and "delicate." Sons were seen as "strong," "alert," "hardy," and "coordinated" (J. Z. Rubin, Provenzano, & Luria, 1974). A replication of this study two decades later found that U.S. parents continue to perceive their infants in gender-stereotyped ways, although less so than in the 1970s (Karraker, Vogel, & Lake, 1995). Parents also tend to engage in rougher physical play with infant sons than with infant daughters and use subtle differences in tone of voice and different pet names, such as "Sweetie" versus "Tiger" (MacDonald & Parke, 1986; Tauber, 1979).

EXHIBIT 5.1 ● Do Parents Want Boys or Girls?

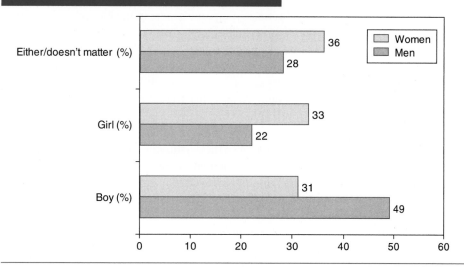

Source: Newport, 2011.

Such differences are also reflected in the kinds of information parents seek *about* their children later on. A recent analysis of data from Google searches found that parents with daughters are significantly more likely to submit queries about their child's weight and physical attractiveness while parents with sons are more likely to search for information about whether their child has above average intelligence or shows signs of being a leader (Stephens-Davidowitz, 2014).

New parents can be very sensitive about the correct identification of their child's sex. Even parents who claim to consider sex and gender irrelevant may spend a great deal of time ensuring that their child has the culturally appropriate gender appearance. Parents of a girl baby who has yet to grow hair (a visible sign of gender in many cultures) will sometimes tape pink ribbons to their bald daughter's head to avoid potential misidentification. In many Latin American countries, families have infant girls' ears pierced and earrings placed in them to provide an unmistakable marker of the child's sex and gender.

In a culture where sex and gender are centrally important and any ambiguity is distasteful, the correct gender identification of babies maintains social order. When my elder son was an infant, I dressed him on several occasions in a pink, frilly snowsuit in order to observe the reactions of others. (Having a sociologist for a father can be rather difficult from time to time!) Inevitably, someone would approach us and start playing with the baby. Some variation of the following interchange would always ensue:

"Oh, she's so cute! What's your little girl's name?"
"Zachary."
"Isn't Zachary a boy's name?"
"He's a boy."

At this point, the responses would range from stunned confusion and awkward laughter to nasty looks and outright anger. Clearly, people felt that I had emotionally abused my son somehow. I had purposely breached a fundamental gender norm and thereby created, in their minds, unnecessary trauma (for him) and interactional confusion (for them).

Both boys and girls learn at a very young age to adopt gender as an organizing principle (Hollander, Renfrow, & Howard, 2011). Sometime between 18 and 24 months of age, most children develop the ability to label gender groups, use gender in their speech, and identify themselves as boys or girls (C. L. Martin & Ruble, 2009). To a young child, being a boy or a girl is simply another characteristic, like having brown hair or 10 fingers. The child at this age has no conception that gender is a category into which every human can be placed (Kessler & McKenna, 1978). But by the age of 5 or so, most children have developed a fair number of gender stereotypes (for example, "boys like trucks" or "girls wear dresses") that they then use to guide their own perceptions and activities (C. L. Martin & Ruble, 2009). They also use these stereotypes to form impressions of others. A boy, for instance, may avoid approaching a new girl who's moved into the neighborhood because he assumes that she will only be interested in "girl" things. Acting on this assumption reinforces the original belief that boys and girls are different. Indeed, to children at this age, gender is typically seen as a characteristic that is fixed and permanent. Their views of gender differences reach their "peak rigidity" between 5 and 7 years of age (Trautner et al., 2005). A few years later, though, their attitudes toward gender become considerably more flexible, although such flexibility isn't always reflected in their actual behaviors (C. L. Martin & Ruble, 2009).

It's important to note that gender socialization is not a passive process in which children simply absorb the information that bombards them. As part of the process of finding meaning in their social worlds, children actively construct gender as a social category (Liben & Bigler, 2002). From an early age, they are like "gender detectives," searching for cues about gender, such as who should and shouldn't engage in certain activities, who can play with whom, and why girls and boys differ (C. L. Martin & Ruble, 2004, p. 67).

Parents and other family members sometimes provide children with explicit instructions on proper gender behavior, such as "Big boys don't cry" or "Act like a young lady." More commonly, though, such instruction is subtler. Decades' worth of research shows that parents speak differently to and play differently with their sons and daughters, often without realizing it. For instance, one study of mothers' reactions to their children's misbehaviors found that they tend to be more concerned about injuries and safety issues with their daughters and tend to focus more on disciplinary issues with their sons (Morrongiello & Hogg, 2004). In another study, parents were instructed to tell their children stories about their own childhoods. In doing so, they were more likely to highlight themes of autonomy and independence when they had sons than when they had daughters (Fiese & Skillman, 2000). Fathers spend more time with their sons and engage in more physical play with them than with their daughters, whereas mothers are more emotionally responsive to girls and encourage more independence with boys (Lanvers, 2004; Raley & Bianchi, 2006). Interestingly, parents—especially parents who claim to be gender neutral in the raising of their children— often fail to acknowledge their socializing role and resort to biological explanations about "hard wiring" when their kids behave in gender stereotypical ways (Kane, 2006).

As children grow older, parents may actually encourage increasingly gender-typed activities (Liben & Bigler, 2002). Research consistently shows that teenage children's household tasks differ along gender lines (Antill, Goodnow, Russell, & Cotton, 1996). For instance, boys are more likely to mow the lawn, shovel snow, take out the garbage, and do the yard work, whereas girls are given chores like cleaning the house, washing dishes, cooking, and babysitting their younger siblings (L. White & Brinkerhoff, 1981). These discrepancies are clearly linked to the different social roles ascribed to men and women, which are discussed in more detail in Chapter 12.

Parental gender expectations—both before and after a child is born—can be powerful (Kane, 2009). Here's how one father put it: "I always wanted a son. . . . I wanted to teach

[him] to play basketball, . . . baseball, and so forth." Daughters, by contrast, yield very different expectations: "I wanted [a girl] . . . to dress her up and to buy the dolls. . . . A girl was someone that you could do all the things that you like to do with more than you could a boy" (Kane, 2009, p. 373).

Gender instructions seem to be particularly rigid and restrictive for U.S. boys. Indeed, the social costs for gender nonconformity are disproportionately severe for boys (Risman & Seale, 2010). One study found that girls' play patterns become less stereotypical as they age; boys, however, must remain ardently masculine (Cherney & London, 2006). As one author put it, girls can still be girls, but boys *must* be boys (Orenstein, 2008).

Consider the different implications of the words *sissy* and *tomboy*. The girl who is a tomboy may fight, use profanity, compete in sports, and climb trees, but her entire gender identity is not called in question by the label. Girls, in general, are given license to do "boy things" (Kimmel, 2004). Indeed, "tomboyness," if considered negative at all, is typically defined as temporary—a stage that a girl will eventually grow out of. One study found that tomboy behavior among girls usually begins by age 5 or 6 and ceases, on average, around the age of 12 (B. L. Morgan, 1998). In addition, the persistent devaluation of "female" activities provides girls—and, later on, women—additional incentive to engage in more socially (and perhaps economically) valued "male" activities (England, 2010). In fact, some parents encourage their soccer-playing daughters to be aggressive because they believe that being tough and competitive at an early age will translate to occupational success in adulthood (H. L. Friedman, 2015).

But the chances for boys to play "girl games" without ridicule are rare, and the risks for doing so are steep. The sissy is not simply a boy who enjoys female pursuits. He is suspiciously soft and effeminate. His "sissyness" is likely to be seen as reflective of his sexual essence, a sign to some of his imminent homosexuality.

It's worth noting, however, that not all parents subscribe so tightly to traditional gender expectations when it comes to raising their sons. A small but growing number of parents have begun to advocate a gender-fluid approach to childrearing by, for instance, allowing their sons to wear dresses and high heels, if that's what they want to do. In 2016, the singer Adele became the focus of social media attention when she took her three-year-old son to Disneyland dressed as Anna from *Frozen*. Some parents refer to their children as "pink boys"—males with a strong interest in traditionally female presentation who still identify as boys (Padawer, 2012). They want their children to occupy the "middle space" between traditional boyhood and traditional girlhood. Although they are fully aware of the problems these boys will face when they display their appearance preferences in public (both from other children as well as adults), they argue that nobody fits the dichotomous gender categories perfectly anyway, so why should they crush their children's individuality by forcing them uncomfortably into a traditional gender group? But their battle is an uphill one as they fight against a community of others whose responses range from confused to hostile.

For the most part, parents participate in gender socialization through the things they routinely provide for their children: clothes, adornments, books, videos, and so forth. Clothes not only provide visible markers of gender; they also send messages about how that person ought to be treated and direct behavior along traditional gender lines (Shakin, Shakin, & Sternglanz, 1985). Frilly outfits do not lend themselves easily to rough-and-tumble play. Likewise, it is difficult to walk quickly or assertively in high heels and tight miniskirts. Clothes for boys and men rarely restrict physical movement in this way. Toys and games are an especially influential source of gender information parents provide their children.

MICRO-MACRO CONNECTION

GIRLS' TOYS AND BOYS' TOYS

Like most people over the age of 50, I can remember a time when toys played a very different role in children's lives than they do now. When I was a kid, my friends and I didn't have many toys, and we usually ended up improvising playthings out of available materials like tree branches, empty boxes, and old stringless tennis rackets. When we did receive a new toy, it was usually because it was a special occasion, like a birthday, a holiday, or a cavity-free dental checkup. Every once in a while we'd save up enough money, walk down to the local toy shop, and buy some toy for ourselves that we'd been coveting for months. The toys were simple and straightforward—wagons, fire engines, dolls, balls, trains, board games—and we'd use them until they broke or wore out. When our parents detected a significant spurt in our maturity, they might get us a toy that required special caution: a chemistry set, an Easy-Bake Oven, an electric racing car set.

Today, toys have changed. They are now a multi-billion-dollar business, part of a giant transnational, interconnected industry. It's virtually impossible to buy a toy these days that's not linked to some new film, television show, fast-food restaurant, or other high-powered marketing campaign. Toy companies now regularly produce TV cartoons based on their own products (C. L. Williams, 2006). Parents find it difficult to resist their children's wishes, which are likely to be formed by television advertisements. Try taking a small child to McDonald's without feeling the pressure to buy a Happy Meal with a toy. The quaint, independent toyshop of the past has been replaced by the massive toy mega-warehouse filled with endless aisles stocked from floor to ceiling with boxes sporting eye-popping colors and screaming images. Even serious world events are now linked to toys. Shortly after Navy SEALs killed Osama bin Laden in 2011, toy companies began to manufacture and market "SEAL Team 6" toys, ranging from posable action figures to plastic weapons.

But the current state of the toy industry is not simply a result of profit-hungry corporations trying to find new ways to exploit the child market (G. Cross, 1997). Toys have always played a significant socializing role in teaching children about the prevailing cultural conceptions of gender. In the 1950s—a time in U.S. history when most adults had endless faith in the goodness of technological progress—Erector Sets and chemistry sets were supposed to encourage boys to be engineers and scientists. Dollhouses and baby dolls taught girls to be modern homemakers and mothers during a time when girls typically assumed they'd occupy those roles in adulthood.

Today, a quick glance at Saturday morning television commercials, toy store shelves, or manufacturers' websites reveals that toys and games remain solidly segregated along gender lines. For instance, the website of the retail giant Toys"R"Us gives online shoppers the option of selecting "girls' toys" or "boys' toys." The featured categories for boys include "Action Figures" and "Vehicle, Hobby, and Radio Control Vehicles" while the featured categories for girls include "Dolls" and "Bath, Beauty Accessories." And although both boys' and girls' toys have a category called "Building Sets," the boys' sets include "Star Wars Carbon Freezing Chamber," "Speed Champions Ford Mustang GT," "The Rebel Alliance Battle Pack," and "Minecraft Snow Hideout"; the girls' sets, on the other hand, include "Friends Party Cakes," "Disney Princess Palace Pets Treasure's Day at the Pool," "Belle's Enchanted Castle," and "Elsa's Sparkling Castle."

"Girls' toys" still revolve around themes of domesticity, fashion, and motherhood. They encourage creativity, nurturing, and physical attractiveness. "Boys' toys" emphasize action and adventure and encourage exploration, competition, and aggression (C. L. Miller, 1987; Renzetti & Curran, 2003). Gender-specific toys foster different traits and skills in children and thereby further separate boys and girls into different patterns of social development.

The iconic and highly stereotypical "Barbie" doll has been one of the best-selling girls' toys for 50 years. In recent years, competitors such as "American Girl" dolls have gained in popularity, challenging Barbie's market primacy. These dolls are advertised as celebrating "all that girls can be" and come in a variety of historical characters, each with her own backstory. "Kaya" was an 18th-century Native American girl who respects nature. "Addy Walker" lived in the 19th century and was an escaped slave. "Julie Albright" was a fun-loving girl in the 1970s who struggled to adjust to a new school.

Toy manufacturers also continue to make fortunes promoting war toys, competitive games of strategy, and sports paraphernalia for boys. In 1983, the popular action figure G.I. Joe got his own TV show; by 1988, two thirds of American boys between the ages of 5 and 11 owned G. I. Joes (G. Cross, 1997). Today, the boys' toy market is saturated with the plastic descendants of Joe: high-tech soldiers, muscle-bound action figures from popular comic books and movies, and intergalactic warriors. A live-action G.I. Joe film hit the theaters in 2009.

Video and online games have become a particularly lucrative product in recent years. Although the gender gap is shrinking, young men account for nearly 60% of all those who regularly play computer and video games (Statista, 2015). Among those who are "addicted" to Internet gaming, teenage boys outnumber girls 10 to 1 (Spada, 2014).

Not surprisingly, most of these games are designed by males for other males. Women make up only 22% of employees in the video game industry (cited in Lynch, Tompkins, van Driel, & Fritz, 2016). Although female video game characters in playable leading roles are more likely to be depicted as strong, independent, and capable than they once were (think of the Lara Croft character in *Tomb Raider*), secondary female characters continue to be portrayed as "damsels in distress" or sex objects (Lynch et al., 2016). Not surprisingly, this is especially true in games rated "T for teen" or "M for mature." Female characters in games with titles like *Bayonetta 2, Honey Select, Dead or Alive: Xtreme Beach Volleyball,* and *Lollipop Chainsaw* are provocatively sexual, scantily clad, and voluptuous. In some games, they are targets of violence at the hands of psychopathic male characters. For instance, *Duke Nukem Forever* allows players to slap seminaked women if they don't cooperate. The gender messages in such games may have a detrimental effect on both boys' attitudes toward girls and women and their conceptions of appropriate male behavior.

From time to time, toy manufacturers have attempted—usually only halfheartedly—to blur the lines between boys' and girls' toys. For instance, Mattel, the maker of Barbie, tried to move away from the doll's over-sexualized, hyperfeminine image in 2012 by introducing a construction set for girls called "Mega Bloks Barbie Build 'n Style." However, the set was bubblegum pink and centered on building a dream mega-mansion. Similarly, the popular Lego building blocks that boys have used for decades to make towers and monsters still come in vivid primary colors. But they are also available in more feminine, pastel colors and come in kits that can be used to make jewelry and dollhouses. *Project MC²*, the Netflix original series that promotes girls' involvement in science, technology, engineering, art, and math, has spawned a line of toys related to these themes, like water-powered remote control cars and lab kits. Although the toys encourage girls to design experiments, they still tend to come in distinctly female colors like pink, red, and purple. One version of the lab kit helps girls to create different shades and flavors of lip balm.

For the most part, toy manufacturers are still quick to exploit the gender-distinct roles children are encouraged to pursue when they become adults. They know full well that the few adults who do object to gender-specific toys will face disappointed children scowling at the sight of some gender-neutral alternative (C. L. Williams, 2006). Mattel offers the "Little Mommy" doll, a soft, cuddly baby that drinks from a bottle and comes with a potty seat for toilet training. On the "Little Mommy" (2017) website, visitors can read a poem that sums up the company's philosophy:

A special little girl will say

I want to be like Mom someday

And with her first doll she can play

Like a mommy in her own loving way

Mattel also makes a pregnant version of Barbie's friend Midge (called "Happy Family Midge"). She comes with a distended tummy that, when removed, reveals a 1¾-inch baby nestled in the doll's plastic uterus. The doll comes with everything a girl needs to play out the birth and care of the new baby, including diapers (pink if it's a girl, blue if it's a boy), birth certificate, bottles, rattles, changing table, tub, and crib. All these dolls clearly teach young girls the cultural value of motherhood, a role most girls are encouraged and expected to enter later in life. You'd be hard pressed to find a comparable toy, popular among boys, that prepares them for future roles as fathers.

Institutions and Socialization

It should be clear by now that becoming who we are is a complex process embedded in the larger social structure. We are much more than the sum of our anatomical and neurological parts. Cultural attitudes toward class, race, and gender can dramatically affect our personal identities. But various social institutions—in particular, the educational system, religious organizations, and the mass media—exert considerable influence on our self-concept, our values, and our perspectives as well.

Education

In contemporary industrial societies, the most powerful institutional agent of socialization, after the family, is education. In fact, according to the structural-functionalist perspective, the primary reason schools exist is to socialize young people. Children formally enter the school system around age 5, when they begin kindergarten, although many enter earlier in preschool or nursery school. At this point, the "personalized" instruction of the family is replaced by the "impersonalized" instruction of the school, where children in most developed countries will remain for the next 13 years or longer. No other nonfamily institution has such extended and consistent control over a person's social growth.

Although schools are officially charged with equipping students with the knowledge and skills they need to fulfill various roles in society (e.g., reading, writing, mathematics, science), they also teach students important social, political, and economic values. When students set up simulated grocery stores or banks, they are learning about the importance of free enterprise and finance in a capitalist society; when they hold mock elections, they are being introduced to a democratic political system; when they spend time tending a school garden or setting up recycling bins, they are learning to nurture the earth.

More subtly, schools teach students what they can expect for themselves in the world. In many school districts, children are grouped into different programs, or tracks, based on an assessment of their academic abilities. In a typical high school, for example, some students will take courses designed to prepare them for college, whereas others will take more general or vocational courses designed to prepare them for work after they graduate. **Tracking** clearly determines future outcomes: Students in the higher tracks often go on to prestigious universities; those in the lower tracks may not go to college at all. Tracking can, therefore, ultimately affect employment opportunities, income levels, and overall quality of life.

Not surprisingly, some parents will go to great lengths to increase the likelihood of their children's success in school. For instance, some parents nowadays choose to delay enrolling their children in kindergarten for a year—a practice known as "academic redshirting"—to allow extra time for social, emotional, and intellectual growth as well as to ensure that the child is not the smallest in the class (Gootman, 2006). Between 1968 and 2005, the proportion of American 6-year-olds enrolled in first grade or above dropped from 96% to 84%. It's not that there were fewer 6-year-olds in the population. It was because more 6-year-olds were in kindergarten rather than first grade (Deming & Dynarski, 2008). In 2011, 1 in 11 kindergarten-age children had not started attending school yet (S. Wang & Aamodt, 2011). There is no evidence that children with low cognitive or social abilities are the ones who are more likely to be redshirted. Instead, parents seem to be motivated primarily by concern over their child's relative competitive position among his or her kindergarten peers (Bassok & Reardon, 2013).

The practice of academic redshirting has a fair amount of support. Some research has shown that children who are older than their classmates perform better academically and athletically (cited in E. Weil, 2007). For their part, kindergarten teachers often encourage redshirting because more mature children are better behaved and initially produce better test scores than younger classmates (S. Wang & Aamodt, 2011).

However, others point out that the consequences of redshirting reverberate beyond the kindergarten classroom. For instance, the children most likely to be redshirted are white males from wealthy families (Bassok & Reardon, 2013). Such children are likely to have spent 2 or more years in high quality preschool; hence starting kindergarten a year later will have little negative effect on them academically. But when children from lower income families are redshirted, they tend to be less academically successful later on. By starting school a year later, they lose time at the beginning of their education when teachers can more easily identify and address possible academic deficiencies. And since they are more likely than wealthier students to drop out in high school, they lose time at the end of their educational careers as well.

Ironically, although individual accomplishment is stressed in U.S. schools through grades and report cards, students learn that their future success in society may be determined as much by who they are as by what they achieve. Ample evidence shows that teachers react to students on the basis of race, religion, social class, and gender (Wilkinson & Marrett, 1985). It is in school that many children are first exposed to the fact that people and groups are ranked in society, and soon they get a sense of their own standing in the social hierarchy.

Some sociologists argue that schooling in most cultures is designed not so much to provide children with factual information and encourage creativity as to produce passive, nonproblematic conformists who will fit into the existing social order (Gracey, 1991). This training in conformity involves several different dimensions (Brint, 1998). First, there is *behavioral* conformity. Teachers in the early grades typically keep children in line by controlling their bodily movements, such as making them sit still or forcing them to raise their hands before speaking. Some schools still work to ensure such conformity through strict punishment of misbehavior. According to the U.S. Department of Education, about 110,000 students are subjected to corporal punishment annually in the 19 states where it is allowed (J. B. King, 2016). Second, schools teach *moral* conformity. Teachers often instruct children about virtues such as honesty, courage, kindness, fairness, and respect. Finally, schools teach children to conform to *culturally* approved styles and outlooks. In some societies, teachers reward their students for showing a quick wit; in other societies, children are rewarded for demonstrating thoughtfulness and asking deep, probing questions. Such training socializes students to adopt traits that people consider culturally desirable within that society.

Sometimes these different dimensions overlap. Rules against arguing with the teacher, for instance, teach children the moral "goodness" of respecting authority. But they can also foster passivity and give students their first taste of control by authoritative adults other than their parents. Such classroom regulations, then, help impose discipline; at the same time, they prepare children for what they will face in the larger culture. Obeying the kindergarten teacher today prepares the individual for obeying the high school teacher, the college professor, and the boss tomorrow.

Unfortunately, children who seek ways to express their creativity often become underachievers who resent the constraining structure of the classroom, excessive rules and regulations, and the emphasis on conformity at the expense of independence (K. Kim & Van Tassel-Baska, 2010). Not surprisingly, numerous studies have found that American children's creativity—sometimes referred to as "CQ," or "creativity quotient"—has declined significantly over the past two decades, especially among younger children (cited in Bronson & Merryman, 2010).

Other countries have made childhood creativity a national priority. In 2008, Great Britain revamped its secondary school curricula to emphasize "idea generation" and not just traditional academic subjects. The European Union designated 2009 as "the European Year of Creativity and Innovation." Chinese schools have begun to adopt a problem-solving approach to education rather than drilling and rote memorization (Bronson & Merryman, 2010).

Although American schools still, for the most part, emphasize traditional academic achievement, educators are beginning to pay more attention to the importance of creativity, developing curricula that incorporate innovation and problem solving into all subject areas, not just the arts. An increasingly popular approach to kindergarten, called "purposeful play," involves teachers subtly guiding students to learning goals through games, art, and fun (Rich, 2015). Some schools even work to instill values that seem at odds with existing social arrangements. For instance, in 2016, several California school districts began testing students not only on standard academic subjects like math, science, and reading but also on how well they'd learned social skills like self-control, empathy, positive relationships with others, making good decisions, and so on (Zernike, 2016).

Because formal education is so important in the everyday lives of most children, the agenda of a particular school system, regardless of its philosophy or method, cannot help but influence the types of people they will eventually become.

Religion

As the structural-functionalist perspective tells us, religion is the social institution that tends to the spiritual needs of individuals and serves as a major source of cultural knowledge. It plays a key role in developing people's ideas about right and wrong. It also helps form people's identities by providing coherence and continuity to the episodes that make up each individual's life (Kearl, 1980). Religious rites of passage, such as baptisms, bar and bat mitzvahs, confirmations, and weddings, reaffirm an individual's religious identity while impressing on him or her the rights and obligations attached to each new status (J. H. Turner, 1972).

Religion occupies a complex place in U.S. life. Structural changes in society have made religious affiliation somewhat unstable in recent years. For instance, as people move from one location to another, many of the ties that bind them to the same religion—most notably, networks of family and friends—are broken. About 36% of U.S. residents attend religious services once a week or more, down from 39% in 2007 (Pew Research Center, 2017). A growing number of people see religion's socializing influence as waning (Pew Forum on Religion and Public Life, 2014b). Most U.S. residents are actually quite ignorant about basic religious history and texts (Prothero, 2007). When 3,400 Americans were asked 32 questions about the Bible, world religions, and religious figures, they only got about half of the questions right on average, even when the questions were about their own religion. In fact, self-described atheists and agnostics scored significantly higher on this test of religious knowledge than Protestants and Catholics (Pew Forum on Religion and Public Life, 2010).

Furthermore, the percentage of Americans who identify with *no* religion (atheists, agnostics, and those who say they are spiritual but have no religious affiliation) grew from 16% in 2007 to 23% in 2014. The trend is especially pronounced among those younger than 30. Consequently, over the past decade, many of the most powerful religious groups have experienced a decline in membership (see Exhibit 5.2). Indeed, since 2007, the percentage of Americans who identify as Christian has declined from 79% to 71% (Pew Research Center, 2015b).

However, a decline in membership does not necessarily mean that all religions are losing their socializing effect in U.S. society. Indeed, at the same time that membership in some religions has shrunk over the past decade, that of other churches has increased (see Exhibit 5.2). And membership in a variety of non-Christian religious groups has grown significantly as well. For instance, between 1990 and 2008, the number of Muslims and Buddhists in the United States increased from a little less than 1 million to more than 2.5 million (ProQuest Statistical Abstract, 2017). Immigration has helped fuel this growth. More than four times as many immigrants as native-born Americans report non-Christian

EXHIBIT 5.2 ● Are Americans Becoming Less Religious?

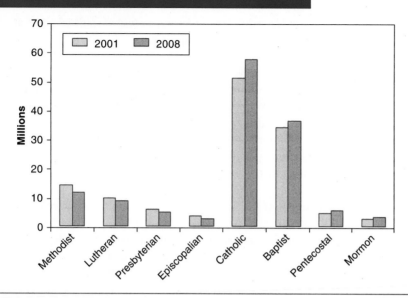

Source: ProQuest Statistical Abstract, 2017, Table 78.

religious affiliations (Pew Forum on Religion and Public Life, 2008). In fact, population experts project that by 2050 the proportion of the population that identifies as Muslim will more than double, and they will overtake Jews as the largest non-Christian religion in the United States (Mohamed, 2016).

Although religion may not look the same as it did 50 years ago, it still remains a fundamental socializing agent in many Americans' lives. Compared with most other Western democracies—such as Canada, Germany, France, Great Britain, and Australia—people in the United States stand out for the depth of their religious beliefs (Zoll, 2005). Consider these facts:

- About 90% of Americans—including those who report no religious affiliation—believe in God (Pew Research Center, 2014d).

- Two thirds of Americans believe that God can supernaturally heal sick people (The Barna Group, 2016).

- Seventy-two percent of U.S. adults believe there is a heaven; 58% believe there is a hell (Pew Research Center, 2014d).

- Sixty-five percent of U.S. adults believe that all of the aspects of the Christmas story—the virgin birth, the journey of the magi, the angel's announcement to the shepherds, and the manger story—reflect events that actually happened (Pew Forum on Religion and Public Life, 2014a).

- Seventy-two percent of Americans say that the display of Christian symbols (like Nativity scenes) on government property should be allowed, either alone or accompanied by symbols of other faiths (Pew Forum on Religion and Public Life, 2014a).

- Two thirds of married Americans had religious weddings and two thirds of Americans, in general, expect to have a religious funeral (Kosmin & Keysar, 2009).

- Eighty-three percent of U.S. adults report feeling a sense of spiritual peace and well-being at least a few times a year (Pew Research Center, 2014d).

Moreover, we still consider ourselves "one nation under God," and our money still proclaims our trust in God. It's virtually impossible these days to watch a sporting event without seeing a boxer pray before a bout, a baseball player cross himself before batting, a football player point skyward after scoring a touchdown, or a basketball player in a postgame interview thank God for guiding the shot that led to his team's victory. Some public schools around the country continue to hold prayer services or Bible studies, in spite of the threat of lawsuits by organizations like the American Civil Liberties Union (Eckholm, 2011a).

Religion is a key component of the American political system, too. Over 90% of members of Congress in 2017 identified as Christian, compared to 71% in the general population (Sandstrom, 2017). Americans are far more likely than people in other industrialized countries to be willing to mix politics and religion. No sitting president would ever dare end a State of the Union speech without asking God to bless the United States of America. As one author put it, "America is the last country left whose citizens don't laugh out loud when their leader asks God to bless the country" (Ignatieff, 2005, p. 47). Nearly half of Americans believe that houses of worship should openly express their views on important social and political issues and about a third think they should openly support particular candidates (Pew Forum on Religion and Public Life, 2014b). Two thirds of Americans feel that it is important that an American president have strong religious beliefs (Pew Forum on Religion and Public Life, 2004). In fact, in some states people who don't believe in God are not eligible to hold public office (Goodstein, 2014a).

Mass Media

Another powerful institutional agent of socialization is the media. Newspapers, magazines, television, radio, film, and the Internet transmit persuasive messages on the nature of reality. They are the gatekeepers of political, economic, and social information, defining what is and isn't important (Marger, 2005). They also tell us the type of person we "should" be, from how we should perform our jobs to how different social classes live to what our sexual relationships and families are supposed to look like. The media teach us about prevailing values, beliefs, myths, stereotypes, and trends (Gitlin, 1979) and provide an avenue through which we learn new attitudes and behavior (Bandura & Walters, 1963).

Media exposure is pervasive in the United States:

- Americans spend about 15.5 hours a day consuming all types of electronic media via television, radio, phone, and computer (University of Southern California Marshall School of Business, 2013).

- Sixty-eight percent of all Americans—whether they are Internet users or not—belong to Facebook and three quarters of them visit the site daily (Greenwood, Perrin, & Duggan, 2016).

- Nearly 80% of teenagers now have cell phones; half of them are smartphones, up from just 23% in 2011. Three fourths of teens access the Internet on their phones, tablets, and other mobile devices (Pew Research Center, 2013b).

VISUAL ESSAY—THANK GOD . . . (OR AT LEAST THE QUARTERBACK)!

Cal Sport Media via AP Images

REUTERS/Paul Hanna

Al Bello/Getty Images Sport/Getty Images

Matthew J. Lee/The Boston Globe/Getty Images

Whether you're a devout Christian or a steadfast atheist, there's no denying that religion occupies a key place in U.S. society. Membership in mainline religious organizations and attendance at traditional religious services may be going down, but people always find other, nontraditional, ways to express their religious devotion. For instance, we've grown accustomed to seeing athletes point to the heavens after hitting a home run or sinking a three-pointer, kneel down to pray after scoring a touchdown or winning a race, or gather for a group prayer with teammates and opponents after a hard-fought game.

Do you think it is appropriate for an athlete to thank God after a successful individual play or a team victory? Some professional sports leagues—like the NFL—now penalize taunting one's opponent or displaying excessive enthusiasm. Should religious gestures likewise be punished? Aside from sports, can you think of other "nonreligious" places or circumstances where people routinely advertise their religious beliefs? Let's look at this issue from a different perspective: Where are expressions of religiosity *never* seen? Why *don't* you see people pointing skyward or dropping to a knee after being approved for a car loan, buying a great loaf of bread, or finding a much-desired pair of pants on sale? In general, what role, if any, do you think religion should play in secular areas of social life?

- Children under the age of 8 are exposed to almost 4 hours of background television each day (times when the television is on but the child is involved in another activity; Lapierre, Piotrowski, & Linebarger, 2012).

- Thirty-eight percent of children *under 2* have used a mobile device to access some type of media (Common Sense Media, 2013).

While U.S. television and other media entertain and expose us to diverse ways of life, they also send powerful messages about important cultural values like individual success. Consider the role of televised sports. Television has reduced the sports experience to a sequence of personal achievements—a cultural value on which the entire U.S. social structure is based. We have grown used to hearing descriptions such as "world record holder," "superstar," and "greatest player of all time." Praise is heaped not only on individuals and the occasional "dynasty" team but also on more specific actions: "best offensive rebounder," "best return of serve," "best at hitting with two outs and runners in scoring position," "best open field tackler," "best chip out of a sand trap." The media emphasis on individual achievement can also be seen in the growing popularity of online fantasy leagues, where participants assemble "teams" of real players and compete against other participants through the performance of those players in actual games. Individual statistics are what matters; a team's wins and losses are irrelevant.

Consider also the most emblematic play in professional basketball today: the slam dunk. It's impossible to watch television highlights of a basketball game without seeing a thunderous, explosive, gravity-defying dunk:

> The dunk is a declaration of power and dominance, of machismo. In a team game, an ensemble of five players a side, it is an expression of self. In a sport devoted to selling sneakers, the dunk is a marketing tour de force, the money shot at the end of every worthy basketball sequence. (Sokolove, 2005, p. 42)

To some observers, though, fans' obsession with acrobatic dunks has made the fundamentals of success—namely, teamwork and sacrifice—seem irrelevant (Sokolove, 2005). In a world where muscled-up athletes, whose only reliable offensive skill is the ability to dunk the ball, can earn millions and where ESPN nationally televises the games of high school phenoms, it's not surprising that individual athleticism has overshadowed the collaborative aspect of the game. Consequently, many young players today are more concerned with perfecting their individual moves than with developing other skills—passing, rebounding, shooting from various spots on the floor, playing defense, and other less glamorous but no less essential elements of a team effort.

The socializing role of the media is especially apparent when it comes to gender. Children's books, for instance, teach youngsters what other little boys or girls in their culture do and what is expected of them. In the early 1970s, Lenore Weitzman and her colleagues studied the portrayal of gender in popular U.S. preschool books (Weitzman, Eifler, Hodada, & Ross, 1972). They found that boys played a more significant role in the stories than girls by a ratio of 11 to 1. Boys were more likely to be portrayed in adventurous pursuits or activities that required independence and strength; girls were likely to be confined to indoor activities and portrayed as passive and dependent. These gender stereotypes in children's books decreased only slightly over the next several decades (S. B. Peterson & Lach, 1990). Recent attempts to publish more nonsexist children's books have had little impact on the overall market. For instance, elementary school reading textbooks still primarily portray males as aggressive, argumentative, and competitive (L. Evans & Davies, 2000). "Gender equality" in children's books usually involves female characters taking on characteristics and roles typically associated with males. These books rarely, if ever, portray male characters exhibiting feminine traits (Diekman & Murnen, 2004).

Similarly, film and television continue to portray males and females in stereotypical ways. Consider these facts (Geena Davis Institute on Gender in Media, 2012, 2014, 2016):

- Only 29% of characters in American films are female, despite the fact that girls and women make up over half the U.S. population.

- Male film characters receive twice the amount of screen time and speak twice as often as female characters.

- In feature films, female characters were more than twice as likely as male characters to be shown in sexually revealing attire and to be thin.

- Comments about appearance were five times more likely to be directed at female film characters than male characters.

Similar gender portrayals exist on television. Girls and women comprise less than 40% of speaking characters on television. Female TV characters are younger than their male counterparts, more likely to be identified by their marital status, and less likely to be seen at work or actually working (Lauzen, 2016). When female characters are shown in an occupation, traditional gender stereotypes remain. On prime-time shows, women comprise 14% of corporate executives, 28% of high-level politicians, 29% of doctors, and 21% of scientists/engineers (S. L. Smith, Choueiti, Prescott, & Pieper, 2012). Even the media coverage of female sports events still tends to focus on the physical appearance and sexual attractiveness of the athletes and not just their competitive accomplishments (Billings, Angelini, & Eastman, 2005; Shugart, 2003). Researchers at Cambridge University Press (2016) have examined about 160 million words found in various media over the past 30 years that deal with sports stories. They found that words like "men" and "man" appear three times as often as "woman" and "women." While male athletes are often described as fast, strong, or big, language around female athletes tends to focus disproportionately on age, marital status, appearance, or clothes. One of the most popular televised events in each Summer Olympics is women's beach volleyball, where athletes' "uniforms" consist of revealing bathing suits.

Media advertising also perpetuates gender stereotypes. Three quarters of the central characters in radio advertisements are men. And men are significantly more likely than women to be portrayed as authorities on products rather than users (Monk-Turner, Kouts, Parris, & Webb, 2007). A study of 467 TV commercials shown between children's cartoons found that, as in the shows themselves, male characters are more likely than female characters to be in a major role, to be active rather than passive, and to be depicted in an occupational setting (S. Davis, 2003). Similarly, an analysis of more than 500 U.S. and Australian commercials targeting children found that girls were much more likely than boys to be portrayed as shy, giggly, and passive (Browne, 1998). The differences were less pronounced in Australia, however, where activists have had more success in countering gender stereotypes in the media than in the United States.

All these gender images have a strong influence on children's perceptions and behaviors (Witt, 2005). Children who watch a lot of television are more likely to hold stereotypical attitudes toward gender, exhibit gender-related characteristics, and engage in gender-related activities than children who watch little television (M. Morgan, 1987; Signorielli, 1990). In one study, girls who did not have stereotypical conceptions of gender to begin with showed a significant increase in such attitudes after 2 years of heavy television watching (M. Morgan, 1982). The more high school students watch talk shows and prime-time programs that depict a lot of sexual activity, the more likely they are to hold traditional sexual stereotypes (Ward & Friedman, 2006).

Conclusion

Becoming the people we are is a complex social process. Those intimate characteristics we hold so dear—our self-concept, our gender, and our racial and ethnic identity—reflect larger cultural attitudes, values, and expectations. Yet we are not perfect reflections of society's values. Despite all the powerful socializing institutions that pull our developmental strings, we continue to be and will always be individuals.

Sometimes we ignore our generalized others and strike out on our own with complete disregard for community standards and attitudes. Sometimes we form self-concepts that contradict the information we receive from others about ourselves. Sometimes we willingly violate the expectations associated with our social class, gender, or race. Societal influence can go only so far in explaining how we become who we are. The rest—that which makes us truly unique—remains a fascinating mystery.

Your Turn

Being a child or an adolescent is not simply a biological stage of development. It is a social identity. People's experiences with this identity emerge from a particular cultural and historical context as well as the process of socialization that takes place within their families.

But many other social institutions assist in the process of raising children, often in ways that aren't immediately apparent.

To see firsthand how such socialization works, visit a large shopping mall. Most malls today have children's clothing stores (e.g., Baby Gap). If yours doesn't, go to one of the large department stores and find the children's clothing section. Start with the infants' clothes. Is there a difference between "girls' clothes" and "boys' clothes"? Note the differences in the style, color, and texture of boys' versus girls' clothes. Collect the same information for clothes designed for toddlers, preschoolers, and elementary school-age children.

Now find a store that specializes in clothes for preteens and teenagers. How do clothing styles and materials differ along gender lines at this age level?

After collecting your data, try to interpret the differences you noticed. Why do they exist? What do these differences say about the kinds of social activities in which boys and girls are expected or encouraged to engage? For instance, which clothes are "rugged" and which are "dainty"? How do such differences reinforce our cultural conceptions of masculinity and femininity? Turning your attention to teenagers, how do popular clothing styles encourage sexuality?

The next stop on your sociological shopping trip is a toy store. Can you detect a boys' section and a girls' section? How can you tell? How do the toys differ? What sorts of interactions with other children do the toys encourage? Competition? Cooperation? Which toys are designed for active play? Which seem to encourage passive play? For what sorts of adult roles do the toys prepare children? Provide specific examples.

Finally, find a bookstore that has a children's book section. Which books are more likely to interest boys? Which will interest girls? Are there different sections for "boy" and "girl" books? What are the differences in the sorts of characters and plots that are portrayed? Does the bookstore have a section that contains books designed to help adolescents through puberty? If so, do these books offer different advice to adolescent boys and girls?

Use your findings in all these areas—clothing, toys, and books—or any others you come across to analyze the role that consumer products play in socializing children into "appropriate" gender roles. Is there more or less gender segregation as children get older? Do you think manufacturers, publishers, retail outlets, and so on are simply responding to market demands (i.e., do they make gender-specific products because that's what people want), or do they play a role in creating those demands?

Chapter Highlights

- Socialization is the process by which individuals learn their culture and learn to live according to the norms of a particular society. It is how we learn to perceive our world, gain a sense of our own identity, and interact appropriately with others. It also tells us what we should and should not do across a range of situations.

- One of the most important outcomes of socialization for an individual is the development of a sense of self. To acquire a self, children must learn to recognize themselves as unique physical objects, master language, learn to take the roles of others, and, in effect, see themselves from another's perspective.

- Socialization is not just a process that occurs during childhood. Adults must be resocialized into a new galaxy of norms, values, and expectations each time they leave or abandon old roles and enter new ones.

- Through socialization, we learn the social expectations that go with our social class, racial or ethnic group, and gender.

- Socialization occurs within the context of several social institutions—family first, and then schools, religious institutions, and the mass media.

Key Terms

agents of socialization: Various individuals, groups, and organizations that influence the socialization process

anticipatory socialization: Process through which people acquire the values and orientations found in statuses they will likely enter in the future

collectivist culture: Culture in which personal accomplishments are less important in the formation of identity than group membership

eugenics: Control of mating to ensure that "defective" genes of troublesome individuals will not be passed on to future generations

game stage: Stage in the development of self during which a child acquires the ability to take the role of a group or community (the generalized other) and conform his or her behavior to broad societal expectations

gender: Psychological, social, and cultural aspects of maleness and femaleness

generalized other: Perspective of the larger society and its constituent values and attitudes

identity: Essential aspect of who we are, consisting of our sense of self, gender, race, ethnicity, and religion

individualist culture: Culture in which personal accomplishments are a more important component of one's self-concept than group membership

looking-glass self: Sense of who we are that is defined by incorporating the reflected appraisals of others

play stage: Stage in the development of self during which a child develops the ability to take a role,

(Continued)

(Continued)

but only from the perspective of one person at a time

reflexive behavior: Behavior in which the person initiating an action is the same as the person toward whom the action is directed

resocialization: Process of learning new values, norms, and expectations when an adult leaves an old role and enters a new one

role taking: Ability to see oneself from the perspective of others and to use that perspective in formulating one's own behavior

self: Unique set of traits, behaviors, and attitudes that distinguishes one person from the next; the active source and passive object of behavior

sex: Biological maleness or femaleness

socialization: Process through which one learns how to act according

to the rules and expectations of a particular culture

total institution: Place where individuals are cut off from the wider society for an appreciable period and where together they lead an enclosed, formally administered life

tracking: Grouping of students into different curricular programs, or tracks, based on an assessment of their academic abilities

SAGE edge™ edge.sagepub.com/newman12e

SAGE edge offers a robust online environment featuring an impressive array of free tools and resources for review, study, and further exploration, keeping both instructors and students on the cutting edge of teaching and learning.

6

Supporting Identity

The Presentation of Self

- Forming Impressions of Others
- Managing Impressions
- Mismanaging Impressions: Spoiled Identities

On Christmas Day, 1981, I met my (former) wife's family for the first time. We had just started dating, so I knew for this group of important strangers, I had to be on my best behavior and say and do all the right things. I wanted to make sure the impression they formed of me was that of a likable fellow whom they'd be proud to call a member of the family someday.

As people busily opened their presents, I noticed the wide and gleeful eyes of a 14-year-old girl as she unwrapped what was to her a special gift—her very own basketball. Being the youngest in a family of eight kids, she didn't have much she could call her own, so this was a significant moment for her. She had finally broken away from a life filled with hand-me-downs and communal equipment. She hugged that ball as if it were a puppy.

I saw my chance to make the perfect first impression. "I'm not a bad basketball player," I thought to myself. "I'll take her outside to the basketball hoop in the driveway, dazzle her with my shooting skills, become her idol, and win family approval."

"Hey, Mary," I said, "let's go out and shoot some hoops." After we stepped outside, I grabbed the new ball from her. "Watch this," I said as I flung it toward the basket from about 40 feet away. We both watched as the ball arced gracefully toward its destination, and for a brief moment, I actually thought it was going to go in. But that was not to be.

As if guided by the taunting hand of fate, the ball struck an exposed bolt that protruded from the supporting pole of the hoop. There was a sickeningly loud pop, followed by a hissing sound as the ball fluttered to the ground like a deflated balloon. It sat there lifeless, never having experienced the joy of "swishing" through a net. For that matter, it had never even been bounced on the ground in its short-lived inflated state.

For a few seconds, we both stood numb and motionless. Then I turned to apologize to the 14-year-old girl, whose once cheerful eyes now harbored the kind of hate and resentment usually reserved for ax murderers and IRS auditors. In a flash, she burst into tears and ran into the house shrieking, "*That guy* popped my ball!" It was hardly the heroic identity I was striving for. As the angry mob poured into the backyard to stare at the villainous and still somewhat unknown perpetrator, I became painfully aware of the fragile nature of the self-images we try to project to others.

We all have been in situations—a first date, a job interview, a first meeting with a girlfriend or boyfriend's family—in which we feel compelled to "make a good impression." We try to present a favorable image of ourselves so that others will form positive judgments of us. This phenomenon is not only an important and universal aspect of our personal lives but a key element of social structure as well.

In this chapter, I examine the social creation of images. How do we form impressions of others? What do we do to control the impressions others form of us? I also discuss the broader sociological applications of these actions. What are the institutional motivations behind individuals' attempts to control others' impressions of them? How do groups and organizations present and manage collective impressions? Finally, what happens when these attempts fail and images are spoiled, as mine was when my errant jump shot murdered a girl's brand-new basketball?

Forming Impressions of Others

When we first meet someone, we form an immediate impression based on observable cues such as age, ascribed status characteristics such as race and gender, individual attributes such as physical appearance, and verbal and nonverbal expressions. This process of **impression formation** helps us form a quick picture of the other person's identity.

Keep in mind that the importance of this information—the value attached to a certain age, race, or gender; the particular physical or personality traits a society defines as desirable; the meaning of certain words and gestures—varies across time and place. Hence, the impressions that people form of others must always be understood within the appropriate cultural and historical contexts. For instance, an emotionally expressive person in the United States may give the impression of being energetic and outgoing; in the United Kingdom such a person may seem boorish and rude; and in Thailand or Japan that person may be considered dangerous or crazy.

Social Group Membership

We can often determine people's age, sex, race, and to a certain degree ethnicity merely by looking at them; social class is less obvious but sometimes becomes known early in an encounter with another person through her or his language, mannerisms, or dress. Our socialization experiences have taught us to expect that people displaying these signs of social group membership have certain characteristics in common. For instance, if all you know about a person you've not yet met is that she's 85 years old, you might predict that she has low energy, a poor memory, and a conservative approach to life. Think about your expectations when you learn that your new roommate is from a different region of this country—or, for that matter, from a different country. Of course, such expectations are rarely completely accurate. Nevertheless, we typically begin social interactions with these culturally defined conceptions of how people from certain social groups are likely to act, what their tastes and preferences might be, and what values and attitudes they are likely to hold.

 This information is so pervasive and so quickly processed that we usually notice it only when it is ambiguous or unavailable. If you spend a lot of time texting or tweeting with strangers, you may have noticed how difficult it can be to form a friendship or carry on a discussion when you don't know whether you are conversing with someone of the same sex or with someone of a different sex or whether the person is much older or much younger than you are. Social group membership provides the necessary backdrop to all encounters between people who have little if any prior knowledge of one another.

Physical Appearance

We confirm or modify early impressions based on social group membership by assessing other characteristics that are also readily perceivable, such as a person's physical appearance (Berndt & Heller, 1986). The way people dress and decorate their bodies communicates their feelings, beliefs, and group identity to others. People's clothes, jewelry, hairstyles, and so on can also indicate their ethnicity, social class, age, cultural tastes, morality, and political attitudes.

But again, our cultural background can influence these impressions. Physical attractiveness is enormously important in U.S. culture. Everywhere we turn, it seems, we are encouraged to believe that if our skin isn't perfect, if we are too short or too tall, if we are over- or underweight, if our hair isn't stylish, if our clothes don't reflect the latest fashion trend, we have fallen short of some attractiveness threshold. Although we readily acknowledge that using a person's physical appearance to form an impression is shallow and unfair, most of us do it anyway.

Is Beauty Only Skin Deep?

The famous Greek philosopher Aristotle said, "[P]ersonal beauty is a greater recommendation than any letter of introduction." Contemporary research confirms that physical appearance affects our perceptions of others. Attractive men are seen as more masculine and attractive women more feminine than their less attractive counterparts (Gillen, 1981). We often assume that good-looking people possess other desirable traits, such as happiness, kindness, strength, and sexual responsiveness (Dion, Berscheid, & Walster, 1972). Such judgments can sometimes be converted to financial gain. Economists have coined the term *beauty premium* to refer to the economic advantages attractive people enjoy:

> Handsome men earn, on average, 5% more than their less-attractive counterparts (good-looking women earn 4% more); pretty people get more attention from teachers, bosses, and mentors. . . . Fifty seven percent of hiring managers [in a recent survey indicated that] qualified but unattractive candidates are likely to have a harder time landing a job, while more than half advised spending as much time and money on "making sure they look attractive" as on perfecting a résumé. (J. Bennett, 2010, p. 47)

But beauty is not always associated with positive impressions and outcomes. For instance, people might assume that those who are extremely attractive are spoiled or aren't particularly intelligent. The (good-looking) actor Rob Lowe said recently, "There's this unbelievable bias and prejudice against quote-unquote good-looking people, that they can't be in pain or they can't have rough lives or be deep or interesting" (quoted in Brodesser-Akner, 2014, p. 12).

In Malawi, a southeast African country with a high rate of HIV infection, women who are *too* beautiful are often subject to suspicious gossip. People who are HIV positive tend to be extremely thin as AIDS takes its toll on the body. Some of the most effective treatments for HIV are antiretroviral drugs (ARVs; see Chapter 14). One of the side effects of the drug is weight gain and smooth skin. Hence, others might presume that women who look *too* healthy must be taking ARVs, meaning that they are HIV positive and not desirable sexual partners (Koenig, 2011).

Impressions based on appearance can also work their way into the legal system. In one study, undergraduate subjects at Cornell University were provided with profiles of defendants in criminal trials and asked to assess their guilt and suggest a punishment. The profiles included information about the defendant's race, gender, height, weight, and eye color, and a high-resolution color photograph, which previous subjects had coded as either attractive or unattractive. In addition, they were given a trial summary (these were all aggravated assault cases), transcripts of the attorneys' closing arguments, and the judge's instructions to the jury. The researchers found that unattractive defendants were 22% more likely to be convicted and, if convicted, spend an average of 22 months *longer* in prison than their better-looking counterparts (Gunnell & Ceci, 2010). The findings of this study did not come as a surprise to the spokesperson for the National Association of Criminal Defense Lawyers, who stated, "We usually want our clients in a suit, with their hair combed and trying to appear as clean-cut as possible. [This study] bears out what many of us knew in our gut" (quoted in Baldas, 2010, p. 1).

On the flip side, ugliness has always occupied a lowly place on the social landscape. In literature and film, ugliness is usually associated with evil and fear, characterizing all manner of monsters, ogres, witches, and villains (Kershaw, 2008). Beyond fictional por-trayals, unattractiveness can have serious everyday consequences. For instance, one study found that even in occupations where looks have no bearing on a person's ability to do his or her job—like computer programming—unattractive workers suffer discrimination (Mobius & Rosenblat, 2006). Many parents these days are becoming less tolerant of any flaw in their children's appearance. Numerous websites now offer retouching services so that parents can airbrush photos of their children to remove blemishes, crooked teeth, and other facial imperfections.

Let's face it though: physical appearance is still a more salient interpersonal and economic issue for women than for men, even though women have more money, political clout, and legal recognition today than ever before. For instance, 61% of hiring managers indicate that it's advantageous for a woman to "show off her figure" in the workplace (cited in J. Bennett, 2010). In 2015, the Montana state legislature adopted a new dress code policy advising female lawmakers to "be sensitive to skirt lengths and necklines" (Healy, 2014, p. 24). No comparable directive exists for men. During the 2016 presidential campaign, Hillary Clinton was routinely scrutinized (and criticized) for her hairstyle and fondness for pantsuits. Here's how one columnist described the way Australians treated that country's first female prime minister a few years back:

> For the three years and three days that Julia Gillard was prime minister of Australia, we debated the fit of her jackets, the size of her bottom, the exposure of her cleavage, the cut of her hair, the tone of her voice, the legitimacy of her rule and whether she had chosen, as one member of Parliament . . . put it, to be "deliberately barren." (Baird, 2013, p. A17)

It's hard to imagine physical appearance being the hub of this kind of attention for male political leaders.

So powerful is the emphasis on women's appearance that it can even influence stan-dard medical procedures. For instance, after female cancer patients undergo mastectomies (the removal of one or both breasts), plastic surgeons and oncologists routinely advise them to have breast reconstruction surgery. Indeed, for years, the medical profession has embraced the idea that breast restoration is a vital component of the cancer treatment itself, even though it is *medically* unnecessary. Despite the toll this surgery can have on women both physically and emotionally, doctors continue to push for it, motivated by the belief that the *appearance* of breasts to others will improve women's quality of life after cancer (Rabin, 2016).

Women routinely inflict serious pain on themselves as they alter their bodies to conform to cultural definitions of beauty. They may pluck their eyebrows, glue on eyelash extensions, use hot wax to strip away "unsightly" body hair, or wear ultra tight-fitting Spanx underwear. Here are a few particularly dangerous practices:

- In China, hundreds of women each year, convinced that being taller would improve their job and marriage prospects, subject themselves to a procedure in which their leg bones are broken, separated, and stretched. Metal pins and screws pull the bones apart a fraction of a millimeter a day, sometimes for close to 2 years. Many Chinese women have lost the ability to walk from this treatment; others have suffered permanent, disfiguring bone damage (C. S. Smith, 2002).

- In the United States, affluent women sometimes undergo potentially dangerous cosmetic foot surgery—called the "Cinderella procedure"—to reduce the size and change the shape of their toes so that they can fit into fashionable, narrow high-heeled shoes (Stover, 2014).

- Girls and women can now wear decorative "circle lenses," brightly colored contact lenses that make eyes appear larger because they cover not just the iris, as ordinary lenses do, but part of the whites as well (Saint Louis, 2010). These lenses, which give wearers a childlike, doe-eyed appearance, are available online without a prescription, much to the chagrin of eye doctors who fear the damage they may cause. A spokesperson for the Food and Drug Administration wrote that consumers risk significant eye injury, even blindness, when they buy contact lenses without a valid prescription.

At the individual level, the emphasis on physical appearance devalues a person's other attributes and accomplishments; at the institutional level, it plays an important role in the nation's economy by sustaining several multibillion-dollar enterprises, including the advertising, fashion, cosmetics, plastic surgery, and weight loss industries.

Sizing People Up

In U.S. society and in most industrialized societies, the negative effects of being considered unattractive are perhaps felt most strongly by those whose body size exceeds cultural standards (Carr & Friedman, 2006). Overall, roughly 17% of children and 36% of adults in this country are obese (Ogden, Carroll, Fryar, & Flegal, 2015). And the number keeps growing, leading various social institutions to adapt their practices. Consider these facts (Taubes, 2012):

- In 2012, the Coast Guard increased its assumption about the average weight of a boat passenger from 160 pounds to 185 pounds.

- Around 25% of Americans between 17 and 24 are unqualified for military service because of their weight.

- Compared to 1960, airlines spend about $5 billion more each year in jet fuel because of the extra power needed to fly heavier Americans. Commercial airlines have obesity seating policies that require a passenger to purchase a second seat if she or he is unable to fit comfortably into a single seat in the ticketed cabin, is unable to properly buckle the seatbelt using a single seatbelt extender, and/or is unable to put the seat's armrests down when seated.

We are just starting to get a picture of the financial toll obesity exacts nationwide. Estimates of medical costs associated with obesity range from $147 billion to $210 billion a year, or over 20% of total medical spending in the United States (The State of Obesity, 2016). In addition, the loss in economic productivity due to medical ailments associated with obesity could run between $390 billion and $580 billion annually by 2030 (Robert Wood Johnson Foundation, 2012). On average, obese adults spend 42% more on direct health care costs and are charged nearly 30% for emergency room visits than nonobese adults (The State of Obesity, 2016). Such figures have led some health insurance companies to charge higher premiums to anyone over a certain body mass index (Singer, 2010), and some employers are now demanding that workers who are overweight pay a greater share of their health care costs (Abelson, 2011b). Not surprisingly, the federal government spends hundreds of millions of dollars annually telling citizens to eat less and exercise more (Taubes, 2012).

Against a cultural backdrop that glorifies thinness, fat is seen not only as unhealthy and costly but as repulsive, ugly, and unclean (LeBesco, 2004). People are likely to judge an overweight person as lacking in willpower and as being self-indulgent, personally offensive, and even morally and socially unfit (Millman, 1980). "Being fat" is the most common reason kids get bullied and picked on in this country, above such traits as race, ethnicity, religion, and physical disability (Bradshaw, Waasdorp, O'Brennan, & Gulemetova, 2011). One study found that mental health caseworkers were more likely to assign negative characteristics (e.g., being too emotional, being unhygienic, engaging in inappropriate behavior) to obese patients than to thin patients (Young & Powell, 1985). Most hospitals don't have CT or MRI scanners that can accommodate extremely large patients. Doctors in such cases are likely to resort to less precise X-rays and hope for the best. Furthermore, overweight patients often complain that doctors criticize them for their weight even when the health problem that brought them to the doctor in the first place is unrelated to their size. For instance, one obese patient went to an urgent care center complaining of shortness of breath. The doctor told her she had a lot of weight pressing on her lungs and that the only thing wrong with her was that she was fat. It turned out that the woman had life-threatening blood clots in her lungs that were unrelated to her size (Kolata, 2016).

It is often said that weight discrimination is the last acceptable form of unequal treatment in the United States (Carr & Friedman, 2006). In the workplace, researchers have found significant discrimination against obese and overweight people at every stage of the employment cycle, including hiring, placement, compensation, promotion, discipline, and discharge (Roehling, 1999). Like unattractiveness in general, research has consistently shown a wage penalty for obese employees, especially women. Researchers at the George Washington University School of Public Health have found that obese men earn on average about $4,772 a year less than normal-weight men and obese women earn $5,826 less than normal-weight women (Newswise, 2011).

In high-visibility occupations such as public relations and sales, overweight people are often regarded as unemployable because they might project a negative image of the company they are working for. Flight attendants have been fired for exceeding airline weight requirements, even though their job-related abilities met company standards (Puhl & Brownell, 2001). A casino in Atlantic City once warned its cocktail waitresses that if they gained more than 10% of their current weight, they'd be suspended without pay for 90 days while they tried to lose the extra pounds. If their weight loss efforts were unsuccessful, they'd be fired (I. Peterson, 2005).

Negative perceptions of obese people are not universal. In Niger, for example, being overweight—ideally with rolls of fat, stretch marks, and a large behind—is considered an essential part of female beauty. Women who aren't sufficiently round are considered unfit for marriage (R. Popenoe, 2005). In Mauritania, girls as young as 5 and as old as 19 years are sometimes forced by their parents to drink five gallons of fat-rich camel's milk each day so they become fat (LaFraniere, 2007). In Botswana, fatness is equated with female fertility and is therefore a positive sign of a woman's marriageability. Large women are said to have "fat eggs" and are therefore fit to bear children (Upton, 2010). In many developing countries, where food supplies are scarce, being overweight is associated with being middle class or wealthy.

Indeed, some anthropologists argue that women's roles in society always influence cultural tastes in body shape. For instance, men tend to prefer larger female bodies in industrial societies where women are economically independent (e.g., Britain and Denmark) and in nonindustrial societies where they bear responsibility for finding food. Only in societies where women are economically dependent on men (such as Japan and Greece) do men have a strong preference for thin, hourglass figures in women. As one anthropologist put it, men's preferences in female body type depend "on the degree to which they want their mates to be strong, tough, economically successful, and politically competitive" (Cashdan, 2008, p. 1104).

Rates of obesity—and accompanying maladies associated with obesity, like diabetes—have been rising worldwide, due principally to the increased production of more processed and affordable food than ever before (Murray & Ng, 2014; Swinburn et al., 2011). At the same time, though, Western images of thinness—and perhaps the stigmatization of obesity as well—have begun to infiltrate places that once had positive attitudes toward large bodies, such as Mexico, Tanzania, and Puerto Rico (Brewis, Wutich, Falletta-Cowden, & Rodriguez-Soto, 2011). An Indian businesswoman recently stated, "I think all around the ideal of beauty is skinny thin. I had a highly educated friend confess that she would prefer for her children to be anorexic rather than overweight" (quoted in Parker-Pope, 2011, p. A3).

In the United States, the value attached to body size is linked to race and social class. By official measures, 67% of Whites are either overweight or obese. Among African Americans and Latino/as, the figures are about 76% and 78%, respectively (The State of Obesity, 2014). As in contemporary developing countries, obesity was once considered a sign of wealth and high status in the United States, but today it's just the opposite. Being overweight is likely to be equated with poverty, where sedentary lifestyles and high-fat diets can be commonplace (Gilman, 2004; D. Kim & Leigh, 2010). Weight problems are compounded in poor communities because the key determinants of physical activity—safe playgrounds, access to high-quality, low-cost food, and transportation to play areas—are either inadequate or nonexistent. And because of poor grocery distribution in low-income neighborhoods, fresh fruits and vegetables are actually more expensive than in suburban stores. Poor black and racially mixed neighborhoods have significantly fewer large-chain supermarkets, natural food stores, fruit and vegetable markets, and bakeries than wealthier white neighborhoods. What they have more of are local grocery stores, convenience stores, and fast-food restaurants—all of which provide fewer healthy choices and tend to charge higher prices for the healthier food they do offer (M. Lee, 2006). These areas are sometimes referred to as "food deserts" because of their nutritional isolation and the lack of mainstream, high-quality grocery stores.

In addition, fast-food companies have grown more aggressive in targeting poor, inner-city neighborhoods. Researchers have found that obesity rates among ninth graders increase by an average of 5% when their school is located within one tenth of a mile of a fast-food restaurant (Currie, DellaVigna, Moretti, & Pathania, 2009). Another study found that lower-income black adults who live closer to fast-food restaurants have higher body mass indexes than those who live farther away (Reitzel et al., 2014). The problem became so acute that in 2008 the Los Angeles City Council adopted legislation mandating a 1-year moratorium on the building of new fast-food restaurants in an inner-city area with a 30% obesity rate (Kurutz, 2008). In 2012, the mayor of New York tried (and failed) to restrict the sale of super-size sugary drinks in fast-food restaurants.

As with physical appearance in general, U.S. women feel the contemporary distaste for obesity particularly strongly. Clothing companies contribute to women's heightened weight concern through the way they size women's clothes. Several companies now manufacture size zero outfits. In 2007, the fashion designer Nicole Miller became the first to introduce a "subzero" size for women with 23-inch waists—roughly the circumference of a junior soccer ball—and 35-inch hips (the average U.S. woman has a 34-inch waist and 43-inch hips; Schrobsdorff, 2006). It is feared that "0" and "00" sizes will become a status symbol among young girls who glorify razor-thin bodies. For older women, clothing companies also engage in a common practice known as "vanity sizing," whereby garments with the same size number become larger over time. In the 1930s, a woman with a 32-inch bust would have worn a size 14; in the 1960s, she'd have been an 8; today, she'd be a size 0 (Clifford, 2011). Such a practice allegedly makes older women feel better about themselves because it gives the illusion that they are thinner than they really are.

But all U.S. women do not share weight concerns equally. Eighty-two percent of African American women and 77% of Latina women are overweight or obese, compared with 63% of white women (The State of Obesity, 2014). Yet white women are significantly more likely than women of color to express concerns about their weight and to exhibit disordered eating behaviors (Abrams, Allen, & Gray, 1993). In one study of 11- to 17-year-olds, white girls were more likely than Latina and black girls to think they were overweight, even though their actual weight was in the "normal" range. Indeed, young black women were far more likely than other groups to consider themselves "good looking" (Mikolajczyk, Iannotti, Farhat, & Thomas, 2012).

Likewise, adult African American women, especially poor and working-class women, worry less than women of other races about dieting or about not being thin enough (Molloy & Herzberger, 1998). One study found that although African American women are more likely than white women to weigh more than 120% of their recommended body weight, they are much less likely to perceive themselves as overweight or to suffer blows to their self-esteem as a result (Averett & Korenman, 1999). When black women do diet, their efforts to lose weight are more realistic and less extreme than white women's attempts.

However, researchers have recently begun to challenge the suggestion that women of color are somehow immune to body weight concerns (e.g., Beauboeuf-Lafontant, 2009). Some have suggested that women of color have always suffered from body dissatisfaction and disordered eating but have largely been overlooked by researchers because they are less likely than white women to seek treatment (Brodey, 2005). Others speculate that body dissatisfaction among women of color has actually increased recently because they are more likely than their predecessors to be exposed to and adopt for themselves dominant white

VISUAL ESSAY—THERE SHE IS, MISS AMERICA...

Bettmann/Bettmann/Getty Images

AP Photo/Chris Polk

Martha Holmes/The LIFE Picture Collection/Getty Images

AP Photo/Isaac Brekken

It should be obvious by now that whether we like it or not, we frequently judge people's character by their size, shape, and attractiveness. Furthermore, you've seen that meeting cultural standards of beauty has always been a more treacherous endeavor for women than for men. What makes things even trickier is that the standards of physical attractiveness can shift over time. For instance, the idealized female body type has become thinner and thinner over the years.

What better place to see the "shrinkage" of feminine beauty than in national pageants like the Miss America contest. Here are photos of the Miss America winners from 1936, 1947, 1999, and 2009. Aside from the obvious changes in fashion styles, do you notice any differences between the bodies of these women? How do you think definitions of beauty in the 1930s compare to definitions of beauty today? Could Katie Stam (Miss America, 2009) have competed successfully in the 1936 pageant? Do you think the appearance standards used to judge contestants in a competition like the Miss America pageant *reflect* broader cultural tastes or do they *determine* those tastes?

preferences, attitudes, and ideals about beauty and weight. One study found that the risk of disordered eating increases for African American women who have a strong desire to assimilate into the dominant white culture (Abrams et al., 1993). Concern over weight shows how powerful cultural beliefs are in the formation of self-concepts. At best, the failure to meet broad cultural standards of thinness can lower self-esteem and generate antagonism toward one's own body. At worst, it can lead to life-threatening eating disorders. Such drastic responses indicate the importance of body size—and physical appearance in general—in forming impressions of other people.

Verbal and Nonverbal Expression

Aside from physical appearance, another important piece of information we use in forming impressions of others is what people express to us verbally or nonverbally. Obviously, we form impressions of others based on what they choose to tell us about themselves. But beyond speech, people's movements, postures, and gestures also provide cues about their values, attitudes, sentiments, personality, and history (G. P. Stone, 1981). Sometimes people use these forms of communication purposely to convey meaning, as when they put on a smile so that others will find them approachable. Professional sign language interpreters know that facial expressions are an integral component of sign language. According to one interpreter:

> The only way you can do a question is with your eyebrows. A major way to do an adverb is with mouth movements. Even in [formal speech] there's often irony, which you show on your face. (quoted in Schulman, 2014, p. 19)

However, some physical expressions, such as a shaky voice, a flushed face, and trembling hands, are difficult to control. They transmit an impression whether we want to or not.

Most of us are quite proficient at "reading" even the subtlest nonverbal messages. We learn early on that a raised eyebrow, a nod of the head, or a slight hand gesture can mean something important in a social encounter. So crucial is this ability in maintaining orderly interactions that some psychologists consider a deficiency in it to be a learning disability akin to severe reading problems (Goleman, 1989).

Managing Impressions

From the previous discussion of impression formation, it's clear that at the same time we're making judgments about others, we're also trying to manipulate information about ourselves to sway how others judge us. This ability to influence the impressions others make of us is the defining feature of human interaction. We often try to create impressions of ourselves that give us advantages—by making us seem attractive or powerful or otherwise worthy of people's attention and esteem. Of course, we're not always good at it. Remember my ill-fated jump shot with my future sister-in-law's new basketball?

The process by which people attempt to present a favorable public image of themselves is called **impression management**. Erving Goffman (1959), the sociologist most responsible for the scholarly examination of impression management, portrays everyday life as a series of social interactions in which a person is motivated to "sell" a particular image to others. The primary goal of impression management is to project a particular identity that will increase the likelihood of obtaining favorable outcomes from others in particular social situations (E. E. Jones & Pittman, 1982; Stryker, 1980). To do so, we can strategically furnish or conceal information. At times, we may need to advertise, exaggerate, or even fabricate our positive qualities; at other times, we conceal or camouflage behaviors or attributes that we believe others will find unappealing.

The prominent role that social media now plays in our lives has created new challenges for impression management. Recall our discussion of role taking in Chapter 5. In our "offline" lives, we interact with various people each day: family, acquaintances, coworkers, friends from different corners of our lives. Consequently, we have the opportunity to express multiple selves and manage different impressions that suit our different immediate needs. You're probably not the same person with your friends as you are with your grandparents. As long as you keep these disparate groups apart, you're OK. But online—when, say, we're posting photos of ourselves on our Facebook page—we have one shot at managing the impression we want others to form of us. And it's an impression various people who have come to know us under very different circumstances could have access to. Perhaps you know someone who posted half-naked drunken photos from his or her 21st birthday party only to have them seen, with much dismay, by unsuspecting parents. Similarly, on Twitter, once we tweet some rant or intimate self-disclosure, it's out there forever, remaining in the feed of whoever is following us. That's a lot of pressure. Facebook seems to acknowledge the necessity for managing multiple selves by allowing users to customize impressions to particular selected audiences through privacy settings and friend lists.

Whether it occurs online or offline in face-to-face interaction, obtaining favorable outcomes through impression management is usually associated with a desire for social approval—that is, with being respected and liked by others. However, different circumstances may require projecting different identities (E. E. Jones & Pittman, 1982). Maybe you've been in situations where you've tried to appear helpless or meek in order to get someone else to do a task you really didn't want to do. A famous actress once said of her director, "He wins us over by being humble, so we help him with this thing he's making" (quoted in Friend, 2017, p. 32). Or perhaps you've tried to appear mean and fearsome to intimidate someone or "played dumb" to avoid challenging a superior (Gove, Hughes, & Geerkin, 1980). Because of our capacity for role taking, we are able to tailor our images to fit the requirements of a particular situation.

Goffman argues that impression management is not just used to present false or inflated images of ourselves. Many authentic attributes we possess are not immediately apparent to others; sometimes our actions may be misinterpreted. Imagine yourself taking the final exam in your sociology course. You look up from your paper and make brief eye contact with the instructor. You're not cheating, but you think the instructor may interpret your wandering eyes as an indication of cheating. What do you do? Chances are you will deliberately overemphasize your noncheating behavior by acting as though you're deep in thought or by glancing up at the clock to highlight your "law-abiding" image.

Frequently people try to present a favorable image of themselves by strategically altering their physical appearance. Clothing and body adornment can be used to manipulate and manage the impressions others form of us. People can dress to convey the impression that they are worthy of respect or, at the very least, attention (Lauer & Handel, 1977). Some research has shown that women who dress in a traditionally masculine way during a job interview are more likely to be hired. Likewise, students perceive teachers who dress formally as more intelligent than teachers who dress casually (cited in Blakeslee, 2012).

Children often signal their entry into the world of adolescence by wearing the clothing of their peers and refusing to wear the clothing chosen by their parents (G. P. Stone, 1981). The purveyors of various music subcultures like pop, hip-hop, metal head, emo, indie, dance/house/techno, and goth use clothing and hairstyle as an expression of identity and social rebellion. And as you are well aware, fashion is a significant element of the student subculture on most college campuses. In short, by what they wear, people tell one another who they are, where they come from, and what they stand for.

HAJO ADAM AND ADAM GALINSKY

CAN YOUR CLOTHES MAKE YOU SMARTER?

We all know that clothes affect how others perceive us. Books like *Dress for Success* and TV shows like *What Not to Wear* confirm the impression management beliefs we all have: people treat us differently depending on what we're wearing. We receive more respect—from friends, clients, and customers—when we are dressed formally than when we are dressed casually. Not surprisingly, when we wear formal clothing, we tend to perceive *ourselves* differently, too, thinking we're more competent and rational than when we're wearing shorts and a T-shirt (Peluchette & Karl, 2007).

But is it possible that the type of clothing people wear can also affect the way they act and process information? A growing scientific field called "enclothed cognition" argues that the answer is a resounding "yes." In one study, when subjects wore expensive, tailored suits, they were more likely than those dressed casually to forgo a $12 reward that day in order to receive a $20 reward the next day. The researchers argued that these subjects were demonstrating better abstract processing, the kind of big-picture thinking CEOs and managers are required to perform on a daily basis. On the flip side, when subjects wore uniforms associated with lower-level workers, they demonstrated greater levels of the "machine-like" thinking required for repetitive tasks (Slepian, Ferber, Gold, & Rutchick, 2015).

Social psychologists Hajo Adam and Adam Galinsky designed a series of experiments to address this question further. They gave subjects long white coats and told some of them the garment was a "lab coat." Others were told it was a "painter's coat." The ones wearing "lab coats" performed better on an array of cognitive tasks that required close attention. In one task, subjects were shown a series of letters on a computer screen for a brief second and asked to immediately identify whether the letters were in blue or red. In some trials, the letters were congruent: R-E-D printed in red and B-L-U-E printed in blue. In others, however the letters were incongruent: R-E-D in blue and B-L-U-E in red. The subjects in "painter's coats" made about twice as many mistakes in the incongruent trials as the subjects wearing "lab coats." Even when they were given an actual painter's coat but *told* it was a lab coat, subjects outperformed others on tasks requiring sustained attention and memory (Adam & Galinsky, 2012).

Research on enclothed cognition can have real-world utility. For instance, does wearing the robe of a judge make people behave more ethically? Can putting on the uniform of a firefighter make someone more courageous? A few years ago, the Utah Department of Corrections decided it had to do something about the unruly, noncompliant, and violent inmates in its women's prisons. Operating on the contention that uniforms make prisoners more likely to disobey rules (Ash, 2009), it provided the inmates with brand-new, plum-colored uniforms and lifted its ban on cosmetics. However, shortly afterward, disciplinary problems plummeted. Some believe that thanks to the new uniforms, the women no longer saw themselves as prisoners but as people (Neilson, 2016).

Dramaturgy: Actors on a Social Stage

"All the world's a stage, / And all the men and women merely players: / They have their exits and their entrances; / And one man in his time plays many parts," wrote William Shakespeare in *As You Like It*. Analyzing social interaction as a series of theatrical performances—what sociologists call **dramaturgy**—has been a staple of symbolic interactionism for decades. Like Shakespeare, Goffman (1959) argues that people in everyday life are similar to actors on a stage. The "audience" consists of people who observe the behavior of others, "roles" are the images people are trying to project, and the "script" is the content of their communication with others. The goal is to enact a performance that is believable to a particular audience and that allows us to achieve the goals we desire. Just about every aspect of social life can be examined dramaturgically, from the ritualized greetings of strangers to the everyday dynamics of our family, school, and work lives.

Front Stage and Back Stage

A key structural element of dramaturgy is the distinction between front stage and back stage. In the theater, front stage is where the performance takes place for the audience. In contrast, back stage is where makeup is removed, lines are rehearsed, and performances are rehashed, and where people can fall "out of character."

In social interaction, **front stage** is where people maintain the appropriate appearance as they interact with others. For workers in a restaurant, front stage is the dining room where the customers (the audience) are present. Here, the servers (the actors) are expected to present themselves as upbeat, happy, competent, and courteous. **Back stage**, however, is the region where people can knowingly violate their impression management performances. In the restaurant, back stage is the kitchen area where the once courteous servers now shout, shove dishes, and even complain about or mock the customers.

As in the theater, the barrier between front and back stage is crucial to successful impression management because it blocks the audience from seeing behavior that would ruin the performance. During a therapy session (front stage), psychiatrists usually appear extremely interested in everything their patients say and show considerable sympathy for their problems. At a dinner party with colleagues or at home with family (back stage), however, they may express total boredom with and disdain for their patients' disclosures. If patients were to see such back stage behavior, not only would it disrupt the performance, but it would damage the psychiatrist's professional credibility and reputation as well. One study found that beneath their mask of neutrality, many psychiatrists harbor strong and professionally inappropriate feelings—including hatred, fear, anger, and sexual arousal—toward their patients (cited in Goleman, 1993).

Props

Successful impression management also depends on the control of objects, called props, that convey identity. In the theater, props must be handled deftly for an effective performance. A gun that doesn't go off when it's supposed to or a chair that unexpectedly collapses can destroy an entire play. The same is true in social interaction. For instance, in preparation for an upcoming visit from their parents, college students may make sure their schoolbooks are in clear view and beer bottles disposed of. Similarly, someone may spend a great deal of time setting a romantic mood for a dinner date at home—the right music, the right lighting, pictures of former lovers hidden from view, and so on.

Sometimes people use props to create an environment that reinforces some individuals' authority over others. Note the way props were used to intimidate this professor as he testified before Congress:

And then I was called to the witness stand. Now, the chair is something nobody talks about. It is low and extremely puffy. When you sit in it your butt just keeps sinking, and suddenly the tabletop is up to your chest. The senators peer down at you from above, and the power dynamic is terrifying. (H. Jenkins, 1999, p. 21)

Props needn't be inanimate objects. To convey to potential clients and investors what they believe will be an air of prestige, money, and crucial global connections, some Chinese companies "rent" white foreigners to pose as fake employees. The companies hope that the presence of these individuals will help to secure a contract or simply support the company's claim of being internationally successful. An ad in a Chinese newspaper for a company called Rent-a-*Laowai* (Chinese for "foreigner") read: "Occasionally companies want a foreign face to go to meetings and conferences or to go to dinners and lunches and smile at the clients and shake people's hands" (quoted in Farrar, 2010, p. 1).

Viewing impression management from a dramaturgical perspective reminds us that our everyday actions rarely occur in a social vacuum. Indeed, our behaviors are often structured with an eye toward how they might be perceived by particular "audiences."

Image Making

In our individualistic, competitive society, appearances can sometimes provide a critically important edge. A person's desire to maximize prestige, wealth, and power can be the driving force behind a thorough makeover. Two prominent examples are Americans' pursuit of improved looks through the invasive alteration of their bodies and politicians' pursuit of a popular identity through a carefully controlled public image. As you will see, these efforts are not things a person undertakes on his or her own. Whole industries have evolved that are devoted to making and remaking images for the public eye.

The Surgical Alteration of Appearance

The desire to manage impressions by changing physical appearance motivates some people to do far more than try a new hairstyle, get a tattoo, or buy a new outfit or two. Even in economic hard times, people in the United States are willing to spend huge sums of money to medically alter their looks. According to the American Society of Plastic Surgeons (2016), there were 1.7 million cosmetic surgery procedures and 14.2 million minimally invasive, nonsurgical procedures (such as Botox injections, cellulite treatments, and chemical peels) in the United States in 2015. Ninety-two percent of the patients were women. These figures represent a 115% increase over 2000. The overall cost for these procedures was about $13.4 billion. Exhibit 6.1 shows recent trends in the popularity of cosmetic procedures.

The desire to surgically alter one's appearance is not unique to the United States:

- Doctors perform more plastic surgeries per capita in South Korea than anywhere else in the world; the United States ranks sixth. It's estimated that one in five women in Seoul have had some kind of cosmetic surgery (International Society of Aesthetic Plastic Surgery, 2016). The most common cosmetic procedure in Korea is blepharoplasty, an eyelid surgery that gives a rounder, more "Western" look to the eye.

- Brazil leads the world in the number of head and facial procedures performed each year (International Society of Aesthetic Plastic Surgery, 2016). In 2001, the Brazilian contestant in the Miss Universe contest scandalized many non-Brazilians by speaking freely and publicly about her breast implants, cheekbone reconstruction, silicone remolding of her chin, pinned-back ears, and liposuction. She told reporters, "I have to work on my figure to get it where I want it. It's something I need for my profession. . . . I have a doctorate in body measurement" (Kulick & Machado-Borges, 2005, p. 128).

- In China, the growing cosmetic surgery industry takes in over $2.4 billion a year as people with newfound affluence rush to go under the knife. As one Chinese student put it, "In China we say there are no ugly women, only lazy women" (quoted in Savacool, 2009, p. 62). The number of Chinese receiving cosmetic plastic surgery doubles each year. As in South Korea, the most commonly requested procedure is one designed to make the eyes appear larger and more "Western" (LaFraniere, 2011). In fact, China hosts an annual *Renzao Meinu* or "artificial beauty" contest, where people from all over the globe compete to become the world's most beautiful product of plastic surgery (Savacool, 2009).

EXHIBIT 6.1 ● I'm Having Some Work Done: More and More People Are Choosing Cosmetic Surgery

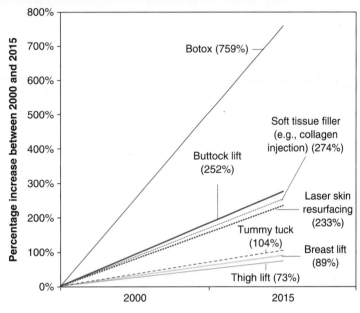

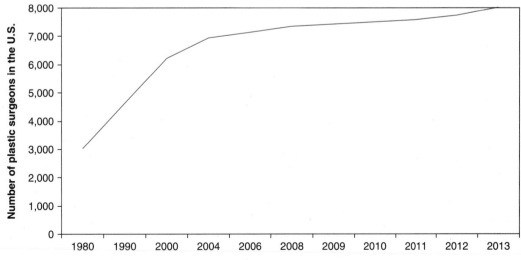

Sources: American Society of Plastic Surgeons, 2016; ProQuest Statistical Abstract, 2017, Table 172.

The growing popularity of cosmetic surgery reflects an alarming level of discontent among people about the way they look. Researchers estimate that 30% to 40% of U.S. adults have concerns about some aspect of their physical appearance (Gorbis & Kholodenko, 2005). And over 2% of the population is so self-conscious about their looks that their lives are constricted in some significant way, from feeling inhibited during lovemaking to becoming homebound or even suicidal (American Psychiatric Association, 2013). About half of these individuals seek some sort of professional medical intervention, like surgery or dermatological treatment (Gorbis & Kholodenko, 2005). Indeed, the number of Americans undergoing weight reduction surgery, such as stomach banding, has increased sevenfold over the past decade, at a cost of over $6 billion annually (cited in Hartocollis, 2012b).

Political Portraits

If you have ever seen a U.S. political party's national convention the summer before a presidential election, you have witnessed a highly professional, meticulously planned effort at impression management. Music, balloons, lighting, logos, colors, even individual delegates in the audience are all transformed into props that are manipulated to project images of patriotism, unity, organization, strength, and, above all, electability. At the center is the candidate, who must personally present an image (also professionally crafted) that will appeal to the voting public. Campaign staffs are concerned as much with ensuring that their candidate "appears presidential" as they are with his or her positions on key political issues.

Consider the images Barack Obama had to craft during his two presidential campaigns. During his first election in 2008, he had to deal with problems in "looking presidential," such as not wearing an American flag lapel pin (which he started doing), "fist bumping" his wife on the campaign trail (which he stopped doing), and having the middle name "Hussein" (which he could do nothing about). He successfully managed his most obvious image problem—his race and ethnicity—by repeatedly telling audiences on the campaign trail that he didn't look like the presidents on our currency and acknowledging that he had a funny name. In doing so, he neutralized opposition attempts to paint him as un-American. By 2012, Obama's political enemies were still trying to paint him as an alien threat, calling attention to his "exotic" upbringing and questioning his religious affiliation, his ability to govern for "all" Americans, or even whether he was a U.S. citizen.

The impression management dilemma many candidates running for office face is how to downplay their affluence. Privileged backgrounds don't provide the "up-from-nothing" life story many candidates these days seem to want (Leibovich, 2014). Every election cycle, we watch all manner of exceedingly wealthy candidates go through the charade of altering their clothing, mannerisms, tastes, and vocabulary to show voters that "they're less loftily removed from the so-called common man than they really are" (Bruni, 2012, p. 3). They'll highlight the dishwashing job or hardscrabble home life they had when younger. Even when they have no such story of early struggles, candidates will work hard to craft an image that they're "just like" everyone else. This explains why they'll eat burgers or bowl with blue-collar folk to convince voters that they're one of them.

For some candidates, whose massive wealth can't be ignored, such attempts can seem far-fetched. Donald Trump, one of the richest presidential candidates in history, was able—through rough tell-it-like-it-is language and baseball caps—to persuade poor and working-class voters that he could empathize with their suffering. Even though he is an Ivy League graduate, real estate tycoon, reality TV star, and an heir to vast inherited wealth who once compared himself to Jesus, Trump claimed he was just like everybody else.

"I love blue collar workers," he said during the campaign, "[a]nd I consider myself in a certain way to be a blue collar worker" (quoted in Edelman, 2016, p. 1).

Once elected, a president, with the help or hindrance of the media, must play simultaneously to international and domestic audiences (P. Hall, 1990). The international audience consists of foreign allies and adversaries, whom he must convince of his authority and his ability to fulfill commitments. The domestic audience is the voting public, whom he must impress through the portrayal of "presidential character": good health, decisiveness, control, a stable home and family life, and so forth. Like all politicians, a president must be prepared to use impression management throughout his tenure to get a favorable result in an opinion poll or a desired vote in Congress or some international body, like the United Nations.

Moreover, the president is but one member of an entire administration made up of various departments, commissions, and agencies, each of which must engage in its own impression management so as not to reflect poorly on the government. For instance, the Counterterrorism Communications Center provides detailed directives for how government officials ought to talk about our military involvements worldwide. Here we see the importance of projecting a trustworthy, knowledgeable image:

> Try to limit the number of non-English terms you use. . . . Mispronunciation could make your statement incomprehensible and/or sound ill-informed. If you must use such a word, make sure your pronunciation is validated by an expert. Don't use words that require use of consonants that do not exist in English and whose nearest English approximation has a totally different meaning. (Counterterrorism Communications Center, 2008, p. 2)

The White House, no matter who is in office, has an entire staff of media and public relations consultants to ensure that images and messages are tightly controlled so as to depict the president in the most favorable light possible. Whenever the president travels—whether it be an excursion to a small town in the heartland or a major state trip to Asia—a small advance team arrives at the location days or perhaps weeks beforehand to coordinate every logistical component of the trip. But it's not just about making sure limousines arrive on time or security personnel know their duties. The advance team functions as an impression management extension of the president by making sure every factory he visits, every walk he takes, and every meal he eats at a local diner runs as smoothly as possible (The White House Blog, 2010). Advance teams must even develop plans for dealing with demonstrators and protestors, should they be present (Office of Presidential Advance, 2002).

Often a president's goals are accomplished through "gesture politics"—actions or initiatives that are largely symbolic and convey, whether purposefully or not, particular characteristics. National leaders frequently find themselves judged not so much by the effectiveness of their policies as by how the public responds to their gestures:

> At least one European newspaper described [former] President Bush's effort to aid tsunami victims [in 2004] as a bid to show U.S. compassion. What was important was not the particulars of Bush's own aid plan, but whether the public would find it convincingly noble. . . . In the public mind [programs] are secondary to (and their success is dependent on) the personal gestures that accompany them. (Caldwell, 2005, p. 11)

Like all of his predecessors, Barack Obama had his share of "gesture politics" appearances following such tragedies as floods in the Mississippi Delta; tornadoes in Tuscaloosa, Alabama,

Joplin, Missouri, and Moore, Oklahoma; a school shooting in Newtown, Connecticut; the aftermath of Superstorm Sandy in New York and New Jersey; the bombing at the Boston Marathon; or the massacre at Charleston's Emanuel African Methodist Episcopal Church. At each of these events, Obama was judged more by the comfort and sympathy his gestures symbolized than by the specific details of his plans. But "gesture politics" always carry the risk of criticism if actions fail to convey the precise level of empathy, sympathy, or strength the general public thinks is appropriate. President Donald Trump faced a harsh media backlash in 2017 for "helping" Puerto Rican victims of Hurricane Maria by throwing rolls of paper towels at them when he visited the island two weeks after the storm devastated it.

Social Influences on Impression Management

Up to this point, I've described impression management and dramaturgy from the viewpoint of individual actors driven by a personal desire to present themselves in the most advantageous light possible. But social group membership may also influence the sorts of images a person tries to present in social interaction. The elements of one's identity—age, gender, race and ethnicity, religion, social class, occupational status—influence others' immediate expectations, which can be self-fulfilling. In other words, members of certain social groups may manage impressions somewhat differently than nonmembers because of society's preconceived notions about them. Race or ethnicity and social status are among the most notable influences on impression management.

Race and Ethnicity

In a society where race is a primary source of inequality, people of color often learn that they will be rewarded if they assimilate to "white norms" and hide the elements of their ethnoracial culture. According to Kenji Yoshino (2006), a law professor, the pressure to "act white" means that people of color must suppress the nonwhite aspects of their hairstyle, clothing, and speech. They must also monitor their social activities, participation in ethnic or race-based organizations or political causes, and friendship networks. The comedian Dave Chappelle once said that African Americans must be "bilingual" if they want to make it in this society. In other words, they become adept at identifying situations, like job interviews, where they must eliminate "black" patterns of speech and "speak white" (Chaudhry, 2006).

Such impression management strategies may increase the likelihood of economic benefit, but they are not without social costs. As then-senator Barack Obama said in a 2004 speech at the Democratic National Convention, "Children [of color] can't achieve unless we raise their expectations and . . . eradicate the slander that says a black youth with a book is acting white" (quoted in Fryer, 2006, p. 53). People of color who "act white" in some situations but perform a different version of their identity when with others like themselves run the risk of being considered sellouts or tagged as "Oreo cookies," "bananas," or "coconuts"—that is, black or yellow or brown on the outside and white on the inside—by members of their ethnoracial communities (Chaudhry, 2006).

Moreover, it's only the relatively affluent who have the opportunity to learn how to act white. Others—Pakistani cab drivers, Latina housekeepers, Korean grocery store clerks, to name a few—have no such option. Indeed, living up (or down) to certain ethnoracial stereotypes may be one of the few ways people can participate actively in public life while retaining their own cultural identity. In the past, for example, Native Americans often complained that in interactions with members of other ethnoracial groups, they were expected to "act Indian" by wearing traditional garb or speaking in the stilted manner of media stereotypes. Contemporary rap and hip-hop stars are often criticized for conforming to unflattering black stereotypes in order to appeal to white, middle-class audiences. But while individuals from disadvantaged groups may appear to fit common racial or ethnic stereotypes in public (front stage), an analysis of private (back stage) behavior often indicates that they are keenly aware of the identities they've been forced to present. Impression management is obviously an important survival tactic.

ELIJAH ANDERSON
THE PUBLIC FACES OF YOUNG BLACK MEN

Sociologist Elijah Anderson carried out observational research in a racially, ethnically, and economically diverse area of Philadelphia he called Village Northton. The area is home to two communities: one black and poor, the other middle to upper income and predominantly white. Anderson was particularly interested in how young black men—the overwhelming majority of whom were civil and law abiding—managed public impressions to deal with the assumption of Village Northton residents that all young black men are dangerous.

Anderson discovered that a central theme for most area residents was maintaining safety on the streets and avoiding violent and drug-related crime. Incapable of making distinctions between law-abiding black males and others, people relied for protection on broad stereotypes: Whites are law abiding and trustworthy; young black men are crime prone and dangerous.

Residents of the area, including black men themselves, were likely to be suspicious of unknown black men on the street. Women—particularly white women—clutched their purses and edged up closer to their companions as they walked down the street. Many pedestrians crossed the street or averted their eyes from young black men, who were seen as unpredictable and menacing.

Some of the young black men in the area developed certain dramaturgical strategies to overcome the assumption that they were dangerous. For instance, many came to believe that if they presented a certain appearance or carried certain props with them in public that represented law-abiding behavior (e.g., a briefcase, a shirt and tie, a college identification card), they would be treated better in contacts with the police or others in the neighborhood. In addition, they often used friendly or deferential greetings as a kind of preemptive peace offering, designed to advise others of their civil intentions. Or they went to great lengths to behave in ways contrary to the presumed expectations of Whites:

I find myself being extra nice to Whites. A lot of times I be walking down the streets . . . and I see somebody white. . . . I know they are afraid of me. They don't know me, but they intimidated. . . . So I might smile, just to reassure them. . . . At other times I find myself opening doors, you know. Holding the elevator. Putting myself in a certain light, you know, to change whatever doubts they may have.
(E. Anderson, 1990, pp. 185–186)

Such impression management requires an enormous amount of effort and places responsibility for ensuring social order on this man. He feels compelled to put strangers at ease so he can go about his own business. He understands that his mere presence makes others nervous and uncomfortable. He recognizes that trustworthiness—an ascribed characteristic of Whites—is something Blacks must work hard to achieve.

Other young black men, less willing to bear the burden of social order, capitalized on the fear they knew they could evoke. Some purposely "put on a swagger" or adopted a menacing stance to intimidate other pedestrians. Some purposely created discomfort in those they considered "ignorant" enough to be unnecessarily afraid of them. According to Anderson, law-abiding youth have an interest in giving the impression that they are dangerous: It is a way to keep others at bay. The right looks and moves ensure safe passage on the street.

The irony of such survival tactics is that they make it even more difficult for others to distinguish between those who are law abiding and those who are crime prone. By exhibiting an air of danger and toughness, a young black man may avoid being ridiculed or even victimized by his own peers, but he risks further alienating law-abiding Whites and Blacks. Members of racial and ethnic minorities face many such special dilemmas in impression management, whether they attempt to contradict stereotypes or embrace them.

Socioeconomic Status

A person's relative economic position in society can also influence impression management. Like the young black men in Anderson's study, some working-class youths, frustrated by their lack of access to the middle-class world and their inability to meet the requirements of "respectability" as defined by the dominant culture, may present themselves as malicious or dangerous. A tough image helps them gain attention or achieve status and respect within their group (Campbell, 1987; A. K. Cohen, 1955).

Conversely, those who occupy the dominant classes of society can get the attention and respect we all want with very little effort (Derber, 1979). They get special consideration in restaurants, shops, and other public settings. They monopolize the starring roles in politics and economics and also claim more than their share of attention in ordinary interactions. By displaying the symbolic props of material success—large homes, tasteful furnishings, luxury cars, expensive clothes and jewelry—people know that they can impress others and thereby reinforce their own sense of worth and status.

Prior to the recent economic recession, the visual trappings of social class had become harder to spot. When credit was easily available, more U.S. adults had access to the traditional high-end props of the well-to-do. A middle-class family could own a flat-screen television or a fancy sports car. Just a few years ago, 81% of respondents in one study indicated that they had felt some pressure to buy high-priced goods (cited in Steinhauer, 2005). So the extremely wealthy ratcheted up the visual display of social status, buying even more expensive products, such as $130,000 cars, $7,000 smartphones, and $400 bottles of wine, and using posh services like personal chefs and private jets. Tougher times, however, led even the super rich to become a bit more discreet in their public displays of wealth:

> Fabulous home theaters are tucked into the basements of plain suburban houses. Bespoke jeans that start at $1,200 can be detected only by a tiny red logo on the button. The hand-painted Italian bicycles that flash across Silicon Valley on Saturday mornings have become the new Ferrari. (Sengupta, 2012, p. A1)

Indeed, for a time, ostentatious displays of wealth became the object of public anger and ridicule. You may recall the firestorm that erupted in the media in 2009, when the chief executives of the major U.S. automakers flew to Washington, DC, in their private jets to appeal for federal bailout money. In fact, some public figures—like Facebook CEO Mark Zuckerberg and his trademark hoodie—take great pains to distance themselves from their upper-class status.

With the election of a multibillionaire as president, it remains to be seen whether or not ostentatious displays of wealth will make a comeback. The popularity of social media sites like "Rich Kids on Instagram" and "Private School Snapchats" as well as Twitter hashtags like #blessed or #donthateappreciate indicates that perhaps they already are.

Status differences in impression management permeate the workplace, too. Those at the very top of an organization need not advertise their high status because it is already known to the people with whom they interact regularly. Their occupational status is a permanently recognized "badge of ability" (Derber, 1979, p. 83). Others, however, must consciously solicit the attention to which they feel they are entitled. For example, physicians in hospitals may wear stethoscopes and white lab coats to communicate their high-status identity to patients; female doctors are especially inclined to wear the white coats so they will not be mistaken for nurses. These status markers become especially powerful when compared with patients, who are often required to shed their own clothes and don revealing hospital-issue garments. It's hard to appear powerful and be taken seriously in a conversation with a doctor when you're barefoot and naked under a paper gown (D. Franklin, 2006). Some indicators of occupational status have become the source of conflict, however. In recent years, thousands of nurses have returned to school to earn their PhDs in nursing. As a result, they are entitled to—and often do—refer to themselves as "Doctor So-and-So" while at work in hospitals. Needless to say, many physicians oppose the use of such titles, seeing it as a threat to their professional authority and stature (G. Harris, 2011a). And they're fighting back. A bill proposed in the Florida state senate would bar nurses from calling themselves doctors, no matter what their degree. In Arizona and Delaware, nurses, pharmacists, and other health care providers who aren't physicians are forbidden from referring to themselves as "Doctor" unless they immediately identify their profession (Waldrop, 2013).

Impression management plays a prominent role in the socialization process within many professions (A. R. Hochschild, 1983). Managers and CEOs in large companies, for instance, become acutely aware through their rise up the corporate ladder of the image they must exude through their dress and demeanor. Salespeople are trained to present themselves as knowledgeable, trustworthy, and, above all, honest. Medical students learn how to manage their emotions in front of patients and to present the image of "competent physicians." New teachers learn what images are most effective in getting students to comply. This teacher's assessment of the importance of impression management more than 50 years ago still rings true today:

> You can't ever let them get the upper hand on you or you're through. So
> I start out tough. The first day I get a new class in, I let them know who's
> boss. . . . You've got to start off tough, then you can ease up as you go along. If
> you start out easygoing, when you try to be tough, they'll just look at you and
> laugh. (E. Goffman, 1959, p. 12)

More generally, in any given interaction, one person is likely to have more power than others (Wrong, 1988). When we first hear the word *power*, we think of it in terms of orders, threats, and coercion. But noncoercive forms of power—the signs and symbols of dominance, the subtle messages of threat, the gestures of submission—are much more common to impression management in social encounters (Henley, 1977). The humiliation of being powerless is felt by people who are ignored or interrupted, are intimidated by another's presence, are afraid to approach or touch a superior, or have their privacy freely invaded by another.

The norms that govern the way people address each other also reflect underlying power differences. For instance, the conversations that take place between friends or siblings are commonly marked by the mutual use of informal terms such as first names or nicknames. When status is unequal, though, the lower-status person is often required to use terms of respect such as *Sir* or *Ma'am* or *Doctor*. In the South in years past, every white person had the privilege of addressing any black person by first name and receiving the respectful form of address in return. A former president's fondness for making up funny nicknames for people on his staff or members of Congress may have appeared amiable and friendly, but it also reinforced power differences. These people were still required to address him as "Mr. President."

Status differences are even more clearly institutionalized in some languages. In Spanish, *tu* is the familiar word for "you," which is used when one is talking to a subordinate or to a person of equal status. *Usted* also means "you," but it is the formal version, used when one is addressing a person of superior status. The terms we use to address others may on the surface appear simply to be forms of etiquette. However, forms of address convey a great deal of information about who we think we are in relation to the others we encounter.

Collective Impression Management

We often find ourselves in situations that require a "couple," "group," or "organizational" image of some sort. These impressions are more complex than individual ones, and their management often requires the help and cooperation of others. For example, business partners often present a united front and a joint image of trustworthiness to their clients. E. Goffman (1959) uses the term **performance team** to describe individuals who intimately cooperate in staging a performance that leads an audience to form an impression of one or all of the team members.

Team members are highly dependent on one another and must show a fair amount of trust and loyalty, because each member has the power to disrupt or "give away" the performance at any moment. Individuals who can't be trusted—such as political advisers who have worked for another party or people who are emotionally unstable—thus make poor teammates.

One of the most obvious performance teams is the married couple. Couples are socially obligated to present a believable and cooperative image, particularly if the audience does not know them very well. Few things are as uncomfortable as being in the presence of a couple who are openly fighting, bickering, or putting each other down. The cultural value of marriage—and, by extension, the institution of family—is publicly reinforced by the ability of couples to collectively project contented images of a loving relationship.

Like individual impression management, successful teamwork depends on maintaining the boundary between front stage and back stage. If a couple's teamwork is cohesive and the performance believable, the partners can give the impression that they are happy and content even if they have had a bitter fight moments before going out in public. But the boundary between front stage and back stage is fragile, and third parties may undermine the best efforts at team impression management. Imagine a dinner guest being informed by a precocious 4-year-old that "Mommy and Daddy were yelling the f-word at each other before you got here." Young children who can speak but are not yet schooled in the social conventions of everyday interaction are not, from a dramaturgical perspective, trustworthy performance teammates. They are often too honest to maintain a front. They are naturally inclined to let audiences back stage, thereby disrupting both the order of the situation and the identities the actors have attempted to claim.

The ability to go back stage periodically is crucial to maintaining a sound team relationship. Not only does it give the team a place to rehearse public performances, but it also provides a refuge from outside scrutiny. For married couples, tensions can rise if they must constantly be "on" for an audience. This is precisely why out-of-town houseguests become a burden after a long visit or why living with one or the other partner's parents becomes so difficult. The couple has no back stage, no chance for privacy, no place to go to escape the demands of audience expectations.

Organizations must carefully manage their impressions, too, as a way of establishing their legitimacy (Ginzel, Kramer, & Sutton, 2004). Those that depend on public approval for their survival have to develop effective team performances to manage public perceptions (S. Taylor & Bogdan, 1980). Take, for instance, the way U.S. law enforcement organizations present high-profile crime suspects to the public. The suspect being transported from one place to another is usually in shackles, with armed officers on either side. Occasionally the officers halfheartedly try to hide the alleged perpetrator's face with a coat or a hat, even though we are likely to know who she or he is. If the suspect is well known, a raincoat will often be draped over her or his handcuffs. The "perp walk," as it is known, is a decades-long American tradition designed not only to satisfy the press but to give the police an opportunity to gloat over their latest capture and, in the process, humiliate the suspect (S. Roberts, 2011). Moreover, if staged well, the perp walk makes the suspect look dangerous—the kind of person who would mail letter bombs, blow up federal office buildings, or commit sexual assault. If prisoners are left unshaven and unkempt and presented in orange prison jumpsuits at a court hearing, the public gets the impression that they've already been convicted.

Individual impression management and organizational impression management are governed by the same principles (A. R. Hochschild, 1983). Take, for instance, the management of props and physical space. Hospitals usually line their walls with soothing paintings designed to calm, not agitate; children's wards are often filled with colorful images of familiar cartoon characters. Other types of physical structures may be managed to convey images of power and dominance. For instance, the White House is symbolically the center of world politics. Some of the most important international decisions are made within its walls. But at the same time,

> the building itself—with its white walls, serene proportions, classical Greek tympanum and colonnade—has become the symbol of a power that radiates not only strength but also peace, freedom, and harmony. The rich and positive symbolism has been daily reinforced by the media broadcasting throughout the world pictures of this resplendent mansion, the opulent elegance of the Oval Room, the . . . professionalism and impeccable white shirts of the president's men, the beautiful green lawns with a cheerful and self-confident president and his playful dog nimbly stepping out of the helicopter as if he were a Greek God alighting from Olympus. (Hankiss, 2001, p. 1)

In any society, people often find themselves in situations where they must depend on others for the successful performance of the roles they play as individuals. Without teamwork, many individual and organizational performances would fail, interactions would fall apart, and ultimately social order would be threatened (Henslin, 1991).

Mismanaging Impressions: Spoiled Identities

While impression management is universal, it's not always successful. We may mishandle props, blow our lines, mistakenly allow the audience to peek back stage, or otherwise destroy the credibility of our performances. Some of us manage to recover from ineffective impression management quite quickly; others suffer an extended devaluation of their identities. What happens when impression management is unsuccessful? What do we do to regain identities and restore social order?

Embarrassment

A common emotional reaction to impression mismanagement is **embarrassment**, the spontaneous feeling we experience when the identity we are presenting is suddenly and unexpectedly discredited in front of others (E. Gross & Stone, 1964). An adolescent boy trying to look "cool" in front of his friends may have his tough image shattered by the unexpected arrival of his mother in the family minivan. We can see his embarrassment in the fixed smile, the nervous hollow laugh, the busy hands, and the downward glance that hides his eyes from the gaze of others (E. Goffman, 1967). Embarrassment can come from a multitude of sources: lack of poise (e.g., stumbling, saying something stupid, spilling a drink, inappropriately exposing body parts), intrusion into the private settings of others (a man walking into a women's restroom), improper dress for a particular social occasion (wearing shorts and flip-flops to a formal dinner party), and so on.

Embarrassment is sociologically important because it has the potential to destroy the orderliness of a social situation. Imagine being at your high school graduation. As the class valedictorian is giving the commencement address, a gust of wind blows her note cards off the podium. As she reaches down to collect them, she hits her head on the microphone and tears her gown. In front of hundreds of people she stands there, flustered, not knowing what to say or do. The situation would be uncomfortable and embarrassing not only for her but for you and the rest of the audience as well.

Because embarrassment is disruptive for all concerned, it is in everyone's best interest to cooperate in reducing or eliminating it. To call attention to such an act may be as embarrassing as the original episode itself, so we may pretend not to notice the faux pas (Lindesmith, Strauss, & Denzin, 1991). By suppressing signs of recognition, we make it easier for the person to regain composure (E. Goffman, 1967). A mutual commitment to supporting others' social identities, even when those identities are in danger, is a fundamental norm of social interaction.

At times, however, embarrassment is used strategically to disrupt another person's impression management. Practical jokes, for instance, are intentional attempts to rein in conceit or overconfidence and cause someone to lose identity. More seriously, groups and organizations may use embarrassment or the threat of embarrassment (e.g., hazing) to encourage a preferred activity or discourage behavior that may be damaging to the group. In that sense, embarrassment reasserts the power structure of the group, because only certain people can legitimately embarrass others. A low-status employee, for instance, has much less freedom to embarrass a superior or make him or her the target of a joke than vice versa (Coser, 1960).

Organizations themselves may also experience embarrassment from time to time:

- In 2012, McDonald's launched two Twitter hashtags, #McDStories and #Meetthe Farmers, which were intended to solicit adoring tweets from loyal McDonald's customers. Instead, it had the opposite embarrassing effect as thousands of people chimed in to complain about the restaurant and its food with tweets like, "I once got food poisoning from eating a Big Mac" and "McDonalds is where dreams of being healthy and fit go to die" (Kuperinsky, 2012).

- In a collectivist culture like Japan, organizational misdeeds or mistakes can create considerable public humiliation, shame, and embarrassment for top officials. In 2010, Toyota faced worldwide condemnation and was forced to recall some 8 million vehicles when it could no longer deny published reports of fatal accidents in which accelerator pedals had gotten stuck at high speeds. A year later, some officials in Japanese government agencies were forced to resign for trying to downplay the public health crisis that occurred after a nuclear reactor sustained major damage from the earthquake and tsunami.

• Sony Corporation faced a massive public relations disaster in 2014 when a group calling itself "Guardians of Peace" (#GOP) hacked into its computer system and posted highly sensitive documents and internal correspondences between executives that revealed disturbing examples of casual racism, star bashing, and a multitude of other embarrassing secrets (Richards, 2014).

When events challenge an organization's public image, leaders are often compelled to engage in activities that protect, repair, and enhance that image (Ginzel et al., 2004). For example, every year, publications like *U.S. News & World Report* and *The Princeton Review* issue their rankings of the top American universities. Schools that receive high rankings boast of that fact in their recruitment materials and on their websites. When a university falls in its ranking from one year to the next, though, officials face the unenviable task of scrambling to mend the school's reputation so that alumni continue to donate money and prospective students still consider applying. Typically, schools that have dropped in the rankings opt to downplay the survey's relevance and criticize the magazine's methodology and ranking criteria, which only a year earlier (when they were ranked higher) were considered sound and trustworthy.

Most government agencies and large corporations like McDonald's, Toyota, and Sony now have massive public relations departments or full-time crisis management teams that carefully oversee the organization's image by controlling negative publicity.

Remedies for Spoiled Identities

Organizations and governments can enlist the aid of experts to overcome the debilitating effects of negative images, but individuals are usually left to their own devices. Fixing a spoiled identity is not easy. The mere knowledge that we are being evaluated negatively can impede our thoughts, speech, and action. Nevertheless, the major responsibility for restoring order lies with the person whose actions disrupted things in the first place.

To restore social order and overcome a spoiled identity, the transgressor will use an **aligning action** (Stokes & Hewitt, 1976). Sometimes aligning can be done easily and quickly. If you step on a person's foot while standing in line at a cafeteria, a simple apology may be all that's needed to avoid the impression that you're a clumsy oaf.

By apologizing, you acknowledge that such an act is wrong and send the message that you are not ordinarily a breaker of such social norms. Other situations, however, call for more detailed repair:

• An **account** is a verbal statement designed to explain unanticipated, embarrassing, or unacceptable behavior (C. W. Mills, 1940; M. Scott & Lyman, 1968). For example, an individual may cite events beyond her or his control ("I was late for the wedding because there was a lot of traffic on the highway") or blame others ("I spilled my milk because somebody pushed me"). An alternative is to define the offending behavior as appropriate under the circumstances, perhaps by denying that anyone was hurt by the act ("Yeah, I stole the car, but no one got hurt"), by claiming that the victim deserved to be victimized ("I beat him up, but he had it coming"), or by claiming higher, unselfish motives ("I stole food, but I did it to feed my family").

- A **disclaimer** is a verbal assertion given before the fact to forestall any complaints or negative implications (Hewitt & Stokes, 1975). If we think something we're about to do or say will threaten our identity or be used by others to judge us negatively, we may use a disclaimer. Phrases such as "I probably don't know what I'm talking about, but . . ." or "I'm not a racist, but . . ." introduce acts or expressions that ordinarily might be considered undesirable. As long as a disclaimer is provided, a self-proclaimed nonexpert can pretend to be an expert and a person claiming to be nonracist feels he or she can go ahead and make a racist statement.

Accounts and disclaimers are important links between the individual and society. We use them to explicitly define the relationship between our questionable conduct and prevailing cultural norms. That is, by using aligning actions, we publicly reaffirm our commitment to the social order that our conduct has violated and thereby defend the sanctity of our social identities and the "goodness" of society.

Other people may also try to deal with a transgressor's spoiled identity through a process called **cooling out** (E. Goffman, 1952): gently persuading someone who has lost face to accept a less desirable but still reasonable alternative identity. People engaged in cooling out seek to persuade rather than force offenders to change. It's an attempt to minimize distress. The challenge is to keep the offender from realizing that he or she is being persuaded.

Cooling out is a common element of social life; it is one of the major functions of consumer complaint departments, coaches, doctors, and priests. Cooling out also plays a major part in informal relationships. A partner who terminates a dating or courting relationship might persuade the other person to remain a "good friend," gently pushing the person into a lesser role without completely destroying her or his self-worth.

Cooling out is often motivated by institutional pressures. Consider the environment of higher education. The aspirations of many people in U.S. society are encouraged by open-door admission policies in some universities and most community colleges (Karabel, 1972). There is a widely held cultural belief that higher education is linked to better employment opportunities and that anyone can go to college. Discrepancies, however, inevitably arise between people's aspirations and their ability to succeed. If educational institutions simply kicked unqualified students out of school, the result would likely be widespread public pressure and anxiety over the system itself. Hence, most community colleges opt for a "soft response" of cooling out the unqualified student (B. Clark, 1960). A counselor may direct a poor student toward an alternative major that would be easier but "not that different" from the student's original goal—for example, nurse's aide instead of registered nurse. Or the counselor might encourage the student to seek employment after graduation from a 2-year program rather than transfer to a 4-year university (Rosenbaum, Deil-Amen, & Person, 2006). That is, the student is gently persuaded to redefine himself or herself.

Institutional cooling-out processes such as these are inherent in a system that doesn't have clear selection criteria. In the United States, admission into college is based on some combination of achievement (course grades), aptitude (standardized test scores), and personality traits (interviews, letters of recommendation). In contrast, educational selection in China is based on the *gaokao*, or "high test"—a national college-entrance examination that is administered every June over 2 or 3 days (depending on the province), and is the sole determinant of admission to all Chinese universities (Larmer, 2015). Because one's eligibility for college study is so clearly and quickly defined, Chinese higher education has no need for an institutionalized cooling-out process.

Stigma

The permanent spoiling of someone's identity is called **stigma**. A stigma is a deeply discrediting characteristic, widely viewed as an insurmountable obstacle preventing competent or morally trustworthy behavior (E. Goffman, 1963). Stigmas spoil the identities of individuals regardless of other attributes those individuals might have. According to Goffman, the three types of stigma are (1) defects of the body (e.g., severe scars, blindness, paralyzed or missing limbs), (2) defects of character (e.g., dishonesty, a weak will, a history of imprisonment or substance abuse), and (3) membership in devalued social groups, such as certain races, religions, ethnicities, or social classes. The impression management task when faced with stigma is not so much to recapture a tarnished identity as to minimize the social damage.

Some stigmas are worse than others. For instance, the use of eyeglasses to compensate for one sensory deficiency (poor vision) is usually considered far less stigmatizing than the use of hearing aids to compensate for a different sensory deficiency (poor hearing). Contemporary hearing aids are designed to be as small and unnoticeable as possible. Eyeglasses, on the other hand, have become a common fashion accessory, often sold in their own trendy boutiques.

Stigma varies across time and culture as well. For instance, being a Christian in the 21st century is very different from being one in AD 100, and being a Christian in the United States is different from being one in the Arab Middle East (Ainlay, Becker, & Coleman, 1986). Ancient Mayans considered being cross-eyed desirable, so parents encouraged babies to focus on objects that forced their eyes to cross (Link & Phelan, 2001). In contemporary Sierra Leone, the stigma of epilepsy is so severe that those who suffer from the condition are considered uneducable, unemployable, and unmarriageable (Baruchin, 2011). And as you saw earlier in this chapter, obesity is stigmatized in contemporary Western societies but was seen as desirable, attractive, and symbolic of status and wealth in the past and is still seen that way in some other cultures today.

Even different situations within the same culture can yield different perceptions of stigma. For example, in the business world, *non*drinking can stigmatize people and limit their career trajectory. Those who abstain often find it harder to get ahead than those willing to drink with coworkers or clients. On Wall Street, nondrinkers complain that they have difficulty closing deals or negotiating with clients simply because they don't drink. In fact, some research suggests that nondrinkers have a harder time climbing the corporate ladder than moderate drinkers. As one director of an alcohol treatment program put it, "If you say you don't drink, you have to deal with the suspicion that you can't play the game" (quoted in Quenqua, 2012a, p. 1).

Interactions between the stigmatized and the nonstigmatized—called "mixed contacts"—can sometimes be uneasy. We have all felt uncomfortable with people who are "different" in appearance or behavior. Stigma initiates a judgment process that colors impressions and sets up barriers to interaction (E. E. Jones & Pittman, 1984).

Whether intentionally or not, nonstigmatized individuals often pressure stigmatized people to conform to "inferior" identities. A person in a wheelchair who is discouraged from going camping is not given the chance to develop important skills and is thus kept dependent. Some have suggested that sightless people learn to *be* blind (that is, to be helpless and reliant on others) as a consequence of the low expectations sighted people have of them (R. Scott, 1981).

Nonstigmatized people often avoid mixed contacts because they anticipate discomfort and are unsure how to act (E. Goffman, 1963). In 2014, the owners of a luxury condominium complex in New York City came under fire after it was revealed that the building had a separate entrance for its lower-income residents that allowed its wealthier residents to avoid awkward exchanges. Research shows that when interacting with a person who is physically disabled, an able-bodied person is likely to be more inhibited and more rigid and to end the interaction sooner than if the other person were also able bodied (Kleck, 1968; Kleck, Ono, & Hastorf, 1966). On the one hand, the able-bodied person may fear that showing direct sympathy or interest in a disabled person's condition could be regarded as rude or intrusive. On the other hand, ignoring it may make the interaction artificial and awkward or create impossible demands (Michener, DeLamater, & Schwartz, 1986).

As for people with stigmatizing conditions, they often sense that others are evaluating them negatively. One study of people diagnosed with a mental disorder found that they had all at one time or another been shunned, avoided, patronized, or discriminated against when others found out about their condition (Wahl, 1999). Consider also the case of Mark Breimhorst, a Stanford University graduate. Mr. Breimhorst has no hands. When he was applying to business schools in 1998, he was given 25% more time to complete the Graduate Management Admission Test. His results were mailed to prospective graduate schools with the notation "Scores obtained under special circumstances." Mr. Breimhorst was not admitted to any of the business schools to which he applied. He filed a federal lawsuit against the testing service, challenging the way they flagged the scores of students who needed accommodations. Such notations, he argued, were stigmatizing because they created suspicion that the scores were less valid than others (Lewin, 2000). In 2003, the testing service stopped flagging the results of students who receive special accommodations.

Faced with the strong possibility of discrimination, people with stigmatizing conditions often use coping strategies to establish the most favorable identity possible. One strategy is to try to hide the stigma. People who are hard of hearing, for instance, may learn to read lips or otherwise interact with people as if they could hear perfectly; those with bodily stigmas may opt for surgery to permanently conceal their condition.

Some stigmatized individuals, particularly those whose conditions are not immediately observable, use a strategy of selective disclosure. Sociologist Charlene E. Miall (1989) interviewed and surveyed 70 infertile women, nearly all of whom characterized infertility as something negative, an indication of failure, or an inability to function "normally." Most of the women were concerned that others' knowledge of their infertility would be stigmatizing. So they engaged in some form of information control. Many simply concealed the information from everyone except medical personnel and infertility counselors. Others used medical accounts, saying, "It's beyond my control." Some disclosed the information only to people they felt would not think ill of them. Some even used the disclosure of their infertility to gain control of a situation by deliberately shocking their "normal" audience (Miall, 1989).

Of course, not all stigmas can be hidden. Some individuals can only minimize the degree to which their stigmas intrude on and disrupt the interaction. One tactic is to use self-deprecating humor—telling little jokes about their shortcomings—to relieve the tension felt by the nonstigmatized. Others may try to focus on attributes unrelated to the stigma. For instance, a person in a wheelchair may carry around esoteric books in a conspicuous manner to show others that he or she still has a brain that works well. Still others with stigmas boldly call attention to their condition by mastering areas thought to be closed to them (such as mountain climbing for an amputee).

And some organize a movement to counter social oppression. For instance, organizations like the National Association to Advance Fat Acceptance and the Council on Size and Weight Discrimination help fat people (*fat* is their preferred adjective, by the way) cope with a society that hates their size by lobbying Congress and state legislatures to combat "size discrimination" and promote "weight diversity" (Saulny, 2009). They have organized civil rights protests in Washington, DC; lobbied health care professionals for tolerance and acceptance; encouraged colleges and universities to consider "size diversity" along with race, class, gender, sexual orientation, and disability status as a component of an inclusive campus; publicly condemned weight-loss TV shows like *The Biggest Loser* for bullying overweight contestants; and organized campaigns against insurance discrimination and the dubious "science" of weight loss programs (LeBesco, 2004; National Association to Advance Fat Acceptance, 2016).

But overcoming the problems created by stigma cannot be accomplished solely through individual impression management or collective demonstrations. Long-lasting improvements can be accomplished only by changing cultural beliefs about the nature of stigma (Link, Mirotznik, & Cullen, 1991). As long as we hold stigmatized individuals solely responsible for dealing with the stigma, only some of them will be able to overcome the social limitations of their condition.

Conclusion

After reading this chapter, you may have an image of human beings as cunning, manipulative, and cynical play actors whose lives are merely a string of phony performances carefully designed to fit the selfish needs of the moment. The impression manager comes across as someone who consciously and fraudulently presents an inaccurate image in order to take advantage of a particular situation. Even the person who seems not to care about her or his appearance may be consciously cultivating the image of "not caring."

There's no denying that people consciously manufacture images of themselves that allow them to achieve some desired goal. Most of us go through life trying to create the impression that we're attractive, honest, competent, and sincere. To that end, we carefully manage our appearance, present qualities we think others will admire, and hide qualities we think they won't. When caught in an act that may threaten the impression we're trying to foster, we strategically use statements that disclaim, excuse, or justify it.

So who is the real you? If people freely change their images to suit the expectations of a given audience, is there something more stable that characterizes them across all situations?

If you are aware that the impression you are managing is not the real you, then you must have some knowledge of what *is* the real you. And what you are may, in fact, transcend the demands of particular situations. Some basic, pervasive part of your being may allow you to choose from a repertoire of identities the one that best suits the immediate needs of the situation. As you ponder this possibility, realize that your feelings about impression management reflect your beliefs about the nature of individuals and the role society and others play in our everyday lives.

Your Turn

Impression management is a tool most of us use to present ourselves as likable people. Occasionally, however, our attempts fail. Survey several friends or classmates and have them describe their most embarrassing moment. Prompt them for specific details: What were the circumstances surrounding the incident? What identities were they trying to present at the time? How did their attempt to claim these identities fail? How did

(Continued)

(Continued)

these people immediately react, physically and behaviorally, to the embarrassment? How did they try to overcome the embarrassment and return order? Did they offer some sort of account? Were the consequences of the failed impression management temporary or permanent? What did the witnesses to the embarrassing incident do? Did their reactions alleviate or intensify the embarrassment your respondents felt?

Once you've gathered a substantial number of stories (about 10 or 15), see if you can find some common themes. What are the most frequent types of embarrassing situations? What are the most frequent reactions? If your class is large, your instructor can have

you report your results to a small group of fellow students or to the entire class. What kinds of patterns can you identify in the embarrassing stories people tell? Are there gender, ethnic, or age differences in what people find embarrassing?

Sociologists Edward Gross and Gregory Stone have written, "In the wreckage left by embarrassment lie the broken foundations of social transactions" (1964, p. 2). What do you suppose they meant by that? Use your results to discuss the sociological importance of embarrassment (and, more important, reactions to embarrassment) in terms of the maintenance of interactional and social order.

Chapter Highlights

- A significant portion of social life is influenced by the images we form of others and the images others form of us.

- Impression formation is based initially on our assessment of ascribed social group membership (race, age, gender, etc.), individual physical appearance, and verbal and nonverbal messages.

- While we are gathering information about others to form impressions of them, we are fully aware

that they are doing the same thing. Impression management is the process by which we attempt to control and manipulate information about ourselves to influence the impressions others form of us. Impression management can be both individual and collective.

- Impression mismanagement can lead to the creation of damaged identities, which must be repaired in order to sustain social interaction.

Key Terms

account: Statement designed to explain unanticipated, embarrassing, or unacceptable behavior after the behavior has occurred

aligning action: Action taken to restore an identity that has been damaged

back stage: Area of social interaction away from the view of an audience,

where people can rehearse and rehash their behavior

cooling out: Gently persuading someone who has lost face to accept a less desirable but still reasonable alternative identity

disclaimer: Assertion designed to forestall any complaints or negative reactions to a behavior or statement that is about to occur

dramaturgy: Study of social interaction as theater, in which people ("actors") project images ("play roles") in front of others ("the audience")

embarrassment: Spontaneous feeling experienced when the identity someone is presenting is suddenly and unexpectedly discredited in front of others

front stage: Area of social interaction where people perform and work to maintain appropriate impressions

impression formation: The process by which we define others based on observable cues such as age, ascribed status characteristics such as race and gender, individual attributes such as physical appearance, and verbal and nonverbal expressions

impression management: Act of presenting a favorable public image of oneself so that others will form positive judgments

performance team: Set of individuals who cooperate in staging a performance that leads an audience to form an impression of one or all team members

stigma: Deeply discrediting characteristic that is viewed as an obstacle to competent or morally trustworthy behavior

SAGE edge™ edge.sagepub.com/newman12e

SAGE edge offers a robust online environment featuring an impressive array of free tools and resources for review, study, and further exploration, keeping both instructors and students on the cutting edge of teaching and learning.

Building Social Relationships

Intimacy and Families

- Life With Others
- Social Diversity and Intimate Choices
- Family Life
- Family and Social Structure
- Family Challenges

So far, the 21st century has been a challenging time for the types of close relationships we commonly think of as the foundation of social life:

- Among college students, traditional dating has seemingly been replaced by *hooking up*—in which two people hang out in a dorm room or meet at a party, go somewhere private, and engage in some form of sexual behavior, ranging from kissing to intercourse (England & Thomas, 2007). Alcohol is often involved. Intimacy and romance? Not so much.

- With a simple swipe of the screen, smartphone apps like Tinder, Hinge, and Grindr allow people—mostly young people—to scan their immediate vicinity for quick potential hook ups . . . based on a few photos and a couple of words (Reich, 2014). Tinder claims it "matches" 12 million people a day (a match is when two people indicate an interest in one another; M. Wood, 2015).

- Over 41 million adults have tried online dating via websites like eHarmony and Match.com or mobile apps like OKCupid and Coffee Meets Bagel. Twenty percent of current committed relationships began online and 17% of marriages that began in 2014 were between people who had met online (Statistic Brain, 2014). The majority of Americans now say that online dating sites or mobile dating apps are a good way to meet people (Smith & Anderson, 2016) and usage has tripled among 18- to 24-year-olds and doubled among 55- to 64-year-olds over the past several years (Smith, 2016).

- There are 34.8 million single-person households in the United States, up from 26.7 million in 2000 (ProQuest Statistical Abstract, 2017). Barely half of all U.S. adults are married—the lowest percentage on record (D. Cohn, Passel, Wang, & Livingston, 2011), although about half of unmarried people say they want to get married sometime in the future (K. Parker, Wang, & Rohal, 2014).

- In 2016, for the first time in modern history, living with one's parents became the most common living arrangement for 18- to 34-year-olds (Fry, 2016a). These households include people who have never left home and those who have left and returned, sometimes more than once. According to one survey, 13% of parents with grown children said that one of their sons or daughters had moved back home within the past year (W. Wang & Morin, 2009).

- About 8.3 million households consist of unmarried opposite sex couples with children (ProQuest Statistical Abstract, 2017). That's a 12-fold increase since 1970. Children are now more likely to have parents who have never married than divorced parents (cited in Tavernise, 2011a).

- In 1970, 11% of all births in the United States were to unmarried mothers; today that figure is almost 41% (ProQuest Statistical Abstract, 2017). About 58% of these births occur within cohabiting relationships (Haub, 2013).

- On June 26, 2015, in the case of *Obergefell v. Hodges*, the Supreme Court ruled that two people of the same sex have the constitutional right to legally marry. Today there are 335,000 married same-sex couples (ProQuest Statistics Abstract, 2017).

Some people might see these events as "proof" that society is going downhill fast; others may see them as signs that intimate and family relationships are strong and simply keeping up with a changing culture.

Like every other aspect of our individual lives, intimacy and family must be understood within the broader contours of our society. This chapter takes a sociological peek into their private and public aspects and explores the role that close relationships, especially family bonds, play in our everyday experience. Why are these relationships so important to us? How do societal factors such as social institutions, gender, race, and social class affect our perceptions of intimacy and belonging? How do they affect family life? And why are the desirable aspects of these relationships so often outweighed by the negative aspects, such as family violence?

Life With Others

The quality and quantity of our relationships with others are the standards against which many of us judge the well-being of our lives. As one journalist recently put it,

> We humans are an exquisitely social species, thriving in good company and suffering in isolation. More than anything else, our intimate relationships, or lack thereof, shape and define our lives. (Murphy, 2017, p. 1)

We spend a tremendous amount of time worrying about these relationships, contemplating new ones, obsessing over past ones, trying to make current ones more satisfying, or fretting over how to get into or out of one. In fact, being in a relationship is so important that there is now an app, called "Invisible Boyfriend (or Girlfriend)" that generates fictitious texts, voice mail messages, and pictures to give uncoupled users "believable social proof" that they actually have a boyfriend (or girlfriend).

Although we hunger for closeness in our lives, it can often be a challenge to maintain. For more than a century, sociologists have been writing that people who live in complex, urban, industrial, or postindustrial societies gradually become less integrated and connected to others (Durkheim, 1893/1947; Riesman, 1950; Tönnies, 1887/1957). In 1985, nearly half of American adults said they had a close friend at work; by 2004, that figure had dropped to only 30% (Grant, 2015). In the late 20th and early 21st centuries, membership in church-related groups, civic organizations (e.g., Red Cross, Boy Scouts, PTA), and fraternal organizations (e.g., Lions, Elks, Shriners) decreased (Putnam, 1995). According to one study, only 42% of Americans know all or most of their neighbors by name (A. Smith, 2010).

Because we're more mobile in our careers and more willing to relocate, we are more likely to break social ties than people were, say, a century ago. In the United States, the number of people who have friends and family they can talk to about important matters has declined dramatically over the past two decades. In fact, a U.S. adult today is much more likely than an adult two decades ago to be completely isolated from others (McPherson, Smith-Lovin, & Brashears, 2006).

Some sociologists attribute these trends to U.S. culture's emphasis on individualism, which takes away a sense of community, diminishes our ability to establish ties with others, and makes it easier for people to walk away from groups they see as unfulfilling (Bellah, Madsen, Sullivan, Swidler, & Tipton, 1985; Sidel, 1986). The high value that contemporary society places on self-reliance and individual achievement can sometimes make social relationships, even family relationships, seem expendable.

In contrast, in collectivist societies such as China and Japan, group ties play a more substantial role in people's everyday lives. There, people consider duty, sacrifice, and compromise more desirable traits than personal success and individual achievement. They assume that group connections are the best guarantee for an individual's well-being. Hence, feelings of group loyalty and responsibility for other members tend to be strong.

On occasion, governments act to ensure family duty. Six centuries ago, the Chinese scholar Guo Jujing wrote *The 24 Paragons of Filial Piety,* a collection of stories that celebrate family sacrifice. One story tells of a woman who cut out her own liver to feed her sick mother; another tells of a boy who sat awake shirtless all night to draw mosquitoes away from his sleeping parents. Fearing that young people were drifting away from their traditional familial responsibilities, the government issued a revised version of the book in 2012 that calls on adults to spend holidays with their parents, cook them meals, and call them weekly (Jacobs & Century, 2012).

Despite the inevitable conflicts in close relationships and the difficulties of maintaining these ties in an individualistic, mobile, high-tech society, people still place a high value on belonging and intimacy and take great pains to achieve them. For instance, many older women who are single, widowed, or divorced, find support not through marriage but through long-term friendships with other women who are at a similar stage in their lives (J. Gross, 2004a). Similarly, we spend more time than ever at work—half of all American workers now spend over 40 hours on the job each week (Saad, 2014)—perhaps to the detriment of relationships with our families. But for many people, forming ties with coworkers can be just as emotionally fulfilling (Wuthnow, 1994). And many of us spend a great deal of time in local hangouts (such as bars and coffee shops), where we can find comfort and good company (Oldenburg & Brissett, 1982). Many people find the sense of belonging they crave in these small groups of friends and like-minded neighbors and coworkers.

MICRO-MACRO CONNECTION
THAT'S WHAT (FACEBOOK) FRIENDS ARE FOR

How have contemporary communication and information technologies—smartphones, social media, FaceTime, Skype, and so on—influenced people's connections to others? At this time, the question is open.

For instance, some research points to a serious isolating effect of these technologies. One study found that users of social media are 28% less likely to seek out their neighbors as sources of companionship than nonusers (cited in Blow, 2010). Others argue that because so much of their social lives are lived on their smartphones, young people today date less, hang out with friends less, have less sex, and are more unhappy than teens in previous generations (Twenge, 2017). As one author put it, "[W]e've become accustomed to being 'alone together'" (Turkle, 2012, p. 1). The more digitally connected we are, the less emotionally connected we become. The more we expect from technology, the less we expect from each other:

> We are offered. . . a whole world of machine-
> mediated relationships on networked devices. As
> we instant-message, e-mail, text, and Twitter,
> technology redraws the boundaries between
> intimacy and solitude. . . . Teenagers avoid making
> telephone calls, fearful that they will "reveal too
> much." They would rather text than talk. Adults, too,
> choose keyboards over the human voice. . . . After
> an evening of avatar-to-avatar talk in a networked
> game, we feel, at one moment, in possession of a
> full social life and, in the next, curiously isolated,
> in tenuous complicity with strangers. We build
> a following on Facebook. . . and wonder to what
> degree our followers are friends. . . . Sometimes
> people feel no sense of having communicated after
> hours of connection. (Turkle, 2011, pp. 11–12)

With over 1.79 billion active Facebook users worldwide and over a billion more on Twitter, Pinterest, LinkedIn, and Instagram (Digital Insights, 2014; Statista, 2016b), social media may be hitting its saturation point. Not surprisingly, more and more people have chosen to steer clear of it primarily because they feel it makes their lives less private and more alienated. We've all had the experience of standing in a crowd of people—in an airport, train station, or academic quad—where just about *everyone* is typing, tapping, swiping, or texting on her or his phone. One student put it this way: "I wasn't calling my friends anymore. I was just seeing their pictures and updates and felt like that was really connecting to them" (quoted in Wortham, 2011, p. B1).

However, other evidence suggests that these technologies merely give people an additional way to establish important interpersonal ties both within and outside their immediate neighborhoods. Rather than isolating people, social media may instead allow already "isolated people to communicate with one another and marginalized people to find one another" (Deresiewicz, 2011, p. 311). They can often provide a meaningful substitute for or enhancement of traditional types of interpersonal involvement, thereby expanding the scope of people's social support networks. The Internet, for instance, allows people to obtain support from a social circle that extends far beyond their geographic community. In addition, it gives people an opportunity to establish more diverse personal networks:

> Social media activities are associated with several
> beneficial social activities, including having
> discussion networks that are more likely to
> contain people from different backgrounds. For
> instance, frequent Internet users, and those who
> maintain a blog are much more likely to confide in
> someone who is of another race. Those who share
> photos online are more likely to report that they
> discuss important matters with someone who is
> a member of another political party. (Hampton,
> Sessions, Her, & Rainie, 2009, p. 3)

To illustrate the dramatically different ends of this debate, consider the following two letters that appeared several years ago in the same edition of the *New York Times* in response to an earlier column on the perils of new communication technologies. The first is from an eighth grader, the second from a high school junior:

> I feel it detracts from my "real" relationships.
> I have never had an interesting conversation
> over social networking. . . . Often when I try to
> have an in-person conversation with someone
> about a real-world event, they are looking at a
> screen, their mind somewhere else, and even as
> they are eternally "connected," I can feel them
> drifting away from me. (Grossbard, 2011, p. 8)

(Continued)

(Continued)

Never before could a high-school student so brazenly reach out to a Harvard graduate student and ask for mentorship on his research paper. Never again will we think it odd for someone from the farthest corner of the globe to be exchanging witticisms on Twitter with a well-known celebrity. (Kaufman, 2011, p. 8)

So, has technology enhanced or destroyed our ties to others? Is a weekly Skype chat or exchange of tweets with your best friend from high school any more or less gratifying than going out to lunch with him or her every Friday? Is texting any more or less personal than an actual phone call? Is upgrading your relationship status on Facebook any more or less meaningful as a sign of commitment and exclusivity than holding hands in public or the exchange of rings? Certainly all would agree that wireless digital technology has changed the way we establish and maintain close relationships. But does that mean that the importance of others in our everyday lives—be they neighbors, coworkers, fellow students, teammates, family members, or personal friends—has diminished?

Social Diversity and Intimate Choices

Our bonds with coworkers, neighbors, relatives, and friends (real or virtual) are certainly an important part of our social lives, but the sense of belonging and closeness that comes from intimate, romantic relationships has become one of the prime obsessions of the 21st century. Magazines, self-help books, supermarket tabloids, websites, blogs, and talk shows overflow with advice, warnings, and pseudoscientific analyses of every conceivable aspect of these relationships.

Most people in the United States assume that love is all they need to establish a fulfilling, long-lasting relationship. But their intimate choices are far from free and private. The choices they make regarding who to date, live with, or marry are governed by two important social rules that limit the field of eligible partners: exogamy and endogamy.

Exogamy

At any given time, each of us is a member of many groups simultaneously. We belong to a particular family, a friendship group, a set of coworkers, a religion, a race, an ethnicity, an age group, a social class, and so on. Entering into intimate relationships with fellow members of some of these groups is considered inappropriate. So society follows a set of customs referred to as **exogamy** rules, which require that an individual form a long-term romantic or sexual relationship with someone *outside* certain social groups to which she or he belongs. For instance, in almost all societies, exogamy rules define marrying or having sex with people in one's own immediate family—siblings, parents, and children—as incest. Presumably, these rules exist in order to prohibit procreation between people who are genetically related, thereby reducing the chance that offspring will inherit two copies of a defective gene.

Exogamy prohibitions typically extend to certain relatives outside the immediate family, too, such as cousins, grandparents, aunts, uncles, and, in some societies, stepsiblings. In the United States, 25 states completely prohibit marriage between first cousins, 19 states allow it, and 6 others allow it only under certain circumstances, such as when both partners are over 65 or when one is unable to reproduce (National Conference of State Legislatures, 2009).

Informally, opposition to romantic relationships between coworkers, between college students who live on the same dorm floor (called "dormcest"), or between athletes who participate in the same sport (for instance, "swimcest") illustrates a common belief that relationships work best when they occur between people who aren't in constant close proximity. A college advice blog once identified some of the pitfalls of dormcest—mismatched expectations, seeing sex partners at their worst, nonexclusivity in a shared living space, keeping things fresh—and provided some strategies to overcome them (A. Jones, 2010).

Different cultures apply the rules of exogamy differently. For example, in South Korea, it was once illegal to marry someone with the same surname—not a trivial law, considering that 55% of the population is named Kim, Park, Lee, Choi, or Chong (WuDunn, 1996). This rule originated centuries ago as a way of preventing marriages between members of the same clan and was written into Korean law in 1957. The ban was deemed unconstitutional in 1997. However, most single people still try to avoid lovers with the same name. As one college student put it, "When I'm introduced to someone, I very casually ask what her name is, and if I find out that it's the same as mine, it puts a mark against her right there" (WuDunn, 1996, p. A4).

In other places, exogamy rules are based on proximity. The Igbo of Nigeria, for instance, forbid inhabitants of the same village to marry because of the possibility they might be kin (Dzimiri, 2014). On occasion, the violation of such exogamy rules can lead to severe sanctions. In 2003, a young Indian couple was beaten to death by members of their own families for being lovers. In their community, it was considered incest for two people from the same village to fall in love. A resident of the village said, "In our society all the families living in a village are all sons and daughters of the whole village. We are like brothers and sisters. The marriage of brothers and sisters is not accepted" (quoted in Waldman, 2003, p. A4).

Endogamy

Simultaneously, less formal, but just as powerful, are the rules of **endogamy**, which limit people's intimate choices to those *within* certain groups to which they belong. The vast majority of marriages in the United States, for example, occur between people from the same religion, ethnoracial group, and social class. These rules of endogamy—or what some sociologists call "assortive mating"—increase the likelihood that the couple will have similar backgrounds and therefore share common beliefs, values, and experiences. But more important, from a sociological point of view, rules of endogamy reflect our society's traditional distaste for relationships that cross social-group boundaries.

Religious Endogamy

Throughout history, many societies have had endogamy rules relating to religion: Only people with the same religious background were allowed to marry. Marrying outside one's religion is more common than it once was in industrialized countries, however, because greater mobility and freer communication bring people from diverse religious backgrounds into contact. In the United States, it's estimated that between one quarter and one half of all marriages occur between people of different religions (B. A. Robinson, 1999).

Nevertheless, religious leaders—from most religious traditions—still actively discourage interfaith marriages. They worry about maintaining their religion's influence over how people identify themselves within a diverse and complex society (M. M. Gordon, 1964). The situation facing U.S. Jews provides a good example of the consequences of marriages that break rules of religious endogamy. Although only 10% of American Jews married non-Jews in 1945, about 58% (and 71% of non-Orthodox Jews) do so today (Goodstein, 2013). A lower birth rate among Jews compared with other groups, coupled with the likelihood that interfaith couples will not raise children as Jews, explains, in part, why the Jewish population has been dropping steadily (Goodstein, 2003). Between 1990 and 2008, the number of Jews in the U.S. population declined from 3.1 million to 2.6 million (Kosmin & Keysar, 2009). Many Jewish leaders fear that the outcome of this trend will be not only the shrinking of the Jewish population but also the erosion and perhaps extinction of an entire way of life.

Racial and Ethnic Endogamy

Racial and ethnic endogamy is a global phenomenon, forming the basis of social structure in most societies worldwide (Murdock, 1949). The issue is an especially volatile one in U.S. society, however, given how racially and ethnically diverse we are. The first law against interracial marriage was enacted in Maryland in 1661, prohibiting Whites from marrying Native Americans or African slaves. Over the next 300 years or so, 38 more states put such laws on the books, expanding their coverage to include Chinese, Japanese, and Filipino Americans. It was believed that a mixing of the races (then referred to as "mongrelization") would destroy the racial purity (and superiority) of Whites. The irony, of course, is that racial mixing had been taking place since the 17th century, much of it through white slave owners raping and impregnating their black slaves.

Legal sanctions against interracial marriage persisted well into the 20th century. In 1958, for example, when Richard Loving (who was white) and his new wife, Mildred Jeter Loving (who was black), moved to their new home in Virginia, a sheriff arrived to arrest them for violating a state law that prohibited interracial marriages. The Lovings were sentenced to one year in jail but then learned that the judge would suspend the sentence if they left the state and promised not to return for 25 years. At the time, the majority of states, including California, Oregon, Indiana, all the mountain states, and every state in the South, legally prohibited interracial marriage (Liptak, 2004). The Lovings found a home in Washington, DC, where interracial marriage was not prohibited, and had three children. While there, they embarked on an appeal of their conviction. In 1967, the U.S. Supreme Court ruled in favor of the Lovings, concluding that using racial classifications to restrict freedom to marry was unconstitutional.

Over a half-century later, attitudes are becoming more tolerant, and people are no longer banished for violating racial endogamy rules. Although the vast majority of U.S. marriages remain racially endogamous, relationships that cross racial or ethnic lines are becoming more common. The number of interracial and interethnic marriages in the United States has grown dramatically, from 3.2% of all existing marriages in 1980 to 9.2% today (ProQuest Statistical Abstract, 2017). These figures grow each year. Of all the marriages that began in 2016, 17% consisted of two people of different racial or ethnic groups, up from 6.7% of marriages that began in 1980 (Cashin, 2017; Pew Research Center, 2012a).

Attitudes toward interracial marriage have steadily improved over the past 60 years (see Exhibit 7.1). Over 40% of people say that an increase in interracial marriages has been a change for the better in U.S. society, compared to 11% who think it has hurt society (Pew Research Center, 2012a).

Nevertheless, people involved in interracial relationships still face some problems. Several contemporary websites offer advice to interracial couples on issues like open hostility and intimidation; negative stereotyping; derogatory comments, stares, and slights; a sense of isolation; and possible family rejection. About half of the black–white couples in one study felt that biracial marriage makes things harder for them, and about two thirds reported that their parents had a problem with the relationship, at least initially (Fears & Deane, 2001). Some interracial couples—especially black–white couples—experience a lack of family support

EXHIBIT 7.1   ●   People Have Grown More Accepting of Interracial Marriage

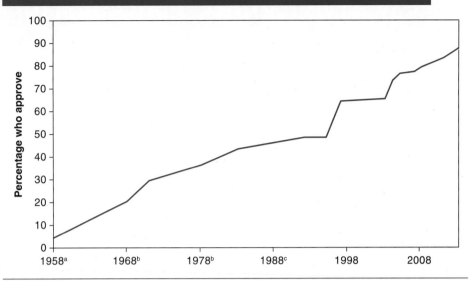

Source: Newport, 2013.

[a]1958 wording: ". . . marriages between whites and colored people"
[b]1968–1978 wording: ". . . marriages between whites and nonwhites"
[c]Wording after 1983: ". . . marriage between blacks and whites"

when choosing to marry each other (R. Lewis & Yancey, 1997). Everyday activities may require more time and effort for interracial couples than for couples of the same race. For instance, when planning vacations, interracial couples often have to do extensive advance research of potential leisure destinations to see how accepting they are of relationships like theirs (Hibbler & Shinew, 2005). As one woman in an interracial marriage put it, "In a perfect world, race wouldn't matter, but that day's a while off" (quoted in Saulny, 2011, p. 4).

Social Class Endogamy

If we based our ideas about the formation of romantic relationships on what we see in movies, we might be tempted to conclude that divisions based on social class don't matter in U.S. society or perhaps don't exist at all. Popular films of the past three or four decades such as *Titanic, The Wedding Planner, Maid in Manhattan, Good Will Hunting, Sweet Home Alabama, The Princess Bride, Pretty Woman,* and, of course, *Cinderella* send the message that the power of love is strong enough to blow away differences in education, pedigree, resources, and taste. When it comes to love, Hollywood's United States is a classless society.

In reality, however, social class is a powerful determinant of whom we choose to marry. Around the world, people face strong pressures to choose marital partners of similar social standing, based on wealth, income, and educational attainment (H. Carter & Glick, 1976; Kalmijn, 1994). For instance, one study found that only 2% of college-educated men married women with less than 12 years of formal schooling (cited in Dzimiri, 2014). And while it might have been the case in the past that women often "married up" (that is, found spouses of higher socioeconomic standing), contemporary heterosexual marriages look as if they are becoming more class endogamous. As women's income relative to men's has increased, the pay gap between spouses in opposite-sex couples has shrunk (C. C. Miller & Bui, 2016). Even if two individuals from different races, ethnic groups,

VISUAL ESSAY—TYING KNOTS, CROSSING LINES

There was a time in our not-too-distant past when interracial marriages were illegal. Jack Johnson, the first African American heavyweight boxing champion, was married three times—all to white women. In 1913, after marrying his first wife, he was convicted of violating the Mann Act, which made it a crime to transport women across state lines for "immoral" purposes. Mildred and Richard Loving of Virginia were arrested shortly after they got married in 1958. Their case made it all the way to the Supreme Court, which ruled in 1967 that state laws barring interracial marriage were unconstitutional.

Today things seem to be different. Bill de Blasio's marriage to a black woman didn't prevent him from being elected mayor of New York City in 2014. No one seemed to care about race when Mark Zuckerberg, founder of Facebook, married Priscilla Chan in 2012. But marriages that cross racial lines still don't receive the level of taken-for-grantedness that within-race marriages unquestionably enjoy.

Why do you think the United States has had such a troubled, and sometimes outwardly hostile, history regarding interracial intimacy? Why is it still hard for some people to accept romance that crosses racial lines? Do you think that people who marry outside their race or ethnicity (or religion, for that matter) are being "disloyal" to their group? To what extent should people consider the possible impact on their larger racial/ethnic/religious community of choosing someone of a different racial group to marry?

or religions marry, chances are they will come from similar socioeconomic backgrounds (think Kanye West and Kim Kardashian; Rosenfeld, 2005). Certainly some people do marry a person from a different social class, but the class tends to be an adjacent one—for instance, an upper-middle-class woman may marry a middle-class man. Cinderella-like marriages, between extremely wealthy and extremely poor people, are quite rare.

One reason this occurs is because individuals of similar social classes are more likely to participate in activities together, where they come into contact with people who share their values, tastes, goals, expectations, and backgrounds (Kalmijn & Flap, 2001). Our education system plays a particularly important role in bringing people from similar class backgrounds together. The proportion of married couples who share the same level of schooling is the highest it's been in 40 years. The odds of someone with only a high school education marrying a college graduate have been decreasing since the 1970s (C. R. Schwartz & Mare, 2005).

Moreover, neighborhoods—and thus neighborhood schools—tend to be made up of people from similar social classes. College often continues this class segregation. People from upper-class backgrounds are considerably more likely to attend costly private schools, whereas those from the middle class are most likely to enroll in state universities and those from the working class are most likely to enroll in community colleges. These structural conditions increase the odds that the people with whom college students form intimate relationships will come from the same class background.

Family Life

To most people's way of thinking, committed intimate romantic relationships form the cornerstone of families. Of all the groups we belong to, family is usually the most significant. Our ancestors provide us with a personal history, and they, along with the families we build later in life, provide much of our identity. Because of its importance in everyday life, sociologists consider family one of the main social institutions, a social structure that addresses not only our personal needs but also the fundamental needs of society (see Chapter 2).

Defining Family

Ironically, as important as family is, it can be an elusive term to define. When most people hear the word **family**, they usually think of **nuclear family**: a unit consisting of parents and siblings. Others may focus on **extended family**: other kin, such as grandparents, aunts, uncles, and cousins. In everyday usage, people may use the word *family* more loosely to describe those with whom they've achieved a significant degree of emotional closeness and sharing, even if they're not related. If I choose to think of my father's best friend, my barber, and even my dog as members of my family, I can.

But we don't live our lives completely by ourselves, and so we don't have complete freedom to define our own families. Not only do we come into fairly regular contact with people who want to know what our family looks like, but we also must navigate a vast array of organizations and agencies that have their own definitions of family and may, at times, impose them on us. Local, state, and federal governments manage many programs that provide certain benefits only to groups they officially define as "families."

The federal government regularly compiles up-to-date statistics on the number of individuals, married couples, and families that live in this country. Obviously it must have some idea of what a family (or what a marriage) is before it can start counting. In its official statistics, the U.S. Bureau of the Census distinguishes between households and families. A **household** is composed of one or more people who occupy the same housing unit. A **family** consists of "two or more persons, including the householder, who are related by birth, marriage, or adoption, and who live together as one household" (U.S. Bureau of the Census, 2005). Not all households contain families. If we accept this narrow definition of family, then other arrangements—people living alone, roommates, unmarried cohabitors, and various forms of group living—cannot be considered families in the strict sense of the word. Such a definition is reflected in many people's beliefs. In a recent national study, respondents were twice as likely to identify unmarried couples (both heterosexual and homosexual) *with* children as families as they were to identify unmarried couples *without* children as families (B. Powell, Bolzendahl, Geist, & Steelman, 2010). According to the government's definition, about 43% of U.S. households are not families (see Exhibit 7.2).

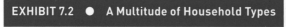

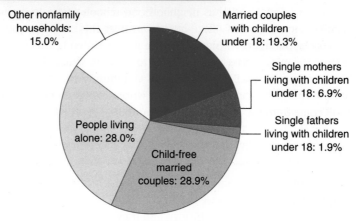

EXHIBIT 7.2 ● A Multitude of Household Types

Source: ProQuest Statistical Abstract, 2017, Table 60.

Having one's living arrangement legally defined as a family has many practical implications. Benefits such as parental rights, inheritance rights, insurance coverage, spousal immigration benefits, savings from joint tax returns, the ability to make medical decisions for another person, and visitation rights in prisons and hospital intensive care units are determined by marital or family status. Members of relationships not defined as family relationships, no matter how committed, economically interdependent, or emotionally fulfilling, are not eligible. For instance, at the time of the terrorist attacks of 2001, no state recognized the legal status of same-sex relationships. So long-term, same-sex partners of victims of the September 11 attack on the Pentagon were not eligible for the same survivor benefits in the state of Virginia that surviving heterosexual spouses were entitled to (Farmer, 2002).

Historical Trends in Family Life

Many functionalist sociologists have voiced concern over the current state of family as a social institution. Over time, they argue, the family has lost many, if not all, of its traditional purposes (Lasch, 1977). Historically, the family was where children received most of their education and religious training. It was where both children and adults could expect to receive emotional nurturing and support. It was the institution that regulated sexual activity and reproduction. And it was also the economic center of society, where family members worked together to earn a living and support one another financially.

But as the economy shifted from a system based on small, privately owned agricultural enterprises to one based on massive industrial manufacturing, the role of family changed. Economic production moved from the home to the factory, and families became more dependent on the money that members earned outside the home. Schools began to take over the teaching of skills and values that were once a part of everyday home life. Even the family's role as a source of emotional security and nurturing began to diminish as it became less able to shield its members from the harsh realities of modern life (Lasch, 1977).

For all these reasons, many people are concerned about the survival of the contemporary family. Anxiety over the future of families has generated some strident calls for a return to the "good ol' days" of family life. The belief in a lost "golden age" of family has led some to depict the present as a period of rapid decline and inevitable family breakdown (Coontz, 2005; Hareven, 1992; Skolnick, 1991). Critics often pessimistically cite high divorce rates, large numbers of out-of-wedlock births, changing gender roles (most notably, the increase in working mothers), and a de-emphasis on marriage as signs of trouble for contemporary families (The National Marriage Project, 2010). However, although marriage is no longer the only relationship where people can make lifelong commitments, most Americans still marry eventually (Coontz, 2013a). Moreover, families have always been diverse in structure and have always faced difficulties in protecting members from economic hardship, internal violence, political upheaval, and social change. Calls for a return to the "good ol' days" are calls for a return to something that has never truly existed. By glorifying a mythical and idealized past, we artificially limit ourselves to an inaccurate image of what we think a "normal" family ought to look like.

Trends in Family Structure

The reality of U.S. family life has never quite fit its nostalgic image. According to sociologist William J. Goode (1971), the traditional family of the past that people in the United States speak so fondly of and want to re-create is somewhat of a myth. He calls the idealized image of the past "the classical family of Western nostalgia":

> It is a pretty picture of life down on grandma's farm. There are lots of happy children, and many kinfolk live together in a large rambling house. Everyone works hard. Most of the food to be eaten during the winter is grown, preserved, and stored on the farm. . . . Father is stern and reserved and has the final decision in all important matters. . . . All boys and girls marry, and marry young. . . . After marriage, the couple lives harmoniously, either near the boy's parents or with them. . . . No one divorces. (p. 624)

Like most stereotypes, this one is not altogether accurate. In the 19th century, U.S. adults had a shorter life expectancy than adults today, so due to the death of a parent, children were actually more likely then than they are now to live in a single-parent home (Kain, 1990). Even children fortunate enough to come from intact families usually left home to work as servants or apprentices in other people's homes. Furthermore, although nearly 20% of U.S. children live in poverty today (Proctor, Semega, & Kollar, 2016), a comparable proportion lived in orphanages at the beginning of the 20th century—but not just because their parents had died. Many were there because their parents simply couldn't afford to raise them. Rates of alcohol and drug abuse, domestic violence, and school dropouts were also higher a century ago than they are today (Coontz, 1992).

Also contrary to popular belief, father-breadwinner/mother-homemaker households were not the only family form in the 19th and early 20th centuries. For instance, by 1900, one fifth of U.S. women worked outside the home (Staggenborg, 1998). But the experiences of employed women varied along class and race lines. For middle- and upper-class white women, few professions other than teaching and nursing were available. Because their income was probably not essential for the survival of the household, most could enter and exit the labor force in response to family demands. In contrast, poor women were likely to work long hours, mostly in unskilled jobs in clothing factories, canning plants, or other industries.

Family life for women of color was even more affected by economic necessity. Black domestic servants, for instance, were often forced to leave their own families and live in their employer's home, where they were expected to work around the clock. And most of them had little choice. Throughout U.S. history, black women have rarely had the luxury of being stay-at-home spouses and parents. In 1880, 73% of black single women and 35% of black married women reported holding paid jobs. Only 23% of white single women and 7% of white married women reported being in the paid labor force at that time (cited in Kessler-Harris, 1982).

Trends in Household Size

Perhaps the most pervasive myth regarding U.S. families of the past is that of the primacy of the extended family with several generations living under the same roof. Today's more isolated nuclear family—which consists, on average, of 2.53 people (U.S. Bureau of the Census, 2016b)—is often compared unfavorably with the image of these large, close-knit support networks. But research shows that U.S. families have always been fairly small and primarily nuclear (Blumstein & Schwartz, 1983; W. J. Goode, 1971; Hareven, 1992). Even in the early 1960s—the heyday of the "Baby Boom" era—the average household consisted of only about 3.3 people (U.S. Bureau of the Census, 2016b). The United States has no strong tradition of large, extended multigenerational families living together. In fact, the highest proportion of extended-family households ever recorded existed between 1850 and 1885 and was only around 20% of all households (Hareven, 1978). Because people didn't live as long then as they do today, most died before ever seeing their grandchildren. Even in the 1700s, the typical family consisted of a husband, a wife, and approximately three children.

When households of the past were large, it was probably due to the presence of non-family members: servants, apprentices, boarders, and visitors. The reduction in average household size we've seen over the past several centuries was caused not by a decline in the number of extended relatives but by a decrease in the number of nonfamily members living in a household, a reduction in the number of children in a family, and an increase in the number of young adults living alone (Kobrin, 1976).

As people migrated to the United States from countries that did have a tradition of extended families, such as China, Greece, and Italy, often their first order of business was to leave their extended family members so they could create their own households. Reducing the size of their families was seen as a clear sign that they had become American. Large, multigenerational families simply didn't make economic sense. Being able to move to a different state to pursue a job would be next to impossible with a bunch of grandparents, aunts, uncles, and cousins in tow.

In addition, it's not at all clear that families today are as isolated as some people make them out to be. More U.S. residents than ever have grandparents alive, and most adults see or talk to a parent on the phone at least once a week (Coontz, 1992). The average distance adult Americans live from their mothers is 18 miles, and more than half of people over the age of 65 have at least one child who lives within 10 miles (National Institute on Aging, 2015). Family members may not live under the same roof, but they do stay in contact and provide advice, emotional support, and financial help when needed (K. Newman, 2005).

Trends in Divorce

Another oft-cited indicator of the demise of the U.S. family based on faulty conceptions of the past is the current high divorce rate. Many observers fear that the intact middle-class family depicted in 1950s television shows such as *Ozzie and Harriet*, *Father Knows Best*, and *Leave It to Beaver* has crumbled away forever. The rise in the divorce rate in the late 20th century has been attributed to the cultural movement toward "swinging singles, open marriages, alternative lifestyles, and women's liberation" in the 1960s and 1970s (Skolnick, 1991). True, this was a revolutionary period in U.S. history, and norms governing all aspects of social life were certainly changing.

What these conclusions overlook, however, is the longer historical trend in divorce in this country. Until World War II, it had been increasing steadily for more than 100 years. It rose sharply right after the war, most likely because of short courtships before the young men shipped out and the subsequent stress of separation. In the 1950s, the rate dropped just as sharply. The high divorce rates of the late 1960s and 1970s, then, represented a return to a national trend that had been developing since the beginning of the 20th century. Indeed, since the mid-1980s, the overall rate has actually been declining (see Exhibit 7.3). But it's important to note that divorce rates vary by age. Among young couples the rate has been stable or declining for the past three decades, principally because young people these days are slower to marry and more selective when they do. In contrast, the divorce rate for people over 35 has actually more than doubled since 1980 (S. Kennedy & Ruggles, 2014).

Furthermore, the rate of "hidden" marital separation 100 years ago was probably not that much less than the rate of "visible" separation today (Sennett, 1984). For financial or religious reasons, divorce was not an option for many people in the past. For instance, divorce rates actually fell during the Great Depression of the 1930s. With jobs and housing scarce, many couples simply couldn't afford to divorce. Rates of marital unhappiness and domestic violence increased. A significant number of people turned to the functional equivalents of divorce—desertion and abandonment—which have been going on for centuries. So you can see that the divorce rate may have been lower in the past, but families found other ways to break up. The image of a warm, secure, stable family life in past times is at odds with the actual history of U.S. families (Skolnick, 1991).

EXHIBIT 7.3   ●   The Ups and Downs of Divorce Over Time

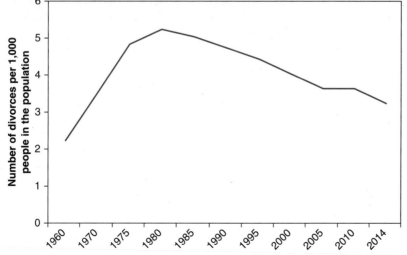

Sources: ProQuest Statistical Abstract, 2017, Table 82.

Cultural Variation in Intimacy and Family

Families can be found in every human society, and from a structural-functionalist perspective, they all address similar societal needs. However, the way families go about meeting these needs—their structure, customs, patterns of authority, and so on—differ widely across cultures. Thus, ideas about what a family is and how people should behave within it are culturally determined.

Most of us take for granted that **monogamy**, the practice of being married to only one person at a time, is the fundamental building block of the family. Of course, some families do exist without a married couple, and some people may have several spouses over their lifetimes. But monogamous marriage remains the core component of our image of family (Sudarkasa, 2001).

In the United States, monogamous marriage is the one adult intimate relationship that is legally recognized, culturally approved, and endorsed at the federal level by the Internal Revenue Service. It's still the only relationship in which sexual activity between the partners is not only acceptable but expected. No other relationship has yet achieved such a status. Despite the growing number of couples choosing nonmarital cohabitation over marriage and overall public concern regarding the disintegration of marriage, monogamous marriage remains the cultural standard against which all other types of intimate relationships are judged.

The primacy of marriage can create biases against those people who are single. They pay more for health and car insurance than married people, don't get the same kind of tax advantages, and may not qualify for certain forms of housing. According to one author, systematic discrimination against people who are single is common but largely unrecognized and unchallenged (DePaulo, 2007). Pastors in some Christian denominations often find it difficult to land a permanent position if they are not married. In conservative, evangelical churches, only 1 pastor in 20 is single; among mainline Protestant denominations, the figure is 1 in 6. In fact, there are more female pastors in mainline churches—about 28%—than there are single male pastors. One minister, who had more than 50 (unsuccessful) job interviews, said, "They often acted like I'm not quite whole because I'm single" (quoted in Eckholm, 2011b, p. A3). Only two never-married people—James Buchanan and Grover Cleveland—have ever been elected president . . . and Cleveland got married while he was in office.

It may be hard to imagine a society that is not structured around the practice and primacy of monogamy, but many societies allow an individual to have several husbands or wives at the same time. This type of marriage is called **polygamy**. Some anthropologists estimate that about 75% of the world's societies prefer some type of polygamy, although few members within those societies actually have the resources to afford more than one spouse (Murdock, 1957; Nanda, 1994). Often polygamy is an adaptation to population or economic conditions. In Russia, for instance, some people, mostly women, have lobbied the government to legalize polygamy because of population pressures: The Russian population is falling by 3% each year and there are only 87 men for every 100 women (by contrast, the ratio in the United States is 98 men for every 100 women; Gao, 2015). Polygamy would give more women, particularly in rural areas, an opportunity to have a husband and therefore legal rights to his financial and physical support as well as legitimacy for their children. According to one anthropologist, the scarcity of potential husbands has led many Russian women to conclude that "half a good man is better than none at all" (quoted in Katbamna, 2009, p. 3).

Even in the United States, certain groups practice polygamy. Although exact numbers are hard to come by, it's estimated that tens of thousands of members of a dissident

Mormon sect in the western United States live in households that contain one husband and two or more wives (T. McCarthy, 2001). Although these marriages are technically illegal, few polygamists are ever prosecuted. In fact, in 2013, a federal judge ruled that parts of Utah's anti-polygamy law were unconstitutional because they violated the First Amendment guarantee of free exercise of religion (J. Schwartz, 2013). Most of the time, practitioners are tolerated as long as they keep to themselves. However, every once in a while media portrayal brings attention to the practice. The popularity of recent television shows such as *Big Love* and *Sister Wives* has sparked public interest in the private everyday lives of American polygamists. In fact, the proportion of Americans who find polygamy "morally acceptable" increased from 7% in 2001 to 16% in 2015 (Newport, 2015).

Societies differ in other taken-for-granted facets of family life as well. Take living arrangements, for example. In U.S. society, families tend to follow the rules of **neolocal residence**; that is, young married couples are expected to establish their own households and separate from their respective families when financially possible. However, only about 5% of the world's societies are neolocal (Murdock, 1957; Nanda, 1994). In most places, married couples are expected to live with or near either the husband's relatives (called "patrilocal" residence) or the wife's relatives (called "matrilocal" residence).

Even the belief that members of the same nuclear family ought to live together is not found everywhere. Among the Kipsigis of Kenya, for instance, the mother and children live in one house and the father lives in another. The Kipsigis are polygamous, so a man might have several homes for his several wives at one time (Stephens, 1963). Among the Tsonga of southern Africa, children live with their grandmothers once they stop breastfeeding. They remain there for several years and are then returned to their parents. On the traditional Israeli kibbutz, or commune, children are raised not by their parents but in an "infants' house," where they are cared for by a trained nurse (Nanda, 1994).

Child-rearing philosophies vary cross-culturally, too. Most people in the United States believe that young children are inherently helpless and dependent: They feel that if parents attend to the child's drives and desires with consistency, warmth, and affection, that child will learn to trust the parents, adopt their values, develop a sturdy self-concept, and turn out to be a well-rounded, normal individual. Most U.S. child development experts believe that neglect and physical punishment can deaden the child's spirit and lead to violence later in life (Dugger, 1996). In contrast, in the highlands of Guatemala, parents believe that their child's personality is determined by the date of birth. Parents in this region are almost entirely uninvolved in the child's life, standing aside so he or she can grow as nature intended. In many societies—Nigeria, Russia, Haiti, the Dominican Republic, and Mexico, to name a few—most parents think that the best way to teach children to be respectful and studious is to beat them when they misbehave. Despite these dramatic differences in child-rearing practices, most children in all these cultures grow up equally well adapted to their societies.

Family and Social Structure

All of us have experience with families of one form or another, so it's very tempting to look at this topic in individualistic, personal terms. However, the sociological imagination encourages us to think about how social forces affect this aspect of our private lives. As you will see, a focus on the influence of social structure—social institutions as well as sources of social inequality, such as gender, race, and class—can help us understand some of the dilemmas facing contemporary families.

How Other Institutions Influence Family

As a social institution, family is connected to other institutions in important ways. Consider, for instance, the effect that the wars in Iraq and Afghanistan have had on family life. For as long as there have been wars, military families have been disrupted when one parent—almost always the father—either shipped out to sea or was deployed in another part of the world. But the structure of U.S. families had changed in many ways by the time the current wars began. Single parents with custody of a child are prohibited from enlisting in the military. In order to join, therefore, they must get a court order to transfer custody to someone else. However, if one becomes a single parent *after* enlisting—due to divorce or death of a spouse—they are allowed to remain. Approximately 8% of all military personnel today are single parents (Powers, 2016). The military as an institution has no special programs in place to assist such parents when they are deployed. Raising a child in the military has always been hard, but being a single parent creates special challenges and difficult choices, not the least of which is what to do with the children while the parent is gone. According to the Servicemembers' Civil Relief Act, military personnel cannot be evicted or have their property seized during deployment. But this law does not protect them from losing custody of their children, if that's what a judge decides. In 2010, a single mother was days away from her yearlong deployment in Afghanistan when her mother backed out of the court order that identified her as the 10-month-old's guardian while his mother was away. With no other choice, she stayed home and missed her flight to Afghanistan. She was immediately arrested by military police and faced court-martial charges and jail time until she agreed to a "less-than-honorable discharge" (Dao, 2010a).

The legal, political, religious, and economic forces that shape society are perhaps the institutions that most influence the identities and actions of individuals within family relationships. Keep in mind that individuals within families can act to influence society as well.

The Influence of Law and Politics

The relationship between the family and the law is obvious. Marriage, for instance, is a legal contract that determines lawful rights and responsibilities. In the United States, each state legislature determines the age at which two people can marry, the health requirements, the length of the waiting period required before marriage, rules determining inheritance, and the division of property in case of divorce (Baca Zinn & Eitzen, 1996). Sometimes the legislature sets limits on specific types of marriage. For instance, to protect noncitizens from potential abuse, the U.S. Congress enacted the International Marriage Broker Regulation Act, which requires that men who seek foreign brides over the Internet disclose information about their criminal record and marital history before any contracts are signed (Porter, 2006).

MICRO-MACRO CONNECTION
I NOW PRONOUNCE YOU . . . SHIFTING PUBLIC SUPPORT FOR LEGAL SAME-SEX MARRIAGE

In the case of same-sex unions, the law's power to either forbid or grant family rights and privileges has been especially obvious . . . and controversial. At the time of this writing, nearly 30 other countries—Argentina, Australia, Austria, Belgium, Brazil, Canada, Colombia, Denmark, England/Wales, Finland, France, Germany,

Greenland, Iceland, Ireland, Luxembourg, Malta, the Netherlands, New Zealand, Norway, Portugal, Scotland, South Africa, Spain, Sweden, and Uruguay—grant gay men and lesbians the right to legally marry. Many other European countries allow same-sex couples to enter "civil unions" (sometimes called "domestic partnerships" or "registered partnerships"), which grant them many of the legal protections and economic benefits and responsibilities of heterosexual marriage. Israel and Mexico recognize marriages between same-sex couples, but only if they are performed in other countries (Freedom to Marry, 2014).

The matter was only recently resolved in the United States. Back in 1996, the federal Defense of Marriage Act—written at a time when three quarters of Americans disapproved of same-sex marriage and *no* state allowed it—formally defined marriage as the union of one man and one woman; authorized all states to refuse to accept same-sex marriages from other states where it could become legal; and denied federal benefits such as Social Security survival payments and spousal burials in national military cemeteries to same-sex couples. But between 2004 and 2014, 36 individual states legalized same-sex marriage, creating a confusing patchwork of recognized legal status. In 2013, the U.S. Supreme Court ruled that the Defense of Marriage Act was unconstitutional, meaning that gay and lesbian couples who live in states where same-sex marriage is legal are entitled to all the federal marriage benefits that heterosexual

EXHIBIT 7.4   ●   Support of Same-Sex Marriage Is on the Rise

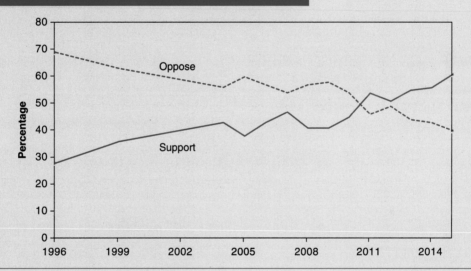

Sources: McCarthy, 2014; Pew Research Center, 2015h.

couples are entitled to. It took 2 more years for the U.S. Supreme Court to rule once and for all that state bans on same-sex marriage were unconstitutional.

The Court's decision reflected a massive historical shift in public opinion (see Exhibit 7.4). In fact, in the last decade support for legalizing same-sex marriage increased in *every* state by an average of 13.6% (Flores & Barclay, 2013). Younger people are especially inclined to support it. In one survey, 73% of people younger than 34 support same-sex marriage rights,

compared with 39% of people over 70 (Pew Research Center, 2015h).

Favorable attitudes toward legal same-sex marriage can even be found in segments of society that one would consider more traditional in their attitudes toward marriage, such as the military, religion, and conservative politics. In 1993, the U.S. Department of Defense enacted the "Don't ask, don't tell" policy. According to this rule, military personnel could not be asked about their sexual orientation. However, openly professing

(Continued)

(Continued)

one's homosexuality or engaging in sexual conduct with a member of the same sex could still constitute grounds for discharge. In 2010, President Obama signed a law repealing the "Don't ask, don't tell" policy. Three years later, the Undersecretary of Defense (2013) issued a memorandum stating, "The Department will work to make the same benefits available to all spouses, regardless of whether they are in same-sex or opposite sex marriages, and will recognize all marriages that are valid in the place of celebration" (p. 1).

It's certainly the case that the overwhelming majority of Evangelical Christians were opposed to the legalization of same-sex marriage (Pew Research Center, 2015d). You may recall the case of Kim Davis, the county clerk for Rowan County, Kentucky, who made headlines in 2015 for refusing to issue marriage licenses to same-sex couples because she felt it was against God's will. However, even before the 2015 Supreme Court ruling, a majority of mainline Protestants and Catholics favored legalization. In fact, 75% of self-identified Catholics between the ages of 18 and 29 supported it (Lipka, 2014). In 2014, the Presbyterian Church (U.S.A.) voted in its General Assembly to change the definition of marriage from "a man and a woman" to "two people" and to allow its ministers to perform same-sex marriage ceremonies in those states where it is legal (Goodstein, 2014b). Other religions—the United Church of Christ, the Quakers, the Unitarian Universalist Association of Congregations, and the Reform and Conservative movements in Judaism—took similar actions. A majority of U.S. Christians now say that homosexuality should be accepted rather than discouraged (Murphy, 2015).

Even in the realm of conservative politics, the public expression of support for or at least tolerance of legal same-sex marriage is growing. While it's true that people who identify as politically liberal are still more likely to approve of legal same-sex marriage than those who

identify as politically conservative (N. Cohn, 2013) and Republicans are more than twice as likely as Democrats to support the rights of wedding-related businesses to refuse services to same-sex couples if they find such service morally objectionable (Suls, 2016), the gap has shrunk. Even before the Supreme Court's decision, equal numbers of Republicans and Democrats (about 72%) felt that legalization was inevitable (Pew Research Center, 2015d).

Incidentally, it's not only gays and lesbians seeking to marry that have had to fight for legal recognition. Nonmarital cohabitors—both gay and straight—have also faced some difficulty achieving legal rights. Although public attitudes have grown more accepting of unmarried couples living together, the law has been slower to adjust. Massachusetts did repeal a 1784 law banning "lewdly and lasciviously associating and cohabitating without the benefit of marriage"—but not until 1987 (J. Yardley, 2000). New Mexico and Arizona didn't repeal their "unlawful cohabitation" laws until 2001. In 2008, voters in Arkansas approved a proposition that bans people who are "cohabiting outside a valid marriage" from serving as foster parents or adopting children (Savage, 2008, p. A31). In some states, landlords can legally refuse to rent to unmarried couples (Hertz, 2014). In fact, some legal scholars have voiced concern that the legalization of same-sex marriage could result in the reduction or even abolition of certain benefits for unmarried gay partners (known as domestic partners). Even before the Supreme Court's 2015 ruling, several large companies—Verizon, Delta Airlines, and IBM, to name a few—had already rescinded health care coverage for unmarried cohabiting partners of employees in states that had legalized same-sex marriage and replaced it with spousal coverage. These companies told their employees that they had to marry within a certain period of time—usually one year—or lose the benefit (T. S. Bernard, 2015).

Law, politics, and family are interconnected in various ways. Consider, for instance, who gets to be a parent. The 2015 Maine Parentage Act established that children in the state can have more than two legal parents. By court order, a third person—referred to as a "de facto parent"—can be granted the same legal rights as the biological or adoptive parents if he or she has been "acting as a parent" to the child. Evidence for such a determination includes living with the child for a significant amount of time, regularly taking care of the child, developing a "parent-like" relationship with the child, and taking on complete and permanent responsibilities for the child (Pine Tree Legal Assistance, 2017).

The Influence of Religion

You saw in Chapter 5 that religion is an important feature of everyday life and a powerful agent of socialization. Religion can also play a role in virtually every stage of family life. One of the key aspects of religion is that it constrains people's behavior, or at the very least encourages them to act in certain ways. This normative aspect of religion has important consequences for people's family experiences. For instance, all the major religions in the United States are strong supporters of marriage and childbearing.

In recent years, more churches have begun requiring engaged couples to participate in premarital counseling and education programs before the wedding. In addition, religions almost universally prohibit sexual relations outside marriage. Some religions prohibit divorce or don't permit remarriage after divorce. In highly religious families, a sacred text such as the Bible, the Qur'an, or the Talmud may serve not only as a source of faith but as a literal guidebook for every aspect of family life, from dating, marriage, and sexuality to child discipline, responses to illness and death, and household division of labor.

Religion's influence on family life needn't be so direct, however. For example, among Muslims and members of certain Christian denominations, families are expected to tithe, or donate, a certain amount of their income (10% in most cases) to support their religious establishment. Although it is a charitable thing to do, tithing obligations can create problems for families that are already financially strapped.

Most evidence suggests that religious involvement has positive effects, especially for families raising children, such as higher levels of marital commitment (Larson & Goltz, 1989) and more positive parent–child relationships (L. D. Pearce & Axinn, 1998; Petts, 2014; Wilcox, 2000). "Spiritual wellness" is often cited as one of the most important qualities of family well-being (Stinnett & DeFrain, 1985).

However, in some situations the link between religious beliefs and actual family behavior may not be as strong as we might think. Even in highly religious families, the practical demands of modern life can make it difficult for people to always subscribe to religious teachings. For instance, although fundamentalist Christians believe wives should stay at home and submit to the authority of their husbands, many fundamentalist women do work outside the home and exert powerful influence over family decisions (Ammerman, 1987). Moreover, although many religions stress the value of keeping families intact, increased religious involvement does not do much to strengthen troubled marriages (Booth, Johnson, Branaman, & Sica, 1995). It may slightly decrease thoughts about divorce, but it doesn't necessarily enhance marital happiness or keep spouses from fighting.

The Influence of Economics

The economy affects virtually every aspect of family life, from the amount of money coming into the household to the day-to-day management of finances and major purchasing decisions. Money matters are closely tied to feelings of satisfaction within family relationships. When couples are disappointed with how much money they have or how it is spent, they find all aspects of their relationships less satisfying (Blumstein & Schwartz, 1983). Sustaining a supportive, nurturing family environment is nearly impossible without adequate income or health care. When economic foundations are weak, the emotional bonds that tie a family together can be stretched to the breaking point.

Financial problems are not just private troubles. Rather, they are directly linked to larger economic patterns. A deep recession and a high unemployment rate can have obvious effects on family life. At the global level, the competitive pressures of the international marketplace have forced many businesses and industries to make greater use of so-called disposable workers—those who work part time or on a temporary contract. These jobs offer no benefits and no security and therefore make family life less stable. Other companies have reduced their costs by cutting salaries, laying off workers, or encouraging early retirement. Some businesses end up relocating either to other countries or to other parts of the United States where they can pay lower wages (see Chapter 10 for a more detailed discussion). Relaxed rules on foreign investment and export duties have made it easy for U.S. companies to relocate their assembly plants abroad, where wages are lower. The companies obviously benefit from higher profits, and the impoverished workers in these countries benefit from more job opportunities and added income. But displaced U.S. workers and their families may suffer.

MICRO-MACRO CONNECTION

BALANCING ACTS: COMPETING WORK AND FAMILY DEMANDS IN DUAL-EARNER HOUSEHOLDS

The financial strains of living in the 21st century have made it difficult for most couples to survive on only one income. For instance, it's estimated that it will cost a two-parent, middle-income family with two children about $233,610 to raise each child from birth to age 17, up from $25,229 in 1960 (Lino, Kuczynski, Rodriguez, & Schap, 2017). Since the mid-1970s, the amount of an average family budget earmarked for mortgage payments increased 69%. To make matters worse, the cost of a college degree has increased 1,120% over the past three decades (Jamrisko & Kolet, 2012).

But incomes have not risen proportionately (see Chapter 10 for more detail). In fact, in constant dollars, median household incomes haven't changed all that much since 1990 (ProQuest Statistical Abstract, 2017). Consequently, in over 60% of married couple families with children, both parents work (U.S. Bureau of Labor Statistics, 2016c), and about 27% of children under the age of 15 live with a stay-at-home parent, compared to half in 1975 (Glynn, 2012; ProQuest Statistical Abstract, 2017).

Balancing the needs of one's family with workplace obligations is a constant struggle for people in dual-earner couples from all income levels (Sullivan, 2015). But it is especially pressing for middle- and low-income couples. Some sociologists feel that the single most important step society could take to help these dual-earner families would be to assist them with childcare demands. The Family and Medical Leave Act (FMLA), signed into law by President Clinton in 1993, was a step in that direction: It guarantees some workers up to 12 weeks of unpaid sick leave per year to attend to their own medical issues; for the birth or adoption of a child; or to care for a sick child, parent, or spouse without fear of losing their job. When the employee returns to work, she or he must be restored

to the same job as before the leave was taken. If that's not possible, the worker must be restored to an equivalent job (one that is similar in terms of pay, benefits, hours, and location; U.S. Department of Labor, 2012).

However, FMLA has some important qualifications that seriously limit its usefulness to the working population:

- The law covers only workers who have been employed continuously for at least one year and who have worked a total of at least 1,250 hours (or about 25 hours a week). So temporary and part-time workers are not eligible.

- The law only covers companies that employ more than 50 workers who live within 75 miles of the worksite.

- The law allows an employer to deny leave to a "key" employee—that is, one who is in the highest-paid 10% of its workforce—if allowing that person to take the leave would create "substantial and grievous injury" to the business's operations.

In 2008, FMLA was amended to permit a spouse, child, parent, or next of kin to take up to 26 weeks of unpaid leave to care for a member of the Armed Forces who is undergoing medical treatment for a serious injury or illness. Other than that, FMLA provisions have not changed in 25 years.

Currently, only about 59% of the civilian U.S. workforce is eligible for FMLA benefits. Of those workers, about 13% actually take the leave they're entitled to (U.S. Department of Labor, 2014). Most of those who actually take leave under FMLA do so to attend to their own illness. Only 21% of employees take leave for the birth or adoption of a child and only 18% do so to care for a sick spouse, child, or parent. And nearly half of those who take leave do so for 10 days or less (Klerman, Daley, & Pozniak, 2013).

Not surprisingly many of those who *don't* take leave are people who may need the time off but can't afford to go without a paycheck. According to one survey, of those eligible workers who needed leave but didn't take it, 78% cited the inability to afford unpaid leave as the principal reason. In fact, 1 out of 10 workers who take unpaid leave under FMLA ends up going on public assistance to make up for the lost wages (National Partnership for Women and Families, 2005). Moreover, relatively few private employers go beyond the minimum unpaid leave policies mandated by FMLA. Despite evidence showing that *paid* family leave policies increase worker productivity and improve morale, loyalty, and retention (National Partnership for Women and Families, 2014), only about 12% of U.S. workers have access to *paid* family leave through their employers (ProQuest Statistical Abstract, 2017).

And although working women (especially those with college degrees) have more access to maternity leave than ever before (Tsai, 2012b), taking advantage of such opportunities can make them vulnerable to discrimination. For instance, employers might be hesitant to hire people who might leave for a year at a time (F. D. Blau & Kahn, 2013).

Sadly, the United States lags behind other countries in its support of dual-earner families. Of the nearly 200 countries examined in a recent study, 180 offer guaranteed paid leave to new mothers, and 81 offer paid leave to fathers. In addition, 175 countries *require* paid annual leave for all workers (not just new parents) and 162 limit the maximum length of the workweek. Only Suriname, Liberia, Palau, Papua New Guinea, Nauru, Western Samoa, Tonga . . . and the United States offer none of these protections (Heymann, 2013). And among the 41 most industrialized countries in the world, the United States is the *only* one that doesn't require paid leave for new parents (Livingston, 2016). In contrast, some countries such as Estonia, Bulgaria, Hungary, Japan, Lithuania, Austria, Czech Republic, Latvia, Norway, and Slovakia guarantee a year or more of paid leave. All member countries of the European Union must allow parents—both mothers and fathers—to request part-time, flexible, or home-based work arrangements in addition to paid leave (Rampell, 2013). They are also prohibited from paying part-time workers lower wages than full-time workers and from limiting paid leaves to full-time workers. In contrast, American workers who reduce their hours typically lose their benefits and take an hourly wage cut (Coontz, 2013b).

If we are truly concerned about preserving and helping families, then perhaps we need to find more effective ways to reduce the conflict between work life and family life. The American workplace has always valued people who put their work ahead of other (translation: family) obligations. But perhaps that is starting to change. Some states as well as some private companies have devised programs to provide more assistance to working families. For instance, in 2017, Washington passed a paid leave law that gives workers 16 weeks to care for babies, themselves, or relatives. New Jersey voted to double its *paid* family leave to 12 weeks, pay workers more while they're on leave, and use the leave in more types of situations (C. C. Miller, 2017b). In 2014, Apple announced that it would include egg freezing and storage, extended maternity leave, adoption assistance, and infertility treatments in its benefits package for female employees.

At the federal level, some calls for change have been heard. In 2009, a bill called the Healthy Families Act was introduced in Congress. This bill would guarantee workers in businesses with 15 or more employees one paid hour off for every 30 hours they work, enabling them to get up to 7 paid sick days a year. They could use their days to care for a sick child, parent, or spouse, or anyone else close to them. However, business groups have fought the legislation, arguing that in tight economic times it would impose added financial hardships on employers (S. Greenhouse, 2009). The bill has never come to a vote. Another piece of legislation, the Federal Employees Paid Parental Leave Act, was also introduced in 2009. This bill would have given all federal employees 4 weeks of *paid* leave each year for the birth or adoption of a child. It was approved by the House of Representatives but never came to a vote in the Senate and, hence, never became law. In 2015, President Obama recommended that federal agencies give their employees up to 6 weeks of *paid* leave after the birth or adoption of a child, a benefit he wanted to extend to all American workers. And during the 2016 presidential campaign, then-candidate Donald Trump made a similar recommendation, though he wanted to limit such leave to mothers. To date, none of these steps have been approved and implemented.

How Social Diversity Influences Family

We cannot talk about structural influences on family life without discussing the role of gender, class, and race. Gender is especially influential, explaining a variety of phenomena in family relationships, such as the way people communicate, how they express themselves sexually, how they deal with conflict, and what they feel their responsibilities are. Culturally defined gender expectations in families are certainly changing. But men and women are still likely to enter relationships with vastly different prospects, desires, and goals.

As you learned in Chapter 5, traditional gender role socialization encourages women to be sensitive, express affection, and reveal weakness, whereas men are taught to be competitive, strong, and emotionally inexpressive. These stereotypes have some basis in fact. Research has consistently shown that women have more close friends than men and are more romantic in their intimate relationships (Perlman & Fehr, 1987). Furthermore, women have been shown to be more concerned about, attentive to, and aware of the dynamics of their relationships than men are (see, e.g., Fincham & Bradbury, 1987; Rusbult, Zembrodt, & Iwaniszek, 1986). Women even think more and talk more about their relationships than men do (Acitelli, 1988; Holtzworth-Munroe & Jacobson, 1985).

Ironically, such female attentiveness and concern do not necessarily translate into more relationship satisfaction. In fact, the opposite may be true. According to one sociologist, every heterosexual marriage actually contains two marriages—"his" and "hers"—and "his" seems to be the better deal (J. Bernard, 1972). Both married men and married women live longer and healthier lives than their single counterparts, but husbands typically are sick less often and have fewer emotional problems (Gove, Style, & Hughes, 1990; Ross, Mirowsky, & Goldstein, 1990; Waite & Gallagher, 2000). They are more likely to receive regular checkups, maintain healthy diets, and exercise regularly than unmarried men (Fustos, 2010b). One study found that compared with married women, married men have lower rates of back pain, headaches, serious psychological distress, and physical inactivity (Schoenborn, 2004).

The reason for these differences may lie in the relationship between cultural gender expectations and family demands. Because of the continued pressures of gender-specific family responsibilities, married women are more likely than married men to experience the stresses associated with parenthood and homemaking. Men have historically been able to feel they are fulfilling their family obligations by simply being financial providers. Some, however, suggest that these gender differences—and hence different health benefits derived from marriage—may be disappearing (Strohschein, 2016). They argue that a society in which most women stay at home to raise children no longer exists. As we saw earlier, in most families today, both spouses tend to be employed. Consequently, some evidence suggests that fathers struggle just as much as mothers in balancing work and family obligations (Harrington, Van Deusen, & Ladge, 2010).

Nevertheless, traditional family attitudes and expectations die slowly. Many people still interpret a father's long hours on the job as an understandable sacrifice for his family's sake. Fathers rarely spend as much time worrying about the effect their work will have on their children as mothers do. In contrast, even in the relatively "liberated" United States, women's employment outside the home is often perceived as optional or, more seriously, as potentially damaging to the family. Even though women work for the same reasons men work—because they need the money—and are now either the primary breadwinners or co-breadwinners in two thirds of families with children (Glynn, 2012), they have traditionally had to justify why working outside the home is not an abandonment of their family duties. Despite the evidence showing that children who spend time in high quality day care when young are more cognitively, socially, and financially successful as adults than children who don't go to day care (J. L. García, Heckman, Leaf, & Prados, 2016), beliefs about the disadvantages and even dire consequences of children spending time away from their mothers still persist (Carey, 2007).

Social class has a substantial effect on family life, too. You saw in Chapter 5 that social class can determine the lessons that parents instill in their children. Social class affects families in other ways, too. All families, no matter what their class standing, face the same issues: work, leisure, child rearing, and interpersonal relations (L. Rubin, 1994). But beneath the similarities, we see dramatic differences in how these issues are handled. For example, because of heightened concern over class boundaries, ancestry, and maintenance of prestige, upper-class parents exert much more control over the dating behaviors of their children than lower-class parents do (Domhoff, 1983; M. K. Whyte, 1990). Upper-class families are also better able to use their wealth and resources in coping with some of the demands of family life. Finding adequate childcare arrangements will probably not pose much of a dilemma to parents who can afford a full-time, live-in nanny. The picture for middle-class families, though, can be different, especially when it intersects with race.

MARY PATTILLO-MCCOY

PRIVILEGE AND PERIL IN MIDDLE-CLASS BLACK FAMILIES

Concerned about how the combination of race and social class affects family life, sociologist Mary Pattillo-McCoy (1999) spent 3½ years in a middle-class black Chicago neighborhood she called "Groveland." She interviewed residents of all ages, including children. The only people she wasn't able to interview were the young adults who had gone off to college. As a black middle-class woman herself, Pattillo-McCoy quickly developed an affinity with the people she studied. She even had friends in common with some of her interviewees.

In many respects, the Groveland families were just like families in any other middle-class neighborhood. Parents saw their children's development into self-sufficient adults as their primary family goal. And they had the financial and social resources to help achieve this goal. Most of them had the wherewithal to pay for private schools, sports equipment, dance lessons, and other enriching activities for their children. Groveland children had access to technology and other resources that their counterparts in poor black neighborhoods did not.

Pattillo-McCoy also found that the Groveland middle-class families had to deal with problems markedly different from those of their white counterparts. For one thing, she found that the neighborhoods where many urban, middle-class African Americans live are likely to be adjacent to poor neighborhoods. In contrast, white middle-class neighborhoods are typically geographically separated from poor areas. In Chicago, for example, 79% of middle-class Blacks were likely to be living within a few blocks of a neighborhood where at least one third of the residents are poor; only 36% of white middle-class Chicago dwellers lived so close to a poor neighborhood (Pattillo-McCoy, 1999).

Thus, Groveland parents had to spend a lot of time trying to protect their children from the negative influences found in the nearby poor, inner-city areas. In doing so, they faced some challenges other middle-class parents were unlikely to face:

> Groveland parents . . . set limits on where their children can travel. They choose activities—church youth groups, magnet schools or accelerated programs in the local school, and the Boy Scouts and Girl Scouts—to increase the likelihood that their children will learn positive values and associate with youth from similar families. Still, many parents are working long hours to maintain their middle-class incomes. They cannot be with their children at all times. On their way to the grocery store or to school or to music lessons, Groveland's youth pass other young people whose parents are not as strict, who stay outside later, who have joined the local gang, or who earn enough money being a lookout at a drug house to buy new gym shoes. They also meet these peers in school and at the park. . . . For some teenagers, the fast life looks much more exciting than what their parents have to offer them, and they are drawn to it. The simple fact of living in a neighborhood where not all families have sufficient resources to direct their children away from deviance makes it difficult for parents to ensure positive outcomes for their children and their neighborhood. (Pattillo-McCoy, 1999, pp. 211–212)

Pattillo-McCoy found that, in many other respects as well, black middle-class families face social realities that are quite different from those faced by white middle-class families. Still, her research also shows that most families within a particular social class face many of the same opportunities and barriers.

Family Challenges

Given all the pressures on families from the society around them, it should be no surprise that some families experience serious problems. Those problems include divorce and its aftereffects and family violence.

Divorce

Although divorce is more common and more acceptable in some places than in others, virtually all societies have provisions—legal, community, or religious—for dissolving marriages (McKenry & Price, 1995). Only the Philippines legally prohibits divorce (although citizens there can acquire legal annulments or separations). As a general rule, divorce rates worldwide tend to be associated with socioeconomic development. The developing countries of Latin America, Asia, and the Middle East have substantially lower divorce rates than the developed countries of Western Europe and North America (United Nations, 2014a).

Iran provides a vivid example of how development and modernization can influence divorce rates, even in a restrictive environment. Economic development in the early 2000s created more job opportunities for women than ever before. Indeed, female college undergraduates now outnumber males two to one. Hence, more women now see divorce as an available way out of an unsatisfying marriage. As one Iranian sociologist put it,

> This economic freedom has had an effect on the behavior of women in the home. In the past, if a housewife left her home, she would go hungry; now there is a degree of possibility of finding a job and earning an income. (quoted in Yong, 2010, p. A4)

Consequently, between 2000 and 2010, the number of Iranian divorces per year tripled, particularly in urban areas.

Even in societies that we would consider modern and developed, powerful religious forces can sometimes suppress divorce. For instance, in 1995, the Irish government began a campaign against the Catholic Church over the country's constitutional ban on divorce. The government estimated at that time that at least 80,000 people were trapped in broken marriages and that they deserved the right to end them and remarry. The Catholic bishops launched a massive advertising counterattack, arguing that even unhappily married people have an obligation to keep their marriages intact to provide a good example for society. The referendum passed by a minuscule margin, and in 1997, for the first time, people in Ireland had the right to legally divorce.

Although the dissolution of marriage is virtually universal, no society values divorce highly. In fact, in most societies, people who divorce are somehow penalized, either through formal controls such as fines, prohibitions against remarriage, excommunication, and forced alimony and child support or through informal means such as censure, gossip, and stigmatization.

The Normalization of Divorce

Fifty years ago, divorce was a topic people talked about in whispers if they talked about it at all. Today, of course, things are quite different. You'd be hard pressed to find an 8-year-old who doesn't know what the word *divorce* means or who hasn't witnessed the end of a marriage, either that of her or his parents or of someone close. Divorce has become a part of everyday life. It's in our movies, television shows, and novels. The children's sections of bookstores stock picture books showing little dinosaurs or bears worrying about the possibility of their parents divorcing. There are even greeting cards for parents whose children live elsewhere. Even the Vatican has begun to re-examine the Catholic Church's historically unsympathetic treatment of divorced parishioners.

As you saw earlier in this chapter, the U.S. divorce rate has declined a bit since reaching a peak in 1981 (Stevenson & Wolfers, 2007). Yet it still remains high, especially compared with other industrialized countries (see Exhibit 7.5). Consider these statistics:

- Roughly 2.2 million U.S. adults divorced in 2014 (the last year for which statistics were available; ProQuest Statistical Abstract, 2017). That works out to just under 19 divorces per 1,000 existing marriages.

- By the age of 46, about 39% of Americans have experienced a divorce. Of those who remarry, 36% will experience another divorce (U.S. Bureau of Labor Statistics, 2013).

- About 23% of marriages—not to mention 55% of cohabitations—end in divorce or separation within the first 5 years (Fustos, 2010a).

- Eighty-three percent of women who married between 1960 and 1964 reached their fifth anniversary, but only 74% of women who married between 1990 and 1994 did so (Kreider & Ellis, 2011).

- The average duration of a marriage before divorce is about 9 years (U.S. Bureau of Labor Statistics, 2013).

Such figures frighten people who are about to enter a "lifetime" relationship and distress those already married who want some sense of permanence.

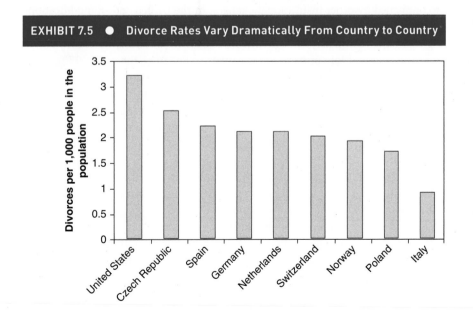

EXHIBIT 7.5 ● Divorce Rates Vary Dramatically From Country to Country

Source: Eurostat, 2016a; National Center For Health Statistics, 2015b.

Despite the traditional "family values" rhetoric we hear so much about these days, divorce in the United States tends to be unaffected by religious restrictions or political conservatism. For instance, several studies have found that born-again Christians are just as likely as anyone else to divorce (cited in Belluck, 2004). In addition, divorce rates are lowest in the so-called liberal states of the Northeast and upper Midwest and are highest in the conservative, heavily religious states of the South, such as Alabama, Arkansas, Oklahoma, and Kentucky (ProQuest Statistical Abstract, 2017). Some sociologists argue that other factors more commonly found in these states—namely younger age at marriage, less education, and lower socioeconomic status—render religiosity irrelevant. No matter how religious they are, young people who drop out of school and marry quickly not only lack emotional maturity but are highly susceptible to the economic strains that can create insurmountable problems in a marriage.

At a cultural level, the causes of the high divorce rates in Western societies include things such as the weakening of the family's traditional economic bonds and the stress of shifting gender roles (D. Popenoe, 1993). One particularly important factor has been a cultural change in the perception of marriage. Marriage has become a voluntary contract system that can be ended at the discretion of either spouse. In the past, when economic needs—not to mention constraints such as parental expectations or religious norms—held couples together, people "made do" with loveless, unsatisfying marriages because they had to. But when these constraints do not exist, people are less willing to make do (Coontz, 2005). Women's increasing earning power and decreasing economic dependence on men have made it easier to end an unsatisfying marriage.

In addition, people's overall attitudes toward divorce have become more accepting. In the 1960s, a divorced politician didn't stand a chance of being elected in the United States. Today, many of our most influential lawmakers are divorced. The current president, Donald Trump, has been divorced twice (and married three times). Most people now recognize that a divorce may be preferable to an unhappy marriage. In short, divorce is as much a part of U.S. family life as, well, marriage.

Changing perceptions of marriage and changing cultural attitudes toward divorce are typically accompanied by other institutional changes. In the United States, modifications of existing divorce laws in the past four decades have made it easier for people to end an unsatisfying marriage. Historically, evidence of wrongdoing—adultery, desertion, abuse, and so forth—was required for courts to grant a divorce. But since the early 1970s, every state has adopted a form of no-fault divorce. No-fault laws have eliminated the requirement that one partner be found guilty of some transgression. Instead, marriages are simply declared unworkable and terminated. Furthermore, no-fault divorce can reduce various forms of personal distress. For instance, whenever a state adopted a no-fault divorce law, rates of female suicide and domestic violence dropped significantly in that state (Stevenson & Wolfers, 2007).

Many critics argue that these laws and innovations have made divorce *too* easy and *too* quick. Indeed, there seems to be a desire in some areas of the country to return to more restrictive divorce laws. Some states, like Vermont, New Jersey, North Carolina, and South Carolina, have mandatory "cooling off" periods that require couples to be separated for 6 months to a year before filing for divorce. Arkansas requires an 18-month period of separation. Some states, like Rhode Island and Nebraska, have mandatory waiting periods of several months between when a couple files for divorce and when it can be finalized (Stonington & McIntyre, 2011). In 1997, the Louisiana state legislature passed a measure requiring engaged couples to choose between a standard marriage that permits no-fault divorce and a "covenant marriage," which can be dissolved only by a mutually agreed-on

2-year separation (2½ years if children are present) or proof of fault—chiefly adultery, abandonment, or abuse (Fee, 2013). Arizona followed suit in 1998, as did Arkansas in 2001. Critics of such measures note that instead of having a positive impact on family life, the result might be an increase in contentious, expensive, potentially child-harming divorces and unhappy, perhaps even dangerous marriages.

Children, Divorce, and Single Parenting

More than 1 million U.S. children see their parents divorce each year (D. Elliott & Simmons, 2011). When we combine divorce, separation, widowhood, and out-of-wedlock births, a significant number of children grow up living with one parent. In 1960, 91% of children under 18 lived with both their parents; by 2015, the figure had fallen to 69% (ProQuest Statistical Abstract, 2017; U.S. Bureau of the Census, 2011b). In fact, 8% of children who live with their mothers will witness three or more maternal partnerships (either marriage or cohabitation) by the time they reach 15 (Fustos, 2010a). The odds of growing up in a single-parent family (and not just because of divorce) are higher for some racial groups than for others (see Exhibit 7.6).

Although divorce can be traumatic for adults, most recover after a period of years. Children, however, have a more difficult time adjusting. For them, divorce may set a series of potentially disruptive changes in motion. They may have to move to a new home in a new neighborhood, make new friends, and go to a new school. Because the overwhelming majority of children of divorced parents live with their mothers (D. Newman, 2009), they often experience a decline in their standard of living. The earning capacity of women is generally lower than that of men to begin with. Furthermore, noncustodial fathers do not always pay child support. In 46% of divorces in which mothers have sole physical custody, fathers are required to pay child support (ProQuest Statistical Abstract, 2017). Of these, only 46% receive the full amount they are awarded, 28% receive partial payments, and 26% receive nothing. Hence, more than half of divorced mothers with custody of children don't receive all the financial assistance they have been granted.

The relationship that children have with their noncustodial parent also tends to deteriorate over time. Some research indicates that noncustodial fathers rarely see their children regularly or maintain close relationships with them (Furstenberg & Harris, 1992). What contact they do have with their children often diminishes over time (W. D. Manning & Smock, 1999). One study found that 75% of noncustodial fathers never attend their child's school events, 85% never help them with their homework, and 65% never take them on vacations (Teachman, 1991). Another found that fewer than one in five noncustodial fathers have a significant influence over their children's health care, education, religion, or other matters important to their welfare (Arendell, 1995).

What are the long-term effects of divorce on children? A substantial body of research shows that regardless of race or education of parents, children raised in single-parent homes have more problems at every stage of life than children from two-parent families. An extensive review of studies published during the 1990s found that children from divorced families fare worse in terms of academic success, psychological adjustment, self-concept, social competence, and long-term health than children from intact, two-parent families (Amato, 2000). When they reach adulthood, they are at greater risk of low socioeconomic attainment, increased marital difficulties, and divorce (Diekmann & Engelhardt, 1999).

These differences are typically attributed to factors such as the absence of a father, increased strain on the custodial parent to keep the household running, and emotional stress and anger associated with the separation. However, the causes of these problems

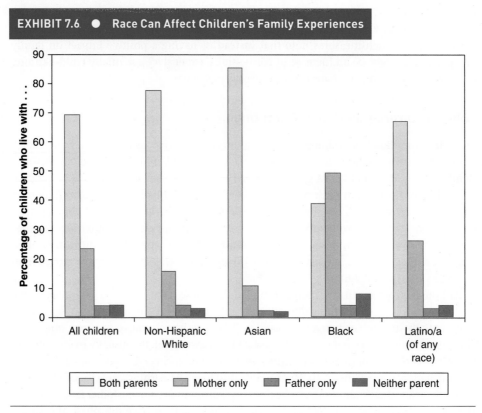

EXHIBIT 7.6 ● Race Can Affect Children's Family Experiences

Source: ProQuest Statistical Abstract, 2017, Table 67.

are just as likely to be factors found in two-parent families: low income, poor living conditions, lack of parental supervision, and marital discord (Amato & Sobolewski, 2001; Cherlin, 1992).

Some critics argue that the standard research design in studies on the impact of divorce on children—comparing children whose parents have divorced with children in happy, intact families—is flawed. Indeed, if we compare kids from divorced families with kids from intact families whose parents are unhappily married or whose families experience a great deal of conflict, we find that the type and frequency of emotional and interpersonal problems are similar for both sets of children (Cherlin et al., 1991). In fact, children who grow up in intact families marked by frequent conflict may actually suffer more. This research suggests that behavioral problems are caused not by the divorce itself but by exposure to conflict between the parents both before and after the divorce (A. J. Stewart, Copeland, Chester, Malley, & Barenbaum, 1997). In short, the simple fact of growing up in a single-parent family may not be as important in the development of a child as the way parents relate to each other and to the child.

Remarriage and Stepfamilies

Sixty four percent of divorced men and 52% of divorced women have remarried, and today 4 out of every 10 weddings involves at least one person who has been previously married (Livingston, 2014). This statistic suggests that although people are quite willing to escape a bad marriage, they have not necessarily given up on the concept of marriage entirely.

Although they are fairly common, remarriages are not without their difficulties. The divorce rate for remarriages is comparable to the rate for first marriages. In the United States, about 25% of remarriages end in divorce within 5 years, compared with 23% of first marriages (Bramlett & Mosher, 2002; Fustos, 2010a).

Remarriages may be somewhat unstable because the traditional roles, relationships, and norms of family don't apply. We have no institutionalized expectations for relationships between former and current spouses, between stepparents and stepchildren, between step- and half-siblings, and with extended kin (Ahrons & Rodgers, 1987). Laws and customs have been slow to catch up. For instance, do stepchildren have legal claims to their stepparents' property? Do incest rules apply to stepsiblings?

Remarriage is particularly difficult when children are involved. Although many stepparents build strong, durable, loving relationships with their partner's children, others face difficulties. When a new stepparent enters the formerly single-parent family, the entire system may be thrown out of balance. He or she may be seen as an outsider or, worse, an intruder. Stepsiblings may be asked to share bedrooms or other possessions. They may see their connection to their biological parent as giving them greater claim on that parent's affection and resources. Rules and habits change and, for a time, confusion, resentment, and hostility may be the norm. Conflict is common in all types of families, but conflict over issues such as favoritism, divided loyalties, the right to discipline, and financial responsibility is particularly likely in stepfamilies.

The high divorce rate of remarriages and the high levels of conflict that can occur within some stepfamilies are not simply an outgrowth of people's psychological inability to sustain intimate relationships, as some analysts have claimed. The fact that remarriages are not fully institutionalized makes them susceptible to difficulty. The lack of clear role definitions, the absence of established societal norms, and the increased complexity of the family structure itself increase the likelihood of tension and turmoil. Perhaps as we develop standard ways of defining and coping with reconstructed families, remarriage will become more institutionalized and less problematic. Until then, remarriage will continue to create a great deal of tension and confusion.

Family Violence

Ironically, relationships in families—with the people who are supposed to nourish us when the outside world has sucked away our life energy—can also be some of the most violent relationships in a society.

Intimate-Partner Violence

According to the World Health Organization, women everywhere face the greatest threat of violence in their own homes (Garcia-Moreno, Jansen, Ellsberg, Heise, & Watts, 2006). Worldwide, nearly one third of women who have been in a relationship have experienced physical and/or sexual violence at the hands of an intimate partner. The rates are highest in the low-income regions of Africa, the Middle East, and Southeast Asia (World Health Organization, 2013a). In some countries—Indonesia, Ghana, India, and Uganda, for instance—it's not unusual for female victims themselves to condone the violence against them. They are actually more likely than men to believe that it's acceptable for a husband to beat his wife if she argues with him or refuses to have sex with him (Population Reference Bureau, 2011).

Exact statistics about the prevalence of violence among intimates are notoriously difficult to collect. In the United States, domestic violence typically occurs in private, beyond the watchful eyes of relatives, neighbors, and strangers. Even with the more stringent rules for police reporting that have been instituted in the past decade or two, most incidents of domestic violence are never reported; others are dismissed as accidents. It's been estimated that only about half of the cases of nonlethal violence against women are reported to the police (Rennison & Welchans, 2000).

The statistics on intimate-partner abuse that *do* exist indicate that it is a widespread problem, although it has declined somewhat over the past two decades. According to the Centers for Disease Control and Prevention (2011), 36% of women—and 28% of men—in the United States have experienced violence, sexual assault, or stalking by a current or former spouse, boyfriend, girlfriend in their lifetimes and nearly half of all men and women have experienced psychological abuse. In addition, about 5% of men and 6% of women (or over 12 million individuals) report being victimized in the past 12 months. About 85% of intimate partner violence victims were women, and 76% of these women were previously victimized by the same offender (Catalano, 2012).

Tragically, intimate partner violence can sometimes be lethal. According to the FBI, about 2,000 people in the United States are killed by an intimate partner each year; two thirds of these victims are women (cited in Fox, 2012). Often these murders are not isolated incidents but are the culmination of a pattern of violence. For instance, one study found that almost half the women murdered by their intimate partners had visited the emergency room within the 2 years before they were killed (Crandall, Nathens, Kernic, Holt, & Rivara, 2004).

But women don't just suffer disproportionate physical consequences. Female victims of intimate violence are also more likely than male victims to suffer psychologically (e.g., from depression, anxiety, or low self-esteem) and socially (e.g., isolation from friends). The economic costs can be steep, too. It's estimated that intimate violence costs the country about $6 billion a year in direct costs (medical and mental health care) and indirect costs (lost productivity due to time away from work; cited in Harjani, 2013). Women who experience severe forms of abuse are also more likely than women who experience less serious forms of abuse to lose their jobs or to go on public assistance.

Although domestic violence between heterosexual partners gets most of the attention, same-sex couples are not immune to the problem. Indeed, same-sex intimate violence is as widespread as it is in heterosexual relationships. It's estimated that the lifetime prevalence of rape, physical violence, or stalking by an intimate partner is about 44% for lesbians and 26% for gay men (Walters, Chen, & Breiding, 2013). In fact, some researchers claim that more violence occurs in long-term homosexual relationships than in heterosexual relationships (Stiles-Shields & Carroll, 2014).

Child Abuse and Neglect

Children are even more likely to be victims of intimate violence than adult family members. In some poverty-stricken countries, children may be consigned to unpleasant and dangerous labor, sold to buy food for the rest of the family, or even murdered in infancy if their parents don't want them or can't afford them. In the United States, there were about 700,000 victims of some form of child maltreatment in 2014 (U.S. Department of Health and Human Services, 2015). About 75% of these children were victims of neglect, 17% were physically abused, and around 8% sexually abused. Because the vast majority of child abuse incidents involve victims who can't protect themselves or report the abuse and remain hidden from the police and social service agencies, many researchers think the actual figure is much higher. And if we take violence against children to mean any act of physical aggression directed by an adult toward a child—including spanking and slapping—perhaps as many as 9 of every 10 U.S. children under the age of 3 have been the object of violence, neglect, or verbal mistreatment by their parents or caretakers (Straus & Gelles, 1990).

Because of the small size of victims compared to their abusers, child abuse can sometimes be fatal. It's estimated that 1,580 children nationally died from abuse or neglect in 2014, and about 80% were killed by one or both parents. About 84% of these victims were 4 years old or younger at the time of their death (U.S. Department of Health and Human Services, 2015).

Intimate Violence in a Cultural Context

Individual-level factors such as frustration over money, stress, and alcohol and drug use are frequently cited as major causes of domestic violence. To some analysts, batterers are either psychopaths or people who are just plain prone to violence. Although it would be comforting to believe that domestic violence is rare and occurs only in families that harbor a "sick" partner, parent, or spouse, it actually happens with alarming frequency and is likely to be committed by people we would otherwise consider "normal." Intimate partner abuse and child abuse—not to mention abuse of elders and violence between siblings—occur in every culture, class, race, and religion. It is not an aberration; it is a fundamental characteristic of the way we relate to one another in private, intimate settings. So to fully understand domestic violence, we must take a look at some important characteristics of the society in which it occurs.

The United States is fundamentally committed to the use of violence to achieve desirable ends (Straus, 1977). For many people, violence is considered the appropriate means by which to resolve certain problems. Furthermore, violence pervades the culture. It is in our schools, our movies, our toy stores, our video games, our spectator sports, our government, and even our clothes. It's in our everyday language, too. How many times have you heard a parent "playfully" warn a misbehaving child that she or he is "cruisin' for a bruisin'"?

In addition to the pervasiveness of violence in the culture, families have several characteristics that increase the probability of conflict. For instance, we spend a lot of time with family members and interact with them across a wide range of situations. The intimacy of these interactions is intense. Emotions run deep. The anger we may feel toward a stranger or an acquaintance never approaches the intensity of the anger we feel toward a spouse—or for that matter, toward a sibling or a child.

Moreover, we also know more about family members than we know about other people in our lives. We know their likes and dislikes, their fears, and their desires. And they know these things about us, too. If someone in your family insults you, you know immediately what you can say to get even. Spouses usually know the "buttons" they can push to hurt or infuriate each other. Arguments can escalate into violence when one partner focuses on the other's vulnerabilities and insecurities.

Finally, family life contains endless sources of stress and tension. For one thing, we expect a lot from our families: emotional and financial support, warmth, comfort, and intimacy. When these expectations aren't fulfilled, stress levels escalate. Life circumstances also contribute to family tension (Gelles & Straus, 1988). The birth and raising of a child, financial problems, employment transitions, illness, old age, death, and so on are all events that potentially increase stress. Indeed, a pregnant or recently pregnant woman is more likely to be the victim of a homicide than to die of any other cause (Horon & Cheng, 2001).

And while intimate violence occurs in all types of relationships and across all genders, women are still more likely to be victimized than men. So we must also look at the broader conceptions of gender that exist within a society. Male dominance in human societies has a long and rather infamous history. Roman law, for instance, justified a husband's killing his wife for reasons such as adultery, wine drinking, and other so-called inappropriate behaviors (Steinmetz, Clavan, & Stein, 1990). Most societies in the world remain dominated by and built around the interests of men. Men typically occupy the high-status positions, make important decisions and exercise political power, tend to dominate interpersonal relationships, and occupy the roles society defines as most valuable (see Chapter 12).

Men who beat their partners are not necessarily psychotic, deranged, "sick" individuals. Rather, they are often men who believe that male dominance is their birthright. Such men are actually living up to cultural prescriptions that are cherished in many societies—aggressiveness, male dominance, and female subordination (Dobash & Dobash, 1979). We have a deeply entrenched tendency to perceive domestic violence as "normal"—as something that, although not necessarily desirable, is not surprising or unexpected, either. Consequently, much of the research in this area has focused on the victims rather than on the perpetrators.

Personal and Institutional Responses to Intimate Violence

One question that has captured the attention of many marriage and family researchers is why people, especially women, stay in abusive relationships in societies where divorce is readily available. During the 1960s, the *masochism thesis*—that is, that women like being humiliated and hurt—was the predominant reason offered by psychiatrists (see, e.g., L. Saul, 1972). Even today, many psychiatrists believe that women who stay in abusive relationships are suffering from some sort of diagnosable personality disorder. Other contemporary explanations focus on the woman's character flaws, such as a weak will or a pathological emotional attachment.

All these explanations focus on the individual victim while paying little attention to her social situation. From a conflict perspective, we can see that in a society reluctant to punish male abusers, many women may perceive that they have no alternatives and may feel physically, economically, and emotionally trapped in their relationships. Many of them leave, sometimes on several occasions, but find that the opportunities outside the relationship are not sufficient and end up returning (D. J. Anderson, 2003). Indeed, the broader economic structure conspires to keep vulnerable women in abusive relationships. Women who are unemployed and cannot support themselves financially are significantly less likely to leave an abusive marriage than women who are employed and who therefore have their own source of income (Strube & Barbour, 1983).

The perception that battered women simply sit back and take the abuse, thinking they somehow deserve it, is inaccurate. One study of 1,000 battered and formerly battered women nationwide found that they had tried a number of active strategies to end the violence directed against them (Bowker, 1993). They tried to talk men out of beating them, extracted promises that the men wouldn't batter them anymore, avoided their abuser or avoided certain volatile topics, hid or ran away, and even fought back. Many of these individual strategies had limited effectiveness, however, and so most of these battered women eventually turned to people outside the relationship for informal support, advice, and sheltering. From these informal sources, the women generally progressed to organizations in the community, such as the police, social service and counseling agencies, women's groups, and battered women's shelters. Some of these women were able, eventually, to end the violence; others weren't. In any case, as the study points out, most women actively try to end their victimization.

If women who are being victimized are reluctant to seek help or contact law enforcement, other professionals may get involved. For years, teachers and pediatricians have been trained to recognize the signs of abuse in the children they deal with. Today, people in various service occupations who come into contact with battered women during the course of their work are undergoing similar training. For instance, the state of Illinois recently enacted a new law that requires beauty salon workers to take a course every 2 years to help them recognize signs of abuse and assault in their customers. They will also be provided a list of resources so they can refer their customers for help. The law was driven by the observation that salons are "safe places" where women often drop their guard and confide in others about their life (Hauser, 2016).

It's important to keep in mind that leaving the relationship doesn't always end the violence. In fact, it may escalate it. One study found that victims who temporarily leave an abusive relationship suffer increased violence compared with those who never leave. Moreover, almost three quarters of visits battered women make to hospital emergency rooms occur after a separation (D. J. Anderson, 2003). About 90% of U.S. women who are killed by ex-husbands or ex-boyfriends were stalked prior to their murders (S. A. D. Moore, 2003).

In some cases, the social organizations and institutions that are designed to help battered women contribute to their inability to escape abuse. As recently as 30 years ago, for instance, emergency room workers routinely interviewed battered women about their injuries with their husbands present. The courts, too, historically treated spousal violence less seriously than other crimes, making it even more difficult for women to seek help. Even today, about 80% of domestic violence victims don't have lawyers to guide them through the legal process (Prah, 2006). Most states require that volunteers who work on domestic violence hotlines complete 40 to 50 hours of training, but no such training is required for police personnel, lawyers, and judges (Prah, 2006).

Sometimes the resources in place to assist battered women are simply inadequate. Several states have waiting lists of intimate violence victims in need of counseling. If shelters are filled—as is often the case—victims may have to be bused hundreds of miles away to a place where shelter is available. This remedy may get them out of harm's way, but it may also wreck their work lives, endanger welfare checks, take them away from the support of extended family and friends, and disrupt their children's schooling. Many women who walk away from abusive relationships are left with no place to live and no way to support themselves. Hence they sometimes end up homeless. In New York alone, more than a quarter of all people seeking shelter cite abuse as the cause of their plight (Navarro, 2014).

In sum, the decision to stay in an abusive relationship is the result not of irrationality or mental dysfunction but of rational choices women make in response to an array of conditions, including fear of and harassment by the abuser, the everyday realities of dependence, and the lack of institutional support (P. L. Baker, 1997). Broader societal circumstances may also play a role. In the months following the September 11, 2001, attacks, for instance, many battered women made the decision not to leave their relationships, clinging to familiar surroundings and coming to believe that a bad home was better than none in such unstable times. As a consequence, shelters reported dwindling demand for beds in their facilities in the immediate aftermath of the attacks (Lewin, 2001). In their need to acknowledge such realities, battered women are no different from any other individuals seeking to negotiate the complexities of social life.

Conclusion

Close relationships form the center of our personal universes. Life with intimates provides us with the sense of belonging that most of us need. However, although these relationships are the principal source of identity, community, happiness, and satisfaction for many, they can be the source of tremendous anguish and suffering for others.

Family, the most structured and culturally valued intimate relationship, is simultaneously a public and a private institution. True, most intimate and family behavior occurs away from the watchful eyes of others; we alone have access to our thoughts, desires, and feelings regarding those with whom we are intimately involved. But friends, neighbors, the government, and even society as a whole have a vested interest in what happens in our intimate lives.

The social institutions and culture that make up our society also shape the very nature and definition of "family." Today, the boundaries of that definition are being pushed by rapidly increasing numbers of what were once considered "nontraditional" families—dual-earner couples, single-parent households, unmarried cohabitors, same-sex married couples, and so on.

Every family relationship, whether it violates or conforms to current social norms, reflects the dominant ideals and beliefs regarding what a marriage or a family ought to look like. Although each relationship is unique, this uniqueness will always be bounded by the broader constraints of our cultural, group, and institutional values.

Your Turn

There is no universal definition of "family." Our ideas about what a family is depend on the culture we grew up in. Within a particular culture, people may also debate what a family is and which groups get to be defined as a family.

With so much disagreement, it would be interesting to find out how people actually define a family. Go to a spot on campus with a lot of foot traffic and ask passersby for their definition of the word *family*. See if you can find any patterns in people's responses. Do you see a tendency to focus on blood or legal relations, or is the emotional component of family more important? Do definitions of family require children?

To delve deeper into the diversity of family definitions and experiences, pose the following questions to several friends or classmates. You don't have to ask all of them or ask them exactly as they appear here. These are merely suggestions. You can add your own questions if you'd like. Try to acquire as diverse a sample of respondents as possible by talking to people from different cultural, racial, ethnic, religious, gender, and age groups:

- How do you define the word *family*?

- Did you live with both of your biological parents throughout your entire childhood? Prior to coming to college, did you spend any time living with one parent? Or neither parent? Explain the circumstances.

- How many brothers and sisters do you have? What are their ages? (Do you have any half-siblings? Step-siblings?)

- If any of your siblings are younger than you, did your parents/guardians expect you to help take care of them when they were little?

- Did you share a bedroom with any of your siblings while you were growing up?

- How many different homes did you live in while growing up (before coming to college)?

- Did you live in close proximity to any extended family (aunts, uncles, cousins, etc.)? Explain.

- Before coming to college, how often did you see your grandparents? How often do you see them now? How would you characterize the relationship you have with your grandparents?

- Did your grandparents or other relatives ever live in your house for an extended period of time?

- How would you characterize your family's treatment of delicate issues (e.g., sex, nudity around the house, etc.)?

- Who was primarily responsible for disciplining you when you got into trouble? What was the most common form of discipline?

- Do you expect to help financially support your parents when you are older?

Did you notice any interesting trends in people's responses? What do their answers say about the structure of their families? Did you find any consistent differences across cultural, gender, class, race, or age lines? For instance, does the likelihood of sharing a room with a sibling differ for people who grew up in different eras? Do members of different ethnic groups maintain different degrees of contact with grandparents or other relatives? Do age and class affect the likelihood of growing up with one or both parents? Do people have different expectations about supporting their parents in the future? What do these different responses tell us about the broader structural context within which we live our family lives?

Chapter Highlights

- In this culture, close relationships are the standard against which we judge the quality and happiness of our everyday lives. Yet in complex, individualistic societies, they are becoming more difficult to establish and sustain.

- Many people in the United States long for a return to the "golden age" of the family. But the image of the U.S. family of the past is largely a myth.

- Although monogamous marriage is the only sexual relationship that has achieved widespread cultural legitimacy in the United States, other forms of intimacy (e.g., extra- and premarital sex, polygamy) are considered legitimate in other societies.

- Although we like to think that the things we do in our family relationships are completely private experiences, they are continually influenced by large-scale political interests and economic pressures. Furthermore, our choices of romantic partners are governed to some degree by cultural rules that encourage us to form relationships within certain social groups and outside others.

- Divorce is not a solely private experience, either. It occurs within a cultural, historical, and community context. The high rate of remarriage after divorce indicates that people still view the institution of marriage as desirable.

- Instead of viewing domestic violence (spouse abuse and child abuse and neglect) as a product of "sick" individuals, sociologists are likely to view it as the product of a culture that tolerates violence in a variety of situations, traditionally grants men authority over women in family roles, and values family privacy and autonomy over the well-being of individual members.

Key Terms

endogamy: Marriage within one's social group

exogamy: Marriage outside one's social group

extended family: Family unit consisting of the parent–child nuclear family and other relatives, such as grandparents, aunts, uncles, and cousins

family: Two or more persons, including the householder, who

(Continued)

(Continued)

are related by birth, marriage, or adoption and who live together as one household

household: Living arrangement composed of one or more people who occupy a housing unit

monogamy: The practice of being married to only one person at a time

neolocal residence: Living arrangement in which a married couple sets up residence separate from either spouse's family

nuclear family: Family unit consisting of at least one parent and one child

polygamy: Marriage of one person to more than one spouse at the same time

SAGE edge™ edge.sagepub.com/newman12e

SAGE edge offers a robust online environment featuring an impressive array of free tools and resources for review, study, and further exploration, keeping both instructors and students on the cutting edge of teaching and learning.

8

Constructing Difference

Social Deviance

- Defining Deviance
- Explaining Deviant Behavior
- Linking Power, Deviance, and Social Control

In 1984, 22-year-old Kelly Michaels moved to New York to pursue her dream of becoming an actress. She was a mild-mannered, devout Catholic who loved children. To support herself, she began working at the Wee Care Preschool in a New Jersey suburb. By all accounts, the kids there loved her (Hass, 1995).

Two weeks after Michaels left Wee Care for a better-paying job at another preschool, a 4-year-old boy who was enrolled at Wee Care was taken to a doctor. A nurse rubbed his back and explained that she was going to take his temperature rectally. He said something like, "That's what teacher [Michaels] does to me at nap time." Although it was unclear exactly what he meant by this—Michaels sometimes rubbed children's backs to get them to sleep and did take their temperature with a plastic forehead strip—the boy's alarmed mother, who happened to be the daughter of a local judge, called the school and the police (Michaels, 1993). The police questioned the child, as well as other children at Wee Care, searching for evidence that Michaels had sexually abused them. As word spread of the investigation, worried parents phoned other parents to share stories about the latest allegations. The police encouraged parents to seek state-funded psychological help for themselves as well as their children. In turn, the therapists encouraged the parents to cooperate with authorities in investigating Michaels.

That casual comment made by one little boy in a doctor's office touched off a 16-month investigation by the Division of Youth and Family Services, which eventually ended in a 235-count indictment against Michaels. During the investigation, scores of parents became convinced that Michaels had raped their children with silverware, wooden spoons, Legos, and light bulbs; that she had played "Jingle Bells" on the piano while naked; and that she had licked peanut butter off children's genitals, made them drink her urine, and forced them to eat excrement off the floor (Hass, 1995). By the time the trial began, Kelly was already being called the "most hated woman in all of New Jersey."

From the start, the case was filled with a host of inconsistencies and questionable legal tactics. For instance, an analysis of interview transcripts found that investigators manipulated the children by introducing suggestive information, providing them with praise when they said things that implicated Kelly Michaels, expressing disbelief when they said good things about her, and inviting them to pretend or speculate about alleged events (Schreiber et al., 2006). Prosecutors never provided any substantiated evidence of abuse, yet they portrayed Michaels as "actressy" and "deviously charming." Everything she did was interpreted from the assumption that she was a "monster." For instance, if she was kind and patient with the children, that meant she was trying to seduce them.

None of the other teachers at the day care center had heard or seen anything, even though most of the alleged abuse supposedly took place during the children's naptime in a room set off only by a plastic curtain. The judge in the trial allowed the children to testify on closed circuit TV while seated on his lap and denied the defense attorneys the opportunity to cross-examine them. One of the prosecution's witnesses—a child therapist—testified that the children who denied being molested by Ms. Michaels suffered from something called "child sexual abuse accommodation syndrome," a psychological condition that made them deny the abuse. In fact, the more the children denied it, the more certain the child therapist was that the abuse had actually happened.

After 13 days of deliberation, the jury found Michaels guilty of 115 counts of assault, sexual abuse, and terrorist threats against 19 children between the ages of 3 and 5 and sentenced her to 47 years in prison. As if to add insult to injury, while in prison she received a bill from the Essex County public defenders office charging her $800,000 in legal fees (L. Manning, 2007). In 1993, after she had spent 5 years in prison—including an 18-month stint in solitary confinement ostensibly for her own protection—a state appellate court overturned the conviction. Later, the New Jersey Supreme Court upheld the appellate court's decision, decrying the original conviction with outrage. The court wrote that all the children who testified against Michaels had been led, bribed, or threatened (Hass, 1995).

You might think that a formal declaration of innocence from such a powerful body as a state supreme court would change people's feelings about Kelly Michaels. Yet she remained a target of hate. Several civil suits were filed against Michaels by parents who still believed their children had been sexually abused. One mother said she would try to kill Michaels with her bare hands if she had the chance. To date, no Wee Care parents have ever publicly retracted their accusations against their child's former teacher (L. Manning, 2007).

Why was it so hard for people to admit that Michaels was innocent? For one thing, at a time when child molestation was becoming a national obsession, the case reflected our darkest collective fears. The terrifying message was that our children could be hurt not only by creepy, middle-aged men but also by seemingly safe, 22-year-old college women. In the frenzy over children's safety, no one seemed willing to protect the principle that a defendant is presumed innocent until proven guilty.

Even more striking about this case is what it says about the way people think. Once members of the community concluded that Kelly Michaels had committed these horrible acts, no amount of conflicting evidence was going to sway them to believe otherwise. Deviant labels and what they imply in people's minds can overshadow everything else about that person. When Michaels was convicted and formally tagged a criminal, the public degradation acquired legal legitimacy. From that point on, she would never again be able to reclaim a normal life and in many people's minds would forever be a "child molester." Long after Michaels's conviction on sexual abuse charges had been overturned, the media continued to identify her as a criminal. An Associated Press news release about her thwarted attempt to sue the county and the state was titled "Sex Offender's Case Denied in Court" (2001).

Few of us have spent 5 years in prison as a wrongly convicted child molester. But people are unjustifiably tagged as deviant all the time. Perhaps there have been times in your life when you acquired some sort of unflattering but inaccurate reputation that you couldn't shed. In this chapter, I examine several questions related to this phenomenon: What is deviance? How does society attempt to control deviant behavior? Who gets to define what is and is not deviant? And what are the consequences of being identified by others as deviant?

Defining Deviance

In its broadest sense, **deviance** is socially disapproved behavior—the violation of some agreed-on norm that prevails in a community or in society at large. Staring at a stranger in an elevator, talking to oneself in public, wearing outlandish clothes, robbing a bank, setting off two bombs at the finish line of the world's most famous marathon, and methodically shooting hundreds of concert-goers from the window of a high-rise Las Vegas hotel can all be considered deviant acts. If we define deviance simply as any norm violation, then most deviance is rather trivial—even "normal"—like driving over the speed limit or walking across an intersection when the light is red. Most of us, at some point in our lives, occupy statuses or engage in behaviors that others could regard as deviant. But most sociologists focus on deviant acts that are assaults on mores, the most serious of a society's norms. It's this type of deviance to which I will devote most of my attention in this chapter.

The determination of which behaviors or characteristics are deviant and which are normal is more complex than you'd think. We usually assume there's a fair amount of agreement in a society about what and who is deviant. For instance, no one would challenge the notion that child abuse is bad and that child abusers ought to be punished. But the level of agreement within a given society over what specific acts constitute child abuse can vary tremendously. Spanking may be a perfectly acceptable method of discipline to one person but be considered a cruel form of abuse by another.

To further complicate the issue, some sociologists who are identified with structural functionalism (e.g., Durkheim, 1895/1958; Erikson, 1966) argue that deviance, as a class of behaviors, is not always bad for society and may actually serve a useful purpose. As you recall from Chapter 4, norm violations help define the cultural and moral boundaries that distinguish right from wrong and increase feelings of in-group togetherness among those who unite in opposition to deviance from group norms. At the surface level, individual acts of deviance disrupt everyday life and generate varying degrees of social condemnation, but at a deeper level, they can contribute to the maintenance and continuity of society. Deviance can also create needed change (Durkheim, 1895/1958). During the 1950s and 1960s, civil rights protestors purposely disobeyed laws they considered discriminatory, such as those that prevented Blacks from entering certain establishments or attending certain schools. These acts of deviance eventually helped convince many voters and politicians to support legislation ending legal segregation.

As you may have guessed, sociologists usually don't judge whether a given behavior should or shouldn't be considered deviant. Instead, they examine how deviance comes about and what it means to society. One of their primary concerns is whether people respond to deviance from the perspective that all human behavior can be classified as essentially good or bad (absolutism) or from the perspective that definitions of deviance are socially constructed (relativism).

Absolutist Definitions of Deviance

According to **absolutism**, there are two fundamental types of human behavior: (1) that which is inherently proper and good and (2) that which is intrinsically improper, immoral, evil, and bad. To those who subscribe to such a position, the distinction is clear and identifiable. The rightness or wrongness of an act exists prior to humanly created rules, norms, and customs and independently of people's subjective judgments (Erich Goode, 1994).

Absolutist definitions of deviance are often accompanied by strong emotional reactions toward those considered deviant. Speaking about the issue of same-sex marriage (over a decade before the U.S. Supreme Court legalized it), the televangelist Jimmy Swaggart once expressed these sentiments:

> I'm trying to find the correct name for it, . . . this utter absolute, asinine, idiotic stupidity of men marrying men. . . . I've never seen a man in my life I wanted to marry. And I'm gonna be blunt and plain; if one ever looks at me like that, I'm gonna kill him and tell God he died. (Brutally Honest, 2004, p. 1)

Such extreme reactions might seem at odds with what appears today to be a growing cultural acceptance of LGBT people. Homosexuals, for instance, have gone from being criminalized and closeted in the 1960s to being granted the right to legally marry in all 50 states in 2015. There are more openly gay characters on television—most notably on shows like *Orange Is the New Black, Grace and Frankie,* and *Modern Family*—than ever before. The NBA player Jason Collins made headlines in 2013 when he disclosed his homosexuality, becoming the first male athlete in a major team sport to come out while still an active player. Fifty-six openly gay, bisexual, or transgender athletes competed in the 2016 Summer Olympics (Outsports, 2016). In addition, nearly two thirds of Americans say homosexuality should be accepted by society and less than 30% say it should be discouraged (Fingerhut, 2016). Gay couples appear in mainstream advertisements for products ranging from e-readers to painkillers. Major cruise lines, tour companies, and hotel chains offer (and openly advertise) vacation packages for gay, lesbian, bisexual, and transgender travelers. Marketing researchers estimate that the annual economic impact of LGBT travelers is around $70 billion a year (Rosenbloom, 2014). In 2015, the World Economic Forum addressed global gay and lesbian rights, the first time this issue has ever been a part of the organization's formal agenda.

A recent nationwide survey found that an overwhelming share of lesbian, gay, and bisexual people (92%) say that society has become more accepting of them in the past decade. About the same proportion expect such acceptance to grow even more in the next decade (Pew Research Center, 2013a). In 2015, a New Jersey court ruled that groups offering "gay conversion therapy"—an intervention program designed to "cure" men of their homosexual urges—violated the state's Consumer Fraud Act and could no longer be practiced (Eckholm, 2015b).

Yet many people still see homosexuals and transgender people as absolutely deviant. According to the International Lesbian and Gay Association, 2.7 billion people today live in countries where homosexuality is a crime punishable by imprisonment, beatings, or even death (cited in Ball, 2014). Consider these examples:

- In 2012, legislators in the Ukraine introduced a bill that would make it a crime punishable by imprisonment for producers of television shows and movies to depict homosexuals sympathetically ("Ukraine Bill Proposes Prison," 2012).

- In Nigeria, people who "directly or indirectly" make a "public show" of same sex relationships, participate in gay clubs, societies, and organizations, or who simply support those organizations can be thrown into prison for as long as 10 years (Nossiter, 2014).

- In 2017, two Indonesian men were sentenced to public lashing for having sex with each other. The men received 85 lashes rather than the maximum of 100 because they renounced their actions (Emont, 2017).

- Afghanistan, Iran, Mauritania, Nigeria, Oman, Qatar, Saudi Arabia, Somalia, Sudan, and Yemen have a statutory death penalty for homosexuality (Cameron & Berkowitz, 2016).

- A few years ago, the Sultan of Brunei signed into law a new penal code that prescribes death by stoning for gay sex (M. Garcia, 2014).

Closer to home, lesbian, gay, bisexual and transgender individuals in the United States still face many obstacles stemming from absolutist attitudes:

- Now that same-sex marriage is legal, gay couples who obtain a public marriage license in a state that doesn't provide nondiscrimination protection could still be at risk in other aspects of their lives. In 15 states, gays and lesbians lack virtually any explicit legal protections in areas such as job protection, establishing credit, housing, and even parenting (T. S. Bernard, 2015; Human Rights Campaign, 2017b). For instance, state, not federal, laws determine who is and who can be a parent. In some states, adoption agencies are prohibited from discriminating on the basis of sexual orientation. But other states have laws that create religious exemptions for adoption providers, allowing agencies to refuse placement in situations that violate the groups' religious beliefs. That means gay couples can be respected and protected as parents in one state, and be complete legal strangers to their children in another. As one woman put it, "We won marriage, and people thought the fight was over. But having to adopt your own child feels way more invasive, upsetting, and disturbing (quoted in E. A. Harris, 2017, p. 7).

- The workplace also remains a perilous place for gays and lesbians. According to the Human Rights Campaign (2014a; 2017a), 91% of Fortune 500 companies provide explicit nondiscrimination protections based on sexual orientation and 82% provide such protections to transgender employees. But corporate policies don't always translate into individual behavior. In many areas of the labor force, open homosexuality is still considered a liability. Despite the corporate protections, over half of gay, lesbian, and bisexual employees nationwide hide their sexual orientation at work and 35% lie about it. And one in four open LGBT employees feel that coworkers become uncomfortable when the topic of sexual orientation comes up or report hearing negative comments about LGBT people at work (Human Rights Campaign, 2014b).

- In the past several years, legislators in at least 25 states have proposed more than 100 bills limiting LGBT rights (Surowiecki, 2016). Some of these laws (called "Religious Restoration Acts") allow business owners to deny service to gays and lesbians if such actions impose a "substantial burden" on their religious beliefs. As one Oklahoma state senator put it, "[Homosexuals] don't have the right to be served in every single store. People need to have the ability to refuse service if it violates their religious convictions" (quoted in Fausset & Blinder, 2015, p. A18).

- In December of 2015, the Food and Drug Administration lifted its lifetime ban on blood donations from all gay and bisexual men (McNeil, 2015). This policy was first instituted in 1983, in the early days of the AIDS crisis before tests for HIV in donated blood, which could easily identify the presence of the virus, became standard. However, the FDA will continue to prohibit donation of blood from gay and bisexual men who have had sex with another man within the past 12 months. Hence, an HIV-negative, married, monogamous, gay man would have to abstain from sex with his spouse for 1 year to be eligible to donate blood.

- In 2013, the Boy Scouts of America ended its ban on openly gay youths participating in its activities; in 2015, it ended its ban on openly gay troop leaders. However, the organization continues to bar transgender boys from joining. In 2016, an 8-year-old New Jersey boy was kicked out of his Cub Scout pack a month after joining because he was transgender (Victor, 2016b).

Absolutist definitions of deviance imply something about society's relationship with the person who is considered deviant. Many people consider "deviants" to be psychologically, and perhaps even anatomically, different from ordinary, rule-abiding people. The attribute or behavior that serves as the basic reason for defining a person as deviant in the first place is considered pervasive and essential to his or her entire character (Hills, 1980). Respectable, conventional qualities become insignificant. It doesn't matter, for instance, that the "sexual deviant" has an otherwise ordinary life, that the "drug addict" no longer uses drugs, or that the violent act of the "wife batterer" was completely atypical of the rest of his life. In short, the deviant act or trait determines the overall worth of the individual (Katz, 1975). Being defined as deviant means being identified as someone who cannot and should not be treated as an ordinary member of society.

There's another element of unfairness involved in the absolutist approach to deviance. People routinely make judgments about deviants based on strongly held stereotypes. If you ask someone to imagine what a typical drug addict looks like, for instance, chances are she or he will describe a dirty, poor, strung-out young man living on the streets and resorting to theft to support his illegal habit. The image probably wouldn't be one of a middle-class, stay-at-home mother or hardworking businessperson hooked on prescription painkillers, even though these groups constitute a higher percentage of drug addicts than any other in U.S. society (Pfohl, 1994).

Absolutist images of deviants are often oversimplified and fall short of accounting for every individual. The vast majority of African Americans do not commit crimes, just as the vast majority of Latino/as are not in gangs, the vast majority of Italians are not involved in the Mafia, and the vast majority of Muslims are not terrorists. Nevertheless, the degree to which an entire group is characterized by an absolutist stereotype is important, because it determines individual and societal responses. If affluent housewives and businesspeople who abuse drugs are not considered typical drug addicts, they will never be the focus of law enforcement attention, collective moral outrage, political rhetoric, or public policy.

Furthermore, sometimes more pressing business concerns can override absolutist positions on a particular form of deviance. In 2016, executives at more than 80 companies—including Apple, Microsoft, and Marriott—signed a public letter condemning laws that discriminated against lesbian, gay, bisexual, and transgender people. When Georgia's state legislature passed a law allowing commercial businesses to discriminate against gays and lesbians under the cloak of protecting religious freedom, Disney said it would stop making movies in the state. Coca-Cola and Google issued similar threats. It was estimated that the state would have lost $1 billion if the bill became law (Blinder & Robertson, 2016). The governor vetoed it. When Citigroup and Wells Fargo opposed a similar law in South Dakota, the governor there vetoed it as well. (Surowiecki, 2016).

Relativist Definitions of Deviance

Reliance on a strict absolutist definition of deviance can lead to narrow and often inaccurate perceptions of many important social problems. This shortcoming can be avoided by employing a second approach to defining deviance, **relativism**, which draws from symbolic interactionism and the conflict perspective. This approach—which parallels the more general "cultural relativism" discussed in Chapter 4—states that deviance is not inherent in any particular act, belief, or condition; instead, it is socially constructed, a creation of collective human judgments and ideas. Like beauty, it is in the eye of the beholder. Consequently, no act is universally or "naturally" deviant. The relativist approach is useful when the focus of study is the process by which some group of people or some type of behavior is defined as deviant.

For the relativist, complex societies consist of different groups with different values and interests. Sometimes these groups agree and cooperate to achieve a common goal, as when different segments of society join together to fight a foreign enemy. But more often than not there is conflict and struggle among groups to realize their own interests and goals.

Different people or groups can thus have dramatically different interpretations of the same event. In 1995, a 35-year-old white ex-Marine named William Masters was taking his usual armed, late-night walk through a barren neighborhood in Los Angeles. He came upon two young Latino men spray painting graffiti beneath a freeway overpass. Masters wrote down the license number of their car on a small piece of paper. When the men saw him and demanded the paper, Masters pulled out his 9-millimeter pistol and shot them, wounding one and killing the other. He told the police that the men had threatened him with a screwdriver and he had acted in self-defense, even though both were shot in the back. He was not charged with murder. Eventually, he was found guilty on one count of carrying a concealed gun in public and one count of carrying a loaded gun in public—charges that carried a maximum of 18 months in jail and a $2,000 fine.

Shortly after his arrest, Masters made a case for why his actions shouldn't be defined as deviant. He told one interviewer he was sure people were glad that he, the intended victim, had gotten away and that no jury would ever convict him (Mydans, 1995). Many people agreed. Callers to radio talk shows and letters to newspapers applauded him for his vigilant antigraffiti efforts and for his foresight in carrying a weapon for self-protection. A few suggested that society would be better off with more people like William around (Mydans, 1995). But others expressed dismay at the verdict and argued that Masters was simply a racist out looking for trouble. They felt he was a deviant who literally got away with murder.

All those who expressed opinions on this case would likely agree on one thing: "Murder" is a deviant act at the far end of the spectrum of social acceptability. However, their perceptions of whether William Masters was a "murderer" were quite different. Was he a "hero" or a "killer"? The answer lies not in the objective act of purposely taking another's life but in the way others define and respond to such an act.

To fully understand the societal and personal implications of deviance designations, we must look at how these definitions are created and perpetuated. One key factor to consider is who is doing the defining. One person's crime is another person's act of moral conscience; one group's evil is another group's virtue; one culture's terrorist is another culture's freedom fighter.

Definitions of deviance are also relative to particular cultural standards:

- In Singapore, a young vandal is a serious deviant (punishable by caning), as is a person who leaves chewed gum where it can be stepped on. The fine for bringing one stick of gum into Singapore is $10,000.

- In Thailand, it is illegal to step on a *baht*, the nation's currency, or insult the king in any way.

- In Malaysia, a Muslim woman can be whipped for drinking alcohol in public or arrested for snacking during the daylight fasting hours of Ramadan.

- In some Indonesian cities, it is illegal for women to straddle motorbikes or hold on to a male driver while riding on the back of one.

- In Japan, a drunk driving conviction carries the possibility of a 3- to 5-year prison sentence, depending on the level of intoxication, and passengers who either provide the alcohol or provide the vehicle face criminal charges as well.

Deviance definitions undergo changes over time as well. For instance, in Great Britain, some laws that were established as far back as the 13th century are only now being repealed. Among them are statutes that prohibit the firing of a cannon within 300 yards of a dwelling and the beating of a carpet in public (Castle, 2015). In the United States, several states at one time had laws designed specifically to protect women's virtue. Florida had a law that prohibited women from parachuting on Sundays. Michigan law made it a crime for men to use profanity in front of women. In Texas, it was a crime for women to adjust their stockings in public. The state of Washington still has a law on the books that makes it illegal to call a woman a "hussy" or "strumpet" in public (Kershaw, 2005).

The absolutist approach assumes that certain individual characteristics are typical of all deviants, but the relativist approach acknowledges that there is no typical deviant. In fact, the same act committed by two different people may yield very different community responses. In 1980, a Bayonne, New Jersey, teacher named Diane Cherchio was caught kissing and groping a 13-year-old male student at an eighth-grade dance. A few years later, after being promoted to guidance counselor, she had sex with an 11th grader, became pregnant, and eventually married him upon his high school graduation in 1985. Yet instead of being fired or even reprimanded, she was allowed to continue working in the public school district for two decades. When the son she gave birth to grew to be a teenager, Ms. Cherchio began having sex with one of his friends. She used her school authority to rearrange the boy's schedule so they had time for their sexual trysts. When that boy's parents found out and complained to the police, she was arrested. Again, she was not fired. School officials instead allowed her to take an early retirement package that increased her pension. They even gave her a gala farewell party. When she finally pled guilty to sexual assault charges in 2005, glowing references from coworkers convinced the judge to sentence her to probation and to spare her from registering as a sex offender (Kocieniewski, 2006).

Cherchio was eventually punished, as have been other older women who've had sexual relationships with teenage boys. Nevertheless, it's hard to imagine a school accommodating or defending a male teacher who seduced teenage girls in such a way. Because she was a young, attractive, intelligent woman whose victims were willing teenage boys, people in her community looked the other way. When *she* did it, somehow it wasn't so bad. One author summed up the public response to such incidents: "A teenage boy who gets to live his fantasy? What can be the harm?" (Levy, 2006, p. 2).

From a relativist approach, immediate situational circumstances, such as the time and location of an act, can also influence definitions of deviance. For example, drinking alcohol on the weekend is more acceptable than drinking during the week, and drinking in the evening is more acceptable than drinking in the morning. Twenty-four states have "stand your ground" laws, which justify deadly force if people feel threatened not just in their home but in any other place they have "a right to be" (Currier, 2012). Had William Masters lived in any of these places instead of Los Angeles, he wouldn't have faced even minor criminal charges; he would have simply been a citizen exercising his legal right. These laws came under national scrutiny in 2012 when an unarmed Florida teenager named Trayvon Martin was gunned down on a Sanford, Florida, sidewalk by a neighborhood watch captain who claimed he felt threatened by the boy and was acting in self-defense. A jury agreed, finding the man not guilty of the second-degree murder charge he faced.

If deviance is relative, then even acts of extreme violence may be defined as acceptable under certain circumstances. Killings committed under the auspices of the government—shooting looters during a riot, killing enemy soldiers during wartime, or executing convicted murderers—fall outside the category of behaviors deemed deviant and problematic in society. However, a relativist approach to defining deviance doesn't mean that we can't be upset by activities that some people consider acceptable:

> Relativity does not require moral indifference, and it does not mean that one can never be . . . horrified by what one experiences in another group or culture. . . . [It] just reminds us that our personal beliefs or our cultural understandings are not necessarily found everywhere. (Curra, 2000, p. 13)

Relativists, like absolutists, acknowledge that every society identifies certain individuals and certain behaviors as bothersome and disruptive and therefore as justifiable targets of social control, whether through treatment, punishment, spiritual healing, or correction. However, to a relativist the main concerns in defining deviance are not so much what is committed but rather who commits the act, who labels it, and where and when it occurs. Some people have the wherewithal to avoid having their acts defined as deviant; others may fit a certain profile and be defined as deviant even if they've done nothing wrong. Definitions of deviant behavior change over time, and certain acts are acceptable to some groups and not others. The definitions most likely to persevere and become part of the dominant culture are those that have the support of influential segments of the population or have widespread agreement among the members of that society.

The Elements of Deviance

The two perspectives on defining deviance raise some complex and controversial issues. The definition of deviance most applicable to both perspectives is this: behavior (how people act), ideas (how people think), or attributes (how people appear) that some people in society—though not necessarily all people—find offensive, wrong, immoral, sinful, evil, strange, or disgusting.

VISUAL ESSAY—HOMOPHOBIA AROUND THE WORLD

REUTERS/Maxim Shemetov

Isaac Kasamani/AFP/Getty Images

REUTERS/Adnan Abidi

AP Photo/David McFadden

Given that same-sex marriage is now legal and gender nonconformity in popular culture and in everyday life is more visible than ever before, it's tempting to think that people in the United States no longer consider nonheterosexual identities to be deviant. But this is not yet the case. Many people continue to oppose same-sex marriage and many states still allow workplace discrimination based on sexual orientation.

It's even worse in some other countries where homosexuality is not only considered deviant, it is a crime punishable by death. Here we see images of anti-gay violence (in Ukraine) and anti-gay protests in India, Uganda, and Jamaica.

Is it a government's responsibility to define some forms of sexual expression as acceptable and other forms as deviant? If yes, what is the overriding societal interest in legitimizing some Intimate relationships and delegitimizing—or even criminalizing—others? With the concepts of absolutism and relativism in mind, consider whether or not a foreign government or international agency (such as the United Nations) ought to step in and protect the rights of gays and lesbians who are being persecuted in other countries.

This definition has three important elements (Aday, 1990):

- *An expectation:* Some sort of behavioral expectation must exist, a norm that defines appropriate, acceptable behavior, ideas, or characteristics. The expectations may be implicit or explicit, formal or informal, and more or less widely shared.

- *A violation:* Deviance implies some violation of normative expectations. The violation may be real or alleged; that is, an accusation of wrongdoing may be enough to give someone the reputation of being a deviant.

- *A reaction:* An individual, group, or society must react to the deviance. The reaction can take several forms: avoidance, criticism, warnings, punishment, or treatment. It may accurately reflect the facts, or it may bear little relation to what really happened, as when people are punished or ostracized for acts they did not commit.

Deviance, then, cannot exist if people don't have some idea of what's appropriate, if someone hasn't been perceived as or accused of violating some social norm, and if others haven't reacted to the alleged transgression.

MICRO-MACRO CONNECTION
SEXUAL ABUSE AND THE CLERGY

Some waves of deviance are considered so horrible that they fundamentally change previously positive perceptions of the individuals and institutions involved. In 2002, the *Boston Globe* published a story about a Catholic priest who had sexually molested children in six Boston parishes between 1962 and 1993 (cited in Jost, 2002). It wasn't the first time such behavior had received media or Church attention. For decades, stories about priests sexually abusing children had periodically popped up in the press.

What gave the 2002 *Boston Globe* story unusual impact was that it focused on the Church's handling of sexual abuse allegations over the years. In the past, priests had routinely been allowed to remain in their posts despite repeated accusations and even admissions of sexual misconduct. In other cases, the Church quietly reassigned abusive priests to different parishes. The 2002 story pointed out that Church officials had known of this particular priest's behavior since 1984, 9 years before he was finally removed from his last parish. Further investigation revealed that the Archdiocese of Boston had quietly settled suits against 70 priests over the preceding decade, often stipulating that in exchange for financial settlement, the victims were not to discuss the cases publicly (Jost, 2002). Under mounting public pressure, the Boston archdiocese agreed to

give prosecutors the names of 100 other priests who had been accused of sexual molestation.

Eventually, similar stories began appearing all over the country. Since that first newspaper story was published, over 5,000 priests have faced accusations of sexual abuse (U.S. Conference of Catholic Bishops, 2011) and about 3,400 have either been defrocked or subject to lesser punishment (Child Rights International Network, 2014). The majority of victims (51%) were between the ages of 11 and 14 at the time of the abuse, and 81% were male (Terry, 2004). Often the most vulnerable children made the easiest victims. One Wisconsin priest molested as many as 200 deaf boys from the 1950s to the 1970s.

Reports of clergy sexual abuse began to surface in other countries, too, like Canada, New Zealand, and Great Britain. A government commission in Ireland found that between 1930 and 1990, thousands of children were sexually abused by Catholic priests in orphanages and reform schools (Jordan, 2009). In 2013, the Catholic Church in Germany released a report indicating that abusive priests had carefully planned their assaults on children and frequently abused the same children over a span of several years (Eddy, 2013). And in 2017, the scandal finally reached the Vatican when Cardinal George Pell, a close adviser to

(Continued)

(Continued)

Pope Francis, faced multiple charges of sexual abuse stemming from his days as a local priest in Australia. What many had hoped was an isolated problem of a few individual bad priests has now become a full-scale, international scandal.

One sociologically interesting element of clergy sexual abuse is that it clearly shows the limitations of relying on absolute stereotypes about what "deviants" look like. If there is any profession that fails to fit the image of "deviance," it's the clergy. Priests—not to mention ministers, nuns, rabbis, and imams—are often the most respected individuals in their communities. Most of them are able to credibly preach against sin and extol a virtuous life. Like Kelly Michaels or even Diane Cherchio, they don't fit the stereotype of the sleazy, drooling "child molester."

So it's no surprise that there wasn't much of an institutional response or even considerable public outrage when allegations of clergy abuse were reported decades ago. Even today when such charges are substantiated, the collective response tends to be that these were "sick" priests, glaring exceptions to the stereotype of the clergy as benevolent shepherds. In 2010, the Vatican secretary of state, Cardinal Tarcisio Bertone, linked the sexual abuse to the "pathological" homosexuality of a few wayward priests (Donadio, 2010a). They were troubled individuals who, with enough compassion and psychiatric treatment, could change their ways. One church official in the 1960s even put a down payment on a Caribbean island that he planned to use as a retreat to sequester sexually predatory priests (Goodstein, 2009). Interestingly, however, according to a massive 5-year study of the scandal commissioned by the U.S. Conference of Catholic Bishops (2011), less than 5% of abusive priests exhibited behavior consistent with a psychiatric diagnosis of pedophilia. In other words, this phenomenon is not simply a matter of a few "bad apples."

Consequently, these kinds of "sympathetic" responses to abusive priests have drawn widespread public outrage as more and more charges of institutional deception and cover-ups continue to surface. In 2011, a Kansas City bishop was indicted for his failure to report suspected abuse, marking the first time the leader of a diocese was held criminally responsible for the actions of a priest he supervised (Sulzberger & Goodstein, 2011). In fact, for years, the Church has been fighting state legislatures around the country to beat back victim-supported attempts to lengthen or abolish the statute of limitations in sex abuse cases

(Goodstein & Eckholm, 2012). The scandal has created an ongoing calamity within the Church that pits those who support the traditional approach of protecting bishops and priests above all else against those calling for more openness and accountability (Donadio, 2010b). While these internal battles rage, devout Catholics have found their everyday lives shattered and their faith in their Church challenged. As one theologian put it,

> This is the greatest crisis in the modern history of the Catholic Church. It raises serious questions about the integrity of its priesthood, and the Catholic Church just can't function without a priesthood that has the support and trust of its people. (quoted in Jost, 2002, p. 395)

The financial fallout from this scandal has been steep. By 2015, the U.S. Catholic Church had paid out over $4 billion in victim compensation (Ruhl & Ruhl, 2015). In addition to monetary settlements, nearly one third of U.S. Catholics in a nationwide survey said they had withheld weekly monetary offerings to the Church in the wake of the scandal (cited in Mulrine, 2003). With shrinking financial support, several dioceses around the country have been forced to close down churches. In the past decade, 11 U.S. dioceses and 2 religious orders have filed for bankruptcy protection (J. L. Thomas, 2014).

Victims' advocacy groups continue to put pressure on the Church to adopt a "zero tolerance" policy. As a result, changes have occurred in the way the Church deals with the problem. Proven perpetrators are now removed from ministry, and church personnel are trained to detect and investigate abuse allegations (T. D. Lytton, 2007). In 2002, the U.S. Conference of Catholic Bishops drafted the *Charter for the Protection of Children and Young People*, which requires churches to implement "safe environment" programs designed to ensure the security of all children as they participate in church and religious activities. In 2014, Pope Francis publicly declared clergy sexual abuse "a leprosy in our house" (quoted in Pullella, 2014, p. 1).

When there are only a few cases of deviance, they're easy to dismiss as individual anomalies. However, when they occur by the thousands, all across the world and in a variety of settings, they come to represent a glaring problem at the institutional level and thus become more likely to provoke serious societal reaction.

Explaining Deviant Behavior

The question of how certain acts and certain people come to be defined as deviant is different from the question of why people do or don't commit acts that are considered deviant. Psychological or biological theories addressing this question might focus on the personality or physical characteristics that give rise to deviant behavior, such as psychological proneness to violence or addiction, genetic predispositions, chemical imbalances, or neurological defects. Most sociological theories, however, focus on the environmental forces that act upon people and the effectiveness of various methods to control them.

The structural-functionalist perspective, for instance, tells us that it is in society's interest to socialize everyone to strive for success so that the most able and talented people will come to occupy the most important positions. Sociologist Robert Merton's "strain theory" (1957) argues that the probability of committing deviant acts increases when people experience a strain or contradiction between these culturally defined success goals and access to legitimate means by which to achieve them. The despair and hopelessness that accompany sudden economic hardship can sometimes evoke anger and blame, leading to violence. Some criminologists noted an unprecedented spike in mass murders in 2009 during the height of the economic recession. For instance, in the span of one month, there were eight mass murders that took the lives of 57 people (cited in Rucker, 2009).

More commonly, though, those who believe that being wealthy and achieving the "American dream" are important goals but have no money, employment opportunities, or access to higher education will be inclined to achieve the goal of financial success through illegitimate means (Merton, 1957). One of the most consistent findings in criminal research is the correlation between unemployment (a factor closely associated with economic disadvantage) and property crime (Hagan, 2000). In this sense, people who sell, say, illegal drugs or stolen cell phones to get rich are motivated by the same desire as people who sell real estate or flat-screen TVs to get rich. But people who lack access to legitimate means to achieve success may also reject the culturally defined goal of success and retreat from society altogether. According to Merton, deviants such as vagrants, chronic drunks, drug addicts, and the mentally ill fall into this category.

Another sociologist, Edwin Sutherland, bases his theory of deviance (Sutherland & Cressey, 1955) on the symbolic interactionist principle that we all interpret life through the symbols and meanings we learn in our interactions with others. Sutherland argues that individuals learn deviant patterns of behavior from the people with whom they associate on a regular basis: friends, family members, peers. Through our associations with these influential individuals, we learn not only the techniques for committing deviant acts (e.g., how to pick a lock or how to snort cocaine) but also a set of beliefs and attitudes that justify or rationalize such behavior (Sykes & Matza, 1957). To commit deviant acts on a regular basis, we must learn how to perceive those acts as normal.

Deterring Deviance

Some sociologists have turned away from the issue of why some people violate norms to the issue of why most people don't (see, e.g., Hirschi, 1969). Their concern is with the mechanisms society has in place to control or constrain people's behavior. **Deterrence theory** assumes that people are rational decision makers who calculate the potential costs and benefits of a behavior before they act. If the benefits of a deviant act (e.g., money or psychological satisfaction) outweigh the costs (e.g., getting caught and punished), we will be inclined to do it. Conversely, if the costs exceed the benefits, the theory predicts that we'll decide it's not worth the risk (van den Haag, 1975).

The controversy surrounding capital punishment is, essentially, a debate over its true capacity to deter potentially violent criminals. According to deterrence theory, a punishment, to be effective, must be swift as well as certain and severe. However, capital punishment is anything but swift. Currently, about 3,000 inmates are on death row in the United States, but only 1,443 prisoners have been executed since 1977, when the death penalty was reinstated (Death Penalty Information Center, 2017). On average, death row inmates spend 15½ years awaiting execution, a figure that has been growing steadily for three decades (Snell, 2014; see Exhibit 8.1).

In addition, opponents of the death penalty argue that violent offenders are often under the influence of drugs or alcohol or are consumed by passion when they commit an act of violence; their violence is more or less spontaneous. Hence, they may not be thinking rationally (weighing the potential benefits of the act against the costs of punishment) at the time of the crime. The threat of being condemned to death may not deter such people when they are committing the act. Researchers have, indeed, found little empirical support for the argument that the threat of capital punishment reduces murders (W. C. Bailey, 1990; Galliher & Galliher, 2002). Nor have they found that well-publicized executions deter homicides. For instance, 80% of executions take place in the southern states, yet perennially this region has the highest murder rate in the country (Death Penalty Information Center, 2017). According to one study, 9 out of 10 leading criminologists don't think the death penalty deters homicides (Amnesty International, 2013),

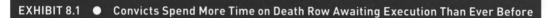

EXHIBIT 8.1 ● Convicts Spend More Time on Death Row Awaiting Execution Than Ever Before

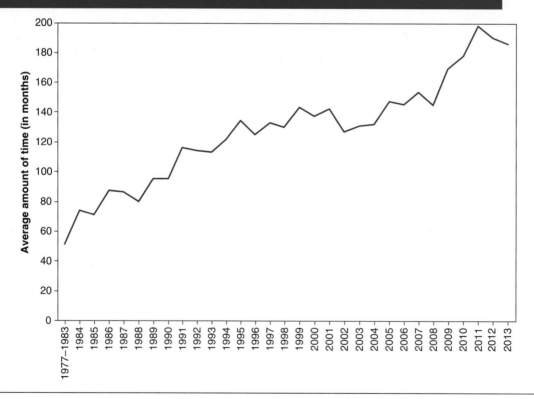

Source: Snell, 2014, Table 10.

Most societies around the world have abandoned the use of capital punishment for both moral and practical reasons: It's inhumane, and it doesn't deter crime. Even in China, a country responsible for most of the world's court-ordered executions, legislators voted in 2006 to bar all but the nation's highest court from approving death sentences ("China Changes," 2006). In the United States, there has been a steady decline in death sentences and executions. In 1996, there were 315 death sentences; in 2016 there were 30, the lowest number since 1977. The 20 executions in 2016 were the fewest since 1991 (Death Penalty Information Center, 2016). And public support has dropped from 80% in 1994 to 49% in 2016 (Oliphant, 2016). Some state legislatures have pushed bills to reduce or even abolish the death penalty. However, such efforts are often motivated by economic realities and not moral concerns or claims of deterrence. During the recent recession, lawmakers in several states argued that capital punishment cases cost states nearly three times as much as homicide cases where the death penalty was not sought (Urbina, 2009).

Labeling Deviants

These theories help us explain why some people engage in deviant acts and others don't, but they bypass the question of why certain acts committed by certain people are considered deviant in the first place. **Labeling theory** attempts to answer this question by characterizing a deviant person as someone—such as the preschool teacher Kelly Michaels—to whom the label "deviant" has been successfully applied (Becker, 1963; Lemert, 1972). According to this theory, the process of being singled out, defined, and reacted to as deviant changes a person in the eyes of others and has important life consequences for the individual. Once the label sticks, others may react to the labeled deviant with rejection, suspicion, withdrawal, fear, mistrust, and hatred (A. K. Cohen, 1966). A deviant label suggests that the person holding it is habitually given to the types of undesirable motives and behavior thought to be typical of others so labeled. The "ex-convict" is seen as a cold-blooded and ruthless character incapable of reforming, the "mental patient" as dangerous and unpredictable, the "alcoholic" as weak willed, the "prostitute" as dirty and immoral.

The problem, of course, is that such labels overgeneralize and can be misleading. For instance, psychologists recently found that upper-class individuals behave more unethically than lower-class people. They are more likely to break the law while driving, take things from others, lie in negotiations, and cheat to increase the chances of winning a prize (Piff, Stancato, Côté, Mendoza-Denton, & Keltner, 2012).

The type of deviant who receives the harshest expressions of public outrage changes with some regularity. At various times, child molesters, crack addicts, and drug dealers have claimed the title of society's most despised deviant. Currently, foreign terrorists, greedy Wall Street executives, steroid-fueled athletes, and white supremacists fit the bill. Often, collective hostility is directed toward people who don't seem to pose a grave societal threat, like those who talk loudly on cell phones in public places or people who drive too slowly on highways. Cigarette smoking used to be seen as a sign of sophistication; nowadays many people consider smoking filthy and disgusting, and smokers are often banished from buildings and forced to keep their distance from entryways. Across the country, landlords of privately owned multiple housing units have begun to forbid smoking *inside* people's apartments. In 2014, a Massachusetts city tried to ban the sale of *all* products containing tobacco or nicotine including cigarettes, chewing tobacco, and e-cigarettes.

Cities around the country sometimes use humiliating labels as an alternative to incarceration. For example, a Cleveland woman who had driven her SUV on a sidewalk to avoid stopping for a school bus was ordered by a judge to stand on a street corner holding a sign that read, "Only an idiot would drive on the sidewalk to avoid a school bus"

(Palmer, 2012). Some cities post the pictures of drug offenders, deadbeat dads, even public urinators on billboards. In some states, convicted drunk drivers have to put special license plates on their cars, and convicted shoplifters must take out ads in local newspapers that use their photograph and announce their crimes. The Chicago police department posts on its website photographs and partial addresses of men arrested for soliciting prostitution, even though they've not yet been convicted. Kansas City posts this information on a government-owned local television station.

Public shaming isn't just for people who've broken laws anymore. In today's wireless age, anyone who violates everyday expectations risks being called out, humiliated, and vilified on social media. A few years ago, a woman named Justine Sacco traveled from New York City to Johannesburg, South Africa. As her flight was taking off, she tweeted "Going to Africa. Hope I don't get AIDS. Just kidding. I'm white!" She then turned off her phone and went to sleep. By the time her flight landed in South Africa, tens of thousands of people had angrily retweeted her initial post; some even threatened her with death. She was immediately fired from her job at an Internet company (Ronson, 2015).

Whether the norms that are being violated are formal (that is, laws) or informal, such penalties are designed to shame the labeled individuals into behaving properly and to deter others from committing such acts. In the process, they satisfy the public's need for dramatic moral condemnation of deviants.

Deviant labels can impair an individual's eligibility to enter a broad range of socially acceptable roles. Many state penal systems use an instrument called the "Psychopathy Checklist–Revised" to decide if an inmate should be awarded parole. The battery of questions yields a score that allegedly determines if the individual is a "psychopath" or not. If an inmate is found to be a "psychopath" and therefore not eligible for parole, the label stays on his or her permanent record, rendering future positive parole decisions unlikely or even impossible ("This American Life," 2011). Indeed, some psychologists believe that fledgling psychopaths can be identified as early as kindergarten. Others, however, feel that branding a child at such an early age can be devastating:

> This isn't like autism, where the child and parents will find support. Even if accurate it's a ruinous diagnosis. No one is sympathetic to the mother of a psychopath (quoted in Kahn, 2012, p. 35).

Consider also the impact of the 1994 Federal Crime Bill on convicted sex offenders. This law requires states to register and track convicted sex offenders for 10 years after their release from prison and to privately notify police departments when the sex offenders move into their community. A website, Family Watchdog, provides information on released sexual offenders in all 50 states, including their names, addresses, convictions, and photographs. Many states have "sexually violent predator" statutes that give officials the power to commit violent sex offenders to mental hospitals involuntarily or to retain them in prison indefinitely *after* their prison terms are up. Because of laws that allow registered sex offenders to live in towns as long as their residence is more than 2,000 feet from a school or park, some communities around the country have found a new way of excluding these individuals from their midst: they've begun creating "pocket parks" out of tiny parcels of land in the community, thereby forcing sex offenders who live nearby to move. These parcels, which can be as small as 1,000 square feet, are often parks in name only, containing no playground equipment or even children. Their sole purpose is to keep sex offenders out of the neighborhood (Lovett, 2013).

In 20 states, convicted rapists, child molesters, and other sex offenders who have completed their prison sentences are forced to remain in prison, indefinitely, under a policy known as "civil commitment." The intent is to provide "treatment" to those individuals deemed to be "sexually dangerous" by the courts until it is safe for the public to let them go. Yet in Minnesota, where more than 700 sex offenders have been civilly committed over the past two decades, *none* have been released (Davey, 2015).

In all these cases, convicts have "paid their debt" to society by serving their mandated punishment. But convicted sex offenders can never fully shed their deviant identity. Finding a decent place to live, a decent job, or even getting out of prison may be a problem for the rest of their lives.

And it's not just sex offenders who must navigate the stigmatizing effects of their deviant labels. Several states are seeking to establish online registries for offenders who engage in a wide range of crimes including arson, drunk driving, methamphetamine production, and animal cruelty (Erica Goode, 2011). The appeal of these laws is hard to understate. According to one law professor, "You'd be hard pressed to find a more politically popular movement in recent years. Whether it's actually good public policy is a distinct and independent question from whether it's politically popular and makes us feel good" (quoted in Erica Goode, 2011, p. A12).

All ex-offenders experience the "stickiness" of labels to some degree, despite legislative efforts to help them. In 2007, Congress passed the Second Chance Act, which funds a variety of services and resources for ex-offenders in hopes of aiding their reentry into society. Nevertheless, potential employers still commonly refuse to hire ex-convicts, even when the crime has nothing to do with the job requirements. Like the public at large, many employers believe that prisons do not rehabilitate but actually make convicts more deviant by teaching them better ways to commit crimes and by providing social networks for criminal activity outside the prison (R. Johnson, 1987). In the past decade or so—particularly in the wake of the attacks of September 11, 2001—the criminal background check industry has grown dramatically. The public now has greater access to criminal history records of ex-offenders than ever before through such websites as CriminalSearches .com and Dirtsearch.org. Nine out of 10 companies—both large and small—now use criminal background checks as part of their hiring process. An examination of jobs posted on Craigslist found several hundred ads that contained statements that the company wouldn't consider applicants with criminal records: for example, "Do not apply with any misdemeanors/felonies," "You must not have any felony or misdemeanor convictions on your record. Period," and "We are looking for people with . . . spotless background/ criminal history" (M. N. Rodriguez & Emsellem, 2011).

In addition, being labeled as deviant may actually increase the probability that the behavior itself will stay the same or become worse (Archer, 1985). A great many ex-convicts in the United States do return to prison. According to the U.S. Department of Justice, about 68% of ex-convicts released in 2005 were arrested for a new offense within 3 years, 45% were convicted again, and 22% ended up back in prison (see Exhibit 8.2). In fact, 16% of released prisoners are responsible for nearly half of all arrests that occur over a 5-year period.

Deviant labels are so powerful that a mere accusation of dangerous activity can taint a person's character. In 2009, two Muslim immigrants from Morocco enlisted in the Army National Guard. They both successfully completed basic training, but just prior to leaving the base in South Carolina, they were questioned by military investigators who suspected them and three other Moroccan immigrants of plotting to poison fellow soldiers. They were placed under military arrest. For the next month and a half, the Army prevented them from calling their families without military personnel present, barred them from speaking to each other in Arabic, and required them to go to the mess hall and bathroom with an escort.

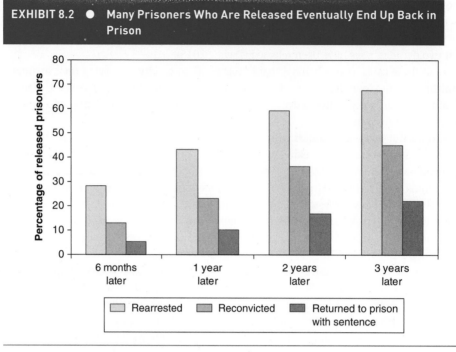

EXHIBIT 8.2 ● Many Prisoners Who Are Released Eventually End Up Back in Prison

Source: Durose, Cooper, & Snyder, 2014, Tables 6 & 16.

It wasn't until a year later that the Army concluded that the allegations against them were completely unfounded. However, despite their innocence, the FBI kept its investigation open. As a result, the two men were unable to receive security clearances, become citizens, obtain concealed weapons permits, or get government jobs (Dao, 2011).

NANCY HERMAN

BECOMING AN EX-CRAZY: HOW FORMER MENTAL PATIENTS STRUGGLE TO OVERCOME A LABEL

Sociologist Nancy Herman (1993) was interested in how labeling can weaken a person's self-image, create "deviant" patterns of behavior, and lead to social rejection. She was especially concerned about how former mental patients are reintegrated into society after their release from a psychiatric hospital. She decided to study ex-mental patients because her father had been an occupational therapist at a large psychiatric institute in Ontario, Canada. She spent most of her childhood and adolescence roaming the halls talking to patients. From time to time, the patients would spend Thanksgiving and Christmas with her family.

For this study, she conducted in-depth interviews with 146 former nonchronic mental patients (hospitalized in short intervals for less than 2 years) and 139 former chronic mental patients (hospitalized continuously for 2 or more years). She interviewed them in a variety of settings, such as coffee shops, malls, and their own homes. Many subjects invited her to their self-help group meetings and therapy sessions.

Herman found that these ex-patients, on release, noticed right away that friends, neighbors, coworkers, and family members were responding to them on the basis of their "mental illness" label and not on the basis of their identity prior to hospitalization. Although their treatment was complete (i.e., they were "cured" of their "illness"), others still saw them as defective. They were often made to feel like failures for not measuring up to the rest of "normal" society. As one woman put it,

When I was released, I presumed that I could resume with the "good times" once again. I was treated—I paid my dues. But I was wrong. From the first moment I set foot back onto the streets of "Wilsonville" and I tried to return to my kids . . . I learned the hard way that my kids didn't want nothing to do with me. They were scared to let me near the grandkids—that I might do something to them. They told me this right to my face. . . . Having mental illness is like having any other illness like heart troubles, but people sure do treat you different. If you have heart troubles, you get treated, and then you come out good as new and your family still loves you. But that's not so with mental illness. . . . [Y]ou come out and people treat you worse than a dog! (quoted in Herman, 1993, p. 303)

On release, some of the former patients Herman interviewed were quite open about their illness and attempted to present themselves in as "normal" a way as they could. Others became political activists who used their "ex-mental patient" label to try to dispel common myths about mental illness or to advocate for patients' rights. But most of the former patients spent a great deal of time selectively concealing and disclosing information regarding their illness and treatment. Strategies of concealment included avoiding certain individuals, redirecting conversations so that the topic was less likely to come up, lying about their absence, and withdrawing from social interaction. Constant concern that people might "find out" created a great deal of anxiety, fear, and frustration, as described by this 56-year-old woman:

> It's a very difficult thing. It's not easy to distinguish the good ones from the bad ones. . . . You've gotta figure out who you can tell about your illness and who you better not tell. It is a tremendous stress and strain that you have to live with 24 hours a day! (quoted in Herman, 1993, p. 306)

The stickiness of the "crazy" label is difficult for former mental patients. However, Herman's research also shows that ex-patients are not powerless victims of negative societal reactions, passively accepting the deviant identity others attribute to them. Rather, they are strategists and impression managers who play active roles in transforming themselves from "abnormal" to "normal."

Linking Power, Deviance, and Social Control

Because deviance is socially defined, the behaviors and conditions that come to be called "deviant" can at times appear somewhat arbitrary. Sociologists working from the conflict perspective would say that definitions of and responses to deviance are often a form of social control exerted by more powerful people and groups over less powerful people and groups. In U.S. society, the predominant means of controlling those whose behavior does not conform to the norms established by the powerful are criminalization and medicalization. Labeling people either as criminals or as sick people gives socially powerful individuals, groups, and organizations a way to marginalize and discount certain people who challenge the status quo. Criminalization and medicalization also have economic and other benefits for certain powerful groups.

The Criminalization of Deviance

Presumably, certain acts are **criminalized**—officially defined as crimes—because they offend the majority of people in a given society and pose the greatest danger. Most of us trust our legal institutions—legislators, courts, the police, and prisons—to regulate social behavior in the interest of the common good. But according to the conflict perspective, the law is not merely a mechanism that protects good people from bad people; it is a political instrument used by specific groups to further their own interests, often at the expense of others' (W. Chambliss, 1964; Quinney, 1970). Law is, of course, determined by legislative action. But legislatures are greatly influenced by powerful segments of society, such as lobbying groups, political action committees, wealthy campaign contributors, and so on.

Tellingly, the acts that threaten the economic or political interests of the groups that have the power to influence public policy are more likely to be criminalized (and more likely to be punished) than are the deviant acts members of these groups are likely to commit. For instance, it's against the law to fail to report income on one's annual tax return. But poor working people are far more likely to be audited by the Internal Revenue Service (IRS) than wealthy people (Johnston, 2002). That's not surprising, given that the IRS looks for tax cheating by wage earners much more closely than it does for cheating by corporations or by people whose money comes from their own businesses, investments, partnerships, and trusts.

Through the mass media, dominant groups influence the public to look at crime in ways that are favorable to them. The selective portrayal of crime plays an important role in shaping public perceptions of the "crime problem" and therefore its "official" definition. For instance, decades of research show that the crimes depicted on television are significantly more likely to be violent than actual crimes committed in the real world (cited in Reiman & Leighton, 2013). When politicians talk about fighting the U.S. crime problem or when news shows report fluctuations in crime rates, they are almost always referring to street crimes (illegal drug use, robbery, burglary, murder, assault, etc.) rather than corporate crimes, governmental crimes, or crimes committed by people in influential positions.

The strategy has worked well. Sixty-five percent of respondents in one study said that the criminal justice system is not tough enough on crime (only 6% felt it was too tough; Kiefer, 2004). Governments at the state and federal level have since responded to this popular sentiment by "getting tough on crime"—cracking down on drug users and dealers, reviving the death penalty, scaling back parole eligibility, lengthening prison sentences, and building more prisons.

Not surprisingly, the inmate population in this country has grown dramatically in the last half century. In 1970, there were fewer than 200,000 people in state and federal prisons; today that figure is about 2.1 million (International Centre for Prison Studies, 2017). Another 4.6 million Americans are on probation and parole (Kaeble & Glaze, 2016), meaning that over 6.7 million people, or about 2% of the population, experience some sort of criminal justice supervision. This situation is less a function of some staggeringly high number of evil people in this country than it is of the "tough on crime" policies that have taken hold in the last few decades. In 2016, the U.S. incarceration rate was 693 prisoners per 100,000 people (International Centre for Prison Studies, 2017). Although the number of U.S. prisoners has actually gone down in recent years, no other industrialized country comes close to this figure (see Exhibit 8.3).

The Social Reality of Crime

But within the United States, certain types of people have always been more likely than others to be defined as deviant in the first place. According to the conflict perspective, most societies ensure that offenders who are processed through the criminal justice system are members of the most disadvantaged groups. In particular, poor people are more likely to get arrested, be formally charged with a crime, have their cases go to trial, get convicted, and receive harsher sentences than more affluent citizens (Reiman & Leighton, 2013). In some places, people who can't afford to pay fines—say, for speeding tickets—often end up in jail (Bronner, 2012). And poor defendants who can't afford bail

EXHIBIT 8.3   ●   The United States Puts More People in Prison Than Any Other Country

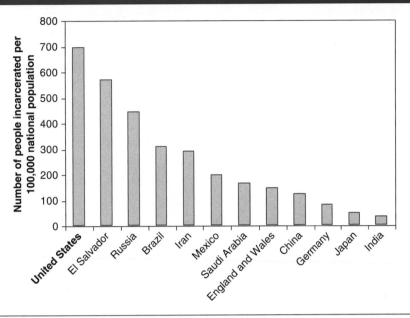

Source: International Centre for Prison Studies, 2017.

are sometimes detained awaiting trial for a longer amount of time than if they'd been convicted right away (Dewan, 2015). Furthermore, although the accused have a constitutional right to an attorney even if they can't afford one, many poor people still face legal proceedings alone. It turns out that this constitutional provision only applies to criminal cases, not civil ones. Hence in civil matters like home foreclosures, job loss, and child support, poor people often end up representing themselves, which usually means they lose because they don't present necessary evidence, commit procedural mistakes, and fail to examine witnesses thoroughly. It's estimated that 80% of the legal needs of the poor in the United States go unmet (Bronner, 2013).

Poor people of color are likely to fit the public image of the "typical criminal" whose actions threaten not only people's personal safety but also the well-being of the entire society (see Chapter 11 for more detail). When such a perception becomes common, official action against them becomes a justifiable and necessary response:

> Poor, young, urban, (disproportionately) black males make up the core of the enemy forces in the crime war. They are the heart of a vicious, unorganized guerrilla army, threatening the lives, limbs, and possessions of the law-abiding members of society, necessitating recourse to the ultimate weapons of force and detention in our common defense. (Reiman & Leighton, 2013, p. 69)

Hovering police helicopters and video cameras mounted on streetlights have become the ubiquitous markers of poor urban neighborhoods. As a consequence, a climate of fear and suspicion has gripped these communities. In such an environment, life for everyone is anxious and unsettled: "Family members and friends are pressured to inform on one another and young men live as suspects and fugitives, with the daily fear of confinement" (A. Goffman, 2009, p. 353).

The past few years have also seen a steady stream of cases in which police officers have used lethal force against unarmed individuals who fit the racially tinged image of a dangerous criminal. Among those that have gotten the most media attention are

- Timothy Russell and Malissa Williams, the Cleveland couple killed in a hail of police bullets after their car backfired. Police fired 137 shots into the car, hitting both Russell and Williams two dozen times;

- Michael Brown, the black teenager and robbery suspect shot to death in the street by a police officer in Ferguson, Missouri, in 2014;

- Eric Garner, the 44-year-old black man from Staten Island, New York, killed in 2014 as a result of an illegal chokehold used by police officers to subdue him;

- Tamir Rice, a 12-year-old black boy shot and killed by police in 2014 after they'd received a dispatch call describing a "young, black male" brandishing a gun (the gun was a toy);

- Walter Scott, a 50-year-old black man shot from behind in 2015 by a police officer in North Charleston, South Carolina, as he fled on foot following a traffic stop for a nonfunctioning brake light;

- Freddie Gray, a 25-year-old black man in Baltimore who died in 2015 from spinal injuries sustained while he was being transported in a police van after being arrested;

- In 2016, after receiving reports of an armed robbery in the area, two Baton Rouge, Louisiana, police officers pinned Alton Sterling, a 37-year-old black man, to the ground after ordering him out of his car. Though he seemed completely unable to move, one of the police officers yelled, "He's got a gun!" Within seconds, an officer shot Sterling to death even though he was still pinned to the ground.

Such actions seem to be motivated less by the objective presence of threat, and more by preconceived notions about who *looks* threatening. So powerful is this image that those who don't conform to it become the exception to the rule. In 2017, a black teenager named Jordan Edwards was killed when a Dallas police officer shot into a car in which he was a passenger. Shortly afterward, online expressions of sympathy highlighted the fact that Jordan was "a great kid" with "awesome parents." The father of one of his friends told a local TV station that he "was not a thug. This shouldn't have happened to him" (quoted in Eligon, 2017, p. A11). Notice how such a statement reinforces the belief that most other black people killed by the police *were* thugs who were up to no good, which somehow played a role in them being shot.

People who don't fit the racially-tinged profile of the "typical criminal" often have a very different experience with law enforcement. For instance, in stark contrast to cases described above, consider this 2016 incident in New Orleans: a white motorist named Ronald Gasser engaged in a verbal altercation with a black driver and ex-NFL player Joe McKnight. When the two cars stopped next to each other at a red light, McKnight got out and approached Mr. Gasser's window. McKnight was unarmed. Gasser pulled out a handgun and shot McKnight three times, killing him. When police arrived, Gasser admitted to them that he had killed McKnight. Nevertheless, the police let him go. It wasn't until 4 days later, after widespread national outrage, that Gasser was arrested and charged with manslaughter (Victor, 2016a).

So it shouldn't come as a surprise that Latino/as and African Americans make up nearly three quarters of all convicted offenders in U.S. federal prisons even though they compose only about one quarter of the general population (U.S. Sentencing Commission, 2016). African American men are incarcerated at a rate 5 times that of Whites; in some states it's 10 times greater (U.S. Sentencing Project, 2016). Black men have a 32% chance of spending time in prison, compared to 17% for Latinos and 6% for white men (U.S. Sentencing Project, 2014).

Although some people may see such figures as clear evidence of higher rates of minority involvement in crime, other statistics seem to suggest something different. For instance, African Americans make up about 13% of the population, but they account for 38.3% of all arrests for violent crime, 29.5% of arrests for property crimes, and 31.7% of arrests for drug violations. Blacks are nearly four times more likely than Whites to be arrested on charges of marijuana possession, even though the two groups use the drug at comparable rates (cited in Urbina, 2013a). In addition, African Americans account for 39% of convictions for violent crimes, 34% of convictions for property crimes, and 46% of convictions for drug crimes (U.S. Bureau of Justice Statistics, 2013).

The effects of race on incarceration extend beyond how people end up in prison in the first place. A recent analysis of parole decisions in the state of New York found that fewer than 1 in 6 black or Latino men are released at their first hearing; the rate for white men is 1 in 4. The difference is especially pronounced for those prisoners who pose the least danger to society: small time offenders who commit property crimes (Winerip, Schwirtz, & Gebeloff, 2016).

Even when they are released, poor black and Latino ex-offenders are significantly less likely than their counterparts of two decades ago to find jobs and stay out of the kind of trouble that leads to further imprisonment (Butterfield, 2000). Many states have sharply curtailed education, job training, and other rehabilitation programs inside prison. In addition, parole officers are quicker to rescind a newly released inmate's parole for relatively minor infractions, such as failing a drug test.

Furthermore, when facing the death penalty, poor defendants of color are often represented by public defenders, who have fewer resources available for investigative work and who may have little, if any, experience in such matters. Not surprisingly, since the death penalty was reinstated in 1977, nearly 43% of defendants who have been executed have been Latino/a or African American, and 55% of the current death row population is Latino/a or African American (Death Penalty Information Center, 2017). Supreme Court Justice Ruth Bader Ginsburg summed up the situation this way:

> People who are well represented at trial do not get the death penalty. . . . I have yet to see a death case among the dozens coming to the Supreme Court on eve-of-execution stay applications in which the defendant was well represented at trial. (quoted in Death Penalty Information Center, 2013, p. 1)

The race of the *victim* plays an even bigger role in death penalty decisions. Over 75% of the murder victims in cases resulting in the death penalty were white, even though nationally only 50% of murder victims are white. In contrast, only 15% of those executed were convicted of killing Blacks, and 7% involved Latino/a victims (Death Penalty Information Center, 2017).

It's important to remember that persistent imbalances in the justice system go beyond the way disadvantaged people are treated by the police, judges, attorneys, and juries. If they were simply a matter of discrimination, the situation would be relatively easy to address. Instead, they occur because the actions of poor individuals are more likely to be criminalized in the first place.

Wealthy, Corporate, and White-Collar Crime

The criminal justice system can look quite a bit different from the other end of the racial/socioeconomic spectrum. In 2013, a white 16-year-old in Texas drove his pickup truck 30 miles per hour *over* the speed limit and ran into a group of pedestrians, killing four of them and injuring two people riding in the truck with him. His blood alcohol level was three times the legal limit for an adult. The prosecutor sought a 20-year prison sentence but the young man received only probation. During the trial, his attorney successfully argued that he had impulse control problems that came from having wealthy, privileged parents who made his life too easy by never setting limits for him. A psychologist testified "he had freedoms that no young man would be able to handle" (quoted in "Affluenza," 2013, p. 19).

More generally, people in the United States tend to take for granted that urban street crime is our worst social problem and that corporate crime is not as dangerous or as costly (Reiman & Leighton, 2013). Unsafe work conditions; dangerous chemicals in the air, water, and food; faulty consumer products; and unnecessary surgery actually put people who live in the United States in more constant and imminent physical danger than do ordinary street crimes (Mokhiber, 1999). Approximately 14,249 Americans were murdered in 2014, less than half the homicide rate in 1990 (ProQuest Statistical Abstract, 2017). At the same time,

- About 4,800 Americans died on the job in 2015 (U.S. Bureau of Labor Statistics, 2016e).

- It's estimated that 3% to 6% of all cancers are caused by exposure to carcinogens in the workplace. This means that in 2012 (the most recent year available), there were between 45,872 and 91,745 new cancer cases in the United States that were caused by exposure in the workplace (Centers for Disease Control and Prevention, 2015c).

- Approximately 1.7 million health-care–associated infections occur in U.S. hospitals each year, resulting in 99,000 deaths (Centers for Disease Control and Prevention, 2015d).

Add in the 3.7 million Americans who suffer from *nonfatal* workplace injuries and illnesses each year (U.S. Bureau of Labor Statistics, 2015) and you can see that violent street crime is not the biggest threat to our health and safety.

Organizational misbehaviors and white-collar crimes also pose greater economic threats to U.S. citizens than does street crime. The FBI estimates that burglary and robbery cost the United States $3.8 billion a year. Unnecessary medical treatments alone, such as unwarranted scans, blood tests, and surgical procedures, cost at least $210 billion annually (cited in Parker-Pope, 2012b). And the total cost of white-collar crimes like corporate fraud, bribery, embezzlement, insurance fraud, and securities fraud amounts to close to $680 billion a year (Reiman & Leighton, 2013).

To be fair, some people actually do view certain types of corporate malfeasance as a more serious form of deviance than street crimes (Huff, Desilets, & Kane, 2010). Indeed, the financial crisis that first gripped the nation in 2008 created a firestorm of public anger that cast unprecedented scrutiny on white-collar misconduct. President Obama vowed to crack down on Wall Street bankers for their "reckless practices" (P. Baker & Herszenhorn, 2010). Across the country, attorneys began to indict loan processors, mortgage brokers, and bank officials on various types of financial fraud. Congress and the Department of Justice plotted strategies for an all-out federal attack (Segal, 2009).

In a few high-profile cases, executives convicted of corporate crimes have, indeed, received harsh prison sentences:

- Bernie Ebbers, CEO of WorldCom, was accused of defrauding the company of $11 billion in 2005 and sentenced to 25 years in prison.

- In 2009, a wealthy stockbroker and financial adviser named Bernard Madoff pled guilty to charges of securities fraud, investment fraud, mail fraud, wire fraud, money laundering, and theft from an employee benefit plan, to name a few. Prosecutors estimated that these schemes cost his clients about $65 billion. The judge called Madoff's actions "extraordinarily evil" and sentenced him to 150 years in prison, an act that was largely symbolic since Madoff was 71 years old at the time (Henriques, 2009).

- In 2011, billionaire hedge fund manager Raj Rajaratnam was found guilty of securities fraud and conspiracy. He was sentenced to 11 years in prison (though the government recommended a sentence twice that long).

But responses like these have been directed largely at individual white-collar criminals. Corporations themselves rarely receive heavy criminal punishment when their dangerous actions violate the law (Reiman & Leighton, 2013). For example, even after it was revealed that Bayer AG—a German pharmaceutical company—had failed to disclose the results of a study showing that a widely used heart surgery medicine increases the risk of death and stroke, the Food and Drug Administration (FDA) did not take the drug off the market (G. Harris, 2006). In 2004, the pharmaceutical company GlaxoSmithKline agreed to settle a $2.5 million lawsuit brought by New York State alleging that the company had hidden the results of drug trials showing that its antidepressant Paxil might have deadly side effects, such as increasing suicidal thoughts in children.

At congressional hearings, lawmakers berated executives from GlaxoSmithKline and other drug companies for hiding study results that challenged the effectiveness of their drugs. In response, the companies promised to do better. But according to studies financed by the National Institutes of Health, crucial facts about many clinical trials continue to be withheld from the FDA (cited in Berenson, 2005).

To ease the inconvenience of prosecution for corporate wrongdoers, the U.S. Department of Justice has instituted a form of corporate probation called *deferred prosecution*. Several major companies that have been charged with billions of dollars' worth of accounting fraud, bid rigging, and other illegal financial schemes—including American International Group, PNC Financial Services Group, Merrill Lynch, AOL-Time Warner, and American Express—have agreed to deferred prosecutions, in which they accept responsibility for wrongdoing, agree not to fight the charges, agree to cooperate with investigations, pay a fine, and implement changes in their corporate structure to prevent future criminal wrongdoing. If a company abides by the agreement for a specified time—usually 12 months—prosecutors will drop all charges (Mokhiber & Weissman, 2004). Since 2007, the Department of Justice has made over 150 deferred prosecution agreements with companies accused of criminal activity

(Henning, 2012). In 2014, Toyota Motors entered into a deferred prosecution agreement with the U.S. Department of Justice after it was revealed that the company had knowingly manufactured vehicles with a safety defect that caused cars to suddenly accelerate, leading to at least 12 deaths. In exchange for avoiding criminal prosecution, Toyota agreed to accept responsibility, admit that it misled the public, cooperate with any future investigations, and pay a $1.2 billion fine to the U.S. government (U.S. Department of Justice, 2014).

Such arrangements are meant to avoid more drastic punishment, which could destroy these companies and cost thousands of innocent lower-level employees their jobs. For instance, when the government aggressively prosecuted the Arthur Andersen accounting firm in 2002 for its criminal role in the famous Enron scandal, 28,000 employees lost their jobs (Lichtblau, 2008).

But the penalties companies do receive are usually relatively minor and don't do much to deter their future law violations. Fines of hundreds of millions of dollars or even several billion dollars may sound like a hefty sum to you and me, but for companies that earn *hundreds of billions* of dollars annually, they barely make a dent. For instance, in the 5 years leading up to the 2010 Gulf of Mexico drilling rig explosion that killed 11 people and dumped nearly 5 million barrels of oil into the water, British Petroleum had received more than $550 million in fines for violations of safety codes, environmental laws, and antitrust statutes. Those fines added up to one tenth of a percent of its revenue over that period. In 2010, the Securities and Exchange Commission imposed a $550 million fine on Goldman Sachs for securities fraud. It was the largest penalty ever paid by a Wall Street firm. However, the company earned $51.7 billion that year, so the fine worked out to about 4 *days* of earnings ("Do Fines Ever Make Corporations Change?" 2010). In 2012, GlaxoSmithKline (yes, the same drug company that had gotten into trouble 8 years earlier) pled guilty to charges that it had promoted unapproved uses of its best-selling antidepressants and had failed to report safety data about its top diabetes drug. The company agreed to pay $3 billion in fines, the largest settlement involving a drug company to date. However, some industry observers argue that even fines of this magnitude will do little to prevent drug companies from such unlawful behavior in the future (K. Thomas & Schmidt, 2012). It's no wonder that many large corporations consider the punishments they receive for wrongdoing simply a cost of doing business.

The imbalance in the legal response to these crimes versus street crimes is glaring. If you were an individual thief who had robbed a bank at gunpoint, a shop owner who had defrauded your customers of millions of dollars, or a small businessperson who had knowingly manufactured a potentially lethal product, it's highly unlikely that you would be allowed to avoid any criminal prosecution simply by "cooperating with the investigation." Our massive law enforcement and criminal justice machinery would no doubt mobilize its vast resources to see that you were prosecuted to the fullest extent of the law. Yet large corporations engage in such activities every day, largely without much public outcry or moral panic. In fact, most aren't even prosecuted under criminal statutes. Between 1982 and 2002, about 170,000 American workers died on the job. During that same period, federal and state workplace safety agencies investigated 1,798 fatality cases in which companies had *willfully* violated workplace safety laws—for instance, by removing safety devices to speed up production, denying workers proper safety gear, or simply ignoring explicit safety warnings. But only 104 of these cases were ever prosecuted. And of those, only 16 resulted in criminal convictions (Barstow, 2003).

Why aren't these dangerous and costly corporate acts considered deviant the way face-to-face street crimes are? According to sociologists Jeffrey Reiman and Paul Leighton (2013), the answer resides in the perceived circumstances surrounding these acts. People typically see the injuries caused by corporate crime as unintentional, indirect, and a consequence of an endeavor culturally defined as legitimate or socially productive: making a profit. In most people's minds, someone who tries to harm someone else is usually considered more evil than someone who harms without intending to. Moreover, harming someone directly seems more deviant than harming someone indirectly. Finally, harm that results from illegitimate activities is usually considered more serious than harm that is a by-product of standard business activities.

The Menace of "Illegal" Drugs

Different cultures show varying levels of tolerance when it comes to drug use. For instance, throughout the South Pacific, people commonly chew betel nuts for their stimulant effects. In the Bolivian and Peruvian Andes, people chew coca leaves during their ordinary workday. The Huichol of central Mexico ingest peyote—a small cactus that produces hallucinations—as part of their religious rituals.

In the United States, we wink at the use of many substances that alter people's state of mind, such as coffee, chocolate, and alcohol. In 2011, companies began marketing baked goods with names like "Lazy Cakes," "Kush Cakes," and "Lulla Pies" that contain the sleep-inducing substance melatonin. The pastries bear labels warning against operating heavy machinery or driving after eating them. One consumer said, "It knocks you out—in a good way, not a bad way. For me, it's not to chill. For me, it's to get a good night's sleep" (quoted in Saint Louis, 2011, p. 4). Nevertheless, because they look and taste like sweet desserts, these products are considered food, not drugs.

But when it comes to illegal drugs, U.S. attitudes change dramatically. Like the term *terrorist*, the term *drugs* is an easy and popular scapegoat on which to heap our collective hatred. The United States has been characterized as a *temperance culture* (Levine, 1992)—one in which self-control and industriousness are perceived as desirable traits of productive citizens. In such an environment, drug-induced states of altered consciousness are likely to be perceived as a loss of control and thus feared as a threat to the economic and physical well-being of the population.

The United States has been in an ill-defined, undeclared, but highly publicized "war" against illegal drugs for more than 40 years. The Drug Enforcement Administration, the FBI, and the U.S. Customs Service seized 4.3 million pounds of illegal drugs in 2012, about twice as much as was seized in 2000 (ProQuest Statistical Abstract, 2017). Federal spending on antidrug campaigns increased from $420 million in 1973 to $26 billion in 2015; an additional $25 billion was spent at the state and local levels (Katel, 2006; Drug Policy Alliance, 2015).

With so much attention and resources now focused on border patrol, terrorism, and homeland security, it would seem that the fight against drug dealers and users is no longer a national priority. Indeed, cuts in the federal budget have reduced the availability of resources devoted to drug enforcement, and some antidrug programs and agencies have been folded into antiterrorism efforts. Nevertheless, there remains a widespread belief that although terrorists pose an external danger, drug users and drug dealers are slowly destroying the country from within and therefore need to be stopped.

Many conflict sociologists, however, argue that antidrug campaigns and legislative activities are driven chiefly by political interests (see, e.g., Erich Goode, 1989). The war on drugs in the United States has permitted greater social control over groups perceived to be threatening, such as young minority men, and has mobilized voter support for candidates who profess to be "tough" on drugs. Capitalizing on the "drug menace" as a personal and societal threat is a common and effective political tactic (Ben-Yehuda, 1990). Indeed, behind the phrase "war on drugs" is the assumption that illegal drugs (ecstasy, cocaine, methamphetamine, heroin, etc.) are the most dangerous substances and the ones that must be eradicated. However, the difference between legal and illegal drugs is not necessarily a function of their relative danger.

For instance, 30% of 12- to 17-year-olds have drunk alcohol (ProQuest Statistical Abstract, 2017). In 2015, about 1,825 U.S. college students died from alcohol-related injuries and car accidents, 97,000 were victims of alcohol-related sexual assault and rape, 696,000 were assaulted by another student who has been drinking, and 600,000 were injured in alcohol-related accidents (National Institute on Alcohol Abuse and Alcoholism, 2015). But alcohol is big business: Sales of alcoholic beverages exceeded $176 billion in 2014 (ProQuest Statistical Abstract, 2017). Hence, efforts to completely criminalize it are few and far between. While most colleges now offer "alcohol-free" housing, encourage students to "drink responsibly," or sponsor alcohol-free social events, few have become "dry" campuses, banning alcohol outright.

And even though it is technically a drug, alcohol rarely enters into conversations on "drug abuse." Indeed, the U.S. Drug Enforcement Administration's website contains detailed fact sheets on heroin, cocaine, methamphetamine, ecstasy, oxycodone (OxyContin), hydrocodone, steroids, LSD, inhalants, and marijuana (even though its recreational use is now legal in eight states) but makes no mention of alcohol.

Tobacco is an even clearer health risk than alcohol—or marijuana and heroin for that matter (Reiman & Leighton, 2013). But aside from some age restrictions, it is legally available to anyone. According to the World Health Organization (2015), nearly 6 million people around the world die each year from tobacco-related causes. In the United States, the death rate among smokers is two to three times higher than that of nonsmokers (B. Carter et al., 2015). Cigarette smoking is responsible for one in five deaths annually, or about 480,000 deaths a year (Centers for Disease Control and Prevention, 2016b). That means that more people die from smoking-related causes than from HIV/AIDS, illegal drug use, alcohol use, motor vehicle injuries, suicides, and murders *combined*. Ten times as many U.S. citizens have died prematurely from cigarette smoking than have died in all the wars fought by the United States during its history. Tobacco significantly increases the risk of respiratory disease, cataracts, stroke, low-birth-weight babies, six categories of cardiovascular disease, and roughly 12 different types of cancer. The costs of smoking are financial as well as physical. It's estimated that smoking and exposure to tobacco smoke cost nearly $170 billion in direct medical costs and $151 billion in lost productivity each year (Xu, Bishop, Kennedy, Simpson, & Pechacek, 2015).

And tobacco doesn't just affect those who choose to consume it directly. According to the Centers for Disease Control and Prevention (2014b), about 88 million nonsmoking U.S. residents over the age of 3 are exposed to secondhand smoke at home, in vehicles, at work, and in public places each year. Such exposure, even for brief periods, can cause health problems. Nonsmokers who inhale secondhand smoke at work or at home increase their risk of heart disease, stroke, and lung cancer by 20% to 30% (Centers for Disease Control and Prevention, 2014b). Almost 50,000 of the above-cited 443,000 cigarette-related deaths are the result of exposure to secondhand smoke (Centers for Disease Control and Prevention, 2014b). Public health experts are now paying close attention to the effects of "thirdhand" smoke—the residue of tobacco smoke left on walls, furniture, clothes, and house dust—as well as e-cigarettes, which tripled in popularity among middle- and high school students between 2013 and 2014 (Tavernise, 2015).

Yet knowing the hazards of smoking cigarettes has not prompted our society to outlaw them entirely, as we have cocaine use. It's true that some cities and states have enacted restrictive smoking bans in bars, restaurants, and other enclosed public places and some places have banned outdoor smoking as well (Springen, 2006). In 2009, President Obama signed into law the Family Smoking Prevention and Tobacco Control Act, which gives the FDA more power to impose stricter controls on the production and sale of cigarettes (D. Wilson, 2009b). But this bill stopped short of completely criminalizing tobacco, which would have had a disastrous impact on many large corporations and on several states whose economies depend on this crop.

The tobacco industry has one of the most powerful political lobbies in Washington. As efforts to limit or prohibit smoking in this country become more successful (the proportion of Americans who currently smoke has fallen by more than half since 1964; U.S. Surgeon General, 2014), tobacco companies are stepping up efforts to combat regulations in other parts of the world. They have fought advertising limits in Great Britain, larger health warnings in South America, and higher taxes in the Philippines and Mexico (D. Wilson, 2010). Even the U.S. Chamber of Commerce supports the American tobacco industry by fighting antismoking laws in places like Australia, Jamaica, Nepal, and Uruguay (Hakim, 2015b). Worldwide, the tobacco industry spends tens of billions of dollars each year on advertising, promotion, and sponsorship (World Health Organization, 2013b).

The response to illegal drug users also shows how conceptions of deviance are socially constructed. Take, for instance, discrepancies in prison sentences for the possession and use of cocaine. Although the two types of cocaine—powdered and crack—cause similar physical reactions, the sentences for those convicted of selling them are vastly different. The average length of a sentence for selling crack cocaine is over 2 years longer than the average sentence for selling powdered cocaine (96 months vs. 79 months; United States Sentencing Commission, 2014a, 2014b). According to federal law, possession of 28 grams of crack cocaine yields a 5-year mandatory minimum sentence for a first offense; it takes 500 grams of powder cocaine to prompt the same sentence (Drug Enforcement Administration, 2015).

Many law enforcement officials argue that the different levels of punishment are justified because crack cocaine is more closely associated with violence than powdered cocaine, it is more dangerous to the user, and it is more likely to cause birth defects in babies whose mothers use it while pregnant. However, a study of the physiological and psychoactive effects of different forms of cocaine found that they are so similar as to make the existing discrepancy in punishment "excessive." In addition, other research has found that the effects of crack use by pregnant women on fetuses are no different from those of tobacco or alcohol use (cited in Coyle, 2003).

Some sociologists argue that the problems associated with crack use have as much to do with class and race as with the drug itself. Harsh sentences for crack offenses have had a disproportionate effect on black men in poor urban areas, where crack is much more common than the powdered cocaine favored by white users. In 2013, 93% of those convicted of crack possession were black and Latino/a; less than 6% were white. By contrast, 31.2% of those convicted of powdered cocaine possession were black, 10% were white, and 58% were Latino/a (though most of these individuals are white; U.S. Sentencing Commission, 2013). In 2010, President Obama signed into law the Fair Sentencing Act, which aims to reduce these sentencing disparities. In 2011, the U.S. Sentencing Commission voted unanimously to reduce the unfairly long sentences for crack offenders already in prison so that they are more in line with shorter terms given powder cocaine offenders (Serrano, 2011).

Meanwhile, little has been accomplished in the way of stopping the illegal activities of the rich and powerful interests that participate in the drug industry. Established financial institutions often launder drug money, despite laws against it (Parenti, 1995). Massive international crime organizations that ensure the flow of illicit drugs into the country have grown bigger and richer, despite a decades-long attempt to stop them (Bullington, 1993). Unlike low-status users and small-time dealers of illegal drugs, these organizations wield tremendous economic power and political influence (Godson & Olson, 1995).

The Medicalization of Deviance

One of the most powerful forces in defining deviance in the United States today is the medical profession. Throughout the 20th century, the medical profession gained in prestige, influence, and authority. This professional dominance gave medicine jurisdiction over anything that could be designated "healthy" or "sick" (Conrad & Leiter, 2004). This trend, what sociologists call **medicalization**, is the process through which deviant behavior is defined as a medical problem or illness and the medical profession is mandated or licensed to provide some type of treatment for it (Conrad, 2005). Each time we automatically refer to troublesome behavior or people as "sick," we help to perpetuate the perception that deviance is like an illness. Many physicians, psychologists, psychiatrists, therapists, and insurance agents, not to mention the entire pharmaceutical industry, benefit from a medicalized view of certain deviant acts.

According to some, we're currently in the midst of an "epidemic of diagnoses" (Welch, Schwartz, & Woloshin, 2007), meaning that more and more actions that were once categorized simply as misbehaviors are being redefined as psychiatric diseases, disorders, or syndromes. Between 1952 and 2000, the number of mental disorders officially recognized by the American Psychiatric Association increased from 110 to close to 400 (P. J. Caplan, 1995; Horwitz, 2002). Many of these designations seem to have nothing to do with illness. Take, for instance a malady called "conduct disorder," a diagnosis restricted to children and adolescents. According to the American Psychiatric Association (2013), the "symptoms" of this disorder include bullying or threatening behavior toward others, physical cruelty, destruction of property, theft, and violations of other rules like staying out late despite parental prohibition. In another era, this sort of misbehavior was called juvenile delinquency.

To accommodate the growth in behaviors being defined as "illnesses," the number of psychiatric professionals has almost tripled over the past two decades, as has the number of people seeking psychiatric help. The combined indirect and direct costs of serious mental "illness" in this society, including lost productivity, lost earnings due to illness, disability benefits, and health care expenditures, are estimated to exceed $317 billion annually (National Institute of Mental Health, 2010). According to the National Alliance on Mental Illness (2013), about 20% of U.S. adults (61.5 million people) suffer from a diagnosable mental disorder in a given year. Along with alcoholism, drug addiction, and serious mental illness, these disorders now include overeating, undereating, shyness, school stress, distress over a failed romance, poor performance in school, hoarding, addiction to using the Internet, public tantrums, and excessive gambling, shopping, and sex.

For their part, drug companies sometimes create medicalized conceptions of deviance by influencing the way conditions are defined and then by marketing disorders and selling drugs to treat them. According to one study, 56% of psychiatrists involved in defining disorders for the latest revision of the American Psychiatric Association's *Diagnostic and Statistical Manual* had financial ties to drug companies (Cosgrove, Bursztajn, & Krimsky, 2009).

In 1997, Congress passed the Food and Drug Administration Modernization Act, allowing drug companies to advertise directly to consumers and create heightened demand for their products. Between 1996 and 2000, drug company spending on television advertising increased by 600%, to $2.5 billion, and it's been rising ever since: Drug companies spent over $5.2 billion on prescription drug advertising in 2015 (Robbins, 2016). And 9 out of the largest 10 drug companies spend more on the advertising and marketing of prescription drugs than they do on research (A. Swanson, 2015).

In the early 2000s, GlaxoSmithKline sought FDA approval to promote the antidepressant drug Paxil as a treatment for what at the time was a relatively obscure condition called social anxiety disorder. In general, the principal symptoms of this "disorder" are excessive worry and anxiety in social and performance situations where embarrassment may occur. After receiving FDA approval, the company spent millions to raise public visibility of these conditions. Before this campaign, diagnoses of these disorders had been relatively rare. Today, some mental health organizations maintain that perhaps as many as 30 million people suffer from one of these problems and are in need of diagnosis and pharmaceutical treatment (Mental Health Channel, 2007).

In 2014, the Irish drug company, Shire, began a massive media campaign to market a condition called binge-eating disorder, which was only officially recognized by the American Psychiatric Association 2 years earlier. The company employed the former tennis star Monica Seles to make the rounds of the most popular television talk shows to discuss her struggles with binge eating. Patient advocacy groups—paid by Shire—directed social media traffic to a company website that contained advice on how people should raise the issue of binge eating with their doctors. By 2015, it had won FDA approval to market its top-selling Vyvanse to treat this "new" disorder (M. Thomas, 2015).

Why has the medicalized view of deviance become so dominant? One reason is that medical explanations of troublesome social problems and deviant behaviors appeal to a society that wants simple explanations for complex social problems. If violent behavior is the result of a dysfunction in a person's brain, it then becomes a problem of defective, violent individuals, not of the larger societal context within which violent acts occur. Likewise, when our doctor or therapist tells us our anxiety, depression, crabbiness, and insecurity will vanish if we simply take a drug, we are spared the difficult task of looking at the social complexities of our lives or the structure of our society.

The medicalization of deviance also appeals to our humanitarian values. The designation of a problem as an illness replaces legal punishment and moral scrutiny with therapeutic treatment (Zola, 1986). The alcoholic is no longer a sinner or a criminal but a victim, someone whose behavior is an "illness" beyond her or his control. Children who have trouble learning in school aren't disobedient and disruptive, they are "sick." If people are violating norms because of a disease that has invaded their bodies, they should not be held morally responsible. Medicalization creates less social stigma and condemnation of people labeled deviant.

Despite its enormous public appeal, the tendency to medicalize deviance has serious social consequences (Conrad & Schneider, 1992). These include the individualization of complex social issues and the depoliticization of deviance.

MICRO-MACRO CONNECTION
THE PHARMACEUTICAL PERSONALITY

The antidepressant drug Prozac arrived on the scene in 1987 and was immediately hailed as a miracle cure. Not only was it effective and easy to prescribe, it was relatively free from the weight gain, low blood pressure, irregular heart rhythms, and other side effects common with earlier antidepressant drugs. By 1990, Prozac had become the top-selling antidepressant in the world, a position it held until 2000. At its peak, it brought in $3 billion in annual revenues (Zuckoff, 2000). Sales have dipped recently as cheaper, generic versions have entered the market. Nevertheless, Prozac and chemically similar antidepressant drugs such as Zoloft, Paxil, Celexa, and Wellbutrin earn $8.7 billion a year in U.S. sales alone ("Top Antidepressant Drugs," 2015). GlaxoSmithKline spent more money—$91 million—advertising Paxil in 1 year than Nike spent advertising its top shoes (C. Elliott, 2003). At one point, 8.5% of the entire U.S. civilian, noninstitutionalized population had a prescription for an antidepressant (Stagnitti, 2005).

Antidepressants quickly grew to be more than just treatments for depression, however. In a common practice known as "off-label" use (that is, the prescribing of a drug for conditions other than those for which it was originally approved), they are now regularly prescribed for people with eating disorders, obsessive-compulsive disorders, anxiety disorders, social phobias, obesity, gambling addiction, and family problems. A version of Prozac called Sarafem is prescribed for women complaining of premenstrual difficulties. Some people use antidepressants to enhance job performance, improve their alertness and concentration, overcome boredom, think more clearly, become more assertive, or get along better with their mates.

Clearly, the therapeutic realm of antidepressants has expanded beyond clinical depression to include more of what were once thought of as ordinary life stresses. In his influential book *Listening to Prozac* (1997), psychiatrist Peter Kramer—an avid proponent and energetic prescriber of the drug—argues that Prozac can (and perhaps should) also be used to remove aspects of our personality we find objectionable. He likens the use of Prozac to overcome undesirable psychological traits to the use of cosmetic surgery to overcome undesirable physical ones.

Many people who have benefited from antidepressants describe them in adoring, almost worshipful terms. They weren't healed; they were transformed.

Shy introverts report turning into social butterflies, mediocre workers turn into on-the-job dynamos, the bored become interested and alert—even the unattractive begin to feel more beautiful. Some people see drugs like Prozac as nothing short of a divine creation:

> As my husband and I watched the results of Prozac, we knew that the medication was God's gift to us. Breakthroughs . . . like Prozac are evidence of His grace. I now *feel* God's love for me as I never have before. . . . I believe that it is helping me be more true to the person God created me to be. (quoted in Tapia, 1995, p. 17)

According to Kramer (1997), his patients feel "better than well" shortly after they begin taking the drug. They report improvement in their popularity, business sense, self-image, energy, and sexual appeal. One patient was having trouble at work and had recently broken up with her boyfriend. Kramer prescribed Prozac. Within weeks, she was dating several men and handling her job demands smoothly. She even received a substantial pay raise. Convinced that the drug had created these improvements in her life, she happily referred to herself as "Ms. Prozac."

Antidepressants are appealing for economic reasons, too. Because traditional psychotherapy (patients talking to therapists about their problems) is time consuming and expensive, efforts to cut health care costs work against its use. A psychiatrist can earn $150 for three 15-minute medication visits compared with $90 for a 45-minute talk therapy session (G. Harris, 2011c). Furthermore, many health care plans limit or exclude extensive talk therapy in their coverage, thereby indirectly encouraging greater use of antidepressant drugs. According to one government survey, only about 11% of psychiatrists provide talk therapy to all their patients, even though recent evidence suggests that such an approach may be as good as or better than drugs in the treatment of depression (G. Harris, 2011b).

Despite claims by some that antidepressants increase suicidal tendencies, they've certainly helped tens of millions of people in serious need. But their popularity raises fundamental sociological questions about the role all sorts of prescription drugs ought to play in everyday life. Critics fear that antidepressants—as well as other drugs that can modify character—are aimed not just at "sick patients" but at people who already function at a high level and want enriched memory, enhanced intelligence, heightened concentration, and a transformation of bad moods into good ones. In a fast-paced, achievement-oriented society such as the United States, the motivations for gaining a competitive edge—whether in school, on the job, or in interpersonal relations—are obvious. Those who earn higher grades, sell more cars, or come across as more charming and attractive can reap enormous financial and social benefits. At high schools around the country, pressure over grades and competition to get into college have driven more and more students to use stimulants like Adderall, Vyvanse, and Concerta. More than one in three college students admit to using such drugs to improve their academic performance ("Adderall Statistics," 2012). Here's how one author described the appeal:

> Now I could study all night, then run 10 miles, then breeze through that week's *New Yorker*, all without pausing to consider whether I might prefer to chat with classmates or go to the movies. It was fantastic. I lost weight. . . . I didn't know how long it had been since I'd slept more than five hours. Why bother?
> (C. Schwartz, 2016, p. 57)

Ten years ago, off-label use of stimulants became the second most common form of illicit drug use on college campuses, trailing only marijuana in popularity (C. Schwartz, 2016). As one columnist put it, in competitive high schools, the use of such drugs to boost grades has gone from "rare to routine" (Schwarz, 2012, p. A1).

And there is growing evidence that the illicit use of stimulants is spilling into the workforce. One Pennsylvania dentist prescribed herself Adderall for years, saying that it enabled her to see "15 patients a day rather than 12" (quoted in Schwarz, 2015a, p. 17).

But once people begin to use a drug to chemically enhance performance, those who do not use the drug—whether for reasons of principle or because they can't afford it—risk losing out and becoming the less rewarded and less valuable members of the community (President's Council on Bioethics, 2003). Would we, as a society, have to resort to legal regulation—much like the ban on athletic performance enhancers such as anabolic steroids—to prevent a desperate race to keep up?

On a more profound level, if we can use existing pharmaceutical technology to chemically eradicate sadness and despair, why would anyone ever put up with emotional discomfort? In the past, people simply assumed that misery and suffering were part of the human condition. Just as physical pain prevents us from burning ourselves if we get too close to a fire, perhaps mental pain, too, serves a purpose, such as motivating us to change life situations that are getting us into trouble. There's the spiritual element as well: "One reconceives sadness as sickness only by emptying it of psychic or spiritual significance and turning it into a mere thing of the body" (President's Council on Bioethics, 2003, p. 261).

But people today are more inclined to believe they have a right not to be unhappy. Sadness is inconvenient and prevents us from reaching our potential. And if there's a drug to get rid of it quickly and cheaply, then why not use it? And it's not just in the form of pills. Researchers in Japan recently found that prefectures with higher naturally occurring levels of lithium in their water—a mineral that helps balance mood swings—have lower suicide rates than other areas (Ohgami, Terao, Shiotsuki, Ishii, & Iwata, 2009). This finding has led some to speculate that perhaps adding lithium to water supplies can build up a community's resistance to depression, not unlike adding fluoride to water supplies has reduced levels of tooth decay.

Mood-altering drugs have not yet completely redefined society. Quite possibly depression, unlike polio or smallpox, will never be essentially wiped out. But the technological possibilities not only of antidepressants but of brain-scanning techniques, genetic modification, and drugs as yet unknown raise important issues about the role of medicine in defining deviance, controlling behavior, constructing personality, and ultimately determining social life and the culture that guides it.

Individualizing Complex Social Issues

As you've seen throughout the first part of this book, U.S. culture often emphasizes the individual over the social structure. Instead of seeing certain deviant behaviors as symptoms of a faulty social system—blocked economic opportunities, neighborhood decay, or unattainable cultural standards—people in the United States tend to see such behaviors as expressions of individual traits or shortcomings. In short, bad or weird people do bad or weird things. Hence, they can be remedied only through actions aimed at the individual (Kovel, 1980). For instance, consider the growing tendency we have to label various forms of hatred or bigotry as medicalized "phobias": homophobia, islamophobia, transphobia, fatphobia, and so on. The American Psychiatric Association (2013) defines phobias as irrational fears and anxieties associated with a specific object or situation that lead to avoidance behaviors. Hence discrimination aimed at a feared object—say gay people or Muslims—becomes the expression of an individual disorder in need of treatment. As one psychologist put it, "[C]oding anti-gay behavior as a personality problem obscures the religious and political beliefs that are spurring anti-gay attitudes" (quoted in Hess, 2016, pp. 14–15).

Individualistic medical explanations of deviance are not necessarily wrong. Some violent people do have neurological diseases, and some people diagnosed with clinical depression do have imbalances of chemicals in their brains. But when we pursue these explanations for everyone whose behavior diverges from social expectations, the solutions we seek focus on the perpetrator to the exclusion of everything else.

Consider attention-deficit/hyperactivity disorder (ADHD), one of the most commonly diagnosed maladies among U.S. children today. A child diagnosed with ADHD is difficult to deal with at home and in the classroom. He or she fidgets and squirms, has difficulty remaining seated, can't sustain attention in tasks or play activities, can't follow rules, talks excessively, and is easily distracted (American Psychiatric Association, 2013).

Fifty years ago, such children were considered troublemakers and would have received punishment or even expulsion from school. Today, however, most hyperactive behavior is diagnosed as a symptom of a mental disorder. Somewhere between 4% and 12% of all school-aged children in the United States will be diagnosed with ADHD at some point in their youth, and three quarters of these children are boys (Getahun et al., 2013). From 2000 and 2010, diagnoses of ADHD increased from 6.2 million to 10.4 million (IMS Health, 2012).

Drugs (with recognizable names like Ritalin, Concerta, and Adderall) are far and away the treatment of choice for people diagnosed with ADHD. The number of prescriptions for drugs to treat ADHD is growing at a faster rate than for any other drug; more prescriptions are written for them than for antibiotics or asthma medication (Conrad, 2005).

Interestingly, recipients of these drugs are getting both younger and older. The American Academy of Pediatrics now recommends diagnosing ADHD for children under 4. More than 10,000 toddlers between 2 and 3 years of age are now medicated for ADHD (Schwarz, 2014). Some predict these numbers will soar even higher as more states begin expanding access to early education (a policy referred to as "Universal Pre-K"). Introducing millions of 3- to 5-year-olds to the behavioral demands of classrooms will mean that more distracted kids will catch the attention of their teachers (Hinshaw & Scheffler, 2014).

At the same time, psychiatrists are making more diagnoses of late-onset ADHD in adolescents and adults (Agnew-Blais, Polanczyk, and Danese, 2016). Not surprisingly prescriptions for adults over 20 increased by 60% between 2008 and 2012 (Schwarz, 2013). All total, annual sales of ADHD drugs have more than quintupled in the last decade from under $2 billion in sales to over $9 billion (cited in Schwarz, 2013). The overall cost of treating ADHD is now between $36 billion and $52.4 billion a year (Getahun et. al., 2013).

This growth is part of an alarming trend toward the increased childhood drug prescriptions in general. For instance, between one quarter and one half of all kids who attend summer camps take some type of daily prescription medications (J. Gross, 2006). From 2013 to 2014, there was a 50% increase in prescriptions for powerful antipsychotics and a 23% increase in antidepressant prescriptions for children under the age of 2 (Schwarz, 2015b). Critics worry not only about the safety of these drugs but also about the mixed messages children receive when they are handed a daily pill to medicate away their troublesome behavior while at the same time they are told to "say no" to other drugs (Koch, 1999).

Despite occasional adverse side effects, the drugs used to treat ADHD are generally successful in quieting unruly and annoying behavior (Whalen & Henker, 1977). And certainly a medical response to ADHD is preferable to harsh punishment. But are we ignoring the possibility that hyperactive behavior may be a child's adaptation to his or her social environment (Sroufe, 2012)? Some pediatricians, for instance, argue that the symptoms of ADHD may just be children's natural reaction to living in a fast-paced, stressful world (Diller, 1998). According to one neuroscientist, the inability to sustain attention, regulate rage, or tolerate normal types of sensory input may be as much a function of living in a "culture of excess and self-indulgence" as faulty brain wiring (cited in Warner, 2010). Others have argued that ADHD may, in part, be a response to an educational system that discourages individual expression (Conrad, 1975), demands more homework and provides less unstructured free time than ever before (Koerth-Baker, 2013), or that expects more self-control from young children than they're capable of exercising (Duncan, 2007). Narrowly defined norms of acceptable behavior make it difficult if not impossible for children to pursue their own desires and needs.

I'm not suggesting that all children who are diagnosed with ADHD are disruptive simply because they live in a multitasking society, are bored in school, or have had their individual creativity and vitality squashed by unsympathetic teachers. Some children do have neurological disorders that create debilitating behavioral problems in need of treatment. The point is that from an institutional perspective, the tendency to label disruptiveness simply as an individual disorder protects the school system's legitimacy and authority. The institution simply cannot function if disruptiveness is tolerated (Tobin, Wu, & Davidson, 1989). But imagine if our educational system promoted and encouraged free individual expression rather than obedience and discipline. In such an environment, overactivity wouldn't be considered disruptive and wouldn't be a problem in need of a medical solution.

When inconvenient or annoying behavior is translated into an individual sickness, medical remedies (usually drugs) become a convenient tool for enforcing conformity and upholding the values of society. When parents say they want "better children," they typically mean they want children who are in line with our culture's values: "well adjusted, well-behaved, sociable, attentive, high-performing, and academically adept" (President's Council on Bioethics, 2003, p. 73). Parents who *don't* want their children to have these characteristics become objects of suspicion.

So it's not surprising that we have come to rely on drugs to help us through many of our common problems in living. One in six Americans now takes a prescription psychiatric drug (antidepressants, antianxiety agents, or antipsychotics; T. J. Moore & Mattison, 2016). Antidepressant drugs, in particular, have become so popular that they are a prominent feature of the culture.

Depoliticizing Deviance

The process of individualizing social problems robs deviant behavior of its power to send a message about malfunctioning elements in society. Disruptive behaviors or statements automatically lose their power to prompt social change when they are seen simply as symptoms of individual defects or illnesses. We need not pay attention to the critical remarks of an opponent if that opponent is labeled as mentally ill. Totalitarian regimes often declare political dissidents insane and confine them to hospitals in an attempt to quiet dangerous political criticism. In 2007, a Russian activist was held in a psychiatric clinic for months after publishing an article detailing the harsh treatment of patients in the same hospital. In China, people who file complaints against local government officials often find themselves involuntarily committed to mental institutions. Although there are no reliable statistics on how often these confinements occur, human rights activists say they're increasing because local authorities are under intense pressure to quell social unrest these days. One woman, who was confined for 7 months after complaining that she had been unfairly denied a government job, said, "What they are trying to do is completely destroy your mind and weaken your body to the point where you go crazy. That's when you will stop petitioning, they hope" (quoted in LaFraniere & Levin, 2010, p. A14). Such practices are not found only in foreign countries. In the early 1990s, a Dallas Morning News investigation discovered that high-ranking U.S. military commanders were trying to discredit and intimidate subordinates who reported security and safety violations or military overpricing by ordering them to undergo psychiatric evaluations or sending them to a mental ward (Timms & McGonigle, 1992). When a low-ranking naval officer reported that fellow sailors had raped three women while stationed in Bermuda, he was committed to a psychiatric hospital for a week (Zwerdling, 2004). An officer in the Air Force contended that his forced hospitalization was part of retaliation for reporting payroll abuses at the Dallas Naval Air Station. He insightfully describes the power of medical labels to discredit his political criticism:

> What happened was nobody would speak to me. Let's face it. After someone has gone to a mental ward, you kind of question what's going on. It was a nice ploy, and it worked. What they did was totally neutralize me. (quoted in Timms & McGonigle, 1992, p. F1)

Creating the image of deviants as sick people who must be dealt with through medical therapies is a powerful way for dominant groups in society to maintain conformity and protect themselves from those whom they fear or who challenge the way "normal" social life is organized (Pfohl, 1994). The seemingly merciful medical labels not only reduce individual responsibility but also reduce the likelihood that such potentially contagious political criticism will be taken seriously (Hills, 1980).

Conclusion

When we talk about deviance, we usually speak of extreme forms: crime, mental illness, substance abuse, and so on. These activities are indeed troublesome, but for most people they remain comfortably distant phenomena. I think most of us would like to cling to the belief that deviants are "them" and normal people are "us."

The lesson I hope you take away from this chapter, however, is that the issue of deviance is, essentially, an issue of social definition. As a group, community, or society, we decide which differences are benign and which are dangerous. Standards and expectations change. Norms come and go. The consequence is that each of us could be considered deviant to some degree by some audience. We have all broken unspoken interactional norms; many of us have even broken the law. To a lesser degree, we are all potentially like Kelly Michaels, subject to being erroneously labeled deviant and unfairly treated as a result. Given the right—or wrong—circumstances, all of us risk being negatively labeled or acquiring a bad reputation.

This chapter has examined deviance as both a microlevel and a macrolevel sociological phenomenon, as something that plays a profound role in individual lives and in society as a whole. Although sociologists are interested in the broad social and political processes that create cultural definitions of deviance, they are also interested in the ways these definitions are applied in everyday life. Societal definitions have their most potent effect when expressed face to face. We can talk about powerful institutions such as medicine creating definitions of deviance that are consistent with broader political or economic interests, but if these definitions aren't accepted as appropriate to some degree by the majority, they will be ineffectual. Again, we see the value of developing the sociological imagination, which helps us understand the complex interplay between individuals and the culture and community within which they live.

Your Turn

People's perceptions of deviant acts and individuals are a crucial element of our understanding of deviance. From a conflict perspective, these perceptions are usually consistent with the goals and interests of those in power. But what exactly are people's perceptions of deviance?

Make copies of the following list, and find 20 to 30 people who would be willing to read it and answer a few questions. Try to get an equal proportion of males and females and younger and older people. Have each person rank the following "deviant" acts in order from 1 to 19, with 19 being the most serious and 1 the least serious. Do not define for them what you mean by "serious."

- Catching your spouse/partner with a lover and killing them both
- Embezzling money from your employer
- Robbing a supermarket with a gun
- Forcibly raping a stranger in a park
- Selling alcohol to minors
- Killing a suspected burglar in your home
- Practicing medicine without a license
- Soliciting for prostitution
- Blowing up a building with people in it for religious reasons
- Hitting your child
- Taking stimulants before a final exam
- Selling cocaine

- Manufacturing and selling cars known to have dangerous defects
- Forcibly raping a former romantic partner or spouse
- Cyberstalking
- Being drunk in public
- Killing a person for a fee
- Smoking cigarettes in a supermarket
- Conspiring to fix the prices of machines sold to businesses

(Many of the items in this exercise are adapted from P. Rossi, Waite, Bose, & Berk, 1974.)

After the volunteers are finished, ask them how they decided on their rankings. What criteria did they use for judging the seriousness of each act? Where did their perceptions come from? Why do they think the "less serious" acts on the list are against the law?

After collecting all your data, compute the average ranking for each of the 19 items (for each item, add all the ranking scores and divide by the number of responses). The larger the average score, the greater the perceived seriousness of that act. Which acts were considered the most serious and which the least serious? Was there a fair amount of agreement among the people in your sample? Were there any differences between the ratings of men and women? Between older and younger people? Between people of different racial or ethnic groups? Use the conflict perspective to discuss the role these perceptions play in the nature and control of deviance.

Chapter Highlights

- According to an absolutist definition of deviance, there are two fundamental types of behavior: that which is inherently acceptable and that which is inherently unacceptable. In contrast, a relativist definition of deviance suggests that it is not a property inherent in any particular act, belief, or condition. Instead, deviance is a definition of behavior that is socially created by collective human judgments. Hence, like beauty, deviance is in the eye of the beholder.

(Continued)

(Continued)

- The labeling theory of deviance argues that deviance is a consequence of the application of rules and sanctions to an offender. Deviant labels can impede individuals' everyday social life by forming expectations of them in the minds of others.

- According to conflict theory, the definition of deviance is a form of social control exerted by more powerful people and groups over less powerful ones.

- The criminal justice system and the medical profession have had a great deal of influence in defining, explaining, and controlling deviant behavior. Criminalization is the process by which certain behaviors come to be defined as crimes. Medicalization is the depiction of deviance as a medical problem or illness.

Key Terms

absolutism: Approach to defining deviance that rests on the assumption that all human behavior can be considered either inherently good or inherently bad

criminalization: Official definition of an act of deviance as a crime

deterrence theory: Theory of deviance positing that people will be prevented from engaging in a deviant act if they judge the costs of such an act to outweigh its benefits

deviance: Behavior, ideas, or attributes of an individual or group that some people in society find offensive

labeling theory: Theory stating that deviance is the consequence of the application of rules and sanctions to an offender; a deviant is an individual to whom the identity "deviant" has been successfully applied

medicalization: Definition of behavior as a medical problem, mandating the medical profession to provide some kind of treatment for it

relativism: Approach to defining deviance that rests on the assumption that deviance is socially created by collective human judgments and ideas

SAGE edge™ edge.sagepub.com/newman12e

SAGE edge offers a robust online environment featuring an impressive array of free tools and resources for review, study, and further exploration, keeping both instructors and students on the cutting edge of teaching and learning.

Social Structure, Institutions, and Everyday Life

Up to this point, I have been discussing how our everyday lives are constructed and ordered. But that is only part of the picture. What does social life look like from the top down? Once the architecture is constructed and in place, what influence does it exert on our everyday lives? To answer these questions, the remaining chapters investigate the organizational and institutional pressures on everyday life and the various sources of structural inequality in society: social class and wealth, race and ethnicity, and gender. Global institutions and population trends are other structural influences on everyday life. These facets of society may seem ominous and impenetrable. However, you will see that our lives don't completely fall under the control of the social structure. As the concept of the sociological imagination suggests, the collective actions of individuals often bring about fundamental changes in society.

9

The Structure of Society

Organizations, Social Institutions, and Globalization

- Social Structure and Everyday Life
- Social Dilemmas: Individual Interests and Structural Needs
- The Structure of Formal Organizations
- Organizations and Institutions
- Globalization and Social Institutions

History will no doubt mark the 2000 presidential election as one of the most bizarre political events of all time. Even today, over a decade and a half later, the effects of this event can still be felt in our national electoral system.

The chaos began on election night. Early in the evening, Al Gore, the Democratic candidate, was projected as the winner of Florida's 25 electoral votes, giving him the inside track to the presidency; a few hours later, that projection was rescinded, and Florida was labeled "too close to call." In the early morning hours of the following day, George W. Bush, the Republican candidate, was projected as the winner of Florida and therefore of the election, only to have that projection withdrawn when Florida, again, was declared "too close to call." The ensuing month brought a daily dose of street protests, charges of voter fraud, recounts, debates over absentee votes, lawsuits, countersuits, and legal rulings. On November 26, the Florida state canvassing board certified that George Bush was the winner. The Florida Supreme Court overruled and ordered another recount. But on December 13, the U.S. Supreme Court issued its definitive ruling, on a 5–4 vote, that the Florida recount was unconstitutional. George W. Bush was thus declared the next president of the United States, even though he had received over half a million fewer votes nationwide than Gore.

To listen to the domestic and foreign news media describe it at the time, the most powerful country in the world was in a state of utter political confusion. The situation was described in either mocking or apocalyptic terms. U.S. citizens were losing their moral authority to lecture other countries about the virtues of democracy. We were about to face a "constitutional crisis" that could paralyze the government. We were going to be a country without a leader. We were on the brink of anarchy.

More recently, the 2016 presidential election was marked by charges of unfairness and illegitimacy. Nearly 2.9 million more voters cast their ballots for the Democratic candidate, Hillary Clinton, than for the winner, Donald Trump. Yet, by virtue of acquiring 306 electoral votes (to Clinton's 232), Trump became the 45th president. Soon after the election, various U.S. intelligence agencies reported that Russia had attempted to influence the outcome by hacking the Democratic National Committee and other political organizations of the Democratic Party. Those hacks led to the public release of thousands of stolen e-mails, many of which included damaging revelations about Clinton. Scores of legislators boycotted Trump's inauguration claiming his election was illegitimate. The following day, millions of people around the country (as well as some other countries) marched to protest the new president. Again, it seemed as if the country was teetering on chaos. At the time of this writing, the ties between Russia and the Trump campaign continue to be investigated.

So why didn't the country collapse during these electoral traumas? To answer that question, we must turn to one of the key concepts of this book: social structure. Despite strong emotions, dire predictions, and confrontational behavior, the political system remained intact. Whether we agreed with the ultimate outcomes of these elections or not, our legal and political institutions worked as they were designed to. From local precincts and campaign organizations to state legislatures to the highest court in the land, the system continued to function. To be sure, the motives of some of the individual players were highly partisan. But the structure itself rose above the actions of these individuals and prevented the sort of large-scale catastrophes media pundits predicted. As one journalist put it following the 2000 election, "The apparatus of government is still in place, skilled politicians and career civil servants still keep things running, and ultimately nothing apocalyptic is likely to happen. . . . The system will work and life will go on" (Belluck, 2001, p. A9).

In the aftermath of both these elections, buses, trains, and planes still ran on time. All of our national tourist attractions remained open. Food was still delivered to grocery store shelves. Municipal services were still provided. Even the stock market remained solid. The majority of Americans simply went about their business, pausing now and then to witness the political spectacle, fret over the direction of the country, or debate with friends, family, and coworkers. Society simply kept going.

One of the great sociological paradoxes of human existence is that we are capable of producing a social structure that we then experience as something other than a human product. It is ironic that we spend most of our lives either within or responding to the influence of larger structural entities—particularly in a society such as the United States, which so fiercely extols the virtues of rugged individualism and personal accomplishment.

This chapter focuses on our relationship with the social structure we construct and maintain, both locally and globally. This focus requires us to examine the structure not only from the individual's perspective but also from the macrosociological perspective of the organizations and institutions themselves. Many important social issues look quite different depending on the perspective we use to understand them.

Social Structure and Everyday Life

As you recall from Chapter 2, **social structure** is the framework of society that exists above the level of individuals and provides the social setting in which individuals interact with one another to form relationships. It includes the organizations, groups, statuses and roles, cultural beliefs, and institutions that add order and predictability to our lives. The concept of social structure is important because it implies a patterned regularity in the way we live and in the way societies work. We could not draw any meaningful conclusions about human behavior if we started with the notion that society is haphazard and that things occur by chance alone.

You can see social structure everywhere. Consider, for instance, the components of social structure that affect the experience of going to high school. Within this broad U.S. educational institution, there are examples of every component of social structure:

- *Organizations:* National Education Association, state teachers' associations, accrediting agencies, local school boards, school districts, and so on

- *Groups:* faculty, administrators, classes, clubs, teams, cafeteria staff, and so on

- *Statuses:* teacher, student, principal, vice principal, counselor, nurse, secretary, custodian, coach, librarian, and so on

- *Role expectations:* teaching, learning, disciplining, making and taking tests, advising, coaching, feeding, and so on

- *Cultural beliefs:* for example, the belief that education is the principal means of achieving financial success, that it makes possible a complex division of labor, and that it makes a technologically advanced society possible

- *Institutionalized norms:* for example, the expectation that everyone attend school until at least the age of 16, school rules that determine acceptable behavior (not running in the halls, not screaming in class, staying on the school grounds until classes are over; Saunders, 1991)

The massive structure of the educational system is a reality that determines life chances and choices. You can choose which science class to take in high school, whether to go on to college, and what to major in once you get there. But the admissions policies of potential colleges and the availability of jobs to people with and without a college degree are factors beyond your control. You're reading this book right now not because of your fondness for fine literature but because of the structural requirements of being a college student. You know you must graduate to increase your chances of getting a good job, and to graduate you must get good grades in your classes. To get good grades in your classes, you must keep up with the material so you're prepared for exams. You probably would rather be doing a number of other things right now—reading a better book, watching TV, texting, tweeting, blogging, sleeping, staring into space—but personal preferences must take a backseat for the time being to the more immediate structural demands of college life.

The structural requirements of the educational system have a broader impact as well. Course grades, standardized test scores, and class rankings are emphasized so much and create such personal anxiety for students that they may actually eclipse learning and intellectual growth:

Throughout our school years, we are taught to believe from society that grades display intelligence. Because of this, our motivation, learning, and personal growth are placed second to attaining the ultimate goal—the grade. . . . We are programmed to imitate what the teacher wants. If we don't, we get a bad grade. . . . Imitation, competition, and fear of grades hinders our discovery. (I. Bell & McGrane, 1999, p. 2)

This competitive atmosphere can sometimes create incompatibility between the needs of the individual student and the needs of the educational system. Suppose your sociology instructor told you that she was going to give everyone in the class an A as long as they showed up each day. Your immediate reaction might be joy, because such a grade would no doubt improve your grade point average (GPA). But what if all instructors in all courses at your school decided to do the same thing? Every student who simply showed up for all her or his classes would graduate with a perfect GPA. How would you feel then? Your joy would no doubt be tempered by the knowledge that the reputation of your school would suffer. As long as our educational system is structured on the principle of "survival of the fittest"—the assumption that only the smartest or hardest-working students earn the top grades—outsiders would perceive such changes as a sign that your school is academically inferior. Hence, your long-term personal interests may actually be best served by a highly competitive system that ensures that some of your fellow students will get lower grades than you.

Beyond your personal outcomes, the competitive educational structure also influences how schools and teachers are assessed. Consider, for instance, the role of standardized testing. In 2001, the No Child Left Behind Act required that all public schools receiving federal funding administer a statewide standardized test annually to all students to determine if they were making adequate progress. If the schools continually failed to meet their performance goals, administrators risked losing their jobs and the schools faced the possibility of being taken over. Low-income schools risked losing their financial aid if students consistently performed poorly. Given such pressures, it's not surprising that more and more schools focused their curricula on standardized testing. For instance, Florida schools spent between 60 and 80 days out of the 180-day school year on testing, and in some districts, tests were given every day (L. Alvarez, 2014).

The problems associated with No Child Left Behind led directly to a new policy, Every Student Succeeds in 2015. According to this law, states still have to test students in reading and math once a year in Grades 3 through 8, as well as once in high school (U.S. Department of Education, 2017). However, the act clearly reduces the emphasis on frequent standardized testing and removes incentives for schools to provide instruction to students solely with the goal of performing well on these tests in mind.

Even when it's operating as it's designed to, social structure can cause problems. Mistakes are sometimes the result of a chain of events set in motion by a system that either induces errors or makes them difficult to detect and correct. For instance, it's estimated that as many as 25% of hospitalized patients a year will experience a preventable medical error of some sort (Landrigan et al., 2010), and as many as 250,000 will die as a result (Makary & Daniel, 2016). That would make avoidable medical mistakes the third leading cause of death in the United States behind only heart disease and cancer.

Some people are particularly vulnerable. An annual study of the experiences of Medicare patients in U.S. hospitals estimates that between 2007 and 2009, there were more than 700,000 safety incidents and close to 80,000 preventable deaths attributable to medical errors such as anesthesia complications, drug mix-ups, infections due to medical care, accidental lacerations, and various other postoperative complications (Health Grades, 2011). To make matters worse, only about one out of every seven errors, accidents, or other events that harm these patients is actually reported (Pear, 2012).

The tendency to hold individual doctors or nurses responsible in such cases demonstrates an overwhelming cultural perception that these errors are caused by personal incompetence. But what appear to be obvious errors in human judgment or ineptitude are sometimes, on closer inspection, linked to broader structural failures. An analysis of 334 drug errors in hospitals found that structural failure was responsible for most of them—for example, poor dissemination of drug knowledge to doctors, inadequate availability of patient information, faulty systems for checking correct dosage, and inefficient hospital procedure (Leape & Bates, 1995). One organization estimates that a system-wide shortage of nurses—which leads to a dangerously high patient-to-nurse ratio—is responsible for tens of thousands of hospital deaths each year (cited in Robbins, 2015). Even the institutional method of training doctors may bear some responsibility. One study found that the overall adequacy and quality of medical care in hospitals decreases significantly in the summer months, not because doctors are distracted by thoughts of beach vacations but because of the timing of new physician residency programs. Summer is when brand new residents fresh out of medical school begin to learn how to care for patients; and they inevitably make mistakes (Young et al., 2011). This problem is so well known in the health care system that it even has a nickname: the July Effect.

Twenty years ago, a report by the Institute of Medicine (1999) recognized that the problem of unnecessary hospital injuries and deaths lies beyond the actions of individual health care workers. It recommended that the health care system build safety concerns into its operations at all levels. It suggested creating a national center for patient safety, establishing a mandatory nationwide reporting system, placing greater emphasis on safety and training in licensing and accreditation evaluations, and developing a "culture of safety" that would help make the reduction of medical errors a top professional priority.

To date, however, the United States, unlike some European countries, has no federal agency charged specifically with hospital oversight. Instead, responsibility for protecting the health and safety of hospital patients lies with a patchwork of state health departments and a nonprofit group called the Joint Commission, which sets quality standards. As a result, bad hospitals are rarely closed and are seldom hit with significant financial penalties for patient suffering (Berenson, 2008). Furthermore, hospitals may actually profit from their own mistakes because insurance companies usually pay for the longer stays and extra care that result from preventable errors (Eappen, 2013).

Some structural improvement is taking place. For instance, to curb the incidence of medical errors, many hospitals around the country have switched to electronic medical record systems and have invested heavily in tablets, smartphones, and other devices to give medical staff instant access to patients' data, drug information, and case studies. However, between 2012 and 2013, only 3.5% of American hospitals improved their safety ratings significantly (The Advisory Board Company, 2013).

MICRO-MACRO CONNECTION
CAN SOCIAL STRUCTURE OVERCOME CATASTROPHE?

People's dependence on social structure is illustrated most clearly when they face calamitous, life-threatening situations. In 2010, 33 Chilean miners were trapped 2,300 feet underground for over 2 months. They all survived and most were surprisingly unscathed after the ordeal. Sure, their physical survival required impressive levels of individual stamina, the diligent efforts of rescuers, a constant flow of food and supplies, effective medical advice from doctors at the surface, and some really good luck. But without the well-organized subterranean social structure they created, they never would have made it.

Early on in the crisis, the trapped miners determined that every decision they made, no matter how large or small, would be put to a majority vote. They developed a

(Continued)

(Continued)

clear authority structure, with every individual assigned to a particular role, such as food organizer, medic, pastor, environmental assistant, communications specialist, and media director. They designated places for eating, exercise, and waste disposal. They split into three groups of 11, each with its own leadership and assigned tasks. They abided by a regular daily schedule that included meals, showers, exercise, "house" cleaning, and chores done in three shifts around the clock (J. Franklin, 2010). To many observers, the remarkably good shape the miners were in when they emerged could be attributed to all this organization. Social structure literally helped save their lives.

Let's turn the clock ahead to the spring of 2011 and the massive Japanese earthquake and tsunami that devastated the country's northern coast and killed tens of thousands of people. Many villages were wiped off the map. One such place was the tiny fishing hamlet of Hadenya in the town of Minamisanriku. After the tsunami hit, homes were destroyed and loved ones disappeared. Bridges were washed out, vehicles crushed, boats stranded. Electricity and cell phone services were nonexistent. Two hundred and seventy survivors huddled in the frigid cold at a hilltop community center. They had very little food, no fuel, and no news from the outside world. It took nearly 2 weeks for the military to finally reach them. But they were all alive. Like the Chilean miners, the people of Hadenya realized that the only way they could survive was to create their own social structure, quickly reorganizing themselves along the lines of the original community:

> Almost as soon as the waters receded . . . they began dividing tasks along gender lines, with women boiling water and preparing food, while men went scavenging for firewood and gasoline. Within days . . . they had re-established a complex community, with a hierarchy and division of labor, in which members were assigned daily tasks.

> They had even created a committee that served as an impromptu government body for this and five other nearby refugee centers. . . . Representatives from the centers met daily to swap supplies and assigned tasks. (Fackler, 2011, p. A11)

It soon became apparent that Hadenya wasn't unique. Refugees in scores of other small hamlets all along the coast created similar makeshift organizations to aid their survival. The groups were so successful that when the local government began to plan for the eventual relocation of all the survivors into temporary housing miles away, officials realized that the spontaneous group organizations might have some lasting use:

> [The mayor] said the town had originally planned to put people into housing as quickly as possible. Now he thought it best to keep these organizations intact, to help people adapt to new and different living environments.

> "They are like extended families," [the mayor] said. "They provide support and comfort." (Fackler, 2011, p. A11)

But social structure is not always a savior during catastrophes. It can sometimes overwhelm individuals' best efforts to exercise their will. Take, for example, an even bigger tsunami disaster that hit 7 years earlier, killing more than 200,000 people in South Asia and Eastern Africa and leaving millions homeless. Ordinary people all around the world pledged to help the victims, alongside promises of billions of dollars in aid and military assistance made by 19 nations. Close to 30% of U.S. citizens donated money to the cause, and another 37% indicated that they intended to do so (Lester, 2005). Two weeks after the disaster, the charitable organization Save the Children had received more than $10 million in donations over the Internet alone. In a typical month, the organization receives between $30,000 and $50,000 (Strom, 2005).

But such spectacular individual benevolence was hobbled and almost crushed at the organizational level. When two dozen government and aid organizations arrived in the hardest-hit regions of Indonesia a week or two after the tsunami hit, they found that looters and black market traders had already descended on the wreckage. Some devastated areas had yet to see any relief workers, while others were swarming with doctors and nurses. Moreover, the presence of foreign military and relief workers soon created resentment in the Indonesian government. In response, it imposed travel restrictions on foreign aid workers, citing security concerns, and demanded that all foreign military personnel leave the country within 3 months. In one of the hardest-hit areas, Banda Aceh, relief organizations found themselves in the middle of a civil war, operating alongside paramilitary rebels (officially regarded as terrorists by the U.S. government) and an Indonesian military known for its corruption and rights abuses (Wehrfritz & Cochrane, 2005). Despite the presence of thousands of caring and generous individuals who came to help, these structural factors conspired to slow down the relief process.

Social Dilemmas: Individual Interests and Structural Needs

Although social structure can clearly affect the lives of individuals, individual actions can also have an enormous effect on social structure and stability. Sometimes those actions are coordinated to benefit a collection of individuals, and sometimes they're undertaken independently and for personal gain. Let's say a group of residents want to make sure that their neighborhood is free of crime. Each individual could go on a personal crusade to stop crime, but it seems more logical and efficient for everyone to volunteer at some point to "patrol" at night or to chip in money to improve street lighting.

In actuality, though, people seldom voluntarily act to achieve a common objective. Instead, they usually act to ensure their own personal interests (J. Cross & Guyer, 1980; Dawes & Messick, 2000; Olsen, 1965). Say that your neighbors decide to fight crime by improving street lighting. They ask people in the community for voluntary donations. Some residents may decide that the rational thing to do is not to donate money for a new streetlight because they figure others will do so. That way, they could enjoy the benefits of safer, well-lit streets without spending their own money. But if every person individually decides not to donate, they may save some cash in the short run, but the new streetlights will never be purchased, and everyone will suffer in the long run. The experience of each person in a group pursuing his or her self-interest regardless of the potential ruin for everyone is known as a **social dilemma** (Messick & Brewer, 1983).

Major social problems, such as environmental pollution, can be understood as stemming, at least in part, from social dilemmas. If I fling one bag of trash out of my car window and onto the highway, it won't seem significant or destructive. Large numbers of people doing the same thing, though, would be very destructive.

But social dilemmas aren't just the result of selfish or inconsiderate motives. Legitimate economic worries can also create them. For instance, during the recent economic recession, more and more individuals chose not to seek medical care or postponed elective surgeries because they couldn't afford them. According to the American Hospital Association (2009), 60% of hospitals reported moderate or significant decreases in elective procedures over the previous year and 55% reported moderate or significant decreases in admissions. At the individual level, delaying such procedures sometimes led to serious medical consequences, as when a benign cyst turned into a tumor because a patient didn't have a routine diagnostic procedure. Many young people who lacked health insurance and couldn't afford medical care borrowed leftover prescriptions from friends, self-diagnosed online, or even set their own broken bones (Buckley, 2009). Indeed, hospitals reported that emergency rooms sometimes saw critically ill patients whose conditions could have been avoided had they not deferred earlier procedures.

Although health insurance companies save money in the short term when patients postpone or forgo care (Abelson, 2011a), these individual choices may also trigger a chain of events that can have dangerous long-term structural consequences. Elective procedures represent perhaps as much as 25% of a hospital's income (Sack, 2009). The loss of revenue that occurs when large numbers of people decide to cancel or postpone nonurgent surgeries—estimated to be close to a million dollars a year in an average teaching hospital (Caramenico, 2012)—can force some hospitals to trim costs by laying off workers, delaying expansions, canceling equipment updates, and reducing services like post acute care, clinics, and patient education. As a result, the quality of hospital care may begin to deteriorate, creating potentially hazardous consequences for all patients.

At an even higher level, if we think of nations as individual actors and the planet as the community to which they belong, many problems that have global significance—including energy shortages, massive climate change, and species extinction—can be understood from this perspective. Two important types of social dilemmas, at both the local level and broader levels, are the tragedy of the commons and the free-rider problem.

The Tragedy of the Commons

The term *commons* was originally used to describe the public pasture ground, often located in the center of medieval towns, where all the local herders could bring their animals to graze. When villagers used the commons in moderation, the grass could regenerate, resulting in a perpetual supply of food for the herds (Hardin & Baden, 1977). However, each herder soon realized that she or he could benefit individually by letting the animals eat as much as they wanted, thereby increasing their size and the price they could fetch at market. Unfortunately, when many of the herders came to this same conclusion and allowed their herds to eat without limit, the grass in the commons could not regenerate fast enough to feed them all. The tragic result was that the commons collapsed and the herds that grazed on it died or were sold off. The short-term needs of the individual overshadowed the long-term collective needs of the group.

In this illustration, the common resource was grazing land, and the group was relatively small. However, the **tragedy of the commons** model can be applied to any situation in which indispensable but finite resources are available to everyone. Fisheries in international waters offer a nice contemporary example. If not overfished, they can last forever because there will always be fish around to reproduce. However, without imposed limits, a fisher can take a large amount of fish for himself or herself. The individual obviously benefits, but in doing so he or she does irreparable damage to the stocks and destroys their long-term viability. If nobody else is overfishing, people will be inclined to fish in moderation. However, once others start to overfish, the urge to keep up is powerful. Consequently, the stocks will be damaged and the fish will cease to regenerate. In short, every single person did what was in her or his own best interests, which produced an outcome that was worse for everyone: no more fish.

Or consider the aggravating slowdowns we sometimes experience when accessing wireless data networks. These networks, like any other common resource, are not unlimited. Once they reach their bandwidth capacity—at, say, peak usage times—there's not enough to go around and everybody suffers. Cell phone companies and network operators usually respond by expanding carrying capacity and building more cell towers. But these remedies cost money (which means higher rates for consumers) and will inevitably bump up against further electromagnetic limits, known as the "spectrum crunch." So as long as we continue to use our devices whenever we want to text a friend who's standing 10 feet away, seek GPS assistance when we already have directions, or search for the nearest microbrewery when we should be studying for a sociology exam, we will have to deal with the inevitable and inconvenient "tragedy" of wireless congestion and slow connection speeds.

The impulse to seek individual gain over the collective good becomes particularly tempting when personal well-being is at stake. In the flood-prone summer of 1993, a river overflowed its banks in Des Moines, Iowa, wiping out a filtration system and making the municipal water supply unsafe. To restore full water service, the system had to be refilled with clean water. The situation was urgent. Without full water pressure in the city's water pipes, not only were the residents without regular water service but fire engines also couldn't use the hydrants. Local officials asked everyone to voluntarily refrain from using tap water in their homes and businesses for a few days. If all the city's residents had complied, everyone in the community would have had water within a couple of days. For some individuals, however, the temptation to use water secretly in the privacy of their own homes was too hard to resist. So many residents violated the city's request that the resumption of full water service had to be delayed for many more days (Bradsher, 1993). The entire community suffered as a result of individuals seeking their own short-term benefits.

Why do such dilemmas occur? Part of the problem is lack of communication and lack of trust among individual members of a community. I may want to be a good citizen and conserve water by using it sparingly, but if I think my neighbors are hoarding it, I too will hoard it to make sure I don't go without. Hence, I may follow a line of action that results in a positive outcome for me in the short run but that may eventually have a negative outcome for the community in the long run.

The problem is made worse when individuals think that meeting their individual needs won't have a noticeable effect on the community. "Is my fondness for long showers during a drought *really* going to harm the community?" The tragedy of the commons arises when everyone, or at least a substantial number of people, conclude that it will not. As we collectively ignore or downplay the consequences of our actions, we collectively overuse the resource and pave the way for disasters that none of us has caused individually (Edney, 1979).

The Free-Rider Problem

Social dilemmas can also occur when people refrain from contributing to a common resource because the resource will be available regardless of their contribution. Why pay for something that's available for free? For example, it is irrational, from an individual's point of view, to donate money to public television and radio. I can enjoy *Sesame Street, Antiques Road Show,* and *Downton Abbey* without paying a penny. My small personal donation wouldn't be more than a tiny drop in public broadcasting's budgetary bucket anyway. I have no incentive to incur any costs when I don't have to. If everyone acted this way, however, we would all eventually lose the resource. If public television and radio depended solely on voluntary donations made during those annoying fund drives, it would have disappeared a long time ago. Member station fees, grants from universities and the federally funded Corporation for Public Broadcasting, and corporate sponsorships actually keep it going.

Sociologists sometimes refer to this type of social dilemma as the **free-rider problem** (Olsen, 1965). As the term implies, a free rider is an individual who acquires goods or services without risking any personal costs or contributing anything in return. Free-rider behavior can be seen in a variety of everyday activities, from reading a magazine at a newsstand without buying it to downloading music files for free from other people's online collections. We all enjoy the benefits our tax dollars provide—police, firefighters, smooth roads, and many other municipal services. But if taxes were voluntary, would anyone willingly pay for these services?

We can see evidence of the free-rider problem at the national level. People often talk about children as a vital resource on whom the future of the country and the planet depend. The care and education of all children can be seen as a public resource. The whole society benefits when children are well educated and in good physical and psychological health. Yet taxpayers—especially those without children—often protest against tax increases to improve schools, raise teachers' salaries, or hire more youth social workers because they fail to see how such increases will benefit them personally in the long run.

Solutions to Social Dilemmas

Social dilemmas can be solved or at least reduced in several ways. Some sociologists and economists argue that privatization is the best solution. When people own a particular resource, the argument goes, they'll be motivated to preserve it. But privatization creates other problems. For one thing, it's difficult to divide up and sell off resources like air and water. In addition, parties that own a large chunk of a resource may have little interest in seeing that it is shared equitably. For example, several years ago, city leaders in Cochabamba, Bolivia, decided that the best way to save a crumbling municipal water supply system was to sell it to a private corporation that would be motivated to keep it in good repair. But the sale led to exorbitant water bills for city residents and eventually to riots by poor people, who could no longer afford drinkable water (G. Gardner, 2005).

Establishing communication among individuals is another way in which the negative effects of social dilemmas can be reduced. When everybody knows what everybody else is up to, they may be less likely to hoard a resource and more likely to pay their fair share. In addition, when individual actions are identifiable, feelings of personal responsibility are likely to increase (Edney & Harper, 1978). Back in 1993, the city government of Des Moines set up an emergency hotline that people could call to anonymously turn in violators of the water rules I described earlier. If a city crew found the water meter running, the valve at the curb would be turned off for a week. No appeals were allowed, and water users were never told who turned them in. In addition, the offenders' names and addresses were immediately made known to reporters under Iowa's open records rules and spread across the state by newspapers, radio, and television (Bradsher, 1993).

As you might suspect, modern technology has added a new wrinkle to this sort of neighborly surveillance. An app called Nextdoor provides a means by which people can share information about—and perhaps keep an eye on—neighbors. Drones can transcend ground-level privacy and provide visual evidence of other people's activities. When California experienced severe drought conditions a few years ago, residents had to live under some very strict water conservation guidelines that sought to significantly reduce household consumption. But even though state officials defined water wasting as a crime punishable by fines of up to $500 a day (Weiser, 2014), infractions were often hard to detect and punish. So ordinary citizens took to social media to publicly expose water wasters. The company Vizsafe provided a link called "Drought" on its community safety app that allowed users to anonymously report water offenders in their neighborhood. At #droughtshaming, Twitter users posted pictures, videos, and street addresses of violators (E. A. Moore, 2015).

Another solution is centralized control of resources, usually by the government. For instance, a few years ago, because of over-harvesting and climate change, the shrimp supply in the Gulf of Maine reached record lows. In 2011, about 350 boats caught $10.6 million worth of shrimp; in 2013, about 200 boats were only able to catch a little over $1 million worth (Bidgood, 2013). So the Atlantic States Marine Fisheries Commission closed the entire 2014 shrimping season in the region to give the depleted shrimp supply time to recover.

Often, centralized control of a resource involves coercion—through restrictive rules or laws—to prevent people from seeking their self-interested goals. Requiring people to pay taxes is one example. Another is setting up union "closed shops," meaning that to work in a company an employee must join the union and pay union dues. Without this requirement, individual employees would be able to enjoy the benefits provided by the union—higher wages, shorter hours, and better working conditions—without having to pay anything for them.

The Structure of Formal Organizations

Social life has far more complex functions than simply trying to balance individual and collective interests. Those of us who live in a complex society are all, to varying degrees, organizational creatures. We are born in formal organizations, are educated in them, spend most of our adult lives working for them, and will most likely die in them (E. Gross & Etzioni, 1985). Organizations help meet our most basic needs.

Think about the food on your dinner plate. The farm where the food is produced is probably a huge organization, as are the unions that protect the workers who produce the food and the trucking companies that bring it to your local stores. And all this is controlled by a vast network of financial organizations that set prices and by governmental agencies that ensure the food's safety.

To prepare the food that is produced, delivered, and sold, you have to use products made by other organizations—a sink, a refrigerator, a microwave, a stove. To use those appliances, you have to make arrangements with organizations such as the water and power departments, the gas company, and the electric company. And to pay those bills, you must use still other organizations—the postal service, your Internet provider, your bank, credit companies, and so on.

Most likely, the money to pay the bills comes from a job you or someone in your household has. If you are employed, you probably work for yet another organization. And when you receive a paycheck, the Internal Revenue Service steps in to take its share.

What about the car you use to get to that job? No doubt a huge, multinational corporation manufactured it. Such corporations also produced and delivered the fuel on which the car runs. The roads you travel on to get to your destinations are built and maintained by massive organizations within the state and federal governments. You aren't even allowed to drive unless you are covered by insurance, which is available only through an authorized organization.

And what if things aren't going well? If you become sick, have an accident, or have a dispute with someone, you have to use organizations such as hospitals, police departments, and courts to rectify the situation.

You get the picture? Life in a complex society is a life touched by public and private organizations at every turn. In such a society, things must be done in a formal, planned, and unified way. For instance, the people responsible for producing our food can't informally and spontaneously make decisions about what to grow and when to grow it, and the people responsible for selling it to us can't make its availability random and unpredictable. Imagine what a mess your life would be if you didn't know when your local supermarket would be open or what sorts of food would be available for purchase. What if one day it sold nothing but elbow macaroni, the next day only mangoes, and the day after that just salad dressing?

In a small-scale community where people grow their own food and the local mom-and-pop store provides everything else, the lack of structure might not be a problem. But this type of informal arrangement can't work in a massive society. There must be a relatively efficient and predictable system of providing goods and services to large numbers of people. The tasks that need to be carried out just to keep that system going are too complex for a single person to manage. This complexity makes bureaucracy necessary.

Bureaucracies: Playing by the Rules

The famous 19th-century sociologist Max Weber (VAY-ber) was interested in understanding the complexities of modern society. He noted that human beings could not accomplish feats such as building cities, running huge enterprises, and governing large and diverse populations, without bureaucracies. Bureaucracies were certainly an efficient and rational means of managing large groups of people, although Weber acknowledged that these qualities could easily dehumanize those who work in and are served by those organizations.

Today we tend to see bureaucracies primarily as impersonal, rigid machines that trespass into our personal lives:

> Living in the modern world means passing, with some frequency, through . . . bureaucratic nonplaces: waiting rooms, security checks, government offices. Inside, we are compelled to perform strange rituals. We submit to fingerprints, recite Social Security numbers, put on paper gowns. . . . We find ourselves reduced and distilled and assessed; our most invisible attributes . . . become visible; some higher power determines whether we are worthy of the favor we are hoping will be conferred. (S. Anderson, 2017, p. 13)

Bureaucracies conjure up images of rows of desks occupied by faceless workers, endless lines and forms to fill out, and frustration over "red tape" and senseless policies. Indeed, the word *bureaucrat* has taken on such a negative connotation that simply to be called one is an insult. Keep in mind, however, that in a sociological sense, a **bureaucracy** is simply a large hierarchical organization that is governed by formal rules and regulations and that has a clear specification of work tasks.

The bureaucratic organization has three important characteristics:

- *Division of labor:* The bureaucracy has a clear-cut **division of labor**, which is carefully specified by written job descriptions for each position. Theoretically, a clear division of labor is efficient because it employs only specialized experts, every one of whom is responsible only for the effective performance of his or her narrowly defined duties (P. M. Blau & Meyer, 1987). Division of labor enables large organizations to accomplish more ambitious goals than would be possible if everyone acted independently. Tasks become highly specific, sometimes to the point that it is illegal to perform someone else's task. In hospitals, for instance, orderlies don't prescribe drugs, nurses don't perform surgery, and doctors don't help patients fill out their insurance forms.

- *Hierarchy of authority:* Not only are tasks divided in a bureaucracy, but they are also ranked in a **hierarchy of authority** (Weber, 1946). Most U.S. bureaucracies are organized in a pyramid shape with a small number of people at the top who have a lot of power and many at the bottom who have virtually none. In such a chain of command, people at one level are responsible to those above them and can exert authority over those below. Authority tends to be attached to the position and not to the person occupying the position, so that the bureaucracy will not stop functioning in the event of a retirement or a death. The hierarchy of authority in bureaucracies not only allows some people to control others but also justifies paying some people higher salaries than others. When applied to political organizations, the hierarchy of authority can create an **oligarchy**, a system in which many people are ruled by a privileged few (Michels, 1911/1949). In such a setting, leaders can often distance themselves from the public, becoming less accountable for their actions in the process.

- *Impersonality:* Bureaucracies are governed by an elaborate system of rules and regulations that ensure a particular task will be done the same way by each person occupying a position. Rules help ensure that bureaucrats perform their tasks impartially and impersonally. Ironically, the very factors that make the typical bureaucrat unpopular with the public—an aloof attitude, lack of genuine concern—actually allow the organization to run more efficiently. We may want the person administering our driver's license examination to be friendly and to care about us, but think of how you'd feel if the examiner had decided to stop for a bite to eat with the person who was taking the driver's test before you.

Your school is a clear example of a bureaucratic organization. It has a definite division of labor that involves janitors, secretaries, librarians, coaches, professors, administrators, trustees, and students. The tasks that people are responsible for are highly specialized. Professors in the Spanish department don't teach courses in biology. In large universities, the specialization of tasks is even more narrowly defined. Sociology professors who teach criminology probably don't teach courses on family.

Although the power afforded different positions varies from school to school, all universities have some sort of hierarchy of authority. Usually, this hierarchy consists of janitors, groundskeepers, and food service workers at the bottom, followed by students, staff employees, teaching assistants, part-time instructors, professors, and department chairs. At the administrative level are associate deans, deans, vice presidents, and ultimately the president of the university and the board of trustees.

In addition, universities are governed by strict and sometimes exasperating rules. There are rules regarding when and how students register for classes, graduation requirements, behavioral policies, and when professors must turn in grades. Strict adherence by university employees to these rules and policies is likely to give universities their final bureaucratic characteristic: impersonality.

As people are fitted into roles within bureaucracies that completely determine their duties, responsibilities, and rights, they often become rigid and inflexible and are less concerned about the quality of their work than about whether they and others are playing by the rules. Hence, people become oriented more toward conformity than toward problem solving and critical thinking. They are the source of frustrating procedures and practices that often seem designed not to permit but to prevent things from happening (G. Morgan, 1986). In 2015, life-endangering delays caused by bureaucratic customs procedures prevented tons of relief supplies (such as food, drinkable water, clothing, and tents) from reaching earthquake victims in Nepal. Government officials there insisted that a strict list of inspection rules be followed, even for these emergency provisions. In fact, some of these officials feared that if they didn't meticulously document all aid distributions, they could later face accusations that they'd kept the goods for themselves (G. Harris, 2015).

Closer to home, bureaucratic obstacles similarly blocked relief efforts after Hurricane Katrina decimated the Gulf Coast in 2005 (Goodman, 2005):

- Out-of-state doctors were told they needed a Louisiana license to practice before they could help Katrina victims in New Orleans.

- In cities as far away as Dallas and Houston, attempts to provide shelter were thwarted by building codes and zoning restrictions.

- Both before and after the storm, car owners who offered to haul people out of New Orleans for $5 or $10 were told they were breaking local laws.

- When it came to housing, medical care, and transportation, poor people—as is always the case—did not have the resources to purchase these services on their own and so had to rely on large bureaucratic organizations to provide them, which meant long delays.

Although Weber (1947) stressed the functional necessity of bureaucracies in complex Western societies, he warned that they could take on a life of their own, becoming impersonal "iron cages" for those within them. He feared that bureaucracies might one day dominate every part of society, locking people into a system that allows movement only from one dehumanizing bureaucracy to another. Weber's fears have been largely realized. The bureaucratic model pervades every corner of modern society. The most successful bureaucracies not only dominate the business landscape but have come to influence our entire way of life.

GEORGE RITZER

THE MCDONALDIZATION OF SOCIETY

Sociologist George Ritzer (2008) uses the McDonald's restaurant chain as a metaphor for bureaucratization. In 2015, revenues from McDonald's restaurants exceeded $25 billion (McDonald's Corporation, 2016). The 36,000 McDonald's restaurants worldwide can be found in nearly every significant town and city across the United States and on the main thoroughfares in most major foreign locales. Sixty-nine million people eat at a McDonald's restaurant somewhere in the world each day.

For Ritzer (2008), **McDonaldization** is "the process by which the principles of the fast food restaurant are coming to dominate more and more sectors of American society as well as of the rest of the world" (p. 1). Indeed, the phenomenal success of McDonald's has spawned countless other fast-food chains that emulate its model. Its formula has also influenced many other types of businesses, among them Toys-"R"Us, Starbucks, Great Clips, Jiffy Lube, Panera Bread, PetSmart, and the Gap. The model is so powerful that nicknames reflecting McDonald's influence have become ubiquitous: Newly constructed houses in expensive subdivisions are called "McMansions," drive-in medical facilities are called "McHospitals," huge houses of worship with enormous congregations are called "McChurches," and low-paying positions in which a worker serves as a faceless cog in a corporate machine are called "McJobs."

The success of McDonald's is more than just McDonaldization. McDonald's has become a sacred institution, occupying a central place in popular culture. The "golden arches" of McDonald's are among the most identifiable symbols in society today.

McDonald's appeals to us in a variety of ways:

The restaurants themselves are depicted as spick-and-span, the food is said to be fresh and nutritious, the employees are shown to be young and eager, the managers appear gentle and caring, and the dining experience itself seems to be fun-filled. Through their purchases, people contribute, at least indirectly, to charities such as the Ronald McDonald House for sick children. (Ritzer, 2008, pp. 8-9)

According to Ritzer (2008), McDonald's (and every company that imitates it) has been so successful primarily because it fits Weber's model of the classic bureaucracy. It has a clear division of labor and a uniform system of rules that make it highly efficient and predictable. No matter where you are, you know what to expect when you go into a McDonald's. Even without looking at the overhead menu, you know what your choices will be; and once you've ordered your hamburger, you know that the ketchup will be in the same place on the sandwich as it always has been. The appeal of such predictability is unmistakable. As one observer put it, McDonald's customers "are not in search of 'the best burger I've ever had' but rather 'the same burger I've always had'" (Drucker, 1996, p. 47).

In addition, if you've ever watched the workers behind the counter, you know that each has specialized tasks that are narrowly defined:

The McDonald's corporation has broken the jobs of griddleman, waitress, cashier and even manager down into small, simple steps. . . . The corporation has systematically extracted the decision-making elements from filling French fry boxes or scheduling staff. . . . They relentlessly weed out all variables that might make it necessary to make a decision at the store level, whether on pickles or on cleaning procedures. (Garson, 1988, p. 37)

McDonaldization is likely to continue, and even spread, for several reasons:

- It is driven by economic interests: Profit-making enterprises will go on emulating the McDonald's bureaucratic model because the increased use of nonhuman technology and the uniformity of its product reap greater efficiency and therefore higher profits.

- It has become a culturally desirable process: Our need for efficiency, speed, predictability, and control often blinds us to the fact that fast foods (as well as their household equivalent, microwavable prepared foods) actually cost us more financially and nutritionally than meals we prepare ourselves from scratch. Moreover, most of us have soothing emotional memories of McDonald's: It's where we went after Little League games, hung out as teenagers, stopped on the way to the hospital for the birth of a first child, and so on.

- It parallels other changes occurring in society: With the increasing number of dual-earner couples, families are less likely to have someone with the time or the desire to prepare a meal and clean up afterward. Furthermore, a society that emphasizes mobility is one in which the fast-food mentality will thrive.

But McDonaldization does have a downside. Although the efficiency, speed, and predictability of this model may be appealing and comforting to some, the system as a whole has made social life more homogeneous, more rigid, and less personal. The smile on the face of the employee taking your order is a requirement of the position, not a sign of his or her sincere delight in serving you. To make matters worse, the routinization that characterizes this sort of bureaucratization sometimes turns consumers into unpaid employees who do the work traditionally performed by paid workers (McDonaldization, 2015). Think of the times you've had to bus your own table at a fast-food restaurant, pump your own fuel at a gas station, bag your own groceries at a supermarket, assemble your own furniture, or navigate your own way through an automated telephone menu.

The fast-food model has robbed us of our spontaneity, creativity, and desire for uniqueness, trapping us in Weber's "iron cage"—a bureaucratic culture that requires little thought about anything and leaves virtually nothing to chance.

The Hierarchical Makeup of Organizations

Given the previous descriptions, you might think that everyone within a bureaucracy feels alienated, depersonalized, or perhaps even exploited. But a person's experience in a large bureaucracy depends in part on where she or he fits into the overall hierarchy of the organization. As the conflict perspective points out, although some people are dehumanized by their place in the hierarchy, others may actually benefit from theirs.

The Upper Echelons

People at the top of large organizations have come the furthest within the bureaucracy, are the fewest in number, and get the most out of their position. One interesting and disturbing characteristic of bureaucracies is that, despite the recent influx of women and people of color into executive positions around the world, executives still tend to be homogeneous: predominantly male, members of the dominant ethnic group, and middle or upper class (DiMaggio & Powell, 1983; Kanter, 1977; W. H. Whyte, 1956; Zweigenhaft, 1987). According to the U.S. Bureau of the Census (ProQuest Statistical Abstract, 2017), close to 90% of chief executives in the United States are non-Hispanic whites and 72% are men. Over 95% of the chief executive officers in the S&P 500 Companies are men (Catalyst, 2017).

In addition, executives' educational, social, and familial experiences are remarkably similar (Kanter, 1977; C. W. Mills, 1956). This homogeneity is caused not only by historical prejudices in hiring and promotion practices but also by the nature of top-level jobs.

Upper-level executives don't have clearly bounded jobs with neatly defined responsibilities. The executive must be prepared to use his or her discretion and be flexible enough to deal with a variety of different problems at all times. However, the bulk of the executive's time is spent not in creating, planning, and making important decisions but in attending meetings, writing memos, responding to phone messages and e-mails, delegating responsibilities to underlings, and participating in company-related social gatherings.

Because the role of the executive is, by nature, vague, no clear-cut criteria exist by which to evaluate whether a person is performing the job effectively. Things such as sales and production figures or profit margins can provide only indirect indicators of an executive's competence. When asked what makes an executive effective, top-level employees mentioned imprecise factors such as the ability to communicate and to win acceptance (Kanter, 1977). In such an environment, a common language and a common understanding among executives are important. So, from the perspective of the organization, the best way to ensure efficiency is to limit top-level jobs to people who have had similar experiences and who come from similar backgrounds. One recent survey found that 80% of employers cited "cultural fit"—the idea that the best workers and managers are like-minded—as the top priority in hiring (cited in Rivera, 2015). The result is a closed circle of executives who resemble one another culturally but who are insulated from the rest of the organization.

The Middle Ground

The middle is in some ways the most depressing segment of a formal organization (Kanter & Stein, 1979). Often, the morale of people in the middle is sustained by their belief that they have a shot at the top. If I believe I have a chance to be promoted at some point in the future, my boring and unfulfilling job as a middle-level manager may hold different meaning for me than if I expect to remain in the same position forever (McHugh, 1968). Unpleasant tasks may be minor inconveniences, but they are the price I have to pay. This hope of future promotion may drive people in the middle to concentrate on accumulating bits of status and privilege so they can make enough of an impact to gain recognition from those above.

For most middle-level employees, however, the hope of upward mobility is just that— hope. Because of the pyramid-shaped structure of most large organizations, the vast majority of middle-level employees will never move up. Many simply fail in the increasingly competitive push for advancement into the upper echelons of the company. Others are stuck in jobs that provide little or no opportunity for advancement. Some people are able to develop a comfortable niche in the middle (Kanter & Stein, 1979), but others may grow bitter, angry, and alienated; these feelings can sometimes manifest themselves in attempts to retaliate and punish the company.

The structure of most large organizations often forces middle-level managers to become cautious in their approach to their jobs. Unwilling to jeopardize the limited privileges they have attained, middle-level managers may become controlling, coercive, and demanding in their relationships with the people they supervise (Kanter & Stein, 1979).

For some people in the middle, membership in the organization becomes the focus of their life, often to the detriment of other roles and relationships. Over 60 years ago, sociologist William H. Whyte (1956) described how the personal lives of rising young executives were often overshadowed by their desire to succeed in the corporate world. Large organizations instilled in their employees a corporate social ethic—a belief that "belongingness" to the group was of the utmost importance to their success in the job. Such beliefs encouraged total commitment to the organization and made a person's private life irrelevant.

Whyte's (1956) depiction of the private costs of organizational life still rings true today. Organizations continue to value team players, middle-level employees who place a company's interests above their own (Jackall, 1988). To be a good team player, one must avoid expressing strong political or moral opinions, sacrifice one's home life by putting in long hours, and be obedient to one's superiors. Being seen as a loyal and effective group member and sticking to one's assigned position are also important. Distinctive characteristics such as being abrasive or pushy are dangerous in the bureaucratic world. According to one study, one of the most damaging things that can be said about a middle-level manager is that she or he is brilliant. This judgment usually signals that the individual has publicly asserted her or his intelligence and is perceived as a threat to others (Jackall, 1988).

Interestingly, individuals today seem to be less willing to sacrifice their personal lives and beliefs for the organization than they once were. Two sociologists, Paul Leinberger and Bruce Tucker (1991), interviewed the sons and daughters of the original "organization men" whom Whyte had interviewed back in the 1950s. Leinberger and Tucker found that these individuals were very different from their parents in values and attitudes. They tended to be individualists, more inclined to pursue self-fulfillment than a feeling of belongingness to the organization. Given recent social trends, this finding is not surprising. In an era when corporate mergers, relocations, and downsizing are commonplace, organizational loyalty makes less sense for the individual.

Although few people want to go back to a past when middle-level employees sacrificed everything for their career aspirations, Leinberger and Tucker (1991) point out that today's cultural emphasis on individualism has also created other problems, such as feelings of isolation, an inability to commit to others, and the absence of a sense of community.

The Lower Echelons

Those who stand lowest in the organization's hierarchy are paid the least, valued the least, and considered the most expendable (Kanter & Stein, 1979). The real sign that someone is at the bottom is the degree to which he or she is controlled by others. People at the bottom typically don't have the right to define their occupational tasks themselves. They have little discretion, autonomy, freedom, or influence. In the university bureaucracy, for example, students usually don't have much say over the content of their courses, the curriculum of their major, the price of tuition, or the requirements necessary for graduation.

Most corporations are still organized in terms of ideas developed in the early 1900s. The fundamental principle is that a highly specific division of labor increases productivity and lowers costs. Hence, managers usually subdivide the low-level work tasks in a bureaucratic organization into small parts that unskilled workers can perform repetitively. This structure provides management with the maximum control over workers' jobs.

Technological advancements often coincide with the subdivision of low-level jobs and a decline in the level of skills required to do them (Hartmann, Kraut, & Tilly, 1989). For example, in the insurance industry, the skilled work of assigning risks and assessing people's claims has been increasingly incorporated into computer software programs. What once required a great deal of human judgment and discretion is now almost completely routinized. Less skilled, less experienced, and lower-paid clerks can now perform the work once performed by skilled workers and professionals (Hartmann et al., 1989).

This process, called **de-skilling**, creates jobs that require obedience and passivity rather than talent and experience. De-skilling provides organizations and even entire industries with clear financial benefits, but it also creates low levels of job satisfaction among employees. Dull and repetitive tasks that offer little challenge, such as assembly line work, account for a substantial amount of the discontent experienced by workers at the bottom of large bureaucracies.

Not surprisingly, lower-level workers are often subjected to a different set of rules and expectations than their managerial counterparts. Some observers characterize the situation as a two-tier system of morality (Ehrenreich, 2002). Low-paid employees are required to work hard, abide by the law, and respect the company's rules. Their personalities are psychologically scrutinized during the application process, and they may be subjected to random drug tests and various forms of monitoring once they're hired. In addition, low-wage workers' time is valued quite differently than those above them. For instance, some companies engage in a practice called "just-in-time scheduling" in which they adjust workers' schedules at will, often with little notice and without consulting the affected workers. Unpredictable hours not only create problems for workers who have other commitments, like family obligations, to attend to, but they also produce an atmosphere of frustration and demoralization (Rauch, 2017).

On the other hand, when workers can take an active role in their jobs—such as making decisions and providing input to superiors on a regular basis—they feel much less alienated and find their jobs more rewarding and satisfying than do workers who lack such autonomy (Hodson, 1996). For instance, over the past few decades, some U.S. hospitals have experimented with redesigning their low-wage, low-skill occupations, such as food service workers, housekeepers, and nursing assistants. These hospitals seek to stabilize the workforce and improve patients' experiences by increasing skill training, diversifying the sorts of tasks workers are responsible for, and creating more autonomy and flexibility. These measures have been shown to reduce turnover and increase job satisfaction (Appelbaum, Berg, Frost, & Preuss, 2003).

Without such workplace innovations, the task facing many workers at the bottom is to make their occupational lives tolerable and more dignified by exerting some kind of control over their work (Hodson, 2001). Lower-level employees are rarely completely powerless and can at times be self-directed, even creative, in their positions. The sheer size of large corporations makes it next to impossible for managers to supervise lower-level workers directly and continuously. Thus, substantial opportunities exist, even in the most highly structured and repetitive jobs, for workers either to redefine the nature of their tasks or to willingly and secretly violate the expectations and orders of superiors. For instance, one study found that clerical, service, and manual workers often figure out ways to do required chores in less than the time allotted by management. They can then spend the rest of their time doing what they want (Hodson, 1991). In workplaces with a union presence and a history of conflict between workers and supervisors, collective worker resistance (such as organized strikes) and individual resistance (such as absenteeism and work avoidance) can give lower-level workers a sense of control (Roscigno & Hodson, 2004).

In sum, lower-level workers are not necessarily powerless automatons whose lives are totally structured from above. In fact, the authority of middle-level managers thoroughly depends on their subordinates' willingness to cooperate and abide by the management's directives. Any sort of worker resistance can be disastrous for the manager and for the organization as a whole (Armstrong, Goodman, & Hyman, 1981). When they are organized, lower-level workers can even exert tremendous influence over the policies of a company through strikes, slowdowns, and collective bargaining arrangements.

The Construction of Organizational Reality

According to the symbolic interactionist perspective, organizations are created, maintained, and changed through the everyday actions of their members (G. Morgan, 1986). The language of an organization is one of the ways it creates its own reality.

At one level, new members must learn the jargon of the organization to survive within it. To function within the military system, for example, a recruit must learn the meaning of a dizzying array of words, phrases, slang, sounds, and symbols that are unintelligible to outsiders (Evered, 1983). More important, language helps generate and maintain the organization by marking boundaries between insiders and outsiders.

For an organization to work well, everyone must also internalize the same rules, values, and beliefs. But people still have their own ideas and may develop their own informal structure within the larger formal structure of the organization (Meyer & Rowan, 1977). One of the ironies of large complex organizations is that if everyone followed every rule exactly and literally, the organization would eventually self-destruct. For example, the goal of the highly bureaucratized criminal court system is to ensure justice by punishing those who have violated society's laws. The U.S. Constitution's Sixth Amendment guarantees each person accused of committing a serious crime a timely court trial by a jury of peers. However, public defenders, district attorneys, private attorneys, and judges actually work closely together to bypass the courtroom and move offenders through the system in an orderly fashion (Sudnow, 1965). In the 1970s, about 8% of felony cases went to trial; today it's estimated that 3% of federal cases and 6% of state cases go to trial (cited in Erica Goode, 2012).

If judges and attorneys followed the procedural rules to the letter and provided all their clients with the jury trial that is their constitutional right, the system would break down. The courts, already overtaxed, would be incapable of handling the volume of cases. As one author put it, "If everyone charged with crimes suddenly exercised his [or her] constitutional rights, there would not be enough judges, lawyers, or prison cells to deal with the ensuing tsunami of litigation" (Alexander, 2012, p. 5). Thus, the informal system of plea bargaining has taken root, allowing the courts to continue functioning. Those who play exclusively by the rules, such as a young, idealistic public defender who wants to take all her or his cases to trial, are subjected to informal sanctions by judges and superiors, such as inconvenient trial dates or heavier caseloads.

In sum, organizational life is a combination of formal structural rules and informal patterns of behavior. Codified rules are sometimes violated and new, unspoken ones created instead. Stated organizational goals often conflict with the real ones. Despite what may appear to be a clear chain of command, the informal structure often has more of an impact on how things are done.

Organizations and Institutions

Understanding the influence of organizations on our everyday lives tells only part of the story. Organizations themselves exist within a larger structural context, acting as a sort of liaison between people and major social institutions such as the economic system, government, religion, health care, and education. As we saw in Chapter 2, institutions provide the foundation for behavior in certain major areas of social life. They are patterned ways of solving the problems and meeting the needs of a particular society.

Organizational Networks Within Institutions

Like individual people, organizations are born, grow, become overweight, slim down, migrate, form relationships with others, break up, and die. They interact with one another, too, cooperating on some occasions and competing on others, depending on the prevailing economic and political winds. They even lie, cheat, and steal from time to time. As with people, some organizations are extremely powerful and can dictate the manner in which other organizations go about their business.

The state of Texas accounts for about 15% of the entire national textbook market (Stille, 2002). A provision in the Texas Education Code states that textbooks should promote decency, democracy, patriotism, and the free enterprise system. A coalition of various watchdog organizations in Texas scours textbooks each year in search of material they consider inappropriate or offensive. For instance, in 2004, the Texas Board of Education approved new high school health textbooks that emphasized abstinence and contained no mention of condoms. Over the past few years, the Texas Board of Education has also asked publishers to delete favorable references to Islam, discussions of global warming, references to evolution, and illustrations of breast and testicular self-examinations (Simon, 2009; E. Smith, 2010). In 2010, the board approved a social studies curriculum that requires history and economics textbooks to stress the superiority of American capitalism, highlights Christian influences of the Founding Fathers, and presents conservative political philosophy in a more positive light (McKinley, 2010; Shorto, 2010). One textbook adopted by the state described the Atlantic slave trade not as forced relocation and enslavement but as the transport of millions of *immigrant workers* to plantations in the American South (Collier, 2015). At one time, of the 28 members of a Board of Education panel responsible for adopting biology textbooks, 6 openly rejected the concept of evolution (Rich, 2013). The economic importance of Texas forces many publishers to write and rewrite their books with that state's rules in mind.

Similarly, when giant corporations, such as General Electric, Apple, Exxon-Mobil, and Coca-Cola, decide to downsize or expand their operations, the effects are felt throughout the entire financial community. But even powerful organizations like these cannot stand alone. Massive networks of organizations are linked by common goals and needs. The networks are often so complex that organizations from very different fields find themselves dependent on one another for survival.

MICRO-MACRO CONNECTION
GOING TO THE HOSPITAL: THE INDIVIDUAL PATIENT MEETS THE MASSIVE HEALTH CARE SYSTEM

Consider the U.S. health care system, one of our most important social institutions. Think about the vast networks of organizations that are necessary for a single patient in a single hospital to receive treatments. First of all, the hospital is tightly linked to all the other hospitals in the area. A change in one hospital, such as a reduction in the number of patients treated in the emergency room or the opening of a new state-of-the-art trauma center, would quickly have consequences for all the others. The linkage among hospitals enables the transfer of equipment, staff, and patients from one to another when necessary.

To be accredited and staffed, the hospital must also connect to formal training organizations, such as medical schools, nursing schools, and teaching hospitals. These organizations usually affiliate with larger universities, thus expanding the links in the network. And, of course, the American Medical Association and various licensing agencies oversee the establishment of training policies and credentials.

To survive financially, the hospital must also make connections to funding organizations. Hospitals have traditionally been owned and operated by a variety of governmental, religious, nonprofit, and for-profit organizations. They must operate under a set of strict regulations, which means they must also link to the city, state, and federal governmental agencies responsible for certification, such as the Joint Commission. Add to these relationships their links to the medical equipment industry, the pharmaceutical industry, food service providers, the legal profession, charities, political action committees working on health care legislation, patients' rights groups, and most notably health insurance companies, and the system becomes even more complex. Indeed, the highly contentious debate over repealing "Obamacare" and replacing it with a new health care insurance system is essentially a fight to protect competing economic, political, and personal interests.

The vast network of organizations within the health care system must also work together in response to broader societal demands and crises. For instance, in the wake of the 1995 Oklahoma City bombing, the attacks of September 11, 2001, and the anthrax attacks in the fall of 2001, the Institute of Medicine (2003) published a report warning that the nation's mental health, public health, medical, and emergency systems were not equipped to respond to terrorism. At the organizational level, gaps exist in the coordination of agencies and services, the training and supervision of professionals, and the dissemination of information to the general public. The report concluded that only a multilayered approach—involving the federal Departments of Health & Human Services and Homeland Security; state and local disaster planners; and relevant professionals in all areas of health care—could stave off potential catastrophe.

But despite the health care system's complexity, size, and importance, when patients go to a hospital they don't see it as a node in a vast network. Patients are obviously much less interested in the hospital's organizational links than they are in whether their nurse is friendly, the food is good, the bed is comfortable, and their doctor is competent. Yet in a 2003 study, one out of three doctors reported purposely withholding information from patients about potentially helpful treatments because those treatments weren't covered by the patient's health insurance (Wynia, VanGeest, Cummins, & Wilson, 2003). The needs of the larger system can sometimes clash with an individual's health care needs, making even face-to-face interactions problematic and, possibly, even detrimental to the patient's health.

Institutional Pressures Toward Similarity

If you think about how many varieties of organizations exist in the world, you might be tempted to focus on their obvious differences. Some are large, others small. Some are formal and complex, others informal and simple. Some have a pyramid-shaped chain of command; others are more egalitarian (E. Gross & Etzioni, 1985). Sociologists have long been interested in the unique ways in which different organizations adapt to changing political, economic, cultural, or environmental circumstances. However, organizations seem to be more similar than different and even tend to imitate one another's actions as they become established in a particular institution (DiMaggio & Powell, 1983).

Organizational similarity is not really that surprising. Because of the nature of the problems that organizations in the same industry have to address, they come to adopt similar methods of dealing with them. When Apple sought to corner the electronic gadget market a few years ago with the popular iPad, it was inevitable that other companies would follow suit with their own tablet devices. The same thing could be said for hybrid cars, Greek yogurt, energy drinks, smart watches, and e-cigarettes.

Often the similarities become overwhelming. There's an old adage among Hollywood filmmakers that goes, "There's no success like a previous box office hit" (Dargis, 2011). Likewise, the major U.S. commercial television networks—NBC, ABC, CBS, and Fox—see the profits one network makes with a particular kind of program and try to attract viewers in much the same way. As you well know, the perceived popularity of a certain type of television show creates an irritating avalanche of similar shows on other networks—like shows where people compete with one another to see who will perform the grossest or the most fearsome feats (*Survivor* and *Fear Factor*), glorified talent contests (*American Idol, America's Got Talent, The Voice,* and *Dancing With the Stars*), cooking competition shows (*Hell's Kitchen* and *Top Chef*), model/fashion shows (*Project Runway* and *America's Next Top Model*), home improvement shows (*Fixer Upper* and *Property Brothers*), and weight loss shows (*Biggest Loser* and *Extreme Weight Loss*). In short, instead of adjusting directly to changes in the social environment, such as the shifting tastes of the television-viewing public, organizations end up adjusting to what other organizations are doing (DiMaggio & Powell, 1983).

The surprising fact is that the imitated practices are not necessarily more effective or successful. After once-novel strategies have spread throughout an industry, they may no longer improve the organization's performance. Viewers eventually get sick of seeing the same types of shows. The net effect of the imitations is to reduce innovation within the industry.

The tendency for organizations to emulate one another is especially strong in times of institutional uncertainty (DiMaggio & Powell, 1983). When new technologies are poorly understood, when the physical environment is undergoing dramatic changes, or when local, state, and federal governments are creating new regulations or setting new agendas, organizations are likely to be somewhat confused about how things ought to be done. Just as individuals look to one another to help define ambiguous situations and determine an appropriate course of action, so do organizations.

One social institution that is particularly susceptible to uncertainty is politics. A massive industry of polling organizations exists to weigh the public's mood about particular social issues or voting preferences. Pollsters often engage in a practice known as "herding," which refers to the tendency to announce results similar to those other organizations have already published. Sometimes they may even alter their own results to align with previous polls. Since polling organizations are judged by the accuracy of their projections, they may be motivated to copy the results of other organizations by the fear of being wrong. This trend tends to intensify in the weeks prior to presidential elections (N. Cohn, 2015). The danger of such a practice is that the entire polling industry reproduces inaccuracies and collective biases that could artificially transform public opinion or even sway elections. Some political analysts have argued that "herding" may have contributed to the overwhelming majority of national polls incorrectly predicting a Hillary Clinton victory in the 2016 presidential election (Saunders, 2016).

Organizations also resemble one another because those who run them, particularly professionals, tend to come from similar training backgrounds. In many institutions, the professional career track is so closely guarded that the individuals who make it to the top are practically indistinguishable from one another (DiMaggio & Powell, 1983). For example, medical schools are important centers for the development of organizational norms among doctors. The fact that most doctors belong to the American Medical Association creates a pool of individuals with similar attitudes and approaches across a range of organizations. When these doctors become administrators, they will likely bring this common approach to running a hospital.

Certain organizational forms dominate not necessarily because they are the most effective means of achieving goals but because social forces such as institutional uncertainty and the power of professions to provide individuals with a single normative standard create pressures toward similarity. Such similarity makes it easier for organizations to interact with one another and to be acknowledged as legitimate and reputable within the field (DiMaggio & Powell, 1983). But this homogeneity is not without its costs. When organizations replicate one another, institutional change becomes difficult and the iron cage of bureaucracy becomes harder to escape.

Globalization and Social Institutions

You've seen in this book so far the enormous effect that globalization is having on everyday life. Many of our important social institutions have become international in scope—notably economics, education, and religion. How do such global institutions meet the needs of human beings around the world?

Economics

Looking around my office at this moment, I notice that my desk and chair were made in the United States, my watch in Switzerland, my stapler in Great Britain, my calculator in Taiwan, my shoes in Korea, my pants in Hong Kong, my bottled water in Italy, my briefcase in Indonesia, the frame holding my kids' picture in Thailand, and my paper clips, scissors, computer, travel mug, and iPhone in China. Because of the rapid increase in economic links among producing nations in recent years, your life is probably similarly filled with products made in other countries. A few years ago, Japan experienced a troubling shortage of bluefin tuna—the most desirable fish used in sushi—because of growing demand in the United States, Europe, and other countries in Asia (Issenberg, 2007).

Economic globalization is more than just a matter of more goods being shipped from one place to another. For instance, there's a pretty good chance that if you talk to someone online to prepare your taxes, provide legal advice, track your lost luggage, solve your software problem, or review your long-distance phone bill, you'll be dealing with someone working at a call center in India or the Philippines. The large pool of English-speaking, technologically savvy workers willing to work for low wages has attracted the phone service operations of companies such as American Express, Sprint, Citibank, Capital One, General Electric, Ford, Hewlett-Packard, and IBM (Lakshmi, 2005). Some giant American technology companies—Amazon, Google, Microsoft, Facebook, and Yahoo—have established data centers in about two dozen countries worldwide (Benko, 2015).

If a product wasn't entirely produced in another country, it's a good bet that some of its components were. Even run-of-the-mill domestic products can have a complex international pedigree. Take, for instance, an ordinary T-shirt. Chances are that the cotton from which it is made was grown somewhere in the southern United States. The cotton is then spun into yarn in Indonesia; the yarn is made into fabric in Bangladesh; and the fabric is sewn into shirts in Colombia or one of several countries in South Asia (National Public Radio, 2014).

The economic processes involved in globalization have made national boundaries less relevant. **Multinational corporations**, businesses that have extended their markets and production facilities globally, have become increasingly powerful over the past several decades. U.S.-based multinational corporations alone employ more than 37 million workers worldwide (ProQuest Statistical Abstract, 2017). These companies control a significant portion of the world's wealth, heavily influence the tastes of people everywhere, and don't owe their allegiance to any one country's political authority or culture. At the same time, international financial organizations, such as the World Bank, the World Trade Organization, and the International Monetary Fund, loan money to countries all over the world to finance development and reconstruction projects. (For more on the global economic impact of international financial organizations and multinational corporations, see Chapter 10.) With the costs of communication and computing falling rapidly, barriers of time and space that traditionally separated national markets have also been falling. Even the most remote rural villagers are linked to the global economy as they carry out transactions over the Internet and send and receive goods around the world.

A global economy has its everyday advantages. Goods manufactured and services provided in a country where wages are lower are less expensive for consumers in other countries. Universally accepted credit cards make international travel more convenient. Snack bars in overseas airports accept American money, as do foreign establishments around the world that are near U.S. borders or military bases. Global economic influence has also enabled a significant portion of the world's population to be healthier, eat better, and live longer than the royalty of past civilizations (Kurtz, 1995).

We may barely be aware of how the taken-for-granted elements of our daily lives connect to the economic well-being of people in faraway places. For instance, for years mining companies have been extracting billions of dollars worth of lithium from several impoverished regions in Chile. Lithium, a silvery-white metal, is essential for the lithium-ion batteries that power smartphones, laptops, and electric cars. One mining company agreed to pay the communities between $9,000 and $60,000 a year for exclusive land and water rights. The company expects to generate $250 million a year in lithium sales (T. C. Frankel, 2016).

Similarly, today's popular electronic devices couldn't work without a little-known gritty, super-heavy mud called columbite-tantalite (coltan, for short). Once coltan is refined in U.S., Japanese, and European factories, it becomes tantalum, a remarkably heat-resistant conductor of electricity. Capacitors made of tantalum can be found inside practically every laptop, tablet, video game system, smart watch, and smartphone in the world. But there isn't nearly enough coltan in the United States, Europe, or Japan to meet these needs. Its largest quantities lie in the rain forests of eastern Congo, where it is mined in much the same way gold was mined in California in the 1800s. Miners spend days in the muck, digging up mud and sloshing it around in plastic tubs until the coltan settles to the bottom. On a good day, a miner can produce about a kilogram of the stuff. Miners earn up to $50 a week, quite a high figure considering that most people in this region live on the equivalent of $10 a month ("What Is Coltan?" 2002).

But global trade has also created some interesting everyday dilemmas. For centuries, workers in Spain and Mexico have enjoyed the workday *siesta*, a long afternoon nap or an extended lunch, sometimes lasting until 5 P.M. But the owners of factories and retail stores have realized that shutting down operations every afternoon so workers can take their siestas is incompatible with growing integration into the global economy. As the president of a Spanish research group that advocates doing away with the siesta put it, "In a globalized world, we have to have schedules that are more similar to those in the rest of the world so we can be better connected" (quoted in R. McLean, 2005, p. 4). Mexico officially cut lunch breaks from 3 hours to 1 hour for government workers in 1999 (R. McLean, 2006). Spain did so in 2006.

Global financial institutions must also keep close track of holidays around the world to avoid trying to do business on nonbusiness days. In some countries, holidays are determined by the lunar calendar, which not only varies from year to year but may vary from area to area within a country based on local customs. In other countries, such as France, the dates of some bank holidays are a matter of negotiation between the banks and the unions that represent their employees. Even weekends are defined differently in different countries. In Taiwan, the weekend consists of every Sunday and the second and fourth Saturdays of each month. In Malaysia, it is every Sunday and only the first Saturday of every month. And in Lithuania, one-day weekends are occasionally followed by four-day weekends (Henriques, 1999).

Economic globalization has fostered more serious social problems as well, including higher levels of unemployment in developed countries, and environmental degradation and the exploitation of workers in poor, developing countries. The result is a worldwide system of inequality whose problems are often invisible to consumers (see Chapter 10). For instance, the speed with which existing tech devices become obsolete and new ones produced to replace them has produced nearly 42 million metric tons of toxic e-waste, most of which is broken down by unprotected workers at dumps in rural China and other developing countries (Benko, 2015).

Despite having a policy that prohibits doing business with foreign companies that exploit their workers, the U.S. government spends over $1.5 billion a year on clothing (shirts for

VISUAL ESSAY—GLOBAL CLOTHES

© Carolyn Jenkins/Alamy

© Anatoly Vartanov/Alamy

AP Photo/David Goldman

JBsports / Alamy Stock Photo

There's no denying that the world is shrinking and that our lives have become more global and interconnected than at any other time in human history. It is no longer possible for people to exist and thrive without *any* contact with other societies. Despite the rhetoric we often hear about our patriotic duty to buy things "made in America," we've gotten to a point where we simply take for granted that many of the products we enjoy in our everyday lives were likely made someplace else. These photos show a random selection of the tags found inside the clothes Americans commonly wear.

As you've seen in this chapter, the fact that much of our clothing is manufactured in Bangladesh or Cambodia or Egypt means that we can pay lower prices for these goods than would be the case if they were made here. By the way, the same goes for much of our furniture, office supplies, appliances, technological gadgets, athletic equipment, and so on. The question isn't whether or not these things *are* made elsewhere. That's a given. The question is what *should* we think and do about it? Does it matter to you that much of what you own was made halfway around the world? Do you have an obligation to care about the conditions under which workers produced these goods? If you found out that the people who assembled your smartphone or manufactured your favorite sweater were being mistreated and exploited, what would you do? What should you do?

airport security workers, uniforms for forest rangers, shirts and pants sold on military bases, and so on) that is manufactured overseas by laborers working under harsh sometimes dangerous conditions (Urbina, 2013b). For instance, child laborers make up a third of the workforce at the Bangladeshi factory that manufactures shirts with Marine Corps logos. The Thai company that makes clothing sold in the Smithsonian Institution pays its workers roughly $10 a day and docks their pay for every mistake they make. Workers at a Cambodian factory that manufactures clothes sold by the Army and Air Force are denied bathroom breaks that lead some to soil themselves at their sewing machines.

We may wish to do our part to make life better for poor workers around the world, but it's hard to take any effective action. For instance, boycotts of exploitative manufacturers are a double-edged sword. The origin of products is seldom clear-cut, and local workers are typically glad to have jobs they wouldn't have had otherwise. Pressure to compete in the global marketplace also erodes the ability of governments to set their own economic policies, protect national interests, or adequately protect workers and the environment.

Education

The prospect of international competition in a global economy can foster changes in a country's educational system. For instance, students in other industrialized countries consistently outperform U.S. students in fields such as math and science (see Exhibit 9.1). Only 9% of American eighth graders reach the advanced level in math, compared to 40% of eighth graders in Singapore and 55% in Shanghai, China (National Center for Education Statistics, 2014b). And a recent analysis found that the average math performance of U.S. high school seniors actually dropped between 2013 and 2015 (National Assessment of Educational Progress, 2015). Such educational gaps can have long-lasting effects. According to data from the National Center for Education Statistics (2013a), American adults between the ages of 16 and 65 lag behind adults in most other industrialized nations in basic job skills like literacy, working with numbers, and using technology to solve problems.

Concern over our ability to compete in the global marketplace has led to nationwide calls for educational reforms such as heavier emphasis on math and science; more time spent on foundational skills, such as reading and writing; increased computer literacy; and training in political geography and international relations. To address this concern, the National Math and Science Initiative provides cash incentives and other forms of support to faculty and students in over 400 schools around the country. Students in participating schools earn $100 for every Advanced Placement (AP) exam they pass while teachers earn salary bonuses for each of their students who passes an AP exam (Matthews, 2012).

Pressures to achieve academically are present from the beginning. Children as early as kindergarten spend significantly more time on lessons and testing these days than on play, exercise, and imagination. According to a study of New York and Los Angeles kindergartens (E. Miller & Almon, 2009), children spend four to six times as long being instructed and tested in math skills and literacy (2 to 3 hours a day) as in free play (20 to 30 minutes a day). Play materials like blocks, sand, water tables, and props for dramatic play have largely disappeared from the classroom. Some school districts in Florida, Wisconsin, and Maryland have recently opted to eliminate recess from the daily schedule. However, a growing body of research says there is little evidence that more time on formal educational instruction and less time in play actually improves young children's long-term achievement. In fact, it may slow emotional and cognitive development, cause elevated levels of stress, and even squash kids' desire to learn (cited in D. Kohn, 2015).

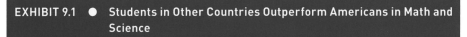

EXHIBIT 9.1 ● Students in Other Countries Outperform Americans in Math and Science

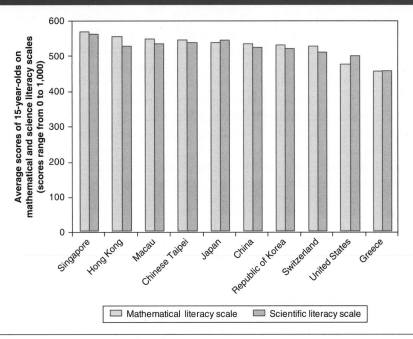

Source: National Center for Education Statistics, 2016, Tables M1 and T2.

Education reformers have consistently called for longer school days and shorter vacations so U.S. students can catch up to their peers elsewhere in the world. Some point out that the school calendar—with its 6½-hour day and 180-day year—was created for the farm-based economy of the past, not today's high-tech one (Ubiñas & Gabrieli, 2011). At his confirmation hearing in 2009, former secretary of education Arne Duncan stated, "Our school day is too short, our school week is too short, our school year is too short" (quoted in Dillon, 2011, p. A14). In response, according to the National Center on Time and Learning (2013), over 1,000 schools have expanded their school days by an average of 1.1 hours a day over conventional schools. And other schools have extended their calendars to 190 or even 200 days a year. Approximately 14% of traditional public schools have adopted a 12-month school year (Kolbe, Partridge, & O'Reilly, 2015).

Some critics feel that we already place far too much emphasis on performance and achievement in this society and that children and young adults end up suffering as a result (Mannon, 1997). Competitive pressures have become so great in some schools that administrators have been forced to make students slow down. For instance, school districts across the nation are addressing concerns about stressed-out children by limiting the amount of homework students do on weeknights and banning it altogether on weekends and holidays (Hu, 2011). In college, anxiety has surpassed depression as the most common mental health diagnosis among students. According to one national study, 59% of undergraduates report feeling overwhelmed by anxiety during the past 12 months and 82% felt exhausted for reasons other than physical activity (American College Health Association, 2016).

Other critics point to the dangerous effects of performance pressure seen elsewhere. For instance, in China entry into college is determined by one standardized exam, called the *gaokao*. Each year, 9 million Chinese high school students take it (by comparison, less than 3.5 million students take *either* the SAT or ACT exam in the United States each year). The pressure to start preparing for this exam begins when children first enter elementary school, where they are grilled on mathematics, science, and proper Chinese and English syntax (Larmer, 2015). As the exam approaches, some will spend 16 hours a day, 7 days a week, studying for *gaokao* in so-called "cram schools." Some public high-school classrooms even provide intravenous drips to students to give them the strength to keep studying. But securing a place in a university often comes at a steep price. Teenage suicide rates in China routinely rise as the test date approaches.

Few people in the United States would argue that we should emulate the pressurized Chinese educational model. At the same time, though, the demands of the global economy and concerns over Americans' ability to compete internationally will continue to exert influence on legislators and education reformers.

Religion

Another institution influenced by globalization is religion. Despite the enormous variety of cultures and ethnicities that exist today, nearly two thirds of the world's population belong to just three major religions—Christianity, Hinduism, and Islam—which have successfully crossed national boundaries for centuries. Exhibit 9.2 shows how dominant these world religions are.

EXHIBIT 9.2   ●   Which Religions Are the Largest Worldwide?

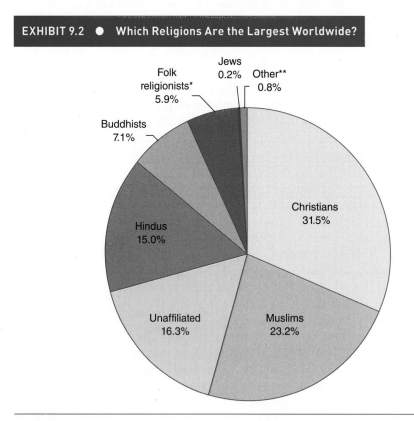

Source: Pew Research Center 2015.

*Includes followers of African traditional religions, Chinese folk religions, Native American religions, and Australian aboriginal religions.

**Includes Bahais, Jains, Sikhs, Shintoists, Taoists, followers of Tenrikyo, Wiccans, Zoroastrians, and other faiths.

Islam is now the fastest growing global religion. By 2050, the number of Muslims will nearly equal the number of Christians worldwide. When taking migration into account, the Muslim population in Europe will nearly double in the next three decades. And despite some efforts to limit their migration to this country, Muslims will soon be the largest non-Christian religion in the United States (Pew Research Center, 2015d).

Some religions are globalizing to deal with shrinking memberships in the countries where they originated. For example, outside the United States and Canada, the Church of Jesus Christ of Latter-Day Saints has grown by over 500% since 1980 (cited in Kress, 2005). The Methodist Church lost 1 million U.S. members between 1980 and 1995 but gained about 500,000 elsewhere, mostly in Africa (Niebuhr, 1998). Indeed, during the 20th century, the population of Christians in Africa grew from 10 million to 360 million. The Anglican Church, in particular, is growing faster in Africa than in its traditional bases, Great Britain and North America; Nigeria alone has 25% of the world's Anglicans (Rice, 2009).

Ironically, this globalization of religion is creating crises for religious communities. Exposure to competing worldviews challenges traditional beliefs. In some cases, religions have reacted with a forceful revitalization of ancient, fundamentalist traditions (Kurtz, 1995). Witness the growing trend toward governments defining themselves in narrowly religious terms. The ascension of fundamentalist Islamic government in Iran, the growing influence of Orthodox Jews in Israeli politics, and the continuing conflict between Hindus and Muslims in Kashmir and between Sunni and Shiite Muslims in Iraq attest to the fact that many people today believe religion cannot be separated from a nation's social and political destiny.

The rise of religious nationalism around the world has created an obvious threat to global security. The attacks of September 11, 2001, and many others since, are the most glaring illustration. Radical elements, like al Qaeda, the Taliban, Boko Haram, and ISIS, sometimes use religious texts—in this case the Qur'an—as justification for violence against societies that they blame for moral decline and economic exploitation. Elsewhere, the possibility of violence by supporters of religious nationalist movements has brought down political regimes, changed the outcomes of elections, strained international relations, and made some parts of the world dangerous places for travelers (Juergensmeyer, 1996).

But religion has also played a positive role in world affairs and has created dramatic social changes. According to Max Weber (1904/1977), the spread of Protestant beliefs throughout Europe made the growth of modern capitalism possible. Protestantism maintained that worldly achievements, such as the accumulation of wealth through hard work, are a sign of God's favor. But the early Protestants also believed that God frowns on vulgar displays of wealth, such as big houses, fancy clothes, and so forth.

So people were motivated to save and reinvest their wealth rather than spend it frivolously. You can see how such beliefs made large-scale and long-term economic growth possible (Weber, 1904/1977). A study of 59 Christian, Buddhist, Muslim, and Hindu countries found that strong religious beliefs tend to stimulate economic growth because of their association with individual traits like honesty, work ethic, thrift, and openness to strangers (Barro & McCleary, 2003).

The influence of religious movements on social life continues. In the 1960s, television pictures of Buddhist monks setting themselves on fire in Vietnam to protest the war fed the growing antiwar movement in the United States. In the 1970s and 1980s, images of Catholic priests and nuns challenging government policies in Central and South America provoked a heightened awareness worldwide of the plight of indigenous people there. In 2007, tens of thousands of Buddhist monks in Myanmar marched in the streets to protest against that country's oppressive military regime. Their actions sparked organized protests in more than two dozen Asian, European, and North American cities. In the early 2000s, followers of the Dalai Lama raised global awareness of the plight of Tibetans who seek independence from China, leading to the establishment of the worldwide International Campaign for Tibet. Since 2009, 135 Tibetan monks have set themselves on fire to protest China's control of Tibet (Tibet Society, 2015).

Conclusion

More than three centuries ago, John Donne wrote, "No man is an island, entire of itself; every man is a piece of the continent, a part of the main." The same can be said of contemporary social life. We are not isolated individuals whose lives are simply functions of personal characteristics and predispositions. We are social beings. We are part of aggregations of other social beings. We have a powerful need to belong to something larger than ourselves. As a result, we constantly affect and are affected by our associations with others, whether face to face or in well-structured groups, massive bureaucratic organizations, or all-encompassing social institutions.

Throughout Part II of this book, I discussed how society and culture affect everyday experiences and how those experiences help to construct and maintain social order. The development of self and self-controlled behavior, the influence of cultural norms, responses to deviance, and so on are all topics that provide insight into how we are able to live together in a relatively orderly and predictable way. In this chapter, however, you can see that the social structure, though created and maintained by the actions of individuals, is more than just the sum of those actions. Organizations interact at a level well above the individual; institutions are organized in a massive, global system.

Social structure is bigger than any of us, exerts enormous control over our lives, and is an objectified reality that appears to exist independently of us. But it cannot exist without us. I'm reminded of a skit from the old British comedy show *Monty Python's Flying Circus,* in which a high-rise apartment building remained strong, solid, and safe only because its inhabitants believed in it. When they doubted its existence, it began to crumble. Like that building, social structure requires constant human support. Once we as a society are no longer able to sustain our organizations or believe in our institutions, they fall apart.

Your Turn

One of the major criticisms of complex contemporary society is its sometimes dehumanizing way of life. To see this consequence of bureaucratization firsthand, visit several fast-food restaurants close to your home (McDonald's, Taco Bell, Kentucky Fried Chicken, Chipotle's, etc.). Observe the overall structure of the establishment. How is the work area situated in relation to the customer area? Are the cooking facilities hidden from public view? Note the number of employees and the gender and age configuration of the staff. Observe the way customers are processed. Can you detect a "script" that the employees follow? How do they address customers? How are orders filled? Is there any room for

"ad-libbing"? Does each worker seem responsible for a single task (grilling burgers, bagging fries, operating the cash register, cleaning tables, etc.)? Do male employees seem to work in areas different from female employees? Is there an apparent hierarchy among the workers? What is the manager's role? Are you able to detect the ways in which ordinary workers might "resist" on a daily basis (breaking the group's norms, sabotage, labor-management conflicts, etc.)?

Compare your findings across the different restaurants you observed. How much similarity in routine is there? Is some common procedure characteristic of all fast-food restaurants, or does each restaurant have a unique way of running? How do diversity and creativity fit into the procedure?

Once you've observed several fast-food restaurants, go to other retail businesses in your area. See if you can find any similarities between the way these stores operate and the way the fast-food restaurants function.

Drawing from this chapter's discussion of the features of bureaucracies and the notion of McDonaldization, discuss how the systems employed in these businesses maximize efficiency at the cost of dehumanizing the people involved, both workers and customers.

Chapter Highlights

- Social structure is both a source of predictability and a source of problems in our everyday life. Sometimes individual interests coincide with structural needs; other times they conflict.

- By virtue of living in society, we are all organizational creatures. We are born in organizations, are educated in them, spend most of our adult lives working in them, and will probably die in them.

- A common form of organization in a complex society is the bureaucracy. A bureaucracy is a large hierarchical organization that is governed by a system of rules and regulations, has a clear specification of work tasks, and has a well-defined division of labor.

- The everyday experience of bureaucratic organizations is determined by where one fits into the hierarchical structure. Bureaucracies look very different depending on whether one is situated at the top, middle, or bottom.

- Organizations are more than structures, rules, policies, goals, job descriptions, and standard operating procedures. Each organization, and each division within an organization, develops its own norms, values, and language.

- Organizations exist within highly interconnected networks. In times of institutional or environmental uncertainty, organizations tend to imitate one another, adopting similar activities, policies, and goals.

- As national borders become increasingly permeable, cultures and social institutions become more global in nature.

Key Terms

bureaucracy: Large hierarchical organization governed by formal rules and regulations and having clearly specified work tasks

de-skilling: Subdivision of low-level jobs into small, highly specific tasks requiring less skilled employees

division of labor: Specialization of different people or groups in different tasks, characteristic of most bureaucracies

free-rider problem: Tendency for people to refrain from contributing to the common good when a resource is available without any personal cost or contribution

hierarchy of authority: Ranking of people or tasks in a bureaucracy from those at the top, where there is a great deal of power and authority, to those at the bottom, where there is very little power and authority

McDonaldization: Process by which the characteristics and principles of the fast-food

(Continued)

(Continued)

restaurant come to dominate other areas of social life

multinational corporation: Company that has manufacturing, production, and marketing divisions in multiple countries

oligarchy: System of authority in which many people are ruled by a privileged few

social dilemma: Potential for a society's long-term ruin because of individuals' tendency to pursue their own short-term interests

social structure: Framework of society—social institutions, organizations, groups, statuses and roles, cultural beliefs, and

institutionalized norms—that adds order and predictability to our private lives

tragedy of the commons: Situation in which people acting individually and in their own self-interest use up commonly available (but limited) resources, creating disaster for the entire community

SAGE edge™ edge.sagepub.com/newman12e

SAGE edge offers a robust online environment featuring an impressive array of free tools and resources for review, study, and further exploration, keeping both instructors and students on the cutting edge of teaching and learning.

10

The Architecture of Stratification

Social Class and Inequality

- Stratification Systems
- Sociological Perspectives on Stratification
- Class Inequality in the United States
- Global Development and Inequality

If you've seen the popular 1997 Hollywood film *Titanic*, you know that the famous ship had every amenity and comfort: Turkish baths, the finest orchestras, intricately tiled walls, the best cuisine. What it didn't have when it hit an iceberg and began to sink was enough lifeboats for everyone on board. There was room in the boats for only 1,178 of the 2,207 passengers and crew members. Over the span of 2 hours on that cold April night in 1912, as the "unsinkable" ocean liner was engulfed by the frigid waters of the North Atlantic, more than 1,500 people lost their lives.

This part of the story is pretty well known. What is less known is that some of the passengers actually had a much better chance of survival than others. More than 60% of the people from the wealthy first-class deck survived, compared with 36% of the people from the second-class deck and 24% of the people from the lowest, or "steerage," class. The figures were even more striking for women and children, who, by virtue of mannerly tradition, were entitled to be spared first. In first class, 97% of the women and children survived; in second class, 89% survived. However, only 42% of the women and children in steerage were saved (W. Hall, 1986).

The main reason why so many wealthier passengers survived was that the lifeboats were accessed from the higher first- and second-class decks. The locked doors and other barriers erected to keep third-class passengers from venturing to the upper decks during the cruise remained in place when disaster struck. In addition, little effort was made to save the people in steerage. Some were forcibly kept down by crew members standing guard.

For passengers on the *Titanic*, social inequality meant more than just differences in the comfort of accommodations or the quality of the food. It literally meant life or death. This situation serves as a metaphor for what many people face in today's society. Those at the top have easy access to various societal "lifeboats" in times of natural or economic disaster; others face locked gates, segregated decks, and policies that make simple survival exceedingly difficult (Sidel, 1986).

Let's turn the clock ahead to the summer of 2005, when Hurricane Katrina killed more than 1,000 people in the Gulf Coast region of the U.S. South. Most of these people died not because of the hurricane's torrential rains and high winds but because of the flooding that occurred when the levees that ordinarily protect the low-lying areas of New Orleans (which were in need of repair to begin with) were breached. In addition to the fatalities, hundreds of thousands of people lost everything they owned and were forced to relocate. Many never returned.

Like the *Titanic* disaster, the storm and its aftermath did not affect all residents equally. The neighborhoods that experienced catastrophic flooding had a lower median income, a higher poverty rate, and a higher percentage of households without a vehicle than the areas that experienced little or no flooding (J. Schwartz, Revkin, & Wald, 2005). Those of us watching the tragedy unfold on television could not help but notice that the vast majority of the evacuees who suffered for days in the sweltering darkness of the Louisiana Superdome and convention center in New Orleans were poor people of color who came from the most vulnerable parts of the city. They either didn't have the necessary transportation to evacuate prior to the hurricane or stayed behind to tend to sick and elderly relatives who couldn't be moved. For years after the hurricane, poor, displaced children who were forced to live in ramshackle government trailer parks continued to suffer from various ailments, including anemia, respiratory infections, and depression (Carmichael, 2008). Again we see how lack of economic resources can have direct, physical consequences in people's lives.

In this chapter, I look at class inequality and stratification. In subsequent chapters, I explore two other facets of inequality: race and/or ethnicity and gender. Please keep in mind that although class, race and ethnicity, and gender are covered in separate chapters, these components of our identities are not experienced separately. They are all interrelated, and they combine to determine individuals' positions in society. For instance, a person doesn't live his life just as a working-class person, just as a man, or just as an Asian American. He is all these things—and more—simultaneously (D. Newman, 2017).

STRATIFICATION SYSTEMS

Inequality is woven into the fabric of all societies through a structured system of **stratification**, the ranking of entire groups of people that perpetuates unequal rewards and life chances in a society. Just as geologists talk about strata of rock, which are layered one on top of another, the "social strata" of people are arranged from low to high. All societies, past and present, have had some form of stratification, although they vary in the degree of inequality between strata. The four main sources of stratification that sociologists have identified—all of which continue to exist in contemporary societies—are slavery, caste, estate, and social class systems.

Slavery

One of the oldest and most persistent forms of stratification in the world is slavery. **Slavery** is an economic form of inequality in which some people are the property of others. Because slaves are owned and controlled, they are denied the rights and life chances other people take for granted. One can become a slave in a variety of ways: through birth, military defeat, debt, or, as in the United States until the mid-19th century, capture and commercial trade (Kerbo, 1991). The Walk Free Foundation (2016) estimates that nearly 46 million adults and children in 167 countries around the world are enslaved today. And it's not just a foreign problem. In the United States, some 58,000 people are exploited as forced laborers.

Slavery has occurred in various forms almost everywhere in the world at some time. Mexico, Great Britain, France, Russia, and Holland all abolished slavery before the United States did in 1863; Spain, Korea, Cuba, and Brazil did so afterward (D. B. Davis, 2006). Several Middle Eastern countries—Saudi Arabia, Yemen, Oman, United Arab Emirates—didn't abolish slavery until the latter part of the 20th century. Though theoretically against the law, tens of thousands of people in the West African nations of Niger, Burkina Faso, Mali, and Mauritania are born into slavery today ("A Continuing Abomination," 2008). Nearly 60% of those living in slavery today can be found in five countries—India, China, Pakistan, Bangladesh, and Uzbekistan (The Walk Free Foundation, 2016).

Sex trafficking is one of the most common forms of slavery today. It's estimated that some 21 million adults and children worldwide are bought and sold into sexual servitude and 98% of them are women and girls (Equality Now, 2017). Some are sold into prostitution, sex tourism, or forced marriage. Through phone calls, e-mails, and online reports, the National Human Trafficking Hotline (2017) estimates that perhaps as many as 67,000 women were trafficked in the United States between 2007 and 2016. In 2017, law enforcement authorities arrested 21 people in Chicago who were part of an elaborate sex-trafficking operation that had existed for 8 years, involved hundreds of Thai women, and netted tens of millions of dollars (Davey, 2017). And it's not just non-Americans who are trafficked in this country. The National Center for Missing and Exploited Children (2017) estimates that due to their mental, physical, and financial vulnerability, between 100,000 and 300,000 youth are "at risk" for commercial sexual exploitation annually in the United States. Indeed, about 1 in 6 American child runaways is a victim of sex trafficking.

Caste Systems

Some societies today retain a second form of stratification: a **caste system**. Traditionally, one's caste, which determines lifestyle, prestige, and occupational choices, was fixed at birth and couldn't be changed. Ancient Hindu scriptures, for instance, identified the strict hierarchy of elite, warrior, merchant, servant, and untouchable castes. The rights and duties associated with membership in each caste were clear. In India, "untouchables"—members of the lowest caste—were once required by law to hide from or, if that wasn't possible, to bow in the presence of anyone from a higher caste. They were routinely denied the right to enter Hindu temples or to draw water from wells reserved for members of the higher castes, who feared they would be contaminated if they touched or otherwise came in contact with an untouchable.

According to Human Rights Watch (2009b), more than 260 million people—mostly in India, Nepal, Bangladesh, Pakistan, and Sri Lanka but also in Japan, Yemen, and several African countries—continue to suffer severe caste discrimination. They are victims of exploitation and violence and face massive obstacles to their full attainment of civil, political, economic, and cultural rights.

Things are beginning to change, however. In India, for instance, where 16% of the population belongs to so-called Scheduled Castes (or *Dalits*, as they prefer to be called; Human Rights Watch, 2012), laws have been passed that prohibit caste-based discrimination. More *Dalits* now vote than members of the upper caste (Dugger, 1999). In fact, the benefits *Dalits* now receive—such as reserved spaces in universities and governmental jobs—have prompted members of the next highest caste of farmers and shepherds to lobby the government to have its caste status *downgraded* so as to be eligible for these benefits (Gentleman, 2007).

But the caste system still serves as a powerful source of stratification. For instance, despite anti-discrimination laws, *Dalits* are sometimes forced to work as "manual scavengers," collecting human excrement and carrying it away in baskets for disposal. Women from this caste typically clean dry toilets in homes, while men do the more physically demanding cleaning of sewers and septic tanks. They face barriers when trying to leave, such as threats of violence and eviction from local residents as well as harassment and unlawful withholding of wages by local officials (Human Rights Watch, 2014). Even Indians living in the United States find that caste sometimes colors their experiences with friends and business associates (J. Berger, 2004).

Estate Systems

A third form of stratification is the **estate system**, or **feudal system**, which develops when high-status groups own land and have power based on their noble birth (Kerbo, 1991). Estate systems were most commonly found in preindustrial societies. In medieval Europe, the highest "estate" in society was occupied by the aristocracy, who derived their wealth and power from extensive landholdings. The clergy formed the next estate. Although they had lower status than the aristocracy, they still claimed considerable status because the Catholic Church itself owned a great deal of land and exerted influence over people's lives. The last, or "third," estate was reserved for commoners: serfs, peasants, artisans, and merchants. Movement between estates was possible, though infrequent. Occasionally, a commoner might be knighted, or a wealthy merchant might become an aristocrat.

Some reminders of the estate system can still be seen today. In Great Britain, for instance, Parliament's House of Lords is still occupied primarily by people of "noble birth," and a small group of aristocratic families still sit at the top of the social ladder, where they enjoy tremendous inherited wealth and exercise significant political power. For a moment, this system seemed to be changing. In 2007, the British House of Commons (the so-called lower house) voted overwhelmingly to introduce elections to the House of Lords. It also voted to remove the last remaining "hereditary peers," whose presence in the House of Lords is based solely on their noble lineage (Cowell, 2007). A week later, the House of Lords soundly rejected the measure.

Social Class Systems

Stratification systems in contemporary industrialized societies are most likely to be based on social class. A **social class** is a group of people who share a similar economic position in society based on their wealth and income. Class is essentially, therefore, an economic stratification system. It is a means of ranking people or groups that determines access to important resources and life chances. Less obviously, perhaps, social class provides people with a particular understanding of the world and where they fit into it compared with others.

Class systems differ from other systems of stratification in that they raise no legal barriers to **social mobility**—the movement of people or groups from one level to another. Theoretically, all members of a class system, no matter how destitute they are, can rise to the top. In practice, however, mobility between classes may be difficult for some people. For instance, where you live can influence your chances of upward mobility. Climbing the income ladder is less common in the Southeast and industrial Midwest and more likely in the Northeast and West where poor people have a greater chance of living in mixed-income neighborhoods with better elementary schools and high schools and more civic engagement (Leonhardt, 2013).

In addition, some economists say that it often takes five or six generations to erase the advantages or disadvantages of a person's economic origins (Krueger, 2002). Within the span of a single generation, there isn't much social mobility—wealthy parents tend to have wealthy children; poor parents tend to have poor children. In fact, the United States has significantly less social mobility than comparable nations. For instance, 42% of Americans who grew up in the bottom fifth of incomes stay there as adults. In Denmark, the figure is 25% and in Britain it's 30% (Jäntti, 2006). Likewise, race and gender have historically combined with class to determine a person's access to educational, social, and employment opportunities. Women of color are especially likely to face barriers to upward mobility, in terms of both economic disadvantage and lack of emotional support from their families (Higginbotham & Weber, 1992).

Sociological Perspectives on Stratification

Sociologists have long been interested in explaining why societies are stratified. Two theoretical perspectives—the structural-functionalist perspective and the conflict perspective—offer insights into the sources and purposes of social inequality. They are often presumed to be competing views, but we can actually use them together to deepen our understanding of why social inequality exists, how it develops, and why it is so persistent.

The Structural-Functionalist View of Stratification

From a structural-functionalist perspective, the cause of stratification lies in a society's inevitable need for order. Because social inequality is found in some form in all societies and thus is apparently unavoidable, inequality must somehow be necessary for societies to run smoothly.

The efficient functioning of society requires that various tasks be allocated through a strictly defined division of labor. If the tasks associated with all social positions in a society were equally pleasant and equally important and required the same talents, it wouldn't make a difference who occupied which position. But structural functionalists argue that it does make a difference. Some occupations, such as teaching and medicine, are more important for the well-being of society than others and require greater talent and training. Society's dilemma is to make sure that the most talented people perform the most important tasks. One way to ensure this distribution of tasks is to assign higher rewards—better pay, greater prestige, more social privileges—to some positions in society so that they will be attractive to people with the necessary talents and abilities (K. Davis & Moore, 1945). Presumably, if these talented people were not offered sufficiently high rewards, they would have no reason to take on the difficult and demanding tasks associated with important positions. Think about it. Why would someone go through the agony and costs of many years of medical school, for instance, without some promise of compensation and high prestige?

Just because a position is important, however, does not mean it is generously rewarded (K. Davis & Moore, 1945). Imagine what our society would be like without people who remove our trash. Not only would our streets be unsightly, but our collective health would suffer. Therefore, garbage collectors serve a vital social function. But they don't get paid very much—on average, about $35,000 a year, according to the U.S. Bureau of Labor Statistics (2016f)—and trash removal is definitely not a prestigious job.

Why aren't garbage collectors higher up in the hierarchy of occupations? According to the structural-functionalist perspective, it is because we have no shortage of people with the skills needed to collect garbage. Physicians also serve the collective health needs of a society. But because of the unique skills and training needed to be a doctor, society must offer rewards high enough to ensure that qualified people will want to enter the medical profession. Doctors—even those just starting out—can expect to make, on average, six times more than garbage collectors (U.S. Bureau of Labor Statistics, 2016f).

This explanation makes some sense. But when we examine the pay scales of actual occupations more closely, it comes up short. For instance, despite the fact that they're in the same profession and have gone through similar training, a registered nurse in a doctor's office can make close to four times as much as a registered nurse working in a high school or junior college. A plumber at a city hospital makes more than twice what a plumber at a decent-sized hotel makes (Davidson, 2011).

But let's not stop there. One look at the salary structure in today's society reveals obvious instances of highly paid positions that don't seem as functionally important as positions that receive lower wages. For instance, Taylor Swift earns nearly $170 million a year. The novelist James Patterson pulls in $95 million a year. The soccer player Christiano Ronaldo and the TV therapist Dr. Phil both make over $88 million a year (*Forbes* Magazine, 2017). You might say that pop singers, TV personalities, authors, and soccer players serve vital social functions by providing the rest of us with a recreational release from the demands of ordinary life; and the best entertainers and athletes do have rare skills, indeed. However, society probably can do without another concert, piece of escapist fiction, televised therapy session, or soccer match more easily than it can do without competent physicians, scientists, computer programmers, teachers, or even trash collectors, who earn substantially less in a year than what many celebrities earn in a day.

Furthermore, the structural-functionalist argument that only a limited number of talented people are around to occupy important social positions is probably overstated. Many people have the talent to become doctors. What they lack is access to training. And why are some people—women and members of racial and ethnic minorities—paid less for or excluded entirely from certain jobs? The debates over equal employment opportunity and equal pay for equal work are essentially debates over how the functional importance of certain positions is determined.

Finally, when functionalists claim that stratification serves the needs of society, we must ask, whose needs? A system of slavery obviously meets the economic needs of one group at the expense of another, but that doesn't make it acceptable. In a class-stratified society, individuals who receive the greatest rewards have the resources to make sure they continue receiving such rewards. Over time, the competition for the most desirable positions will become less open and less competitive. The offspring of "talented"—that is, high-status—parents will inevitably have an advantage over equally talented people who are born into less successful families. Hence, social background and not personal aptitude may become the primary criterion for filling important social positions (Tumin, 1953).

The structural-functionalist perspective gives us important insight into how societies ensure that all positions in the division of labor are filled. Every society, no matter how simple or complex, differentiates people in terms of prestige and esteem and possesses a certain amount of institutional inequality. But this perspective doesn't address the fact that stratification can be unjust and divisive, a source of social *disorder* (Tumin, 1953).

The Conflict View of Stratification

In contrast, conflict theorists argue that social inequality is neither a societal necessity nor a source of social order. They see it as a primary source of conflict, coercion, and unhappiness. Stratification ultimately rests on the unequal distribution of resources—some people have them, others don't. Important resources include money, land, information, education, health care, safety, and adequate housing. Those high in the stratification system can control these resources because they are the ones who set the rules. The conflict perspective takes it as a fundamental truth that stratification systems serve the interests of those at the top and not the survival needs of the entire society.

Resources are an especially important source of inequality when they are scarce. Sometimes, their scarcity is natural. For instance, there's only a finite amount of land on earth that can be used, inhabited, and owned. At other times, however, the scarcity of a resource is artificially created. For instance, in 1890, the founder of De Beers, the South African company that currently controls two thirds of the international diamond market, realized that the sheer abundance of diamonds in southern Africa would make them virtually worthless on the international market. So he decided to carefully limit the number of diamonds released for sale each year. This artificially created rarity, coupled with a carefully cultivated image of romance, is what made diamonds so expensive and what continues to make companies such as De Beers so powerful today (Harden, 2000).

Rich and politically powerful individuals frequently work together to create or maintain privilege, often at the expense of the middle and lower classes (Phillips, 2002). The U.S. Congress is dominated by members—both Republicans and Democrats—who are far richer than the citizens they represent. The median net worth of a member of Congress is about $1.03 million, 18 times more than that of a typical American household (Choma, 2015). Over half of Congress members are millionaires. The current president is a multi-billionaire. Thus, from the conflict perspective, it's not at all surprising that politicians would make decisions that benefit the wealthy over others. For instance, in 2014, the U.S. Supreme Court ruled that placing limits on the amount of money individuals could contribute to national candidates for office was unconstitutional. That year, only about 32,000 wealthy people—roughly one one hundredth of 1% of the population—provided $1.2 billion in federal campaign contributions (Olsen-Phillips, Choma, Bryner, & Weber, 2015).

Furthermore, while Congress continues to search for ways to cut spending on programs designed to help low-income Americans, such as Medicaid (the health insurance system that covers poor adults and their dependents), low-income housing programs, food stamps, legal services for the poor, and supplemental nutrition for poor families, the wealthiest 20% of the population gets over half of the overall savings from breaks in the U.S. tax code (for things like mortgage interest and rental expenses; Congressional Budget Office, 2014). In fact, Americans earning over $1 million a year receive about $30 billion a year in federal grants and subsidies (D. Stone & Colarusso, 2011). A 2017 tax cut bill slashed the federal tax rate on corporate profits from 35% to 21% and wealthy corporations can reduce that rate even further due to an array of favorable legal deductions and loopholes. Indeed, when called upon to provide financial relief to the victims of natural disasters like hurricanes and tornadoes, many members of Congress favor paying for the aid only by cutting the budgets of existing social programs that help other needy citizens rather than by repealing tax cuts for upper-class Americans (Pappas, 2013).

There's some evidence that a growing number of Americans perceive tensions between those at the top and the rest of the population, as the conflict perspective would predict. A recent poll by the Pew Research Center (2014a) found that 62% of Americans believe that the economic system unfairly favors the powerful and 78% believe that too much influence is concentrated in the hands of a few large companies. In addition, nearly 6 in 10 people believe that the rich pay too little in taxes and 55% believe that rich people are more likely than the average person to be greedy (cited in Kohut, 2012).

What the conflict perspective gives us that the structural-functionalist perspective doesn't is an acknowledgment of the interconnected roles that economic and political institutions play in creating and maintaining a stratified society.

The Marxian Class Model

Karl Marx and Friedrich Engels (1848/1982) were the original proponents of the view that societies are divided into conflicting classes. They felt that in modern societies, two major classes emerge: *capitalists* (or the bourgeoisie), who own the **means of production**—land, commercial enterprises, factories, and wealth—and are able to purchase the labor of others, and *workers* (or the proletariat), who neither own the means of production nor have the ability to purchase the labor of others. Workers, instead, must sell their own labor to others in order to survive. Some workers, including store managers and factory supervisors, may control other workers, but their power is minimal compared with the power exerted over them by those in the capitalist class. Marx and Engels supplemented this two-tiered conception of class by adding a third tier, the *petite bourgeoisie,* which is a transitional class of people who own the means of production but don't purchase the labor power of others. This class consists of self-employed skilled laborers and businesspeople who are economically self-sufficient but don't have a staff of subordinate workers (R. V. Robinson & Kelley, 1979). Exhibit 10.1 diagrams the positions of the three classes.

Capitalists have considerable sway over what and how much will be produced, who will get it, how much money people will be paid to produce it, and so forth. Such influence allows them to control other people's livelihoods, the communities in which people live, and the economic decisions that affect the entire society. In such a structure, the rich inevitably tend to get richer, to use their wealth to create more wealth for themselves, and to act in ways that will protect their interests and positions in society.

Ultimately, the wealthy segments of society gain the ability to influence important social institutions such as the government, the media, the schools, and the courts. They have access to the means necessary to create and promote a reality that justifies their exploitative actions. Their version of reality is so influential that even those who are harmed by it come to accept it. Marx and Engels called this phenomenon **false consciousness**. False consciousness is crucial because it is the primary means by which the powerful classes in society prevent protest and revolution. As long as large numbers of poor people continue to believe that wealth and success are solely the products of individual hard work and effort rather than structured inequalities in society—that is, they believe what in the United States has been called the American Dream—resentment and animosity toward the rich will be minimized and people will perceive the inequalities as fair and deserved (R. V. Robinson & Bell, 1978).

Neo-Marxist Models of Stratification

In Marx's time—the heyday of industrial development in the mid-19th century—ownership of property and control of labor were synonymous. Most jobs were either on farms or in factories. Lumping all those who owned productive resources into one class and all those who didn't into another made sense. However, the nature of capitalism has changed a lot since then. Today, a person with a novel idea for a product or service,

EXHIBIT 10.1 ● Karl Marx's Model of Social Class

	Control labor of others	Do not control labor of others
Own means of production (land, factories, etc.)	*Capitalists*	*Petite bourgeoisie*
Do not own means of production	*Workers*	*Workers*

high-speed Internet access, and a smartphone can go into business and make a lot of money. Corporations have become much larger and more bureaucratic, with a long, multilevel chain of command. Ownership of corporations lies in the hands of stockholders (foreign as well as domestic), who often have no connection at all to the everyday workings of the business. Thus, ownership and management are separated. The powerful people who run large businesses and control workers on a day-to-day basis are frequently not the same people who own the businesses.

In light of changing realities, more contemporary conflict sociologists, such as Ralf Dahrendorf (1959), have offered models that focus primarily on differing levels of authority among the members of society. What's important is not just who owns the means of production but who can exercise influence over others. **Authority** is the possession of some status or quality that compels others to obey (Starr, 1982). A person with authority has the power to order or forbid behavior in others (Wrong, 1988). Such commands don't require the use of force or persuasion, nor do they need to be explained or justified. Rulers simply have authority over the ruled, as do teachers over students, employers over employees, and parents over children. These authority relationships are not fixed, of course: Children fight with their parents, students challenge their teachers, and workers protest against their bosses. But although the legitimacy of the authority may sometimes be called into question, the ongoing dependence of the subordinates maintains it. The worker may disagree with the boss, and the student may disagree with the teacher; but the boss still signs the paycheck, and the teacher still assigns final grades.

Like Marx and Engels, Dahrendorf believed that relations between classes inherently involve conflicts of interest. Rulers often maintain their position in society by ordering or forcing people with less authority to do things that benefit the rulers. But by emphasizing authority, Dahrendorf argued that stratification is not exclusively an economic phenomenon. Instead, it comes from the social relations between people who possess different degrees of power.

Dahrendorf's ideas about the motivating force behind social stratification have since been expanded. Sociologist Erik Olin Wright and his colleagues (Wright, 1976; Wright, Costello, Hachen, & Sprague, 1982; Wright & Perrone, 1977) have developed a model that incorporates both the ownership of means of production and the exercise of authority over others. The capitalist and petite bourgeoisie classes in this scheme are identical to those of

EXHIBIT 10.2 ● Erik Olin Wright's Model of Social Class

	Exercise authority	Do not exercise authority
Own means of production	Capitalists	Petite bourgeoisie
Do not own means of production	Managers	Workers

Marx and Engels. What is different is that the classes of people who do not own society's productive resources (Marx and Engels's worker class) are divided into two classes: managers and workers (see Exhibit 10.2).

Wright's approach gives us a sense that social class is not simply a reflection of income or the extent to which one group exercises authority over another. Lawyers, plumbers, and cooks, for instance, could each conceivably fall into any of the four class categories. They may own their own businesses and hire assistants (placing them in the capitalist class), work for a large company and have subordinates (placing them in the manager class), work for a large company without any subordinates (placing them in the worker class), or be self-employed (placing them in the petite bourgeoisie; R. V. Robinson & Kelley, 1979).

Wright's approach also emphasizes that class conflict is more than just a clash between the rich and the poor. Societies have, in fact, multiple lines of conflict—economic, political, administrative, and social. Some positions, or what Wright calls **contradictory class locations**, fall between two major classes. Individuals in these positions have trouble identifying with one side or the other. Middle managers and supervisors, for instance, can align with workers because both are subordinates of capitalist owners. Yet because middle managers and supervisors can exercise authority over some people, they may also share the interests and concerns of owners.

Weber's Model of Stratification

Other conflict sociologists have likewise questioned Marx's heavy emphasis on wealth and income as the sole factors that stratify society. Max Weber (1921/1978) agreed with Marx that social class is an important determinant of stratification. However, he observed that the way people are ranked is not just a matter of economic inequality. Weber added two other dimensions—status (or what he called prestige) and power—to his model of stratification, preferring the term **socioeconomic status**—the prestige, honor, respect, and power associated with different class positions in society—rather than class to describe social inequality (Weber, 1970).

The existence of these other dimensions makes the conflict model of class stratification more complex than simply a battle between the rich and the poor. **Prestige** is the reverence and admiration given to some people in society. It is obviously influenced by wealth and income, but it can also be derived from *achieved* characteristics, such as educational attainment and occupational status, and from *ascribed* characteristics, such as race, ethnicity, gender, and family pedigree. While wealth and prestige often go hand in hand, they don't necessarily have to. Drug dealers, for example, may be multimillionaires, but they aren't well respected and therefore aren't ranked high in the stratification system. On the flip side, professors may earn a modest salary, but they can command a fair amount of respect. **Power**, for Weber, is a person's ability to affect decisions in ways that benefit him or her. Again, power is usually related to wealth and prestige, but it need not be. Sometimes low-income individuals can band together and influence decisions at the societal level, as happened in 2012 when several thousand janitors effectively shut down the city of San Francisco by going on strike and marching through the streets to demand higher wages and better working conditions.

Class Inequality in the United States

One of the ideological cornerstones of U.S. society is the belief that all people have equal opportunities and that only individual shortcomings can impede a person's progress up the social ladder. After all, the United States is billed as the "land of opportunity." Our folklore is filled with stories of disadvantaged individuals who use their courage and resolve to overcome all adversity. We don't like to acknowledge that class inequality exists or that some people face immovable obstacles on the path to success that others will never have to face. But sociologists tell us that our place in the stratification system determines the course of our lives, in obvious and subtle ways.

Class and Everyday Life

Class standing in the United States has always determined a whole host of life chances, including access to higher education; better-paying jobs; and healthier, safer, and more comfortable lives:

- In fire-prone regions of the country, insurance companies offer "premium" protection plans to wealthy policyholders. At the first sign of a wildfire in the vicinity, someone will come and spray special fire retardant on the policy owner's house to prevent it from burning (W. Yardley, 2007).

- A study of street repair work in Indianapolis found that the average time it took between the filing of a complaint and the fixing of a pothole was 11 days in neighborhoods with an average annual income of more than $55,000; in neighborhoods with an average income of less than $25,000, it took an average of nearly 25 days (T. Evans & Nichols, 2009).

- In high-tech, affluent Silicon Valley, some wealthy executives spend millions of dollars trying to ensure their survival in the event of an apocalyptic catastrophe. Some purchase vacation homes in other countries that could serve as escape havens; others keep gassed-up helicopters on the premises (and pilots on call) just in case they need to get away quickly; still others build elaborate (and expensive) underground bunkers with state-of-the-art air filtration systems (Osnos, 2017).

- As those with limited financial means fight simply to have access to any form of health care—for instance, the average wait for an appointment with a family care physician is 29 days (Schwartz, 2017)—those at the top enjoy luxurious personal medical attention. For an annual fee, ranging from a few thousand to as much as 80 thousand dollars, wealthy individuals can buy "boutique" or "concierge" medical care, which includes 24/7 access to their physician; same-day appointments with a guaranteed waiting time of no more than 15 minutes; medical examinations at home, at work, or even in airports; nurses to accompany them when they go to see specialists; and routine physicals that are so thorough they can last up to 3 days (Belluck, 2002; Garfinkel, 2003; Ody, 2012; Schwartz, 2017; Zuger, 2005). For those wealthy individuals who end up in the hospital, the pampering continues. New York-Presbyterian/Weill Cornell Hospital offers a luxury penthouse wing whose deluxe accommodations rival the world's best hotels: chef-prepared gourmet menus, the finest Italian bed linens, a marble bathroom, and a butler (N. Bernstein, 2012).

● If you've been on an airplane recently, you've seen how painfully obvious class distinctions have become. While airlines have reduced the space between coach section seats by about 10% since the 1990s (Mouawad & White, 2013), more affluent passengers can indulge in the spacious first-class section that often includes flatbed seats. First-class cabins usually contain more flight attendants per person than coach, and first-class attendants respond more quickly to call buttons. In addition, most airlines now have special express security lines for first-class passengers so as to avoid inconvenient delays. And it's not just about shorter waits, better service, and roomier seats. Emirates Airlines offers first-class passengers their own enclosed suites—complete with minibar, 19-inch television, bed, and "dine on demand" room service—as well as access to one of two shower spas on board (Rosato, 2004). When its wealthiest passengers change planes in Atlanta, New York, and other hubs, Delta Airlines chauffeurs them between terminals in a Porsche . . . what the airline calls "surprise and delight" service (N. D. Schwartz, 2016).

Such exclusive personal attention reinforces feelings of power and privilege. On the other side of the coin, people who are less well off routinely face frustrating barriers in their daily lives. They must often make use of public facilities (health clinics, Laundromats, public transportation, etc.) to carry out the day-to-day tasks that wealthier people can carry out conveniently and privately.

Social class also determines access to everyday resources that can contribute to long-term advantages. Poor families spend, on average, 60% of their income on food, clothing, and housing, leaving less money available for leisure activities as well as things geared toward the future, like insurance and savings. As one author put it, "[T]hinking about the future is a form of luxury" (D. Thompson, 2013, p. 1). Consider also something we all now take for granted: Internet access. It would seem as if the Internet has become a truly universal resource. Over the last decade, inexpensive access over wireless phone lines has brought the Internet to millions of working-class people who may not have been able to afford it in the past. However, the emergence of services like video on demand, videoconferencing, online medicine, and web classrooms has restratified digital access. These functions require the kind of high-speed connections that tend to be available only through expensive contracts. Eighty-one percent of people earning between $60,000 and $100,000 a year own smartphones compared to 47% of those who earn less than $29,000 (Barone, 2014). Half of middle and high school students from higher-income families have high-speed Internet access at home, compared to 20% of middle-income children and only 3% of poor children (cited in C. Kang, 2013). High-speed wireless access can provide many educational, technological, occupational, and quality-of-life opportunities that lower-speed connections can't. As a result, those with slower connection speeds may experience lower-quality health services, entertainment outlets, career opportunities, and education options (Crawford, 2011). In addition, lower-income middle school students lag behind more affluent students in their ability to find, evaluate, and discuss information they find online (Leu, Forzani, Rhoads, Maykel, Kennedy, & Timbrell, 2015).

We can see similar imbalances when it comes to college admissions. Most of us would like to think that admissions decisions are based solely on a student's merit: high academic achievement (reflected in high school grades) and strong intellectual potential (reflected in scores on standardized aptitude tests like the SAT). What could be fairer than the use of these sorts of objective measures as the primary criteria for determining who gets an elite education that will open doors for a lifetime?

Would it disturb you to know that your SAT score may depend as much on your parents' financial status as on your own intellect? Obviously, simply coming from a well-to-do family doesn't guarantee a high score on the SAT, but it can help. If you were fortunate enough to attend high school in an affluent, upper-class neighborhood, chances are your school offered SAT preparation courses. In some of these schools, students take practice SAT exams every year until they take the real one in their senior year. Even if a school doesn't provide such opportunities, private lessons from test preparation coaches are available to those who can afford them. Access to these opportunities pays off (see Exhibit 10.3).

But social class is not just about differences in access to technological, educational, or economic opportunities. People create and maintain class boundaries through their perceptions of moral, cultural, and lifestyle distinctions (Lamont, 1992). For example, some communities forbid residents to dry their clothes outdoors on clotheslines because it gives the neighborhood a shabby appearance. A few years ago, the town of Wilson, North Carolina, voted to prohibit people from keeping old sofas on their front porches (Bragg, 1998). For generations, poor people in the area—unable to purchase expensive outdoor furniture—

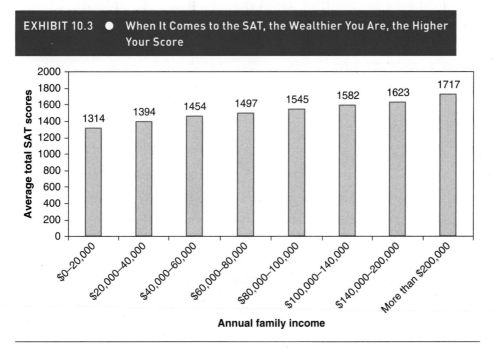

EXHIBIT 10.3 ● When It Comes to the SAT, the Wealthier You Are, the Higher Your Score

Source: National Center for Fair and Open Testing, 2016.

had kept their worn-out sofas and chairs on the porch, where they could still be used. But more affluent residents saw the practice as "low class" and approved the ban to make neighborhoods more presentable.

In the end, class is a statement about self-worth and the quality of one's life:

> It's composed of ideas, behavior, attitudes, values, and language; class is how you think, feel, act, look, dress, talk, move, walk; class is what stores you shop at, restaurants you eat in; class is the schools you attend, the education you attain; class is the very jobs you will work at throughout your adult life. Class even determines when we marry and become mothers. . . . We experience class at every level of our lives; class is who our friends are, where we live . . . even what kind of car we drive, if we own one. . . . In other words, class is socially constructed and all-encompassing. (Langston, 1992, p. 112)

Class Distinctions

Although the boundaries between social class categories tend to be fuzzy and subjective, distinct class designations based on typical occupational patterns and incomes remain a part of everyday thinking, political initiatives, and social research. When we think of social classes, we usually talk about the upper class, the middle class, the working class, the near-poor, and the poor (see Exhibit 10.4)

EXHIBIT 10.4   ●   Social Classes in the United States

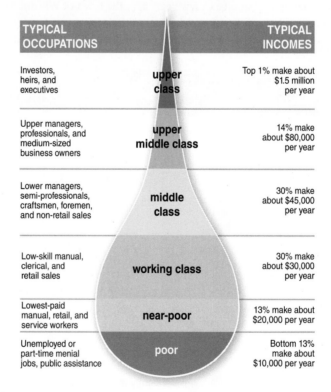

TYPICAL OCCUPATIONS		TYPICAL INCOMES
Investors, heirs, and executives	**upper class**	Top 1% make about $1.5 million per year
Upper managers, professionals, and medium-sized business owners	**upper middle class**	14% make about $80,000 per year
Lower managers, semi-professionals, craftsmen, foremen, and non-retail sales	**middle class**	30% make about $45,000 per year
Low-skill manual, clerical, and retail sales	**working class**	30% make about $30,000 per year
Lowest-paid manual, retail, and service workers	**near-poor**	13% make about $20,000 per year
Unemployed or part-time menial jobs, public assistance	**poor**	Bottom 13% make about $10,000 per year

Source: Adapted from Gilbert, 2015.

VISUAL ESSAY—THE BENEFITS OF CLASS

AP Photo/Kamran Jebreili, File

Jose Giribas/Bloomberg via Getty Images

Big Cheese Photo LLC / Alamy Stock Photo

©iStockphoto.com/recep-bg

Robert Daemmrich/Corbis Historical/ Getty Images

Horizons WWP / TRVL / Alamy Stock Photo

In a chapter about stratification and inequality, it's very easy to get bogged down (even overwhelmed) by statistics. We can talk about unemployment figures, median household incomes, net worth, wage disparities, and rates of health care coverage all we want. But in the end, inequality plays itself out most obviously in how people go about meeting their day-to-day needs. Here we see images of a few common aspects of everyday life (getting an education, traveling by air, traveling by land) from the perspective of those at "the top" and those who are not as fortunate.

As you look at these pairs of photos I want you to think about the larger implications of these different experiences. For instance, aside from comfort, what difference does it make whether you take an intercontinental flight in a private three-room suite or elbow-to-elbow with the stranger next to you in the cramped coach section? Similarly, what other feelings of advantage (or disadvantage) get reinforced when traveling in a chauffeur-driven limousine versus taking a crowded public bus like this one in Japan? Finally, how would your learning experience change if you attended a public high school in the South Bronx where textbooks are out-of-date and the ceilings are caving in versus a private high school in Austin, Texas, where the facilities are state-of-the-art and every student gets an iPad? As you ponder these imbalances, think of a bigger question: is it true—as our folklore would have us believe—that everyone in this society has the same opportunities to live a good life? Do you think everyone *should* have the same opportunities? Why?

The Upper Class

The **upper class** in the United States is a small, exclusive group that occupies the highest levels of status and prestige. For some, membership in the upper class is relatively recent, acquired through personal financial achievement. These families are usually headed by high-level executives in large corporations and highly compensated lawyers, doctors, scientists, entertainers, and professional athletes. Such individuals may have been born into poor, working-class, or middle-class families, but they have been able to climb the social ladder and create a comfortable life. They are sometimes called "the new rich."

Others, however, are born into wealth gained by earlier generations in their families (Langman, 1988). The formidable pedigree of "old wealth," not to mention the wealth itself, provides them with insulation from the rest of society. Their position in society is perpetuated through a set of exclusive clubs, resorts, charitable and cultural organizations, and social activities that provides members with a distinctive lifestyle and a perspective on the world that distinguishes them from the rest of society.

Although "old wealth" families enjoy upper-class status across generations, most American families go through a wide range of economic experiences that can move them from one class level to another. For instance, it's estimated that 73% of American families will spend at least 1 year in the top fifth of income earners (Rank, 2014).

Sociologists G. William Domhoff (1983, 1998) and C. Wright Mills (1956) have made the case that members of the upper class can structure other social institutions to ensure that their personal interests are met and that the class itself endures. They control the government, large corporations, the majority of privately held corporate stock, the media outlets, universities, councils for national and international affairs, and so on (Domhoff, 1998). Hence, members of this class enjoy political and economic power to a degree not available to members of other classes.

For example, the educational system plays not only a key socializing role (see Chapter 5) but also an important role in perpetuating or reproducing the U.S. class structure. Children of the upper class often attend private schools, boarding schools, and well-endowed private universities (Domhoff, 1998). In addition to the standard curriculum, these schools tend to emphasize "essay-text literacy"—the ability to read, evaluate, analyze, and synthesize written texts—in their curricula. Such a skill enables students to communicate in precise language and to formulate, examine, and defend arguments. Important social institutions such as governments, corporations, and professions are built upon essay-text literacy (Finn, 2012).

Required attendance at school functions; participation in esoteric sports such as lacrosse, squash, and crew; the wearing of school blazers or ties; and various "character-building" activities are designed to teach young people the unique lifestyle of the ruling class. Students also learn the vocabulary, inflection, fashion, aesthetic tastes, values, and manners of the upper class (R. Collins, 1971). In many ways, boarding schools function like "total institutions" such as prisons and convents (E. Goffman, 1961), isolating members from the outside world and providing them with routines and traditions that are highly effective agents of socialization.

In a study of more than 60 elite boarding schools in the United States and Great Britain, Peter Cookson and Caroline Persell (1985) showed how the philosophies and programs of boarding schools help transmit power and privilege. This school experience forms an everlasting social, political, and economic bond among all graduates, and the schools act as gatekeepers into prestigious universities. After graduates leave these universities, they connect with one another at the highest levels in the world of business, finance, and government. The director of development at Choate, an elite prep school in Connecticut, said this:

> There is no door in this entire country that cannot be opened by a Choate graduate. I can go anywhere in this country and anywhere there's a man I want to see . . . I can find a Choate man to open that door for me. (quoted in Cookson & Persell, 1985, p. 200)

The privileged social status that is produced and maintained through the elite educational system practically guarantees that the people who occupy key political and economic positions will form a like-minded, cohesive group with little resemblance to the majority whose lives depend on their decisions. As one columnist put it:

> There is an archipelago of affluent enclaves clustered around the coastal cities, Chicago, Dallas, and so on. If you're born into one of them, you will probably go to college with people from one of the enclaves; you'll marry someone from one of the enclaves; you'll go off and live in one of the enclaves. (D. Brooks, 2012, p. A23)

The Middle Class

In discussing the U.S. class system, it is tempting to focus on the very top or the very bottom, overlooking the chunk of the population that falls somewhere in the ill-defined center: the **middle class**. Ironically, the middle class has always been important in defining U.S. culture. Every other class is measured and judged against the values and norms of the middle class. It is a universal class, a class that supposedly represents everyone. According to one recent survey, 9 out of 10 Americans consider themselves middle class regardless of the size of their income (cited in P. Cohen, 2015). Not surprisingly, the middle class is a coveted political constituency. Liberal and conservative politicians alike court it. Policies are proclaimed on its behalf.

But the lofty cultural status of the middle class in U.S. society belies the difficulties it experiences. Economists, pundits, and sociologists have long been fond of talking about the middle class being "under assault," "endangered," or "fragile" (T. A. Sullivan, Warren, & Westbrook, 2000). Median household incomes rose steadily throughout the 1980s and 1990s, were stagnant during the 2000s, and have only recently begun to increase. In 1980, the median household income (in current dollars) across all ethnoracial groups in the United States was $44,059. By 2016, it had increased to $59,039 (U.S. Bureau of the Census, 2017).

However, despite this growth, many middle income workers across the country are seeing their hours cut—for instance, by being moved from full time to part time or by losing opportunities for overtime. According to data from the U.S. Bureau of Labor Statistics (2017b), in 2017, about 5.5 million workers had to cut their hours to fewer than 35 a week due to slack work conditions or the inability to find full-time work. Even as unemployment has dropped to prerecession levels, the number of people working part time involuntarily is 45% higher than it was in 2007, leading one researcher to call part-time work in the United States the "new normal" (Golden, 2016).

According to the U.S. Bureau of the Census, in 1967, 53% of households were defined as "middle income" (that is, they earned between $35,000 and $100,000 a year); in 2013, that figure dropped to 43% (cited in Searcey & Gebeloff, 2015). Moreover, between 1970 and 2014, the share of the nation's income earned by middle class households dropped from 62% to 43% (Pew Research Center, 2015a).

Today, even families with good incomes live close to the financial edge, one layoff or medical emergency away from financial crisis. Consequently, Americans now see a middle class with fewer opportunities to get ahead, less disposable income, and lower job security than the middle class of previous generations. According to one recent poll, 85% said it was more difficult now than a decade ago to maintain their standard of living (cited in Blow, 2013).

Some economists predict that even as the economy improves, the job market will continue to be weak in part because companies have learned to produce more cost-efficiently with a smaller workforce. Since 2010, equipment and software prices have dropped 2.4% while labor costs have risen 6.7%. So when companies grow, they quickly realize that it's much cheaper to buy new machines than to hire more people (Clifford, 2013). In 1999, the typical new business started with 7.7 employees; today that figure is 4.7 (cited in Rampell, 2012). Said one executive, "I want to have as few people touching our products as possible. Everything should be as automated as it can be" (quoted in Rampell, 2011, p. A1). Consequently, the number of middle-income jobs has dropped. There were 74% fewer word processor/typist jobs, 70% fewer computer operators, 46% fewer travel agents, and 29% fewer accountants and bookkeepers in 2013 compared to 2000 (Rattner, 2014). Moreover, employers are increasingly turning to temporary rather than full-time, permanent workers, who would be eligible for benefits.

It's worth noting, however, that some economists and tech experts see this trend toward temporary work as the wave of the future, citing the growing popularity of freelance, short-term "contract" jobs (like Uber, Thumbtack, and TaskRabbit) that individuals coordinate through mobile apps (Heller, 2017; Irwin, 2016). But while these nontraditional jobs offer a level of flexibility that lots of people these days want, they typically don't offer the benefits (employer-based health insurance, paid leave, pensions, unemployment insurance, and so on) that more conventional employment offers.

And so it's no wonder that even though the economy has been improving, many middle-class adults feel like they're on a treadmill that constantly threatens to throw them into a less desirable social class (Blow, 2013). Compared to two decades ago, a smaller percentage of Americans believe it is possible to start out poor, work hard, and get rich (Sorkin & Thee-Brenan, 2014). Moreover, only half of Americans in their 30s today earn more than their parents did at the same age; in the 1970s, that figure was 92% (Leonhardt, 2016).

The Working Class

Members of the **working class**—people who work in factory, clerical, or low-paying sales jobs—are even more susceptible to economic fluctuations than those in the middle class. Most working-class people have only a high school education and earn an hourly wage rather than a weekly or monthly salary. Although they may earn enough money to survive, they typically don't earn enough to accumulate significant savings or other assets. Under the best circumstances, they usually have difficulty buying a home or paying for a child's education. When times are bad, they live their lives under the constant threat of layoffs, factory closings, and unemployment.

The working class always suffers disproportionately from downturns in the U.S. economy. Consequently, they are far more pessimistic about their futures than wealthier Americans. For instance, one survey found that people who make less than $30,000 a year are more likely than people earing middle incomes to expect to be laid off or take a pay cut and to say they have had trouble paying for medical care or paying the rent (Pew Research Center, 2011).

In addition, this group is more likely to say the country is headed in the wrong direction and that the economy is getting worse. Consequently, they fear losing their jobs more than any other income class (Green, 2015). Most political experts agree that such discontent fueled Donald Trump's presidential victory in 2016.

To survive psychologically in an economically unstable world, many working-class people resort to defining their jobs as irrelevant to their core identity. Instead of focusing on the dreariness or the insignificance of their work, they may come to view it as a noble act of sacrifice. A bricklayer put it simply: "My job is to work for my family" (Sennett & Cobb, 1972, p. 135). Framing their work as sacrifice allows them to escape the disappointment of an unfulfilling job and orient their lives toward their children's and grandchildren's futures, something that gives them a sense of control they can't get through their jobs.

But it is especially difficult for working-class parents to sacrifice "successfully." Upper-class and middle-class parents make sacrifices so their children will have a life *like* theirs. Working-class parents sacrifice so their children will *not* have a life like theirs. Their lives are not a "model" but a "warning." The danger of this type of sacrifice is that if the children do fulfill the parents' wishes and rise above their quality of life, the parents may eventually become a burden or an embarrassment to them. Thus, people who struggle to make ends meet are sometimes caught in a vicious trap. In addition, they must deal with public perceptions of them and their work that are decidedly negative.

MIKE ROSE

"UNSKILLED" JOBS REQUIRE LOTS OF COMPLEX SKILLS

Author Mike Rose (2004) grew up in a modest home, the son of working-class immigrants. Most of the adults in his family and in his neighborhood never graduated from high school, and all of them worked in blue-collar or service jobs their whole lives. He was fully aware, early on, that these manual laborers did not occupy a particularly valued place in American society. Low-paying jobs are often labeled "unskilled." Such workers are consistently marginalized, either by more affluent people who treat them as if they are invisible or by widely held cultural stereotypes that they are unintelligent and unrefined. Because their work doesn't usually require advanced educational credentials, there's a belief that those who do it aren't that bright.

Rose set out to examine these stereotypes. He observed working-class people on the job—waitresses, hair stylists, plumbers, welders, and so on—and took detailed notes of their activities. Once he became aware of the rhythms of their work, he began asking them questions, casual ones to start with and more specific ones as he got to know them better.

What he found was that apparently "mindless" working-class occupations require high levels of skill, judgment, and intelligence. Hair stylists, for example, must show an astonishing amount of aesthetic and mental agility when they turn vague requests ("I want something light and summery") into an actual hairstyle pleasing to the client. They must also have command of a remarkable range of knowledge—nutrition, hair growth patterns, the biology of skin, hair treatment chemicals, and popular images of beauty—in order to provide their clients not only with a look they want but with advice on how to maintain a stylish appearance. As one stylist described it,

> You've got to add up all these pieces of the puzzle, and then at the end you've got to come up with a thought, OK, it's gotta be this length, it's gotta be layered here, it's gotta be textured there. . . . It's not like we just start cutting. By the time I take my client to the shampoo bowl, after the consultation, I already have a little road map as to how I'm going to cut this haircut. (quoted in Rose, 2004, p. 33)

(Continued)

(Continued)

Similarly, working-class women who wait on tables in inexpensive diners and coffee shops must have advanced information-processing skills, including a sharp memory and the ability to make lightning-fast mathematical calculations. On the surface, restaurant work seems highly structured and routine—from the physical layout that guides people's movements to the norms of dining that are well known to customers and waitstaff. Once seated, customers expect a series of events to unfold along a familiar time line. Indeed, their satisfaction (and the size of the tip they leave) is based on the manner in which the service meets these expectations.

On closer inspection, however, the restaurant environment is exceedingly complex and unpredictable. For instance, customers enter at different times and make requests at different stages of their meals, so each table proceeds at a different pace. This staggering of schedules maximizes the restaurant's flow of trade, but it increases the physical and cognitive demands on waitresses, especially during peak hours or when customers are particularly demanding. The meals themselves develop under their own different timetables. Some items cook quickly; others take a long time. Some meals have only a limited amount of time in which they can be served. So servers must also be aware of the temporal rhythm of the kitchen. And since the restaurant's profit depends on the constant turnover of customers, all this occurs under the pressure to move people along quickly.

Our collective failure to acknowledge the qualities and skills that even lower-status jobs require has helped to undermine a large chunk of the American working-class population. Rose's research is less of an objective assessment of these occupations than it is a plea to broaden our definitions of intelligence and to see dignity in the jobs that keep American society running.

The Poor

In an affluent society like the United States, the people at the very bottom of the social class structure face constant humiliation in their everyday lives. You've heard the old saying "Money can't buy happiness." The implication is that true satisfaction in life is more than just a matter of being wealthy. Indeed, research shows that compared with others, people with high incomes aren't happier, don't spend more time in enjoyable activities, and tend to be more tense (Kahneman, Krueger, Schkade, Schwarz, & Stone, 2006). Yet such information provides little comfort to the **poor**, those people who are chronically unemployed or underemployed and who can't pay their bills, don't know where their next meal is coming from or whether their job will exist tomorrow, suffer from ill health, or have no home. The legendary vaudeville singer Sophie Tucker once said, "I've been rich and I've been poor—and believe me, rich is better."

What Poverty Means in the United States

We hear the word *poverty* all the time. In common usage, poverty is typically conceived in monetary terms, as the lack of sufficient funds to ensure an adequate lifestyle. Sociologists, though, often distinguish between absolute and relative poverty. The term **absolute poverty** refers to the minimal requirements a human being needs to survive. The term **relative poverty** refers to one's economic position compared with the living standards of the majority in a given society. Absolute poverty means not having enough money for minimal food, clothing, and shelter. But relative poverty is more difficult to gauge. It reflects culturally defined aspirations and expectations. Poor people "generally feel better if they know that their position in life does not compare too badly with others in society" (quoted in D. Altman, 2003, p. 21). An annual family income of $10,000, which would constitute abject poverty in the United States, is perhaps five times higher than the *average* income in many developing countries. As Kentucky senator and presidential candidate Rand Paul once said, "The poor in our country are enormously better off than the rest of the world"

(Paul, 2010, p. 16). Although such a statement reflects a common perception that life in a U.S. slum is comfortable when compared with life in destitute regions in other parts of the world, it overlooks the very real suffering associated with American poverty.

The Poverty Line

The U.S. government uses an absolute definition of poverty to identify people who can't afford what they need to survive. The U.S. **poverty line** identifies the amount of yearly income a family requires to meet its basic needs. Those who fall below the line are officially poor. The official poverty line is based on pretax cash income only, which doesn't include food stamps, Medicaid, public housing, and other noncash benefits. The line varies by family size, and it's adjusted each year to account for inflation. But it doesn't take into account regional differences in cost of living. In 2016, the official poverty line for a family of four—two parents and two children—was an annual income of $24,339.

That dollar amount is established by the U.S. Department of Agriculture and for decades has been based on something called the Thrifty Food Plan. This plan, developed in the early 1960s, is used to calculate the cost of a subsistence diet, which is the bare minimum a family needs to survive. This cost is then multiplied by three because research at the time showed that the average family spent one third of its income on food each year. The resulting amount was adopted in 1969 as the government's official poverty line. Even though the plan is modified periodically to account for changes in dietary recommendations, the formula itself and the basic definition of poverty have remained the same for nearly five decades.

Many policymakers, economists, sociologists, and concerned citizens question whether the current poverty line provides an accurate picture of basic needs in the United States. Several things have changed since the early 1960s. For instance, today food costs account for about 13% of the average family's budget because the price of other things, such as housing and medical care, has increased at much higher rates (U.S. Bureau of Labor Statistics, 2016a). In addition, there were fewer dual-earner and single-parent families in the past, meaning that fewer families had to pay for childcare. In short, today's family has many more expenses and therefore probably spends a greater proportion of its total income on nonfood items. The consequence is that the official poverty line is probably set too low and therefore underestimates the hardships that struggling Americans experience (Swarns, 2008a).

In 2011, the U.S. Census Bureau proposed a new way of determining the poverty line called the Supplemental Poverty Measure. This new formula is based on an estimate of expenditures on food, clothing, shelter, and utilities. It also takes into consideration medical spending, taxes, commuting costs, and childcare. Using this model, the poverty line for a family of four would rise by around $2,000 and about 1.4 million more people would be considered poor (Short, 2015). Others have proposed a measure, called the Self-Sufficiency Standard, that uses of the costs of *all* basic needs—housing, utilities, food, childcare, health care, transportation, taxes, and so on—to compute a poverty threshold (D. Pearce, 2014). These costs are adjusted for geographic variation in cost of living. Using either of these alternative models would likely raise the poverty threshold for a family of four to an annual income of around $30,000.

Some economists suggest that the exclusive focus on income in setting the poverty line underestimates the harmful long-term effects of poverty. Obviously, when families don't have enough income, they can't buy what they need—adequate food, clothing, and shelter. But when families don't have any assets, such as savings and home equity, they lose economic security and their ability to plan, dream, and pass on opportunities to their children (Block, Korteweg, & Woodward, 2013; Shapiro, 2008).

Deciding who is and isn't officially poor is not just a matter of words and labels. When the poverty line is too low, we fail to recognize the problems of the many families who have difficulty making ends meet but who are not officially defined as poor. A needy family earning an amount slightly above the poverty line may not qualify for a variety of public assistance programs, such as housing benefits, Head Start, Medicaid, or Temporary Assistance for Needy Families. As a result, its standard of living may not be as good as that of a family that earns slightly less but qualifies for these programs.

The Near-Poor

Interestingly, the government seems to agree implicitly that the poverty line is set too low. The U.S. Bureau of the Census defines the 14 million people who earn up to 25% more than the official poverty line amount as the **near-poor** or **working poor** (Proctor, Semega, & Kollar, 2016). These individuals and families are not "officially" poor, but face difficulties making ends meet. Those who fall into this category can be eligible for certain government assistance programs. For instance, the Affordable Health Care Act (also known as "Obamacare") extends Medicaid coverage to people earning 38% above the official poverty line.

The existence of the near-poor is fraught with irony. For one thing, they tend to defy stereotypes of how poor people live. Half live in married-couple households, 49% live in the suburbs, 42% have private health insurance, and 28% work full time (DeParle, Gebeloff, & Tavernise, 2011). And because of the recent recession, they tend to be older and better educated than the near-poor were 30 years ago. In 1979, 26% of low-wage workers (those earning less than $10 an hour) were teenagers and 25% had some college experience; today teenagers make up only 12% of low-wage workers and 43% have spent some time in college (Dube, 2013).

When nothing out of the ordinary happens, the near-poor can manage. But an unexpected event—a sickness, an injury, the breakdown of a major appliance or automobile, a layoff—can destroy a family financially and sink it into poverty. As one near-poor mother of two put it, "We're O.K. unless something—anything at all—goes wrong" (quoted in Davey, 2011, p. A22). A recent study found that 47% of Americans either could not pay for an emergency expense costing $400 or would have to sell something or borrow money to cover it (Federal Reserve, 2015).

Near-poor families must sometimes juggle scarce resources simply to survive. According to one study (Feeding America, 2014), about 69% of food bank client households across the country have to choose between paying for utilities and paying for food (referred to as the "heat or eat dilemma"). Most choose heat. A study of 34,000 people nationwide found that during the cold winter months, families spend less on food and reduce their caloric intake by an average of 10% in order to pay their fuel bills (Bhattacharya, DeLeire, Haider, & Currie, 2003). Imagine being a poor single mother with a sick child. One trip to the doctor might cost an entire week's food budget or a month of rent. Dental work or an eye examination is easily sacrificed when other pressing bills need to be paid. If she depends on a car to get to work and it breaks down, a few hundred dollars to fix it might mean not paying the electric bill that month. When gasoline prices skyrocket—as they did for a while in 2012 when a gallon of gas cost nearly $5—many near-poor families find that they have to cut down on food purchases so they can afford to drive to work. These are choices that wealthier families never face.

Institutional responses to this sort of dilemma are often unsympathetic. Take, for instance, the reactions schools have to students whose parents have not paid their lunch bill. In 2014, the Department of Agriculture found that nearly half of all school districts used some form of "lunch shaming" to humiliate the child and compel parents to pay the unpaid lunch bill. In some schools, cafeteria cashiers will throw away the child's hot lunch and replace it with a cold one. In Alabama, a cafeteria worker stamped "I need lunch money" on a child's arm (Siegel, 2017).

The Poverty Rate

The **poverty rate**—the percentage of residents whose income falls below the official poverty line—is the figure that the U.S. government uses to track the success of its efforts to reduce poverty. Exhibit 10.5 shows how the poverty rate has fluctuated over the past few decades. In 2015, 13.5% of the population—or 43.1 million Americans—fell below the official poverty line, up from 11.3% in 2000 but down from over 15% in 2012. Indeed, due to the recent economic recovery, millions of people nationwide have climbed out of poverty (P. Cohen, 2016). But, as we saw earlier, inching above the official poverty line does not guarantee a comfortable or even sustainable life. Hence if we add the near-poor to those officially counted as poor, the number of people who suffer financially in this country increases to over 57 million, or about 18% of the population (Proctor, Semega, & Kollar, 2016).

When used to describe national trends in poverty, the overall poverty rate can obscure important differences among subgroups of the population. In 2015, 9.1% of people who identify themselves as non-Hispanic Whites and 11.4% of Asian Americans fell below the poverty line. That same year, 24.1% of Blacks and 21.4% of Latino/as (who could be of any race) were considered poor. The poverty rate in the South (15.3%) and West (13.3%) is higher than the rate in the Midwest (11.7%) and Northeast (12.4%). In addition, poverty is higher in rural areas (16.7%) than in metropolitan areas (13.0%), although it's highest in inner cities (16.8%). Finally, people with disabilities are nearly three times as likely to be poor than those without disabilities (Proctor, Semega, & Kollar, 2016).

Although racial and ethnic minorities have consistently been rated among the poorest Americans, other groups have seen their status change over time. Before Social Security was instituted in 1935, many of the most destitute were elderly. As recently as 1970, 25% of U.S. residents over the age of 65 fell below the poverty line. Today, only 8.8% of the people in this age group are poor (Proctor, Semega, & Kollar, 2016). Exhibit 10.6 shows how the poverty rate of older Americans has declined.

Children's fortunes have gone in the reverse direction. About 14.5 million American children under the age of 18 (19.7%) live in households that are officially poor. This is a disproportionate share of the people in poverty. As you would suspect, poverty figures for children vary dramatically along ethnoracial lines. About 33% of African American and 29% of Latino/a children under 18 live in poverty—compared with 17.2% of non-Hispanic White children and 12.3% of Asian children (ProQuest Statistical Abstract, 2017).

The United States has one of the highest child poverty rates of any industrialized nation (UNICEF, 2014a). To put that 19.7% figure into perspective, the average child poverty rate in the 33 other member nations of the Organization for Economic Cooperation and Development (2014) is 13%. Rates in Scandinavian countries are especially low, ranging from 3.7% to 7.0% (Bertelsmann Stiftung, 2011).

To make matters worse, about 10.1 million poor American children now live in "high-poverty" neighborhoods (defined as areas with poverty rates of 30% or more). That marks a 25% increase since 2000. Growing up in these neighborhoods increases the risk of health problems, teen pregnancy, dropping out of school, and a host of other social and economic problems that limit a child's ability to successfully transition into adulthood (Annie E. Casey Foundation, 2015).

EXHIBIT 10.5 ● How Has the Poverty Rate Changed Over Time?

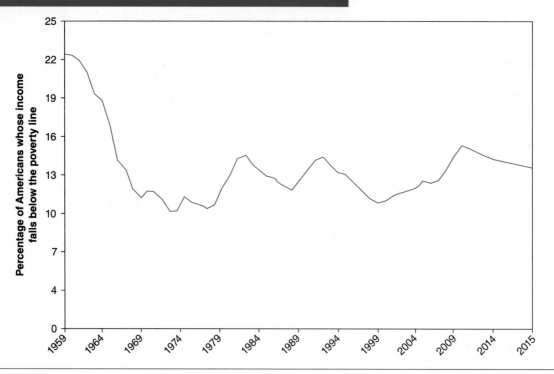

Source: DeNavas-Walt, Proctor, & Smith, 2010, Table 4; DeNavas-Walt & Proctor, 2014, Table 3. Proctor, Semega, & Kollar, 2016, Table 3.

EXHIBIT 10.6 ● When It Comes to Poverty, the Elderly Have an Advantage

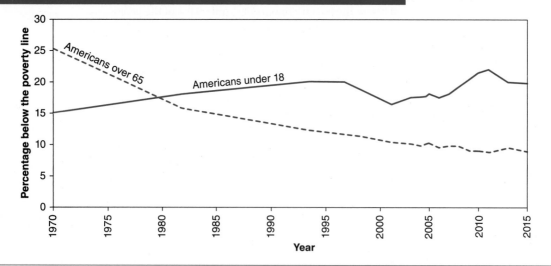

Source: 1970–1999 data from U.S. Bureau of the Census, 2000; 2001 data from Proctor & Dalaker, 2002; 2003 data from DeNavas-Walt, Proctor, & Lee, 2006; 2006–2007 data from DeNavas-Walt, Proctor, & Smith, 2008; 2008–2009 data from DeNavas-Walt, Proctor, & Smith, 2010; 2010 data from DeNavas-Walt, Proctor, & Smith, 2011; 2013 data from DeNavas-Walt & Proctor, 2014; 2015 data from Proctor, Semega, & Kollar, 2016.

Several factors explain why the poverty rate among U.S. children is high compared with that of older U.S. residents. For one thing, family structure is closely related to child poverty. The poverty rate for families headed by single mothers is 28.2%, compared with 14.9% for families headed by single fathers and 5.4% for married-couple families (Proctor, Semega, & Kollar, 2016). In addition, government spending on programs for the elderly (Medicare, Social Security) has increased dramatically over the past four decades (Mishel, Bivens, Gould, & Shierholz, 2013), while spending on families and children (cash assistance, health care, food and nutritional aid, etc.) has dropped and will continue to drop into the foreseeable future (Davey, 2011; Steuerle, 2007). Not surprisingly, young families with children are six times as likely to be poor as elderly families (cited in Tavernise, 2011b). Worldwide, there is a strong correlation between the amount of money a country spends on social programs and rates of poverty (see Exhibit 10.7).

EXHIBIT 10.7 ● When Governments Spend More on Social Programs, Poverty Goes Down

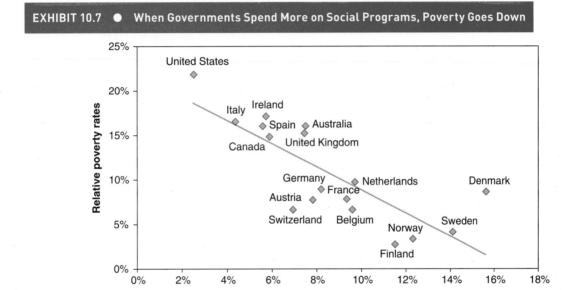

Source: Reprinted from L. Mishel, J. Bivens, E. Gould, & H. Shierholz, 2013, *The State of Working America.*

The Consequences of Poverty

Poverty isn't just about rates, trends, and official definitions. It is a never-ending burden borne on the shoulders of those who are least equipped to endure it. Being poor clearly influences people's physical and intellectual well-being.

Poverty and Health

With each step down the income ladder comes increased risk of headaches, varicose veins, respiratory infection, hypertension, stress-related illness, low-birth-weight babies, stroke, diabetes, and heart disease (Krugman, 2008; Pérez-Peña, 2003; Shweder, 1997). Recent studies have found a troubling increase in tropical parasitic diseases like Dengue fever and typhus in poverty-stricken areas of the U.S. South and Southwest that were heretofore confined to poor countries in Latin America. These parasites thrive where there is poor street drainage, plumbing, sanitation, and garbage disposal (Hotez, 2012).

Among children, decades of research show that rates of chronic illness, injury, ear disease, asthma, and physical inactivity all increase as socioeconomic status decreases (Chen, Matthews, & Boyce, 2002). Some researchers point out that poverty begins to affect a child's health even before he or she is born. Poor pregnant women are less likely to receive quality prenatal care and more likely to be exposed to environmental toxins that can harm fetal development than wealthier women (Furstenberg, 2011).

It might be tempting to attribute such class disparities to the unhealthy lifestyle choices of people on the bottom socioeconomic rungs of society. For instance, those below the poverty line are significantly more likely to smoke cigarettes and smoke them more heavily than those above the poverty line (Centers for Disease Control and Prevention, 2017). However, it is impossible to ignore the institutional activities that aggravate the problem. For instance, consider rules that determine eligibility for government programs for the needy (see Chapter 6). Poor children whose Supplemental Nutrition Assistance Program benefits are cut or reduced because their parents' income rises slightly above the eligibility threshold are significantly more likely to be in poor health, be at risk for developmental delays, and experience child food insecurity than those whose families remain eligible to receive benefits (Children's Health Watch, 2013).

Even after controlling for age, sex, race, family size, and education, the risk of death steadily increases as income goes down (Chetty, Stepner, & Abraham, 2016). And the gap is growing. According to data analyzed by the Social Security Administration (cited in Tavernise, 2016), among men born in 1920, there was a 6-year difference in life expectancy between those in the top 10% of income earners and those in the bottom 10%. Among men born in 1950, that difference more than doubled to 14 years. For women, the gap in life expectancy grew from 4.7 years to 13 years. The health status of poor people in the United States is so bad that volunteer medical groups that were created to provide free medical services in destitute third-world countries like Ghana, Tanzania, and Haiti sometimes set up mobile medical facilities in poor rural areas of the United States (Towell, 2007).

Not only do people without sufficient economic means face greater health risks than others, but they may also lack the ability to get effective medical care when they need it. According to the most recent data from the National Center for Health Statistics (Cohen, Martinez, & Zammitti, 2016), 8.6% of the U.S. population was uninsured in 2016. While this represents a substantial decrease compared to 2013 (Sanger-Katz, 2014) and the lowest level since 2008 (principally due to subsidies provided by the Affordable Care Act), it means that about 27.3 million Americans still have no health insurance. At the time of this writing, Congress was debating a replacement to the Affordable Care Act and President Trump was seeking other ways to fulfill his campaign promise of dismantling the program.

The effects of being able to afford health insurance can't be overstated. A nationwide study found that uninsured people experience a 40% increase in their risk of dying, which, according to one study, translates into about 45,000 deaths annually (Wilper et al., 2009). When the state of Massachusetts adopted mandatory health care coverage for all its residents in 2006, the death rate in the state dropped significantly. The decline was steepest in those counties that had the highest proportion of poor and uninsured people prior to the adoption of the law (Sommers, Long, & Baicker, 2014).

In addition to inadequate or nonexistent health care, approximately 12.7% of American households are "food insecure"—meaning that some members don't have enough to eat or the family uses strategies like eating less varied diets, participating in food assistance programs, or getting emergency food from community food pantries (ProQuest Statistical

Abstract, 2017). That means that about 29.1 million adults and 13.1 million children live in households that experience hunger or the risk of hunger.

As you will recall from Chapter 6, lower-income families actually pay higher-than-average prices for food (Brookings Institution, 2006). Large supermarket chains, for example, hesitate to open stores in very poor neighborhoods because of security fears. Hence, residents who are without transportation must rely on small neighborhood grocery stores, which usually charge more for food than large supermarkets do.

Poverty and Education

The educational deck is likewise stacked against poor people. A recent report by the Education Trust (Ushomirsky & Williams, 2015) showed that nationally the highest poverty school districts receive about 10% (or about $1,200) less state and local funding per student than the lowest poverty districts. That might not sound like much, but for a 1,000-student high school, that works out to $1.2 million in missing resources every year. Moreover, teachers in poor districts tend to be less experienced and are paid less than teachers in more affluent districts (LaCoste-Caputo, 2007). Without adequate resources, teachers become frustrated and do not teach; children become cynical and do not learn.

The consequences of such imbalances are striking. Children in school districts that have the highest concentrations of poverty perform an average of *four grades* below children from the wealthiest districts (Rich, Cox, & Bloch, 2016).

Even if they manage to graduate from high school, most poor children can't afford to attend college. Those who do are more likely to attend community colleges or state universities, which are less expensive but lack the prestige, and often the quality, of their more expensive counterparts. Despite nationwide efforts to increase access to higher education, universities have not been particularly successful in recruiting and retaining poor students (Pérez-Peña, 2013). An examination of 38 elite colleges in the United States found that more students come from families in the top 1% of the income scale than come from the entire bottom 60%. Moreover, children from the top 1% are 77 times more likely to attend an Ivy League college than children whose parents are in the bottom 25% (Chetty, Friedman, Saez, Turner, & Yagan, 2017). Of course, students without family wealth do sometimes attend top universities with the help of need-based scholarships. But these schools, by and large, have no systematic plans for identifying, recruiting, or admitting low-income students.

Furthermore, once they get into college, poor students don't fare as well as their more affluent counterparts. In a National Center for Education Statistics study that has been tracking college students for over a decade, 14% of those from the most disadvantaged quarter of the population earned a bachelor's degree. In contrast, 60% of those from the most advantaged quarter earned a degree (cited in Dynarski, 2015).

Such a gap is especially significant because a bachelor's degree is essential in today's global economy where 6 out of every 10 jobs require postsecondary education and training (Mather & Jarosz, 2014). According to the U.S. Bureau of the Census (ProQuest Statistical Abstract, 2017), people with some college experience but no degree earn, on average, about $36,000 a year. College graduates on average earn more than $65,000 a year. These numbers demonstrate that the educational system often seals the fate of poor people instead of helping them succeed within the U.S. class structure.

Out on the Streets

The most publicly visible consequence of poverty is homelessness. No one knows for sure exactly how many homeless people live in the United States. The National Alliance to End Homelessness (2016) estimates that on any given night, there are more than 564,000 homeless people; another 7 million are doubled up with family or friends, the most common living situation prior to becoming homeless. Approximately 63% of homeless people are single adults, 37% are people in families, and 6.5% are unaccompanied youth and children. Of homeless adults, 18% are employed, and 13% are military veterans (U.S. Conference of Mayors, 2014).

The causes of homelessness in the United States are typically institutional ones: stagnating wages, changes in welfare programs, the gentrification of old neighborhoods, and, perhaps most important, lack of affordable housing. Nearly three quarters of homeless families cite lack of affordable housing as the principal cause of their homelessness (U.S. Conference of Mayors, 2014). When rising wealth at the top of society drives up housing prices, the poor are left unable to afford decent housing (Shipler, 2004).

According to the federal government, housing is considered "affordable" if it costs no more than 30% of a family's income. The poorest fifth of the population spend about 78% of their wages on housing. By comparison, the wealthiest fifth of the population spend only 19% of their income on housing (cited in Swartz, 2007). In 2016, the nationwide median housing wage—the minimum amount of money a person would have to make to afford a modest two-bedroom apartment—was $20.30 an hour (or an annual income of over $42,000, assuming full-time, year-round employment). That's nearly three times the federal minimum wage ($7.25 an hour) and almost $5 more than the average wage earned by renters nationwide ($15.42 an hour). Nowhere in the United States does a full-time, minimum-wage job provide enough income to afford adequate housing, and in some states—California, New York, New Jersey, New Hampshire, Virginia, Maryland, and Massachusetts to name a few—a household would need the income of at least three minimum-wage jobs. In Hawaii, three minimum-wage jobs still wouldn't be enough (National Low Income Housing Coalition, 2016).

Why Poverty Persists

Even in the best of times, a prosperous country such as the United States has a sizable population of poor people. Why, in such an affluent society, is poverty a permanent fixture? To explain the persistence of poverty, we must look at enduring imbalances in income and wealth, the structural role poverty plays in larger social institutions, and the dominant cultural beliefs and attitudes that help support it.

Enduring Disparities in Income and Wealth

One obvious reason poverty is so persistent in the United States is the way income and wealth are distributed. According to the U.S. Bureau of the Census (ProQuest Statistical Abstract, 2017), the average annual income of the top 5% of U.S. households is $214,462 while the average annual income of the bottom 20% of households is under $22,800.

This wide income gap between the richest and poorest segments of the population has been growing steadily over the past few decades (see Exhibit 10.8). The most affluent 20% of American households now account for over half of all the income earned in a given year, up from 43% in 1965 (Russell Sage Foundation, 2016). Indeed, over the past four decades, incomes of the richest 1% of American households have grown 275%; during the same time, incomes for the bottom 20% have grown only 18% (Congressional Budget Office, 2014).

Meanwhile, compensation for those at the very top continues to soar. In 1964, the average compensation for a top executive in an American company was about $822,000. In 2016, chief executives at the S&P 500 companies averaged $13.1 million in total

EXHIBIT 10.8 ● The Gap Between the Haves and the Have-Nots Is Getting Wider

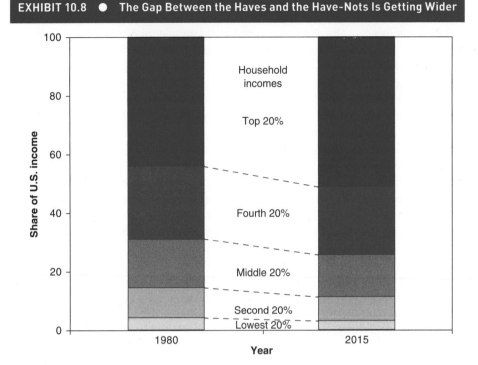

Source: ProQuest Statistical Abstract, 2017, Table 721.

compensation. To put it another way, in the early 1980s, corporate executives earned $42 for every $1 earned by the average production worker; by 2016, that figure had increased to $347 (AFL-CIO, 2017). We may want to believe that personal effort and hard work solely determine our success, but it's hard to imagine that a CEO of, say, an electronics company works 347 times harder than a person who actually assembles the TVs and cell phones.

Over the past few years, the public has become increasingly angry over the escalation of executive pay. A 2011 Harris poll found that two thirds of adults do not believe that successful Wall Street executives deserve to make the kind of money they earn (Harris Interactive, 2011). In 2010, Congress passed what are known as the Dodd-Frank reforms, which give shareholders greater voice in determining executives' salaries and bonuses. But to date, executive compensation remains disproportionately high. In 2015, the bonus pool for Wall Street executives was nearly double the *total* earnings of all Americans working full time at the federal minimum wage (which is $7.25 an hour; S. Anderson, 2015).

Tax laws also work to the advantage of those at the top. The rich do pay a lot of taxes as a total percentage of all taxes collected; however, they don't pay a lot of taxes as a percentage of what they earn and can afford. In the 1940s, the tax rate for the wealthiest tax bracket was about 90%; in 1980, it was 49%. Today, it's 37%. Incidentally, the income threshold for individuals in that top bracket is $500,000. Any earnings above that are taxed at the same rate. In other words, someone making $40 million a year pays the same tax percentage as someone making $501,000 a year (Tax Foundation, 2017). At the state and local level, the effective tax rate for the poorest fifth of households is about 11%; for the wealthiest tier of earners, it's only 5.4% (Institute on Taxation and Economic Policy, 2015).

As a result, the United States has the greatest income disparity between poor and wealthy citizens of any industrialized nation (Mather & Jarosz, 2014). As we've seen, the wealthiest fifth of U.S. families earn almost nine times more than the poorest fifth (ProQuest Statistical Abstract, 2017). In France, the richest fifth earn seven times more than the poorest fifth, and in Japan, they earn four times more (Phillips, 2002). But to be fair, the income gap between rich and poor is worse in some developing countries. For example, in Thailand, Indonesia, and the Philippines, the richest 10% of residents earn over three quarters of their country's income (Kulikowski, 2014). Similar disparities exist in Latin American countries and in most of sub-Saharan Africa.

Inequalities in income lead to even more striking inequalities in wealth. A lifetime of high earnings and inheritance from privileged parents creates a lasting advantage in ownership of property; of durable consumer goods such as cars, houses, and furniture; and of financial assets such as stocks, bonds, savings, and life insurance. The wealthiest 1% of U.S. households controls 36% of all the country's wealth. By comparison, the bottom 90% controls only 23% of all the wealth (Saez & Zucman, 2016). We will never live in a society with a perfectly equal distribution of income and wealth. Some people will always earn more, have more, and maybe even deserve more than others. But the magnitude of the gap between rich and poor in the United States challenges the notion that we live in a society where everyone is valued equally. As disparities in income and wealth grow, so does the gap in quality of life and access to opportunity between those at the top of society and those at the bottom.

MICHAEL NORTON AND DAN ARIELY

WEALTH INEQUALITY IN THE UNITED STATES: WHAT WE THINK, WHAT WE WANT, AND WHAT WE ACTUALLY HAVE

With such a wide wealth disparity in this country, you might be wondering why more people don't try to do something to change it. One possible reason could be that most people don't actually know the magnitude of the wealth gap between the richest and poorest Americans. You will recall from Chapter 3 that "perceived" reality can sometimes have a greater impact on people's lives than "actual" reality. Several years ago, a Harvard business professor and a Duke psychology professor surveyed about 5,500 Americans online to see what they thought about wealth in the United States. The sample consisted of men and women, conservatives and liberals, rich and poor people (Norton & Ariely, 2011). They asked the respondents two basic questions: (1) What do you think the distribution of wealth is in the United States? And (2) What do you think the distribution of wealth *ideally should* be? To ensure that all respondents had the same thing in mind, the authors provided them with a clear definition of wealth:

Wealth . . . is defined as the total value of everything someone owns minus any debt that he or she owes. A person's net worth includes his or her bank account savings plus the value of other things such as property, stocks, bonds, art, collections, etc., minus the value of things like loans and mortgages. (p. 9)

What they found was striking. Americans, of all political persuasions, ideally prefer a distribution of wealth more along the lines of countries like Sweden where those at the top have a modest amount of wealth and those at the bottom account for a larger share of the country's assets than is the case in the United States. Second, they found that people drastically underestimate the actual magnitude of the American wealth imbalance (see Exhibit 10.9). The authors conclude that these erroneous perceptions of wealth inequality may lead to overly optimistic beliefs about poor people's access to opportunities for social mobility, hence impeding any meaningful or effective effort to change the situation.

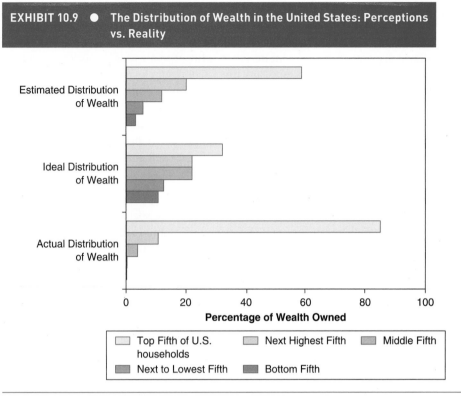

EXHIBIT 10.9 ● The Distribution of Wealth in the United States: Perceptions vs. Reality

Source: Norton & Ariely, 2011

The Social "Benefits" of Poverty

Recall the structural-functionalist assertion that stratification is necessary because it ensures that the most qualified and valuable people in society will occupy the most important positions. Social conditions exist and persist only if they are functional to society in some way. But functional for whom? If you were to survey people on the street and ask them if poverty is a good or bad thing, most, I'm sure, would say, "Bad." Yet according to sociologist Herbert Gans (1971, 1996), within a free-market economy and competitive society such as the United States, poverty plays a necessary institutional role. Although structural functionalism has often been criticized for its propensity to justify the status quo, Gans combines it with conflict thinking to identify several economic and social "functions" served by poverty that benefit all other classes in society:

- Poverty provides a ready pool of low-wage laborers who are available to do society's "dirty work." Poor people work at low wages primarily because they have little choice. When large numbers of poor people compete for scarce jobs, business owners can pay lower wages. The company responsible for the hazardous task of cleaning up the toxic and radioactive waste at a Japanese nuclear plant ravaged by the 2011 earthquake targeted poor and unskilled workers in its recruitment ads (Tabuchi, 2014).

- Poverty ensures that there will be enough individuals to populate an all-volunteer military. To people with limited educational and occupational opportunities, military service holds the promise of an escape from poverty through stable employment, comprehensive insurance coverage, a living wage, free schooling, and the development of marketable skills. Historically, American armed forces have drawn disproportionately from the lower socioeconomic rungs of society (Asoni & Sanandaji, 2013). That's especially true when unemployment and economic uncertainty are high (Kelty, Kleykamp, & Segal, 2010; Kriner & Shen, 2010). During the height of the wars in Iraq and Afghanistan, American casualties were overwhelmingly from families of modest means who lived in sparsely populated rural counties (Cushing & Bishop, 2005; Golway, 2004). By 2006, 34% of U.S. military personnel killed in Iraq came from the poorest quarter of families, while only 17% came from the richest quarter (cited in "Price Paid," 2006).

- Poverty supports occupations that either serve the poor or protect the rest of society from them: police officers, welfare workers, social workers, lawyers, pawnshop owners, and so on. Even drug dealers and loan sharks depend on the presence of a large population of poor people willing to pay for their illegal services.

- Poverty is the reason some people purchase goods and services that would otherwise go unused: secondhand appliances; day-old bread, fruits, and vegetables; deteriorated housing; dilapidated cars; care from incompetent physicians; legal advice from inept attorneys; and so forth. In 2002, dozens of Coca-Cola employees in Texas revealed that, for years, they had been required to sell expired Coke to stores in poor neighborhoods. They were instructed to strip cans from their boxes, stuff them into fresh boxes with new dates stamped on the side, and stock them on store shelves in poor neighborhoods as if they were new (Winter, 2002). Clearly, this merchandise had little or no monetary value outside the poverty market; it was believed that the beverages couldn't be sold to wealthier Coke drinkers because they'd have noticed the difference.

- Poverty is a visible reminder to the rest of society of the "legitimacy" of the conventional values of hard work, thrift, and honesty. By violating, or seeming to violate, these mainstream values, the poor reaffirm these virtues. If poor people are thought to be lazy, their presence reinforces the ethic of hard work; if the poor single mother is condemned, the two-parent family is idealized.

- Poverty provides scapegoats for society's institutional problems. The alleged laziness of the jobless poor and the anger aimed at street people and beggars distract us from the failure of the economic system to adequately deal with the needs of all citizens. Likewise, the alleged personal shortcomings of slum dwellers and the homeless deflect attention from shoddy practices within the housing industry.

This explanation of poverty's persistence can easily be dismissed as cold and heartless. We certainly don't want to admit that poor people allow the rest of us to avoid unpleasant or even dangerous tasks and enjoy comfortable and pleasant lifestyles. Yet this explanation is quite compelling. Just as society needs talented people to fill its important occupational positions, it also needs a stable population of poor people to fill its "less important" positions. If society fostered full equality, who would do the dirty work?

If we are truly serious about reducing poverty, we must find alternative ways of performing the societal functions it currently fulfills. But such a change will assuredly come at a cost to those who can now take advantage of poverty's presence. In short, poverty will be eliminated only when it becomes dysfunctional for people who *aren't* poor.

The Ideology of Competitive Individualism

Poverty also persists because of cultural beliefs and values that support the economic status quo. An important component of this value system in U.S. society is the belief in **competitive individualism** (Feagin, 1975; M. Lewis, 1978; Neubeck, 1986). As children, most of us are taught that nobody deserves a free ride. The way to be successful is to work hard, strive toward goals, and compete well against others. We are taught that we are fully responsible for our own economic fates. Rags-to-riches stories of people who rose above terrible conditions to make it to the top reinforce the notion that anybody can be successful if she or he simply has the desire and puts in the necessary effort.

The dark side of the U.S. belief in competitive individualism is that it all too easily justifies the unequal distribution of rewards and the existence of poverty. If people who are financially successful are thought to deserve their advantages, allegedly because of individual hard work and desire, then the people who are struggling financially must likewise deserve their plight—because of their *lack* of hard work and desire. People in the United States have an intense need to believe that good things happen to good people and bad things happen to bad people (Huber & Form, 1973; Lerner, 1970). In short, most of us want to believe that if a poor person is suffering, he or she "must have" done something to deserve it. The people who succeed, in contrast, "must have" been born smarter, stayed in school longer, or worked harder. The belief in competitive individualism gives people the sense that they can control their own fate.

But the depth of such beliefs sometimes depends on people's political leanings. For instance, a recent national poll found that a majority of people who identify as conservative say that poverty is due to lack of effort, while those who identify as liberal are significantly more likely to cite circumstances beyond one's control as the cause (Pew Research Center, 2014c). Similarly, socioeconomic status can influence these attitudes. When asked why people succeed, lower-income people are more likely than wealthy people to downplay competitive individualism and cite things like "coming from a wealthy family" or "knowing the right people." Upper-class individuals, on the other hand, are more likely than their lower-income counterparts to contend that opportunities for success and advancement are available to everyone, meaning that success is a result of individual merit. They are likely to cite "natural ability," "a good education," and "hard work" as factors that are essential to getting ahead in life. Hence, they can justify inequality by emphasizing equal chances (cited in J. Scott & Leonhardt, 2005). Notice, in the following passage, how one economist blames poverty on the willful actions of poor people who decide not to take advantage of available economic opportunities:

> Some poor people may choose not to work as hard as investment bankers working 70 hours a week. . . . One of the most amazing phenomena of recent years is why so many people . . . have not responded to the opportunities out there. (quoted in Stille, 2001, p. 19)

The belief system that such a comment reflects ignores the possibility that the competition itself may not be fair. Competitive individualism assumes that opportunities to learn a high-level trade or skill or enter a profession are available to everyone. Every person is supposed to have the chance to "be all that she or he can be." But the system may be rigged to favor those who already have power and privilege.

The Culture of Poverty

A variation of the belief in competitive individualism is the argument that poor people as a group possess beliefs, norms, values, and goals that are significantly different from those of the rest of society and that perpetuate a particular lifestyle that keeps them poor. Oscar Lewis (1968), one of the earliest proponents of this **culture-of-poverty thesis**, maintained that poor people, resigned to their position in society, develop a unique value structure to deal with the unlikelihood that they will ever become successful by the standards of the larger society. This culture is at odds with the dominant culture—in the United States, the middle-class belief in self-discipline and hard work.

According to Lewis, although the culture of poverty may keep people trapped in what appears (to the outside observer) to be an intolerable life, it nevertheless provides its own pleasures. Street life in the inner city is exhilarating compared with a world where jobs are dull, arduous, and difficult to obtain and hold (P. Peterson, 1991). It's more fun to hang out, tell exaggerated stories, and exhibit one's latest purchases and conquests than to work and struggle in the "conventional" world. This extreme "present-orientedness"—the inability to live for the future (Banfield, 1970)—and not the lack of income or wealth is the principal cause of poverty, according to this view.

Once the culture of poverty comes into existence, Lewis argued, it is remarkably persistent: You can take the child out of the inner city, but you can't take the inner city out of the child—that sort of thing. Furthermore, it is passed down from generation to generation. By age 6 or 7, he said, most children have absorbed the basic values and attitudes of their subculture, rendering them unable to take advantage of any opportunities that may present themselves later in life. Others have argued that a poor family with a history of welfare dependence tends to raise children who lack ambition, a solid work ethic, and self-reliance (Auletta, 1982).

But the contention that there is a stable, enduring culture of poverty may be overstated. For instance, according to one sociologist, 54% of Americans between 25 and 60 will experience poverty or near-poverty for at least 1 year during the course of their lives (Rank, 2013). In other words, most people tend to move in and out of poverty.

Furthermore, not all poor people become dependent on public assistance. According to the U.S. Bureau of the Census (Irving & Loveless, 2015), only 61% of families that fall below the poverty line receive any form of government aid. And people who do receive such assistance tend to enter and leave the system, making it difficult to sustain a tradition of dependence across generations. Less than 10% of poor families receive monetary government assistance for more than 3 years.

Critics of the culture-of-poverty approach also contend that behavior that seems to be characteristic of poor people is likely to be caused by institutional impediments, such as a tradition of racial or ethnic prejudice and discrimination, residential segregation, limited economic opportunities, and occupational obstacles against advancement (W. J. Wilson, 1980). Poor African Americans, for example, still struggle to overcome the disadvantages of slavery and the Jim Crow laws that subjugated their ancestors. Other root causes of poverty include skyrocketing health care costs, the growing lack of affordable housing, and a changing economy that has all but eliminated entire classes of high-paying, low-skilled jobs.

Nevertheless, despite the lack of supportive evidence, the culture-of-poverty explanation remains popular. Many people strongly believe that poor people live by a different set of moral standards and therefore will remain in poverty unless forced to change their values and attitudes. In 2017, Secretary of Housing and Urban Development Ben Carson echoed these sentiments when he referred to poverty as a state of mind: "You take somebody with the wrong mind-set, you can give them everything in the world—they'll work their way right back down to the bottom" (quoted in Alcindor, 2017, p. 1).

If poverty is a "way of life," as this statement implies, then giving poor people enough money to raise them out of poverty is not the answer; changing their troublesome "mindset" culture is. Most Americans—particularly those who identify as conservative—feel that government aid to the poor does more harm than good (Pew Research Center, 2014c). During the 2012 presidential campaign, the current Speaker of the House of Representatives (who was the Republican vice presidential candidate at the time) echoed these sentiments when he proposed a sharp reduction in government assistance programs: "We don't want to turn the safety net into a hammock that lulls able-bodied people to lives of dependency and complacency, that drains them of their will and their incentive to make the most of their lives" (quoted in McAuliff, 2012, p. 1).

So it follows that the contemporary U.S. welfare system reflects the belief that the best way to reduce poverty is to change poor people's lifestyles. In 1994, more than 5 million U.S. families received government assistance in the form of cash payouts. By 2017, that figure had dropped to 1.1 million (U.S. Department of Health and Human Services, 2017). You might think that such a drop reflects the fact that fewer citizens need government aid, but much of the reduction was actually due to the eligibility limitations of a new welfare system that began in 1996. This system includes a mandatory work requirement (or enrollment in vocational training or community service) after 2 years of receiving assistance and a 5-year lifetime limit to benefits for any family. Despite soaring unemployment rates and the worst economic recession in decades, 16 states have cut their welfare caseloads since 2008, sometimes by as much as 50% (cited in DeParle, 2012).

Contrary to popular belief, the financial help that people receive on public assistance is not enough to sustain a life that is remotely comfortable. According to the Center on Budget and Policy Priorities (2016), cash benefits (called Temporary Assistance to Needy Families) fall below half the poverty line in every state. Thirty-three states provide payments below 30% percent of the poverty line and, in 16 of those states, benefit levels are below *20%* of the poverty line, or about $336 a month for a family of three.

Some of the people who leave welfare do, in fact, find sustained employment (Duncan & Chase-Lansdale, 2001). However, more than half of the decrease in welfare rolls in the first decade after welfare reform went into effect reflected a decline in government assistance to families that were poor enough to qualify for aid rather than an increase in the number of families who no longer needed the assistance.

You'd think that with all the political rhetoric over "ending welfare as we know it," the welfare system would be the largest drain on the federal budget. However, programs to assist the poor constitute only about 11% of the entire federal budget. In 2017, the federal government spent approximately $281 billion on welfare assistance, including Temporary Assistance for Needy Families, food and nutrition programs, and housing assistance. That same year, it spent more than $1.6 *trillion* on Social Security, unemployment insurance, and Medicare—the government-subsidized health care program for the elderly (usgovernmentspending.com, 2017).

Nonetheless, the assumptions behind welfare reform are clear: Making work mandatory will teach welfare recipients important work values and habits, make poor single mothers models of these values for their children, and cut the nation's welfare rolls. The underlying idea is that hard work will lead to the moral and financial rewards of family self-reliance. It will cure poverty and welfare dependence and ensure that new generations of children from single-parent families will be able to enter the American mainstream. Like competitive individualism, however, this ideology protects the nonpoor, the larger social structure, and the economic system while blaming poor people for their own plight.

Global Development and Inequality

As you've seen elsewhere in this book, it is becoming increasingly difficult to understand life in any one society without understanding that society's place in the larger global context. The trend toward globalization (see Chapter 9) may have brought the world's inhabitants closer together, but they are not all benefiting equally. Nations have differing amounts of power to ensure that their interests are met. The more developed and less developed countries of the world experience serious inequalities in wealth that have immediate consequences for their citizens.

The Global Economic Gap

Just as an economic gap exists between rich and poor citizens within a single country, economic gaps exist between rich and poor countries. Consider these facts:

- The average per-capita yearly income in Western Europe, the United States, Canada, Japan, and other developed countries is $39,963; in the less developed countries of the world, it's $8,936 (Population Reference Bureau, 2016).

- About 0.13% of the world's population controls 25% of the world's financial assets. On the other end of the economic spectrum, about 2.2 billion people in less developed countries live on the equivalent of less than $2.00 a day (World Hunger Education Service, 2015).

- The wealthiest 20% of the world accounts for about 77% of all private consumption; the poorest fifth, only 1.5% (Shah, 2013a). Twelve percent of the world's population (who happen to reside in developed countries) uses 85% of its water.

MICRO-MACRO CONNECTION
THE CHANCES OF LIVING A HEALTHY LIFE VARY TREMENDOUSLY AROUND THE WORLD

People around the world are living longer and healthier lives than ever before because of changes in public health policies over the past century—disease control, safe drinking water, effective medical treatment, and the like. Infant mortality rates worldwide are at an all-time low, less than half of what they were in 1970 (Population Reference Bureau, 2016). But these improvements have not been shared equally by all the planet's inhabitants. For the more than 1 billion people worldwide living in extreme poverty, basic health services remain virtually nonexistent (World Hunger Education Service, 2015). They lack safe drinking water, decent housing, adequate sanitation, effective birth control, sufficient food, health education, professional health care, trustworthy transportation, and secure employment. Ninety-eight percent of people worldwide who go hungry live in the less developed world (World Hunger Education Service, 2015).

Not surprisingly, poor countries lag behind wealthier countries on most important measures of health: infant and child mortality, stunted growth, malnutrition, childhood vaccinations, prenatal and postnatal care, and life expectancy (Population Reference Bureau, 2016; UNICEF, 2009). According to the organization Save the Children (2017), the 10 worst countries to be a child—in terms of threats to physical and emotional health, exposure to violence, and so on—are all in destitute countries of sub-Saharan Africa. In contrast, the best countries to be a child are the wealthy, developed countries of northern Europe. The risk of a woman dying from childbirth complications is 14 times higher in less developed countries than it is in developed countries (Population Reference Bureau, 2014). Over half of all women worldwide who die during pregnancy and childbirth are African; and for every African woman who dies, another 20 suffer from debilitating complications (cited in Grady, 2009).

HIV/AIDS presents one of the most troubling global health imbalances. Although significant progress has been made in the past few years with rates of new infections on the decline worldwide (UNAIDS, 2016a), the vast majority of HIV-infected people around the world remain those who are poor and lack access to the effective but extremely expensive drug treatments. Nearly 70% of people living with HIV/AIDS worldwide live in sub-Saharan Africa, and three quarters of people who die from AIDS-related causes come from this region (UNAIDS, 2016a).

The effect HIV/AIDS has had on overall life expectancy is staggering. In the developed regions of North America and Europe, male babies born today can expect to live until they are 76 and girl babies can expect to live to 82. In those African countries with high rates of HIV infection (like Lesotho and Swaziland), life expectancy is about 50 (Population Reference Bureau, 2016). Such startling figures will have severe long-term consequences as millions of the world's poorest children become orphaned and face a lifetime of despair.

Even susceptibility to natural disasters is stratified. Globally, the poorest regions are at the greatest risk for life-threatening drought, tropical storms, earthquakes, tsunamis, and floods (Marsh, 2005). Four out of five poor people in Latin America and over half of the poor people in Asia and Africa live on land that is highly vulnerable to natural degradation and disaster. These people often have no choice but to occupy the least valuable and most disaster-prone areas, such as riverbanks, unstable hills, and deforested lands. Developing countries contain 90% of the victims of natural disasters and bear 75% of the economic damage they cause (DeSouza, 2004).

Politics may sometimes get in the way of improving the health of people in developing countries. Wealthy countries could easily afford to provide regular vaccines, mosquito nets, soil nutrients, sufficient food, and clean water supplies to poor countries to address treatable problems like malaria and malnutrition. In fact, in 2005, the United Nations declared that ending world hunger and disease was "utterly affordable" and would only require that wealthy countries commit one half of 1% of their total incomes to aid poor countries. However, many of these nations have been reluctant to provide such assistance. The United States, for example, provides less than two tenths of 1% of its total income, the smallest percentage among major donor countries (Shah, 2009). As long as expenditures for public health measures in poor countries remain a politically unpopular budget item in wealthy countries, the global health divide will persist.

Explanations for Global Stratification

How has global stratification come about? The conflict perspective explains not only stratification within a society but also stratification between societies. One way a country can use its power to control another is through **colonization**—invading and establishing control over a weaker country and its people in order to expand the colonizer's markets. Typically, the native people of the colony are forced to give up their culture. The colony serves as a source of labor and raw materials for the colonizer's industries and a market for their high-priced goods. Much of North and South America, Africa, and Asia were at one time or another under the colonial control of wealthier nations:

Arid Spain and Portugal siphoned off South America's gold; tiny Holland dominated vast Indonesia. Britain, barren except for coal, built an imperial swap shop of grain, lumber, cotton, tea, tobacco, opium, gems, silver and slaves. Japan, less than a century out of its bamboo-armor era, conquered much of China for its iron and coal. (McNeil, 2010, p. 5)

Although the direct conquest of weak countries is rare today, wealthy countries are still able to exploit them for commercial gain. Powerful countries can use weaker countries as a source of cheap raw materials and cheap labor. They can also exert financial pressure on poorer nations by setting world prices on certain goods (Chase-Dunn & Rubinson, 1977). Because their economic base is weak, poor countries often have to borrow money or buy manufactured goods on credit from wealthy countries. The huge debt they build up locks them into a downward spiral of exploitation and poverty. They cannot develop an independent economy of their own and thus remain dependent on wealthy countries for their very survival (A. G. Frank, 1969).

Global Financial Organizations

It's not just powerful nations that have the ability to hold poor nations in their grip. International financial organizations play a significant role in determining the economic and social policies of developing countries. For instance, the World Bank funds reconstruction and development projects in poor countries through investments and loans. It spends about $35 billion annually to better the lives of destitute people worldwide (World Bank, 2012). Similarly, the International Monetary Fund (IMF) tries to foster economic growth and international monetary cooperation through financial and technical assistance. The World Trade Organization (WTO) oversees the rules of trade between nations.

These organizations spend a lot of money to improve the standard of living in many poor countries by funding projects such as new roads or water treatment plants. And they've been somewhat successful. Funding from the World Bank helped cut the proportion of the world's population living in extreme poverty from 43% in 1990 to 21% in 2010 (Lowrey, 2013a).

But global financial organizations may, from time to time, do more harm than good. The WTO, for example, can impose fines and sanctions on debtor countries that don't act as it dictates. It has, in the past, forced Japan to accept greater levels of pesticide residue on imported food, prevented Guatemala from outlawing deceptive advertising on baby food, and eliminated asbestos bans and car emission standards in various countries (Parenti, 2006).

In fact, countries that receive the aid of these organizations sometimes end up even more impoverished than before. When the World Bank and the IMF provide development credit, they do so with certain conditions attached. The conditions, referred to as **structural adjustments**, typically reflect a Western-style, free-market approach: reducing government spending, lifting import and export restrictions, privatizing public services, removing price controls, increasing interest rates, eliminating food subsidies, and devaluing the country's currency (Shah, 2013b). For instance, countries might be required to lift trade restrictions, enhance the rights of foreign investors, cut social spending, increase exports, or balance their budgets in exchange for aid.

Conditions like these have at times threatened the welfare of citizens in recipient nations (Brutus, 1999; U.S. Network for Global Economic Justice, 2000):

- In Haiti, the IMF and World Bank blocked the government from raising the minimum wage and insisted that government services, such as sanitation and education, be cut in half. The desperate Haitian government complied, despite the fact that life expectancy is only 61 years for Haitian men and 65 years for women and that the infant mortality rate is 10 times higher than in the United States (Population Reference Bureau, 2014).

- In Mexico, the World Bank advised the government to abolish constitutionally guaranteed free education at the national university, making it virtually impossible for poor Mexicans to go to college.

- In Zimbabwe, the World Bank persuaded the government to shift production supports from food crops such as corn to export crops such as tobacco. As a result, malnutrition increased and infant mortality doubled.

You can see that global financial relationships between international lending institutions and poor countries are a double-edged sword. The countries certainly receive much-needed financial assistance. But in the process, they sometimes become even more dependent and less able to improve conditions for their citizens.

Multinational Corporations

Global stratification has been made even more complex by the growth of massive multinational corporations, which can go outside their countries' borders to pursue their financial interests if domestic opportunities aren't promising. They can invest their money in more lucrative foreign corporations or establish their businesses or factories abroad. U.S.-based multinational corporations employ over 26 million people worldwide and have total assets of nearly $38 trillion (ProQuest Statistical Abstract, 2017).

But such success often comes at a price. The largest U.S.-based multinational corporations continue to achieve record earnings while hiring fewer American workers than ever. The United States has lost about 5 million manufacturing jobs since 2000 (Long, 2016). Between 2009 and 2011, 35 of the largest U.S.-based multinational corporations—including Walmart, International Paper Company, and United Parcel Service—added 446,000 jobs, a growth rate substantially higher than other U.S. companies. However, three quarters of these new jobs went to workers overseas (Thurn, 2012).

With their ability to quickly shift operations to friendly countries, multinational corporations find it easy to evade the governance of any one country. Their decisions reflect corporate goals and not necessarily the well-being or interests of any particular country. In fact, the largest multinational corporations have accumulated more wealth than many entire countries, as Exhibit 10.10 shows.

From a structural-functionalist perspective, a U.S. company locating a production facility in a poor country would seem to benefit everyone involved. The host country benefits from the creation of new jobs and a higher standard of living. The corporation, of course, benefits from increased profits. And consumers in the country in which the corporation is based benefit from paying lower prices for products that would cost more if manufactured at home. Furthermore, the entire planet benefits because these firms form alliances with many different countries and therefore might help pressure them into settling their political disputes peacefully.

Multinational corporations are indeed a valuable part of the international economy, as we saw in Chapter 9. However, the conflict perspective argues that in the long run, multinationals can actually perpetuate or even worsen global stratification. One common criticism of multinationals is that they exploit local workers and communities. Employees in foreign plants or factories often work under conditions and for wages that wouldn't be tolerated in wealthier countries. For instance, garment workers in Cambodia earn, on average, about $126 a month; in Bangladesh, such workers earn about $91 a month (Center for American Progress, 2013).

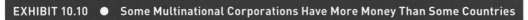

EXHIBIT 10.10   ●   Some Multinational Corporations Have More Money Than Some Countries

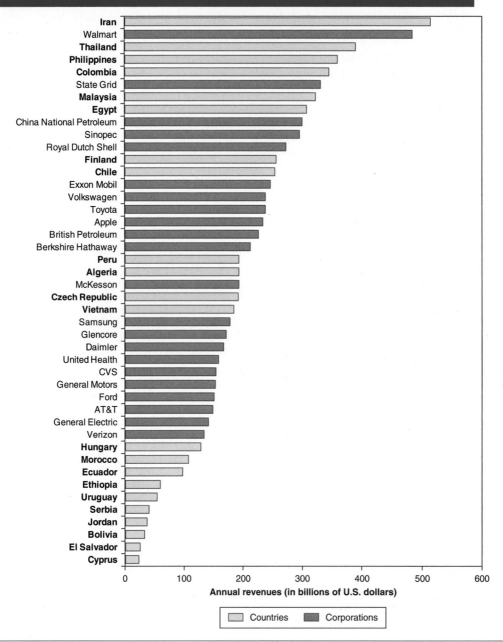

Source: Gross national income data from World Bank, 2017; multinational sales data from *Fortune*, 2017.

In addition, environmental regulations and occupational safety requirements that tend to drive up the cost of finished products, such as protection against dangerous conditions or substances, sometimes don't exist in other countries. Hence, local workers may become sicker and the environment more polluted when foreign manufacturers set up facilities. Conditions in foreign factories were so bad and criticism from human rights organizations so strong that a 1997 presidential task force created a code of conduct on wages, working conditions, and child labor for apparel factories that U.S. companies own and operate around the world.

The host countries themselves are equally likely to be exploited. The money multinational corporations earn is rarely reinvested in the host country. In fact, 85% of the profit from exported products ends up in the hands of the multinational corporations, bankers, traders, and distributors (Braun, 1997). For example, in Brazil, one of the world's largest agricultural exporters, shipments abroad of fruits, vegetables, and soybeans have grown considerably over the past several decades. During the same period, however, the number of Brazilians who were undernourished grew from one third to two thirds of the population (Braun, 1997).

Local economies can suffer, too. For instance, supermarket chains owned by large multinational corporations have revolutionized food distribution worldwide. They are popular with consumers all over the world because of their lower prices and greater variety and convenience (Dugger, 2004). But these stores tend to get their produce from large conglomerates that have more money and marketing know-how than small, local suppliers and can therefore provide cheaper fruits and vegetables. Hence, the livelihoods of millions of struggling small farmers have been destroyed, widening the gap between the haves and the have-nots in developing countries.

Multinational corporations can also perpetuate global inequality by their decisions on when to develop certain products and where to market them. A case in point is the global pharmaceutical industry. A significant proportion of medical research today is devoted to drugs that are likely to sell in the lucrative markets of developed countries. These drugs are usually either "blockbuster" drugs (those that can earn billions of dollars a year) or "lifestyle" drugs (those that enhance the lives of generally healthy people). The astounding popularity—and profit-making capacity—of erectile dysfunction drugs like Viagra and Cialis and baldness drugs like Propecia and Rogaine are recent examples. Impotence and baldness can be characterized as lifestyle troubles or embarrassing inconveniences but certainly not life-threatening illnesses.

This trend has global significance. Of the new drugs registered between 2000 and 2011 by the world's largest pharmaceutical companies, only 4% were created to combat "neglected tropical diseases" (deadly and disabling diseases that affect populations in mainly low-income countries; Pedrique et al., 2013).

Not all multinationals are hard-hearted organizations that ignore the well-being of their workers abroad, the well-being of the workforce at home whose jobs are being exported to other countries, or the health and welfare of poor people in developing nations. For many multinationals, relocating manufacturing facilities to another country where labor is less expensive is a necessary response to global economic pressures as well as the demands of domestic consumers for inexpensive products. But the processes that drive corporate decisions do sometimes drive individuals out of work, contribute to environmental and health problems, and reinforce global inequality.

Conclusion

In Chapter 1, I pondered the question of how free we really are to act as we wish. I described some of the personal, interpersonal, and structural considerations that limit or constrain our choices. In this chapter, you have seen how this fundamental issue is affected by social stratification and inequality. Simply put, certain groups of people have a greater capacity to control their own lives than others. Your position in the stratification system can determine not only your ability to influence people and exert authority but a whole host of life chances as well, from financial stability to housing, education, health care, nutrition, and day-to-day comfort. The unequal distribution of economic resources, whether between wealthy and poor individuals in the same society or between wealthy and poor countries worldwide, has created a seemingly indestructible system of haves and have-nots.

The profound imbalances in wealth, power, and prestige that exist in the United States are especially ironic given how loudly and frequently U.S. citizens boast of their cultural commitment to the values of equality and justice. Nevertheless, the U.S. system is set up, like most others in the world, to promote, enhance, and protect the interests of those who reside at or near the top of the stratification system. Authority, wealth, and influence grant rights that are unknown to the vast majority of people.

It's rather shocking that in a country as wealthy as the United States, a comfortable, healthy, and stable life is well beyond the reach of tens of millions of people. Constant media images of wealth remind poor and working-class people that they are outsiders who can only watch and long to be part of that affluent world. And when disaster strikes, poor people receive the message once again that their marginal status in society can have deadly consequences.

We speak of the poor as if they were an unchanging and faceless group to be pitied, condemned, or feared. To talk of the "poverty problem" is to talk about some depersonalized, permanent fixture on the U.S. landscape. But poverty is people. It's people standing in soup kitchen lines and welfare lines. It's people living in rat-infested projects. It's people sleeping on sidewalks. It's people struggling to acquire things the rest of population takes for granted. It's people coming up short in their quest for the American Dream.

When we look at the institutional causes of poverty, we see that the personality or "cultural" traits often associated with poverty—low ambition, rejection of the work ethic, inability to plan for the future—might be better understood as the consequences of poverty rather than its causes. As long as the structural obstacles to stable employment, adequate wages, and a decent education continue to exist, so will the characteristic hopelessness associated with poverty.

Your Turn

Even people whose income is above the poverty line can sometimes find it difficult to make ends meet. Imagine a family of four living in your hometown. Suppose that both parents work, that one child is 7 years old and in elementary school, and that the other is 3 and must be cared for during the day.

Make a list of all the goods and services this family needs to function at a minimum subsistence level—that is, at the poverty line. Be as complete as possible. Consider food, clothing, housing, transportation, medical care, child care, entertainment, and so on. Estimate the minimum monthly cost of each item. If you currently live on your own and must pay these expenses yourself, use those figures as a starting point (but

remember that you must estimate for a family of four). If you live in a dorm or at home, ask one of your parents (or anyone else who pays the bills) what the expenses are for such goods and services. Call a local day care center to see what it charges for child care. Go to the local supermarket and compute the family food budget. For expenses that aren't divided on a monthly basis (e.g., clothing and household appliances), estimate the yearly cost and divide by 12.

Once you have estimated total monthly expenses, multiply by 12 to get the annual subsistence budget for the family of four. If your estimate is higher than the government's official poverty line (around $24,339), what sorts of items could you cut out of the budget for the family to be defined as officially poor and therefore eligible for certain government programs? By looking for ways to cut expenses from your minimal subsistence budget, you will get a good sense of what everyday life in poverty is like.

Describe the quality of life of this hypothetical family that makes too much to be officially poor and too little to sustain a comfortable life. What sorts of things are they forced to do without that a more affluent family might simply take for granted (e.g., annual vacations, pocket money, a savings account, a second car, eating out once a week)? What would be the impact of poverty on the lives of the children? How will the family's difficulty in meeting its basic subsistence needs translate into access to opportunities (education, jobs, health care) for the children later in life?

Source: Adapted from M. V. Miller, 1985.

Chapter Highlights

- Stratification is a ranking of entire groups of people, based on race, gender, or social class, which perpetuates unequal rewards and life chances in society.

- Social class is the primary means of stratification in many societies, including the United States. Contemporary sociologists are likely to define one's class standing as a combination of income, wealth, occupational prestige, and educational attainment. Social class is more than an economic position; it is a way of life that affects how we experience every facet of our lives.

- The structural-functionalist explanation of stratification is that higher rewards, such as prestige and large salaries, are afforded to the most important positions in society, thereby ensuring that the most qualified individuals will occupy the highest positions. Conflict theory argues that stratification reflects an unequal distribution of power in society and is a primary source of conflict and tension.

- The official U.S. poverty line, the dollar cutoff point that defines the amount of income necessary for subsistence living, may actually be set too low, thereby underestimating the proportion of the population that is suffering financially.

- Poverty persists because it serves economic and social functions. The ideology of competitive individualism—that to succeed in life all one has to do is work hard and win in competition with others—creates a belief that poor people are to blame for their own suffering. In addition, poverty receives institutional "support" from a distribution of wealth and income that is growing increasingly unequal.

- Stratification exists not only among different groups within the same society but also among different societies within a global community. Wealthy nations are better able to control the world's financial resources than poor nations are.

Key Terms

absolute poverty: Inability to afford the minimal requirements for sustaining a reasonably healthy existence

authority: Possession of some status or quality that compels others to obey one's directives or commands

caste system: Stratification system based on heredity, with little movement allowed across strata

(Continued)

(Continued)

colonization: Process of expanding economic markets by invading and establishing control over a weaker country and its people

competitive individualism: Cultural belief that those who succeed in society are those who work hardest and have the best abilities and that those who suffer don't work hard enough or lack the necessary traits or abilities

contradictory class locations: Individuals, such as middle managers and supervisors, whose positions place them between two major classes, making it difficult to identify with one side or the other

culture-of-poverty thesis: Belief that poor people, resigned to their position in society, develop a unique value structure to deal with their lack of success

estate system (feudal system): Stratification system in which high-status groups own land and have power based on noble birth

false consciousness: Situation in which people in the lower classes come to accept a belief system that harms them; the primary means by which powerful classes in society prevent protest and revolution

means of production: Land, commercial enterprises, factories, and wealth that form the economic basis of class societies

middle class: In a society stratified by social class, a group of people who have an intermediate level of wealth, income, and prestige, such as managers, supervisors, executives, small business owners, and professionals

near-poor: Individuals or families whose earnings are between 100% and 125% of the poverty line (see also **working poor**)

poor: In a society stratified by social class, a group of people who work for minimum wage or are chronically unemployed

poverty line: Amount of yearly income a family requires to meet its basic needs, according to the federal government

poverty rate: Percentage of people whose income falls below the poverty line

power: Ability to affect decisions in ways that benefit a person or protect his or her interests

prestige: Respect and honor given to some people in society

relative poverty: Individuals' economic position compared with the living standards of the majority in the society

slavery: Economic form of inequality in which some people are legally the property of others

social class: Group of people who share a similar economic position in a society, based on their wealth and income

social mobility: Movement of people or groups from one class to another

socioeconomic status: Prestige, honor, respect, and lifestyle associated with different positions or groups in society

stratification: Ranking system for groups of people that perpetuates unequal rewards and life chances in society

structural adjustments: Conditions that global financial organizations attach to countries to whom they provide development aid

upper class: In a society stratified by social class, a group of people who have high income and prestige and who own vast amounts of property and other forms of wealth, such as owners of large corporations, top financiers, rich celebrities and politicians, and members of prestigious families

working class: In a society stratified by social class, a group of people who have a low level of wealth, income, and prestige, such as industrial and factory workers, office workers, clerks, and farm and manual laborers

working poor: Employed people who consistently earn wages but do not make enough to survive (see also **near-poor**)

SAGE edge™ edge.sagepub.com/newman12e

SAGE edge offers a robust online environment featuring an impressive array of free tools and resources for review, study, and further exploration, keeping both instructors and students on the cutting edge of teaching and learning.

11

The Architecture of Inequality

Race and Ethnicity

- Race and Ethnicity: More Than Just Biology
- Histories of Oppression and Inequality
- Racial and Ethnic Relations
- Global Perspectives on Racism

Just like millions of other Americans, I sat transfixed in front of my television on the night of November 4, 2008, watching the presidential election results trickle in. At about 11:00 P.M. Eastern time, the networks made the astounding projection: Barack Obama—a man with a black Kenyan father, a white American mother, and a "foreign-sounding" name—would be the 44th president of the United States. I sat in semi-disbelief. Had this country, one with such a difficult, painful, and deadly racial history, really just elect a black man to the highest office in the land? A development that would have been unthinkable 50, 25, or even 10 years earlier had just happened. People of all colors and classes here and abroad danced in the streets. Jesse Jackson, Oprah Winfrey, Colin Powell, and countless other less famous people wept with joy. Parents named their newborns "Barack." One African American columnist wrote a letter to her 4-month-old son that night:

> What does Barack Obama's election mean to you? When you are older we will talk about how African American children, like their parents and grandparents, have struggled to overcome the feeling that no matter how hard they study and work and try, there are barriers—some visible, others hidden but still there— that block their way. The feeling that we can rise, but only so far. I did not want you to grow up believing that bitter remnants of the past could hold power over your future. I wanted to be able to tell you that it wasn't true—that you could be anything you wanted to be. But I couldn't quite believe it myself. Now I do. (Kelley, 2008, p. 29)

Sociologists, columnists, and political analysts quickly tried to find the most memorable and most articulate way to capture the historical significance of the moment. Some speculated that it might finally mark the end of racial division and exclusion in this country:

> It was a moment. It was *the* moment. Obama was biological proof of some kind of progress—the product of an interracial relationship, the kind that was outlawed in some states as recently as 1967 but was normalized. He seemed to absolve us of original sin and take us past this stupid, dangerous race stuff. What if suddenly anything was possible? What if we could be and do whatever and whoever we wanted? In that moment, the country was changing. *We* were changing. (Morris, 2015, pp. 52–53)

Others wondered if we'd become a "postracial" society, where traditional racial categories no longer mattered. In a national poll the day before Obama's first inauguration, more than two thirds of African Americans said they believed that Martin Luther King's famous 1963 dream (of a country where race and ethnicity are losing their status as major criteria for judging the content of a person's character) had been fulfilled (CNN.com, 2009). And surveys the first few years of his administration consistently showed that college-age Blacks were as optimistic and upbeat about their economic futures as Whites (Cose, 2011).

As I sit here now and think back to what took place that night 10 years ago, I think about the other important but less dramatic educational, economic, political, and cultural gains that people of color have made recently:

- Close to half of all Latino/as and Blacks between 18 and 24 are now enrolled in college (Pérez-Peña, 2012a). The percentage of African American and Latino/a college graduates has also risen steadily over the past 15 years, as has the proportion of ethnoracial minority families that could be considered middle or upper class.

- According to the Centers for Disease Control and Prevention (2016c), African Americans born in 2014 can expect to live between 6 and 9 years longer than those born in 1980. Although a life expectancy gap still exists between Whites and Blacks, over the past four decades, it has decreased from 7 to 3.4 years.

- Black artists like Jay-Z, Beyoncé, Drake, and Nicki Minaj have achieved remarkable crossover success. The most successful athlete in what was once an exclusively white sport, tennis, is black: Serena Williams. Three out of every 10 major league baseball players today is Latino. In the NBA, 30% of head coaches and 44% of assistant coaches are people of color (Lapchick, 2017).

Yet a decade after that historic election, I can't get past a very different reality. Despite the progress they've attained, African Americans, Latino/as, and Native Americans still remain, on average, the poorest and most disadvantaged of all groups in the United States. Their average annual income is still substantially lower than that of Whites and Asian Americans. Working-class black households earn about 55% of what working-class white households earn, a gap that is exactly the same as it was in 1967 (Campos, 2017). The poverty rate for Blacks and Latinos is still more than double what it is for Whites (Proctor, Semega, & Kollar, 2016). The unemployment rate of Blacks is twice as high as that of Whites and Asians. And the rate of home ownership among Blacks and Latino/as is well below 50%, compared to almost 70% among Whites (ProQuest Statistical Abstract, 2017). Of all ethnoracial groups in this society, African Americans have the highest rate of infant mortality; highest rates of most cancers, diabetes, heart disease, high blood pressure, and HIV/AIDS; and highest rates of death from treatable illnesses, violence, and drug- or alcohol-induced causes (American Sociological Association, 2005; Centers for Disease Control and Prevention, 2016c; ProQuest Statistical Abstract, 2017). Even though Blacks and Whites use marijuana at similar rates, Blacks are four times as likely to be arrested for possession (American Civil Liberties Union, 2013). Indeed, it's estimated that there are 1.5 million fewer black men between the ages of 25 and 54 in everyday society than there should be because of high rates of imprisonment, homicide, and other forms of early death (Wolfers, Quealy, & Leonhardt, 2015).

I also think of specific incidents in the recent past that further belie the image of racial progress and harmony:

- In the summer of 2015, a 21-year-old avowed white supremacist opened fire in an African Methodist Episcopalian church in Charleston, South Carolina, killing nine people who were there for a Bible study meeting. Witnesses said that before he began shooting, he shouted out a series of racial epithets. In the weeks following the massacre, fires destroyed six black churches in five southern states.

- In 2016, a white man in Olympia, Washington, stabbed an interracial couple after seeing them kiss in public (Wootson, 2016b).

- That same year, a waiter in a Southern California restaurant refused to serve four Latina women until they provided him with "proof" that they were citizens (Wootson, 2016a).

- In 2017 on a commuter train in Portland, Oregon, a 35-year-old man shouted racial and ethnic slurs at a 16-year-old woman and her Muslim friend. When three bystanders tried to intervene, he stabbed them, killing two and wounding one (Wang, 2017a).

- Also in 2017, a white man opened fire on two Indian immigrants in a Kansas bar after shouting ethnic slurs and questioning their immigration status. One of the men died, the other was seriously injured (Stevens, 2017).

- According to the Southern Poverty Law Center (SPLC; 2016a), in the first few weeks after the 2016 presidential election, schools around the country reported a significant increase in the use of racial slurs and incidents involving swastikas, Nazi salutes, and confederate flags among students. Public libraries experienced a similar uptick of incidents involving the defacing of books about Islam (Mele, 2016). Ku Klux Klan flyers were found on the Long Island Railroad. White supremacists openly and violently marched on the streets of Charlottesville, Virginia. The Anti-Defamation League reported that anti-Semitic crimes rose by more than a third in 2016, and the Council of American-Islamic Relations cited a 50% increase in anti-Muslim attacks (Coll, 2017). The SPLC (2016b) also pointed out that 37% of documented anti-immigrant and racist hate crimes directly referenced either President Trump or his campaign slogans.

So how far have we really come? Which is the real United States? Is it the one that overcame centuries of racial conflict and elected a black president? Or is it the one perpetually plagued by economic inequality, prejudice, and hatred?

In the previous chapter, I examined the class stratification system. But social class doesn't create unequal life chances on its own. This chapter focuses on another important determinant of social inequality: race and ethnicity.

Race and Ethnicity: More Than Just Biology

To most people, **race** is a category of individuals labeled and treated as similar because of common physical traits, such as skin color, skeletal structure, color and texture of hair, and shape of eyes, nose, or head (Desmond & Emirbayer, 2009). It is widely assumed that people who are placed in the same racial category share behavioral, psychological, and personality traits that are linked to their physical similarities. But sociologists typically use the term **ethnicity** to refer to the nonbiological traits—such as shared culture, history, language, patterns of behavior, and beliefs—that provide members of a group with a sense of common identity. Whereas ethnicity is thought to be something that we learn from other people, race is commonly portrayed as an inherited and permanent biological characteristic that can be used to divide people into mutually exclusive groups.

But the concept of race isn't nearly so straightforward. For instance, people who consider themselves "white" may actually have darker skin and curlier hair than some people who consider themselves "black." In addition, some groups have features that do not neatly place them in one race or another. Australian Aborigines have black skin and "Negroid" facial features but also have blond, wavy hair. The black-skinned !Kung, who live in the Kalahari Desert of southern Africa, have epicanthic eye folds, a characteristic typical of East Asian peoples.

Not surprisingly, there are no universal racial categories. Brazilians have three primary races—*branco* (white), *prêto* (black), and *pardo* (mulatto)—but use dozens of more precise terms to categorize people based on minute differences in skin color, hair texture and length, and facial features. South Africa has four legally defined races—black, white, colored, and Indian—but in England and Ireland the term *black* is used to refer to all people who are not white. In one small Irish town that experienced an unprecedented influx of refugees in the late 1990s, anyone who wasn't Irish was considered black. As one resident put it, "Either Romanians or Nigerians, we don't know the difference. They're all the same. They're all black" (quoted in Lyall, 2000, p. A6). Conversely, some African Americans visiting Ghana are shocked when people there refer to them as *obruni*, or "white foreigner" (Holliday, 2014).

In some places, race concepts and racial identification are fluid, reflecting changes in economic standing, not skin color:

- Brazilians who climb the class ladder through educational and economic achievement may find themselves in a different racial category, as illustrated by popular Brazilian expressions such as "Money whitens" or "A rich Negro is a white man, and a poor white man is a Negro" (Marger, 1994, p. 441). Educated nonwhite parents in Brazil are significantly more likely to classify their children as white than are less-educated nonwhite parents (Schwartzman, 2007).

- In Ecuador, infertile women pursuing in vitro fertilization assistance frequently seek white egg donors as a means of improving the racial identity (and social status) of their baby (E. F. S. Roberts, 2012).

- In Puerto Rico, a U.S. territory, conceptions of race are markedly more fluid than they are in the United States. Race is seen as a continuum of categories with different shades of color as the norm and classifications that can change as one's socioeconomic circumstances change (C. E. Rodriguez & Cordero-Guzman, 2004).

- In the United States, over a third of African Americans in a nationwide survey indicated that because of a widening gap between middle-class and poor Blacks, "black" can no longer be thought of as a single race (cited in Gates, 2007).

The complex issue of defining race points to a complicated biological reality. Since the earliest humans appeared, they have consistently tended to migrate and interbreed. For instance, a recent genetic study of 160,000 Americans found that, on average, European genes account for almost one quarter of the DNA of those who identify as African American; Latino/as were, on average, 65% European. The researchers also estimate that over 6 million European Americans have some African ancestry (Bryc, Durand, Macpherson, Reich, & Mountain, 2015). Indeed, there is no gene that is 100% of one form in one race and 100% of a different form in another race (P. Brown, 1998).

That is not to say that race has absolutely *no* connection to biology. Geneticists and public health officials have known for quite a while that some diseases are not evenly distributed across racial groups. For instance, sickle cell anemia occurs in about 1 out of every 365 African American births. By contrast it occurs in 1 out of every 16,300 Latino/a births (Centers for Disease Control and Prevention, 2016e). Hemochromatosis, a digestive disorder that causes the body to absorb too much iron, affects Whites of Northern European descent much more frequently than people of color. Among African Americans, Asian Americans, Latino/as, and American Indians, the disease is virtually nonexistent. Among Whites, about 5 people out of 1,000—0.5%—carry two copies of the hemochromatosis gene and are susceptible to developing the disease. One out of every 8 to 12 Whites is a carrier of one abnormal gene (National Digestive Diseases Information Clearinghouse, 2011). However, no disease is found *exclusively* in one racial group. Furthermore, it's unclear whether these differences are solely due to some inherited biological trait or to the life experiences and historical, geographical, and/or environmental location of certain groups.

For most sociologists (e.g., Desmond & Emirbayer, 2009; Gans, 2005)—and a growing number of biologists (e.g., Yudell, Roberts, DeSalle, & Tishkoff, 2016)—race is more meaningful as a symbolic category than as a biological or genetic one. That is, the characteristics a society selects to distinguish one ethnoracial group from another shape social rankings and determine access to important resources. But these categories have less to do with innate physical differences or genetic predispositions than with what the prevailing culture defines as socially and historically significant (American Sociological Association, 2002). For instance, Jews, the Irish, Italians, and even some Germans were once defined as members of inferior races. They came to be seen as "white" only when they entered the mainstream culture and gained economic and political power (Bronner, 1998). Sociologists have noted that more and more U.S. adults feel comfortable simply shedding the ethnic identities they were born into and taking on new ones (Hitt, 2005).

Historical changes in the categories used by the U.S. government in its decennial population censuses further illustrate shifting conceptions of race (S. M. Lee, 1993):

- In 1790, the first U.S. census used the following classifications: Free White Males, Free White Females, All Other Free Persons, and Slaves.

- In 1870, there were five races: White, Colored (Black), Mulatto (people with some black blood), Chinese, and Indian.

- Race categories in the 1890 census reflected white people's concern about race mixing and racial purity. Eight races were listed, half of them applying to black or partly black populations: White, Colored (Black), Mulatto (people with three-eighths to five-eighths black blood), Quadroon (people with one-fourth black blood), Octoroon (people with one-eighth black blood), Chinese, Japanese, and Indian.

- In 1900, Mulatto, Quadroon, and Octoroon were dropped, so that any amount of "black blood" meant a person had to be classified as "black."

- In 1910 and 1920, Mulatto returned to the census form, only to disappear for good in 1930.

- Between 1930 and 2000, some racial classifications (such as Hindu, Eskimo, part Hawaiian, and Mexican) appeared and disappeared. Others (Filipino, Korean, Hawaiian) made an appearance and have remained since.

- Individuals filling out the 2010 census form had a wide array of racial categories from which to choose: White, Black, American Indian or Alaska Native, Asian Indian, Chinese, Filipino, Japanese, Korean, Vietnamese, Native Hawaiian, Guamanian or Chamorro, or Samoan.

You may have noticed that Latino/a or Hispanic is not included in the list of races on the latest census form. With the exception of the inclusion of "Mexican" in 1930, Spanish-speaking people have routinely been classified as "white." But because Latino/as can be members of any race, "Hispanic origin" appears on the census form, not as a race but as an ethnicity. In fact, the 2010 form explicitly states "Hispanic origins are not races."

This way of thinking has not been received well by all Latino/as. Many do not identify with any of the current racial categories. Census data show that 87% of Americans born in Cuba and 53% born in Mexico identify themselves as white; but a majority of those born in the Dominican Republic and El Salvador refused to identify themselves by any of the racial categories on the census form (cited in S. Roberts, 2010). In the 2010 census, many Latino/as chose to use "American Indian" to identify their race. Consequently, the number of "Hispanic American Indians" tripled between 2000 and 2010 (cited in Decker, 2011). In 2012, the U.S. Census Bureau began looking into a combined "race or origin" question for the 2020 census that would include "Hispanic, Latino, or Spanish Origin" as a category along with "White," "Black, African American, or Negro," "American Indian or Alaskan Native," "Asian," and "Native Hawaiian or Other Pacific Islander" (Haub, 2012).

Similarly, the Census Bureau is also considering adding a "Middle Eastern/North African" category to the 2020 census for the nearly 4 million Arab Americans who are currently categorized as "white" (Krogstad, 2014).

In short, racial categories are not natural, biological groupings. They are created, inhabited, transformed, applied, and destroyed by people and by social institutions (Omi & Winant, 1992; Saperstein, Penner, & Light, 2013). What ties individuals together in a particular racial group is not a set of shared physical characteristics—because there aren't any physical characteristics shared by all members of a particular racial group—but the shared experience of identifying, and being identified by others, as members of that group (Piper, 1992).

In the end, of course, race and ethnicity are matters of self-definition. But are there limits to what we can call ourselves? In theory, we live in a society built on the premise that we can be what we want as long as we don't hurt others or infringe on their rights. Such a cultural value implies that perhaps how we racially identify is solely a matter of individual determination. But you're probably well aware that for some aspects of our identity, those choices are limited and can sometimes be challenged by others. You may recall the firestorm that erupted in 2015 when it was revealed that Rachel Dolezal—a self-identified black woman who was president of the Spokane, Washington, chapter of the NAACP and an instructor of African American Studies at Eastern Washington University—was actually white. She professed deep empathy and sympathy with black people from the time, as a teenager, her parents adopted four black children. She attended a historically black college, Howard University. She married a black man. Her art reflected the black experience. She curled her hair and even darkened her skin. She constructed a reputation as a powerful advocate for civil rights. One acquaintance she knew when she was younger said she seemed like "a black girl in a white body . . . but she was snow white, white-white, lily white" (quoted in K. Johnson, Pérez-Peña, & Eligon, 2015, p. A13). But she wasn't just immersed in black political issues, appearance, and lifestyle; she said she *was* black, even though both of her biological parents are white. This was an identity many people simply couldn't accept. While some called her "transracial," implying that she was creating a new, more fluid conception of race (Morris, 2015), others accused her of "playing black," choosing to adopt an African American heritage and look and to cast off her white racial advantage when it suited her, something actual people of color cannot do (Pérez-Peña, 2015). Blacks have always had a harder time claiming whiteness. Said one black author, "Unlike Rachel Dolezal, I don't have the option of choosing my race" (T. W. Harris, 2015, p. A25).

MICRO-MACRO CONNECTION
WHY ISN'T BARACK OBAMA WHITE?

Definitions of race and the way those definitions are incorporated into people's individual identities are particularly difficult for people whose biological parents are of different races. Former president Obama, as you well know, is biracial. Although he sometimes jokingly refers to himself as a "mutt," he, like so many biracial individuals before him, is typically identified as black. He will forever be known as the first black or African American president, not the first biracial president or the first half-white president. Why?

Since the era of slavery, the United States has adhered to the "one-drop rule" regarding racial identity (F. J. Davis, 1991). The term dates back to a common law in the South that a "single drop of black blood" makes a person black. Sociologists call this a hypodescent rule, meaning that racially mixed people are always assigned the status of the subordinate group (F. J. Davis, 1991). Conversely, mixed-race people in other groups must meet a hereditary threshold in order to claim a particular ethnoracial identity. For instance, some Native Americans carry a document, known as the CDIB (Certificate of Degree of Indian Blood), that indicates whether they have enough Indian blood to be considered Indian (Hitt, 2005).

Most people in the United States still tend to see race in mutually exclusive skin color categories: black, white, red, yellow, brown. Even when faced with ambiguities, people still try to put others into single-color racial groups (A. Holmes, 2015). But the dramatic growth in multiracial children—the proportion of multiracial babies grew from 1% in 1970 to 10% in 2013—has upset traditional views of racial identity and has led more and more people of mixed racial heritage to fight against the traditional "one-drop" thinking and embrace their more complex identity. A recent survey found that 60% of multiracial adults are proud of their mixed race background and feel it makes them more tolerant of other cultures. Only 4% felt it has been a disadvantage (Pew Research Center, 2015f). Interestingly, however, when asked how they identify themselves, only 40% of people with a mixed race background used the term *multiracial*. The rest identified with one race either because they

(Continued)

(Continued)

look like one race or were raised as one race. And one in five said they felt pressure from others to identify as a single race.

In the mid- to late 1990s, individuals with a mixed racial heritage lobbied Congress and the Bureau of the Census to add a multiracial category to the 2000 census. They argued that such a change would add visibility and legitimacy to a racial identity that had heretofore been ignored. Even before this debate emerged, some scholars had been arguing that a multiracial category might soften the racial lines that divide the country (Stephan & Stephan, 1989). When people blend two or more races and ethnicities within their own bodies, race becomes a less potent social divider, thereby presenting a biological solution to the problem of racial injustice (J. E. White, 1997). Such a sentiment is echoed by this columnist (a black woman married to a white man):

> [My son] is the exact shade you'd get if you mixed his father and me up in a paint can—a color I call golden. . . . Perhaps as the number of multiracial Americans continues to grow, there will be a plurality of golden people who are impossible to positively identify as one race or the other. And the rest of us who can be easily categorized will be forced to accept that color does not contribute to the content of one's character because we won't know which set of stereotypes to apply to whom. (Kelley, 2009, p. 41)

Not everyone thought such a change to the census form would be a good idea. Many civil rights organizations objected to the inclusion of a multiracial category (R. Farley, 2002). They worried that it would reduce the number of U.S. citizens claiming to belong to long-recognized ethnoracial minority groups, dilute the culture and political power of those groups, and make it more difficult to enforce civil rights laws (Mathews, 1996). Job discrimination lawsuits, affirmative action policies, and federal programs that assist minority businesses or that protect minority communities from environmental hazards all depend on official racial population data from the census. Even today there is concern with those who self-identify as multiracial. As one author recently put it, "Mixed-race blacks have an ethical obligation to identify as black—and interracial couples share a similar moral imperative to inculcate certain ideas of black heritage and racial identity in their mixed-race children, regardless of how they look" (T. C. Williams, 2012, p. 5).

In the end, the civil rights organizations won. For the 2000 census, the government decided not to add a multiracial category to official forms. Instead, it adopted a policy allowing people, for the first time, to identify themselves on the census form as members of more than one race. According to the 2010 census, 9 million people—or about 3% of the population—identify themselves as belonging to more than one race (Humes, Jones, & Ramirez, 2010).

Some sociologists caution, however, that the Census Bureau's method of measuring multiracial identity—checking two or more race categories—does not adequately reflect the way people personally experience race. As one journalist recently put it:

> As the daughter of an African American father and a white mother, born with olive skin, light eyes and thick, curly hair, I have been aware of a tension between the way the outside world sees me, the way the government sees me . . . , and the way I see myself. (A. Holmes, 2015, p. 14)

Sociologists David Harris and Jeremiah Sim (2002) examined data from the National Longitudinal Study of Adolescent Health, a survey containing information on the racial identity of a nationwide sample of more than 11,000 adolescents. They found that the way people racially classify themselves can change from context to context. Almost twice as many adolescents identify themselves as multiracial when they're interviewed at school as when they're interviewed at home. Furthermore, only 87.6% expressed the same racial identities across different settings. This research is important because it shows that census data on multiracial identity don't necessarily account for people who self-identify as multiracial in everyday situations. Sizable numbers of multiracial adolescents change their racial identity—to that of a single race—as they enter adulthood (Doyle & Kao, 2007). About 3 in 10 adults with a multiracial background say that they have changed the way they describe their race over the years. Some say they once thought of themselves as only one race and now think of themselves as more than one race; others say just the opposite (Pew Research Center, 2015f).

So whether Barack Obama is white, black, mixed, or interracial ultimately depends on how he defines himself. When he filled out his 2010 census form, Obama checked the category "Black, African American or Negro" only, even though others may define him differently. In one poll, 55% of black respondents said the former president is black and only 34% said he was mixed. Among white respondents, 53% said he was mixed, while 24% identified him as black (P. Taylor, 2014b).

VISUAL ESSAY—PICK A COLOR . . . ANY COLOR

Fred W. McDarrah/Getty Images

AP Photo/File

Colin Mulvany/The Spokesman-Review via AP, File

Seemingly every day, we're reminded that race is our national obsession—a topic that just won't go away. For hundreds of years, we've struggled with how to live with racial diversity. But as you've already seen in this chapter, even before we can address the vexing issue of racial inequality, we have to ask a more fundamental question: what is race? To most sociologists, race is less an objective biogenetic trait than it is a social construction. I've presented plenty of evidence in this chapter to support that notion. But can race also be a *personal* construction? Here we see three people (one you may remember; two you've likely never heard of) who claimed a personal racial identity that didn't conform to their heredity or physical traits. In 2015, Rachel Dolezal made national headlines because she said she was black, even though both her parents and all four of her grandparents are white. Effa Manley was a blond haired, hazel-eyed white woman who married a black man in the 1930s and lived her life as a black woman. Because of her work in the Negro Baseball Leagues, she became the first woman elected to the Baseball Hall of Fame. And Anatole Broyard was a mixed-race, Creole-born writer in Louisiana who lived his life as a white man so his books would be more acceptable to a wider reading audience.

In each of these cases, an individual constructed a racial identity that contradicted the hereditary evidence. Should people have the right to claim any race they want or does there need to be some kind of physical "proof" or at least some level of community endorsement? Do cases like these three support or challenge the notion that race is socially constructed?

Histories of Oppression and Inequality

A quick glance at the history of the United States reveals a record of not just freedom, justice, and equality but also of conquest, discrimination, and exclusion. Racial and ethnic inequalities have manifested themselves in phenomena such as slavery and fraud; widespread economic, educational, and political deprivation; the violent and nonviolent protests of the civil rights movement; and racially motivated hate crimes. Along the way, such injustices have constricted people's access to basic necessities, including housing, health care, a stable family life, and a means of making a decent living.

Every ethnoracial minority has its own story of persecution. European immigrants—Germans, Irish people, Italians, Poles, Jews, Greeks—were objects of hatred, suspicion, and discrimination when they first arrived in significant numbers in the United States. For instance, Benjamin Franklin once expressed fear that white Pennsylvanians would be "overwhelmed by swarms of swarthy Germans, who 'will soon so outnumber us, that all the advantages we have will not . . . be able to preserve our language, and even our government will become precarious'" (quoted in S. Roberts, 2008, p. 6). Nineteenth-century newspaper job ads routinely noted, "No Irish need apply." Jews were refused admission to many U.S. universities until the mid-20th century. The National Origins Act of 1924 restricted immigration from southern Europe (mainly Greece and Italy) until the 1960s. Because these groups had the same skin color as the dominant white Protestants, however, they eventually overcame most of these obstacles and gained entry into mainstream society. Most recently, immigrants from Asia, Latin America, and the Middle East have become popular targets of hostility. For people of color in this country, racial equality has always been elusive.

Native Americans

The story of Native Americans includes racially inspired massacres, takeover of ancestral lands, confinement on reservations, and unending governmental exploitation. Successive waves of white settlers seeking westward expansion in the 18th and 19th centuries pushed Native Americans off any land the settlers considered desirable (U.S. Commission on Human Rights, 1992). A common European belief that Native Americans were "savages" who should be displaced to make way for civilized Whites provided the ideological justification for conquering them.

According to the Fourteenth Amendment to the U.S. Constitution, "All persons born or naturalized in the United States, and subject to the jurisdiction thereof, are citizens of the United States and of the state wherein they reside." But despite the broad wording of this amendment, Native Americans were excluded from citizenship. In 1884, the U.S. Supreme Court ruled that Native Americans owed their primary allegiance to their tribe and so did not automatically acquire citizenship at birth. Not until 1940 were all Native Americans born in the United States considered U.S. citizens (Haney López, 1996).

Despite their history of severe oppression and continuing disadvantaged economic status compared with other groups, some Native Americans have shown a remarkable ability to endure and in a few cases to shrewdly promote their own financial interests. In the Pacific Northwest, for instance, some Indian tribes have successfully protected their rights to lucrative fishing waters (F. G. Cohen, 1986). Casinos and resorts have made some tribes wealthy. The Connecticut Sun, a professional women's basketball franchise, plays its home games on the grounds of a casino owned by the Mohegan nation. Elsewhere, organizations have been formed to advance the financial concerns of Native Americans in industries such as gas, oil, and coal, where substantial reserves exist on Indian land (Snipp, 1986). However, intense struggles between large multinational corporations and Native American tribes continue today over control of these reserves.

Latino/as

The history of Latino/as in this country has been diverse. Some groups have had a relatively positive experience. For instance, Cuban immigrants who streamed into this country in the late 1950s, fleeing Fidel Castro's communist political regime, received an enthusiastic welcome (Suarez, 1998). Many early Cuban immigrants were wealthy business owners who, fearing their fortunes would be confiscated by the Cuban government, set up lucrative companies, particularly in South Florida. Today, Cuban American families are the most economically and educationally successful of any Latino/a group.

But other groups have experienced extreme resentment and oppression. For instance, when the United States expanded into the Southwest, white Americans moved into areas already inhabited by Mexicans. After a war that lasted from 1846 to 1848, Mexico relinquished half its national territory to the United States, including what are now the states of Arizona, California, Colorado, New Mexico, Texas, Nevada, and Utah, as well as parts of Kansas, Oklahoma, and Wyoming.

In theory, Mexicans living on the U.S. side of the new border were to be given all the rights of U.S. citizens. In practice, however, their property rights were frequently violated, and they lost control of their mining, ranching, and farming industries. The exploitation of Mexican workers coincided with a developing economic system built around mining and large-scale agriculture, activities that demanded a large pool of cheap labor (J. Farley, 1982). Workers often had to house their families in primitive shacks with no electricity or plumbing for months on end while they performed seasonal labor.

Today, the status of Latino/as is mixed. They account for more than 40% of the 81 million people added to the U.S. population over the last 30 years and now represent a bigger proportion of the U.S. population than Blacks (see Exhibit 11.1). In 2010, 6 of the 15 most common surnames in the United States were of Hispanic origin, compared to zero in 1990 (U.S. Bureau of the Census, 2016a). By 2060, 3 out of every 10 persons in the United States will be Latino/a (ProQuest Statistical Abstract, 2017). Larger numbers mean not only greater influence on the culture but perhaps more political clout as well.

Economically and educationally, however, the situation is less rosy. The average annual income for Latino/a individuals and families is still substantially lower than that of other groups (ProQuest Statistical Abstract, 2017). In addition, Latino/a children are significantly more likely to drop out of school and less likely to go to college than are white, Asian American, or African American children. Their low levels of education, coupled with geographic concentration in economically distressed areas of the country, has made Latino/as, particularly men, especially vulnerable to downsizing and unemployment (Mather & Jacobsen, 2010). Indeed, if current levels of inequality persist in the future, the number of low-income Latino/a youth will increase from 11 million to 16 million by 2050 (Mather, 2016).

African Americans

The experience of African Americans has been unique among ethnoracial groups in this country because of the direct and indirect effects of slavery. From 1619, when the first black slaves were sold in Jamestown, Virginia, to 1865, when the Thirteenth Amendment outlawed slavery, several million Blacks in this country endured the brutal reality of forced

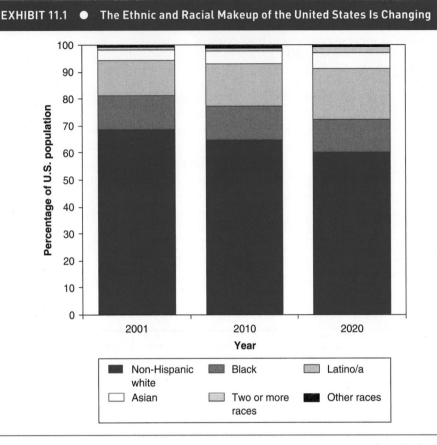

EXHIBIT 11.1 ● The Ethnic and Racial Makeup of the United States Is Changing

Source: U.S. Bureau of the Census, 2002, Table 14; ProQuest Statistical Abstract, 2015, Table 12; ProQuest Statistical Abstract, 2017, Table 13.

servitude. Slave owners controlled every aspect of a slave's life. They determined which slaves could marry and which marriages could be dissolved. Wedding vows among slave couples often substituted the phrase "until distance do us part" for "until death"—or "the white man"—"do us part" (T. W. Hunter, 2011). The economic value of children (i.e., future slaves) meant that slave owners had a financial interest in keeping slave marriages intact. But even the possibility of stable family life was an illusion. When economic troubles forced the sale of slaves to raise money, slave owners didn't hesitate to separate the very slave families they had once advocated. The daily threat of separation hung over every slave family.

We usually assume that slavery only existed in the South, but Northerners benefited from it as well. Slaves were such an economic asset in the 18th and early 19th centuries that many of the nation's largest insurance companies—from as far away as New York—commonly sold Southern slave owners life insurance policies for their slaves. That way, if they were to die prematurely, the owners could recoup up to three quarters of the slaves' value. Northern banks like JP Morgan Chase and Wells Fargo allowed Southerners seeking loans to use slaves as collateral and actually took possession of some of them when their owners couldn't pay off their loans (Swarns, 2016).

Following emancipation, racial mistreatment remained pervasive. Freed Blacks in the South found themselves arrested on trumped-up charges like selling produce after dark or talking loudly to white women in public. Vagrancy was criminalized so that Blacks who

But some college students argue that university responses to things like Halloween costumes are an institutional overreaction to an innocuous tradition. They argue that the university response is less about concern for students' safety and more about oversensitivity to an age-old practice that is motivated neither by maliciousness nor mockery. They say that *any* Halloween costume—gory zombies, Playboy bunnies, etc.—could be offensive to someone somewhere. So why make such a big deal out of it?

What do you think? Is cultural appropriation a sincere and harmless form of flattery or is it a derisive and dangerous form of ethnoracial abuse?

Class, Race, and Discrimination

Some sociologists have argued that discriminatory treatment, as well as the unequal social and political status of some racial groups, is more a function of social class than of race. If this belief were completely accurate, the lives of middle- and upper-class people of color would be relatively free of discrimination. The election and reelection of Barack Obama clearly showed that well-educated, highly qualified members of ethnoracial minorities are no longer barred from the highest positions in society. However, some civil rights advocates believe Obama's victories were isolated successes and fear many people will mistakenly conclude that racial discrimination is over (Swarns, 2008b). As the former chair of the U.S. Commission on Civil Rights put it, "It's like saying that because some poor white person made it, there's no poverty" (quoted in Cose, 2009, p. 43).

Indeed, even for many financially successful people of color, lack of respect, faint praise, low expectations, and outright harassment and exclusion continue to be common features of their lives (Feagin & McKinney, 2003). After a racial slur was spray painted on his house in 2017, the famous basketball star LeBron James put it this way: "No matter how much money you have, no matter how famous you are, no matter how many people admire you, being black in America is tough" (quoted in Kilgore, 2017, p. 1). In the early 1960s, the civil rights activist Malcolm X put it even more bluntly: "What does a white man call a black man with a PhD? A nigger" (quoted in Hartlep, 2013, p. 68).

Minority professionals often bemoan the tendency of others to assume they bring to every interaction the perspective of their entire group. A successful law professor, who happens to be Chinese American, once said, "I suspect . . . that at every appearance . . . my audience continues to see and hear me as a spokesperson on behalf of Asian Americans" (Wu, 2002, p. 37).

Sociologists Joe Feagin and Karyn McKinney (2003) analyzed data from focus group and individual interviews with several hundred middle-class U.S. Blacks to determine the consequences of the discrimination they experienced at work. These individuals, all of whom were college educated and held professional or managerial jobs, agreed that the work-related stresses they felt did not come from the demands of the jobs themselves but from racially hostile workplace environments that often included the mistrust of colleagues, unfair promotion practices, or outright mistreatment through the use of racial epithets and derogatory names.

Everyday life can be trying as well. Wealthy Blacks all over the country sometimes complain that they are watched closely when shopping in upscale stores or that the police view them with suspicion simply because their skin color doesn't match the neighborhood. In 2016, a former employee of the high-end clothing store Versace sued the company over its policy of using a secret code to alert other workers when a black customer entered the store (Cuevas, 2016). Situations like these are disturbing and frustrating not only because of the racist attitudes that lie behind them but also because the people who experience them had come to believe that their upward social mobility protected them from such treatment. A respondent in Feagin and McKinney's (2003) study put it this way:

> I'm always in the process of trying to develop a better and healthier way of working through the inevitable anger about this situation. There's a price you pay in being sensitive and conscious. . . . Have you ever seen a dog really being angry about his condition? If you really were a beast, it wouldn't bother you. The problem is that . . . this treatment bothers you most, because you definitely and clearly aren't what the world thinks you are. (p. 45)

In sum, racial discrimination is still very prevalent in the lives of members of ethnoracial minorities, including those who are financially successful. In fact, such discrimination is more apparent than that experienced by low-income people because the affluent individuals have entered previously inaccessible social spaces (Bonilla-Silva, 2008). One study even found that Blacks with college degrees experience more discrimination than those without degrees (Forman, Williams, & Jackson, 1997).

The days of No Negroes and No Indians signs on public facilities may be gone, but less blatant contemporary expressions of personal racism serve as a constant reminder that in the 21st century, members of ethnoracial minorities—no matter what their class standing—are still stereotyped, prejudged, and discriminated against every day.

The Cultural Ideology of Racism

If I stopped here in my discussion of racism, you might be inclined to consider it an individual-level phenomenon that could best be stopped by changing the way people think or by personal acts of kindness and respect. But the sociologically important thing about racism is that it exists not just in the minds and actions of individuals but in a cultural belief system that both justifies the domination of some groups over others and provides a set of social norms that encourages differential treatment for these groups (O'Sullivan-See & Wilson, 1988). From a conflict perspective, the ideology of racism that exists in our language and in our prevailing cultural beliefs contributes to racial and ethnic inequality.

Racism in Language

Certainly, derogatory racial slurs reflect underlying racism. But racism in language is often less obvious. Consider the use of **panethnic labels**—general terms applied to diverse subgroups that are assumed to have something in common (D. Newman, 2017). Today, we use the general terms *Native American* or *American Indian* to refer to all 560 or so native nations living in the United States, despite their different languages and cultures. *Asian American* refers to a variety of peoples from dozens of countries whose ethnic heritages and lifestyles are quite different from one another. Similarly, *Hispanic* or *Latino* refers to people whose backgrounds include culturally diverse areas such as Mexico, the Caribbean, Central America, and South America. To some, even the term *African American*, which is widely considered to be a positive racial label, glosses over the thousands of ethnic groups, class interests, and indigenous religions that exist on the continent of Africa. Reliance on panethnic labels allows users to overlook and ignore variations within a particular labeled group, thereby reinforcing stereotypes. In response to these concerns, the University of California expanded the number of Asian American categories on its application forms from 8 to 23, allowing prospective students to claim a more specific ethnic identity.

Racial identifiers often become equated with negative meanings. Consider, for instance, connotations of the words *black* and *white*. Among the definitions of *black* in *Webster's New Universal Unabridged Dictionary* are "soiled and dirty," "thoroughly evil," "wicked," "gloomy," "marked by disaster," "hostile," and "disgraceful." The definition of *white*, in contrast, includes "fairness of complexion," "innocent," "favorable," "fortunate," "pure," and "spotless." The pervasive "goodness" of white and "badness" of black affects children at a very young age and provides white children with a false sense of superiority (R. B. Moore, 1992). Young children know the difference between a black lie, which is harmful and inexcusable, and a white lie, which is small, insignificant, and harmless.

Also important are the political implications of racially tinged terminology. Terms such as *economically disadvantaged, underclass, inner city, urban,* and *underdeveloped* sound unprejudiced, but they are often used as code for racial terms (Krugman, 2014). For instance, a study of the 1995 Louisiana gubernatorial election revealed that the white candidate's stated opposition to affirmative action and his discussion of the crime problems in "inner-city" neighborhoods (which everyone knew were black and Latino/a neighborhoods) subtly symbolized his racial attitudes, appealed to many white voters, and thereby contributed to his victory over a black candidate (Knuckey & Orey, 2000).

Language is just a small part of the overall problem of racist ideology in U.S. society. It seemingly pales in comparison with more visible issues such as racial violence and economic discrimination. But remember that language filters our perceptions. It affects the way people think from the time they first learn to speak. Fortunately, efforts are being made today to address the issue of language and its crucial role in maintaining racism and oppression. People are becoming more aware of the capacity of words to both glorify and degrade (R. B. Moore, 1992).

The Myth of Innate Racial Inferiority

Scientific-sounding theories of the innate inferiority of certain ethnoracial groups have long been used to explain why some groups lag behind others in areas such as educational achievement and financial success. These theories combine with the belief in competitive individualism (see Chapter 10) to justify all forms of prejudice and discrimination.

Appeals to biology and nature have been used throughout history to define the existing stratification system as proper and inevitable (S. J. Gould, 1981). What would you think of a person who harbored the following beliefs about Blacks?

> [Blacks] have less hair on the face and body. They secrete less by the kidnies [*sic*], and more by the glands of the skin, which gives them a very strong and disagreeable odour [*sic*]. . . . They are at least as brave, and more adventuresome. But this may perhaps proceed from a want of forethought, which prevents their seeing a danger till it be present. . . . In imagination, they are dull, tasteless, and anomalous. . . . The improvement of the blacks in body and mind, in the first instance of their mixture with the whites, has been observed by everyone, and proves that their inferiority is not the effect merely of their condition of life. . . . I advance it therefore . . . that the blacks . . . are inferior to the whites in the endowments both of body and mind.

A white supremacist? A raving bigot? An ignorant fanatic? How would your assessment of this person change if you found out that this passage was written by none other than Thomas Jefferson (1781/1955, pp. 138–143)? In the 18th and 19th centuries, no white person—not even one apparently committed to protecting people's right to "life, liberty and the pursuit of happiness"—doubted the validity of natural racial rankings: Indians below Whites, and Blacks below everyone else. Other idols of Western culture—George Washington, Abraham Lincoln, Charles Darwin—held similar beliefs about the "natural inferiority" of some races, beliefs that were commonly accepted knowledge at the time but would at the very least be considered racially insensitive today.

The approval given by white scientists to conventional racial rankings arose not from objective data and careful research but from a cultural belief in the "goodness" and inevitability of racial stratification. Such beliefs were then twisted into independent, "scientific" support. Scientists, like everybody else, have attitudes and values that shape what they see. Such thinking is not the result of outright dishonesty or hypocrisy; rather, it is the combination of the way human minds work and the generally accepted knowledge of the day.

The belief in innate racial inferiority is not just a historical curiosity. Two decades ago, the idea reemerged in a book called *The Bell Curve: Intelligence and Class Structure in American Life* (Herrnstein & Murray, 1994). The authors argued that racial and ethnic differences in intelligence—as measured by IQ scores—must be due, at least in part, to heredity. The book set off a firestorm of debate that continues to this day (Pethokoukis, 2014).

From a conflict perspective, beliefs about racial inferiority provide advantages for the dominant group. These beliefs discourage subordinate groups from questioning their disadvantaged status. In addition, they provide moral justification for maintaining a society in which some groups are routinely deprived of their rights and privileges. Nineteenth-century Whites could justify the enslavement of Blacks, and 20th-century Nazis could justify the extermination of Jews and other "undesirables," by promoting the belief that those groups were biologically subhuman.

Despite energetic searches over the centuries, a link between "inferior" race-based genes and certain traits and abilities has not been found (Hacker, 1992). For one thing, comparing racial groups on, say, intelligence overlooks the range of differences within and between groups. Many African Americans are more intelligent than the average white person; many Whites are less intelligent than the average Native American.

Variations such as these are difficult to explain in terms of the genetic superiority of one race. Moreover, treating the more than 250 million "white" people in the United States as a single (and intellectually superior) group is problematic at best and misleading at worst. It can't account for the wide variation in academic achievement among whites of different national backgrounds. For instance, at the time *The Bell Curve* was written, 21% of white Americans of Irish descent completed college, whereas 22% of Italian Americans, 33% of Scottish Americans, and 51% of Russian Americans did so (Hacker, 1994).

Moreover, genetic predispositions cannot account for variations in IQ in a particular ethnoracial group over the span of a generation or two. Psychologist James Flynn (1999) examined IQ scores in various populations over a 60-year period. He found that scores had increased in all countries for which data existed—a phenomenon known as the "Flynn effect" (see Exhibit 11.2). In some countries, average scores had improved by 25 points or more. Increases of such magnitude simply cannot be explained by genetics. Instead, they reflect better education and improvement in things like abstract problem solving across generations.

Finally, such comparisons also ignore a problem I described earlier in this chapter: that race itself is a meaningless biological category. How can we attribute racial differences in intelligence to genes when race itself is not traceable to a single gene?

Nevertheless, the idea that racial inferiority is innate remains appealing. If observable, physical differences among races are inherited, the argument goes, then why not differences in social behavior, intelligence, and leadership ability? Like the belief in competitive individualism we examined in the previous chapter, the belief in innate racial inferiority places the blame for suffering and economic failure on the individual rather than on the society in which that individual exists.

EXHIBIT 11.2   ●   In Many Countries, Average IQ Scores Tend to Go Up Over Time

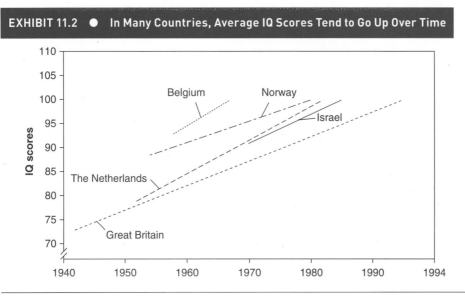

Source: Flynn, 1999, Figure 1.

MICRO-MACRO CONNECTION
WHY ARE BLACK ATHLETES SO DOMINANT?

The flip side of the belief in innate racial inferiority is the notion that some racial groups have a biologically rooted superiority in some areas of life. Take, for instance, the widely held belief that some racial groups are biologically predisposed to be more athletically successful than others. All but one male Boston Marathon winner since 1990 has been either a black Kenyan or Ethiopian, and every male world record holder at every standard track distance is an athlete of African descent (Muscat, 2013). Today, black athletes dominate the highest levels of sports such as football, basketball, and track. In the United States, African Americans make up about 13% of the population but constitute over 69% of players in the NFL (National Football League), 74% of players in the NBA (National Basketball Association), and 69% of players in the WNBA (Women's National Basketball Association; Lapchick, 2017). Not surprisingly, many

people see numbers like these and assume that Blacks must be "naturally" stronger, swifter, and more coordinated than athletes from other races.

In the late 19th century, African Americans were allowed to play professional baseball alongside Whites; boxing, too, was racially integrated. But by the turn of the century, white athletes threatened to quit rather than share the field or the ring with black athletes. Early white heavyweight boxing champions such as John L. Sullivan and Jack Dempsey refused to fight black opponents. In 1888, baseball team owners tacitly agreed not to sign any more African American players. Their formal exclusion lasted until 1947, when Jackie Robinson became the first African American in the 20th century to play baseball in the major leagues (Sage, 2001).

The rationale behind excluding African Americans was not based on their inability to compete. On

(Continued)

(Continued)

the contrary, it was based on the common belief that Blacks were athletically *superior* to Whites. Many 18th- and 19th-century scholars believed black slaves were bred by their owners to be physically strong. In recent decades, such ideas have taken on a scientific cast (Entine, 2000). For instance, some biologists argue that black athletes' muscles are better adapted to hot climates and, therefore, are better at providing energy quickly. Others have cited better power-to-weight ratios and longer Achilles tendons.

Black athletic superiority has become an almost taken-for-granted truth in the sports world. Many athletes have publicly expressed their belief that black success in sports is a consequence of Blacks' physical superiority to Whites. Hall of Fame basketball star Larry Bird (who is white) once voiced his support for the contention that white players don't stack up to black players: "[Basketball] is a black man's game and it will be forever. I mean, the greatest athletes in the world are African American" ("Bird: NBA," 2004, p. 1). Roger Bannister, a British distance runner who was the first to break the 4:00 mile, once said, "I am prepared to risk political correctness by drawing attention to the seemingly obvious but under-stressed fact that black sprinters and black athletes in general seem to have certain natural anatomical advantages" ("Sports Quiz," 2017, p. 6).

The problem with the belief in black athletic superiority is that physical strength (a seemingly positive characteristic) is all too often associated with alleged social, moral, or intellectual deficiency. A nationally known sportscaster once commonly referred to powerful black athletes (but never white athletes) as "thoroughbreds," a term that simultaneously acknowledged their physical prowess and likened them to horses. A while back I heard an ESPN commentator say that Vince Young, a black quarterback who at the time played for the Philadelphia Eagles, was not smart enough to be a starter in the NFL. He said that Young was a gifted and truly phenomenal athlete, but teams need an intelligent leader to be their quarterback. Such comments strengthen the notion that black athletes are athletically superior but deficient in most other ways.

Extending this logic, physically outclassed white athletes must rely on self-discipline, mental acuity, "a tireless work ethic," "fiery determination," and an unwavering attention to discipline and "fundamentals" in order to compete. In this way, successful white athletes become especially praiseworthy because they're able to overcome their "natural" limitations. Such an attitude is reflected in these assessments, the first from

a white college basketball player, the second from the former coach of a white player who was being inducted into the Hall of Fame:

> I know I'm not going to beat them with my quickness so I need to see exactly how they're playing me. . . . You have to study the game and watch every little thing to look for some kind of advantage. (quoted in Hutchens, 2002, p. D8)

> He was one of the most creative players that I've ever seen. He wasn't the most athletic, but he made up for it by being creative with his footwork and always finding a way to get his shot off. (quoted in Wells, 2011, p. C8)

Notice how lack of quickness and athleticism becomes a virtue as it opens the way to a superior intellect and work ethic.

Conversely, Blacks' athletic success is often considered a natural by-product of their physical "gifts," not the result of hard work or intellect (S. Brooks, 2009). Occasionally, the famous tennis player Serena Williams expresses dismay over press coverage of her victories, which commonly emphasize her strength in overpowering her opponents rather than the mental preparation and strategizing required to be the best in the world.

Because of these pervasive stereotypes, the white public often tempers its admiration of black athletic superiority with contempt for what some consider an arrogant, undisciplined style. A few years ago, the NFL decided to penalize players who wore uniforms that didn't conform to tight league regulations, who "trash talked" (taunted opponents), and who choreographed post-touchdown celebrations. These players were almost exclusively black.

Still, the undeniable fact is that Blacks *do* dominate certain professional sports in the United States. One sociological explanation is that such domination results not from innate physical superiority alone but from a complex set of social conditions that channels a disproportionate number of physically talented Blacks into athletic careers (Edwards, 1971). Sport has long been perceived as one of the few avenues of social mobility open to members of certain ethnoracial minorities: baseball for Latinos, football and basketball for African Americans. A national survey found that by a margin of three to one over Whites, Blacks cited financial gain as one of the most important reasons to play sports: "If I am successful at sports, I can make a lot of money" (cited in Price, 1997). Where children from other racial groups are being taught that a good education will pay off, many black children are being taught that a good education may not be enough to overcome the prejudice and discrimination that exist in society. Hence, they are more likely to be encouraged to hone their physical skills and to spend more time perfecting this resource. A high school basketball coach put it this way: "Suburban [white] kids tend to play for the fun of it. Inner-city [black] kids look at basketball as a matter of life or death" (quoted in Price, 1997, p. 35).

Sport has always served as a source of tremendous pride in black and Latino/a communities. Victory is especially sweet because it represents something larger than the athlete herself or himself; it symbolizes the values and aspirations of an entire people (Rhoden, 2006). But highlighting the rags-to-riches stories of a tiny number of successful athletes is a double-edged sword. These high-profile athletes are worthy of celebration, but they disguise the reality of how little social mobility actually results from sports participation. Only 3 in 1,000 high school basketball players are ever *drafted* by an NBA team, let alone become a high-paid star (NCAA, 2013). As one sociologist once remarked,

"You have a better chance of getting hit with a meteorite in the next 10 years than getting work as a professional athlete" (quoted in Sage, 2001, p. 283).

An overemphasis on athletic accomplishments can also discourage academic and occupational achievement in favor of physical self-expression, thereby harming ethnoracial minority communities in the long run. Only about half of black male Division I athletes graduate from college within 6 years, compared to 73% of undergraduate students overall (Harper, Williams, & Blackman, 2013). It might be more useful in the long run to focus on the fact that there are 12 times more black lawyers and 15 times more black physicians than there are black professional athletes (Sage, 2001).

Whether or not the emphasis on sports is a good thing and whether or not black athletes do have some anatomical advantage, we must always remember that so-called black athletic superiority is as much a social product as a biological one. Innate talent is never sufficient in itself to explain athletic excellence (D. F. Chambliss, 1989). If we rely simply on innate superiority to explain black success in sports, we overlook the broader social structural context in which everyday life is embedded.

Institutional Racism: Injustice Built Into the System

If you think about it, anyone can be personally racist, whether overtly or quietly. Members of any ethnoracial group can develop a set of beliefs or a vocabulary that denigrates outsiders. But one form of racism, less obvious and perhaps more dangerous, can work only to the advantage of those who wield power in society: institutional racism. **Institutional racism** consists of established laws, customs, and practices that systematically reflect and produce racial inequalities in society, whether or not the individuals maintaining these practices have racist intentions (J. M. Jones, 1986). Thus, a society can be racist even if only a small proportion of its members harbor personally racist beliefs. Because African Americans, Latino/as, Asian Americans, Muslim Americans, Native Americans, and other groups have historically been excluded from key positions of authority in social institutions, they often find themselves victimized by the routine workings of such structures.

Sometimes institutional racism is obvious and codified into the law. Until the early 1990s, for example, South Africa operated under an official system of *apartheid*: Nonwhite groups were legally segregated and subjected to sanctioned forms of political and economic discrimination. In the United States, the forceful relocation of Native Americans in the 19th century, the repressive Jim Crow laws in the 20th-century South, and the internment of Japanese Americans during World War II are all examples of legislated policies that purposely worked to the disadvantage of already disadvantaged groups.

Understanding less obvious forms of institutional racism, however, is a better test of the sociological imagination. Because it is a built-in feature of social arrangements, institutional racism is often much more difficult to detect than acts of personal racism. At times it is camouflaged behind claims that may on the surface seem quite reasonable. For instance, the U.S. Army has a grooming policy, known as AR670-1, that describes, among many other things, acceptable hairstyles for military personnel. The policy makes no mention of race or ethnicity, but it specifically forbids cornrows, braids, twists, and dreadlocks (Byrd & Tharps, 2014). Since these hairstyles are most likely to be worn by African Americans, the *consequence* of the policy is that it systematically imposes appearance limitations on one racial group and not others and therefore may be institutionally discriminatory.

Consider also New York City's controversial "stop and frisk" policy, which gave police the power to stop and detain someone based on "reasonable suspicion" of involvement in criminal activity. Although the policy was motivated by the need to keep the streets safe and not specifically defined in racial terms, many civil rights groups alleged that it was applied overwhelmingly to young black and Latino men (Harris-Perry, 2012). Between 2004 and 2012, 83% of those stopped and interrogated were black or Latino/a (Bergner, 2014). In 2013, a federal judge ruled that these tactics violated the constitutional rights of people of color. Since then, street stops by New York City police officers have plummeted and the racial disparity has narrowed, though not entirely (A. Baker, 2017).

Institutional racism exists in many corners of civilian life as well. Home delivery businesses, such as pizza parlors, sometimes refuse to deliver to certain neighborhoods. Several years ago, Domino's Pizza was criticized in the media when it was revealed that the company distributed software to its outlets to let them mark addresses on computers as green (deliver), yellow (curbside only), or red (no delivery). The company defended such policies as a rational response to the threat of sending easy-to-spot, cash-carrying delivery personnel into unsafe areas ("Pizza Must Go Through," 1996).

Consider one well-established practice for granting home mortgage or home improvement loans. Many banks use zip codes to mark off the neighborhoods they consider high risk—that is, where property values are low and liable to drop even further. These practices—known as *redlining*—began over 80 years ago as a Federal Housing Administration policy. They make it virtually impossible for individuals in such areas to borrow money to buy or improve a home. Unfortunately, these are precisely the areas where minorities, with lower-than-average incomes, are most likely to find an affordable home to purchase (Coates, 2014). So places where African Americans lived, and even places *near* where African Americans lived, were identified as neighborhoods that were too risky to issue mortgages (Rothstein, 2017). *Redlining* is not just a vestige of the past. In 2015, the Department of Housing and Urban Development entered into a settlement with Associated Bank after finding that the bank had systematically denied mortgage loans to underserved black and Latino/a communities in Chicago and Milwaukee (National Fair Housing Alliance, 2017). You can see that such policies give individual loan officers the ability to claim that they are not denying loans to people because of their race but are merely following their employers' policy. The resulting discrimination, however, is the same.

Sometimes institutional racism that may at first seem inconsequential can create lasting harm to a community. For instance, like many cities, Salinas, California, has a fixed amount of money in its budget for playground repairs. For years, the city spent all this money on renovating playgrounds in mostly white, middle-class neighborhoods. But the playgrounds that were in the worst shape and in most need of repair were in poor Latino neighborhoods. However they were never fixed. The imbalance of attention was not a result of purposeful bigotry. Instead, Salinas had a reactive policy whereby it repaired playgrounds only when residents in those communities complained to the city. In the poor, Latino communities, people either didn't have the time or didn't feel empowered to call and complain. So the equipment was allowed to deteriorate, further harming the neighborhood (T. Murphy, 2017).

Although practices like these might not be *intentionally* racist, their consequences are clearly discriminatory because the people who end up suffering as a result of the policies tend to be people of color. Institutional racism is difficult to address in such situations because there may not be an individual "bad guy" or identifiable bigot who is the source of the discrimination.

MICRO-MACRO CONNECTION
GIMME SHELTER—HOUSING SEGREGATION AND DISCRIMINATION

Fifty years ago, the Fair Housing Act was enacted, prohibiting housing discrimination based on race, color, religion, or national origin. There is some evidence that residential segregation based on race has dropped in recent years (Glaeser & Vigdor, 2012), and some argue that class segregation is now the more serious concern (Kahlenberg, 2017). However, segregation—especially when it comes to Whites—still exists (Crowder, Pais, & South, 2012). For instance, half of Blacks and 40% Latino/as live in neighborhoods with *no* white presence. In contrast, the average white person lives in a neighborhood that is 80% white (National Fair Housing Alliance, 2017).

Residential segregation is not just about people living near others of the same race. Research indicates that for members of ethnoracial minorities, it can be associated with a variety of problems, such as lower income, wealth, homeownership, school performance, and educational attainment; less access to healthy food; greater exposure to environmental hazards; and shorter life expectancy (National Fair Housing Alliance, 2017). In fact, among white and black families with similar incomes, white families are more likely to live in neighborhoods with better schools, more day-care options, nicer parks and playgrounds, and more transportation options (Reardon, Fox, & Townsend, 2015). Racially segregated neighborhoods are also the ones where daily humiliations are a way of life: trash is collected less frequently, streets remain unpaved, and water, power, and sewage services are less reliable (Rothstein, 2014).

The National Fair Housing Alliance (2017) conservatively estimates that there are approximately 4 million fair-housing violations every year in the rental market alone. Apart from incidents of landlords discriminating against people with disabilities, most of these cases involve ethnoracial minorities. On occasion, such housing discrimination is personal, the result of individuals' blatant "we don't want you people here" attitudes. According to one study, white residents prefer to live in communities where there are relatively few Blacks, regardless of their wealth. Consequently, white and black families of similar income levels tend to live in different worlds (Krysan, Couper, Farley, &

Forman, 2009). Nationwide, high-income black families are four times as likely as high-income white families to live in poor neighborhoods (Eligon & Gebeloff, 2016).

More commonly, though, it's institutional, politely and subtly driven by company policies (D. Pearce, 1979). Discriminatory policies include making fewer houses or rental units available to minorities, limiting their access to financial assistance, and steering them toward particular neighborhoods. Because these policies restrict opportunities for people of color, they are much more likely than white families to live in neighborhoods that have a shortage of important commercial, educational, and financial resources (National Fair Housing Alliance, 2017).

In 2001, African Americans, who represent about 13% of the population, received 5% of conventional home loans. By 2012, the figure had dropped to 2%. Latino/a borrowers, roughly 17% of the population, accounted for 8% of conventional loans in 2001, but only 4.5% in 2012 (National Fair Housing Alliance, 2015). To put it another way, 27% of Blacks and 19% of Latino/as applying for mortgage loans are denied, compared to 10% of Whites and Asian Americans. Consequently, the home ownership rate for black and Latino/a households (41% and 47%, respectively) are far lower than the rate for Whites (72%), a gap that has widened since 2004 (Desilver & Bialik, 2017).

When they *do* receive home loans, African Americans and Latino/as are significantly more likely than Whites to have to pay substantially higher "subprime" interest rates (Desilver & Bialik, 2017; Mui, 2012). Some argue that the discrepancy in rates is justified because borrowers who have poor credit histories are higher risks or because Blacks and Latino/as have fewer assets and therefore have less money for down payments than white borrowers (Blanton, 2007). But the discrepancy is even found between minority and white borrowers with similar credit scores (Bocian, Ernst, & Li, 2006). In 2012, the U.S. Justice Department reached a multimillion-dollar settlement with SunTrust and Bank of America over allegations that these institutions imposed loan fees—what some called a "racial surtax"—on black borrowers; white borrowers with similar credit histories and qualifications were not charged these fees (Mui, 2012).

Racial Inequality in the Economic System

Institutional racism is readily apparent throughout the U.S. economy. Consider participation in the labor force. With the exception of Asian Americans, workers of color have always been concentrated in lower-paying jobs (see Exhibit 11.3). African Americans make up 11.9% of the entire civilian U.S. workforce over the age of 16, but only 4.4% of lawyers, 7.5% of physicians, and 5.6% of architects and engineers. Similarly, Latino/as make up 16.7% of the labor force but are underrepresented in the fields of law (5.6%), medicine (5.9%), and architecture/engineering (8.8%; ProQuest Statistical Abstract, 2017). This underrepresentation becomes more acute in the higher echelons of certain professions. For instance, while 17% of attorneys in U.S. law firms are members of ethnoracial minorities, only 5% ever become partners in those firms (cited in Glater, 2006).

Because ethnoracial minorities are occupationally concentrated in low-paying jobs, they are particularly vulnerable to job insecurity, even in times of economic improvement. For instance, the rate of unemployment for Blacks and Latino/as is consistently higher than that of other groups. In the summer of 2017, the unemployment rate for Blacks was 7.5%, compared with 5.2% for Latino/as, 3.7% for Whites, and 3.6% for Asians (U.S. Bureau of Labor Statistics, 2017d).

Members of ethnoracial minorities can sometimes find their employment opportunities limited or blocked by the institutional practices and beliefs common in certain industries. Take, for instance, the restaurant business. Researchers in one study (Restaurant Opportunities Center of New York, 2009) hired white, black, Asian, and Latino/a people to act as job applicants for advertised server positions in 181 upscale New York City restaurants. The applicants were paired up—one white and one nonwhite—and matched for age, appearance, gender, and work experience. They were also trained to have similar mannerisms and answer questions in similar ways. So theoretically, the only thing distinctive about the two people in a pair was their race. Their arrival at restaurants was staggered so that they showed up about 30 minutes apart. This way the restaurant managers had no way of knowing the "applicants" were part of a study. Overall, white applicants were

EXHIBIT 11.3 ● The Most Common Occupations Among Several Ethnoracial Groups		
Blacks:	**Latino/as:**	**Asians:**
Home Health Aide	Drywall installer	Personal appearance worker
Barber	House painter	Software developer
Postal Service Mail Sorter	Roofer	Medical scientist
Bus Driver	Grounds maintenance worker	Computer hardware engineer
Telemarketer	Maid	Pharmacist
Licensed Vocational Nurse	Carpet installer	Gaming services worker
Chauffeur	Sewing machine operator	Tailor/dressmaker/sewer

Source: ProQuest Statistical Abstract, 2017, Table 639.

Note: There is no column for Whites in this exhibit because the U.S. Bureau of the Census does not provide data on the proportion of Whites in specific occupations.

significantly more likely than applicants of color to have their work experience accepted without probing, to be granted an interview, and to be offered a position. The researchers concluded that this differential treatment was not a result of "a few bad apples" with racist intent. Instead, they identified industry-wide trends and practices as the culprit. For instance, a pervasive "culture of informality" exists in the restaurant business. Although such informality creates a casual, "familylike" work environment, it also creates subjective recruitment and hiring practices that rely on word-of-mouth and friendship networks rather than the formal procedures and explicit hiring criteria that could protect against conscious and unconscious biases and stereotypes.

Racial Inequality in the Health Care System

As I pointed out at the beginning of this chapter, the economic and educational advances of ethnoracial minority groups over the past decade or so have been tempered by continuing disparities—and in some cases, worsening disparities—in health and health care. One researcher estimates that more than 83,000 people of color die each year due to disproportionate exposure to unhealthy living conditions, higher levels of discrimination-induced stress, implicit biases among health care providers, and inferior medical treatment (Matthew, 2015). People of color are also less likely than Whites to have access to health insurance. Though their numbers have gone down since the implementation of the Affordable Care Act, 12% of nonelderly Blacks and 17% of Latino/as lack health insurance. By comparison, less than 8% of nonelderly Whites are uninsured (Kaiser Family Foundation, 2016). As the president of the American Medical Association once put it, "When people don't have health insurance, they live sicker and they die younger" (quoted in D. Wilson, 2009a, p. 16).

Recently, public health officials have noted a spike in death rates among non-Hispanic Whites, a rise most attribute not to health care disparities but to an increase in cases of drug and alcohol poisoning (Case & Deaton, 2015), especially overdoses of opioid painkillers (cited in Kolata & Cohen, 2016). Nevertheless, ethnoracial differences in health outcomes are still glaring when it comes to the most serious diseases:

- A study of heart failure among 5,000 black and white men and women over a 20-year period found that Blacks had a rate 20 times higher than Whites (Bibbins-Domingo, 2009).

- In a 2009 study of over 19,000 people with cancer, African American patients with breast, prostate, or ovarian cancer had significantly lower survival rates than white patients (Albain, Unger, Crowley, Coltman, & Hershman, 2009). White women with breast cancer live, on average, 3 years longer than black women with breast cancer (Silber et al., 2013).

- Although rates of new HIV/AIDS cases have dropped among all groups over the past decade, they remain stubbornly high among some groups. African Americans constitute 41% of all people living with HIV/AIDS in the United States (ProQuest Statistical Abstract, 2017). According to data from the Centers for Disease Control and Prevention (cited in Villarosa, 2017), 1 in 2 African American gay and bisexual men will be infected with the HIV virus. By comparison, the risk is 1 in 11 for white gay and bisexual men. Furthermore, death rates from HIV/AIDS also vary widely between different ethnoracial groups (see Exhibit 11.4).

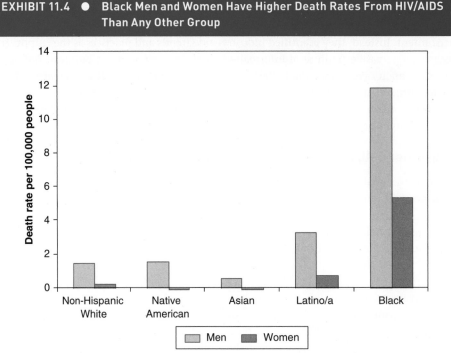

EXHIBIT 11.4 ● Black Men and Women Have Higher Death Rates From HIV/AIDS Than Any Other Group

Source: ProQuest Statistical Abstract, 2017, Table 135.

Sometimes personal racism is to blame for health outcomes. For instance, in one study, doctors described African American patients—no matter what their education and income levels—as less intelligent, less likely to follow medical advice, less likely to participate in rehabilitation, and more likely to abuse alcohol and drugs than white patients (Van Ryn & Burke, 2000). Another study found that doctors often stereotype Asian patients as compliant and "problem free" (cited in American Sociological Association, 2005). When time and medical resources are limited, such beliefs can drive the treatment decisions doctors make.

But we can't simply blame ruthless and bigoted individuals for all racial imbalances in the health care system. Instead, the financial considerations that drive the health care system create a context ripe for institutional racism. Consider racial differences in organ transplants. According to the Organ Procurement and Transplantation Network (2017), the 2017 national kidney transplant waiting list consisted of 36.5% Whites and 32.9% African Americans. (This figure in and of itself is telling: African Americans make up only about 13% of the population yet account for over one third of people in need of kidney transplants.) However, to date Whites have received 56.3% of all kidney transplants, while African Americans have received only 23.9%. Such a discrepancy is likely linked to hospitals' determination of a candidate's ability to pay before approving an expensive procedure. These policies are sometimes referred to as "green screens" or "wallet biopsies." For example, the total cost of a kidney transplant—including preoperative and postoperative care—is about $334,000. A liver transplant can run over $739,000, and a heart transplant costs over $1.2 million (Bentley, 2014). So it's not surprising that most hospitals would screen potential recipients for some kind of evidence up front that their insurance will cover the procedure. Because ethnoracial minorities are less likely than Whites to have medical insurance, they are less likely to receive a referral for transplant surgery (Stolberg, 1998). Financial concerns, not outright racial prejudice, lie at the heart of these policies.

Sometimes the institutional racism underlying threats to people's health is less obvious than ineffective and insufficient medical care. For instance, people in neighborhoods where hazardous waste treatment plants, toxic vacant lots, landfills, fracking test sites, and petrochemical plants or other sources of industrial pollution exist are disproportionately exposed to the unhealthful effects of air pollution, water pollution, and pesticides. The decisions on where to place such facilities are usually based not on the ethnoracial makeup of an area but on factors such as the cost of land, population density, and geological conditions. However, because the less desirable residential areas (and hence more desirable industrial areas) are disproportionately inhabited by poor people of color, these decisions have the effect of discriminating against them (Velázquez, 2002). For instance, Native American reservations, which have less stringent environmental regulations than other areas, have been targeted by the U.S. military for stockpiles of nuclear, chemical, and biological weapons and by private companies for solid waste landfills, hazardous waste incinerators, and nuclear waste storage facilities (G. Hooks & Smith, 2004). When it comes to the federal government cleaning up polluted areas, predominantly white communities see faster action, better results, and stiffer penalties for polluters than do communities where ethnoracial minorities predominate (Bullard, 2001).

All over the country—from sparsely populated rural states to major urban cities—members of ethnoracial minorities are exposed to more pollution than Whites. This difference in exposure may account for approximately 7,000 deaths a year from heart disease alone (L. P. Clark, Millet, & Marshall, 2014). The predominantly Latino/a neighborhoods south of Tucson are exposed to 20 times the acceptable levels of the carcinogenic solvent trichloroethylene, and rates of cancer, birth defects, and genetic mutations in those neighborhoods far outpace national averages (Velázquez, 2002).

Poor African American communities often have the worst conditions. A 100-mile, overwhelmingly African American stretch of towns between New Orleans and Baton Rouge, Louisiana, is known as "Cancer Alley" because it is the polluted home to over 150 petrochemical plants and 17 oil refineries (Flaherty, 2014). Overall, the greater the proportion of black residents in a community, the more likely it is that there will be industrial sources of air pollution within a two-mile radius of people's homes (Perlin, Sexton, & Wong, 1999). Indeed, Blacks are 79% more likely than Whites to live in areas where air pollution levels constitute serious health risks (cited in Little, 2007).

Perhaps the most well-known recent example of environmental danger is taking place in Flint, Michigan. In 2016, the city became engulfed in crisis after it was revealed that officials failed to publicly acknowledge that the water supply had been contaminated with lead and had poisoned local children. Lead poisoning is associated with a variety of illnesses, developmental delays, and behavioral problems (Doleac, 2017). Both Michigan and the federal government declared a state of emergency. A year later, Flint's residents still couldn't drink the water without a filter. Most families continued to rely on bottled water for everything from brushing their teeth to cooking and bathing (Sanborn, 2017). Residents suffered from heightened levels of stress, depression, and trauma, too (Goodnough & Atkinson, 2016). Flint's population is 57% black, and nearly 40% of the citizens live below the poverty line. In 2017, a government-appointed civil rights commission issued a report blaming the crisis on "historical, structural, and systematic racism" (Almasy & Ly, 2017, p. 1). The conclusion the report drew was hard to ignore: Had this been a white, middle-class city, the crisis would have been addressed much sooner and the consequences much less devastating.

MICRO-MACRO CONNECTION
RACIAL GUINEA PIGS AND MEDICAL MISTRUST

Racist ideologies and institutional discrimination in the field of medicine understandably lead to mistrust of the system among some groups. For instance, African Americans were once routinely used as subjects, frequently without their consent, for new medical treatments, experimental procedures, and medical demonstrations (Washington, 2006). During World War II, the U.S. government used Black soldiers as experimental subjects to examine the effects of mustard gas and other chemical agents on American troops. They wanted to see if the effects were different on black skin. They also used Japanese Americans, who served as proxies for the enemy. White soldiers were used too, but they served as scientific control groups. Experimenters used their reactions to establish what was "normal," and then compared them to the minority soldiers. All of the experiments were done in secret and weren't recorded on the subjects' official military records so there is no proof of what they went through. They received no follow-up health care at all. And they were sworn to secrecy about the tests and were threatened with dishonorable discharge and military prison time if they told anyone. So they were not able to receive adequate medical treatment for their injuries, because they couldn't tell doctors what had been done to them (Dickerson, 2015).

The most infamous case was the Tuskegee syphilis study. In 1932, the U.S. Public Health Service initiated a study in Tuskegee, Alabama, to determine the natural course of untreated syphilis in black men. In exchange for their participation, the 400 men—all poor and most illiterate—received free meals, free medical exams, and burial insurance. The men were never told they had syphilis. Instead, they were told that they had "bad blood" and would receive treatment. In reality, they received no treatment. When penicillin became available in the early 1950s—the most effective treatment for syphilis—the men were not treated.

In fact, the Public Health Service actively sought to prevent treatment. Even as the men began to die or to go blind or insane, penicillin was withheld. As soon as the experiment was publicized in 1972, it was stopped. Since then, the federal government has paid out more than $9 million in damages to victims and their families and heirs.

The Tuskegee study was driven not by the outright prejudice of individual medical researchers but by scientific rationale and the dominant, taken-for-granted medical "facts" of the time. Prevailing medical opinion in the 1930s was that Blacks were born with strong sexual appetites and a lack of morality, which made them particularly susceptible to sexually transmitted diseases. This belief, coupled with the equally dominant belief that Blacks wouldn't seek treatment even if it were available, led the researchers to conclude that this segment of the population would provide the best subjects for their study.

Such cases of medical maltreatment in the name of research are not merely vestiges of the past. For instance, a few years ago, the Kennedy Krieger Institute in Baltimore was accused of intentionally exposing black children—some as young as a year old—to high levels of dangerous lead dust in their homes as part of a study exploring the hazards of lead paint. The Institute, which provided no medical treatment for lead poisoning, had assured families that the homes were "lead safe" (T. C. Williams, 2011).

Recently, researchers at the University of Maryland have been trying to examine a new approach to treating trauma victims in inner-city emergency rooms called Emergency Preservation and Resuscitation (EPR). Most people who sustain traumatic injuries (from accidents, stab wounds, or gunshots) die from the blood loss and not from the direct destruction of a vital organ. In other words, with enough time the injuries are fixable. This new procedure involves rapidly cooling the patient's temperature to 50 degrees in hopes that "freezing" the body would preserve the heart, brain, and other organs just long enough to give emergency room doctors a little more time to sew up the holes and stop the blood loss (Twilley, 2016). They would then warm and revive the patient before everything shuts down.

The problem in researching such a new technique is that it is impossible to secure consent from the patients since they are always near or clinically dead. And notifying next-of-kin for consent would take too long. So researchers have turned to a controversial process known as "community consultation" in which they try to get broad community support, instead of permission from individuals. Through community meetings, shopping mall information tables, church events, and other gatherings, researchers ask healthy residents in the community if they would be open to the treatment. People who do not want to participate can opt out by wearing a special bracelet *at all times* that says "NO TO EPR-CAT" (CAT stands for "cardiac arrest from trauma"). If they end up in an emergency room with a traumatic injury, people *not* wearing the bracelet could be treated with EPR. In this low-income community where most trauma cases are gunshot victims and 90% of those victims are black men, it is virtually certain that patients subjected to this experimental procedure would be black. Some black residents, already mistrusting medicine, have shown reluctance to make themselves eligible for EPR because they fear similarities to past cases of medical exploitation (like Tuskegee). According to one medical ethicist, such fears are not unwarranted. As she put it, the community consent approach robs individuals of "an already marginalized group of the ability to say yes or no to a study that might harm them" (quoted in Twilley, 2016, p. 44).

The pervasive distrust of the health care system that many people of color have today can put them at even greater disadvantage. For example, disproportionate numbers of African Americans—as well as Latino/as and Native Americans—avoid participating in medical research (cited in Alvidrez & Areán, 2002), especially in clinical trials involving new and potentially effective treatments for life-threatening illnesses. One study found that 92% of patients involved in trials for a promising new class of drugs to treat lung cancer were white, though they make up only 77% of the population (Borghaei et al., 2015). Such mistrust of the medical field has been cited as one of the reasons African Americans have been slow to come for HIV testing and medical care (Dervarics, 2004), are less likely than Whites to donate organs (Srikameswaran, 2002), and are less likely than Whites to agree to surgery for early stages of cancer (Bach, Cramer, Warren, & Begg, 1999).

Racial Inequality in the Educational System

In 1954, the U.S. Supreme Court ruled in *Brown v. Board of Education of Topeka* that racially segregated schools were unconstitutional because they were inherently unequal. School districts around the country were placed under court order to desegregate. But within the past decade, courts have lifted desegregation orders in at least three dozen school districts around the country. In 2007, the Supreme Court reversed itself and ruled that public school systems could not try to achieve or maintain integration through actions that take explicit account of students' race. At the time of the ruling, such programs were in place in hundreds of school districts around the country (L. Greenhouse, 2007). Some districts have resorted to using integration plans based on children's socioeconomic disadvantage, rather than race, to skirt these restrictions (Bazelon, 2008).

You might assume that the court took this action because desegregation plans based on students' race were no longer needed. However, African American and Latino/a students are actually more isolated from white students today than they were just 15 years ago (Government Accountability Office, 2016). The proportion of all U.S. schools that are more than 90% black or Latino/a has more than tripled since 1988, from 5.7% to 18.6% (Orfield, Ee, Frankenberg, & Siegel-Hawley, 2016). The average black and Latino/a student attends a school in which at least 70% of the students are not white. In contrast, the average white student attends a school in which nearly three quarters of the students are white (Orfield & Frankenberg, 2014).

And it's not just students who are segregated. According to government estimates, 82% of public school teachers and 88% of private school teachers nationwide are white (National Center for Education Statistics, 2013b). In general, white teachers have very little experience with racial diversity. They are likely to teach in schools where almost 90% of their faculty colleagues and over 70% of the students are also white (Frankenberg, 2006).

Schools where the majority of students are not white are likely to be schools where poverty is concentrated. Sixty-one percent of all high-poverty schools (defined as schools where 75% to 100% of students qualify for free or reduced-price lunches) have a predominantly black or Latino/a student body (Government Accountability Office, 2016). Looked at another way, the average black and Latino/a student attends a school where 68% of the students are poor. In contrast, the average white or Asian student attends a school where less than 40% of the students are poor (Orfield, Ee, Frankenberg, & Siegel-Hawley, 2016).

The racial mix of the classroom has important implications for the quality of the education students receive. School segregation has long been associated with lower academic performance and lack of preparation for the interracial world that awaits students of color after graduation (Kleinfield, 2012). Schools in poor communities lack the financial and therefore educational resources that schools in more affluent communities have (see Chapter 10). For instance, poor school districts are less likely than wealthier districts to offer Advanced Placement (AP) programs. And because poor schools tend to be in minority communities, fewer students of color have access to AP courses. So while African Americans make up 14.5% of high school graduates, they constitute only 9% of those taking AP exams and 4.6% of those with passing scores (College Board, 2014). Furthermore, poor, predominantly minority, schools hire fewer teachers with credentials in the subjects they're teaching and have more unstable enrollments, higher dropout rates, and more students with untreated health problems. Despite attempts to rectify the problem, black and Latino/a students still lag behind white and Asian students at all levels of the educational system (see Exhibits 15A, 15B, and 15C).

Lack of money isn't the only thing that impedes academic performance among certain ethnoracial groups. Common institutional assumptions and practices within the educational system can also lead to unequal outcomes. For instance, nationwide, black students are significantly more likely than other students to be subjected to disciplinary practices in school. According to 2012 data from the U.S. Department of Education, black students made up 18% of those enrolled in the schools that were studied, yet they accounted for 35% of one-time suspensions, 46% of multiple suspensions, and 39% of expulsions. The disparity is especially pronounced for black girls who tend to be punished more harshly than their white peers for the same behaviors. For instance, they are more likely to be disciplined for loitering, disobedience, disruptive behavior, and fighting. In addition, they

EXHIBIT 11.5A ● Race and Ethnicity Affect Reading and Math Scores

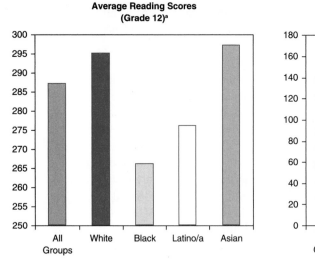

Average Reading Scores
(Grade 12)[a]

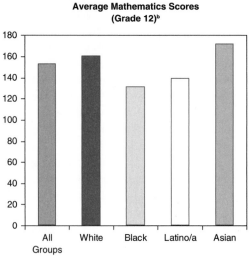

Average Mathematics Scores
(Grade 12)[b]

Source: National Center for Education Statistics, 2017a, Tables 221.10 & 222.10

a. Scale ranges from 0 to 500

b. Scale ranges from 0 to 300

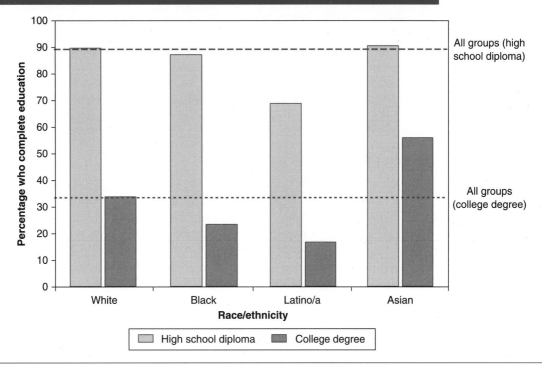

EXHIBIT 11.5B ● **Race and Ethnicity Can Determine the Likelihood of High School and College Graduation**

Source: ProQuest Statistical Abstract, 2017, Table 252.

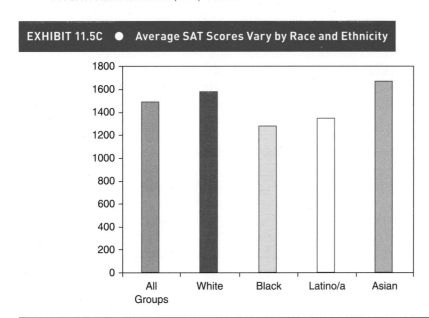

EXHIBIT 11.5C ● **Average SAT Scores Vary by Race and Ethnicity**

Source: National Center for Fair and Open Testing, 2016

are far more likely to be suspended or referred to law enforcement by school officials. One reason for this discrepancy is the way adults perceive black girls. A recent study found that adults tend to view black girls between ages 5 and 14 as less innocent than white girls of the same age. They are believed to need less protection and support and are considered more knowledgeable about sex and other adult topics. The researchers refer to this phenomenon as the "adultification" of black girls (R. Epstein, Blake, and González, 2017). This perception likely contributes to the harsher punishment of black girls by educators and other school resource officers.

Such treatment has long-term consequences. Because of the growing popularity of get-tough, zero tolerance policies, students who are disciplined in school are increasingly likely to wind up in the criminal justice system. Here, too, race plays a role. Nationwide, 70% of students who are arrested for misdemeanor offenses at school or referred to the courts are black or Latino/a (cited in L. Alvarez, 2013).

Remedies for Institutional Racism

If tomorrow all people in the United States were to wake up harboring absolutely no hatred, prejudice, or animosity toward other groups, institutional racism would still exist. It is part of the structure of society. Thus, it requires a structural solution.

You have already seen how the educational system and the legal system are undertaking limited measures to overcome certain types of institutional racism. However, the most far-reaching structural solution to the problem of institutional racism has been **affirmative action**. Affirmative action is a governmental policy, developed in the early 1960s, that requires organizations to draft a written plan on how they will seek out members of minority groups and women for educational or occupational positions from which they had previously been excluded. One assumption is that past discrimination has left certain people ill equipped to compete with others as equals today. Another assumption is that organizations will not change discriminatory policies unless they are forced to do so.

Contrary to popular belief, employers and university admissions officers are not compelled to institute hiring or admissions quotas or to compromise standards to meet affirmative action goals. They are simply required to gather all relevant information on all applicants, to interview qualified minority candidates, and to make sure underrepresented groups have access to needed information. For instance, companies doing business with the government can set numerical hiring goals based on the availability of qualified candidates in the particular field. However, affirmative action guidelines specify that such goals cannot be quotas:

> Numerical goals do not create set-asides for specific groups, nor are they designed to achieve proportional representation or equal results. Rather, the goal-setting process in affirmative action planning is used to target and measure the effectiveness of affirmative action efforts to eradicate and prevent discrimination. . . . The regulations . . . specifically prohibit quota and preferential hiring and promotions under the guise of affirmative action numerical goals. In other words, discrimination in the selection decision is prohibited. (United States Department of Labor, 2011, p. 1)

For close to half a century, affirmative action policies have been successful in helping members of ethnoracial minorities get ahead (Katel, 2008). Businesses, unions, universities, and local governments accused of discrimination in hiring or admissions have been sued under the 1964 Civil Rights Act. In part because of such actions, more than 40% of U.S. colleges and universities reported enrollment gains among African Americans and Latino/as during the mid-1990s (cited in Worsnop, 1996). People of color now hold a greater percentage of management, white-collar, and upper-level blue-collar jobs than ever before. Even young black men—historically the most economically disadvantaged and alienated group in the United States—have made some employment gains (Nasar & Mitchell, 1999). Wages and salaries, relative to those of Whites, have also improved somewhat (although, as we've seen, they still lag behind).

Despite its successes, affirmative action remains highly controversial. In one national survey, for example, 93% of respondents agreed that society has an obligation to help hardworking people overcome disadvantages so they can succeed in life. However, when asked whether a fictitious low-income college applicant who happens to be black should be given preference over a high-income student who happens to be white, only 36% agreed (Carnevale & Rose, 2003).

Opposition to affirmative action comes from all directions. Some politically liberal critics, for example, argue that the lives of people for whom affirmative action policies were originally designed—the poorest and most disadvantaged—remain largely unchanged. Although the percentages of Blacks and Whites earning midrange incomes are roughly the same now, there continues to be a large discrepancy at the top and bottom income levels (ProQuest Statistical Abstract, 2017). And while it's true that U.S. colleges in general are accepting more students of color today than ever before, the nation's top schools are not. Black and Latino/a students are actually more underrepresented at these colleges than they were 35 years ago (Ashkenas, Park, & Pearce, 2017). Furthermore, the students of color who are admitted tend to come from middle- or upper-class backgrounds. For example, of the 8% of Harvard's undergraduates who are black, only a handful are from poor families in which all four grandparents were born in this country and are descendents of slaves (Rimer & Arenson, 2004). In addition, many schools don't provide enough support to ensure that students from historically disadvantaged groups actually graduate. The 6-year graduation rate for Latino/a students is around 50%; for Native Americans and African Americans, it's below 40%. By comparison, 62.1% of white students and 70% of Asian students graduate within 6 years (National Center for Education Statistics, 2014a). Because a college degree is associated with success later in life (bachelor's degree holders earn about twice as much a year as those with high school diplomas), such educational disappointment can have far-reaching social and personal effects.

Conservative critics argue that preferential treatment of any group, even one whose rights have been historically unrecognized, is demeaning to the people it's supposed to help and unfair to everyone else, amounting to a form of "reverse" discrimination. According to one study, such an assessment reflects an attitude held by many Whites that racism is a "zero-sum game," meaning that any *decrease* in bias against members of ethnoracial minorities will be associated with an *increase* in perceived bias against Whites (Norton & Sommers, 2011).

Some go further, arguing that affirmative action isn't needed because discrimination is already illegal and nothing more is required. And others maintain that it's not working because the problems that disadvantaged people face have more to do with economics or with inherent character flaws than with race (Fish, 2000). After five decades of such criticisms, many people have come to believe that affirmative action in all its forms should be abolished.

Over the past decade, several states have passed laws banning race-based affirmative action policies in college admissions. In 2008, a white student who was not admitted to the University of Texas sued the state, charging that the university's affirmative action policy unfairly discriminated against her because she was white. The case went all the way to the U.S. Supreme Court, which ruled in 2016 that affirmative action was *not* unconstitutional thereby allowing colleges and universities to consider an applicant's race in their admissions decisions (Hurley, 2016).

Ironically, other modes of preferential treatment continue to operate with virtually no criticism or challenge. For instance, applicants who are most likely to receive favored treatment when it comes to college admissions are white, affluent "legacies," or children of alumni. Playing favorites with alumni children is a common practice at almost every private college and many public institutions as well. At some highly selective universities, like Harvard and Princeton, legacies are five times as likely to be accepted as unconnected applicants with similar or better credentials (cited in Mandery, 2014). Some schools reserve a certain number of spaces for legacies. In one recent year at Harvard, marginally qualified white legacies outnumbered all African American, Mexican American, Puerto Rican, and Native American students combined.

Clearly, affirmative action remains a divisive issue. In a society with a tradition of racial stratification, what is the best way to overcome institutional inequality? Does it take discriminating in the opposite direction to "make things equal," or is it enough simply to treat people equally from this point on?

Here's one way to think about these questions: Imagine a fictitious championship game of a basketball tournament between University A and University B. The rules of the game clearly favor University A. Its team is allowed five players on the court, but Team B is allowed only four. Team A gets 4 points for every basket made; Team B gets 2. Team A is given 2 points for each free throw made; Team B gets 1. Team A is allowed to physically impede the progress of the opposing players without being called for a foul, and so on. At halftime, Team A leads Team B by a score of 70 to 15. During halftime, tournament officials decide that the current rules have made the game completely unfair and have harmed the interests of Team B. They declare that from now on, each team will have the same number of players on the court and receive the same number of points per basket. But there's a slight problem—when the game resumes after halftime, the score is still 70 to 15!

In other words, just because opportunities have been equalized in the present doesn't mean that the accumulated disadvantages of the past have been entirely overcome (Shapiro, 2008). Such is the problem we face today. We can legislate hiring and admission policies that do away with unfair advantages to any group, but is that action enough to address a long history of exclusion? For a long time to come, members of certain groups will continue to be underrepresented in traditionally white positions. Can U.S. citizens achieve complete equality without forcing those who have benefited historically to give up some of their advantages? The answer to this question is complex, controversial, and emotionally charged and will have a great impact on the nature of ethnoracial relations in the United States in the foreseeable future.

Global Perspectives on Racism

Given the focus of this chapter so far, you might be tempted to conclude that racism and racial inequality are purely U.S. phenomena. Certainly, these problems are very obvious in a society such as the United States, which is so ethnically and racially diverse and which has had such a long history of bitter conflict. But ethnoracial tension is the worldwide rule, not the exception. In fact, in 2016, the United Nations General Assembly (2016) issued a statement expressing concern that racism and xenophobia (intense fear of people from other countries) were growing worldwide.

Like disadvantaged ethnoracial groups in the United States, minority groups in other countries suffer discrimination that limits their opportunities for success:

- During soccer matches all across Europe, black players are routinely subjected to racist taunts, derisive chanting, monkey noises, and hurled bananas from white fans (Garsd, 2015).

- Several countries in Europe, including Belgium, France, and Austria, ban Muslim women from wearing facial veils in public; others, like the United Kingdom and Germany, are considering such bans (Weaver, 2017). The European Union now allows private employers to ban Muslim women from wearing head scarves at work (Bilefsky, 2017).

- In Eastern European countries such as Slovakia, Romania, Hungary, and the Czech Republic, discrimination against the Roma—or Gypsies—is the norm. They have been despised for centuries as thieving subhumans with no respect for the law and are stereotyped as loud, dirty, indecent, and sloppy (Erlanger, 2000). As a result of such attitudes, Roma suffer disproportionately from poverty, interethnic violence, discrimination, illiteracy, and disease (N. Wood, 2005). Such treatment is not confined to countries where Romas have long resided. In 2010, France embarked on a major push to reduce crime and illegal immigration by forcibly expelling some Romas and demolishing the camps they live in, even though such mass expulsion based on ethnicity violates European Union law (Erlanger, 2010; Sayre, 2012). Two-thirds of Roma children in France do not attend school regularly, due in part to bureaucratic obstacles designed to keep them out, such as the required provision of multiple identity documents before being allowed to enroll (de Bourmont, 2017).

- In Mexico, all citizens are considered legally equal under the country's constitution. Yet it is a society deeply divided along racial lines, particularly between dark-skinned people of Indian descent and light-skinned people of Spanish descent. Ironically, most Mexicans are of mixed lineage, so that nearly all of them could be considered at least part Indian. But Mexicans who are considered Indians are the object of severe discrimination. They have significantly lower educational attainment and occupational status than lighter-skinned Mexicans. In addition, they are more likely to live in poverty (Villarreal, 2010).

Sociologists once believed that the global forces of industrialization and modernization would create ethnoracially diverse societies where people's loyalty would be directed to the national society rather than their racial or ethnic community (Deutsch, 1966). But the opposite has happened. At a time when people from every corner of the globe are linked technologically, economically, and ecologically and when mass migrations mix people from different races, religions, and cultures in unprecedented numbers, racial and ethnic hostilities are at an all-time high (Barber, 1992).

It's tempting to view ethnic conflict as the pent-up expression of age-old ethnic loyalties and cultural differences. However, in many areas of the world, the origins of conflict can be traced to the lingering effects of colonialism and the manipulation of political leaders. Consider, for instance, the ethnic violence that occurred between Hutus and Tutsis in Rwanda in the mid-1990s. The way the conflict was presented in the media led many outside observers to assume that these two groups had some deep-seated, centuries-old ethnic hatred of one another that had reached its boiling point. It turns out, though, that prior to German colonization in the 19th century and Belgian colonization in the early 20th century, Rwandans didn't consider themselves Hutu or Tutsi. They saw themselves as one group. People drew their identity from where they were born or by how much wealth they had (J. R. Bowen, 1996). It was the colonizers who decreed that each person had to have an "ethnic identity" that determined their place in society. By pitting one group against another, colonial rulers, whose numbers were always quite small, could seek out allies among certain ethnic groups. Belgian rulers formed such an alliance with the Tutsis. Their suppression of the Hutus created a sense of collective Hutu identity and outrage. In the 1950s, Hutus successfully rebelled against Tutsis. Eventually, Tutsi resentment led to the creation of their own rebel army. The conflict reached its bloody conclusion in the civil war of 1994, in which hundreds of thousands of Tutsis and moderate Hutus were killed.

Regardless of its source, so much ethnic conflict is going on in the world today that we might conclude that hostility between groups is among the most universal of human feelings (Schlesinger, 1992). Look at any online news service these days and you'll see stories of ethnic, religious, or racial conflict: Jews and Palestinians in Israel and Gaza, Buddhists and Muslims in Myanmar, Chechens and Russians in the former Soviet Union, Janjaweed and Darfurians or Sudanese and Nubans in Sudan, Hindus and Muslims or Bengalis and Gurkhas in India, the Han and Uighurs in western China, Lendus and Hemas in the Democratic Republic of the Congo, Georgians and Ossetians in Georgia, Sunis and Shiites in Iraq and Syria, Orma and Pokomo in Kenya, Tajiks and Pashtuns in Afghanistan, the Kyrgyz and Uzbeks in Kyrgyzstan, and the Ijaw and Itsekiri in Nigeria. According to the United Nations High Commissioner on Refugees (2015), nearly 60 million people around the world have been forcibly displaced because of ethnic conflict and/or persecution in their home countries.

Unfortunately, when people feel that their survival is threatened, they often blame others for their problems, particularly newly arrived others who look and act differently. In Great Britain, France, and Germany, loud and sometimes violent resentment occurs between the native born and immigrants from Africa, Eastern Europe, and the Middle East. In the United States, such animosity is likely to be directed toward immigrants from Latin America and Asia (see Chapter 13 for more details).

But global forces don't just increase ethnoracial tension and inequality; sometimes they help to resolve it. In South Africa, for example, the end of apartheid in the early 1990s was the result of an international boycott. In the 1980s, the global media brought the world pictures and stories of the brutal treatment of South African Blacks. When consumers in the United States and other industrial nations stopped buying products from companies that held investments in South Africa, the companies began to withdraw their money. The minority white government felt the sting as domestic economic problems mounted. As a result of these pressures, the white population of South Africa voted to abolish apartheid. Shortly thereafter, the first black president, Nelson Mandela, was elected. In 1996, a new constitution was adopted that officially and peacefully completed South Africa's transition from white supremacy to nonracial democracy. The document renounces the racism of the past and guarantees all South Africans broad freedoms of speech, movement, and political activity (Daley, 1996). Although serious inequalities and animosities remain, the country is well on its way toward unity and stability.

Conclusion

On April 16, 1963, the Reverend Martin Luther King Jr. was arrested and jailed for leading a civil rights demonstration in Birmingham, Alabama. At that time, not only were Blacks being subjected to daily doses of fear, violence, and humiliation, but they also had to constantly fight what Dr. King called "a degenerating sense of nobodiness." Torn between the brutal reality of a racist society and a fierce optimism for the future, he wrote from his jail cell,

Let us all hope that the dark clouds of racial prejudice will soon pass away and the deep fog of misunderstanding will be lifted from our fear-drenched communities and in some not too distant tomorrow the radiant stars of love and brotherhood will shine over our great nation with all of their scintillating beauty. (M. L., Jr. King, 1991, p. 158)

Over 50 years later, our society—like most societies around the globe—still struggles with the debilitating effects of personal and institutional discrimination based on race, religion, and ethnicity. In the United States, state-supported segregation and discrimination have given way to a form of racism that resides not in flagrant exclusion but in the day-to-day workings of our major social institutions. Despite recent gains, people of color still suffer noticeable disadvantages in economics, education, politics, employment, health care, vulnerability to crime, and many other areas. When opportunities to learn, legislate, and make a living are unequally distributed according to race, all facets of life remain unequal.

A half decade after racial segregation was ruled unconstitutional in the United States, the complete integration of fundamental social institutions such as public schools, government, and business has only partially been achieved. And some are questioning the very value of integration. One reason race relations are so problematic today is that public debate over the issue confuses personal racism and institutional racism. Different types of racism require different solutions. We cannot put an end to economic deprivation or massive residential segregation by trying to convince people not to stereotype other groups.

I realize that this chapter has been rather depressing. After reading it, you may have a hard time imagining a society without racial or ethnic stratification, one where skin color is about as relevant in determining people's life chances as eye color. As one columnist recently put it, race is "the issue that won't go away" (Krugman, 2015, p. A17).

We must remember, however, that differences do not have to imply inequality. The transformation from difference to disadvantage is a social construction. The people of every society decide which differences should be irrelevant and which should be the primary criteria for making social and legal distinctions between groups of people. The good news is that because we construct these differences, we can tear them down.

Your Turn

A curious and disturbing feature of prejudice is that many of our beliefs and attitudes about other racial or ethnic groups are formed without any direct contact with members of those groups. The media—most notably television—play a significant role in providing the public with oversimplified and often inaccurate ethnoracial information, which indirectly shapes public attitudes.

For one week, observe several prime-time television shows that feature prominent African American, Latino/a, Asian, or Middle Eastern characters. The shows can be either comedies or dramas. Note the number of characters on each show who are people of color. Pay particular attention to the way the characters are portrayed. For instance, are they college educated? Gainfully employed? Happily married? What is their apparent social class standing? How do their mannerisms, appearances, and speech patterns conform to common stereotypes associated with members of these groups? How frequently do their words or actions refer to their own race or ethnicity? Do the plots of the shows revolve around what you might consider "racial" themes? That is, how often does the issue of race or ethnicity come up during the course of the show?

(Continued)

(Continued)

If you have time, you can expand your analysis to examine the role of race and ethnicity in stand-up comedy. What proportion of comedians of color use race as part of their act compared with white comedians? What are the consequences of comedians such as Kevin Hart, Margaret Cho, George Lopez, Aziz Ansari, and Maz Jobrani playing on ethnoracial stereotypes in their acts?

Interpret your observations sociologically. What are the implicit messages communicated by the portrayal of ethnoracial minorities in American media? What role does humor play in reinforcing or fighting prejudice? Are characters who do not act in stereotypical ways conforming instead to a white, middle-class standard? If so, how will this portrayal ultimately affect public perceptions of race?

Chapter Highlights

- The history of race and ethnicity in U.S. society is an ambivalent one. Famous sayings about equality conflict with the experiences of most ethnoracial minorities—experiences of oppression, violence, and exploitation. Opportunities for life, liberty, and the pursuit of happiness have always been distributed along racial and ethnic lines.

- Personal racism is manifested in the form of bigotry, prejudice, and individual acts of discrimination. Quiet discrimination is expressed not directly but rather indirectly through anxiety about or avoidance of minorities.

- Racism can also be found in language and norms prescribing differential treatment of certain groups.

- Institutional racism exists in established institutional practices and customs that reflect, produce, and maintain ethnoracial inequality. Institutional racism is more difficult to detect than personal racism and hence is more difficult to stop. Because such racism exists at a level above personal attitudes, it will not disappear simply by reducing people's prejudices.

- Ethnoracial conflict is not just an American phenomenon. It is a global reality.

Key Terms

affirmative action: Program designed to seek out members of minority groups for positions from which they had previously been excluded, thereby seeking to overcome institutional racism

colorism: Skin color prejudice within an ethnoracial group, most notably between light-skinned and dark-skinned Blacks

discrimination: Unfair treatment of people based on some social characteristic, such as race, ethnicity, or sex

ethnicity: Sense of community derived from the cultural heritage shared by a category of people with common ancestry

implicit bias: prejudiced attitudes or beliefs that operate at a level below conscious awareness

institutional racism: Laws, customs, and practices that systematically reflect and produce racial and ethnic inequalities in a society, whether or not the individuals maintaining these laws, customs, and practices have racist intentions

panethnic labels: General terms applied to diverse subgroups that are assumed to have something in common

personal racism: Individual expression of racist attitudes or behaviors

prejudice: Rigidly held, unfavorable attitudes, beliefs, and feelings about members of a different group based on a social characteristic such as race, ethnicity, or gender

quiet discrimination: Form of discrimination expressed subtly and indirectly through feelings of discomfort, uneasiness, and fear, which motivate avoidance rather than blatant discrimination

race: Category of people labeled and treated as similar because of allegedly common biological traits, such as skin color, texture of hair, and shape of eyes

racial transparency: Tendency for the race of a society's majority to be so obvious, normative, and unremarkable that it becomes, for all intents and purposes, invisible

racism: Belief that humans are subdivided into distinct groups that are different in their social behavior and innate capacities and that can be ranked as superior or inferior

stereotype: Overgeneralized belief that a certain trait, behavior, or attitude characterizes all members of some identifiable group

SAGE edge™ edge.sagepub.com/newman12e

SAGE edge offers a robust online environment featuring an impressive array of free tools and resources for review, study, and further exploration, keeping both instructors and students on the cutting edge of teaching and learning.

12

The Architecture of Inequality
Sex and Gender

- Sexism at the Personal Level
- The Ideology of Sexism: Biology as Destiny
- Institutions and Gender Inequality
- The Global Devaluation of Women

At a women's convention held in Seneca Falls, New York, participants created a modified version of the Declaration of Independence. They called it the Declaration of Sentiments and Resolutions. Here are some excerpts from that document:

> We hold these truths to be self-evident: that all men and women are created equal. . . . The history of mankind is a history of repeated injuries . . . on the part of man toward woman, having in direct object the establishment of an absolute tyranny over her:

> He has compelled her to submit to laws, in the formation of which she had no voice.

> He has monopolized nearly all profitable [occupations], and from those she is permitted to follow, she receives but a scanty remuneration. He closes against her all the avenues to wealth and distinction which he considers most honorable to himself.

> He has endeavored, in every way that he could, to destroy her confidence in her own powers, to lessen her self-respect, and to make her willing to lead a dependent and abject life.

> In view of their social degradation and in view of the unjust laws above mentioned, and because women do feel themselves aggrieved, oppressed, and fraudulently deprived of the most sacred rights, we insist that they have immediate admission to all the rights and privileges which belong to them as citizens of the United States.

Who were the women who wrote this statement? Women's liberationists of the 1960s and 1970s? Radical feminists of the 1990s and 2000s? Neither. They were participants in the first convention in support of women's rights ever held in the United States—in 1848 (Declaration of Sentiments and Resolutions, 2001, pp. 449–450).

We tend to think that in the past, women were either content with their second-class status or unaware that it could be otherwise. As you can see from the preceding declaration, though, 170 years ago U.S. women were anything but passive, ignorant victims of discrimination.

Many people are also inclined to believe that the battle against gender inequality has been won. Beginning with the civil rights movement of the 1960s and the so-called sexual revolution of the 1970s, a process of liberation has given contemporary U.S. women opportunities that equal men's. After all, as many U.S. women as men work in the paid labor force, the majority of college students these days are women, and women play a more prominent role in business, politics, and entertainment. In 2017, there were 104 women serving in Congress (21 in the Senate and 83 in the House of Representatives), and six states had female governors. Perhaps you will be surprised to learn in this chapter, then, that women's struggle to overcome economic, legal, and social inequality is as relevant in the 21st century as it was in 1848.

In Chapter 5, I discussed the difference between sex and gender and how we learn to become boys and girls and men and women within the appropriate social and cultural contexts. Being placed in a gender category affects everything we do in life. But gender is more than just a source of personal identity that sets societal expectations; it is a location in the stratification system and a major criterion for the distribution of important resources in most societies.

In this chapter, I will address several important questions: What are sexism and gender discrimination? How are they expressed and felt at the personal level? How is inequality based on sex and gender supported by cultural beliefs and symbols? At the institutional level, how is inequality related to family and work roles? What are its legal and economic consequences? And finally, how pervasive is gender inequality around the world?

Sexism at the Personal Level

What do you think of when you hear the word *sexism*? The husband who won't let his wife work outside the home? The construction worker who whistles and shouts vulgar comments at female passersby? The presidential candidate who brags about grabbing women's genitals? Perhaps you think of the woman who consistently mocks men's interpersonal skills or their clumsy attempts at romance? Sexism is all those things, to be sure. But sociologically speaking, **sexism** refers to a system of beliefs that assert the inferiority of one sex and that justify discrimination based on gender—that is, on feminine or masculine roles and behaviors. At the personal level, sexism refers to attitudes and behaviors communicated in everyday interaction.

In male-dominated societies, or **patriarchies**, which exist in every quadrant of the globe, cultural beliefs and values typically give higher prestige and importance to men than to women. Throughout such societies, inequality affects girls and women in everything from the perceptions, ambitions, and social interactions of individuals to the organization of social institutions. Above all, gender inequality in a patriarchy provides men with privileged access to socially valued resources and furnishes them with the ability to influence the political, economic, and personal decisions of others. **Matriarchies**, societies that give preference to women, are rare in the contemporary world. Anthropologists have identified some small societies in China, Indonesia, Ghana, Costa Rica, and India where women hold all positions of authority (Garrison, 2012).

Even the most democratic societies tend to be male dominated to some degree, thereby influencing the types of gender beliefs people have. Research on U.S. gender stereotypes, for instance, has shown that they haven't changed all that much over the years (D. L. Berger & Williams, 1991; Eagly & Karau, 2002; Fine, 2010; C. L. Martin & Ruble, 2009; Rudman & Glick, 1999). Some researchers have shown that women are consistently perceived as more passive, emotional, easily influenced, and dependent than men (Broverman, Vogel, Broverman, Clarkson, & Rosenkrantz, 1972; Deaux & Kite, 1987; Tavris & Offir, 1984). Others have noted the myriad ways personal sexism is expressed in U.S. society, both overtly and subtly, through physical domination, condescending comments, sabotage, and exploitation (Benokraitis & Feagin, 1993). One study found that although some forms of personal sexism are motivated by hostility, others are motivated by benevolence, as when men assume women are helpless and thus feel compelled to offer assistance (Glick & Fiske, 1996). Such attitudes and behaviors not only place women in a lower-status position compared with men but also channel them into less advantageous social opportunities.

Men, of course, aren't the only ones who can be personally sexist. Certainly, some women dislike men, judge them on the basis of stereotypes, hold prejudiced attitudes toward them, objectify them sexually, consider them inferior, and even discriminate against them socially or professionally. We must keep in mind, though, that male sexism occupies a very different place in society from female sexism. The historical balance of power in patriarchal societies has allowed men as a group to subordinate women socially and sometimes legally to protect male interests and privileges. Because men still tend to hold most positions of power, their prejudice and discrimination have more cultural legitimacy, are more likely to be reflected in social institutions, and have more serious consequences than women's sexism.

Sexism and Social Interaction

Everyday social life is fraught with reminders of gender imbalances. Men and women interact with each other a lot, but rarely do these interactions occur between two people who are of equal status (Ridgeway & Smith-Lovin, 1999). The average woman is reminded frequently of her inferior position, through subtle—and sometimes not so subtle—ways. Men often have a hard time understanding women's reactions to uncomfortable personal encounters between the sexes, which might explain why men are less likely than women to believe that going out for a drink or having dinner with a coworker of a different sex is inappropriate (C. C. Miller, 2017d). So just as white people enjoy racial transparency (see Chapter 11), members of the dominant sex take for granted the social arrangements that serve their interests. For example, consider the following tongue-in-cheek quote from a female newspaper columnist:

> By whistling and yelling at attractive but insecure young men, we women may actually help them feel better about themselves, and give them new appreciation of their bodies. Some might say women were descending to the level of male street-corner oafs, but I'm willing to take that risk. If, with so little effort, I can bring joy to my fellow man, then I am willing to whistle at cute guys going down the street. (Viets, 1992, p. 5)

If you're a man, you may wonder why the columnist is bothering to make fun of "wolf whistles." The answer simply is that this behavior means different things when directed at men versus women. Unsolicited sexual attention may be an enjoyable, esteem-enhancing experience for men, but it doesn't have the weight of a long tradition of subordination attached to it, nor is it linked in any way to the threat of violence. One female distance runner, describing the inevitable lewd catcalls she gets from men when she runs, put it this way: "Men are in danger of, at worst, being laughed at by a woman. Women are in danger of being *killed* by men" (quoted in Sagal, 2015, p. 30).

More generally, men aren't subjected to **objectification**—that is, to being treated like objects rather than people—in the same way that women are. Sure, women gawk at and swoon over good-looking men from time to time (just watch old reruns of *Sex and the City* sometime). But men's entire worth is not solely determined by a quick and crude assessment of their physical appearance. For women, who must often fight to be taken seriously in their social, private, and professional lives, whistles and vulgar comments serve as a reminder that their social value continues to be based primarily on their looks. In 2016, the *Harvard Crimson*, the student newspaper at venerable Harvard University, revealed that for several years the men's soccer team had been keeping a "scouting report" in which they rated the school's female soccer players on a scale of 1 to 10 and provided descriptions of their physical traits and musings about their preferred sexual positions (Seelye & Bidgood, 2016).

Communication patterns also show the effects of unconscious personal sexism. Research in the symbolic interactionist tradition suggests that women and men converse in different ways (Parlee, 1989; Tannen, 1990). For instance, women are more likely than men to use a tag question at the end of a statement ("She's a good professor, *don't you think?*") and modifiers and hedges such as *sort of* and *kind of* (Lakoff, 1975). But such techniques may make the speaker sound less powerful and therefore challenge her credibility and qualifications. Imagine if your math professor always said things like, "The answer to the problem is $3x + y$, *isn't it?*" Or if your boss said, "We're going to pursue the Johnson account; *is that OK?*" As one columnist recently noted, the increasingly popular use of *kind of* and *sort of* makes for "wishy-washy . . . speech that lacks clarity, confidence, and authority" (Kurutz, 2014, p. 12).

●
THOMAS LINNEMAN

WHAT CAN "UPTALKING" TELL US ABOUT GENDER?

People ask questions both by the inclusion of certain words (what, when, who, where, how, why) and by a rising intonation at the end of a sentence, known as "uptalking." In the last several decades, uptalking has moved beyond simply signaling a question to become a common component of everyday communication, particularly among young people. Maybe you know someone who consistently (and annoyingly) expresses statements that sound like questions.

Researchers who study language generally agree that uptalking is more common among female speakers than male speakers. However, they disagree as to the meaning of such patterns. Some (e.g., Lakoff, 1975) argue that uptalking is an indicator of female submissiveness that signals uncertainty and lack of conviction in what one is saying. Others, however, argue that uptalking establishes common ground between speaker and listener or acts as a way to make sure listeners are keeping up with a particular story (see Linneman, 2012).

Sociologist Thomas Linneman (2012) decided to examine the relationship between gender and uptalking empirically. Like me, Linneman is a fan of the

(Continued)

(Continued)

TV game show, *Jeopardy!* The show's been on TV for decades, so you probably know the format: Six categories with five clues each appear on a board. The clues have different dollar values. Contestants select a category and dollar value (e.g., "20th Century Authors for $600") and the corresponding clue is revealed. The first person to ring in can provide a response. The twist is that the clues are "answers" and the contestant must provide his or her response in the form of a question. While watching the show one night, Linneman noticed that some contestants uptalked exclusively, others did so occasionally, and still others never uptalked, instead providing their responses with flat, statement-like intonation.

To see whether gender could explain these different uptalking tendencies, Linneman designed a content analysis study in which he coded the intonation of 5,473 responses provided by 300 contestants over the span of 100 episodes. He found that, indeed, uptalking signals uncertainty. When both male and female contestants gave an incorrect response (that is, when they were uncertain), they were significantly more likely to uptalk than when they gave a correct response.

But when gender was included in the analysis, some interesting patterns emerged. Women uptalked nearly twice as often as men. Furthermore, women were actually more likely to uptalk when they were winning on the show than when they were doing poorly. The opposite was the case for men. Linneman speculates that perhaps successful women use uptalking as a "compensatory strategy" to conform their gender performance to traditional expectations. Women who show their knowledge brashly are typically considered unfeminine and unlikeable. By the way, this phenomenon exists beyond TV game shows. In a different study, both male and female subjects rated female executives who voiced their opinions as significantly less competent than their more reserved peers; talkative male executives, though, were seen as more competent (Brescoll & Uhlmann, 2008).

On the other hand, men are much less likely to uptalk when competing against other men than when their opponents are women. Here, too, gender may play a role. Norms of masculine certainty are especially pronounced when men compete with other men. When competing against women, however, they raise their use of uptalking perhaps "as a chivalrous effort to 'protect' women contestants" (Linneman, 2012, p. 101).

Although this study focused on the artificial environment of a television game show, it does illustrate how gender imbalances can be reinforced not only by what we say but also by the way we say it.

The implicit, nonverbal messages of social interaction—body movements, facial expressions, mannerisms, posture—also have more serious implications and consequences for women than for men. For example, femininity is typically gauged by how little space women take up; masculinity is judged by men's expansiveness and the strength of their gestures. Women's bodily demeanor tends to be restrained and restricted (Henley, 1977). What is typically considered "ladylike"—crossed legs, folded arms—is also an expression of submission. Men's freedom of movement—feet on the desk, legs spread, straddling a chair—conveys power and dominance. Such interactional norms place women who are in authoritative positions in a no-win situation. If, on the one hand, they meet cultural definitions of femininity by being passive, polite, submissive, and vulnerable, they fail to meet the requirements of authority. If, on the other hand, they exercise their authority by being assertive, confident, dominant, and tough, their femininity may be called into question (J. L. Mills, 1985).

Nonverbal cues can also play an important role in providing people with information about their social worth. Thus, they sometimes serve to keep women "in their place." It is the rare female subway traveler in New York who hasn't been groped on a crowded train. Preparing for these unwanted encounters is as taken for granted as making sure you have the proper fare:

> Women know the drill. . . . Pull in your backside. . . . Wedge a large bag for protection between yourself and the nearest anonymous male rider. . . . Put on your fiercest face, and brace yourself for contact. (Hartocollis, 2006, p. B11)

The fact that men can more freely touch women than vice versa serves as a reminder that women's bodies are not considered entirely their own. In several countries—Japan, India, Egypt, Iran, Brazil, Indonesia, the Philippines, and Malaysia, to name a few—unwanted fondling has gotten so bad on crowded trains and subways that transportation companies have introduced "women only" cars to protect women. Mexico and Israel provide "women only" bus service.

U.S. women are also routinely exposed to assorted forms of sexual harassment—unwelcome leers, comments, requests for sexual favors, and unwanted physical contact—in a variety of institutional settings, from schools to workplaces. According to the American Association of University Women (2013), 56% of all girls in Grades 7 to 12 experience verbal, physical, or electronic sexual harassment in a given year and 87% say it had a negative effect on them. In addition, about 24% of teenage girls are bullied at school and another 7% report being cyber bullied (ProQuest Statistical Abstract, 2017). And nearly two thirds of female college students experience sexual harassment at some point during their college careers, though fewer than 10% tell a university official and an even smaller number file an official complaint (C. Hill & Silva, 2006).

The U.S. Equal Employment Opportunity Commission (2017a) resolved more than 7,400 cases of workplace sexual harassment in 2016 to the tune of over $40 million in compensation to victims. About 6,100 of these victims were women. But these figures obviously underestimate the problem since they don't include incidents that are never reported. According to a recent national poll, 80% of women said they'd experienced sexual harassment at work, down only slightly from the 92% who reported such experiences *40 years ago* (Mateo & Menza, 2017). The most common forms of harassment they reported were leering, sexual remarks/teasing, sexual pressure, and unwanted touching or pinching.

Some occupations are particularly vulnerable to sexual harassment and assault. For instance, sexual affronts from male guests are an everyday safety hazard for female hotel workers (S. Greenhouse, 2011). They are so common, in fact, that hotel managers routinely provide their housekeeping staff with a list of safety precautions, for example, to always carry a panic button (or Mace) in your pocket, always clean rooms in tandem with another housekeeper, and always prop the door open when cleaning a room (J. Bernstein & Ellison, 2011; McGeehan, 2012). But it's not just powerless women in lower paying jobs who are vulnerable to such harassment. Several dozen female entrepreneurs in the lucrative tech start-up industry report being subjected to sexually suggestive comments and sexual advances by wealthy potential investors (Benner, 2017). In 2017, a parade of well-known Hollywood actresses lined up to accuse the powerful studio executive, Harvey Weinstein, of various forms of sexual harassment. Similar accusations against famous male celebrities, wealthy businessmen, and powerful politicians quickly followed.

From a conflict perspective, cases of sexual harassment are expressions of and attempts to reinforce positions of dominance and power (Uggen & Blackstone, 2004). Indeed, the vast majority of harassment cases involve male assertions of power over women. But women aren't the only victims. Sometimes an overbearing, sexually aggressive female boss may harass a male subordinate; but more commonly, men are victimized when other men create a hostile environment through bullying, hazing, sexual insults, and other boorish behaviors. According to the U.S. Equal Employment Opportunity Commission (2017a), sexual harassment charges filed by men increased from 11.6% of all cases in 1997 to 16.6% of all cases in 2016.

Men can also be victimized in settings where you'd least expect it. The Pentagon estimates that close to 14,000 male service members experienced unwanted sexual contact in 2012, mostly by other men as a form of hazing or intimidation (Dao, 2013). As troubling as this figure is, however, women face a far less welcoming and more dangerous environment in the military.

MICRO-MACRO CONNECTION
FIGHTING TWO WARS: SEXUAL HARASSMENT IN THE MILITARY

The U.S. military has been almost exclusively male for most of its history, except for female medical, clerical, and logistics personnel. In 2013, the Pentagon lifted its ban on women serving in combat positions. But men still make up the vast majority of the armed forces and hold all the highest positions of authority. Even today, depending on the branch of service, women make up a small, albeit growing, percentage of our active military force. In 2016, more than 214,000 women were on active duty in the military and another 590,000 were in the reserves or National Guard (Statistic Brain, 2017). That represents a higher number of women in the armed services than at any other time in history (during the Vietnam War, for instance, women made up 2% of active-duty military) but still accounts for a little less than 15% of all U.S. military personnel.

Misconduct against women is pervasive in the entire military system. According to Department of Defense data, about 25% of female service members experienced severe and persistent sexual harassment in 2016 and another 4% were sexually assaulted (Protect Our Defenders, 2017). These figures represent a decrease compared to 2015. Nevertheless, female soldiers are still statistically more likely to be assaulted by a fellow soldier than killed in combat (Ellison, 2011). And such figures don't even include the countless number of female soldiers who regularly face degradation, hostility, and loneliness instead of the camaraderie every soldier depends on for comfort and survival. Many female military personnel end up waging what amounts to two wars—one against the enemy and one against their fellow soldiers (Benedict, 2009). In just 4% of cases are perpetrators convicted of a sex offense. Not surprisingly, the Department of Defense estimates that 81% of sexual assaults are never reported. One in four survivors of either sexual assault or sexual harassment end up leaving the military as a result (Protect Our Defenders, 2017).

The situation goes beyond individually violent soldiers. As far back as 2004, the Pentagon concluded that the root cause of the problem was a decade's worth of failure on the part of commanding officers to acknowledge its severity (cited in Shanker, 2004). Things got so bad that in 2005, the Department of Defense rewrote its rules so that female soldiers could report sexual assaults confidentially and gain access to counseling and medical services without setting off an official investigation. It now pursues complaints more aggressively and sponsors a Sexual Assault Prevention and Response website to provide "guidance and other information for victims of sexual assault, unit commanders, first responders, and others who deal with this sensitive issue."

However, the military chain of command and the way alleged victims are treated during investigative proceedings continues to deter them from filing formal charges. Nearly 60% of women who report a sexual assault face some sort of retaliation, and in three quarters of these cases the retaliation comes from someone in the victim's chain of command (Protect Our Defenders, 2017). Article 32 of the *Uniform Code of Military Justice* allows defense lawyers to ask aggressive questions of alleged victims that would not be allowed in civilian courts. For example, in 2013 a female Navy midshipman who accused three Naval Academy football players of rape was asked whether she wore a bra, how wide she opened her mouth during oral sex, and whether she'd apologized to another midshipman with whom she'd had sex for "being a ho" (Steinhauer, 2013). And under Article 60 of the code, the convening authority in a sexual assault case has the power to reduce or even dismiss sentences entirely regardless of a jury's decision. In many situations, this individual is the commanding officer of or works closely with the defendant (Draper, 2014).

More generally, politicians' attitudes toward military victims of sexual assault and harassment remain somewhat unsympathetic. During the 2016 presidential campaign, then-candidate Donald Trump attributed the high number of sexual assaults simply to the growing number of women in the military: "What did these geniuses expect when they put men and women together?" (quoted in Steinhauer & Rosenberg, 2016). A bill, which would have allowed victims to bypass the military chain of command and go straight to military prosecutors when reporting sexual assaults, was defeated in the Senate in 2016.

Sexual Orientation

Prejudices expressed at the personal level often combine gender and sexual orientation. For many decades, gays and lesbians have been rejected, ridiculed, and condemned on moral, religious, criminal, or even psychiatric grounds (see Chapter 8). Today, although the number of Americans who identify as LGBT has increased in recent years (A. Brown, 2017), they continue to experience heightened levels of discrimination, interpersonal rejection, or unfair treatment (see Exhibit 12.1). More people file complaints regarding mistreatment in public accommodations (hotels, motels, restaurants, theaters, etc.) due to sexual orientation or gender identity than due to race (Mallory & Sears, 2016).

Sometimes attitudes toward LGBT people are less obviously negative, but can have unforeseen consequences nonetheless. For instance, a recent study of both patients and health care providers found that nearly 80% of doctors and nurses believed that patients would be unwilling to disclose their sexual orientation if asked; however, only 10% of actual patients said they'd refuse to provide such information. Many clinicians believe that information about sexual orientation can be important in understanding a patient's needs and not asking for it risks making medical care less effective (Haider et al., 2017).

Often the attitudes are unabashedly virulent. According to the Federal Bureau of Investigation (2014), there were over 1,400 reported hate crime offenses based on sexual orientation in 2014. Several years ago, a gay college student in Wyoming, Matthew Shepard, was pistol-whipped, tied to a fence, and left to die. At his funeral, protestors from a church in Topeka, Kansas, held up signs reading, "God Hates Fags!" The church's website had a picture of Matthew depicted burning in hell. The same website had a similar photo of a lesbian who was mauled to death by two dogs a few years earlier. Above her picture, it read, "God used literal dogs to kill a figurative dog." More recently, nine attackers lured a 30-year-old gay man into a house, where they stripped him, tied him to a chair, burned his nipples and penis with a cigarette, whipped him with a chain, and sodomized him with a baseball bat while shouting antigay slurs at him (M. Wilson & Baker, 2010). In 2013, a man set fire to a gay nightclub in Seattle after telling a friend that "homosexuals should be exterminated" (M. Carter, 2014). In 2017, a Mississippi gang member who kidnapped and killed a 17-year-old transgender woman was sentenced to 49 years in prison, marking the

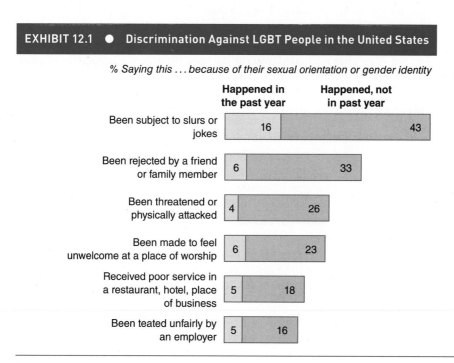

EXHIBIT 12.1   ●   Discrimination Against LGBT People in the United States

% Saying this . . . because of their sexual orientation or gender identity

	Happened in the past year	Happened, not in past year
Been subject to slurs or jokes	16	43
Been rejected by a friend or family member	6	33
Been threatened or physically attacked	4	26
Been made to feel unwelcome at a place of worship	6	23
Received poor service in a restaurant, hotel, place of business	5	18
Been teated unfairly by an employer	5	16

Source: Pew Research Center, 2013a.

first time hate crime sentencing guidelines were applied to a case involving a transgender victim (Federal Bureau of Investigation, 2017).

Gay, lesbian, bisexual, and transgender youth are particularly susceptible to bullying at school. One recent survey found that 82% of LGBT youth had been bullied because of their sexual orientation. Sixty-four percent felt unsafe at school as a result, and 32% indicated that they'd stayed out of school for at least 1 day because they felt unsafe (NoBullying.com, 2015). According to one researcher, gay, lesbian, and bisexual youth are about five times as likely as heterosexuals to attempt suicide (Hatzenbuehler, 2011). In 2010, a rash of suicides among harassed and bullied gay and transgender teenagers in New Jersey, California, Texas, and Indiana focused national attention on the problem. In one Minnesota school district alone, four gay and lesbian teenagers committed suicide in 2011 (Erdely, 2012).

Sexual Violence Against Women

The epitome of sexual discrimination expressed at the personal level is, of course, sexual violence. Forcible rape and other forms of sexual assault exist throughout the world, in the most democratic societies as well as in the most repressive.

In the United States, rape is the most frequently committed but least reported of all violent crimes. According to the Centers for Disease Control and Prevention, about 19.3% of American women have been raped in their lifetimes and another 27% have been subjected to some other form of unwanted sexual contact (Breiding, 2014). But less than a third of these crimes ever come to the attention of the police—compared with 62% of robberies and aggravated assaults; even victims of domestic violence are more likely to report the crime to the police (58%; Truman & Morgan, 2016). Among college students, one in four women experience rape or sexual assault during their college careers but only about 20% of these crimes are ever reported (Association of American Universities, 2015). According to the National Crime Victimization Survey—an annual assessment of crime victimization carried out by the U.S. Bureau of Justice Statistics—more than 431,000 women over the age of 12 said they'd been raped or sexually assaulted in 2015, about triple the 140,000 cases that were reported to the police that year. As you can see in Exhibit 12.2, while the incidence of rape and sexual assault has fluctuated over the past two decades, the percentage of cases that are reported to the police has remained consistently low.

Rape as a Means of Social Control

According to the conflict perspective, stratification along sex and gender lines has long distorted our understanding of rape. Throughout history, women have been viewed socially and legally as the property of men, as either daughters or wives. Thus, in the past, rape was defined as a crime against men or, more accurately, against men's property (Siegel, 2004). Any interest a husband took in another man sexually assaulting his wife probably reflected a concern with his own status, the loss of his male honor, and the devaluation of his sexual possession.

Even when women are not seen as men's property, their lives can be controlled by rape and sexual assault. According to an organization in India called the LGBT Collective, parents of lesbians will sometimes handpick a relative to rape their daughters in hopes it will "cure" them of their homosexuality (Jain, 2015). These violent acts are known as "corrective rapes." In South Africa, such rapes are so common that lesbians there are sexually assaulted twice as often as heterosexual women (Hunter-Gault, 2012). As one woman put it,

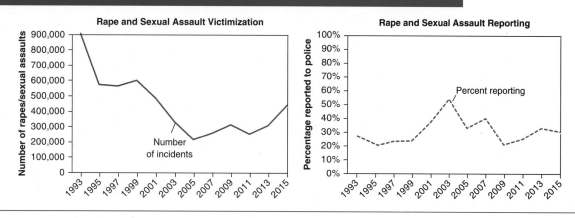

EXHIBIT 12.2 ● The Frequency of Rape and Sexual Assault Fluctuates Over Time; Reporting Does Not

Source: U.S. Bureau of Justice Statistics, 2017.

We get insults every day, beatings if we walk alone, you are constantly reminded that . . . you deserve to be raped, they yell, "if I rape you then you will go straight . . . you will buy skirts and start to cook because you will have learned how to be a real woman." (quoted in ActionAid, 2009, p. 15)

Around the world, rape is a time-tested wartime tactic of terror, revenge, and intimidation (Amnesty International, 2004; Enloe, 1993; Sengupta, 2004):

- In Syria and Iraq, thousands of Yazidi girls—some as young as 9—have been raped, tortured, and held as sex slaves by ISIS terrorists since 2014 (Raven, 2015).

- In Nigeria, hundreds of women and girls kidnapped by Boko Haram, a radical Islamist sect, were repeatedly raped as part of a deliberate strategy to dominate and intimidate rural residents (Nossiter, 2015).

- In Somalia, the militant group Al-Shabab routinely seizes and gang rapes women and girls as a way of supporting its reign of terror in the southern part of the country (Gettleman, 2011).

- In the Democratic Republic of the Congo, bands of soldiers waged "a war of rape and destruction against women" for decades (Herbert, 2009, p. A17). The United Nations estimates that 200,000 Congolese women and children have been raped during the long-simmering war there. In the eastern part of the country alone, as many as 50,000 babies, conceived through rape, have been born over the past two decades (A. Baker, 2016).

The devastation of these atrocities extends beyond the psychological humiliation, physical wounds, and deaths of individual victims. Entire families and neighborhoods are traumatized when husbands are forced to watch their wives being raped, parents their daughters, or children their mothers.

All forms of oppression employ the threat of violence to ensure compliance. The subordination of women in particular depends on the power of men to intimidate and punish them sexually. According to some feminist sociologists, men have used rape and the threat of rape throughout history to exert control over women (Brownmiller, 1975). The mere existence of rape limits women's freedom of social interaction, denies them the right of self-determination, and makes them dependent on and ultimately subordinate to men (Griffin, 1986).

The fear of rape goes beyond simply making life terrifying and uncomfortable for women. It also can restrict their economic opportunities. Women may avoid some neighborhoods with affordable housing because of potential danger. If a woman has a job that requires night work, she may be forced to buy a car to avoid walking at night or using public transportation. The threat of sexual assault restricts where and when she is able to work, thereby limiting her money-earning choices and perhaps keeping her financially dependent on others.

Women are also harmed by the larger cultural ideology surrounding rape. I think most of us are inclined to believe that men who rape must be pathologically violent individuals. Hence all one has to do to avoid being raped is to avoid strange/dangerous guys. However, rapists as a group have not been shown to be any more disturbed than nonrapists (Griffin, 1986; Warshaw, 1988). In fact, most rapists are quite "normal," even "likeable," by usual societal standards (Krakauer, 2015). The vast majority of rapes—about 80%—involve people the victim knows: friends, acquaintances, classmates, coworkers, or relatives (Planty, Langton, Krebs, Berzofsky, Smiley-McDonald, 2013) and only 11% involve weapons (Dobie, 2016). But when rape is generally perceived to be perpetrated by psychologically defective strangers, it doesn't implicate the dominant culture or established social arrangements. In other words, rape isn't considered the fault of society; it's the fault of flawed men who can't abide by society's rules. This assumption may explain why date or acquaintance rape, marital rape, and other forms of sexual violence that don't fit the typical image have, until quite recently, been ignored or trivialized.

We must therefore examine the crime of rape within a broader cultural context that encourages certain types of behavior between men and women (S. Jackson, 1995). When we do so, rape becomes less an act of deviance and more an act of overconformity to cultural expectations, less an act committed by abnormal individuals and more an act of "normal" men taking cultural messages about power and assertiveness to their violent extreme. As one author wrote over two decades ago, rape is the "all-American crime," involving precisely those characteristics traditionally regarded as desirable in American men: strength, power, domination, and control (Griffin, 1989).

Victim Blaming

Globally, cultural beliefs about gender, sexuality, and intimacy influence societal and legal responses to rape and rape victims (Faleiro, 2013; R. Morgan, 1996; A. J. Rubin, 2011):

- In Afghanistan, a married woman who is raped can be charged with adultery and imprisoned; a condition of release is that she marry the man who raped her. In Colombia, a man who rapes a woman—whether he knows her or not—can be absolved of all charges if he simply offers to marry her.

- In Senegal, single women who are rape victims may be killed by their families because as nonvirgins they can no longer command a high dowry; a married woman who's been raped may be killed by her "dishonored" husband.

- In Iran, because Islamic tradition forbids the execution of virgins, any woman condemned to die must first lose her virginity through rape.

- Many political leaders in India attribute that country's increasing incidence of rape to women's use of cell phones and their inclination to go out at night. Said one, "Just because India achieved freedom at midnight does not mean that women can venture out after dark" (quoted in Faleiro, 2013, p. A19).

Arguably, the United States has a more sympathetic reaction to rape victims. But the legal response here still tends to be consistent with men's interests, focusing on women's complicity, blameworthiness, or dishonesty. In rape cases, unlike any other crime, victims typically must prove *their* innocence rather than the state having to prove the guilt of the defendant. As one attorney put it, "If a person was mugged in an alley, would we be skeptical of the victim's testimony . . . because there weren't any eyewitnesses?" (quoted in Krakauer, 2015, p. 292). Typically, after an accuser files a report and submits to a physical examination, police officers will ask her if she wants them to launch an investigation. In many cities, if she doesn't explicitly agree, she is deemed uncooperative and the case is dropped (Pérez-Peña & Bogdanich, 2014).

The institutional fear of women making false allegations often seems to drive the manner in which such cases are handled: "For centuries, it has been asserted and assumed that women 'cry rape,' that a large proportion of rape allegations are maliciously concocted for purposes of revenge or other motives" (Lisak, Gardinier, Nicksa, & Cote, 2010, p. 1318). Some researchers even claim that perhaps half of all rape allegations are false (e.g., Kanin, 1994). In truth, however, fewer than 1 in 10 accusations turn out to be false (Lisak et al., 2010). Despite its infrequency, fear of the false accusation—and the potential stigmatization suffered by those accused—motivated the Department of Education in 2017 to consider overhauling federal policies enacted by the Obama administration in 2011 that had made it easier for colleges to find men accused of sexual assault guilty (Young, 2017).

So it's not surprising that many women who have been victimized come to the conclusion that reporting their experiences would, at best, be embarrassing and useless, and at worst be traumatizing. As one psychiatrist put it, "[I]f one set out intentionally to design a system for provoking posttraumatic stress disorder, it might look very much like a court of law" (quoted in Krakauer, 2015, p. 243).

Consider the way a victim is treated in the immediate aftermath of a rape. When she reports being victimized, she is physically examined, photographed, probed, and swabbed for the assailant's DNA. This process—which can last several hours in a hospital—produces what's known as a "rape kit." The kit is then sent to a crime lab, where, after thorough DNA analysis, it becomes the key piece of physical evidence in criminal proceedings. National studies have found that criminal trials that include a rape kit containing DNA evidence are significantly more likely to lead to a conviction than cases where there is no kit.

You would think that the process that produces such an important component of a legal case would be quick, efficient, and above all used in court. However, hundreds of thousands of these kits sit in storage rooms around the country untested (Joyful Heart Foundation, 2015). According to one study of rape cases in Los Angeles County, there are more than 12,000 *untested* rape kits sitting in police storage facilities; 450 of them have been there for more than 10 years (Human Rights Watch, 2009a). The backlog problem has gotten so bad in Texas that a legislator there introduced a bill that would use public crowdfunding to help pay for a reduction in the backlog of thousands of untested rape kits because the state wasn't (Hauser, 2017).

Such delays can be tragic. California has a 10-year statute of limitations for rape (the maximum period after a crime when a defendant can be prosecuted) that can be lifted only if a rape kit is tested within 2 years of the date of the crime. It's no wonder that so many women are reluctant to report being sexually victimized.

The conflict perspective provides one explanation for the widespread tendency to hold women responsible for their own victimization: The common definition of rape is based on a traditional model of sexual intercourse—penile-vaginal penetration—rather than on the violent context within which the act takes place.

The primary focus on the sexual component of the crime has long required that information about the intimate circumstances of the act and about the relationship between the people involved be taken into consideration—all of which tends to put female rape victims at a disadvantage during criminal proceedings. Research consistently shows that observers attribute more blame to the victims and minimize the seriousness of the assault when the perpetrator is an acquaintance or dating partner (S. T. Bell, Kuriloff, & Lottes, 1994). One study of convicted rapists found that those who assaulted strangers received longer prison sentences than those who were acquaintances or partners of their victims, regardless of the amount of force used or physical injury to the victim (McCormick, Maric, Seto, & Barbaree, 1998).

Moreover, public attitudes toward rape and rapists continue to be influenced by the relationship between the people involved. In 31 states, if a rape leads to pregnancy and a baby, the rapist is entitled to visitation rights (Kristof, 2012). One study of college students found that some people (mostly men) still believe it is acceptable for a man to force his wife to have sex with him, and that when compared with other types of violent offenses, marital rape is considered less serious than rape committed by a previously unknown assailant (Kirkwood & Cecil, 2001). In fact, until 1976, state rape laws defined rape as nonconsensual sexual intercourse between a man and a woman *who was not his spouse*. Although every state at least partially abolished this marital exemption by the early 1990s, many states continue to define spousal rape as a separate offense from stranger rape (Rape, Abuse & Incest National Network, 2009). For instance, most states impose a deadline on the reporting of marital rape (between 30 days and 1 year, depending on the state) that is significantly shorter than the 3-year limit for reporting a nonmarital rape. Other states require proof of threats or force in marital rape cases but only require proof of lack of consent in other rape cases. Oklahoma, for example, requires evidence of "force or violence" if the victim is the "spouse of the perpetrator." Furthermore, the state deems penetration to be rape if "the victim is at the time unconscious," but only if that victim is *not* the perpetrator's spouse (Allen, 2015). In 2014, a candidate for Congress in Virginia stated publicly that he didn't think spousal rape should be a crime at all: "How on earth you could validly get a conviction of a husband-wife rape when they're living together, sleeping in the same bed, she's in a nightie, and so forth, there's no injury, there's no separation or anything" (quoted in Crocker, 2014, p. 1).

Even when rape victims are not married to or living with their attackers, they are often expected to provide clear evidence that they were "unwilling" and tried to resist. Anything short of vigorous and repeated resistance can still call the victim's motives into question. Indeed, research suggests that police, prosecutors, and juries are less likely to believe allegations of rape if there is no evidence of violence (McEwan, 2005).

No other serious crime requires that the victim prove lack of consent. People aren't asked if they wanted their house broken into or if they enticed someone to beat them up and steal their wallet. Yet if women cannot prove that they resisted or cannot find someone to corroborate their story, consent (or even latent desire) may be presumed (Siegel, 2004). In one study of college students, about 17% of women believed a man has a right to assume consent if a woman allows him to touch her in a sexual way; 25% believed that if a woman touches a man in a sexual way, he has a right to assume consent; and 33% believed a man has a right to assume consent if a woman has had an oral sexual encounter with him (B. Johnson, Kuck, & Schander, 1997). Often the assertion that a rape victim "moaned" during the assault is an effective means of persuading police, attorneys, judges, and jurors that the sex was consensual, even though people moan in fear and pain, not just pleasure. In 2014, Jameis Winston, then the Heisman Trophy-winning quarterback of the Florida State Seminoles, was accused of raping a fellow student. When asked in a student conduct hearing what led him to believe she had given consent, he claimed she provided consent by "moaning." He was cleared of the charge (Krakauer, 2015).

Certain states have reconsidered the issue of what constitutes consent. In most states a woman may withdraw her consent to have sex at any time, and if the man continues, he is committing rape. However, in North Carolina, once a woman gives consent, she cannot rescind it. Such an understanding of consent rests on the belief that at a certain point during arousal, a man loses the ability to stop (Lee-St. John, 2007). In 2014, California became the first state to address this matter when its legislature enacted an "affirmative consent" law (sometimes referred to as "the Yes Means Yes Law") that specifies that consent can no longer be inferred from failure or ambiguity about saying "no." Instead consent must be conscious, clear, and voluntary. Silence or lack of protest no longer constitutes consent (California Legislative Information, 2014). About a quarter of all states now say sex is not legal without positive agreement, though some states still require evidence of force or resistance to prove lack of consent (Shulevitz, 2015b).

But public perceptions are slow to change. Many people regard female rape victims as at least partly to blame if they put themselves in risky situations, for instance, by behaving seductively, wearing "provocative" clothing, drinking too much, or telling dirty jokes. In one poll, 26% of respondents said that they thought a woman was partially or totally responsible for being raped if she was wearing sexy or revealing clothing, and 22% held the same view if a woman had had many sexual partners. Similarly, 30% of people said that a woman was partially or totally responsible for being raped if she was drunk, and 37% held the same view if the woman had failed to clearly say "no" to the man (Amnesty International, 2005). The governor of Ohio recently told a college student that if she didn't want to be sexually assaulted she should not "go to parties where there's a lot of alcohol" (quoted in Gittleson, 2016, p. 1).

The important sociological point of these findings is that many men and even some women don't always define violent sexual assault as a form of victimization. They think it is either something women bring on themselves or something men understandably do under certain circumstances. These views have become so entrenched that many women have internalized the message, blaming themselves to some degree when they are assaulted. Apart from fear, self-blame is the most common reaction to rape and is more frequent than anger (Janoff-Bulman, 1979). When rape victims say things such as, "I shouldn't have walked alone," "I should have known better than to go out with him," or "I shouldn't have worn that dress to the party," they are at least partly taking the blame for a crime they didn't commit. Such guilt and self-blame make recovery all the more difficult and tend to increase rates of depression, posttraumatic stress, shame, anxiety, and even suicidal thoughts (Kubany et al., 1995).

As a consequence of victim blaming, women are forced to bear much of the responsibility for preventing rape. I frequently pose this question in my introductory sociology class: What can people do to stop rape from occurring? Students' responses always echo the standard advice: Don't walk alone at night. Don't get drunk at parties where men are present, and if you do drink, know where your drink is at all times. Don't flirt or engage in foreplay if you have no intention of "going all the way." Don't miscommunicate your intentions. Don't wear revealing clothes. Certainly some of these safety measures are smart, sensible things to do. But note how all of these suggestions focus exclusively on things that *women* should avoid in order to prevent rape and say nothing about the things *men* can do to stop it. Confining discussions of rape prevention to women's behavior and vulnerability suggests that if a woman doesn't take these precautions, she is "inviting trouble." And "inviting trouble" implies that violent male behavior either is a natural response to provocation or is likely to happen if precautions aren't taken to discourage it.

Some progress is being made regarding cultural perceptions of rape. Myths are being debunked, the violent sexual exploitation of women in the media is being protested, and the rules governing admissible evidence in rape trials are being changed. Many police departments around the country now require investigators to initially assume that victims are telling the truth rather than lying when they report a rape. Some prosecutors are being trained to provide juries with research on the various—and sometimes counterintuitive—ways that victims respond to trauma to avoid the presumption that "truly innocent" victims respond similarly and predictably (Krakauer, 2015). Moreover, the federal government has recently sought to expand the definition of rape to include forcible anal and oral penetration and penetration with an object or body part other than the penis. And in 2013, the U.S. Department of Justice (2013) issued new victim-centered protocols to improve the way rape victims are treated by first responders and hospital personnel.

However, as long as we live in a culture that objectifies women and glorifies male assertiveness, we will continue to face the problem of sexual violence.

The Ideology of Sexism: Biology as Destiny

The domination of one group over another is always endorsed by a set of beliefs that explains and justifies that domination. You saw in the previous chapter that racial discrimination is often justified by the belief in innate racial inferiority. With sexism, it is the belief that men and women are biologically and naturally different that has been used historically to rationalize unequal treatment (Fine, 2010).

For 19th- and early-20th-century physicians, few "truths" were more incontestable than the fact that women were the products and prisoners of their anatomy. One French scientist noted a century ago that women have smaller brains than men, which explained their "fickleness, inconstancy, absence of thought and logic, and incapacity to reason" (quoted in Angier & Chang, 2005, p. A1). Even today, there's no shortage of books purporting to show that female tendencies in self-control, risk taking, intuition, empathy, anxiety, aggression, emotions, and even decision making can all be traced to the structure and function of their brains (Baron-Cohen, 2003; Brizendine, 2006; Mansfield, 2006).

Likewise, women's reproductive systems have been the object of scientific attention and concern for centuries (Scull & Favreau, 1986). Everything supposedly known about women that made them different from men—their subordinate place in society, their capacity for affection, their love of children and aptitude for child rearing, their "preference" for domestic work, and so on—could be explained by their uterus and ovaries (Ehrenreich & English, 1979; Scull & Favreau, 1986). Scholars in the past warned that young women who studied too much were struggling against nature, would badly damage their reproductive organs, and would perhaps even go insane in the process (Fausto-Sterling, 1985). So the exclusion of women from higher education was not only justifiable but necessary for health reasons and for the long-term good of society.

Some structural-functionalist sociologists have also used the bodily differences between men and women to explain gender inequality. The fact that men tend to be physically stronger and that women bear and nurse children has created many culturally recognized sex-segregated social roles, especially at work and in the family (Parsons & Bales, 1955). This specialization of roles is the most effective way to maintain societal stability, structural functionalists believe. By giving birth to new members, by socializing very young children, and by providing affection and nurturing, women make invaluable contributions to society. The common occupations women have traditionally had outside the home—teacher, nurse, day care provider, maid, social worker, and so on—tend therefore simply to be extensions of their "natural" tendencies.

Similarly, men's physical characteristics have been presumed to better suit them for the roles of economic provider and protector of the family. And if it's true that men are "naturally endowed" with traits such as strength, assertiveness, competitiveness, and rationality, then they are best qualified to enter the serious and competitive world of work and politics (Kokopeli & Lakey, 1992). Sociologist Steven Goldberg (1999) argues that because male rule and male dominance seem to characterize the vast majority of human societies, this gender difference must be rooted in evolutionary biology.

The problem with depicting masculinity and femininity as natural, biologically determined traits is that it confuses sex with gender. The underlying assumption of sexist ideology—that gender is as "unchangeable" as sex—overlooks extensive similarities between the sexes and extensive variations within each sex. The distributions of men and women on most personality and behavioral characteristics generally overlap (Carothers, 2013). For instance, men as a group do tend to be more aggressive than women as a group. But these differences are a matter of degree, not kind. Hence some women are much more aggressive than the average man, and some men are much less aggressive than the average woman. Indeed, social circumstances may have a greater impact on aggressive behavior than any innate, biological traits. Some studies show that when women are rewarded for behaving aggressively, they can be just as violent as men (Hyde, 1984; N. Jones, 2009).

Furthermore, the reliance on biology ignores the wide cultural and historical variation in conceptions of masculinity and femininity. For instance, although every known society has a division of labor based on sex, what's considered "men's work" and "women's work" differs. In most societies, men fish, hunt, clear land, and build boats and houses, but in some societies, women regularly perform these tasks. In most societies, women do the cooking; but in some societies, cooking is typically a male responsibility (Eitzen & Baca Zinn, 1991).

Although women have become prominent in the U.S. workforce, many people still believe that they are less capable than men of performing certain tasks outside the home. Some still may find female doctors or lawyers unusual. Legislators and military officials continue to debate the role of female soldiers in direct ground combat. The controversy in several churches over whether women should be ordained as ministers and priests illustrates the depth and intensity of people's feelings about gender-appropriate career pursuits.

Moreover, as we saw in Chapter 5, the qualities we consider naturally feminine are usually seen as less socially valuable than those considered masculine. Girls do suffer sometimes when their behavior is considered "boylike." But accusing a boy of acting like a girl is the ultimate schoolyard insult. Even when they get older, many men can be easily whipped into aggressive responses by accusations of femininity, such as when coaches call their male players "girls" or "ladies."

The biological rationale for gender inequality—what one psychologist calls "neurosexism" (Fine, 2010)—is difficult to justify these days. Technological advances—including bottled baby formula, contraceptives that give women more choices over childbearing, and innovations that lessen the need for sheer physical strength—have made it possible for women and men to fulfill many of the same responsibilities. Nevertheless, as long as people believe that gender-linked roles and societal contributions are determined by nature, they will continue to accept inequality in women's and men's opportunities, expectations, and outcomes. If people consider it "natural" for women to play nurturing, weak, and dependent roles, then limiting women to such positions seems neither unfair nor oppressive.

Institutions and Gender Inequality

The subordination of women that is part of the everyday workings of social institutions (or **institutional sexism**) has far greater consequences for women as a group than personal expressions of sexism. When sexism in social institutions becomes part of the ongoing operation of large-scale organizations, it perpetuates and magnifies women's disadvantages, making social equality all the more difficult to attain. But not only can social institutions be sexist, they can also be gendered. In other words, institutions and organizations segregate, exploit, and exclude women solely on the basis of their physical characteristics and then compound the impact of their sexism by incorporating values and practices based on traditional expectations for women and men (Kimmel, 2004).

Masculinized Institutions

More often than not, social institutions incorporate masculine values—which is not surprising because, historically, men have developed, dominated, and interpreted most institutions. Take competitive sports, for example. Most of us would agree that to be successful, an athlete must be aggressive, strong, and powerful—attributes typically associated with masculinity. By celebrating these traits, a sport such as football symbolically declares itself an arena that women cannot or should not enter (except, of course, as spectators, cheerleaders, or sideline reporters).

But even sports such as gymnastics and figure skating, which used to value more "feminine" traits like grace, beauty, and balance, have made their judging criteria more masculine in recent years. For a woman to be a world-class gymnast or skater these days, she must also be physically strong and exhibit explosive acrobatic power. Indeed, the popularity of women's team sports in this country coincides with the increasing presence of traditionally male traits such as physical strength and competitive vigor in female athletes.

At the same time, however, individual female athletes who are considered *too* strong or who compete *too* well sometimes face suspicions about their femaleness:

> When men are more talented than others, it is an expression of the beauty of sports. But when women outcompete others, suspicions about eligibility and arguments for a level playing field often arise. (Jordan-Young & Karkazis, 2012, p. D8)

For the 2012 Olympics, the International Olympic Committee established a policy banning women with naturally high levels of testosterone from competition, claiming that such women would have an unfair advantage (Macur, 2017).

But the masculinization of institutions is not just about hormones. In most high schools, student culture revolves around sports, especially football. In such an environment, privilege and power are conferred on successful male athletes. Some sociologists and educators fear that high schools are now being pressured to apply an equally aggressive, competitive, "masculinized" approach to the curriculum as well, through emphases on academic rigor, high-stakes test taking, zero tolerance discipline policies, and increased efforts in math, science, and technology (Lesko, 2008).

The masculine traits necessary for successful athletic and educational competition can be seen in other institutions. For instance, we don't often associate the practice of religion with masculine traits like aggression, strength, and power. However, some evangelical pastors have become disdainful of mainstream American Protestantism for what they perceive as its softening or "feminizing" of Christ. As one Christian blogger put it, "The 'hard' attributes of God like His justice, holiness, wrath, power, and judgment [have been] jettisoned in favor of "soft" attributes like love and mercy" (Vaughan, 2016, p. 1). They believe that too much attention is paid to sensitivity and tolerance and not enough to damnation and salvation:

> What really grates is the portrayal of Jesus as a wimp, or worse. Paintings depict a gentle man embracing children and cuddling lambs. Hymns celebrate his patience and tenderness. . . . The mainstream church . . . has transformed Jesus into a "Richard Simmons, hippie, queer Christ," a "neutered and limp-wristed popular Sky Fairy of pop culture that . . . would never talk about sin or send anyone to hell." (quoted in Worthen, 2009, p. 22)

To counteract this trend, some evangelical churches have begun to incorporate a hypermasculine, hard-edged, smackdown approach to the Gospel into their religious services.

Similarly, most bureaucracies in institutional areas such as business, politics, and the military operate according to taken-for-granted masculine principles. Successful leaders and organizations are usually portrayed as aggressive, goal oriented, competitive, and efficient—all characteristics associated with masculinity in this society.

Take politics, for example. Historically, male candidates branded as unmasculine "wimps" or "pansies" by their opponents have rarely won election. In the 1950s, reporters referred to supporters of the Democratic presidential candidate, Adlai Stevenson, as "lace-cuff liberals" and "lace-panty diplomats" (Hess, 2017, p. 12). Stevenson lost—twice. In 2017, a Montana congressional candidate named Greg Gianforte body-slammed a male reporter at a news conference days before the election in reaction to a question he didn't like. In doing so, he broke the reporter's glasses. Afterward, some political commentators praised the candidate's manhood and sarcastically disparaged the reporter's weak and fragile (read feminine) response: "Crying little snowflake got his glasses broken. Boohoo." "Did anyone get his lunch money stolen today and then run to tell the recess monitor?" (quoted in Hess, 2017, pp. 12–13). Gianforte won the election easily.

And at a structural level, strong governments, prosperous businesses, or efficient military units are rarely described as supportive, nurturing, cooperative, kind, and caring (Acker, 1992). When institutions are gendered in these ways, everyday inequalities become apparent.

Gender Inequality in Health and Health Care

Gender inequality has created some curious discrepancies in the way the medical establishment treats men and women. For instance, prior to the 2014 Affordable Care Act ("Obamacare"), it was legal in most states for insurance companies selling individual policies—those for people who don't have group insurance coverage through their employers—to charge women higher premiums than men for the same medical coverage . . . a practice known as "gender rating." The difference in price ranged from 4% to 48% and collectively cost women about $1 billion annually. The justification for this practice was the belief that women used the health care system more than men because of all the medical procedures associated with pregnancy and childbirth. The Department of Health and Human Services ended the practice of "gender rating" in 2014. However, during the debate over health care reform in 2017, a male congressional representative from Illinois challenged the requirement that insurance companies cover the costs of maternity services by suggesting that it was "silly" for men to have to pay for them (Reilly, 2017).

Ironically, in every developed country, men tend to have more health problems and a shorter life expectancy than women (Read & Gorman, 2010). They occupy more physically demanding jobs and engage in more dangerous activities. Hence, they've historically been at greater risk for various bodily injuries and stress-related ailments. Men also have higher rates of cancer susceptibility (excluding breast, cervical, and ovarian types) than women (Dorak & Karpuzoglu, 2012).

Yet women have historically been the focus of intrusive medical attention more than men (B. K. Rothman, 1984). Women are more likely than men to undergo surgical and diagnostic procedures. Indeed, the three most common short-stay surgical procedures for women—cesarean section, repair of lacerations during childbirth, and hysterectomy—all deal with female anatomy and physiology. The three most common short-stay procedures for men—cardiac catheterization, coronary artery bypass grafting, and reduction of fracture—are not sex specific (ProQuest Statistical Abstract, 2017). Not surprisingly, physicians often specialize in *women's* health care, but rarely do they specialize in *men's*. Obstetricians and gynecologists deal exclusively with the reproductive and sexual matters of female patients. There are no comparable specialties of medicine devoted solely to men's reproductive health (urologists address men's reproductive issues, but they also see female patients).

Normal biological events in women's lives—menstruation, pregnancy, childbirth, and menopause—have long been considered problematic conditions in need of medical intervention. For instance, the American Psychiatric Association (2013) now officially recognizes "premenstrual dysphoric disorder" in its official manual of mental disorders. Indisputably, many women around the world experience irritability, moodiness, and other symptoms related to hormonal cycles. The issue, however, is whether these symptoms ought to be labeled as a medical and/or mental problem (Lander, 1988). To do so not only promotes the selling of drugs to healthy women (C. A. Bailey, 1993; Figert, 1996) but fosters the belief that women, biologically frail and emotionally erratic because of their hormones, cannot be allowed to work too hard or be trusted in positions of authority (Fausto-Sterling, 1985).

From a sociological perspective, it seems highly likely that women's experiences with the "symptoms" surrounding menstruation are related to the place that menstruation occupies in the larger society. We live in a culture that, by and large, has tried either to ignore menstruation or to present it as shameful. Consider the fact that in a social media environment teeming with hypersexualized images of women, officials at Instagram decided that a photo of a clothed woman with what appear to be menstrual stains on her white pants was objectionable and deleted the post (Wortham, 2015).

Only relatively recently—as evidenced by the glut of commercials and advertisements for "feminine hygiene" products—has menstruation come out of the closet. But, of course, the attention we as a culture devote to menstruation continues to be almost exclusively negative, focusing on overcoming bothersome premenstrual symptoms or camouflaging the unsightly or otherwise unappealing by-products of menstruation itself. Television advertisements for sanitary pads still depict absorbency by using blue, rather than the more accurate red, liquid. And most ads continue to reinforce the belief that menstruation should be hidden. Marketing campaigns for brands like Playtex, Tampax, and o.b. often emphasize how inconspicuous their tampons are. In one TV commercial for Tampax, the tampon is so discreet that a teacher mistakes it for a piece of candy when she catches a student passing one to a friend (Beck, 2015a). A website called Beinggirl.com posts advice for adolescent girls on a variety of topics. One blog, titled "Keeping It Quick and Quiet," reinforced the idea that menstruation is shameful by providing advice such as, "Be discreet when you're bringing a tampon into the girls' room. . . . Anyone can bring a purse to the restroom (a classic hiding spot) but try tucking it in your waistband, bra, sock, or cell phone case. No one needs to suspect a thing" and "For better hiding potential, try compact tampons" (Beinggirl.com, 2010).

Given the special attention women's health problems receive, it's ironic that, outside of obstetrics and gynecology, research on women's general health needs has been rather limited. More than 20 years ago, the U.S. Public Health Service reported that a lack of medical research on women limited our understanding of their health concerns (B. K. Rothman & Caschetta, 1999). The reason often given for their exclusion from medical studies was that their menstrual cycles complicated the interpretation of research findings. In addition, medical researchers have historically been reluctant to perform research on women of childbearing age for fear that exposing them to experimental manipulations might harm their reproductive capabilities. In fact, in the 1970s and 1980s, federal policies and guidelines actually called for the blanket exclusion of women of childbearing potential from certain types of drug research. That meant that any woman who was physically capable of becoming pregnant, regardless of her own desire to do so, could be excluded. Concerns were less about threats to women's health than they were about the possibility of liability if reproductive damage due to exposure to the experimental drug occurred (J. A. Hamilton, 1996).

The exclusion of women from medical research became so problematic that Congress passed a law in 1993 stipulating that women must be included in clinical trials in numbers sufficient to provide evidence of the different ways men and women respond to drugs, surgical treatments, and changes in diet or behavior. Nevertheless, medical research still either excludes women entirely or includes them only in limited numbers (P. Johnson, Fitzgerald, Salganicoff, Wood, & Goldstein, 2014). The National Institutes of Health (NIH) reissued a set of policy guidelines in 2013 requiring all applicants for government grants to provide assurance that women are being included in their study design. In 2014, the NIH went further, calling on all laboratories to take steps to include female mice, rats, pigs, and other animals in preliminary drug studies that use non-humans (Rabin, 2014b). That same year, the organization took the unprecedented step of distributing $10.1 million in grants to more than 80 medical researchers for the sole purpose of including more female participants in their studies (Rabin, 2014a).

Gender Inequality in the Media

You saw in Chapter 5 that the media's portrayal of men and women contributes to gender socialization. But the media as an institution can also contribute to the cultural devaluation of women and perpetuate gender inequality.

Worldwide, men tend to control the creation, production, and dissemination of media images and information. Women hold only about 3% of key decision-making positions in mainstream media (The Women's Media Center, 2011). At 20 of the country's top news outlets, women produce only about one third of news reports. When it comes to reporting the news, women are on-camera about 25% of the time, report 38% of stories in newspapers, and write 46% of features online; they also represent about 10% of sports editors and columnists (The Women's Media Center, 2017).

On entertainment television, male writers, creators, and executive producers out-number women four to one and male directors outnumber female directors eight to one. Furthermore, men accounted for 83% of all directors, executive producers, producers, writers, cinematographers, and editors for the 250 most profitable feature films made in the United States in 2016; this figure is the same as it was in 1998 (The Women's Media Center, 2017). Such imbalances in productive and creative control means that what we see on television and in theaters is likely to reflect men's perspectives.

Hence, apart from the occasional powerful female character—like Michonne in *The Walking Dead,* Alicia Florrick in *The Good Wife,* or Olivia Pope in *Scandal*—the portrayal of women in film and on prime-time television remains rather traditional and stereotypical. Although fewer women are portrayed as stay-at-home mothers than in the past, men are still more likely than women to be shown working outside the home (D. Smith, 1997). Women express emotions much more easily and are significantly more likely to use sex and charm to get what they want than are men. An analysis of 18 prime-time television situation comedies found that female characters are significantly more likely than male characters to receive derogatory comments about their appearance from other characters. These comments are typically reinforced by audience laughter (Fouts & Burggraf, 2000).

A glimpse at the portrayal of modern women in U.S. advertising, fashion, television, music videos, and films further reveals a double-edged stereotype. On the one hand, we see the successful woman of the 21st century: the perfect wife/mother/career woman, the triumphant professional who leaps gracefully about the pages of fashion magazines. She is the high-powered lawyer or surgeon that we see on prime-time television: outgoing, bright, and assertive. No occupation is beyond her reach.

Coexisting with this image, though, is the more traditional and more stereotypical image of the "exhibited" woman: the seductive sex object displayed in beer commercials, magazine advertisements, soap operas, and the swimsuit issue of *Sports Illustrated.* When the famous former decathlete and reality TV star, Bruce Jenner, publicly transitioned into Caitlyn Jenner in 2015, the media reaction—while often positive and supportive—tended to focus exclusively on her glamorous and "sexy" new appearance. As Jon Stewart (2015), former host of *The Daily Show,* put it, when Caitlyn was a man, "we could talk about [his] athleticism and business acumen, but now [she's] a woman and [her] looks are really the only thing we care about."

More generally, media continue to present stereotypes that show women as shallow, vain, and materialistic characters whose looks overshadow all else. Popular dating-themed reality shows like *The Bachelor* reinforce the belief that sexual charm and physical attractiveness are lures that women can use to attract men.

In sum, women today are not only expected to achieve educationally and economically at unprecedented levels but they also must look sexy doing it. These images, created mainly by and for men, produce the illusion that success or failure is purely a personal, private achievement and ignore the complex social, economic, and political forces that continue to prevent real-life women from achieving success.

MICRO-MACRO CONNECTION
CAN MEDIA IMAGES MAKE YOU SICK?

What is especially troublesome about media images of female beauty is that they are largely artificial and unattainable. The average American woman is 5'4" tall and weighs 165 pounds. The average fashion model is 5'10" and weighs 107 pounds. Researchers at Johns Hopkins University compiled data on the heights and weights of Miss America pageant winners between 1922 and 1999. They found that the weights of these women steadily decreased, reaffirming the cultural value of thinness (Rubinstein & Caballero, 2000). Recent winners have had a height-weight ratio that places them in the range of what the World Health Organization defines as "undernourished" (J. B. Martin, 2010).

Nonetheless, television, magazine, and Internet images of sticklike models and celebrities continue to appeal to young women who equate thinness with popularity and success. It's not surprising, therefore, that girls and young women who regularly view these images spend a great deal of time and energy trying to emulate them through extreme dieting and other disordered eating patterns (J. L. Wilson, Peebles, Hardy, & Litt, 2006). The following statistics were compiled by the Eating Disorders Coalition (2017) and the National Eating Disorders Association (2011, 2015):

- Forty-two percent of first- to third-grade girls want to be thinner, 51% of 9- to 10-year-old girls feel better about themselves when they're on a diet, and 81% of 10-year-olds are afraid of being fat.

- Eating disorders are the third most common chronic illness among adolescent females.

- Ninety-one percent of college women attempt to control their weight through dieting.

- On any given day, about half of American women are on a diet, even though 95% of them will likely regain the weight they've lost within 1 to 5 years.

- Twenty million American women suffer from a clinically significant eating disorder at some time in their lives.

Although many people view such statistics with alarm, others see them as benign or even positive. An Internet movement called "pro-ana" (for pro-anorexia) or "pro-mia" (for pro-bulimia) encourages young women to view eating disorders not as dangerous medical conditions but as positive lifestyle choices. Hundreds of pro-ana websites and blogs provide young women with dieting challenges, discussion groups, and inspirational messages or "pep talks" about the desirability of limiting food intake and the appeal of extreme thinness. Some contain declarations such as "Food is Poison." Pro-anas also post their messages and pictures celebrating extreme thinness on social network sites like Facebook, Twitter, Pinterest, and Tumblr. Other sites, like YouTube, provide "thinspiration" (or "thinspo") videos, visual celebrations of skeletal women, including some celebrities and models. Soundtracks to these videos include songs with messages like "Skeleton, you are my friend" and "Bones are beautiful" (Heffernan, 2008). The most recent offshoot of this online trend is an Instagram craze called "rib cage bragging" where young women post pictures of themselves clearly designed to expose their ribcages. The thinner they are, the more proudly their ribs protrude (B. Y. Lee, 2017).

Supporters of pro-ana sites argue that they are simply providing young anorexic and bulimic women a place to go where they can get support and not be judged. However, critics worry that the movement glorifies dangerous and potentially life-threatening conditions. Research seems to support this position. A study of 10- to 22-year-olds with diagnosed eating disorders found that those who frequented pro-ana websites remained sicker for longer periods than those who visited prorecovery sites. About 96% said they'd learned new tips for purging and weight loss from the pro-ana sites, and two thirds used these methods (J. L. Wilson et al., 2006). Another study found that 84% of college women reduced their caloric intake within 90 minutes of being exposed to pro-ana sites (Jett, LaPorte, & Wanchisn, 2010). As one 28-year-old Australian woman put it, "At any time I could jump on my phone and have a step-by-step guide on how to be anorexic" (quoted in Rushton, 2016, p. 1). The potential for harm is so great that the Academy for Eating Disorders (2006) has called on government officials and Internet service providers to require warning screens for pro-ana websites much like the warning labels found on cigarette packs.

Incidentally, girls aren't the only ones who may suffer as a result of dangerous media images. The popularity of male celebrities with lean, muscular bodies like Channing Tatum, Ryan Gosling, and Dwayne "the Rock" Johnson have led more and more adolescent boys to become obsessed with weight lifting and body fat percentages. One study found that over 40% of middle school and high school boys regularly exercise to increase muscle mass, 38% use protein supplements, and 6% have tried using steroids (Eisenberg, Wall, & Neumark-Sztainer, 2012). And, like girls, they too have their social network sites—dubbed "fitspo" and "fitspiration" (Quenqua, 2012b).

Gender Inequality in Families

Much of the inequality women face revolves around the traditional view of their family role: keepers of the household and producers, nurturers, and socializers of children. Although in other times and places, women have had different levels of responsibility for homemaking, they have always been responsible for reproduction.

One of the major consequences of the industrial revolution of the 18th and 19th centuries was the separation of the workplace and the home. Prior to industrialization, most countries were primarily agricultural. People's lives centered on the farm, where husbands and wives were partners not only in making a home but also in making a living (Vanek, 1980). Farm couples were interdependent; each person needed the other for survival. It was taken for granted that women provided for the family along with men (J. Bernard, 1981). Although the relationship between husbands and wives on the farm was never entirely equal—wives still did most if not all of the housekeeping and family care—complete male dominance was offset by women's indispensable contributions to the household economy (Vanek, 1980).

With the advent of industrialization, things began to change. New forms of technology and the promise of new financial opportunities and a good living drew people (mostly men) away from the farms and into cities and factories. For the first time in history, the family economy in some societies was based outside the household. Women no longer found themselves involved in the day-to-day supervision of the family's business as they had once been. Instead, they were consigned to the only domestic responsibilities that remained necessary in an industrial economy: the care and nurturing of children and the maintenance of the household. Because this work was unpaid and because visible goods were no longer being produced at home, women quickly found their labor devalued in the larger society (Hareven, 1992).

However, as we saw in Chapter 7, men weren't the only ones who left home each day to work in factories. At the turn of the century, hundreds of thousands of children worked in mines, mills, and factories (Coontz, 1992). And contrary to popular belief, one fifth of U.S. women worked outside the home in 1900, especially women of color (Staggenborg, 1998).

Today, the devaluation of "women's work" is the result of a separation of the public and private spheres (Sidel, 1990). As long as men dominate the public sphere—the marketplace and the government—they will wield greater economic and political power within society and also be able to translate that power into authority at home. Women's work within the relatively powerless private sphere of the home will continue to be hidden and undervalued.

According to the conflict perspective, the problem is not that housewives don't work; it's that they work for free outside the mainstream economy, in which work is strictly defined as something one is paid to do (Ciancanelli & Berch, 1987; Voyandoff, 1990). Ironically, however, domestic work is actually invaluable to the entire economic system.

If a woman were to be paid the minimum going rate for all her labor as mother and housekeeper, including childcare, transportation, housecleaning, laundry, cooking, bill paying, and grocery shopping, her yearly salary would be comparable to that of women who are employed full time, year round. One study found that if we apply average hourly wage rates to the typical daily amounts of childcare mothers of children under 12 provide, a low-end estimate of the monetary value of this work is about $33,000 a year (Folbre & Yoon, 2006). But because societal and family power is a function of who brings home the income, such unpaid work does not afford women the prestige it might if it were paid labor.

Despite the accelerated entry of women into the paid labor force in the past few decades, housework continues to be predominantly female. According to the U.S. Bureau of Labor Statistics (2017a), far more women than men engage in housework and childcare (see Exhibit 12.3). On average, they spend about 1½ hours a day more than men cleaning, preparing meals/cleaning up afterward, buying groceries, and tending to children. Husbands do play a more prominent role in the raising of children than they did two decades ago, and they've increased their contribution to housework somewhat (Bianchi, Robinson, & Milkie, 2006), especially when compared with men in other industrialized countries (Fuwa, 2004). But the household work that husbands do is typically quite different from the work that wives do. Women's tasks tend to be essential to the daily functioning of the household (Fuwa, 2004); men's chores are typically infrequent, irregular, or optional:

> They take out the garbage, they mow the lawns, they play with children, they occasionally go to the supermarket or shop for household durables, they paint the attic or fix the faucet; but by and large, they do not launder, clean, or cook, nor do they feed, clothe, bathe, or transport children. These . . . most time-consuming activities . . . are exclusively the domain of women. (Cowan, 1991, p. 207)

From a structural-functionalist perspective, one could argue that traditional gendered household responsibilities actually reflect an equitable, functional, interdependent division of labor. That is, the husband works in the paid labor force and supports the family financially; the wife takes care of the household work and childcare. Each person provides

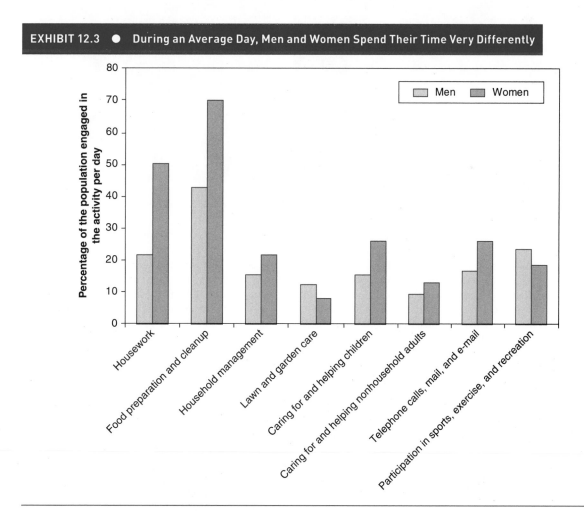

EXHIBIT 12.3 ● **During an Average Day, Men and Women Spend Their Time Very Differently**

Source: U.S. Bureau of Labor Statistics, 2017a, Table A1.

VISUAL ESSAY—THINLY VEILED

Photo by Photofusion/Universal Images Group via Getty Images

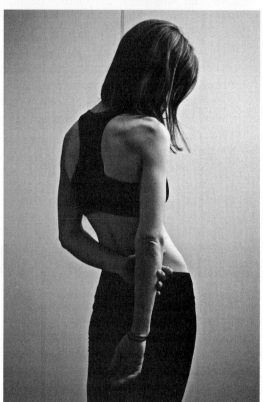

Aaron Lynett/Toronto Star via Getty Images

One of the messages of this chapter is that media images of gender can—and often do—have serious consequences for people. In Chapter 6, you saw how images of female beauty have contracted over the years. Here we look at this issue from a social media angle. Pro-ana websites, blogs, Facebook pages, Twitter feeds, etc. have proliferated over the past decade, bringing with them a seemingly endless supply of "thinspirational" images, quotes, and advice—like the ones you see here—for young women who want to be thin. Some of these sites present themselves as sources of support and encouragement for individuals living an anorexic "lifestyle." Critics, however, charge that the information they post drives young women deeper into body obsession and self-starvation, which can ultimately be lethal.

The images here are a tiny sampling of the thousands that are a mouse click or smartphone swipe away. And they probably aren't perfectly representative of all the posts one can see online. However, they serve as a launching point for several important questions. In general, do you think these images serve as a positive or negative influence on the young people who are likely to view them? Would you answer differently if there were a greater gender balance in the bodies and messages that are portrayed? Can images like these help to alleviate one of this country's most serious public health problems—obesity? Do social networking sites have a duty to withhold such imagery if there's evidence that it could be dangerous, or would that be a violation of free speech?

essential services in exchange for those provided by the other. But research in this area indicates that the gender discrepancy in housework responsibilities does not diminish when women work full time outside the home. On average, when both parents work full time, mothers spend about 23 hours per week on household tasks, while fathers spend only about 12.5 hours (U.S. Bureau of Labor Statistics, 2017a). The hours that women spend on household labor are down from 35 hours in the mid-1960s, and men have increased their contribution from 4 hours per week, but still men contribute only half as much time as women do to the maintenance of the home.

To make matters worse, women's disproportionate involvement in household tasks goes beyond what can be measured by the hours people spend doing things. Fathers may devote more time, say, to coaching their kid's soccer team, but it's the mothers who tend to do the "behind-the-scenes" work that makes the child's participation possible in the first place (sign ups, scheduling, buying gear, etc.; Lareau & Weininger, 2008). Furthermore, women are still far more likely than men to be the household managers, the ones who make sure everything gets done. It's women who tend to be the "designated worriers," a responsibility that can have implications that extend beyond the home. As one author put it:

> Mothers draft the to-do lists while fathers pick and choose among the items. And whether a woman loves or hates worry work, it can scatter her focus on what she does for pay and knock her partway or clean off a career path. This distracting grind of apprehension and organization may be one of the least movable obstacles to women's equality in the workplace. (Shulevitz, 2015a, p. 6)

In sum, the fact that housework and childcare—both in planning and activity—are still predominantly women's work gives us some sense of how pervasive and powerful our sexist ideology continues to be. And belief in this ideology may actually be growing. According to research by the Council on Contemporary Families, men between the ages of 18 and 25 are actually more likely than older men to believe that it would be best for everyone involved if women took care of the home and family (cited in Coontz, 2017).

Gender Inequality in Education

Another institutional setting in which gender inequality persists is education. In elementary school and beyond, teachers are likely to treat their male and female students differently (M. Sadker, Sadker, Fox, & Salata, 2004):

- Girls receive less teacher attention and less useful feedback than boys.

- Girls talk significantly less in class than boys, and when they do speak up, they are more likely than boys to be reminded to raise their hands.

- Girls are more likely than boys to be the focus of unwanted sexual attention in school.

Since it is sometimes quite subtle, most people are unaware of the hidden sexist lessons and quiet losses it creates (D. Sadker, Sadker, & Zittleman, 2009). However, over the course of their school careers, such differential treatment takes its toll on girls.

The harm isn't apparent right away, though. In elementary school and middle school, girls outperform boys on almost every standard measure of academic achievement (Legewie & DiPrete, 2012; Tyre, 2006). Boys are more likely than girls to repeat a grade, drop out, be put in special education, or be diagnosed as having an emotional problem, a learning disability, or attention-deficit disorder (Lewin, 1998). Yet boys have higher expectations for themselves and higher self-esteem than girls, a gap that widens with each passing year in the school system (Freiberg, 1991). As girls make the transition from childhood to adolescence, they are faced with a conflict between the way they see themselves and the way others, particularly teachers, see them (Gilligan, 1990).

These gender-typed patterns pervade high school. Teenage boys' sense of their own masculinity tends to be derived primarily from their achievements, such as participation in organized sports (Messner, 2002). Boys are also likely to be encouraged by counselors and teachers to formulate ambitious career goals. In contrast, prestige and popularity for teenage girls are still likely to come largely from their physical appearance. Indeed, girls are far more likely to face discipline or even suspension for the violation of school dress codes. Such actions are typically motivated by the argument that tight pants, a bare kneecap, or a revealed collarbone are a distraction to boys (B. Alvarez, 2016). So it's not really all that surprising that, by the end of high school, boys outperform girls on standard measures of academic achievement. For instance, although the majority of SAT takers are girls, boys' average total score is higher (1494 for boys vs. 1474 for girls; National Center for Fair and Open Testing, 2016).

Gender differences in academic performance are usually a cultural by-product as opposed to some innate intellectual difference. Take, for instance, the common belief that boys are naturally better at science and mathematics than girls. College-bound senior boys outperform girls on the math section of the SAT by an average of 30 points (there are no gender differences on the reading and writing sections; The College Board, 2014). Evidence indicates, however, that American girls today often have strong mathematical skills and are gaining ground on boys. In the early 1980s, for instance, boys identified as "highly gifted" in mathematics—that is, those who scored in the 90th percentile of the math section of the SAT even though they were still too young to take the test—outnumbered girls 13 to 1. By 2005, that ratio had dropped to less than three to one (Andreescu, Gallian, Kane, & Mertz, 2008). But these girls continue to live in a culture that doesn't value, actively discourages, or even socially penalizes mathematical excellence in girls.

In addition, cross-cultural evidence shows that many Asian and Eastern European countries consistently produce girls with strong mathematical abilities, while other countries (chiefly the United States) do not (Andreescu et al., 2008). In fact, girls in developing countries are far more likely than girls in industrialized countries to indicate that they like math and science and would like to work in those fields (Charles, 2011). In the United States, girls who excel in national and international mathematical competitions are likely to be the daughters of immigrants.

Gender inequality is evident in college, too . . . but not always in the direction you might think. On the one hand, for the past three or four decades, the majority of college students have been women (see Exhibit 12.4). And women earn 57.4% of all bachelor's degrees, 58.5% of all master's degrees, and 51.7% of all doctorates (National Center for Education Statistics, 2017a). Moreover, college women study more and have higher grade point averages than men. They're also more likely to complete their bachelor's degrees in 4 or 5 years (cited in Lewin, 2006).

Yet men are more likely to take courses geared for math and science majors and achieve higher grades in those courses than women (The College Board, 1998). Many of the majors that lead to high-paying or high-prestige careers remain dominated by men (engineering, economics, mathematics, earth sciences, etc.). For instance, women earn only 18% of engineering and computer science degrees, and about 40% of mathematics degrees; but they earn 77% of psychology degrees, 80% of degrees in education, and 85% of nursing degrees (National Center for Education Statistics, 2017a). At tech companies like Apple,

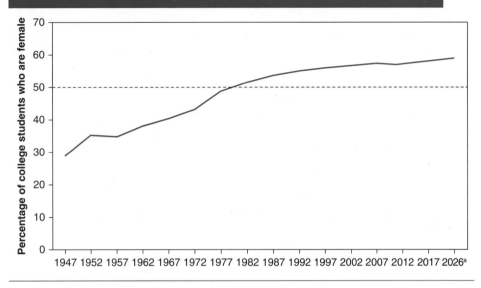

EXHIBIT 12.4   ●   For 40 Years, More Women Than Men Have Gone to College

Source: National Center for Education Statistics, 2017a, Table 303.10.

[a]Projection

Google, and Facebook, fewer than 20% of the technical employees are women (cited in C. C. Miller, 2015). But this is not just an American tendency. Among developed countries worldwide, only 14% of young women entering college for the first time choose a science- or technology-related field; nearly 40% of men do so (Organization for Economic Cooperation and Development, 2015a).

Some evidence suggests that teachers' stereotypical biases may be at least partially responsible for girls' lack of desire to take math and science courses and ultimately on the jobs they get and wages they earn when they become adults. For example, one study found that sixth-grade girls outscored boys on a math aptitude test when the test was graded anonymously. However, when graded by teachers who knew the students' names (and could therefore tell their sex), the boys outscored the girls. By the time they got to high school, the girls who had been discouraged by their elementary school teachers were less likely than boys to take advanced courses in math and science (Lavy & Sand, 2015). In college, science professors continue to see their male students as more competent, hireable, and worthy of mentoring than female students (Moss-Racusin, Dovidio, Brescoll, Graham, & Handelsman, 2012).

To overcome the impact of such differential treatment before students get to college, some educational reformers have advocated sex-segregated private schools as well as single-sex classrooms in coeducational public schools (Rich, 2014). They argue that girls who go to single-sex schools are more assertive, more confident, and more likely to take classes in math, computer science, and physics than girls in coeducational schools. They also have higher career aspirations than girls who attend coeducational schools (Watson, Quatman, & Edler, 2002). Boys in single-sex environments are less likely to get into trouble and more likely to pursue interests in art, music, and drama than their counterparts in coeducational schools (National Association for Single Sex Public Education, 2013).

The Department of Education estimates that there are approximately 750 public schools around the country that offer at least one single-sex class and 850 entirely single-sex public schools (cited in Rich, 2014). In addition, some private schools now offer a combination of mixed-sex and single-sex education, with boys and girls learning together in elementary school and high school but being taught separately during the turbulent middle school years. As one prominent educator put it, "Girls who are 'confident at 11 and confused at 16' will more likely be creative thinkers and risk-takers as adults if educated apart from boys in middle school" (quoted in J. Gross, 2004b, p. A16).

However, not everyone thinks that single-sex education is the answer (Fine, 2010). The American Council for CoEducational Schooling (2011) issued a recent report showing that girls don't learn any better or faster in a single-sex educational environment than they do in a coeducational setting. Furthermore, critics point out that separating girls and boys based on an assumption that girls can't learn effectively when in the presence of boys may actually promote rather than diminish gender stereotypes.

Current trends in college enrollments and innovation in educational policy give us reason to believe that in the future, sex and gender might become less significant factors in determining people's educational tracks.

Gender Inequality in the Economy

Because of their difficulty converting educational achievements into high pay, women have historically been prevented from taking advantage of the occupational opportunities and rewards to which most men have had relatively free access. These days, some men may feel under economic assault and their masculinity threatened when they earn less than their partners (Chira, 2016). But overall women continue to have much less earning power in the labor market than men.

The unequal economic status of women not only results from the personal sexism of potential employers but is tied to larger economic structures and institutional forces. The standard assumptions that drive the typical workplace often work against women, both at work and at home. For instance, during the recent economic recession, many mortgage lenders became skittish about approving home loans for expectant parents. They feared that these couples would inevitably experience a temporary drop in income if the mother went on temporary maternity leave—or perhaps a permanent loss of income if she decided to leave the workforce entirely—and therefore would be unable to make their mortgage payments (T. S. Bernard, 2010).

More generally, think of the things one has to do to be considered a good worker by a boss: put in extra hours, travel to faraway business meetings, go to professional conferences, attend training programs, be willing to work unpopular shifts, or entertain out-of-town clients. These activities assume that employees have the time and the freedom from familial obligations to do them. In many professions, like law and finance, people who work extra-long hours actually get paid higher salaries (Goldin, 2014). Because women, especially mothers, still tend to have the lion's share of responsibility at home, they are less able than their male colleagues to "prove" to their bosses that they are good, committed employees. Even if women are able to commit extra time to work, employers frequently assume that, because they are women, they won't. A famous hedge fund billionaire recently stated that in the world of global trading, babies are a "killer" for women's careers: "As soon as that baby's lips touch that girl's bosom, forget it" (quoted in J. Johnson, 2013, p. 1). Indeed, working mothers continue to earn significantly less than other employed women (Porter, 2012).

Furthermore, even when companies provide "family-friendly" workplace policies—such as flexible work schedules or the opportunity to temporarily reduce hours—women may be penalized for using them. Women who opt for these provisions risk being seen as less competent and less committed to their work. In countries with generous family-friendly work policies, women sometimes end up getting paid less and find their access to management and other high-power positions limited (Goldin, 2014). In the United States, female workers were actually more likely to get promoted *before* the Family and Medical Leave Act of 1993 (see Chapter 7) became law (K. Thomas, 2015). By the way, it's not only women who are affected this way. Men who seek work flexibility may be stigmatized even more than women because employers tend to view them as deviating from traditional male breadwinner expectations. In fact, men who take leave for the birth of a child are less likely than men who don't to get promoted or receive raises (J. C. Williams, Blair-Joy, & Berdahl, 2013).

But in general, women continue to face economic obstacles men never do. For instance, although it is against federal law for a company with 15 or more employees to discriminate against pregnant job seekers, it can be difficult for a woman to get hired if she lets prospective bosses know she's pregnant. Hence some pregnant applicants withhold this information during interviews or wear baggy clothing to conceal it. Their concerns are not unwarranted. Many pregnant women are pushed out of their jobs every year, either by being put on unpaid leave or by being fired outright (cited in Liptak, 2014). The U.S. Equal Employment Opportunity Commission (2017b) received about 6,000 official complaints of such pregnancy discrimination in 2016, up from about 4,000 in 2000.

Such assumptions are present in professional, academic environments, too. In its assessment of the underrepresentation of women in science and engineering positions, the National Academy of Sciences (2007) concluded that the traditional scientific or engineering career rests on the assumption that faculty members will be thoroughly committed to their occupation throughout their working life. It found that attention to other obligations, such as family, is often interpreted as a lack of dedication to one's career. Because the burden of family and household care still generally falls more heavily on women than on men—and because women seldom have substantial spousal support—women scientists and engineers experience greater conflict between their family and professional roles than male scientists and engineers do.

It's not surprising, therefore, that women in these fields experience widespread bias. It's not just that there are relatively few of them in graduate programs, in academic positions, and in leadership positions in professional organizations. They are also often perceived by professional mentors as less competent and less committed than their male counterparts (Moss-Racusin et al., 2012). In 2015, Tim Hunt, a Nobel Prize-winning biochemist, while addressing the World Conference of Science Journalists, said:

> Let me tell you about my trouble with girls. Three things happen when they are in the lab: You fall in love with them, they fall in love with you, and when you criticize them they cry. (quoted in Bilefsky, 2015, p. A4)

As a consequence of such attitudes, women in science and engineering typically receive fewer resources and less institutional support than men (National Academy of Sciences, 2007).

The Sex-Segregated Workplace

In general, though, U.S. women have made progress in overcoming traditional obstacles to employment. In 1950, a little over 30% of adult women were employed in the paid labor force; today, that figure is about 57%, and it increases to 67.6% for married mothers, 72.2%

for single mothers, and 78.2% for widowed, separated, and divorced mothers (ProQuest Statistical Abstract, 2017). Over half of all U.S. workers today are female. A record 40% of all households with children younger than 18 include mothers who are either the sole or primary breadwinners for the family, up from just 11% in 1960 (W. Wang, Parker, & Taylor, 2013). And women have become increasingly more likely to work into their 60s and 70s (Goldin & Katz, 2016).

The increase in female labor force participation has been particularly dramatic in some traditionally male-dominated fields such as medicine and law. For instance, in 1983, 15% of lawyers and 16% of physicians in the United States were women; by 2016, those figures had more than doubled (U.S. Bureau of the Census, 2004; ProQuest Statistical Abstract, 2017).

Although such a trend is encouraging, there are signs that women's economic progress has stalled. Women's overall participation in the paid labor force actually peaked 20 years ago (Covert, 2017). Younger women without college degrees are especially vulnerable, suffering from decreasing wages and increasing unemployment (Jarosz & Mather, 2017). Consider also the persistent sex segregation that exists in the workplace. Women make up 94.6% of all secretaries, 90% of all registered nurses, 94.4% of all childcare workers, 97.1% of all dental hygienists, and 97.5% of all preschool and kindergarten teachers (ProQuest Statistical Abstract, 2017). Despite their increased presence in traditionally male occupations, women still tend to be underrepresented among dentists (34.4%), physicians (38.2%), engineers and architects (14.2%), lawyers (35.7%), police officers (14.1%), and firefighters (3.5%).

In other words, most of the changes that have taken place in the sex distribution of different occupations have been the result of women entering male lines of work, not vice versa. Although women have entered traditionally male occupations at a steady clip since the 1980s, men have not noticeably increased their representation in female-dominated occupations. The number of male nurses, kindergarten teachers, and secretaries has increased only minimally, if at all (ProQuest Statistical Abstract, 2017). There remains a deep stigma attached to men who pursue stereotypically female occupations (you might recall that a running joke in the popular movie *Meet the Parents* was that the main male character, Greg Focker, was a nurse). So it shouldn't surprise us that most men who can afford to do so, choose to avoid "female jobs" (P. Cohen, 2013). Job postings that advertise for applicants who are "sympathetic" or "caring" tend not to attract very many male candidates (C. C. Miller, 2017a) One study even found that some men would rather suffer unemployment than accept "women's jobs," even plentiful high-paying ones, because of the potential damage to their sense of masculinity (C. F. Epstein, 1989). Indeed, the jobs that are most in demand today—nursing, nurse assistants, home health care aides—sit open because many men find them unmanly and demeaning (Chira, 2017). As one sociologist put it, "[W]e have a cultural lag where our views of masculinity have not caught up to the change in the job market" (quoted in C. C. Miller, 2017e, p. 3).

This kind of "one-way" occupational shift may cause problems in the long run. Historically, when large numbers of women enter a particular occupation previously closed to them, the number of men in that occupation decreases. Given that greater value is usually awarded to male pursuits, such occupations become less prestigious as men leave them. In fact, the higher the proportion of female workers in an occupation, the less both male and female workers earn in that occupation (Padavic & Reskin, 2002).

Greater female entry into traditionally male lines of work doesn't necessarily mean gender equality, either. For instance, sex segregation often occurs in specific jobs *within* a profession. In medicine, female physicians are substantially overrepresented in specialties such as family practice, pediatrics, and obstetrics and gynecology and underrepresented in more prestigious and lucrative areas such as surgery and cardiology. As I mentioned, women make up about a third of all practicing physicians. But they account for 62% of pediatricians, 55% of obstetrician/gynecologists, and 52% of child psychiatrists. By contrast, less than 10% of cardiologists, neurosurgeons, thoracic surgeons, and orthopedic surgeons are women (Association of American Medical Colleges, 2016).

Similarly, among lawyers, women are promoted at a lower rate than their male counterparts, and they remain underrepresented in private practice, in law firm partnerships, and in high positions such as judges on the federal courts, district courts, and circuit courts of appeals (Hull & Nelson, 2000).

In sum, although more women than ever work in the paid labor force, we continue to have some jobs that employ almost exclusively women and others that employ almost exclusively men. When people are allocated jobs on the basis of sex rather than ability to perform the work, chances for self-fulfillment are limited (Reskin & Hartmann, 1986). Society also loses, because neither men nor women are free to do the jobs for which they might best be suited. However, segregation is most harmful to individual women, because the occupations they predominantly hold tend to be less prestigious and to pay lower wages than those held predominantly by men.

The Wage Gap

> The Lord spoke to Moses and said, "When a man makes a special vow to the Lord which requires your valuation of living persons, a male between twenty and sixty years old shall be valued at fifty silver shekels. If it is a female, she shall be valued at thirty shekels." (Leviticus 27:1–4)

You don't have to go back to biblical times to find evidence of the practice of setting women's pay at less than men's. Even though the 1963 Equal Pay Act guaranteed equal pay for equal work in the United States, and Title VII of the 1964 Civil Rights Act banned job discrimination on the basis of sex (as well as race, religion, and national origin), a gap in earnings persists. In 2015, the average earnings for all U.S. men working full time, year round was $51,212. All women working full time, year round earned about $40,742 per year (Proctor, Semega, & Kollar, 2016). To put it another way, for every dollar a U.S. man earns, a woman earns only about 80 cents. The wage gap is especially pronounced for women of color. African American women earn about 70 cents for every dollar a man earns; for Latina women, it's 60 cents (Institute for Women's Policy Research, 2016). Although women have been closing the wage gap over the past several decades, progress has been rather slow. At the current rate, they won't achieve full pay equity with men nationally until the year 2059. Black women will have to wait until the year 2124 and Latina women won't achieve full pay equity until 2248 (Institute for Women's Policy Research, 2016).

Today's gender wage gap actually widens with age. At the start of their careers, the gap is small: young college-educated women, for instance, earn about 90% of what college-educated men earn. However, by the time these individuals are fully immersed in their careers, the pay gap has grown. By their early 40s, female college graduates can expect to earn roughly 55% percent less than male college graduates (Barth, Goldin, Kerr, & Olivetti, 2017). To put it another way, the average American woman can expect to lose $530,000 in lifetime earnings compared to men; the average college-educated woman can expect to earn about $800,000 less than men (E. Gould, Schieder, & Geier, 2016). In addition, because women earn less when they're employed, their retirement pensions are also significantly smaller than men's (National Women's Law Center, 2006).

I should point out that the wage gap is a global phenomenon. To varying degrees, in every country around the world, men earn more than women. In Japan and Korea, the gender wage gap is larger than it is in the United States, with women earning around 30% to 40% less than men. In other countries, however, such as Belgium, Greece, Hungary, Italy, New Zealand, and Norway, the wage gap is narrower with women earning 90% or more of what men earn (Organization for Economic Cooperation and Development, 2015b).

Why is the U.S. wage gap so persistent? One reason, of course, is occupational segregation and the types of jobs women are most likely to have. For five of the "most female" jobs (that is, those that are around 95% female)—namely, preschool teacher, teacher's assistant, housekeeper, childcare worker, and dental assistant—the overall average weekly salary is $527. For five of the "most male" jobs (those around 95% male)—namely, airplane pilot, firefighter, aircraft engine mechanic, plumber, and construction worker—the overall average weekly salary is $1,081 (U.S. Bureau of Labor Statistics, 2017e). But segregation isn't the whole story. Even in the same occupations, men's and women's earnings diverge (see Exhibit 12.5).

Some economists and policymakers argue that the wage gap is essentially an institutional by-product that exists because men on the whole work more hours per year, are more likely to work a full-time schedule than women, and have more work experience and training (Dey & Hill, 2007). Now, you will recall from Chapter 10 that due to the lingering effects of the recent economic recession, large numbers of both men and women have been forced to work part time because of workplace cutbacks. But women are particularly susceptible to this trend. According to the U.S. Bureau of Labor Statistics (2017b), 12% of employed men over the age of 16 work part time, compared with 24% of employed women. Not only do part-time workers earn less, but during hard times, they are usually the first ones pushed out of employment—not because they're women but because their jobs are the most expendable.

Even after controlling for differences in experience, age, and education—factors that might justify discrepancies in salary—the wage gap between men and women remains (Weinberg, 2007). For instance, the average income of female workers in the United States is significantly lower than that of men with the same level of educational attainment. Women with bachelor's degrees earn, on average, about 63.6% of what men with bachelor's degrees earn. In fact, women with bachelor's degrees can expect to earn less than men with a 2-year associate's degree (mean annual earnings of $50,856 compared with $51,865). Similarly, women with doctoral degrees (with mean annual earnings of $91,254) earn less than men with only master's degrees (with mean annual earnings of $96,896) (ProQuest Statistical Abstract, 2017).

One possible remedy for the wage gap is to increase women's access to occupations that have traditionally been closed to them. As I noted earlier, this is already happening, to a certain degree, although sex segregation is still the rule. Furthermore, women and their families need enhanced efforts to ensure non-discriminatory hiring and pay practices, better training and career counseling, and improved work-family supports. Broader public policies, like raising the minimum wage, could increase wages in the lowest-paid jobs, which is especially important for women, particularly women of color (Institute for Women's Policy Research, 2016). Five states (Iowa, Minnesota, Montana, Washington, and West Virginia) now have laws that address the gender wage gap by requiring employers to

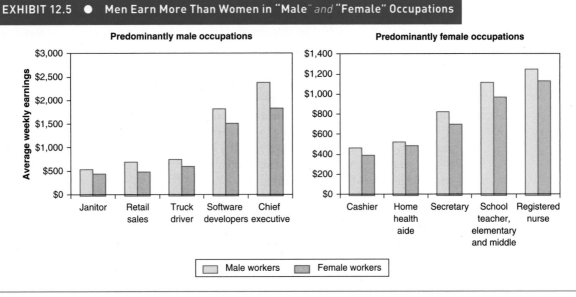

EXHIBIT 12.5 ● Men Earn More Than Women in "Male" *and* "Female" Occupations

Predominantly male occupations

Predominantly female occupations

Source: Hegewisch & Wiliams-Baron, 2017, Tables 1 & 2.

pay workers in different jobs equitable wages if the jobs require comparable levels of skill, effort, and responsibility.

But to date, little has been done to change the situation at the national level. In 2007, a bill was introduced in the U.S. Senate called the Fair Pay Act. It sought to end wage discrimination against those who work in female-dominated jobs by establishing equal pay guidelines for equivalent work. For example, within an individual company, employers could not pay less for jobs held predominately by women than for jobs held predominately by men if those jobs were similarly important to the employer (National Committee on Pay Equity, 2007). However, the bill was defeated. In 2009, President Obama signed into law a stripped-down version of the bill, which makes it easier for women to file equal-pay lawsuits but didn't address the equal pay issue directly. The original bill was introduced again in 2013, but never came to a vote in Congress. In 2016, another bill called the Pay Equity for All Act was introduced but it has yet to come to a vote either.

The Global Devaluation of Women

At first glance, women seem to be making tremendous advances worldwide—becoming better educated and more economically independent than ever before. For instance, the number of girls of primary school age worldwide who did not attend school dropped from 58 million in 2000 to 31 million in 2012 (UNICEF, 2014c). And over the past several decades, women in most regions of the world have increased their representation in most sectors of the paid labor force.

Nevertheless, women remain physically and economically disadvantaged in most societies around the world, especially in developing countries. Worldwide, women make up a little over half of all HIV-infected adults (amFAR, 2016). But in the poor countries of west and central Africa, young women account for 64% of new HIV infections. In the Cameroon, Ivory Coast, and Guinea, adolescent girls are *five times* more likely than boys the same age to be infected (Avert, 2017b). In addition, 86% of all women worldwide who die from childbirth complications come from the developing countries of sub-Saharan Africa and Southern Asia (UN Women, 2015). And while women have made significant strides worldwide in access to education, they still lag far behind men in labor force participation (International Labour Organization, 2017). In the Arab States and Northern Africa, unemployment rates for women exceed 20%, twice the rate of men. And where they are employed, women make up the vast majority of global factory workers in multinational corporations, often working in unsafe and unhealthy conditions at extremely low pay.

In many countries, women do not have the same everyday legal, familial, and bodily protections that men enjoy. According to the United Nations, one in three women worldwide experience some form of intimate violence (UN Women, 2016). Consider the vulnerability women face in these countries:

- In Kyrgyzstan, it's estimated that more than half of all married women were abducted by their soon-to-be husbands in a centuries-old legal custom known as *ala kachuu* (which literally means "grab and run"). If the woman is kept in the man's home overnight, her virginity becomes suspect, her name disgraced, and her future marriage chances destroyed. So most women (about 80%, according to estimates) eventually relent and marry their abductor, often at the urging of their own families (C. S. Smith, 2005).

- In Sri Lanka, hundreds of thousands of women have been forced by economic need to leave their own families and migrate to affluent Persian Gulf countries, where they work as maids for wealthy families. Saudi Arabians refer to Sri Lanka as "the country of housemaids" (Waldman, 2005). These women are considered heroines at home because of their economic contributions to their families, but they are often subjected to severe beatings and mistreatment at the hands of their foreign employers.

- In Afghanistan, wives are sometimes killed by their husbands for having sex outside the marriage or for not bearing a son (Bowley, 2012). And Afghan daughters face likely death at the hands of their families if they return home after eloping (A. J. Rubin, 2015).

- In Syria, girls who bring dishonor to their families by having premarital sex are sometimes killed by relatives. Under Syrian law, these killings, called *ghasalat al arr* ("washing away the shame"), are not considered murder (Zoepf, 2007).

- In 2015, over 7,600 Indian women—an average of 21 a day—were killed by their husbands for not providing adequate dowries (National Crime Records Bureau, 2016). Even though India officially banned dowry (gifts that a woman receives from her parents on marriage) in 1961, it is still an essential part of premarital negotiations and now encompasses the wealth that the bride's family pays the groom.

The globalization of the world economy also helps create a market for the international exploitation of women. In many poor countries, one of the fastest-growing criminal enterprises is forcing naïve and desperately poor women to work as prostitutes in other countries. In some of these countries, prostitution is legal; in others it may be illegal, but enforcement is inconsistent and punishment light. Without any other means of support and often without knowledge of the native language, these women become completely dependent on men who are perfectly willing to exploit them.

However, the public devaluation of women can sometimes hide a very different private reality. Take, for example, the decision by Islamic women in the Middle East to wear *hijabs* (veils that cover their necks and chests) in the presence of men. Such an act may seem to outside observers as a sign of powerlessness and subordination. But many of these women see themselves as political activists who are helping to create a new society by transforming everyday life from within (Luhrmann, 2015).

Similarly, Japanese women have historically occupied a visibly subservient position in society and in families. Women in the workforce suffer discrimination in hiring, salary, and promotion despite the presence of equal-opportunity laws there. Only about 49% of Japanese women currently work outside the home (World Bank, 2015). They are typically expected to clean, cook, and tend to the needs of their husbands within the home. Yet many Japanese wives dominate their husbands. They tend to control the household finances, giving their husbands monthly allowances as they see fit. If a man wants to withdraw money from the family account, the savings bank will usually phone the wife to get her approval. Japanese men are even starting to take on some of the housework responsibilities, which would have been unthinkable a couple of decades ago.

Women are making significant strides in other parts of the world where they have traditionally suffered. In places like Uganda, Burundi, and Tunisia, women now account for around 30% of elected officials. For women in Rwanda, the figure is 56%—the highest in the world—up from just 17% in 2000 (Population Reference Bureau, 2011). Despite persistent victimization and oppression, women in Iran, Afghanistan, Somalia, and Liberia are at the forefront of local and national reform movements (Foroohar, 2010). In Algeria, women make up 60% of university students, 70% of lawyers, and 60% of judges. They also contribute more to household income than men (Slackman, 2007).

To some extent, the improvement of women's lives in some parts of the world can be attributed to global forces for change, which sometimes spread democratic values and humanitarian principles (Giddens, 2005). For instance, following reports of beatings, burnings, and beheadings of female domestic workers at the hands of their bosses in Saudi Arabia, Indonesia, Sri Lanka, and elsewhere, the International Labor Organization adopted a treaty that protects women from such abuse. Observers estimate that such a pact could protect the 50 to 100 million domestic workers who heretofore had very few if any rights (Human Rights Watch, 2011).

In 1979, the United Nations General Assembly adopted a treaty known as the Convention on the Elimination of All Forms of Discrimination Against Women (Division for the Advancement of Women, 2009). By accepting the treaty, countries agreed to take measures to end discrimination against women in all forms by

- incorporating the principle of equality of men and women into their legal systems, abolishing all discriminatory laws, and adopting appropriate ones prohibiting discrimination against women,

- establishing tribunals and other public institutions to ensure the effective protection of women against discrimination, and

- ensuring elimination of all acts of discrimination against women by persons, organizations, or enterprises.

All but 2 of the 189 participant countries of the United Nations have ratified this agreement, which legally binds them to put its provisions into practice (United Nations Treaty Collection, 2017). The only holdouts are the tiny Pacific Island nation, Palau . . . and the United States.

Conclusion

Inequality based on sex and gender goes beyond the degrading media and cultural images of women, the face-to-face interactions that reinforce the devaluation of women, and the stereotypical beliefs of individual people. It is woven into the institutional and cultural fabric of societies around the world. In the 21st-century United States, it is as much a part of the social landscape as baseball, apple pie, and Fourth of July fireworks. Every woman has felt sexism at some level, whether as personal violence, annoying harassment, sexually suggestive leers and comments, fear of going out at night, job discrimination, legal obstacles, or subtle encouragement toward "appropriate" pursuits—whether they be sports, hobbies, or careers.

Men tend to benefit from living in a society where language, identity, intimacy, history, culture, and social institutions are built on gender distinctions, even if the men themselves do not support such inequality. Like most people whose interests are being served by the system, men are largely unaware of the small and large advantages the social structure provides them and therefore tend to underestimate the sexism women feel in their lives (C. C. Miller, 2017c). Thus, most men don't see sex and gender inequality as their problem—it's a "women's issue"—and they are less likely than women to see a need for large-scale social change.

So the first step toward gender equality is that men will have to come to understand their role in the process, even in the absence of blatant, personal sexism. All men are tacitly involved in the oppression of women each time they automatically giggle at sexist jokes, mistake female doctors for nurses, dismiss the sexual objectification of women as harmless "locker room talk," expect less from women on the job or in school, or expect more of them at home.

The next step will require a fundamental transformation of institutional patterns and cultural values. Such a solution sounds too massive to be possible. But today, we are seeing early steps in that direction: changing conceptions of family roles, women's increasing (though not yet equal) participation in the labor force, their growing (but not yet equal) political power, and greater awareness of sexual exploitation and violence worldwide. How far these changes will take us in the future remains to be seen.

Your Turn

To understand how beliefs are translated into action, examine how sexism influences people's activities. One fruitful area of examination is the home. Locate a few of each of the following types of couples in which both partners are employed full time outside the home:

- Newly married couple without children (married less than 1 year)

- Married couple without children (married 10 years or more)

- Married couple (older or younger) with at least one child living at home

- Nonmarital cohabiting couple (heterosexual or homosexual)

- Remarried couple

Ask each person in the couple to make a list of all the household chores that need to be done during the course of a week. Ask each to be as specific and exhaustive as possible (e.g., "cleaning windows" rather than "cleaning the house"). After the lists are completed, ask each person to indicate which of these tasks that person is primarily responsible for, which tasks that person's partner is responsible for, and which are shared. Ask the participants also to estimate the total amount of time spent each week on all these tasks combined. Finally, ask them to estimate how many hours they work at their jobs during a typical week. (*Note:* To ensure that you're gauging each individual's perceptions, interview each partner separately.) Compare people's responses to see if you can find any differences—in terms of time spent doing housework and the number of tasks for which each one is responsible—between

- partners in the same couple
- men and women
- younger and older couples
- married and cohabiting couples
- couples with and without children at home
- married and remarried couples
- heterosexual and homosexual couples

Do women who work outside the home still bear the primary responsibility for housework? Is the traditional gender division of labor absent in certain types of couples? How does the presence of children affect the household division of labor? If partners have different ideas about housework responsibilities, to what do you attribute this lack of agreement? Describe the tensions that men and women experience when trying to balance work and home responsibilities.

Chapter Highlights

- Personal sexism is most apparent during the course of everyday interaction in the form of communication patterns and gestures. It can be particularly dangerous when expressed in the form of sexual harassment and sexual violence.

- Gender stratification is perpetuated by a dominant cultural ideology that devalues women on the basis of alleged biological differences between men and women. This ideology overlooks the equally important role of social forces in determining male and female behavior.

- Institutional sexism exists in the media, in the law, in the family, in the educational system, and in the economy. Women have entered the paid labor force in unprecedented numbers, but they still tend to occupy jobs that are typically considered "female" and still earn significantly less than men.

- Not only are social institutions sexist in that women are systematically segregated, exploited, and excluded, but they are also "gendered." Institutions themselves are structured along gender lines so that traits associated with success are usually stereotypically male characteristics: toughmindedness, rationality, assertiveness, competitiveness, and so forth.

- Despite recent advances worldwide, women still tend to suffer physically, psychologically, economically, and politically in most societies.

Key Terms

institutional sexism: Subordination of women that is part of the everyday workings of economics, law, politics, and other social institutions

matriarchy: Female-dominated society that gives higher prestige and value to women than to men

objectification: Practice of treating people as objects

patriarchy: Male-dominated society in which cultural beliefs and values give higher prestige and value to men than to women

sexism: System of beliefs that asserts the inferiority of one sex and justifies gender-based inequality

SAGE edge™ edge.sagepub.com/newman12e

SAGE edge offers a robust online environment featuring an impressive array of free tools and resources for review, study, and further exploration, keeping both instructors and students on the cutting edge of teaching and learning.

13

Demographic Dynamics
Population Trends

- The Influence of Birth Cohorts
- Demographic Dynamics
- Population Trends in the United States

admit it. I said those seven words I once vowed I'd never say. The ones that tag you as a clueless, over-the-hill relic. No, it wasn't, "Hey, have you guys heard of tweeting?" It was, *"I just don't understand you kids today!"*

It all started over a decade ago when I was arguing with my two sons—teenagers at the time—over what to watch on television. I wanted to watch a rerun of the sixth game of the 1975 World Series. I told them that my choice was a priceless piece of U.S. sports history, the best World Series game ever played, according to many baseball historians. They wanted to watch the X Games. I felt like I had the moral high ground on this one. A classic moment should always take precedence over some new fad. Besides, I didn't quite understand the appeal of the X Games. Sure, I knew it was an annual alternative sports festival based on weird-sounding extreme sports like Skateboard Big Air, Moto X Freestyle, BMX Dirt, Snowboard Super Pipe, Ski Slopestyle, and so on. But I didn't care to know the difference between a "varial heelflip" and a "backside disaster." To me, "grinding" is what you do with coffee beans in the morning and "getting clean air" means moving out of Los Angeles.

They told me that I was a dinosaur and that I had better wake up and smell the 21st century. The X Games, they claimed, were the future. And you know what? They turned out to be right. The extreme sports made famous by the X Games soon became part of an influential youth subculture with its own hard-edged language, fashion, and music. In fact, the word *extreme* is now a modifying adjective for all sorts of activities that push beyond what's commonly accepted. As one journalist put it, "The extreme version of anything is now widely assumed to be an improvement on the original rather than a perverse amplification of it" (Havrilesky, 2014, p. 12). With a simple online search you can find information on extreme camping, extreme bartending, extreme fitness, extreme trampoline, extreme pumpkin carving, extreme chess, extreme tanning, extreme couponing, and even extreme childbirth.

Extreme sports are self-consciously designed to be thrilling, dangerous, subversive, and rebellious. Their appeal resides not so much in grace, strategy, or competitive drive as in the chance for disaster to strike. Between 2000 and 2011, extreme sports participants suffered 4 million injuries, 11% of which were head and neck injuries (Sharma, Rango, Connaughton, & Sabesan, 2014). "The fact that they're called 'extreme' sports means, if you make a mistake, you die," said one admirer (quoted in Clemmitt, 2009, p. 301). And in the 2013 Winter X Games, a freestyle snowmobiler did indeed die after being knocked unconscious during a crash landing.

For the most part, extreme athletes bear little resemblance to athletes in more traditional sports. They tend to despise rules, regulations, and standard conceptions of the competitive spirit. Indeed, many extreme sports don't have objective measures of success—like finishing first in a race or scoring more points than an opponent—but are instead judged on their degree of risk and danger. They don't want merely to improve on what others have done in the past (like hit more home runs, score more goals, or shoot a lower round of golf); they want to do something that's never been done before.

The allure has been powerful. One survey found that more teens and preteens prefer watching extreme sports on television to watching college basketball, college football, auto racing, hockey, tennis, or golf (G. Bennett, Henson, & Zhang, 2003). Indeed, while many traditional sports have witnessed a decline in the number of participants, skateboarding has surged 49% and snowboarding has increased 51% since 1999 (Sharma et al., 2014). More runners now participate in obstacle races—where they must negotiate mud, barbed wire, fire, and other daunting challenges—than in traditional marathons or triathlons. And once these sports become old hat, extreme athletes find new ways to push the limit, through activities like wingsuit BASE jumping, paramotoring, waterfall kayaking, cliff face camping, kiteboarding, or canyon swinglining.

Ironically, although extreme sports appear to be solidly antiestablishment, they have clearly become a multibillion-dollar mainstream business (J. Longman & Higgins, 2005). Nitro Circus—a media firm that organizes an extreme sports traveling show of mind-blowing daredevil jumps and stunts—has a 40-city worldwide tour, a television show on NBC Sports, and a 3D feature film. With annual revenues in the range of $50 million, *Forbes* magazine (2015) recently added the firm to its list of America's Most Promising Companies. Indeed, corporate America has been scrambling to co-opt the language, image, and culture of extreme athletes in order to tap into this booming market. The champion snowboarder Shaun White earns tens of millions of dollars a year from multimillion endorsement deals with companies like Kraft, Burton, Target, Oakley, and Ubisoft. Extreme sports have also achieved a significant degree of societal acceptance. Events like freestyle skiing, snowboarding, mountain biking, and BMX cycling are now in the Olympics.

And yet many older people still fail to understand the attraction of these sports. What my sons didn't realize at the time was that they had identified one of the most crucial dividing lines in society today. They and I may be members of the same family. We may share the same genes, ethnicity, social class, and political views. But we're also members of two extremely different, sometimes antagonistic, social groups that are distinguished by one simple and unchangeable fact: our ages.

In the past several chapters, I examined various interconnected sources of social stratification: social class, race and ethnicity, and sex and gender. You have seen that the distance between the haves and the have-nots—both locally and globally—continues to grow wider as a result of their different levels of access to important cultural, economic, and political resources. But within the United States, as well as most other societies, imbalances between various age groups will also be a defining feature of social life in the decades to come. This chapter examines the relationship between broad population trends—which include not only a changing age structure but also population growth and immigration—and everyday life. How are these changes affecting the ability to provide people with the resources they need for a comfortable life? How are important social institutions functioning as a result of these population shifts?

The Influence of Birth Cohorts

If you're like most college students, you've no doubt asked yourself at least some of these questions: Will I get a job after I graduate? Where will I live? Will I be able to afford a house? Will I have a spouse? Will I ever be a parent? How will I save for my retirement? The answers to these questions are obviously influenced by your personal desires, traits, values, ambitions, and abilities. And as you've already read in this book so far, your social class, gender, race, religion, and ethnicity will shape the answers, too.

But they will also be influenced by your place in the population at a given point in time. **Birth cohorts** are sets of people who were born during the same time period—usually within a span of 10 to 15 years—and who face similar societal circumstances brought about by their position in the age structure of the population. Birth cohorts affect people's everyday lives in two fundamental ways (Riley, 1971):

- People in the same birth cohort tend to experience life course events or social rites of passage—such as puberty, marriage, childbearing, graduation, entrance into the workforce, and death—at roughly the same time. Sociologists call these experiences **cohort effects**. The size of your birth cohort, relative to other cohorts, can have a significant impact on your life experiences: It can determine things like the availability of affordable housing, high-paying jobs, and attractive potential mates and can also affect how satisfied you feel with your own life. One study found that large cohorts in developed countries tend to have higher rates of suicide than small cohorts because people face more economic disadvantage and have more difficulty integrating into their communities when there are large numbers of people in the same age range competing for limited resources (Stockard & O'Brien, 2002).

- Members of the same birth cohort also share a common history. A cohort's place in time tells us a lot about the opportunities and constraints placed on its members. Unexpected historical events (wars, epidemics, natural disasters, economic depressions, etc.), changing political conditions, and major cultural trends, called **period effects**, contribute to the unique shape and outlook of each birth cohort. Many historians, for instance, believe that a period of drought and famine caused the people of the Mayan civilization to abandon their great cities nearly a thousand years ago. Those who were adults when this period began enjoyed comfortable lives, reveled in the high culture of the Mayans, and had tremendous prospects for the future. But for their children, born just a generation later, starvation, death, and social dislocation were the basic facts of life (Clausen, 1986).

Cohort and period effects combine to give each birth cohort its distinctive properties, such as ethnic composition, average life expectancies, and age-specific birthrates. For instance, women who experienced the Great Depression of the 1930s during their peak childbearing years—when they were in their 20s and early 30s—had the lowest birthrate of any cohort during the 20th century. Therefore, women born between 1900 and 1910 tended as a group to have smaller families to rely on in their old age, which for them occurred roughly between 1970 and 1980. These experiences contrasted sharply with those of women born a mere 10 years later, who were too young to have children during the Great Depression and entered their peak childbearing period during the relatively prosperous years after World War II. They tended to have large families and therefore more sources of support in their old age (Soldo & Agree, 1988).

Cohort and period effects can also influence your worldview and self-concept. Think how different your goals and ambitions would be had you experienced childhood during a time of relative affluence, such as the late 1990s, as opposed to a period of severe economic uncertainty, say the late 2000s and early 2010s. Rights and privileges taken for granted by one cohort are likely to be considered unattainable dreams by a different one.

As we grow older, we develop and change in a society that itself is developing and changing. We start our lives in one historical period with a distinct set of social norms, and we end our lives in another. Early in the 20th century, for example, most people went to school for only 6 or 7 years, which yielded an adequate education for the types of jobs their parents and older siblings held. Today, 89% of U.S. residents go to school for at least 12 years (ProQuest Statistical Abstract, 2017). As a result, older cohorts on the whole tend to score substantially lower on standardized intelligence tests than younger cohorts. Because of such test results, social scientists long assumed that intelligence declines markedly with age. But we now know that these differences are the result not of aging but of changing societal values regarding education (Clausen, 1986).

Even the way people personally experience the aging process is affected by the social, cultural, and environmental changes to which their cohort is exposed in moving through the life course. Because of advances in nutrition, education, sanitation, medical treatment, working conditions, transportation safety, and environmental quality, younger cohorts can expect to live longer and healthier than older cohorts.

As you can see, birth cohorts are more than just a collection of individuals born around the same time; they are distinctive generations tied together by historical circumstances, population trends, and societal changes. However, we must also realize that when many individuals in the same cohort are affected by social events in similar ways, the changes in their collective lives can produce changes in society. Each succeeding cohort leaves its mark on the prevailing culture. In other words, cohorts are not only affected by social changes but contribute to them as well (Riley, Foner, & Waring, 1988).

Baby Boomers

The birth cohort that has received the most national attention is, without a doubt, the Baby Boom generation—the 76 million or so people born between 1946 and 1964. They make up around 25% of the entire U.S. population (Pollard & Scommegna, 2014).

The passing of this massive cohort through the life course has been described metaphorically as "a pig in a python." If you've ever seen one of those nature shows on TV where snakes devour and digest small animals, you know how apt the metaphor is. In 1980, the largest age group in the United States consisted of people between 15 and 24 years of age. In 1990, the largest group in the United States consisted of people between 25 and 34 years of age. In 2000, it was 35- to 44-year-olds. In 2010, it was people between 50 and 60

(Colby & Ortman, 2015). So you see that as this cohort bulge works its way through the life course, it stretches the parameters of the relevant social institutions at each stage. Baby Boomers packed hospital nurseries as infants, school classrooms as children, and college campuses, employment lines, and the housing market as young adults (Light, 1988). In middle age, they became prime movers in the burgeoning markets for adventure travel, relaxed-fit fashion, diet, nutrition, and wellness products.

The trend will continue into the future. By the year 2030, there will be over 74 million Baby Boomers of retirement age, compared to about 48 million today (ProQuest Statistical Abstract, 2017). As they reach their golden years, programs concerned with later life—pension plans, Social Security, Medicare—will be seriously stretched. For instance, the number of older Americans covered by Medicare will increase by 30 million over the next two decades (Greenblatt, 2011). And sometime in the middle of the century, there will likely be a surge in business for the funeral industry as this generation reaches the end of its collective life cycle (Schodolski, 1993).

Baby Boomers have left an especially influential mark on the institution of family. Their generation was the first to redefine families to include a variety of living arrangements, such as nonmarital cohabitation and never-married women with dependent children (Wattenberg, 1986). They were also the first to acknowledge the expectation of paid work as a central feature of women's lives. And they were the first to grow up with effective birth control, enabling delayed childbearing, voluntary childlessness, and low birthrates.

Consequently, the Baby Boomers who are now reaching old age have fewer children to turn to for the kind of help they gave their own grandparents and parents (Butler, 1989). Hence, they will be more likely than previous generations to turn to social service and health care organizations to care for them. Not surprisingly, most Baby Boomers are quite pessimistic about their ability to sustain their quality of life (Pew Research Center, 2010).

Generation X

Although Baby Boomers have dominated the cultural spotlight for decades, U.S. society has also taken notice of the generation to follow them, known as Generation X. Today, there are more than 61 million U.S. residents who were born between 1965 and 1979 (ProQuest Statistical Abstract, 2017). The birthrate during the 1970s, when most of these individuals were born, was about half what it was during the post–World War II years of the Baby Boom.

More Generation Xers—roughly 40% of them—experienced the divorce of their parents than any previous generation. As a result, they tend to be emotionally conflicted about marriage. They are less likely to get married than older generations and more likely to delay marriage and childbearing if they do (Carlson, 2009). In addition, they're more likely to be single—with or without children—than previous generations (Sayer, Casper, & Cohen, 2004).

Even more Generation Xers grew up as so-called latchkey children, the first generation of children to experience the effects of having two working parents. For many of these children, childhood was marked by dependence on others—teachers, friends, babysitters, and day care workers.

On many social issues—legalizing marijuana, same-sex marriage, immigration policy, abortion rights, civil liberties—Generation Xers take a more liberal position than older cohorts. But their political leanings are divided. Those who came of age during the Reagan and George H. W. Bush presidencies are more inclined to identify as Republicans; those who grew up during the Clinton and George W. Bush eras are markedly Democratic (Taylor, 2014a).

The Millennium and Post-Millennium Generations

The 85 million or so individuals born between 1980 and 2000 make up the next noticeable cohort, known as the Millennium Generation. This cohort has surpassed the Baby Boom as the largest living cohort (Fry, 2016b). It is qualitatively different as well. For instance, this cohort is more ethnically diverse than previous cohorts; 4 in 10 are not white (P. Taylor, 2014a). They are also more likely than preceding cohorts to grow up in a nontraditional family. One in 4 lived in a single-parent household as a child; 3 in 4 had working mothers, and 4 in 10 had mothers who were primary or sole breadwinners in the family. In addition, compared with older cohorts, they are less religious, less likely to serve in the military, more likely to identify as politically independent, and on track to become the most educated cohort in American history (Pew Research Center, 2014b).

Most notably, the Millennium Generation is more digitally connected than any older cohort. They were the first generation to take wireless connectivity for granted (see Exhibit 13.1). The average Millennial sends or receives about 3,700 texts a month (cited in Dokoupil, 2012). He or she also has about 250 Facebook friends, compared to an average of 50 among older Baby Boomers (Pew Research Center, 2014b). One Millennial journalist put it this way: "It is one thing to own a smartphone, as so many of us do. It is quite another to have mastered its uses at age 10" (Tanenhaus, 2014, p. 7). In contrast, one third of Baby Boomers say they never use the Internet, and half say they don't have home broadband services (M. Anderson & Perrin, 2017).

Although this preoccupation with technology may create a generation less interpersonally adept than generations of the past, the exposure to other cultures that the Internet

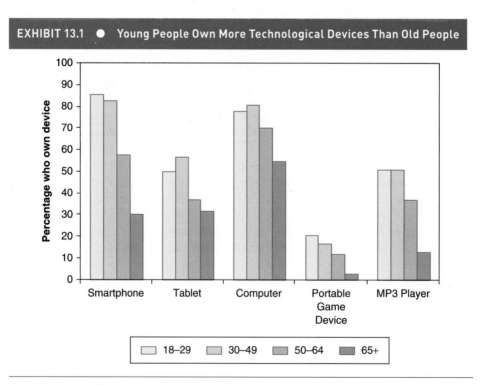

EXHIBIT 13.1 ● Young People Own More Technological Devices Than Old People

Source: M. Anderson, 2015.

provides will make these individuals significantly more worldly than any other generation in history. And as Millennials began to exit college, they came to the workforce with unprecedented technological savvy, forcing employers to think more creatively about how to meet their needs (Trunk, 2007). Indeed, some have argued that this cohort's seemingly constant participation in social networking, online gaming, and video sharing and its perpetual attachment to tablets and smartphones actually give its members the technological skills they'll need to succeed in the contemporary world. They have also become adept at maintaining and navigating intimate connections in an "always on," full-time technological community (Ito et al., 2008).

On some issues, members of the Millennium Generation seem to be less risky than prior generations. For one thing, today's high school seniors smoke cigarettes less, use marijuana less, and drink alcohol less than their 1980 counterparts (Parker-Pope, 2012a). In addition, the proportion of high school students who have ever had sexual intercourse decreased from 54.1% in 1991 to 46.8% in 2013. Of those who have had sex, the percentage who used a condom the last time they had intercourse increased from 46.2% in 1991 to 59.1% in 2013 (Centers for Disease Control and Prevention, 2015f). Indeed, rates of pregnancy, abortion, and births for girls between 15 and 19 have all declined since 1990 (ProQuest Statistical Abstract, 2017).

At the same time, Millennials seem even less eager to get married in their early 20s than either Generation Xers or the Baby Boomers. Forty-eight percent of Baby Boomers were married when they were between 18 and 32 compared to 36% of Generation Xers and 26% of Millennials (cited in Shim, 2014). In addition, compared with older cohorts, they are more inclined to be tolerant of single women having children, people living together without being married, mothers of young children working outside the home, people of different races marrying one another, and gay couples legally marrying and raising children.

Because of their size and consumption tendencies—they will spend an estimated $1.4 trillion a year by 2020—Millennials remain the most coveted generation for corporate marketers. Entire retail industries—from food and clothing to entertainment and digital technology—design their products with this lucrative cohort in mind (Stout, 2015).

The next birth cohort of note will be those born after 2000. Because they have not yet received a significant amount of scholarly attention, there's no agreement about what to call them: Post-Millennials? Generation Z? the iGeneration? (for now I'll call them post-Millennials). This lack of identity hasn't stopped people from speculating about them, however. For instance, even more than Millennials, post-Millennials are "digital natives" (Turner, 2015) who have *never* experienced life without the Internet, social media, or wireless devices (refer back to Exhibit 13.1). It remains to be seen what effect this technological exposure will have on future interpersonal relations and even neurological development.

Others point to the fact that this cohort has not yet experienced the sort of turbulent period effect (September 11 attacks, the Great Recession, etc.) that the Millennials experienced during their formative years. Hence they may be more conscientious, hard-working, and practical—and less self-absorbed—than their predecessors. Compare the serious and studious "Alex Dunphy" character from *Modern Family* (a millennial) to the narcissistic "Hannah Horvath" from *Girls* (a post-millennial; Priestly, 2015; Williams, 2015). One study of 1,200 post-Millennial college students found that although they tend to be disengaged from participation in a political system they find dysfunctional, they are likely to have a "thoughtful worldview" and want to engage in work that has a tangible and lasting impact on social problems (Seemiller & Grace, 2015).

MICRO-MACRO CONNECTION
GENERATION WARS?

As Millennials and post-Millennials mature and begin to control important social institutions, their attitudes and behaviors will eventually shape reality for the rest of society. But for now, older generations, especially Baby Boomers, so dominate the cultural and economic landscape that they have evoked a fair amount of resentment from younger generations. The wealth gap between Baby Boomers and younger generations of Americans is the widest on record. The typical household headed by someone over 65 has a net worth 25 times greater than a household headed by someone under 35 (P. Taylor, 2014a).

The recent recession hit Millennials particularly hard. Their unemployment rate remains significantly higher than that of older cohorts, and more Millennials are burdened with student debt than any previous generation of young adults (Pew Research Center, 2014b). Between 2008 and 2014, the proportion of Millennials who describe themselves as middle class dropped from 53% to 42%, while the proportion who consider themselves lower or lower-middle class increased from 25% to 46% (Pew Research Center, 2014b). Nearly two thirds rely on their parents for financial support after college (Davidson, 2014). According to the Pew Research Center, 15% of 25- to 35-year-old Millennials now live in their parents' home. This is 5 percentage points higher than the share of Generation Xers who lived in their parents' home in 2000 when they were the same age (10%). Moreover, those who live with their parents are doing so for longer stretches of time (Fry, 2017). As one writer put it, the financial crisis that began in 2008 "battered career prospects, drove hundreds of thousands into the shelter of school or parents' basements, and left hundreds of thousands of others in continual underemployment" (Lowrey, 2013b, p. 12).

Perhaps it's not so surprising, then, that many parents—who footed the bill for the skyrocketing price tag of their children's college education—feel justified in claiming a strong continuing stake in their careers. Some employers and job recruiters cite an increase in the number of parents who are actively involved in getting their kids a job or who intervene when they have run-ins with bosses (Scheiber, 2017). Nearly a quarter of employers in one survey had encountered some type of parental involvement in the hiring process, such as submitting their child's resume, making interview arrangements, negotiating salary and benefits, complaining if the company didn't hire the child, or even attending the interview (P. Gardner, 2007).

So common has this sort of parental involvement become that some recruiters ask candidates before they even receive a job offer if they need to talk to their parents before making a decision.

To make matters worse, younger Americans will have to foot the bill for the massive national debt racked up by Baby Boomers. One writer even blames the "greed, shortsightedness, and blind partisanship" of Baby Boomers for bringing "the global economy to its knees" (quoted in Kotkin, 2012, p. 42).

Not surprisingly, about 60% of Americans have doubts that the Millennials and post-Millennials will have the opportunity to live better than their parents (Saad, 2012). The situation has led some to refer to them as "Generation Squeezed" (Samuelson, 2012), "The Go-Nowhere Generation," "Generation Why Bother" (Buchholz & Buchholz, 2012), or "Generation Screwed" (Kotkin, 2012). It's no wonder that many young people today view older generations with disdain. A syndicated columnist described the intergenerational animosity this way:

> We grew up in the shadow of the baby boomers, who still manage, in their [old age], to commandeer disproportionate attention. Every time they hit a life cycle milestone it's worth 10 magazine covers. When they retire, the Social Security system will go under! When they die, narcissism will be so much lonelier. (A. O. Scott, 2010, p. 4)

And such animosity is not only found in the United States. Following the vote to withdraw from the European Union in 2016 (known as "Brexit"), angry Millennials in the United Kingdom blamed older people for what they felt was a disastrous vote. As one banner outside Big Ben proclaimed: "You Stole Our Future From Us!" A twitter user put it this way: "England's geezers just bequeathed their grandchildren a future of impoverished irrelevance." Another said, "Millennials watch in horror as the Baby Boomers continue to destroy the world." But maybe they had only themselves to blame. Voter turnout for people over 55 was 82%; for those under 34, it was only 47% (Zak, 2016).

Yet the news is not all bad. Young people remain significantly more upbeat than their elders. One poll found that only 9% of 18- to 34-year-olds say they don't think they will ever be able to have enough to live the life they want. In contrast, 28% of adults ages 35 and older say they don't anticipate making enough money in the future (Pew Research Center, 2012b).

Demographic Dynamics

Many aspects of our personal lives are influenced by our birth cohort, but our lives are also affected by societywide and worldwide population trends. Sociologists who study fluctuations in population characteristics are called **demographers**. Demographers examine several important and interrelated population processes to explain current social problems or to predict future ones: birth or fertility rates, death or mortality rates, and patterns of migration. These three processes influence a population's growth, overall age structure, and geographic distribution.

Population Growth

The most fundamental population characteristic is, of course, size. Trends in population size are mostly a function of birth and death rates. As long as people are dying and being born at similar rates, the size of the population remains stable (barring large changes caused by migration). But when birthrates increase and death rates decrease, the population grows.

Consider this: It took hundreds of thousands of years, from the beginning of humanity to the early 19th century, for Earth's human population to reach 1 billion. However, it took only an additional hundred years for it to reach 2 billion. Then, 3 billion was reached 30 years later; 4 billion, 16 years later; and 5 billion, a little over 10 years after that. Today's population is 7.5 billion and will likely exceed 9.3 billion by 2050 (Haub & Gribble, 2011; United Nations, 2011; U.S. Bureau of the Census, 2015).

People disagree about the consequences of such growth. In the past, a large population was seen as a precious resource. The Bible urged humanity to be fruitful and multiply. One 18th-century British scholar, referring to the strategic importance of a large population, called a high birthrate "the never-failing nursery of Fleets and Armies" (quoted in Mann, 1993, p. 49).

Although few individuals today sing the praises of massive population growth, some argue that it isn't particularly troublesome. A larger population creates greater division of labor and a larger market to support highly specialized services. More people are available to contribute to the production of needed goods and services.

Others, however, aren't so optimistic. When a particular population is excessively large, people are forced to compete for limited food, living space, and jobs. According to some contemporary demographers, population growth can compound, magnify, or even create a wide variety of social problems, such as pollution, environmental degradation, housing shortages, high inflation, energy shortages, illiteracy, and the loss of individual freedom (Weeks, 1995).

Global Imbalances in Population Growth

On a global scale, population growth widens the gap between rich and poor nations, perpetuates social and economic inequality within nations, gives rise to racial and ethnic separatism, and increases the already high levels of world hunger and unemployment (Ehrlich & Ehrlich, 1993). Environmental threats are growing, too. Humanity's use of once-plentiful natural resources—fossil fuel, rich soil, and certain plant and animal species—is now 50% higher than Earth's biologically productive capacity. In 2012, the equivalent of 1.6 Earths was needed to provide the natural resources and services humanity consumed in 1 year. By 2030, we'll need more than two planets to support the consumption of all humans (World Wildlife Fund, 2016).

The problem, however, is not just that the world population is growing rapidly but also that different countries experience vastly different rates of growth. Populations in poor, developing countries tend to expand rapidly, whereas those in wealthy, developed countries have either stabilized or are declining. The growth rate of the world's population is approximately 1.2% per year (Population Reference Bureau, 2016). But that figure masks the dramatic regional differences that will exist for several decades to come. Consider these facts:

- Today, about 16.9% of the world's population resides in more developed countries. By 2050, only 13.4% of the population will come from these areas. In contrast, the least developed countries of the world are home to 13% of the human population today, but by 2050, nearly 20% of the world's people will live in these countries (Population Reference Bureau, 2016).

- In Africa, the rate of natural population increase (that is, without taking migration into consideration) is about 2.5% each year; Europe, in contrast, is experiencing a growth rate of 0%. Sub-Saharan Africa alone has seen its population triple in the past 50 years (cited in E. Rosenthal, 2012b). If current trends continue, by the middle of the 21st century, the population of Germany will be 10% smaller, Croatia's 20% smaller, and Ukraine's 30% smaller than it is today. In contrast, Mali's population will be 190% bigger, Zambia's, 230% bigger, and Niger's 270% bigger (Population Reference Bureau, 2014).

- In 1950, 5 of the 10 most populous nations were in the industrialized world. In 2016, only 2 industrialized countries were in the top 10: Russia and the United States. By 2050, demographers predict that the United States will be the only developed country among the world's most populous nations. The rest will be developing countries in Asia, Africa, and South America. (Crossette, 2001; Population Reference Bureau, 2016). In fact, by 2050, more people will live in Nigeria than in the United States.

These imbalances will influence how people view one another, affect global and domestic policies, and determine the availability of food, energy, and adequate living space (P. Kennedy, 1993). When the most highly industrialized and economically productive countries begin to experience shrinking populations, their role as major global producers and consumers of goods is thrown into doubt. The result can be economic and political turmoil as other countries jockey for global advantage.

Why would populations in poor, developing countries grow at such a high rate when so many people are already struggling to survive? When societies begin to industrialize, living conditions improve. New technology often means better food supplies and increased knowledge about disease. Societies learn how to keep their water supplies clean and how to dispose of garbage and sewage. So people begin to live longer. In 1990, 33% of all deaths worldwide occurred to people over 70; in 2010, that figure increased to 43%, indicating that infectious and communicable diseases are claiming fewer young victims (cited in Tavernise, 2012).

But for a considerable time after the death rate begins to fall, the birthrate remains high, resulting in a dramatic increase in the size of the population (see Exhibit 13.2). In the developing countries of sub-Saharan Africa, for instance, women will bear an average of 5 children in their lifetimes. By comparison, U.S. women have, on average, 1.8 children. In Canada, the figure is 1.6, and in the countries of Southern Europe, it's a minuscule 1.4 (Population Reference Bureau, 2016).

	World	More Developed Countries	Less Developed Countries
EXHIBIT 13.2 ● **Different Parts of the World Experience Different Rates of Population Growth**			
Births Per Day	403,241	37,575	365,666
Deaths Per Day	157,227	34,467	122,759
Natural Increase Per Day	246,015	3,108	242,907

Source: Population Reference Bureau, 2016.

One of the reasons birthrates are so high in less developed countries is the lack of access to effective contraception. Only 46% of women in these regions use some form of modern contraception, compared with 62% in the more developed world (Population Reference Bureau, 2016). In sub-Saharan Africa, the figure is 26%. In contrast, 68% of U.S. women and 78% of Northern European women use modern contraception. In addition, established laws, customs, and religious norms often continue to exert strong influences on people's reproductive behavior. In less developed nations, children are likely to be perceived as productive assets and "social security" for old age (Mann, 1993).

Politics, Culture, and Population Growth

You may have the impression that population growth is a "natural" process working relentlessly and inevitably on unsuspecting populations. Yet human intervention—government intervention, more specifically—has at times purposefully altered the size or even the configuration of a population for political or economic reasons.

Take China, for example. Because of its massive population of more than 1.38 billion and its limited resources, Chinese leaders have been struggling for decades to limit family size. One of every five humans alive today is Chinese, but China has only 7% of Earth's farmland, much of it of poor quality. To address the problem, the government enacted a strict family planning policy in the early 1970s that limited most families to one child. Couples had to wait until their mid-20s to marry. Provinces and cities were assigned yearly birth quotas. Neighborhood committees determined which married couples could have a baby and which would be subjected to forced sterilizations (Ignatius, 1988; Wong, 2015). They also charted the menstrual cycles and pelvic exam results of every woman of childbearing age in the area (Jian, 2013). Women who lacked approval to be pregnant were often subjected to forced abortions (Kahn, 2007). According to data from the Chinese Health Ministry, since the policy was enacted, Chinese doctors have performed 336 million abortions and 196 million sterilizations (Rabinovitch, 2013).

The effectiveness of China's family planning policy has amazed population experts. The average number of births per woman has decreased from more than 7 in the 1960s to 1.6 today (Population Reference Bureau, 2016). In contrast, the average number of births per woman in India, a country with similar population pressures, is 2.3. The Chinese government estimates that without the policy, the country's population of 1.38 billion would have been 30% larger by now (Rabinovitch, 2013).

But the success of this policy has created some serious social problems. So few babies are being born now—and so many more elderly people are living longer—that the overall age of the population is growing steadily. Chinese officials have noted a phenomenon called the "four-two-one problem"—a generation of only children who will have to find the resources to care for two aging parents and four elderly grandparents ("One Child Left Behind," 2009). Today, there are six Chinese working adults for every one retired person; by 2040, there will be just two (French, 2007). It's estimated that by that same year, China will have an older population than the United States but with only about one fourth the average per capita income (Kahn, 2004). Retirement funds and pension plans are scarce. Only 40% of elderly men and 13% of elderly women receive any kind of support from a pension. And the social networks that once supported aging Chinese are no longer there. Migration to urban areas and the work pressures of an increasingly industrialized economy have fractured family ties (Population Reference Bureau, 2010). The problem became so bad that in 2015 the Chinese government revised the policy so that married couples can now have two children (Buckley, 2015).

Officials in many other countries are now starting to worry that their populations aren't growing enough. In Denmark, for example, Sex and Society, an organization that provides much of the country's sex education in schools, recently shifted its lessons from an emphasis on pregnancy prevention to guidance on how to *get* pregnant (Hakim, 2015a). In contemporary Russia, where population experts estimate that the population will decline by 9% between now and 2050 (Population Reference Bureau, 2014), politicians have promoted a variety of policies to reverse the trend such as a nationwide ban on abortions, financial incentives for couples to have children, increased funds for prenatal care and maternity leave, and a tax on childlessness ("Fearing Demographic Abyss," 2006; Karush, 2001). In one central Russian region, the governor decreed September 12 to be a "Day of Conception," in which couples are given the day off from work to . . . well . . . procreate. Those who have a baby 9 months later receive money, cars, and other prizes ("Baby, and a Car," 2011). Similarly, in 2017, city officials in a town in Sweden proposed a new policy that would give municipal employees an hour-long paid break each week to go home and have sex, thereby increasing the birthrate (Bilefsky & Anderson, 2017).

Other countries have tried direct financial incentives, what some call "baby bounties," to encourage people to have more babies. For instance, in an effort to stem population decline, the president of Chile announced a proposal in 2013 that would pay couples US$200 for their third child, US$300 if they have a fourth child, and US$400 for a fifth (Catholic News Agency, 2013). In 2010, the Taiwanese government announced a nationwide contest for the most creative slogan that would motivate couples to procreate, with a prize of about US$32,000. But 2010 was the Year of the Tiger, an unfavorable year for childbearing according to the Chinese zodiac, so the plan backfired (Haub, 2010).

Cultural tradition also plays a powerful role in people's decisions about having children. Some patriarchal cultures express a deep preference for male children because only they can perpetuate the family line. As one Chinese mother put it, "If you have only girls, you don't feel right inside. You feel your status is lower than everyone else" (quoted in Jacobs, 2009, p. 8).

Parents in such cultures may take extreme measures to have sons rather than daughters. In rural China—where the now-defunct one-child policy coupled with a tradition of favoring boys over girls led many parents to fear they will be left to take care of themselves in old age—the abduction and sale of baby boys continues to be a thriving business (Jacobs, 2009). Elsewhere, female babies are aborted, killed at birth, abandoned, neglected, or given up for foreign adoption (Kristof, 1993). It's estimated that as many as 12 million female fetuses have been aborted over the past three decades as families seek ways to secure male heirs (J. Yardley, 2011). In 2003, India passed a law called the Pre-Conception and Pre-Natal Diagnostic Techniques (Prohibition of Sex Selection) Act, which makes it a crime to determine the sex of an unborn child. However, this law hasn't stopped many prospective parents from wanting to identify the sex of their baby during pregnancy. Indeed, few people are ever prosecuted for violating this law. Between 2003 and December 2014, only 206 doctors were convicted of illegal sex identification (Mascarenhas, 2016).

Practices like these have led to a conspicuous shortage of females in some parts of the world. Under normal circumstances in every society, there are between 103 and 107 boys born for every 100 girls; but higher male infant mortality works to even the distribution of boys to girls. In India, however, there are 109 males for every 100 females, the lowest sex ratio in that country since it achieved independence in 1947 (Jha, 2011). In some areas of China, the ratio is 120 males for every 100 females. There are 32 million more Chinese males under 20 than females; in 2005 alone, there were 1.1 million more boys born than girls (Zhu, Lu, & Hesketh, 2009). Demographers have identified similar shortages of females in South Korea, Pakistan, Bangladesh, Nepal, and Papua New Guinea, and some estimate that about 163 million females are "missing" from Asia's population (Hvistendahl, 2011).

Incidentally, such gender biases are not confined to foreign countries. In this country, a similar bias is found among U.S.-born children of Chinese, Korean, and Indian immigrants. Census data indicate that couples from these ethnic groups will keep trying to have a son—and perhaps make use of sex-selection procedures—if their first and second children are daughters. Among firstborn children, the ratio of male children to female children is relatively equal. But when the firstborn child is a girl, male second children outnumber female second children 117 to 100. And when the first two children are girls, the sex ratio for third children soars to 151 boys for every 100 girls. No such sex imbalance exists in other racial or ethnic groups (Almond & Edlund, 2008).

Age Structure

In addition to population growth, demographers also study the **age structure** of societies—the balance of old and young people. Age structure, like the size of a population, is determined principally by birthrates and life expectancy.

The proportion of old people in the world has been growing steadily for decades. Currently, 8% of the global population is over 65 (Population Reference Bureau, 2016). By 2050, that figure is projected to be 17% (Scommegna, 2012). During the same period, the proportion of the "oldest old" (those over 80) will increase more than fivefold (United Nations Population Division, 2003).

But as with population growth in general, age structures are not the same in all societies. In developing countries where birthrates are high and life expectancy remains relatively low—as in most countries of Southeast Asia, Latin America, the Indian subcontinent, the Middle East, and especially Africa—the age structure tends to be dominated by young people. The number of Indians between 15 and 34 is already larger than the entire populations of the United States, Canada, and Great Britain combined (Sengupta, 2016). Forty-three percent of the population in sub-Saharan Africa is under the age of 15 (Population Reference Bureau, 2016). The median age of the population in the world's three youngest countries—Uganda, Somalia, and Niger—is 16 or below (United Nations, 2017). In contrast, developed countries that are experiencing low birthrates coupled with increasing life expectancy have a very different age structure, as Exhibit 13.3 shows. More old people are living, and fewer people are being born. Only 16% of Europe's population is under 15

(Population Reference Bureau, 2016). The median age of the population in the world's three oldest countries (Italy, Japan, and Germany) is about 46 (United Nations, 2017). In Japan, it's estimated that over the next 25 years, the proportion of elderly people in the population will increase from one in four to one in three (Harney, 2012). Japanese society

EXHIBIT 13.3 ● Populations Tend to Be Younger in Less Developed Than in More Developed Regions

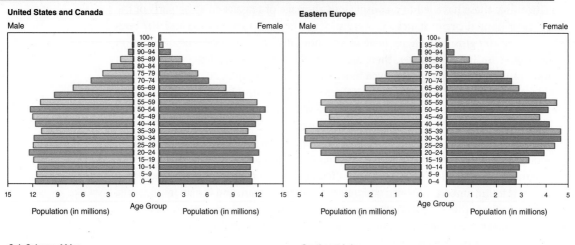

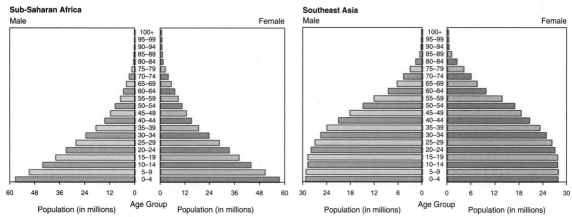

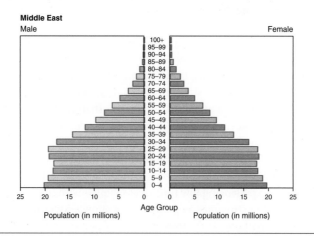

Source: U.S. Census Bureau International Database.

is getting old so quickly and deaths per year among the elderly are rising so fast that families sometimes have to wait for days before having a funeral for a loved one because of the backlog of bodies at crematories (the vast majority of Japanese are cremated). This has led to a growth in *itai hoteru,* or "corpse hotels," where families can stay—and bodies can be stored—at low cost until the crematory is ready (Rich, 2017).

The global implications of these different age structures cannot be understated. In Germany, Austria, France, and other European countries, a decreasing number of young people pay into a pension system that must support a growing number of older people (R. Bernstein, 2003). Governments have reacted to the aging of their populations by reducing social services, including the pensions that millions of retirees have been counting on. A growing proportion of older people can strain economies in other ways. For instance, the World Health Organization (2012) projects that by the middle of the 21st century, the number of people with age-related dementia worldwide will more than triple to 115 million. The cost of caring for these people will approach $2 trillion.

In contrast, when young people outnumber the elderly in a particular country, they are likely to overwhelm labor markets and educational systems (K. Davis, 1976). The result is a steady decline in living standards. When combined with a skewed sex ratio—due to a shortage of young females and an overabundance of young males—the likelihood of instability and even violent political unrest increases (Hvistendahl, 2011). In the spring of 2011, we witnessed massive angry demonstrations in many parts of the Middle East that continue today in places like Syria and Egypt. Not surprisingly, over 60% of the populations in these countries are under 30 years of age (U.S. Bureau of the Census, 2011a). Increasing rates of unemployment leave more and more young people angry and dissatisfied. As one observer put it, "An increase in youth unemployment is a better predictor of social unrest than virtually any other factor" (quoted in Sengupta, 2016, p. 7). Some authors even go so far as to predict that if these young men cannot find spouses or jobs, they will pose such a threat to the internal stability of these countries that their governments may decide they have to go to war with other countries simply to occupy the surplus male population (Hudson & den Boer, 2004).

The obvious consequence of today's trends is that developing nations will have the burden of trying to accommodate populations dominated by young people, whereas developed nations will have the burden of trying to support millions of people over the age of 65.

Geographic Distribution

Many people seek to escape these kinds of problems through **migration**, or moving to another place where prospects for a comfortable life are brighter. Through the centuries, migration has played a crucial role in history as people have contended for territory and the resources that go with it ("Workers of the World," 1998). Today, global media expose people more quickly and more consistently than ever to appealing lifestyles elsewhere. Large-scale migration includes both within-country movement and cross-border movement.

Migration Within a Country

Migration trends within a country can have a considerable effect on social life. In the United States, such internal migration usually consists of people moving from colder to warmer climates or from large cities to outer suburbs (Lalasz, 2006). But in less developed countries these days, in-country migration is more likely to reflect **urbanization**, the process by which people leave rural areas and begin to concentrate in large cities. For instance, today, 54% of the world's population lives in cities; by 2050, it will be 66%

(Population Reference Bureau, 2016). In Asia and Africa, four times more people live in cities today than in 1950. It's estimated that in India alone, 404 million people will move from villages to cities by 2050 (United Nations, 2014b).

This transformation has changed assumptions about what urban living means worldwide. In the past, cities were meccas of commerce and culture and tended to have higher standards of living and better health conditions than rural areas. Even today, legislators in some countries believe that urbanization will spur economic growth and provide people with access to better hospitals, schools, and other services. For instance, in 2013, China announced a massive 12-year plan to relocate 250 million rural residents to newly constructed cities (I. Johnson, 2013).

But when urban populations grow rapidly, as many are now doing in the developing world, cities have a hard time keeping up. The result can be an increase in pollution, environmental degradation, public health problems, and unsustainable patterns of production and consumption (United Nations, 2014b). For instance, over the past 25 years, access to clean piped water has grown dramatically. According to the Population Reference Bureau (2016), 91% of the world's population now has access to safe water compared to 76% in 1990. However, of those who still lack such access, more than half live in cities in sub-Saharan Africa. And more than 2.4 billion people—mostly in southern Asia and sub-Saharan Africa—continue to lack access to improved sanitation facilities. Moreover, cities typically have much higher rates of poverty, crime, violence, and sexually transmitted diseases than rural areas. It's estimated that the number of people living in urban slums increased from about 650 million in 1990 to 863 million in 2012 (UN Habitat, 2014).

Migration From One Country to Another

Population movement from one country to another is equally significant. It's estimated that 244 million people—or 3.3% of the world's population—live outside their countries of birth (United Nations Population Fund, 2016). International migration is encouraged by disparities in opportunities. Poverty, political instability, war, famine, environmental deterioration, high unemployment, and the lure of high wages in richer countries continue to drive the world's poorest people to give up their life savings and risk death to find a better life in more prosperous nations.

You might think that when people migrate from underdeveloped, overcrowded countries to more developed, technologically advanced ones, everyone would benefit. After all, migration lowers population pressures and unemployment at home while offsetting the problems of negative population growth and an aging workforce in developed destination countries. Indeed, the only way Japan and most European countries will be able to sustain a stable population in the future is through immigration.

From a sociological point of view, however, international migration often creates conflict. People seeking opportunities abroad can no longer move to uncharted areas but rather must push into territories where other people already live. Instead of seeing immigrants for their contribution to the overall economy, the people already in residence see immigrants as immediate competitors for scarce resources and a personal threat. The immigrants require jobs, housing, education, and medical attention, all of which are in limited supply. They also bring with them foreign and perhaps bewildering habits, traditions, and norms.

Immigration creates a variety of cultural fears: fear that a nation can't control its own borders, fear that an ethnically homogeneous population will be altered through intermarriage, fear of the influx of a "strange" way of life, and fear that newcomers will encroach on property, clog the educational system, create crime waves, and suck up social benefits largely paid for by "natives" (P. Kennedy, 1993). Many people also express concern that immigrants are responsible for outbreaks of diseases such as HIV/AIDS, tuberculosis, measles, and cholera, which strain health care systems and thus create even more resentment. Above all, they fear that immigrants and their offspring may one day become a statistical majority, rendering the "natives" powerless in their own country.

Even though laws in most countries ban discrimination against immigrants, antiforeigner resentment and prejudice are global phenomena. For instance, legislators in France and Italy continue to look for ways to tighten their borders so they can limit the free flow of immigrants, chiefly from North Africa. The Danish People's Party—a political party based on extreme anti-immigration policy positions—garnered its highest level of popular support ever in the 2015 election. In Great Britain, antipathy toward immigrants, particularly those from South Asia and the Middle East, is credited with fueling nationalist anger and leading to the 2016 vote to leave the European Union (Joseph Rowntree Foundation, 2016). In Australia, politicians talk of being swamped by South and East Asians. In the United States, immigrants from Latin America bear the brunt of the public's anti-immigrant animosity. In Japan, the resentment is directed toward almost anyone who isn't Japanese. Despite a severe labor shortage that could cripple its economy, Japan has done little to loosen its tight restrictions on immigration. In fact, the government actively encourages foreign workers and foreign graduates of its universities to return home as quickly as possible (Tabuchi, 2011).

It's important to note, though, that such hostility is not inevitable. Peaceable contact with immigrants at work, at school, or in the community can reduce feelings of threat and the willingness to expel legal immigrants from the country (McLaren, 2003). In any case, the trend toward greater immigration is unlikely to slow down as long as communication and transportation technologies continue to shrink the globe and economic disparities between countries continue to exist.

Population Trends in the United States

In the United States, two important demographic trends will exert a profound effect on the population in the future: the growing proportion of nonwhite, non–English-speaking immigrants and their children and the shifting age structure of the population, marked by a growing proportion of elderly and a shrinking proportion of young people. These two trends together will strain the social fabric in years to come, raising questions about the fair distribution of social resources.

Immigration and the Changing Face of the United States

Because the U.S. population is currently growing at a manageable rate, Americans may have trouble understanding the impact of population explosions in other countries on their everyday lives here. But as populations burst the seams of national boundaries elsewhere, many of those seeking better opportunities end up in the United States. Newly arrived immigrants believe that chances to get ahead, protection of women's rights, treatment of the poor, and availability of schools are all better here than in their countries of origin (Rieff, 2005). Some arrive legally by plane, boat, or train. Others arrive unlawfully by foot or are smuggled in the backs of trucks or the holds of cargo ships.

The Immigrant Flow

In the mid-1980s, the U.S. Bureau of the Census predicted that by the year 2050 the United States would have a population of 300 million (Pear, 1992). But that number was surpassed over 40 years earlier, in 2007. Subsequently, the Census Bureau has revised its estimate to 398 million by 2050 (ProQuest Statistical Abstract, 2017).

Part of the reason this projection had to be adjusted was that immigration in the late 20th and early 21st centuries increased more than had been anticipated and has remained fairly high ever since. In 2014, 42.4 million immigrants lived in the United States, about 11.4 million of whom were undocumented (ProQuest Statistical Abstract, 2017; Zeigler & Camarota, 2016). The share of the U.S. population that is foreign born rose from 5% in 1967 to 13.4% in 2015 (the highest proportion since 1890) and is expected to hit 18% by 2065 (López & Bialik, 2017; Pew Research Center, 2015e).

Of course, this isn't the first time immigration has increased the size of the U.S. population. In the first decade of the 20th century, nearly 9 million immigrants entered the country. In 1915, foreign-born residents constituted 15% of the population (U.S. Bureau of the Census, 2006). But what makes contemporary immigration different is that fewer of today's newcomers are of European descent (see Exhibit 13.4).

Consequently, the racial and ethnic composition of the United States has changed dramatically over the past century. In 1900, one out of every eight U.S. residents was of a race other than white; in 2014, the ratio was one in three; and by 2060, it is projected to be one in two (Colby & Ortman, 2015). As you can see from Exhibit 13.4, 9 out of 10 documented immigrants come from Asia (which includes the Middle East), Africa, or Latin America. In fact, between 2010 and 2014, new immigration plus births to immigrants after they arrived accounted for 87% of total U.S. population growth (Zeigler & Camarota, 2016). Trends like these will continue to alter the look of the American population into the foreseeable future.

The non-European immigrant population has never been spread evenly across the country. Immigrants have historically tended to settle in large urban areas that serve as ports of entry, such as New York, Los Angeles, Houston, and Miami. California, New York, Texas,

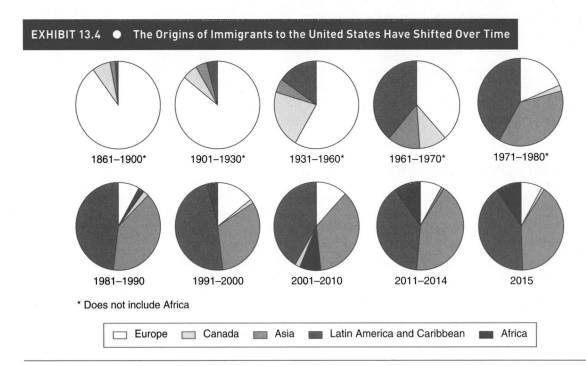

EXHIBIT 13.4   ●   The Origins of Immigrants to the United States Have Shifted Over Time

1861–1900*   1901–1930*   1931–1960*   1961–1970*   1971–1980*

1981–1990   1991–2000   2001–2010   2011–2014   2015

* Does not include Africa

☐ Europe   ☐ Canada   ☐ Asia   ■ Latin America and Caribbean   ■ Africa

Sources: Daniels, 1990; U.S. Bureau of the Census, 2000; ProQuest Statistical Abstract, 2013, Table 50; ProQuest Statistical Abstract, 2017, Table 51; U.S. Department of Homeland Security, 2014, Table 3.

and Florida are home to more than half of foreign-born residents in the United States (Grieco et al., 2012).

But new immigrants can now be found in every corner of the United States. Just like everyone else, immigrants are motivated to go where the jobs are. It might come as a surprise to you, but the states with the largest percentage increases in the number of immigrants over the past several years have been North Dakota (up 45%), Wyoming (up 42%), Montana (up 19%), Kentucky (up 15%), New Hampshire (up 14%), and Minnesota and West Virginia (both up 13%; Zeigler & Camarota, 2016). Questions of how best to integrate immigrants and their children are now being debated in every corner of the country.

Social Responses to Immigrants

U.S. residents have always had a love–hate relationship with immigrants. In good times, immigrants have been welcome contributors to the economy. Early in the 20th century, their labor helped build roads and the U.S. rail system. When the economy is strong, immigrants fill unwanted jobs, open businesses, and improve the lives of many U.S. residents by working cheaply as housekeepers, dishwashers, and gardeners.

When times are bad, however, or when the political winds shift—as they have recently—many U.S. residents are inclined to shut the door and blame immigrants for many of the country's economic and social woes. During these periods, people often describe the influx of immigrants as a "flood," subtly equating their arrival with disaster. As in Europe, immigrants to the United States often find they are targets of a variety of social anxieties, from economic tension to outright hostility.

MICRO-MACRO CONNECTION
THE PECULIAR POLITICS OF IMMIGRATION

Immigration is one of the hot-button political issues of our time. Indeed with frequent legislative and legal debates about restrictive policies, protective border walls, and travel bans, it is probably *the* major political issue today. But it's not one of those concerns where liberals and conservatives line up neatly on opposing sides.

As you might expect, some conservative politicians consider the millions of undocumented immigrants in this country to be invaders who threaten national security, take away jobs from U.S. citizens, commit crimes, and change the culture by refusing to assimilate (Katel, 2005). During the 2016 presidential campaign, Donald Trump openly expressed such hostility:

> When Mexico sends its people, they're not sending their best. They're sending people that have lots of problems and they're bringing those problems to us. They're bringing drugs. They're bringing crime. They're rapists. (quoted in Benen, 2015, p. 1)

Most of the people who voted for him agreed with this sentiment and strongly supported his campaign promise of building an impenetrable wall along the U.S—Mexico border. After his election, President Trump proposed slashing *legal* immigration by 50% in 10 years by cutting the number of visas granted to relatives of citizens and by giving preference to immigrants who speak English or who have advanced degrees (P. Baker, 2017).

Conservative politicians typically favor laws that would provide funds to toughen border security and increase the law enforcement surveillance of immigrants. The number of border patrol agents assigned to the U.S.–Mexico border has increased steadily since the early 1990s. In 1992, there were 3,555 border patrol agents assigned to this region; by 2000, that number had increased to 8,580. Since 2000, the number of agents in the Southwest has more than doubled to over 17,000 agents (Customs and Border Protection, 2016). With improved surveillance technology such as drones,

(Continued)

(Continued)

face recognition software, mobile fingerprint scanners, and cell-site simulators—which mimic cell phone towers to intercept phone data—the identification of undocumented immigrants is easier and will likely become more common in the future (Bedoya, 2017).

In the span of just 2 years, 164 anti-immigration bills were passed around the country by mostly conservative legislatures (I. Gordon & Raja, 2012). Arizona attracted national attention in 2010 when it became the first state to enact a law that makes the failure to carry immigration documents a crime and gives police broad powers to detain anyone who "appears" to be in the country illegally. Polls taken at the time indicated that a majority of Americans supported such a measure, even though they felt it would likely lead to racial profiling (Archibold & Thee-Brenan, 2010). The following year, five more states—Alabama, Georgia, Indiana, South Carolina, and Utah—passed similar laws. Alabama's law cuts off *all* state and local services to undocumented immigrants; makes it a crime to hire, rent property to, or "harbor" unauthorized immigrants; and deputizes local police officers to initiate deportation proceedings if they encounter someone merely suspected of being here without documentation (Symmes, 2012). In 2017, the governor of Texas signed into law a bill outlawing sanctuary cities (which are jurisdictions that pledge to protect immigrants by refusing to fully cooperate with federal immigration authorities) and granting law enforcement officers unprecedented powers in tracking down undocumented immigrants. For instance, the new law allows police to question someone's immigration status during *any* encounter such as a routine traffic stop and not just during a lawful arrest (DeJean, 2017).

But addressing the problem of undocumented immigration is not as simple as locking down borders, detaining people who "look" illegal, kicking individuals out of the country, or not letting them in in the first place. Nearly half of all unauthorized immigrants are parents (Pew Hispanic Center, 2013) and about 350,000 children are born to at least one unauthorized immigrant each year (J. S. Passel & Cohn, 2011). Because the 14th Amendment to the Constitution states that any baby born in the United States, regardless of the citizenship status of his or her parents, is automatically a U.S. citizen, the political desire for deportations can create serious problems for these families. It's estimated that in 2013, 72,000 undocumented immigrants who were deported were the parents of children born in the United States (Foley, 2014). So what should happen to these children? If a child is deported along with her or his parents, then technically the government is deporting an American citizen. On the other hand, if the parents are allowed to remain in the country, they are being given a special—and, in some people's minds, unwarranted—benefit (Falcone, 2009).

Some liberal politicians have also called on the government to limit immigration by sealing the borders. Their primary concern is that foreign immigrants, both authorized and unauthorized, hurt poor U.S. residents by directly competing with them for low-level jobs (Danziger & Gottschalk, 2004). And because they're usually willing to work for less money, some economists point out, undocumented workers depress wages among the less skilled native-born workers (Broder, 2006; T. A. Frank, 2013; Lowenstein, 2006).

In 2011, the Obama administration began cracking down on employers who hire illegal immigrants while at the same time it moved away from arresting the workers themselves (Preston, 2011). In 2013, Congress, with unanimous Democratic support, passed an immigration reform bill that doubled the number of border patrol agents, required the construction of 700 miles of additional fencing, required employers to use an e-Verify system to check the citizenship status of all job applicants, and provided funding for unmanned aerial drones to patrol the border (O'Keefe, 2013).

But *pro*-immigrant sentiment can be found on both ends of the political spectrum, too. For instance, the deportation of the immigrant parents of babies born in the United States may actually conflict with other conservative ideals, such as the primacy of intact, two-parent families. Furthermore, to some fiscal conservatives, immigrants make important contributions to the economy. Forty-nine percent of maids, 47% of taxi drivers and chauffeurs, and 35% of construction laborers are foreign-born (Zeigler & Camarota, 2016). Moreover, immigrants are 30% more likely to start a new business than native-born Americans, and for every 100 foreign-born workers in science and technology, 262 additional jobs are created (cited in D. Brooks, 2013). One study found that a 1% increase in employment in a state due to immigration produces an income increase of 0.5% in that state (Peri, 2009). Struggling cities in the Midwest, like Dayton, Chicago, Cleveland, Indianapolis, and St. Louis, have adopted initiatives that seek to *attract* immigrants—both highly skilled workers and low-wage laborers—in hopes they will stimulate their sluggish local economies (Preston, 2013). In fact, a recent report by the National Academies of Sciences, Engineering, and Medicine (2017) found that nationally, immigration actually increases productivity and economic growth.

Moreover, unauthorized immigrants make up about 5.1% of the nation's labor force. In fact, unauthorized immigrants outnumber U.S.-born workers in hotel, food service, construction, transportation, extraction, and farming jobs (J. S. Passel & Cohn, 2015). As one journalist put it, without undocumented immigrants,

> fruit and vegetables would rot in fields. Toddlers in Manhattan would be without nannies. Towels at hotels in states like Florida, Texas, and California would go unlaundered. Commuters at airports from Miami to Newark would be stranded as taxi cabs sat driverless. Home improvement projects across the Sun Belt would grind to a halt. And bedpans and lunch trays at nursing homes in Chicago, New York, Houston, and Los Angeles would go uncollected. (D. E. Murphy, 2004, p. 1)

Some conservative economists also argue that Social Security would go broke without the $7 billion or so in annual payments from undocumented workers, many of whom—contrary to popular perceptions—pay their share of income taxes (D. E. Murphy, 2004; Porter, 2005).

For many liberal-leaning civil rights organizations and advocates for ethnic minorities, immigration is a human rights issue, and hostility toward immigrants is seen as fundamentally racist (S. A. Holmes, 1995). The recent refugee crisis in places like Syria, Afghanistan, and Somalia has drawn global attention to the plight of the 65 million or so people worldwide who are forced to leave their countries, often under the threat of death (United Nations High Commissioner for Refugees, 2016). Furthermore, liberal immigration advocates point to the fact that immigrants, in general, tend to have lower educational achievement, higher rates of poverty, more families without health insurance, and more families on public assistance than native-born U.S. residents (Camarota, 2004). In 2012, President Obama created a new policy called Deferred Action for Childhood Arrivals (known as "DACA"). This policy was designed to protect individuals who came to this country as children from deportation and provide them with work permits so they can find legal employment. In 2017, to the surprise of many, the Trump Administration issued a statement saying that the program, at least for the time being, would remain in effect.

For their part, the public, too, has mixed feelings about immigration. We are, as two researchers for the Population Reference Bureau put it, "a nation of immigrants unsure about immigration" (P. Martin & Midgley, 2010, p. 6). For instance, in a recent poll, 72% of respondents said that undocumented immigrants currently living in the United States should be allowed to stay in the country legally, if they meet certain requirements. And while roughly half (51%) said immigrants strengthen the country because of their hard work and talents, 41% felt that immigrants are a burden because they take jobs, housing, and health care. In addition, more people felt that legal immigration should be decreased (31%) than felt it should be increased (24%; Pew Research Center, 2015c).

Just how broader economic conditions will affect public attitudes and political action is unclear. Heightened competition over a shrinking supply of jobs could lead to increased hostility against immigrants and louder calls for more restrictive laws or tougher enforcement of existing laws. Government limitations on the number of immigrants entering the country could improve the employment prospects of poor, less educated, native-born workers, who are likely to be hardest hit by economic downturns.

But such political action may be unnecessary. The flow of undocumented immigrants from Latin America into the United States has slowed in recent years. After peaking at 12.2 million in 2007, the number of undocumented immigrants dropped following the economic recession and has stabilized at around 11 million a year ever since. The drop has been particularly steep among undocumented Mexican immigrants (Passel & Cohn, 2016). Experts attribute the decrease not only to economic slowdowns and immigration crackdowns in the United States but also to expanding economic and educational opportunities and declining birthrates in Mexico.

You can see that the immigration issue illustrates a clash of political and economic forces. To politicians of all stripes, immigration is a crucial and sometimes volatile issue. But as long as powerful business interests see the need for a pool of cheap, mobile labor that is willing to work outside union and regulatory constraints, attempts to crack down on illegal immigration will remain ineffective. As long as jobs are available, poor foreigners will continue to come here seeking a better life.

The "Graying" of the United States

At the same time that the United States grapples with the changing ethnic and racial configuration of its population, it also must address its shifting age structure. Perhaps the most important and most problematic demographic trend in the United States today involves the increasing average age of the population. In 1910, 38% of the U.S. population was under 18; today, that figure is 22.9% and will be under 20% by 2050 (U.S. Bureau of the Census, 2014). Two hundred years ago, the median age for U.S. residents was 16; in 1980, it was 30; today, it is 37.8. And it's expected to be over 43 by 2060 (ProQuest Statistical Abstract, 2017).

Two developments in the past few decades have conspired to alter the U.S. age structure. The first has been a decrease in the number of children being born. In 1960, there were approximately 24 births per 1,000 people in the population. By 2016, the rate had dropped to 12 per 1,000 (Population Reference Bureau, 2016). More U.S. women than ever are choosing not to have children at all (Dye, 2008). Like many countries in the developed world, the U.S. fertility rate is barely at the level necessary to replace the current population in the next generation. Most of the conditions that have helped lower fertility—improved educational and employment opportunities for women and more effective contraception, for example—are not likely to reverse in the future.

The other development has been an increase in people surviving to old age. The number of Americans over the age of 65 has nearly doubled in the last four decades (Greenblatt, 2011). Technological advances in medicine and nutrition have extended the lives of countless U.S. residents, whose historical counterparts would not have lived nearly as long. Life expectancy has risen from 67.1 for males and 74.7 for females born in 1970 to 76.4 for males and 81.2 for females born in 2014 (ProQuest Statistical Abstract, 2017). By 2040, old people will constitute a greater proportion of the U.S. population than children (U.S. Bureau of the Census, 2014). The number of people over 85, an age group for which health care costs are exceptionally high, will grow fastest of all, increasing from 1.8% of the population in 2010 to just under 5% in 2050 (Colby & Ortman, 2014). Some demographers project that by 2050, there will be 10 times the number of centenarians (people living to 100) that we have today (cited in Dominus, 2004).

Why should you be concerned about the "graying" of the U.S. population? The answer is that a society with an aging population will inevitably experience increased demands for pensions, health care, and other social services for the elderly. Although older people in the United States tend to be healthier than their counterparts in the past, a significant proportion suffer from health problems and chronic disease and will eventually need some kind of long-term care (National Institute on Aging, 2006). The ability and willingness of society, and in particular the working population, to bear the additional burden of caring for the growing number of elderly people is an open question.

Political debate rages today over how—or even whether—the Social Security system should be transformed to accommodate the growing number of people who will turn 65 in the coming years. One survey found that just 14% of working-age people believe that Social Security will have sufficient funds to provide the current level of benefits when they retire; 39% say there will be enough money to provide reduced benefits and 43% think that, when they retire, the program will be unable to provide any benefits (Pew Research Center, 2014b). Their concerns are not unreasonable. As you probably know, Social Security payments made to retired people come from deductions taken from the paychecks of currently employed working-age people. In 1945, there were 12 older-age adults for every 100 working-age adults. Today there are 21 and by 2030, when all the Baby Boomers will be retired, there will be 35 (Colby & Ortman, 2014). Unless elderly Americans are better able to support themselves financially in the future than they are today, the government will have to play an even larger role in providing health care and other services. To do that, it will have to devote more tax dollars to the needs of older citizens, a prospect that seems unlikely given the current political atmosphere that advocates reduced rather than increased government spending.

VISUAL ESSAY—THERE'S NO PLACE LIKE HOME

REUTERS/Lucy Nicholson

For years, immigration has been one of the most contentious political issues facing both elected officials and candidates seeking office. Although we are, for the most part, a nation of immigrants, there has always been a substantial—and vocal—segment of the population that seeks to curtail immigration, sometimes forcefully. However, immigration will likely always be a component of an open and vibrant society. Here we see a simple montage of street signs found in a single city: Los Angeles.

For much of our history, the ultimate goal for individual immigrants was to shed the cultural trappings of their country of origin (language, mannerisms, diet, clothing, etc.) and assimilate into American society. Yet most large cities have always had informal but nonetheless identifiable ethnic enclaves (known by such names as "Chinatown," "Germantown," "Little Italy," "Little Tokyo," etc.). Judging from these signs, it seems that the current trend is toward even greater ethnic or national identification. Do you think the development and maintenance of ethnic communities like these contribute to or detract from "American culture"? What's to be gained (and also what's to be lost) when groups of immigrants live and work in such homogeneous areas? Would their full assimilation and integration into the larger culture be preferable?

The graying of the United States is challenging businesses and service providers to gear their products and amenities toward older clientele. For instance, some hospitals now provide emergency rooms specifically designed for the elderly. They include more soothing décor, limited medical machinery, and volunteers who circulate among the patients offering reading glasses, hearing aids, and pleasant conversation (Hartocollis, 2012a). Employers may have to restructure the workplace as well. Already, fewer young workers are available to replace retiring workers. Some employers will be forced to pay higher wages or provide additional benefits to attract new workers or will be forced to focus more attention on employee productivity, perhaps turning to machines to replace workers.

On the positive side, however, employers will have to find innovative ways to keep older workers interested in the job. Business owners are beginning to realize that older workers are more stable and trustworthy employees than younger workers. One study found that 54% of employed Millennials would rather be working somewhere else, compared to 21% of older Baby Boomers (that is, those born between 1946 and 1955; cited in Moeller, 2012). Indeed, older workers stay at their jobs longer than younger workers and therefore are more reliable employees. According to the U.S. Bureau of Labor Statistics (2016b), the average amount of time workers between the ages of 55 and 64 are at one job (10.1 years) is more than three times that of workers between 25 and 34 (2.8 years). Also, 55% of workers between 60 and 64 were employed for at least 10 years with their current employer, compared with only 13% of those ages 30 to 34.

So employers are realizing that it makes good business sense to develop new strategies to recruit older employees. CVS Pharmacies, for example, offers a "snowbird" program in which several hundred employees from Northern states are transferred each winter to pharmacies in Florida and other warmer states (S. Greenhouse, 2014). Employers may also have to keep older workers interested in continuing to work by offering substantial bonuses or by creating prestigious and well-paid part-time positions. Michelin Tire Company lets older white-collar workers stretch out their careers by transferring them from often-stressful 50- and 60-hour-a-week jobs to less demanding part-time jobs (S. Greenhouse, 2014).

Conclusion

In discussing current and future demographic trends, I can't help but think about my two Millennial sons and my post-Millennial daughter. The Millennium Generation cohort was the first to reach the teen years during the 21st century and the post-Millennial Generation was the first to be *born* in the 21st century. I wonder what kind of impact their cohorts will have on their lives. Will the world's population reach the predicted catastrophic proportions, or will we figure out a way to control population growth and enable all people to live quality lives? Will the growing ethnic diversity of U.S. society continue to create tension and conflict, or will Americans eventually learn how to be a truly multicultural nation? What will be the single, most definitive "punctuating" event for my sons' cohort: a war, an assassination, a severe economic depression, a terrorist attack, a natural disaster, a political scandal, or some environmental catastrophe? Or will it be world peace, an end to hunger and homelessness, a sustainable environment, or a cure for cancer?

I also wonder how well social institutions will serve my children's generation. Will jobs be waiting for them when they're ready to settle down and go to work? What will be their share of the national debt? How will they perceive family life? Will marriage be an outdated mode of intimacy by the time they reach middle age? What will be a desirable family size?

As a parent, of course, I'm more than a little curious about how these questions will be answered. But as a sociologist, I realize that they will emerge only from the experiences and interactions of my kids, and others their age, as they progress through their lives. Herein lies the unique and fundamental message of the sociological perspective. As powerful and relentless as the demographic and generational forces described in this chapter are in determining my children's life chances, the responsibility for shaping and changing this society in the 21st century ultimately rests in the hands of their generation. This topic—the ability of individuals to change and reconstruct their society—is the theme of the next and final chapter.

Your Turn

Demographers often use population pyramids (refer to Exhibit 13.5) to graphically display the age and sex distributions of a population. These pictures are often used to draw conclusions about a population's most pressing economic, educational, and social needs. To see what these pyramids look like for different countries, visit the U.S. Bureau of the Census website (www.census.gov/population/international/data/idb/informationGateway.php). Once there, you can select a particular country and then click on the "Population Pyramids" tab to display its age and sex distribution.

Using information from the most recent U.S. census (available in the government documents section of your school's library or at www.census.gov), construct population pyramids for several different types of U.S. cities:

- A college town (e.g., Ann Arbor, Michigan; Ithaca, New York)

- A military town (e.g., Norfolk, Virginia; Annapolis, Maryland)

- A large urban metropolis (e.g., New York City, Chicago, Los Angeles)

- A small rural town

- An affluent suburb

- A city with a large elderly retirement community (e.g., St. Petersburg, Florida; Sun City, Arizona)

Exhibit 13.5 is a form you can copy and then use to construct your population pyramids.

After constructing your population pyramids, describe how the age and sex profiles of these cities differ. What other characteristics of these cities do you think would be different as a result of the shape of their populations? Consider the following:

- The nature of the educational system
- The types of businesses that would succeed or fail
- The sorts of recreational opportunities available
- Political issues considered important and the degree of citizen involvement in political activity
- Important health care issues
- Crime rates
- Divorce rates
- Suicide rates

EXHIBIT 13.5 ● Population Pyramid Form

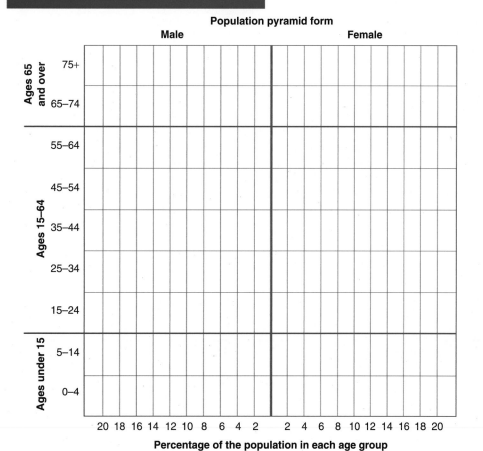

From these differences, draw some general conclusions about how people's lives are influenced by the age and sex distribution of the population in which they live.

Chapter Highlights

- Often overlooked in our quest to identify the structural factors that shape our everyday experiences are the effects of our birth cohort. Birth cohorts are more than just a collection of individuals born within a few years of each other; they are distinctive generations tied together by historical events, national and global population trends, and large-scale societal changes.

- Earth's population is growing at an unprecedented rate. But different countries experience different rates of growth. Poor, developing countries are expanding rapidly, whereas the populations in wealthy, developed countries have either stabilized or, in some cases, declined.

- When the population of a country grows rapidly, the age structure is increasingly dominated by young people. In slow-growth countries with low birthrates and high life expectancy, the population is much older, on average.

- As conditions in developing countries grow worse, pressures to migrate increase, creating a variety of cultural, political, and economic fears in countries experiencing high levels of immigration.

- The changing age structure of the U.S. population—more older people and fewer younger people—suggests that a number of adjustments will have to be made in both employment policies and social programs.

Key Terms

age structure: Population's balance of old and young people

birth cohort: Set of people who were born during the same era and who face similar societal circumstances brought about by their shared position in the overall age structure of the population

cohort effect: Phenomenon in which members of a birth cohort tend to experience a particular life course event or rite of passage—puberty, marriage, childbearing, graduation, entry into the workforce, death—at roughly the same time

demographer: Sociologist who studies trends in population characteristics

migration: Movement of populations from one geographic area to another

period effect: Phenomenon in which a historical event or major social trend contributes to the unique shape and outlook of a birth cohort

urbanization: Process by which people leave rural areas and begin to concentrate in large cities

SAGE edge™ edge.sagepub.com/newman12e

SAGE edge offers a robust online environment featuring an impressive array of free tools and resources for review, study, and further exploration, keeping both instructors and students on the cutting edge of teaching and learning.

14

Architects of Change
Reconstructing Society

- Social Change
- Social Movements
- The Sociological Imagination Revisited

Jonathan Simms, a 17-year-old student from a working-class family in Belfast, Northern Ireland, was a gifted soccer player who some felt had a chance of playing professionally. In September 2001, however, things began to change. He seemed to lose interest in soccer, and his playing suffered. Around the house, he became clumsy and began falling down, dropping things, and slurring his words. His parents suspected that he was drinking or taking drugs.

Within weeks, Jonathan became so weak that he had to be rushed to the hospital. He was diagnosed with a condition called variant Creutzfeldt-Jakob disease, popularly known as mad cow disease. This malady is a debilitating condition that results from eating infected beef. It can incubate in the body for years, even decades, before manifesting itself by attacking the brain (Belkin, 2003). By the middle of 2002, Jonathan could no longer walk or talk. His parents had to bathe him. Soon he became totally unresponsive, lying in bed in a vegetative state.

Doctors told Jonathan's parents that there was no chance he would live more than a year. But his father, Don, refused to accept the prognosis. And so he set out on a single-minded mission: to save his son's life. Don quit his job and spent days on the Internet trying to find doctors, researchers, or anybody else who could commute his son's death sentence.

Don Simms eventually found a researcher, Steven Dealler, who had been experimenting with a powerful and sometimes lethal new drug called pentosan polysulfate (PPS). PPS had shown some effectiveness in treating animals suffering from a similar disease called scrapie but had never been tested on humans. The problem with PPS is that it must be injected directly into the brain to achieve its intended effect. Most doctors were convinced that injecting this drug directly into a human's brain would be fatal.

So Don embarked on another quest: to find someone who would be willing to use this technique on his son. He found Dr. Nikolai Rainov, a neurosurgeon who was an expert on injecting cancer drugs directly into the brain. Dr. Rainov agreed to treat Jonathan, but the board of neurosurgery at Rainov's hospital refused to approve the treatment plan, stating that it was simply too dangerous (Belkin, 2003). Britain's Committee on Safety of Medicines entered the fray, saying that there was no rational basis for prescribing the drug ("Family of VCJD Victim Claim Untried Treatment Is a Success," 2003).

Don didn't give up and eventually found a hospital in Germany that would allow the PPS treatment. He chartered a medical transport plane—at his own expense—and prepared his son for the trip. But days before the family was set to leave, the German Department of Health blocked them. Germany had no cases of mad cow disease and wanted to keep it that way.

Again, Don refused to give up. He hired a lawyer and took the case to court in Great Britain. Numerous legal battles ensued. But in December 2002, 15 months after the initial diagnosis, a High Court judge ruled that the family could proceed with the treatment.

Jonathan began PPS treatments in February 2003. After several months, his doctors noticed that his heart rhythms were improving, that he had regained his ability to swallow, and that he was more responsive to light and pain. There were none of the adverse side effects that critics had predicted. By all accounts, the disease had been brought under control. In 2008, his condition was upgraded from "critical" to "non–life threatening." However, in 2011, Jonathan Simms finally died. Nevertheless, he lived for a decade with the disease—that's about a decade longer than anyone except his father thought possible at the time of his diagnosis. To date, he is the world's longest known survivor of mad cow disease (Yurkiewicz, 2012).

The message of the Jonathan Simms case is sociologically compelling: An individual was able to overcome the institutional obstacles of a massive international medical establishment to find an answer to a seemingly unsolvable problem. As we have seen throughout this book, institutions must operate in a highly structured, standardized, and impersonal way, at a level above the interests and personalities of the individual people they are created to serve. Imagine the chaos that would ensue if the system were set up so that any parent with a terminally ill child could compel researchers, physicians, and hospitals to concoct unique and risky treatments. The entire health care system would quickly collapse. That hasn't stopped some patient advocacy groups from lobbying for laws that would allow the "compassionate use" or "expanded access" of not-yet-approved experimental drugs for seriously ill patients who have run out of other options (Harmon, 2009). The Food and Drug Administration (FDA; 2015) has an entire section on its website devoted to explaining its "expanded access" policy. For instance, the FDA now permits the use of some experimental drugs, but only in extreme emergency cases and with many safeguards and restrictions.

But from an institutional perspective, new drugs must be tested meticulously—and sometimes slowly—to determine their effectiveness and to identify all potentially dangerous side effects before they are made available to the public. A sharp line must be drawn between the need to satisfy the principles of sound scientific method and the desire to help individuals who are suffering (D. J. Rothman & Edgar, 1992). Insurance companies usually won't pay for drugs that have not completed rigorous scientific testing (Harmon, 2009). Indeed, from time to time, the FDA has actually slowed down its drug approval process in response to reports of unsafe drugs on the market (G. Harris, 2005). But Jonathan's story shows that individuals can overcome bureaucratic slowness and actually change a part of the social structure. As a result of his father's actions, the standard medical approach to treating people infected with mad cow disease changed.

In the past, only the most dedicated individuals, such as Don Simms, were able to become highly involved in medical decisions. Today, however, such involvement is becoming routine. At the first appearance of a symptom—even before a doctor mentions a diagnosis or prescribes a drug—people can immediately go online and consult one of the thousands of medical apps, websites, Twitter feeds, or blogs that offer information (some of it more trustworthy than others) on everything from common colds to exotic diseases. And when they do visit their doctors, patients typically arrive with smartphones full of information they've gathered online and often with their own self-diagnoses.

By working together, individuals with the same illnesses or medical concerns have also been able to act as their own best advocates. For instance, in the early 1990s, AIDS deaths were mounting while the slow progress of the government drug approval process kept drugs out of the hands of the people who needed them. But AIDS activists demanded that the FDA loosen rules for clinical trials and speed up the approval process (L. K. Altman, 2011). They were successful and thus altered the way AIDS drugs are developed and regulated. Effective treatments—called antiretroviral therapies (ARVs)—are now being produced more quickly and are making an impact (McNeil, 2011). For many people who are HIV positive, AIDS is now merely a chronic illness, not the inevitable death sentence it once was (D. Brown, 2011).

AIDS activists have also successfully pressured pharmaceutical companies to allow developing countries in sub-Saharan Africa and elsewhere to import cheaper, generic ARVs (Swarns, 2001). As a result, global access to ARVs has expanded dramatically over the last few years, tripling between 2009 and 2015. In 2015, over 17 million people in low- and middle-income countries—and over 13 million in sub-Saharan Africa alone—received this treatment, thereby exceeding the number of people who were eligible for it, but who lacked access (UNAIDS, 2016b). In some African countries with high rates of HIV infection—like Botswana, Swaziland, Zambia, Namibia, Malawi, and Zimbabwe—over 60% of people in need now have access to ARVs (Avert, 2017a). Activists working together magnified the influence that none of them could have had acting individually. The reach of their achievements goes beyond sick individuals to global institutions and concerns.

This theme—the power of individuals acting collectively to change the structural elements of their society—guides this final chapter of the book. I have spent the previous 13 chapters discussing how our society and everything in it is socially constructed and how these social constructions, in turn, shape the lives of individuals. You may feel a little helpless when considering how much control culture, bureaucracies, institutions, and systems of social stratification have over our lives. It's only fitting, then, to end this book on a more encouraging note, with a discussion of social change and the ways individuals can reconstruct their society.

Social Change

Change is the preeminent characteristic of modern human societies, whether it occurs in personal relationships, cultural norms and values, systems of stratification, or institutions. Everywhere you look—your school, your job, your home, your government, and every aspect of your very way of life—institutional and cultural change is the rule, not the exception.

As a result of substantive changes affecting many social institutions simultaneously, the United States and other technologically advanced societies have become what sociologists call **postindustrial societies**. Economies that once centered on farms and agriculture or factories and the production of material goods now revolve around information and service industries, including communication, mass media, research and development, tourism, insurance, banking and finance, and technology. The everyday lives of ordinary people in these societies are qualitatively different from the lives of those in agricultural or industrial societies.

Change is clear when we look at specific institutions. Consider how the nature of higher education has changed in the past half century. If you had taken this sociology course 50 years ago, your instructor would have needed only a few tools: a good collection of books and articles on the subject, a well-stocked library, a typewriter, some pencils, a Ditto machine, a stack of carbon paper, chalk, a slide projector, and a love of the discipline. Good instructors today still need a love of the discipline (I hope!), but it's becoming difficult to teach interestingly, effectively, and efficiently without taking advantage of state-of-the-art technology: high-speed, in-class Internet access; videos, syllabi, and course assignments available online; social networking sites for quick responses to course-related topics; and computerized test banks. Instructors can now choose from dozens of programs and apps that instantaneously grade essay exams (Markoff, 2013) or allow them to monitor whether students are keeping up with their online reading assignments (Streitfeld, 2013). Indeed, the increasing use of massive open online courses (MOOCs) could very well shift the traditional college experience to the virtual world in years to come.

Think about how family life in the United States has changed over the past 50 years. Divorce rates were low in the 1950s, skyrocketed in the 1960s and 1970s, stabilized in the 1980s and 1990s, and have dropped a bit in the 2000s. Women have entered the workforce in unprecedented numbers. People are waiting longer to marry, and once they do, they are having fewer children. Cultural concerns about gender equality have altered the way men and women relate to one another inside and outside the home. Social and sexual rules that once seemed permanent and natural have disintegrated: Same-sex couples can legally marry. Unmarried couples can live openly together, unmarried women can have and keep their babies without community condemnation, and remaining single and remaining childless are acceptable lifestyle options. In short, today's family bears little resemblance to the cultural ideal of the 1950s.

These changes in family life have, in turn, affected other institutions. Because so many families are headed by dual-earner couples these days, children spend less time with their parents than they did in the past, forcing families to depend on others to look after their children: paid caregivers, friends, neighbors, and/or teachers. More parents than ever rely on professional day care centers to watch over their preschool-age children. Many of these centers require that children be toilet trained before they enroll, compelling parents to exert premature pressure on their children to comply. As a result, many pediatricians report an increase in children with toilet training problems, such as lack of daytime and nighttime urine control (Erica Goode, 1999).

Schools are also being called on to address many of the problems families used to deal with at home on their own. They now routinely provide students with training in moral values, technological and financial "literacy," adequate nutrition, and practical instruction to help them avoid drug and alcohol abuse, teen pregnancy, and sexually transmitted diseases.

Not surprisingly, the very nature of childhood is also changing. Contemporary social critics argue that childhood has all but disappeared in the modern world. In the United States, children are exposed to events, devices, images, and ideas that would have been inconceivable to their Baby Boom grandparents or Generation X parents when they were young. For instance, some parents now set their babies up with e-mail accounts,

Instagram feeds, Twitter handles, and other social networking sites within hours of their birth (M. Wood, 2014). More generally, the increasingly competitive nature of childhood is making some parents feel obligated to give their young children every conceivable edge to help them succeed.

MICRO-MACRO CONNECTION
ARE PARENTS PUTTING TOO MUCH PRESSURE ON THEIR CHILDREN TO EXCEL AT SPORTS?

In the past, childhood sports were simply fun and recreational. But youth sports are now a multibillion-dollar business (Greene, 2004). With the promise of lucrative professional careers looming large, parents often encourage young children who show some athletic promise to hone their skills early on. For instance, gymnasts and figure skaters must start training for their athletic futures when they're toddlers if they have any desire to succeed later on. Gyms around the country offer exercise classes for children as young as 4 months.

In communities all across the country, parents encourage and sometimes force their children to specialize in one sport and play it year round, making what were once carefree activities look, for all intents and purposes, like work. When asked how long the baseball season is for his team of 9-year-olds, one coach replied, "Labor Day to Labor Day" (quoted in Pennington, 2003, p. C16). Ironically, such early specialization is making children less athletically well-rounded and more prone to injury (F. Bowen, 2016).

Furthermore, it has become rather common for children to be turned over to professionals for training for future athletic careers. Affluent towns often have youth soccer clubs run by paid directors and coached by professionals rather than parent volunteers. Some parents go even further. At IMG Academies in Bradenton, Florida, for instance, potential sports prodigies—in team sports like baseball, basketball, and soccer as well as individual sports like tennis and golf—practice their sport over 4 hours a day for 5 days a week from September to May. In addition, they participate in hours of intense physical and mental conditioning each week. Depending on the sport, tuition plus room and board can cost over $70,000 a year for first to fifth graders, and that's not counting extras like deluxe meal plans, language tutors, and private coaching sessions, which can cost several thousand dollars more (IMG Academy, 2015). In the end, some parents end up investing hundreds of thousands of dollars in their young children's athletic futures hoping for the next Serena Williams, Bryce Harper, or LeBron James.

Parents who pressure their children to succeed athletically defend their actions by citing studies that show that adolescents involved in sports are less likely to use drugs and are more likely to get good grades in school than children who aren't involved. The ultra-organized model of sports teams, they believe, is a valuable way to teach children qualities they will need down the road, like teamwork, responsibility, and self-reliance.

But not everyone is in favor of specialized, pressurized sports activities for children. Grassroots organizations have sprung up in recent years to help parents and children return relaxation to lives that are crammed with games, practices, and other activities (Tugend, 2006). The American Youth Soccer Organization provides guidance on its website for how communities can establish "Silent Saturdays," days on which coaches are asked not to coach their players and parents are asked not to cheer or guide their children in any way. There is no shouting, swearing, or yelling at referees and, according to supporters, no pressure on children.

As we saw in Chapter 9, the pressure on children to excel at younger and younger ages reflects a growing concern with young people's ability to compete in the global economic marketplace. In the pressure-packed world of contemporary childhood sports, we see the interconnections of large-scale social change and everyday life.

More seriously, children these days seem to have more trouble getting along in society than they once did. More teenagers than ever suffer from severe anxiety and there's been a doubling of hospital admissions for suicidal youth over the last 10 years (Denizet-Lewis, 2017). Harassment, bullying, verbal abuse and disrespect of teachers, and gang activity have become routine elements of many children's school experiences. In 2015, there were about 841,100 nonfatal victimizations (theft and violence) at school and 545,100 non-fatal victimizations away from school involving 12- to 18-year-olds (National Center for Education Statistics, 2017b). In addition, 10% of elementary school and 9% of secondary school teachers have been threatened with injury or physically attacked by a student. The majority of public schools now control access to school grounds, require faculty and staff to wear photo IDs, limit students' access to social networks, forbid student cell phone use at school, or use surveillance cameras on campus. About 4 million public school students in the United States receive in-school suspensions and 3.2 million receive out-of-school suspensions each year.

Nearly 110,000 juveniles were arrested in 2015 for drug offenses or liquor law vio-lations (ProQuest Statistical Abstract, 2017). According to the National Association of School Psychologists (2013), 5% of high school students carried a gun on school property, and another 7% were threatened or injured by a weapon (such as a gun, knife, or club) on school property. No wonder that since the late 1980s, 44 states have adopted new laws enabling courts to try more children as adults. In fact, 91% of youthful offenders are held in adult facilities rather than juvenile detention centers (Minton & Zeng, 2016).

The state of childhood is even more precarious in other parts of the world:

- UNICEF (2010) estimates that between 500 million and 1.5 billion children worldwide experience violence annually. And every year as many as 275 million children witness domestic violence in their own homes.

- Between 1990 and 2013, 223 million children around the world died before their fifth birthday (UNICEF, 2014b).

- The United Nations estimates that about 1.1 million children worldwide are deprived of their liberty and detained in prisons, military facilities, immigration detention centers, welfare centers, or educational facilities (C. Hamilton, Anderson, Barnes, & Dorling, 2011).

- More than 150 million children under 14 are engaged in child labor, many in hazardous conditions involving mines, agricultural chemicals and pesticides, and heavy machinery. In the world's poorest countries, nearly one in four children are engaged in work that is potentially dangerous (UNICEF, 2015).

- Worldwide, 87 million children under the age of 7 have spent their entire lives in war zones (UNICEF, 2016) and 22% of school-age children in these regions are unable to attend school (UNICEF, 2017). More than 250,000 children—sometimes as young as 9—have been exploited as child soldiers and are taking part in armed conflicts in places such as the Central African Republic, Chad, the Democratic Republic of Congo, Somalia, and Sudan. Four out of 10 are girls (War Child, 2015).

Clearly, social change doesn't always make children's lives as carefree as we would wish.

The Speed of Social Change

In the distant past, societies tended to change slowly, almost imperceptibly, during the course of one's lifetime. Family and community traditions typically spanned many gen-erations. Although the traditional societies that exist today still change relatively slowly, change in postindustrial societies is particularly fast paced. Even while writing this book, I've had to revise many examples at the last minute because things have changed so abruptly.

The pre-Facebook, pre-Twitter, pre-Instagram, pre-YouTube, pre-Tinder early 2000s already seem like a nostalgic, bygone era.

Because we live in a world that seems to be in a constant state of technological flux, we're often tempted to believe that social change is an exclusively contemporary issue. Keep in mind, however, that sociologists and other scholars have long expressed deep concern over the effects that social change has on people. The 19th-century sociologist Émile Durkheim (1897/1951) argued that rapid social change creates a vacuum in norms, which he called **anomie**, where the old cultural rules no longer apply. When things change quickly—through sudden economic shifts, wars, natural disasters, population explosions, or rapid transitions from a traditional to a modern society—people become disoriented and experience anomie as they search for new guidelines to govern their lives.

Widespread anomie affects the larger society as well. Durkheim believed that when change disrupts social norms, it unleashes our naturally greedy impulses. Without norms to constrain our unlimited aspirations and with too few resources to satisfy our unlimited desires, we are in a sense doomed to a frustrating life of striving for unattainable goals (Durkheim, 1897/1951). The result, Durkheim felt, is higher rates of suicide and criminal activity as well as weakened ties to family, neighborhood, and friends.

But change isn't always bad. Sometimes speedy change is necessary to effectively address shifting social conditions. For instance, over the span of a few years in the early 2000s, school districts around the country drastically modified their curricula in response to the sudden ascendancy of the Internet in students' everyday lives, forever changing the face of U.S. education. At least 70% of public school teachers now use computers in their classes at least some of the time (National Center for Education Statistics, 2010).

The velocity of change today has affected the way sociologists go about their work, too. When U.S. society was understood to be relatively stable, sociological study was fairly straightforward. Most social researchers in the 1950s believed that one could start a 5- or 10-year study of some social institution, say the family or higher education, and assume that the institution would still be much the same when the study ended (Wolfe, 1991). Today, such assumptions about the staying power of institutions are dubious at best.

There is no such thing as a permanent social institution. Thus, sociologists, like everyone else in contemporary society, have had to adjust their thinking and their methods to accommodate the rapid pace of social change.

Causes of Social Change

The difficulty of pinning down any aspect of society when change is so rapid has led sociologists to study change itself. Following in the footsteps of Durkheim, they ask what causes all these technological, cultural, and institutional changes? On occasion, massive change—in the private lives of individuals as well as in entire social institutions—can result from a single dramatic event, such as the attacks of September 11, 2001, Hurricane Katrina in 2005, the global economic meltdown of 2008, the Japanese earthquake and tsunami of 2011, or massive droughts (in California) and floods (in Texas) in 2015. We can be thankful that such momentous events are relatively rare. Sociologists who focus on change tell us that institutional transformations are more likely to be caused over time by a variety of social forces, including environmental and population pressures, cultural innovation, and technological and cultural diffusion.

Environmental and Population Pressures

As you saw in Chapter 13, the shifting size and shape of the population—globally and locally—is enough by itself to create change in societies. As populations grow, more and more people move either into urban areas, where jobs are easier to find, or into previously uninhabited areas, where natural resources are plentiful.

Environmental sociologists note the complex interplay among humans, social structure, and natural resources as previously undeveloped territories are settled. For instance, one social scientist has argued that many civilizations throughout history—such as the Easter Islanders, the Mayans, and the Norse colony in Greenland—collapsed because deforestation led to soil erosion, which led to food shortages and ultimately political and social collapse (Diamond, 2005).

Even when new areas are developed for food production, environmental damage often occurs. Of course, improved food supplies have obvious benefits for societies around the world. Fewer and fewer people today die from famine and malnutrition than ever before. But the positive effects of a growing global food supply have been tempered by the serious environmental harm that new production techniques have caused. For instance, pesticide use has increased 17-fold over the past several decades, threatening the safety of water supplies. Some insects have developed resistance, which leads to increased pesticide use. New crop varieties often require more irrigation than old varieties, which has been accompanied by increased erosion and water runoff. As demand for meat products increases, cattle ranches expand, destroying natural habitats, displacing native animal species, and polluting water sources. Modern factory farming practices helped spread mad cow disease throughout Great Britain (Cowley, 2003), affecting people like Jonathan Simms.

More broadly, the clearing of forests and the burning of fossil fuels, such as coal, oil, and natural gas, have been implicated as the chief cause of **global climate change**—a steady rise in Earth's average temperature as a result of increasing amounts of carbon dioxide in the atmosphere. We are already seeing the consequences of climate change: Polar ice caps and glaciers are melting; sea levels are rising; storms are becoming more intense and deadly; droughts are becoming more extreme; plants and animals are being forced out of their habitats; and certain diseases, like malaria, are spreading to higher latitudes. Some states, like Louisiana, have already begun making plans to relocate entire coastal communities—referred to as "climate refugees"—whose homes are already being destroyed by floods and rising seas (Davenport & Robertson, 2016).

Many scientists believe that the long-term effects of global climate change may lead not only to unprecedented catastrophic degradation of the environment and natural habitats, but also to the biggest global public health threat of the 21st century. For instance, one study estimates that worldwide in the next century, the number of times people will be exposed to extreme rainfall and floods will quadruple, the number of exposures to extreme drought will triple, and exposure of elderly people to major heat waves will increase by a factor of 12 (N. Watts et al., 2015). The Centers for Disease Control and Prevention (2016a) predicts that as a consequence of these events, we are likely to see worldwide increases in storm-caused injuries, heat-related illnesses, asthma and other respiratory ailments, cardio-vascular disease, malnutrition, vector-borne (that is, those transmitted by mosquitos, ticks, and fleas) maladies, and water-borne diseases.

And it's not just our physical health. Some economists predict that warm weather states could see staggering climate change-related financial losses, such as the destruction of valuable coastal property, increased energy costs due to heavier air-conditioner use, shrinking tourism, and a reduction in labor productivity due to sweltering heat (Hsiang et al., 2017).

Cultural and Technological Innovation

But population and environmental pressures have the potential to create more positive social change in the form of cultural and technological innovation. For example, natural disasters, such as earthquakes, hurricanes, and tornadoes, often inspire improvements in emergency response technology, home safety products, and architectural design that improve everyone's lives. Likewise, concerns about pollution and global climate change have fostered innovative changes in people's behavior (e.g., recycling and conserving energy), the growth of sustainable agricultural practices, the creation of environmentally safe, "green" products and services (low-watt light bulbs, low-flow showerheads, and biodegradable detergent), and the development of energy-efficient hybrid vehicles and nonpolluting energy sources, such as solar power and wind power. The result is felt not only on an individual level but also on a societal level, as eco-efficient environmentally sustainable businesses grow around these innovations and attract investors. The BlueGreen Alliance (2015), a coalition of business, labor, environmental, and community groups, estimates that a $500 billion investment in things like clean energy (wind and solar), energy efficient buildings, green manufacturing, hybrid and electric vehicles, and rebuilding the nation's roads and railways could produce millions of jobs in the next decade.

Sometimes, these scientific discoveries and technological inventions spur further innovations within a society. Improvements in motor vehicle safety, such as air bags, safety belts, child safety seats, and motorcycle helmets, have contributed to large reductions in motor vehicle deaths and fundamentally changed the way we drive. Water fluoridation is credited for a 40% to 60% reduction in tooth loss in adults. Safer and healthier foods have all but eliminated nutritional deficiency diseases such as rickets, goiter, and pellagra in the United States (Centers for Disease Control and Prevention, 1999).

Often, revolutionary innovations seem insignificant at first. Imagine what life would be like without the invention of corrective eyeglasses, which dramatically extended the activities of near- and farsighted people and fostered the belief that physical limitations could be overcome with a little ingenuity (for one thing, instead of reading these wonderful words, you'd be reading strings of random letters and symbols since I wouldn't be able to see what I was typing!). The invention of indoor plumbing, the internal combustion engine, television, telephones, the microchip, nuclear fusion, and effective birth control have been instrumental in determining the course of human history. Sometimes the smallest innovation has the largest impact: According to one author, without the machine-made precision screw—the most durable way of attaching one object to another—entire fields of science would have languished, routine maritime commerce would have been impossible, and there would have been no machine tools and hence no industrial products and no industrial revolution (Rybczynski, 1999).

But social institutions can sometimes be slow to adjust to scientific and technological innovations. Consider, for instance, the medical treatment of infertility. Artificial insemination, in vitro fertilization, surrogate motherhood, and other medical advances have increased the number of previously infertile people who can now bear and raise children. And more and more same-sex couples are utilizing infertility treatments to have children. According to one of the nation's largest sperm banks, about one third of its clients are lesbian couples (Holson, 2011b). Yet these technological developments were changing the face of parenthood well before society began to recognize and address the ethical, moral, and legal issues they raised. For instance, close to half a million embryos created through in vitro fertilization are kept frozen at fertility clinics around the country. Many of them belong to couples that no longer need them because they are finished having children. But it's unclear exactly what should be done with the embryos. Some couples are opposed to destroying them for moral or religious reasons. Most couples don't want to donate them to other couples because of genetic links to their own children. (In fact, state and federal regulations make donation to other couples difficult because they require donors to come back to the clinics to be tested for infectious diseases.) Still others would like to donate them for research, but that option is not always available (Grady, 2008).

The very definition of family and parenthood can change when technology plays a role in childbearing. Surrogacy—an arrangement in which a woman agrees to become pregnant and give birth to a child others will raise—divides motherhood into three distinct roles, which may be occupied by three separate people: the *genetic* mother (the one who supplies the egg from which the fetus develops), the *gestational* mother (the one who experiences pregnancy and gives birth), and the *social* mother (the one who raises the child). Add to the mix the *genetic* father and the *social* father, and you can see how difficult it can sometimes be to establish legal parenthood. There is little uniformity between states about whether to recognize and enforce surrogacy agreements. Some states grant preference to surrogacy contracts; others assume the woman giving birth to the child is the mother and will reverse that determination only when the commissioning couple files a prebirth order to legally adopt the child after he or she is born (Shapo, 2006).

Moreover, some technological innovations that were meant to improve our lives have changed people's behavior in unanticipated, and sometimes dangerous, ways. Consider these examples:

- Without question, antibiotics were a revolutionary advance in the treatment of infectious diseases. But doctors soon began prescribing them for minor illnesses just to be safe. As a result of the overuse of antibiotics, some infectious and highly dangerous organisms have become resistant to the drugs. The Centers for Disease Control and Prevention (2014a) conservatively estimates that each year at least 2 million people acquire serious antibiotic-resistant infections and at least 23,000 people die as a direct result. And many more die from other conditions what were complicated by an antibiotic-resistant infection.

- Smartphones and tablets have provided us with unprecedented access to information and entertainment. But these devices frequently compete with other important tasks for our attention. According to the National Highway Traffic Safety Administration (2017), there were 3,477 people killed and an estimated additional 391,000 injured in motor vehicle crashes involving distracted drivers. Drivers in their 20s make up 24% of all drivers in fatal crashes, but comprise 27% of distracted drivers and 33% of distracted drivers who were using cell phones at the time of the accident. The risk of a driver getting into an accident or near accident is 23 times greater when she or he is texting while driving than when she or he is not doing so (cited in Federal Communication Commission, 2013).

- Not only do hybrid cars reduce air pollution and reliance on fossil fuels, but they also reduce noise pollution. However, pedestrians and bicyclists sometimes have difficulty hearing these cars coming their way, thereby increasing the risk of being struck or run over. At intersections, parking lots, and other places where cars travel slowly, pedestrians and bicyclists get hit by hybrids at up to twice the normal rate. To address the problem, manufacturers market fake car noise so unwary pedestrians and cyclists can hear them coming (Mihm, 2009).

- Drones have changed the way we see and record our world and have made important contributions to disaster recovery, the detection of illegal poaching, and reforestation. But as they become more popular, they've begun to pose a significant public safety threat as they fly ever closer to the airspace of helicopters and commercial airliners.

Computers, in particular, have revolutionized our lives by making purchasing, communicating, and information gathering easy and efficient. Wireless communication technology, in particular, has all but eliminated the constraints of time and place, whether we're conversing with friends, researching a topic of interest for a sociology paper, seeking guidance on an important decision, finding a good Thai restaurant in a new neighborhood, or simply conducting everyday business.

In some ways, the anonymity of the Internet allows people to do or say things they wouldn't do or say if they were identifiable. For instance, anonymity allows dissidents and whistle blowers to post critical comments about powerful individuals and organizations that they would be reluctant to post if their identities were known. But it also invites the posting of inflammatory and sometimes threatening messages online (Bazelon, 2011). Funeral-related websites have become quite popular in the past few years, giving distant mourners opportunities to post remembrances of the dead that range from simple text messages to multimedia presentations (Holson, 2011a). But the anonymity and one-click immediacy of these sites has emboldened some people to say nasty things about the deceased they wouldn't say in a letter or in person. The posting of angry tirades, petty insults, accusations of incest or criminal activity, and revelations of adultery is so common that some sites have been forced to employ full-time screeners to filter out personal attacks and inappropriate comments (Urbina, 2006).

MICRO-MACRO CONNECTION
THE INTERNET NEVER FORGETS: TECHNOLOGY AND THE EROSION OF PERSONAL PRIVACY

Our reliance on wireless telecommunications has also made us much more vulnerable to invasions of privacy, creating what one sociologist calls "a culture of surveillance" (Staples, 2014). Today, our lives are tracked by both public agencies and private companies, sometimes with, but often without our consent. Every time we go online, use our phones, register our cars, or buy something with a credit card, our private information—from religious preferences, political affiliation, annual income, and educational history to our entertainment likes and dislikes and shopping habits—is made public. Companies in the multibillion-dollar data mining industry collect and sell personal and behavioral data to anyone willing to buy them.

In 2013, a former contractor for the National Security Agency leaked details of a large-scale government surveillance program that allegedly included monitoring the phone conversations of American citizens and tapping into e-mails and texts. In addition, the government has been working with research teams from various private companies and universities to develop an automated data collection system (a so-called data eye in the sky) that would focus on patterns of communication, consumption, and movement of populations. It would monitor publicly accessible data including "Web search queries, blog entries, Internet traffic flow, financial market indicators, traffic webcams and changes in Wikipedia entries" (Markoff, 2011, p. 1). In 2014, the U.S. Supreme Court attempted to reverse this trend when it ruled that police must obtain warrants to search the cell phones of people they arrest.

Increased technological surveillance is not limited to actions by the government and local law enforcement. With websites and apps like Net Nanny, Secure Teen, and TeenSafe, parents can track their children's whereabouts and tightly monitor their texts, calls, Internet searches, and social media usage. Everyday citizens now have the technological capability to spy on each other. For instance, the website Nextdoor.com was originally designed to give people a forum for interacting with neighbors, a place to find a local babysitter or report a missing pet. However, it quickly evolved into a place where people easily report "suspicious" activity. Often the site becomes a magnet for racial profiling.

(Continued)

(Continued)

One post warned of "a light-skinned black female" walking her dog and talking on her cell phone. "I don't recognize her," the poster said, "Has anyone described any suspect of crime like her?" (quoted in Medina, 2016, p. A10).

Although most people realize that in today's wirelessly connected world, complete privacy is an illusion—one survey found that 91% of respondents think that we have lost control over how companies gather and use our personal information (Madden, 2014)—our lives remain open digital books. For one thing, it's easy to ignore the fact that the Internet never forgets; it retains every bit of information ever posted, sometimes making it impossible to escape one's past. As one columnist put it:

> Every day, those of us who live in the digital world give little bits of ourselves away. On Facebook and LinkedIn. To servers that store our e-mail, Google searches, online banking and shopping records. (B. Friedman, 2012, p. 5)

If you've applied for a job in the past couple of years, you're well aware that employers routinely scan the Internet for information about job seekers. In the medical field, the Department of Health and Human Services helps potential employers with a website called the National Practitioner Data Bank. Here, state licensing boards, hospitals, and other health care facilities can find out whether a doctor's license has been revoked in another state or if the doctor has ever been disciplined.

In pre-Internet days, people could essentially leave "childish things" and youthful transgressions behind them as they matured into adulthood. No one had to know that when you were younger you smoked a lot of pot, engaged in some petty shoplifting, said really stupid things, followed Phish around the country for a year and a half, or slept with a lot of random people. Today, however, those experiences have an unbounded shelf life.

With so much private material available online, nearly 9 in 10 Internet users have taken steps to remove or mask their digital footprints. However, most still express a consistent lack of confidence about the security of their everyday information (Rainie, 2016). Massive cyber attacks that expose the private information of millions of people—like those that hit Yahoo and the credit-reporting agency Equifax recently—reinforce this lack of public trust.

And it's not just the Internet that invades our privacy:

- Large retail stores like Nordstrom, Cabela's, and Family Dollar use video surveillance and cell phone signals to track shoppers' behavior, including what sections of the store they visit and how much time they look at merchandise before buying it (Clifford & Hardy, 2013).

- Because of advances in miniaturization and inexpensive digital storage, tiny cameras allow for the recording and surveillance of virtually every aspect of our lives—"from nannies and sleeping babies to vandalism-plagued parking lots to fireplaces awaiting Santa" (Hardy, 2014, p. A1).

- Almost three quarters of major U.S. employers use some form of electronic monitoring of their workers, and school districts all across the country give radio frequency ID wristbands to students so they can monitor their movements on campus. These are the same devices prison inmates are forced to wear in several states (Staples, 2014).

- Most American universities now use some type of antiplagiarism service to monitor students and their work so they can detect cheating. When test proctors at the University of Central Florida see what they suspect is student cheating, they can direct an overhead camera to zoom in and photograph the student; images are then burned onto a CD and retained for evidence (Gabriel, 2010).

As you can see, technological innovation can be a double-edged sword. It has the potential to make our everyday lives more efficient, convenient, and productive. But it can also chip away at the thing we hold most dear: our personal privacy.

Diffusion of Technologies and Cultural Practices

Another cause of social change is **cultural diffusion**: the process by which beliefs, technology, customs, and other cultural items spread from one group or society to another. You may not realize it, but most of the taken-for-granted aspects of our daily lives originally came from somewhere else. For instance, pajamas, clocks, toilets, glass, coins, newspapers, and soap were initially imported into Western cultures from elsewhere (Linton, 1937). Even a fair amount of the English language has been imported, as can be seen from the following examples:

algebra (Arabic)

anatomy (Greek)

bagel (Yiddish)

barbeque (Taíno)

boondocks (Filipino Tagalog)

catamaran (Tamil)

coyote, poncho (Spanish)

dynamite (Swedish)

medicine (Latin)

safari (Swahili)

tycoon (Chinese)

vogue (French)

yogurt (Turkish)

Diffusion often occurs because one society considers the culture or technology of another society to be useful. However, the diffusion process is not always friendly, as you may recall from the discussion of colonization in Chapter 10. When one society's territory is taken over by another society, the indigenous people may be required to adapt to the customs and beliefs of the invaders. When Europeans conquered the New World, Native American peoples were forced to abandon their traditional ways of life and become more "civilized." Hundreds of thousands of Native Americans died in the process, not only from violent conflict but also from malnutrition and new diseases inadvertently brought by their conquerors. Whether diffusion is invited or imposed, the effect is the same: a chain reaction of social changes that affect both individuals and the larger social structure.

Social Movements

One danger of talking about the sources of social change or its cultural, environmental, and institutional consequences is that we then tend to see change as a purely macrolevel structural phenomenon, something that happens to us rather than something we create. But social change is not some huge, invisible hand that descends from the heavens to arbitrarily alter our routine way of life. It is, in the end, a phenomenon driven by human action.

Collective action by large numbers of people has always been a major agent of social change, whether it takes the form of a women's march on Washington, DC, to advocate legislation and policies regarding human rights, immigration reform, health care reform, reproductive rights, the natural environment, LGBTQ rights, racial equality, freedom of religion, and workers' rights; people holding a pray-in outside the Capitol building to encourage lawmakers to pass a "moral" budget; or a sit-in by students in the Harvard University president's house to demand higher wages for the school's blue-collar workers. When people organize and extend their activities beyond the immediate confines of the group, they may become the core of a **social movement** that has the ability to alter society:

> The great movements that changed the course of our history . . . forced
> elites to inaugurate reforms that they otherwise would have avoided,
> as . . . when the Thirteenth Amendment was passed during the Civil War
> ending . . . slavery. . . . Or in the 1930s, when the national government finally
> granted workers the right to organize and inaugurated the first government
> income-support programs. Or when the Southern [segregation] system was
> struck down in response to the civil rights movement. Or when the antiwar
> movement helped to force the withdrawal of American forces from Southeast
> Asia. (Piven, 2013, p. 12)

Underlying all social movements is a concern with social change: the desire to enact it, stop it before it begins, or reverse it. That desire may be expressed in a variety of ways, from peaceful activities such as signing petitions, kneeling during the playing of the national anthem, participating in civil demonstrations, and donating money to violent activities such as rioting and overthrowing a government.

Types of Social Movements

Depending on the nature of their goals, social movements can be categorized as reform movements, countermovements, or revolutionary movements. A **reform movement** attempts to change limited aspects of a society but does not seek to alter or replace major social institutions. Take the U.S. civil rights movement of the 1960s. It did not call for an overhaul of the U.S. economic system (capitalism) or political system (two-party democracy). Instead, it advocated a more limited change: opening up existing institutions to full and equal participation by members of minority groups (DeFronzo, 1991). Similarly, the anti–Vietnam War movement challenged government *policy* (and in the process brought down two presidents—Lyndon Johnson and Richard Nixon), but it didn't seek to change the form of government itself (Fendrich, 2003). Other recent examples of reform movements include the women's movement, the nuclear freeze movement, the Black Lives Matter movement, the school prayer movement, and the environmental movement. The Tea Party movement is a reform movement that emerged in 2009, espousing the values of individual liberty and limited government. Their message resonated with enough voters in 2010 that several Tea Party candidates won election to Congress (though they've not been as successful in subsequent elections). However, although adherents express a desire to dismantle the federal government for what they perceive to be out-of-control spending, debt, and deficits, the politicians they helped elect still must enact any change within the confines of the present system of government.

Because reform movements seek to alter some aspect of existing social arrangements, they are usually opposed by some people and groups. **Countermovements** are designed to prevent or reverse the changes sought or accomplished by an earlier movement. A countermovement is most likely to emerge when the reform movement against which it is reacting becomes large and effective in pursuing its goals and therefore comes to be seen as a threat to personal and social interests (Chafetz & Dworkin, 1987; Mottl, 1980). The contemporary Alt-Right and White Nationalist movements, for instance, are aimed at protecting and promoting the rights of white Americans. They emerged in response to a fear that the influence of ethnoracial minorities was growing and gained traction and visibility throughout the Obama presidency.

Countermovements can last so long that they become part of mainstream culture and politics. Consider the emergence in the 1980s and 1990s of a conservative social countermovement often called the "religious right" or the "Christian right." It was initially provoked by a growing perception among its members of enormous social upheaval in U.S. society: the breakdown of traditional roles and values and a concerted challenge to existing institutions such as education, religion, and the family. Although members of the religious right blamed these changes on the civil rights, antiwar, student, and women's movements of the 1960s and 1970s (Klatch, 1991), they perceived the women's movement as particularly dangerous. Indeed, the leaders of the religious right were the first, in modern times, to articulate the notion that the push for women's equality was responsible for the unhappiness of many individual women and the weakening of the American family (Faludi, 1991). Access to legal abortion, the high divorce rate, and the increased number of children who grow up with working mothers are often offered as proof that the moral bases of family life are eroding (Klatch, 1991). Even today, the Christian right's fear of shifting definitions of gender due to earlier reform movements motivates them to action:

> In an era when sexual liberation has saturated American culture, when women are climbing the corporate ladder and bearing fewer children, and mainline churches are ordaining women and homosexuals, conservative evangelicals are escalating their counteroffensive. Many call themselves complementarians, signaling their belief that God ordained complementary—not identical or flexible—roles for men and women. (Worthen, 2010, p. 54)

Over the past few decades, the religious right has had some success in shifting the political and social mood of the country. It first gained legitimacy in 1980, when presidential candidate Ronald Reagan and several Senate candidates who were supported by the group won the election. It reasserted its influence in 1994 with the takeover of Congress by conservative Republicans. And it gained even more power and visibility with the elections of George W. Bush and later Donald Trump, who promote many religious right themes. Today, it remains a formidable and influential wing of the Republican Party.

Recently, the religious right turned its focus to opposing the increasing visibility and political gains of the gay community. Through national organizations such as the Eagle Forum, the Christian Coalition, Christian Voice (USA), the Family Research Council, the Traditional Values Coalition, Concerned Women for America, Focus on the Family, and many smaller regional groups around the United States, it has achieved some notable triumphs at the state and local levels. It has succeeded in influencing public school curricula and promoting anti–gay-rights legislation. Even on the day in 2015 that the U.S. Supreme Court struck down same-sex marriage bans nationwide, various religious right organizations began mounting a strategy to fight back that included a call for stronger legal protections for those who want to avoid any involvement in same-sex marriage based on their religious beliefs (Eckholm, 2015a). In 2017, the Court agreed to hear an appeal from a Colorado baker who was sued for discrimination after refusing to make a wedding cake for a gay couple on religious grounds.

Over the years, the religious right has been especially effective in limiting access to abortion. Even though the majority of U.S. citizens still favor the legal right to abortion (Lipka, 2015), virtually every state in the nation over the past two decades has enacted new restrictions, such as hospital requirements, mandatory waiting periods, compulsory involvement of second physicians, gestational limits, state-mandated counseling, spousal consent, and parental notification (Guttmacher Institute, 2017). In recent years, legislatures in states such as Kansas, Texas, Oklahoma, and Indiana have been successful in passing restrictive laws that make it even more difficult or uncomfortable for women to get abortions, such as requiring doctors to show the woman a picture of the fetus or regulating the amount and type of equipment, drugs, and resources available in clinics. Few medical schools or residency programs in obstetrics and gynecology provide training in abortion techniques, although pressure from medical student advocacy groups has led a few programs to reinstate abortion instruction into the curriculum (Bazelon, 2010). Forty-five states allow individual health care providers to refuse to participate in an abortion (Guttmacher Institute, 2017).

Given such an environment, it's not surprising that abortion services have become less and less available. About 90% of all U.S. counties (and 94% of counties in the South and Midwest) have no abortion provider. These counties are home to 39% of all American women (R. K. Jones & Jerman, 2017). Nationwide, the number of abortion providers decreased by about 47% between 1982 and 2014 (Alan Guttmacher Institute, 2014; Henshaw & Finer, 2003; R. K. Jones & Jerman, 2017; Kaiser Family Foundation, 2008). Five states—Mississippi, Missouri, North Dakota, South Dakota, and Wyoming—have only one clinic that provides abortion services. In addition, rates of legal abortion have declined steadily over the past two decades. In 1990, there were about 27 abortions per 1,000 women between the ages of 15 and 44; today, that figure is 14.6 per 1,000 (R. K. Jones & Jerman, 2017).

The women's movement, the gay rights movement, and the religious right all remain quite active today, creating numerous colorful conflicts in the national political arena. However, it is important to remember that all these movements are pursuing their interests within the existing social system—as do all reform movements and countermovements. In contrast, **revolutionary movements** attempt to overthrow the entire system itself, whether it is the government or the existing social structure, in order to replace it with another (Skocpol, 1979). The American Revolution of 1776, the French Revolution of 1789, the Russian Revolution of 1917, the Iranian Revolution of 1979, and the Afghan Revolution of 1996 are examples of movements that toppled existing governments and created a new social order.

Revolutionary change in basic social institutions can be brought about through nonviolent means, such as peaceful labor strikes, democratic elections, and civil disobedience. However, most successful revolutions have involved some level of violence on the part of both movement participants and groups opposing the revolution (DeFronzo, 1991).

Elements of Social Movements

Whichever type they are, social movements occur when dissatisfied people see their condition as resulting from society's inability to meet their needs. Movements typically develop when certain segments of the population conclude that society's resources—access to political power, higher education, living wages, legal justice, medical care, a clean and healthy environment, and so on—are distributed unequally and unfairly (R. Brown, 1986). People come to believe that they have a moral right to the satisfaction of their unmet expectations and that this satisfaction cannot or will not occur without some effort on their part. This perception is often based on the experience of past failures in working within the system.

As individuals and groups who share this sense of frustration and unfairness interact, the existing system begins to lose its perceived legitimacy (Piven & Cloward, 1977). Individuals who ordinarily might have considered themselves helpless come to believe that as a social movement they have the capacity to change things and significantly alter their lives and the lives of others:

- In 2006, a website called MomsRising.org was launched, bringing mothers together to talk about ways to change public policy. In "house parties" all across the country, small groups of mothers meet regularly to discuss ways to lobby legislators on issues like family leave, pay equity, health insurance, childcare, and after-school activities (St. George, 2007). They now have over a million members nationwide and 3,000 active bloggers and have been influential in changing paid family leave policies in several states (MomsRising.org, 2017).

- In several dozen cities across the country, day laborers—typically immigrants who congregate at well-known locations like street corners or parking lots, waiting for building contractors, landscapers, plumbers, or other potential employers to offer a day's work—organized to set their own minimum wages (S. Greenhouse, 2006).

- Migrant farm workers all across the country have organized to seek improvements in their working conditions: In Vermont, they protested to win vacation days and improved housing in the dairy industry; in California, they've sought to address consumer concerns that produce be grown under nonexploitive conditions; and in Florida, they've persuaded large companies like Burger King, McDonald's, and Walmart to raise wages (S. Greenhouse, 2015).

- In Chicago, public school teachers mobilized parents and won a contract fight with the mayor that not only provided them with more job security but also improved educational quality (Piven, 2013).

Ideology

Any successful social movement must have a compelling **ideology**, a coherent system of beliefs, values, and ideas that justifies its existence (R. W. Turner & Killian, 1987; Zurcher & Snow, 1981). An ideology fulfills several functions. First, it helps frame the issue in moral terms. Once people perceive the moral goodness of their position, they become willing to risk arrest, personal financial costs, or more for the good of the cause. Second, the ideology defines the group's interests and helps to identify people as either supporters or detractors, creating identifiable "good guys" and "villains." Finally, an ideology provides participants with a collective sense of what the specific goals of the movement are or should be.

Consider the antiabortion (or pro-life) movement. Its ideology rests on several assumptions about the nature of childhood and motherhood (Luker, 1984). For instance, it assumes that each conception is an act of God and so abortion violates God's will. The ideology also states that life begins at conception, the fetus is an individual who has a constitutional right to life, and every human life should be valued (Michener, DeLamater, & Schwartz, 1986). This ideology reinforces the view among adherents that abortion is immoral, evil, and self-indulgent.

The power of an ideology to mobilize support for a social movement often depends on the broader cultural and historical context in which the movement exists. For instance, it would have seemed in the 2003 buildup to the invasion of Iraq that antiwar activists would be able to make a strong case against going to war by using an ideology based on a portrayal of the United States as a hostile aggressor. After all, the country we were set to invade, Iraq, posed no direct threat to the United States, hadn't undertaken a large-scale military mobilization, wasn't involved in planning or carrying out the 9/11 attacks that precipitated our military action, and wasn't harboring those who were involved. Internationally, the sympathetic response that we received from other countries immediately after 9/11 was short lived, replaced by a growing perception that the United States was a global bully whose policies ignore the interests of people in other countries. The vast majority of nations around the world—foes and allies alike—were strongly opposed to the invasion.

But the post-9/11 cultural context in this country was a mixture of anger, fear, lingering shock, and heightened patriotism, which made an ideology of military restraint intolerable to many Americans. Enduring memories of earlier antiwar protestors' hostility toward soldiers returning from Vietnam during the late 1960s and early 1970s complicated the task. Reluctant to disrespect the individual soldiers in Iraq who were willing to put their lives at risk, antiwar activists had to walk a thin line between opposing U.S. aggression and expressing support for the young men and women who were being asked to carry out that aggression on the front lines. Against such a backdrop, the ideology of the 2003 antiwar movement—which advocated a diplomatic, reflective, and measured approach—sounded unpatriotic, weak, and inadequate, not to mention disloyal to the thousands who died in the 9/11 attacks. Not surprisingly, the movement failed to prevent the onset of war.

Although an ideology might be what attracts people to a movement, it must be spread through social networks of friends, family, coworkers, and other contacts (Zurcher & Snow, 1981). For some people, in fact, the ideology of the movement is secondary to other social considerations. Potential participants are unlikely to join without being introduced to the movement by someone they know (Gladwell, 2010). The ideological leaders of a social movement might want to believe that participants are there because of "the cause," but chances are the participants have a friend or acquaintance who persuaded them to be there (Gerlach & Hine, 1970; Stark & Bainbridge, 1980).

Sometimes the activities required to promote or sustain a particular movement run counter to the ideological goals of the movement itself. The leaders of successful political revolutions, for example, soon realize that to run the country they now control, they must create highly structured bureaucracies not unlike the ones they have overthrown. Two years after helping to topple a dictatorial regime that had ruled for 30 years, leaders of the Egyptian pro-democracy movement issued an ultimatum calling for the resignation of the new democratically elected president, Mohammed Morsi, who was eventually forced out by the Egyptian military.

Furthermore, an ill-defined, unarticulated ideology—or one that is too broadly defined— may in the end slow any headway the movement is able to make in the first place. For instance, the Occupy Wall Street movement generated significant attention in 2011. Its "We are the 99%" slogan became a popular call for economic justice nationwide. Then-president Obama came out in support of it during his 2012 election campaign; so did House Minority Leader Nancy Pelosi. But the movement has never been able to sustain the same level of interest or effectiveness since. Although its general goal was to reduce economic inequality, it advocated a slew of specific objectives that included a reduction of corporate influence in politics, a more balanced distribution of income, job creation, bank reform, relief for indebted students, housing reform, and so on. In addition, it expanded its interests to include protection of workers in Bangladesh and solidarity for protestors in Turkey, Brazil, and Greece. Some critics, as well as members of the movement itself, argued that its ideological purview has been spread too thin to effectively influence policy.

Participants in reform movements and countermovements may also have to engage in behaviors that conflict with the ideological beliefs of the movement. The religious right movement's pro-family, pro-motherhood positions are clearly designed to turn back the feminist agenda. However, early in the movement, it became clear that to be successful, it would have to enlist high-profile women to campaign against feminist policies. Women on the religious right frequently had to leave their families, travel the country to make speeches, and display independent strength—characteristics that were anything but the models of traditional womanhood they were publicly promoting. Note how the following description of a popular female minister in the Christian right movement could apply to just about any modern-day, female professional:

> Priscilla [Shirer] now accepts about 20 out of some 300 speaking invitations each year, and she publishes a stream of Bible studies, workbooks and corresponding DVDs. . . . Jerry [her husband] does his share of housework and childcare so that Priscilla can study and write. He travels with his wife everywhere. Whenever possible, they take their sons along on her speaking trips, but they often deposit the boys with Jerry's mother. (Worthen, 2010, p. 54)

Ironically, social movements sometimes require the involvement of individuals from outside the group whose interests the movement represents. For example, many of the people who fought successfully for Blacks' right to vote in Alabama and Mississippi during the civil rights movement of the 1950s and 1960s were middle-class white college students from the North. Similarly, it wasn't until mainstream religious organizations, labor groups, and college students got involved that the living wage movement—an effort to require states, cities, and counties to pay their low-wage workers an amount above the federal minimum wage—became successful. About three quarters of Americans now support raising the federal minimum wage from $7.25 an hour to over $12 an hour (National Employment Law Project, 2015). Through protests and public relations blitzes aimed at voters, politicians, and corporations, the Fight for $15 movement has encouraged workers at the bottom of the pay scale all across the country to demand a living wage from their employers. As a result, cities such as Seattle, Los Angeles, and San Francisco have raised their minimum wages to $15. The state of New York plans to do so in most counties by 2021 and California will follow suit statewide by 2022 (S. Greenhouse, 2016). Recently, however, the movement has faced increasing resistance due to some evidence that small businesses in places with a $15 minimum wage are cutting the hours of their low-level workers to make up for the higher wages they have to pay, thereby leaving these workers with less income. One study concluded that despite earning more per hour, wages for these workers has actually fallen by an average of $125 a month because they're not working as much (Jardim et al., 2017).

The ideology of a social movement may gain additional credibility when voiced by those whose interests would seem to be contrary to its goals. In the mid-2000s, opposition to the war in Iraq gained some traction not because people took a second look at the original antiwar ideology or because street protests and rallies suddenly gained their attention. Instead, it grew because many U.S. soldiers who fought there and saw the conditions firsthand started speaking out in opposition, often under the threat of disciplinary action (Houppert, 2005). Combatants knew the reality of war in ways that civilian protestors never could (Utne, 2006). Some even spoke out while on the front lines, posting daily blogs that criticized the condition of military equipment and resources, our lack of understanding of Iraqi insurgents, and ultimately our very involvement in the war (Finer, 2005). Membership in organizations with names like Operation Truth, Gold Star Families for Peace, and Iraq and Afghanistan Veterans of America grew during the early years of the war (N. Banerjee, 2005).

Furthermore, people who are already disadvantaged by particular social conditions may not be as effective as others in promoting their cause because they lack the money, time, skills, and connections that successful movements require. For instance, the people who would stand to benefit the most from environmental improvement—individuals in poor, polluted communities—have historically been uninvolved in the environmental movement. Residents tend to see environmentalists as middle- and upper-middle-class outsiders whose own neighborhoods are relatively unpolluted and who don't appreciate the community's concerns (Bullard, 1993). Nobody wants garbage dumps, landfills, incinerators, or polluting factories in their backyards. But if these are the only ventures that will provide steady employment for residents, poor communities are left with little choice but to support them. Consequently, they often fear that outside environmentalists will take away their jobs and economic livelihoods. Recently, however, many members of poor communities have joined the environmental movement, motivated not by a "Save the earth" ideology but by a more immediately relevant one that emphasizes the unfairness and discrimination to which they are exposed. As one successful local activist put it, "People here aren't going to install solar panels on their roofs or drive a Prius, but they can demand institutional change and decent business practices" (quoted in Breslau, 2007, p. 69). In some developing nations, poor communities have mobilized resistance to commercial tree plantations, oil drilling, mining, or dam construction when these developments are perceived to constitute a threat to people's livelihoods (Martinez-Alier, 2003).

Rising Expectations

You might think that major social movements, particularly revolutionary ones, would be most likely to occur when many people's lives are at their lowest and most desperate point. Certainly, huge numbers of disadvantaged people who see little chance of things improving and who perceive the government as unwilling or unable to meet their needs are necessary for any massive movements for change (Tilly, 1978).

But some sociologists argue that social movements are actually more likely to arise when social conditions are already starting to improve than when they are at their worst (Brinton, 1965; Davies, 1962). Constant deprivation does not necessarily make people want to revolt. Instead, they are more likely to be preoccupied with daily survival than with demonstrations and street protests. Heightened expectations brought about by small improvements in living conditions, however, show those who are deprived that their society is capable of being different, sparking a desire for large-scale change. As one historian put it, "'Ironically, revolutions happen at times when things are getting better'—when people realize they have more control over their lives" (quoted in Dokoupil, 2011, p. 7). When these new expectations aren't met, deprived people become angry. The gap between what they expect and what they have now feels intolerable. Although they may actually be somewhat better off than in the past, their situation relative to their expectations now appears much worse (Davies, 1962). Such frustration makes participation in protest or revolutionary activity more likely.

Resource Mobilization

At any given point, numerous problems in a society need to be fixed, and people's grievances remain more or less constant from year to year. Yet relatively few major social movements exist at any one time. If widespread dissatisfaction and frustration were all that is needed to sustain a social movement, "the masses would always be in revolt" (Trotsky, 1930/1959). What else is needed for a social movement to get started, gain support, and achieve its goals?

According to **resource mobilization theory**, the key ingredient is effective organization. No social movement can exist unless it has an organized system for acquiring needed resources: money, labor, participants, legal aid, access to the media, and so on (J. D. McCarthy & Zald, 1977). How far a movement goes in attaining its goals depends on its ability to expand its ranks, build large-scale public support, and transform those who join into committed participants (Zurcher & Snow, 1981).

Most large, long-term social movements involve a national and even international coalition of groups. Such widespread organization makes the movement more powerful by making recruiting and fundraising more efficient. Movements that historically have lasted the longest—the women's movement, the antiabortion movement, the civil rights movement, the environmental movement—are those supported by large organizational bureaucracies. The National Organization for Women, the Christian Coalition, the National Association for the Advancement of Colored People (NAACP), the Sierra Club, and the like have full-time lobbyists or political action committees in Washington that connect them to the national political system. Few movements can succeed without such connections, because achieving social change often requires changing laws or convincing courts to interpret laws in particular ways.

Highly organized social movements use an established network of communication (J. D. McCarthy & Zald, 1977). Movements need an effective system both for getting information to all participants and for recruiting and fundraising (Tarrow, 1994). The ability to quickly mobilize large numbers of people for, say, a flash mob or a march to the nation's capital depends on the ability to tell them what is going to happen and when and where it will happen. Modern social movements must use websites, social media, direct mailing strategies, and networked phone and computer systems to be successful.

During the so-called Arab Spring in 2011, antigovernment protestors in Egypt, Tunisia, Yemen, Morocco, Libya, Syria, Bahrain, Saudi Arabia, Jordan, and elsewhere used Twitter, Facebook, and YouTube to mobilize collective actions and export images of their plight around the world. Cell phones replaced traditional reporters as the world's "eyes and ears" on the protests (Preston & Stelter, 2011). Media outlets referred to the movement variously as the Facebook Revolution, the Twitter Revolution, and the Keystroke Revolution.

Today, it would be inconceivable for a movement's organizers to attempt to mobilize support *without* Facebook, Instagram, YouTube, or Twitter. Consider recent protests over the excessive use of lethal force by police officers against people of color—what some have called "the first civil rights movement of the 21st century." It started in 2014 with a single online photo that went viral: Michael Brown—the unarmed black man shot by a police officer in Ferguson, Missouri—lying facedown on the street, bleeding from his head. Such incidents have been occurring for decades, but only recently has the movement been able to use social media to successfully convey the message that they represent a national epidemic:

Their innovation has been to marry the strengths of social media—the swift, morally blunt consensus that can be created by hashtags; the personal connection that a charismatic online persona can make with followers; the broad networks that allow for the easy distribution of documentary photos and videos—with an effort to quickly mobilize protests in each new city where a police shooting occurs. (J. C. Kang, 2015, p. 36)

Social media—not to mention more traditional media like television, newspapers, and radio—play an equally important part in the success of a social movement by helping to validate and enlarge the scope of its cause. In other words, these media play a key role in constructing a particular social reality useful to the movement by conveying the message that the movement's concerns are valid and that the movement is an important force in society. A small group of people disrupting a town hall meeting on immigration reform is, for all intents and purposes, a nonevent without media coverage or a witness posting a tweet. Media recognition is often a necessary condition before those who are the targets of influence respond to the movement's claims and demands (Gamson & Wolfsfeld, 1993).

In sum, movements that succeed in enacting substantial social change are not necessarily those with the most compelling ideological positions or the greatest emotional appeal (Ferree, 1992). Instead, they are the ones with the necessary high-level organization and communication networks to mobilize supporters and the necessary media access and technological savvy to neutralize the opposition and transform the public into sympathizers.

Bureaucratization

It makes sense that the most successful social movements are those that are the best organized. However, high-level organization can backfire if it leads to rigidity and turf wars, common to any bureaucracy. When organizations within a movement differ in their philosophies and tactics, tremendous infighting and bickering may break out among organizations ostensibly working toward the same goal.

For instance, the U.S. civil rights movement during the 1950s and 1960s included many diverse, seemingly incompatible organizations. The NAACP was large, racially integrated, legalistic, and bureaucratic in form; the Student Nonviolent Coordinating Committee (SNCC) was younger and more militant in its tactics and after a while excluded Whites from participation; the Southern Christian Leadership Conference (SCLC) was highly structured, had a religious ideology, and was dominated by male clergy; the Black Muslims and the Black Panthers advocated violent methods to achieve civil rights. The ideologies and methods of these diverse civil rights groups often conflicted, which arguably slowed down the extension of civil rights to African Americans.

No matter their shape, size, or motive, social movements require sustained activity over a long period (R. W. Turner & Killian, 1987). Thus, unlike riots, which are of limited duration, social movements may become permanent fixtures in the political and social environment. Ironically, a social movement whose goal is the large-scale alteration of some aspect of society can, in time, become so large and bureaucratic itself that it becomes part of the establishment it seeks to change. For instance, Sinn Féin was a movement founded in 1905 to end British rule in Ireland. Among its offshoots over the years was the Irish Republican Army, which carried out a bombing and terror campaign in Northern Ireland and England for decades. In recent years, most of the violence has been stopped, and the people of Ireland have won some autonomy. Sinn Féin is now the third-largest political party in

VISUAL ESSAY—MARCHING FOR CHANGE

REUTERS/Carlo Allegri

AP Photo/Cliff Owen

Joel Sheakosk/Barcroft Media/Getty Images

Albin Lohr-Jones/LightRocket/Getty Images

David Grossman / Alamy Stock Photo

Tony Karumba/AFP/Getty Images

David McNew/Getty Images News/Getty Images

If there's one thing we can count on in this country it's that when a group of people feels mistreated, wronged, downtrodden, or persecuted, they will take to the streets to demonstrate. Even as our lives become more and more technologized and virtual, a group of people marching in the streets with distinctively low-tech signs and slogans remains the iconic image of protest. It might take Twitter or Facebook or Instagram to mobilize people, but the demonstration itself is always "in person." And as you can see from the images here, the topics and targets of protest are as diverse as the people who participate in them.

As you think about the various issues represented here, do you believe that street protests are an effective means of enacting social change? Have you ever participated in such a protest? What was the cause you were protesting against?

What was the outcome? Have we reached a "saturation" point in which this tactic has become so stale that it's lost its effectiveness? Can you think of a better way to change some aspect of society that you think needs changing?

Ireland, with its own news organization, a highly structured network of local branches, and representatives in both the Irish Parliament and the European Parliament.

In addition, people who devote their lives to a movement come to depend on it for their own livelihood. Hence, social movements organized for the purpose of enacting social change actually provide structure and order in the lives of their members, acting as sources of opportunities, careers, and rewards (Hewitt, 1988).

Political Opportunity Structure

Social movements also depend on conditions outside their control. One such condition is the structure of existing political institutions. Political systems are more or less vulnerable and more or less receptive to challenge at different times (McAdam, McCarthy, & Zald, 1988). These ebbs and flows of political opportunities produce cycles of protest and movement activity. When political systems are firm, unyielding, and stable, people have to deal individually with their problems or air their grievances through existing channels. But when a system opens up and people realize it is vulnerable—that they can actually make a difference—movements are likely to develop.

Sometimes these opportunities are unintentional and exist quite independently of the actions of movement members. For instance, in the 1970s, two antinuclear movements arose in (what was then West) Germany and France. The movements had similar ideologies and used similar mobilization techniques. However, the German movement flourished and remains highly influential in national politics today. The French movement was weak and quickly died off. Why were the outcomes of these two movements so different? In Germany, the government procedure for reviewing nuclear power facilities provided opportunities for those opposed to nuclear power to legally intervene. The procedure in place in France was closed and unresponsive to public sentiment (Nelkin & Pollak, 1981). Similarly, the emergence in the 1970s of the contemporary environmental movement in the United States was possible because government agencies were already sympathetic to environmental concerns (Gale, 1986).

The idea that unintentional political opportunities can encourage social movements for change was dramatically supported during the 1989 pro-democracy movement in the former Soviet Union and Eastern Europe. In the mid-1980s, the Soviet government under Mikhail Gorbachev embarked on a massive program of economic and structural reforms (*perestroika*) as well as a relaxation of constraints on freedom of expression (*glasnost*). The ensuing liberties encouraged open criticism of the political order and created new opportunities for political action (Tarrow, 1994). Protest movements took advantage of these opportunities, leading to the sometimes violent struggles for independence on the part of small, ethnically homogeneous republics that we saw during the 1990s and continue to see today in a few remaining areas. In other words, only when the political structure became less repressive could these monumental changes take place.

Political instability can sometimes spawn less dramatic reform movements. The changing fortunes of a government can create uncertainty among supporters and encourage challengers to try to take advantage of the situation. Consider once more the civil rights movement in the United States in the 1950s and 1960s. During the 1950s, as the first calls for racial equality were being heard, many conservative Southern Democrats defected to the Republican Party, where their segregationist leanings met with more sympathy. The ensuing decline of Southern white support for the Democratic Party, coupled with the movement of African Americans to large cities in the North, where they were more likely to vote, forced the Democrats to seek black support in the presidential election of 1960. The black vote is widely credited with John Kennedy's narrow victory that year (McAdam, 1982). Hence, the Kennedy administration (and later the Johnson administration) felt compelled to campaign for civil rights (Tarrow, 1994). Increased political power, in turn, enhanced the bargaining position of civil rights forces, culminating in two landmark pieces of legislation: the Civil Rights Act of 1964 and the Voting Rights Act of 1965.

At other times, existing political regimes intentionally create or actively support structural opportunities for change. For example, the U.S. anti–drunk-driving movement is strong and influential today because it enjoys substantial support from federal, state, and local governments; state and federal highway agencies; and state and local police departments (J. D. McCarthy & Wolfson, 1992). When in the 1980s the movement advocated a national drinking age of 21, many state legislatures balked, fearing a backlash from powerful alcohol producers, distributors, and retailers. However, the federal government enacted legislation threatening to withhold significant amounts of federal highway funds from states that didn't establish a drinking age of 21—a strong incentive for states to pass such a law.

Political opportunities provide the institutional framework within which social movements operate. Movements form when ordinary citizens respond to changes in the opportunity structure that lower the costs of involvement and reveal where the authorities are vulnerable. Unlike money and power, these conditions are external to the movement. If political opportunities exist, then even groups with fairly mild grievances or few resources can develop a successful movement (see also J. C. Jenkins & Perrow, 1977). In contrast, groups with deep grievances and ample resources—but few political opportunities—may never get their movements off the ground (Tarrow, 1994).

The Sociological Imagination Revisited

In the summer of 1981 with my brand new bachelor's degree in hand (yes, I *am* that old!), I had the good fortune to backpack through Europe. While in Florence, Italy, I made a point of visiting the Galleria dell'Accademia, the museum where one of my favorite works of art, Michelangelo's statue of David, resides. To my eye, it is truly a masterpiece of sculpture, nearly flawless in its detail. I stood there admiring this amazing work of art for close to 2 hours. As I left, I noticed several sculptures that had escaped my attention when I first entered the museum. I soon discovered that they, too, were created by Michelangelo. What made them particularly interesting was that they were all unfinished. Some were obviously near completion, but others looked to me like shapeless blocks of granite. As I looked closer, I could see the actual chisel marks the great sculptor had made. I imagined the plan Michelangelo had in his head as he worked. I envisioned him toiling to bring form to the heavy stone.

These imperfect slabs of rock showed evidence of human creation in a way that the perfect, finished statue of David never could. At that moment, I saw Michelangelo as a real guy who fashioned beauty from shapelessness. I began to admire the genius of the creator and not just the creation. I went back to look at *David* again with a newfound appreciation.

Society isn't nearly as perfect as Michelangelo's *David*, yet we can still fall into the trap of seeing social structure as a product that exists on its own and not as something that people have collectively chiseled. We sometimes forget that many of the realities of our lives that we take for granted were the result, at some point in history, of the handiwork of individuals. One generation's radical changes become another's taken-for-granted features of everyday life. The fact that you can't be forced to work 70 or 80 hours a week, can't be exposed to dangerous working conditions without your knowledge, and are entitled to a certain number of paid holidays a year are a result of the actions of real people in early labor union movements for whom *none* of these protections existed.

Because we are inclined to take so many of our freedoms, rights, and desires for granted, we may not only overlook the struggles of those who came before us but also downplay the extent to which inequities and injustices even existed in the past. For instance, many young women today have never even considered that they are only a generation or two removed from a time when they might have been prohibited from attending the college or pursuing the career of their choice, when they might have been expected to abandon their own dreams and ambitions to provide the support their husbands needed to succeed, or when they might have had to take sole responsibility for household chores and their children's daily care while their husbands focused on work and the outside world. The majority of young women polled in a survey several years ago indicated that they didn't know that abortion was once illegal (Zernike, 2003). Like most beneficiaries of past movements, these young women simply take their freedoms and opportunities for granted, sometimes even expressing contempt for the feminists responsible for winning the rights they so casually enjoy (Stacey, 1991). When word spread online recently that the actress Shailene Woodley did not consider herself a feminist," one critic said, "She's hardworking and talented, and the fact that she can open a movie is feminism in action. Another said, "Dear Young Actresses: Before you sound off on feminists and how you're not one, please figure out what feminism is" (both quoted in Meltzer, 2014, p. E1). A British columnist put it this way:

> When I talk to girls they go, "I'm not a feminist . . ." And I say: "What? You don't want to vote? Do you want to be owned by your husband? Do you want your money from your job to go into his bank account? If you were raped, do you still want that to be a crime? Congratulations: you are a feminist." (quoted in Lyall, 2012, p. 40)

So the irony of social movements, then, is that the more profound and far reaching their accomplishments, the more likely we are to eventually forget the original inequities that fostered them and the efforts of the individuals who produced them.

Fundamentally, societies remain stable because enough individuals define existing conditions as satisfactory, and societies change because enough individuals define situations that were once tolerable as problems that must be acknowledged and solved.

Some influential acts of individuals may at first blush appear rather insignificant. Early in 1960, four black students at North Carolina Agricultural and Technical State University, in Greensboro, engaged in a series of discussions in their dormitory room about the state of the civil rights movement. They came to the conclusion that things weren't progressing quickly enough in the still-segregated South and that it was time for action. So they decided to go to the lunch counter at the local Woolworth's store and order coffee and doughnuts. Now that might not sound like much. But in the early-1960s South, public eating facilities that weren't reserved for Blacks were forbidden by law to serve Blacks. And Greensboro at the time was the sort of place where any act of racial rebelliousness was routinely met with violence (Gladwell, 2010).

After purchasing some school supplies in another part of the store, the four students sat down at the lunch counter and placed their orders. As anticipated, the reply was, "I'm sorry, we don't serve you here" (McCain, 1991, p. 115). They remained seated for 45 minutes, citing the fact that they had been served in another part of the store without any difficulty. They were subjected to the verbal taunts, racial slurs, and even violence of angry Whites in the store.

Their actions attracted the attention of area religious leaders, community activists, and students from other local colleges, both black and white. Despite the abuses they knew awaited them, these four young men returned to Woolworth's a few days later, only this time with more demonstrators. At one point, they and their fellow protestors occupied 63 of the 65 seats available at the lunch counter. This was the first social movement covered by television, too, so word of their actions spread quickly. They received endorsements from religious organizations like the North Carolina Council of Churches. Within weeks, young African Americans and sympathetic Whites had engaged in similar acts in nine states and 54 cities in the South as well as several areas in the North, where stores were picketed. After several months of protests, Woolworth's integrated its lunch counter.

Some historians argue that many of the political movements for change that burst onto the scene in the 1960s—including the women's movement, the antiwar movement, and the student free speech movement—could trace their philosophical and tactical roots to this small act by four students (Cluster, 1979). Admittedly, the participants in all these movements might have developed the sit-in as a tactic on their own, even if in 1960 the four students *had* been served coffee and doughnuts at Woolworth's. The point is, though, that the collective movement that arose from the actions of these seemingly insignificant individuals in 1960 had an enormous impact on the massive changes that occurred in the United States over the next 50 years and probably beyond.

We re-create society not only through acts of defiance and organized social movements but also through our daily interactions. The driving theme throughout this book has been that society and its constituent elements are simultaneously human creations and phenomena that exist independently of us, influencing and controlling our private experiences at every turn.

Organizations and institutions exist and thrive because they implicitly or explicitly discourage individuals from challenging the rules and patterns of behavior that characterize them. Imagine what would happen to the system of higher education if you and others like you challenged the authority of your school. You could establish a new order in which students would dictate the content of courses, take control of the classroom, abolish grading or any other evaluative mechanism used for assessing student performance, do away with tuition, and so on. But because you have an education and a career to gain from the institutional structure as it stands, you're not very likely to do something to jeopardize it.

Does this mean that we are all leaves in the wind, buffeted here and there by the powerful and permanent forces of a structure that dwarfs us? To some extent, the answer is yes. I subscribe to the sociological imagination and strongly believe that to fully understand our lives, we must acknowledge that processes larger than ourselves determine some of our private experiences. Along the way, though, we sometimes lose sight of our important role as shapers of society. Although society presents itself as largely unchangeable, U.S. culture is based at least in part on the "can-do" attitude. I recall, as a child in 1969, sitting in a darkened living room with my parents on a warm July evening. The only light in the room came from the gray-blue glow of our little black-and-white television. I watched with great amazement the fuzzy, almost imperceptible image of astronaut Neil Armstrong taking the first tentative steps on the moon and stating, "That's one small step for man, one giant leap for mankind." I didn't realize at the time how far beyond the space program the power of that statement stretched. But since then, I have come to realize that people do indeed leave footprints on the world in which they live.

Conclusion and Farewell

Sociology is not one of those disciplines that draws from a long-standing body of scientific facts and laws. We do have some useful explanations for why certain important social phenomena happen, and we can make reasonable projections about future developments. But sociology is not inherently a discipline of answers. It's a discipline of questions, one that provides a unique and useful method for identifying the puzzles of your life and your society.

This discipline scrutinizes, analyzes, and dissects institutional order and its effects on our thinking. It exposes the vulnerable underbelly of both objective and official reality and, by doing so, prods us into taking a closer look at ourselves and our private worlds—not an easy thing to do. Sociology makes life an unsafe place. I don't mean that it makes people violent or dangerous; I mean that it makes perceptions of social stability unstable or at least fair game for analysis. It's not easy to admit that our reality may be a figment of our collective minds and just one of many possible realities. We live under a belief system that tells us that our unchallenged assumptions are simply the way things are.

Sociology is thus a "liberating" perspective (Liazos, 1985). It forces us to look at the social processes that influence our thoughts, perceptions, and actions and helps us see how social change occurs and the impact we can have on others. In doing so, sociology also points out the very limits of liberation. We become aware of the chains that restrict our "movements." But sociology also gives us the tools to break those chains. The sociological imagination gives us a glimpse of the world both as it is and as it could be. To be a sociologically astute observer of the world as it is, you must be able to strip away fallacies and illusions and see the interconnected system underneath. Only then can you take full advantage of your role as a co-creator of society.

I leave you with one final thought: If you now look at your life and the lives of those around you differently, if you now question things heretofore unquestionable, if you now see where you fit in the bigger societal picture, if you now see orderly patterns in areas you previously thought were chaotic, or chaos in areas you previously thought were orderly, then you are well on your way to understanding the meaning—and the promise—of sociology.

Your Turn

Reading about people taking an active role in reconstructing a part of their personal lives or of their society is one thing, but it's quite another to see such people in action. Most communities contain people who were at one time active in a major movement for social change: the labor movement, the antiwar movement, the women's movement, the civil rights movement, the antiabortion movement, the Occupy Wall Street movement, and so forth. Find a few people who were actively involved in one such movement. Ask them to describe their experiences. What was their motive for joining the movement? What sorts of activities did they participate in? What

were the goals they wanted to accomplish? Looking back, do they feel the movement accomplished those goals? If not, why not? What else needs to be done?

For purposes of historical comparison, see if you can identify a movement that is currently under way in your community. It might be a drive in support of a broad societal concern, such as environmental awareness or equal access to health care; a group organized to address a political issue of local interest, such as an antismoking ordinance; or an attempt to stop something that some people think might harm the local area, like the construction of a factory or the arrival of a particular type of business.

Try to attend a gathering in which the movement is involved. It might be an organizational meeting, a city council meeting, an open town hall meeting, a protest march, a fundraiser, or a demonstration.

What happened at the gathering? What seemed to be the overall atmosphere? Was it festive, solemn, angry, or businesslike? Was any opposition present?

Interview some of the participants. Ask them the same questions you asked the participants who were in past movements. Do people get involved in social movements for the same reasons they did in the past?

Most social movement organizations now have their own websites on the Internet. Visit some of these sites to get a sense of the kinds of information these organizations provide. Do they tend to be primarily informational, focusing on the history and current state of the issue at hand, or are they primarily recruitment tools, designed to attract new participants and financial donors? How are these sites presented? Do they appeal to the emotions, or do they rely on factual argument? Do these websites contain links to the sites of other organizations that have similar ideologies?

Relate your observations from the interviews and the Internet to the discussion of social movements in this chapter. What are the most effective tactics and strategies? How are resources mobilized? Why do some movements succeed and others fail?

Chapter Highlights

- Whether at the personal, cultural, or institutional level, change is the preeminent feature of modern societies.

- Social change is not some massive, impersonal force that arbitrarily disrupts our routine way of life; it is a human creation.

- Social change has a variety of causes: adaptation to environmental pressures, internal population changes, technological discoveries and innovations, and the importation of cultural practices from other countries.

- Social movements are long-term collective actions that address an issue of concern to large numbers of people.

- Societies remain stable because enough people define existing conditions as satisfactory and they change because enough people define the once accepted conditions as problems that must be solved.

Key Terms

anomie: Condition in which rapid change has disrupted society's ability to adequately regulate and control its members and the old rules that governed people's lives no longer seem to apply

countermovement: Collective action designed to prevent or reverse changes sought or accomplished by an earlier social movement

cultural diffusion: Process by which beliefs, technology, customs, and other elements of culture spread from one group or society to another

global climate change: Steady rise in Earth's average temperature as a result of increasing amounts of carbon dioxide in the atmosphere

ideology: Coherent system of beliefs, values, and ideas

postindustrial society: Society in which knowledge, the control of information, and service industries are more important

(Continued)

(Continued)

elements of the economy than agriculture or manufacturing and production

reform movement: Collective action that seeks to change limited aspects of a society but does not seek to alter or replace major social institutions

resource mobilization theory: A theory of social movements that suggests that no social movement can exist unless it has an organized system for acquiring needed resources: money, labor, participants, legal aid, access to the media

revolutionary movement: Collective action that attempts to overthrow an entire social system and replace it with another

social movement: Continuous, large-scale, organized collective action motivated by the desire to enact, stop, or reverse change in some area of society

SAGE edge™ edge.sagepub.com/newman12e

SAGE edge offers a robust online environment featuring an impressive array of free tools and resources for review, study, and further exploration, keeping both instructors and students on the cutting edge of teaching and learning.

• Glossary •

Absolute poverty: Inability to afford the minimal requirements for sustaining a reasonably healthy existence

Absolutism: Approach to defining deviance that rests on the assumption that all human behavior can be considered either inherently good or inherently bad

Account: Statement designed to explain unanticipated, embarrassing, or unacceptable behavior after the behavior has occurred

Achieved status: Social position acquired through our own efforts or accomplishments or taken on voluntarily

Affirmative action: Program designed to seek out members of minority groups for positions from which they previously had been excluded, thereby seeking to overcome institutional racism

Agents of socialization: Various individuals, groups, and organizations who influence the socialization process

Age structure: Population's balance of old and young people

Aligning action: Action taken to restore an identity that has been damaged

Altruistic suicide: Type of suicide that occurs where ties to the group or community are considered more important than individual identity

Analysis of existing data: Type of unobtrusive research that relies on data gathered earlier by someone else for some other purpose

Anomic suicide: Type of suicide that occurs when the structure of society is weakened or disrupted and people feel hopeless and disillusioned

Anomie: Condition in which rapid change has disrupted society's ability to adequately regulate and control its members and the old rules that governed people's lives no longer seem to apply

Anticipatory socialization: Process through which people acquire the values and orientations found in statuses they will likely enter in the future

Ascribed status: Social position acquired at birth or taken on involuntarily later in life

Authority: Possession of some status or quality that compels others to obey one's directives or commands

Back stage: Area of social interaction away from the view of an audience, where people can rehearse and rehash their behavior

Birth cohort: Set of people who were born during the same era and who face similar societal circumstances brought about by their shared position in the overall age structure of the population

Bureaucracy: Large hierarchical organization governed by formal rules and regulations and having clearly specified work tasks

Caste system: Stratification system based on heredity, with little movement allowed across strata

Coalition: Subgroup of a triad, formed when two members unite against the third member

Cohort effect: Phenomenon in which members of a birth cohort tend to experience a particular life course event or rite of passage—puberty, marriage, childbearing, graduation, entry into the workforce, death—at roughly the same time

Collectivist culture: Culture in which personal accomplishments are less important in the formation of identity than group membership

Colonization: Process of expanding economic markets by invading and establishing control over a weaker country and its people

Colorism: Skin color prejudice within an ethnoracial group, most notably between light-skinned and dark-skinned Blacks

Comparative method: Research technique that compares existing official statistics and historical records across groups to test a theory about some social phenomenon

Competitive individualism: Cultural belief that those who succeed in society are those who work hardest and have the best abilities and that those who suffer don't work hard enough or lack necessary traits or abilities

Conflict perspective: Theoretical perspective that views the structure of society as a source of inequality that always benefits some groups at the expense of other groups

Content analysis: Form of unobtrusive research that studies the content of recorded messages, such as books, speeches, poems, songs, television shows, websites, and advertisements

Contradictory class locations: Individuals, such as middle managers and supervisors, whose positions place them between two major classes, making it difficult to identify with one side or the other

Cooling out: Gently persuading someone who has lost face to accept a less desirable but still reasonable alternative identity

Countermovement: Collective action designed to prevent or reverse changes sought or accomplished by an earlier social movement

Criminalization: Official definition of an act of deviance as a crime

Cultural diffusion: Process by which beliefs, technology, customs, and other elements of culture spread from one group or society to another

Cultural relativism: Principle that people's beliefs and activities should be interpreted in terms of their own culture

Culture: Language, values, beliefs, rules, behaviors, and artifacts that characterize a society

Culture-of-poverty thesis: Belief that poor people, resigned to their position in society, develop a unique value structure to deal with their lack of success

Demographer: Sociologist who studies trends in population characteristics

Dependent variable: Variable that is assumed to be caused by, or to change as a result of, the independent variable

De-skilling: Subdivision of low-level jobs into small, highly specific tasks requiring less skilled employees

Deterrence theory: Theory of deviance positing that people will be prevented from engaging in a deviant act if they judge the costs of such an act to outweigh its benefits

Deviance: Behavior, ideas, or attributes of an individual or group that some people in society find offensive

Disclaimer: Assertion designed to forestall any complaints or negative reactions to a behavior or statement that is about to occur

Discrimination: Unfair treatment of people based on some social characteristic, such as race, ethnicity, or sex

Division of labor: Specialization of different people or groups in different tasks, characteristic of most bureaucracies

Dramaturgy: Study of social interaction as theater, in which people ("actors") project images ("play roles") in front of others ("audience")

Dyad: Group consisting of two people

Egoistic suicide: Type of suicide that occurs in settings where the individual is emphasized over group or community connections

Embarrassment: Spontaneous feeling experienced when the identity someone is presenting is suddenly and unexpectedly discredited in front of others

Empirical research: Research that operates from the ideological position that questions about human behavior can be answered only through controlled, systematic observations in the real world

Endogamy: Marriage within one's social group

Estate system (feudal system): Stratification system in which high-status groups own land and have power based on noble birth

Ethnicity: Sense of community derived from the cultural heritage shared by a category of people with common ancestry

Ethnocentrism: Tendency to judge other cultures using one's own as a standard

Eugenics: Control of mating to ensure that "defective" genes of troublesome individuals will not be passed on to future generations

Exogamy: Marriage outside one's social group

Experiment: Research method designed to elicit some sort of behavior, typically conducted under closely controlled laboratory circumstances

Extended family: Family unit consisting of the parent-child nuclear family and other relatives, such as grandparents, aunts, uncles, and cousins

False consciousness: Situation in which people in the lower classes come to accept a belief system that harms them; the primary means by which powerful classes in society prevent protest and revolution

Family: Two or more persons, including the householder, who are related by birth, marriage, or adoption, and who live together as one household

Fatalistic suicide: Type of suicide that occurs when people see no possible way to improve their oppressive circumstances

Feminist perspective: Theoretical perspective that focuses on gender as the most important source of conflict and inequality in social life

Feudal system: Stratification system in which high-status groups own land and have power based on noble birth

Field research: Type of social research in which the researcher observes events as they actually occur

Folkway: Informal norm that is mildly punished when violated

Free-rider problem: Tendency for people to refrain from contributing to the common good when a resource is available without any personal cost or contribution

Front stage: Area of social interaction where people perform and work to maintain appropriate impressions

Game stage: Stage in the development of self during which a child acquires the ability to take the role of a group or community (the generalized other) and conform his or her behavior to broad societal expectations

Gender: Psychological, social, and cultural aspects of maleness and femaleness

Generalized other: Perspective of the larger society and its constituent values and attitudes

Global climate change: Steady rise in Earth's average temperature as a result of increasing amounts of carbon dioxide in the atmosphere

Globalization: Process through which people's lives all around the world become economically, politically, environmentally, and culturally interconnected

Group: Set of people who interact more or less regularly and who are conscious of their identity as a unit

Heteronormative culture: Culture in which heterosexuality is accepted as the normal, taken-for-granted mode of sexual expression

Hierarchy of authority: Ranking of people or tasks in a bureaucracy from those at the top, where there is a great deal of power and authority, to those at the bottom, where there is very little power and authority

Historical analysis: Form of social research that relies on existing historical documents as a source of data

Household: Living arrangement composed of one or more people who occupy a housing unit

Identity: Essential aspect of who we are, consisting of our sense of self, gender, race, ethnicity, and religion

Ideology: Coherent system of beliefs, values, and ideas

Implicit bias: Prejudiced attitudes or beliefs that operate at a level below conscious awareness

Impression formation: The process by which we define others based on observable cues such as age, ascribed status characteristics such as race and gender, individual attributes such as physical appearance, and verbal and nonverbal expressions

Impression management: Act of presenting a favorable public image of oneself so that others will form positive judgments

Incorrigible proposition: Unquestioned cultural belief that cannot be proved wrong no matter what happens to dispute it

Independent variable: Variable presumed to cause or influence the dependent variable

Indicator: Measurable event, characteristic, or behavior commonly thought to reflect a particular concept

Individualist culture: Culture in which personal accomplishments are a more important component of one's self-concept than group membership

Individualistic explanation: Tendency to attribute people's achievements and failures to their personal qualities

In-groups: The groups to which we belong and toward which we feel a sense of loyalty

Institutionalized norm: Pattern of behavior within existing social institutions that is widely accepted in a society

Institutional racism: Laws, customs, and practices that systematically reflect and produce racial and ethnic inequalities in a society, whether or not the individuals maintaining these laws, customs, and practices have racist intentions

Institutional sexism: Subordination of women that is part of the everyday workings of economics, law, politics, and other social institutions

Intersexuals: Individuals in whom sexual differentiation is either incomplete or ambiguous (also known as people with disorders of sexual development)

Labeling theory: Theory stating that deviance is the consequence of the application of rules and sanctions to an offender; a deviant is an individual to whom the identity "deviant" has been successfully applied

Latent functions: Unintended, unrecognized consequences of activities that help some part of the social system

Looking-glass self: Sense of who we are that is defined by incorporating the reflected appraisals of others

Macrolevel: Way of examining human life that focuses on the broad social forces and structural features of society that exist above the level of individual people

Manifest function: Intended, obvious consequences of activities designed to help some part of the social system

Material culture: Artifacts of a society that represent adaptations to the social and physical environment

Matriarchy: Female-dominated society that gives higher prestige and value to women than to men

McDonaldization: Process by which the characteristics and principles of the fast-food restaurant come to dominate other areas of social life

Means of production: Land, commercial enterprises, factories, and wealth that form the economic basis of class societies

Medicalization: Definition of behavior as a medical problem, mandating the medical profession to provide some kind of treatment for it

Microlevel: Way of examining human life that focuses on the immediate, everyday experiences of individuals

Middle class: In a society stratified by social class, a group of people who have an intermediate level of wealth, income, and prestige, such as managers, supervisors, executives, small business owners, and professionals

Migration: Movement of populations from one geographic area to another

Monogamy: Practice of being married to only one person at a time

Moral entrepreneurs: Groups that work to have their moral concerns translated into law

Mores: Highly codified, formal, systematized norms that bring severe punishment when violated

Multinational corporation: Company that has manufacturing, production, and marketing divisions in multiple countries

Near-poor: Individuals or families whose earnings are between 100% and 125% of the poverty line (see also **working poor**)

Neolocal residence: Living arrangement in which a married couple sets up residence separate from either spouse's family

Nonmaterial culture: Knowledge, beliefs, customs, values, morals, and symbols that are shared by members of a society and that distinguish the society from others

Nonparticipant observation: Form of field research in which the researcher observes people without directly interacting with them and without letting them know that they are being observed

Norm: Culturally defined standard or rule of conduct

Nuclear family: Family unit consisting of at least one parent and one child

Objectification: Practice of treating people as objects

Oligarchy: System of authority in which many people are ruled by a privileged few

Organization: Large, complex network of positions, created for a specific purpose and characterized by a hierarchical division of labor

Out-groups: The groups to which we don't belong and toward which we feel a certain amount of antagonism

Panethnic labels: General terms applied to diverse subgroups that are assumed to have something in common

Participant observation: Form of field research in which the researcher interacts with subjects, sometimes hiding his or her identity

Patriarchy: Male-dominated society in which cultural beliefs and values give higher prestige and value to men than to women

Performance team: Set of individuals who cooperate in staging a performance that leads an audience to form an impression of one or all team members

Period effect: Phenomenon in which a historical event or major social trend contributes to the unique shape and outlook of a birth cohort

Personal racism: Individual expression of racist attitudes or behaviors

Play stage: Stage in the development of self during which a child develops the ability to take a role, but only from the perspective of one person at a time

Polygamy: Marriage of one person to more than one spouse at the same time

Poor: In a society stratified by social class, a group of people who work for minimum wage or are chronically unemployed

Postindustrial society: Society in which knowledge, the control of information, and service industries are more important elements of the economy than agriculture or manufacturing and production

Poverty line: Amount of yearly income a family requires to meet its basic needs, according to the federal government

Poverty rate: Percentage of people whose income falls below the poverty line

Power: Ability to affect decisions in ways that benefit a person or protect his or her interests

Prejudice: Rigidly held, unfavorable attitudes, beliefs, and feelings about members of a different group based on a social characteristic such as race, ethnicity, or gender

Prestige: Respect and honor given to some people in society

Primary group: Collection of individuals who are together for a relatively long period, whose members have direct contact with and feel emotional attachment to one another

Probabilistic: Capable only of identifying those forces that have a high likelihood, but not a certainty, of influencing human action

Qualitative research: Sociological research based on non-numeric information (text, written words, phrases, symbols, observations) that describes people, actions, or events in social life

Quantitative research: Sociological research based on the collection of numeric data that utilizes precise statistical analysis

Quiet discrimination: Form of racism expressed subtly and indirectly through feelings of discomfort, uneasiness, and fear, which motivate avoidance rather than blatant discrimination

Race: Category of people labeled and treated as similar because of allegedly common biological traits, such as skin color, texture of hair, and shape of eyes

Racial transparency: Tendency for the race of a society's majority to be so obvious, normative, and unremarkable that it becomes, for all intents and purposes, invisible

Racism: Belief that humans are subdivided into distinct groups that are different in their social behavior and innate capacities and that can be ranked as superior or inferior

Reactivity: A problem associated with certain forms of research in which the very act of intruding into people's lives may influence the phenomenon being studied

Reflexive behavior: Behavior in which the person initiating an action is the same as the person toward whom the action is directed

Reform movement: Collective action that seeks to change limited aspects of a society but does not seek to alter or replace major social institutions

Relative poverty: Individuals' economic position compared with the living standards of the majority in the society

Relativism: Approach to defining deviance that rests on the assumption that deviance is socially created by collective human judgments and ideas

Representative: Typical of the whole population being studied

Resocialization: Process of learning new values, norms, and expectations when an adult leaves an old role and enters a new one

Resource mobilization theory: A theory of social movements that suggests that no social movement can exist unless it has an organized system for acquiring needed resources: money, labor, participants, legal aid, access to the media

Revolutionary movement: Collective action that attempts to overthrow an entire social system and replace it with another

Role: Set of expectations—rights, obligations, behaviors, duties—associated with a particular status

Role conflict: Frustration people feel when the demands of one role they are expected to fulfill clash with the demands of another role

Role strain: Situations in which people lack the necessary resources to fulfill the demands of a particular role

Role taking: Ability to see oneself from the perspective of others and to use that perspective in formulating one's own behavior

Sample: Subgroup chosen for a study because its characteristics approximate those of the entire population

Sanction: Social response that punishes or otherwise discourages violations of a social norm

Secondary group: Relatively impersonal collection of individuals that is established to perform a specific task

Self: Unique set of traits, behaviors, and attitudes that distinguishes one person from the next; the active source and passive object of behavior

Self-fulfilling prophecy: Assumption or prediction that in itself causes the expected event to occur, thus seeming to confirm the prophecy's accuracy

Sex: Biological maleness or femaleness

Sexism: System of beliefs that asserts the inferiority of one sex and justifies gender-based inequality

Sexual dichotomy: Belief that two biological sex categories, male and female, are permanent, universal, exhaustive, and mutually exclusive

Sick role: Set of norms governing how one is supposed to behave and what one is entitled to when sick

Slavery: Economic form of inequality in which some people are legally property of others

Social class: Group of people who share a similar economic position in a society, based on their wealth and income

Social construction of reality: Process through which the members of a society discover, make known, reaffirm, and alter a collective version of facts, knowledge, and "truth"

Social dilemma: Potential for a society's long-term ruin because of individuals' tendency to pursue their own short-term interests

Social institution: Stable set of roles, statuses, groups, and organizations—such as the institution of education, family, politics, religion, health care, or the economy—that provides a foundation for behavior in some major area of social life

Socialization: Process through which one learns how to act according to the rules and expectations of a particular culture

Social mobility: Movement of people or groups from one class to another

Social movement: Continuous, large-scale, organized collective action motivated by the desire to enact, stop, or reverse change in some area of society

Social structure: Framework of society—social institutions, organizations, groups, statuses and roles, cultural beliefs, and institutionalized norms—that adds order and predictability to our private lives

Society: A population of people living in the same geographic area who share a culture and a common identity and whose members are subject to the same political authority

Socioeconomic status: Prestige, honor, respect, and lifestyle associated with different positions or groups in society

Sociological imagination: Ability to see the impact of social forces on our private lives

Sociology: The systematic study of human societies

Spurious relationships: A false association between two variables that is actually due to the effect of some third variable

Status: Any named social position that people can occupy

Stereotype: Overgeneralized belief that a certain trait, behavior, or attitude characterizes all members of some identifiable group

Stigma: Deeply discrediting characteristic that is viewed as an obstacle to competent or morally trustworthy behavior

Stratification: Ranking system for groups of people that perpetuates unequal rewards and life chances in society

Structural-functionalist perspective: Theoretical perspective that posits that social institutions are structured to maintain stability and order in society

Subculture: Values, behaviors, and artifacts of a group that distinguish its members from the larger culture

Survey: Form of social research in which the researcher asks subjects a series of questions verbally, online, or on paper

Symbol: Something used to represent or stand for something else

Symbolic interactionism: Theoretical perspective that explains society and social structure through an examination of the microlevel, personal, day-to-day exchanges of people as individuals, pairs, or groups,

Theory: Set of statements or propositions that seeks to explain or predict a particular aspect of social life

Total institution: Place where individuals are cut off from the wider society for an appreciable period and where together they lead an enclosed, formally administered life

Tracking: Grouping of students into different curricular programs, or tracks, based on an assessment of their academic abilities

Tragedy of the commons: Situation in which people acting individually and in their own self-interest use up commonly available (but limited) resources, creating disaster for the entire community

Transgender: State in which one's gender expression or identity does not conform to her or his assigned sex

Transsexuals: People who identify with a different sex and sometimes undergo hormone treatment and surgery to change their sex

Triad: Group consisting of three people

Unobtrusive research: Research technique in which the researcher, without direct contact with the subjects, examines the evidence of social behavior that people create or leave behind

Upper class: In a society stratified by social class, a group of people who have high income and prestige and who own vast amounts of property and other forms of wealth, such as owners of large corporations, top financiers, rich celebrities and politicians, and members of prestigious families

Urbanization: The process by which people leave rural areas and begin to concentrate in large cities

Value: Standard of judgment by which people decide on desirable goals and outcomes

Variable: Any characteristic, attitude, behavior, or event that can take on two or more values or attributes

Visual sociology: Method of studying society that uses photographs, video recordings, and film either as a means of gathering data or as sources of data about social life

Working class: In a society stratified by social class, a group of people who have a low level of wealth, income, and prestige, such as industrial and factory workers, office workers, clerks, and farm and manual laborers

Working poor: Employed people who consistently earn wages but do not make enough to survive (see also **near-poor**)

• References •

8 Osaka teachers to be punished for refusal to sing national anthem. (2012, February 25). *Japan Today.* www.japantoday.com/category/national/view/8-osaka-teachers-face-punishment-over-refusal-to-sing-national-anthem. Accessed January 8, 2015.

Abeles, V. (2016, January 3). Is school making our children ill? *The New York Times.*

Abelson, R. (2011a, May 14). Health insurers profit as many postpone care. *The New York Times.*

Abelson, R. (2011b, November 17). The smokers' surcharge. *The New York Times.*

Abrams, K. K., Allen, L., & Gray, J. J. (1993). Disordered eating attitudes and behaviors, psychological adjustment and ethnic identity: A comparison of black and white female college students. *Journal of Eating Disorders, 14,* 49–57.

Academy for Eating Disorders. (2006). *Academy for Eating Disorders calls for warning labels on "pro-ana" Web sites.* www.aedweb.org/public/proana.cfm. Accessed July 10, 2007.

Accord Alliance. (2014). *FAQs—What are major recent changes in terms of "standard of care" for various DSD?* www.accordalliance.org/learn-about-dsd/faqs/. Accessed July 16, 2014.

Achenbach, J. (2015, March). Why do many reasonable people doubt science? *National Geographic Online.* ngm.nationalgeographic.com/2015/03/science-doubters/achenbach-text. Accessed May 19, 2015.

Acitelli, L. (1988). When spouses talk to each other about their relationship. *Journal of Social and Personal Relationships, 5,* 185–199.

Acker, J. (1992). From sex roles to gendered institutions. *Contemporary Sociology, 21,* 565–569.

ActionAid. (2009). *Hate crimes: The rise of "corrective" rape in South Africa.* www.actionaid.org/assets/pdf/CorrectiveRapeRep_final.pdf. Accessed June 3, 2009.

Adam, H., & Galinsky, A. D. (2012). Enclothed cognition. *Journal of Experimental Social Psychology, 48,* 918–925.

Aday, D. P. (1990). *Social control at the margins.* Belmont, CA: Wadsworth.

Adderall Statistics. (2012). Statistic brain. www.statisticbrain.com/adderall-statistics/. Accessed January 22, 2013.

Adler, P. (1985). *Wheeling and dealing.* New York, NY: Columbia University Press.

The Advisory Board Company. (2013). *Leapfrog's new safety grades: 800-plus hospitals get an A, but a few still get Fs.* www.advisory.com/daily-briefing/2013/10/23/new-leapfrog-safety-grades-nearly-all-hospitals-stay-the-same. Accessed May 21, 2015.

"Affluenza": When the wealthy escape justice. (2013, December 27). *The Week.*

AFL-CIO. (2017). *Executive pay watch.* aflcio.org/paywatch. Accessed June 1, 2017.

Agnew-Blais, J. C., Polanczyk, G. V., & Danese, A. (2016). Evaluation of the persistence, remission, and emergence of Attention-Deficit/Hyperactivity disorder in young adulthood. *JAMA Psychiatry, 73,* 713–720.

Ahrons, C. R., & Rodgers, R. H. (1987). *Divorced families: A multidisciplinary developmental view.* New York, NY: Norton.

Ainlay, S. C., Becker, G., & Coleman, L. M. (1986). *The dilemma of difference.* New York, NY: Plenum Press.

Alan Guttmacher Institute. (2014). *Induced abortion in the United States.* www.guttmacher.org/pubs/fb_induced_abortion.html. Accessed June 24, 2015.

Albain, K. S., Unger, J. M., Crowley, J. J., Coltman, C. A., & Hershman, D. L. (2009). Racial disparities in cancer survival among randomized clinical trials patients of the Southwest Oncology Group. *Journal of the National Cancer Institute, 101,* 984–992.

Alcindor, Y. (2017, May 25). Ben Carson calls poverty a "state of mind," igniting a backlash. *The New York Times.*

Alexander, M. (2012, March 11). Go to trial: Crash the justice system. *The New York Times.*

Allen, S. (2015, June 9). Marital rape is semi-legal in 8 states. *The Daily Beast.* www.thedailybeast.com/marital-rape-is-semi-legal-in-8-states. Accessed June 21, 2017.

Allport, G. (1954). *The nature of prejudice.* Reading, MA: Addison-Wesley.

Almasy, S., & Ly, L. (2017, February 18). Flint water crisis: Report says "systematic racism" played a role. *CNN Politics*. www.cnn.com/2017/02/18/politics/flint-water-systematic-racism/index.html. Accessed June 11, 2017.

Almond, D., & Edlund, L. (2008). Son-biased sex ratios in the 2000 United States Census. *Proceedings of the National Academy of Sciences, 105,* 5681–5682.

Altman, D. (2003, April 26). Does a dollar a day keep poverty away? *The New York Times*.

Altman, L. K. (2011, May 31). 30 years in, we are still learning from AIDS. *The New York Times*.

Alvarez, B. (2016, January 6). Girls fight back against gender bias in school dress codes. *NEA Today*. neatoday.org/2016/01/06/school-dress-codes-gender-bias/. Accessed June 16, 2017.

Alvarez, L. (2013, December 2). Seeing the toll, schools revisit zero tolerance. *The New York Times*.

Alvarez, L. (2014, November 10). States listen as parents give rampant testing an F. *The New York Times*.

Alvidrez, J., & Areán, P. A. (2002). Psychosocial treatment research with ethnic minority populations: Ethical considerations in conducting clinical trials. *Ethics and Behavior, 12,* 103–116.

Amato, P. R. (2000). The consequences of divorce for adults and children. *Journal of Marriage and the Family, 62,* 1269–1287.

Amato, P. R., & Sobolewski, J. M. (2001). The effects of divorce and marital discord on adult children's well-being. *American Sociological Review, 66,* 900–921.

American Academy of Pediatrics. (2014). *Let them sleep: AAP recommends delaying start times of middle and high schools to combat teen sleep deprivation.* www.aap.org/en-us/about-the-aap/aap-press-room/Pages/Let-Them-Sleep-AAP-Recommends-Delaying-Start-Times-of-Middle-and-High-Schools-to-Combat-Teen-Sleep-Deprivation.aspx. Accessed January 5, 2015.

American Association of University Women. (2013). *Crossing the line: Sexual harassment at school.* www.aauw.org/files/2013/02/crossing-the-line-sexual-harassment-at-school-executive-summary.pdf. Accessed June 19, 2013.

American Civil Liberties Union. (2013). *The war on marijuana in black and white.* www.aclu.org/sites/default/files/field_document/1114413-mj-report-rfs-rel1.pdf. Accessed July 3, 2015.

American Civil Liberties Union. (2014). *War comes home: The excessive militarization of American policing.* www.aclu.org/sites/default/files/assets/jus14-warcomeshome-report-web-rel1.pdf. Accessed January 6, 2015.

American College Health Association. (2016). *National College Health Assessment: Undergraduate student reference group.* www.acha-ncha.org/docs/NCHA-11 SPRING 2016 UNDERGRADUATE REFERENCE GROUP EXECUTIVE SUMMARY.pdf. Accessed January 27, 2017.

American Council for CoEducational Schooling. (2011). *Evidence-based answers.* lives.clas.asu.edu/access/faq-school achievement.html. Accessed June 21, 2013.

American Council on the Teaching of Foreign Languages. (2016). *Foreign language enrollments in K-12 public schools: Are students ready for a global society?* www.actfl.org/news/reports/foreign-language-enrollments-k-12-public-schools-are-students-ready-global-society. Accessed January 2, 2017.

American Hospital Association. (2009). *The economic crisis: The toll on the patients and communities hospitals serve.* www.aha.org/content/00-10/090427econcrisisreport.pdf. Accessed May 29, 2013.

American Nonsmokers' Rights Foundation. (2016). *Overview list-How many smokefree laws?* www.no-smoke.org/pdf/mediaordlist.pdf. Accessed January 2, 2017.

American Psychiatric Association. (2013). *Diagnostic and statistical manual of mental disorders* (5th ed.). Washington, DC: Author.

American Society of Plastic Surgeons. (2016). *2015 plastic surgery statistics.* www.plasticsurgery.org/news/plastic-surgery-statistics. Accessed January 7, 2017.

American Sociological Association. (2002). Statement of the American Sociological Association on the importance of collecting data and doing social scientific research on race. www.asanet.org/governance/racestmt.htm. Accessed June 18, 2003.

American Sociological Association. (2005, July). *Race, ethnicity, and the health of Americans* (ASA Series on How Race and Ethnicity Matter). Washington, DC: Author.

amFAR. (2016). *Statistics: Women and HIV/AIDS.* www.amfar.org/about-hiv-and-aids/facts-and-stats/statistics—women-and-hiv-aids/. Accessed June 20, 2017.

Ammerman, N. T. (1987). *Bible believers: Fundamentalists in the modern world.* New Brunswick, NJ: Rutgers University Press.

Amnesty International. (2004). *Rape as a tool of war: A fact sheet.* www.amnestyusa.org/women/pdf/rapeinwartime.pdf. Accessed September 4, 2009.

Amnesty International. (2005). *UK: New poll finds a third of people believe women who flirt partially responsible for being raped.* www.amnesty.org.uk/press-releases/uk-new-poll-finds-third-people-believe-women-who-flirt-partially-responsible-being. Accessed June 15, 2017.

Amnesty International. (2013). *The death penalty and deterrence.* www.amnestyusa.org/our-work/issues/death-penalty/us-death-penalty-facts/the-death-penalty-and-deterrence. Accessed January 23, 2013.

Anderson, D. J. (2003). The impact on subsequent violence of returning to an abusive partner. *Journal of Comparative Family Studies, 34,* 93–112.

Anderson, E. (1990). *Streetwise: Race, class and change in an urban community.* Chicago: University of Chicago Press.

Anderson, M. (2015). *The demographics of device ownership.* Pew Research Center. www.pewinternet.org/2-015/10/29/the-demographics-of-device-ownership/. Accessed June 21, 2017.

Anderson, M., & Perrin, A. (2017). *Tech adoption climbs among older adults.* Pew Research Center. www.pewinternet.org/2017/05/17/tech-adoptions-climbs-among-older-adults/. Accessed June 21, 2017.

Anderson, S. (2015). *Off the deep end: The Wall Street bonus pool and low-wage workers.* Institute for Policy Studies. www.ips-dc.org/wp-content/uploads/2015/03/IPS-Wall-St-Bonuses-Min-Wage-2015.pdf. Accessed May 26, 2015.

Anderson, S. (2017, June 18). New sentences. *The New York Times Magazine.*

Andreescu, T., Gallian, J. A., Kane, J. M., & Mertz, J. E. (2008). Cross-cultural analysis of students with exceptional talent in mathematical problem solving. *Notices of the American Mathematical Society, 55,* 1248–1260.

Angier, N. (1997, May 13). New debate over surgery on genitals. *The New York Times.*

Angier, N., & Chang, K. (2005, January 24). Gray matter and the sexes: Still a scientific gray area. *The New York Times.*

Annie E. Casey Foundation. (2015). *Millions of children living in high-poverty areas.* www.aecf.org/blog/millions-of-children-living-in-high-poverty-areas/. Accessed May 31, 2017.

Antill, J. K., Goodnow, J. J., Russell, G., & Cotton, S. (1996). The influence of parents and family context on children's involvement in household tasks. *Sex Roles, 34,* 215–236.

Appelbaum, E., Berg, P., Frost, A., & Preuss, G. (2003). The effects of work restructuring on low-wage, low-skilled workers in U.S. hospitals. In E. Appelbaum, A. Bernhardt, & R. J. Murname (Eds.), *Low-wage America.* New York, NY: Russell Sage.

Archer, D. (1985). Social deviance. In G. Lindzey & E. Aronson (Eds.), *Handbook of social psychology* (3rd ed., Vol. 2). New York, NY: Random House.

Archibold, R. C., & Thee-Brenan, M. (2010, May 4). Poll finds serious concern among Americans about immigration. *The New York Times.*

Arendell, T. (1995). *Fathers and divorce.* Thousand Oaks, CA: Sage.

Ariès, P. (1962). Centuries of childhood: A social history of family life. New York, NY: Vintage Books.

Armstrong, P. J., Goodman, J. F. B., & Hyman, J. D. (1981). *Ideology and shop-floor industrial relations.* London, UK: Croom Helm.

Ash, J. (2009). *Dress behind bars: Criminal clothing as criminality.* London, UK: I.B. Tavris.

Ashkenas, J., Park, H., & Pearce, A. (2017, August 25). Affirmative action yields little progress on campus for Blacks and Hispanics. *The New York Times.*

Asoni, A., & Sanandaji, T. (2013). *Rich man's war, poor man's fight? Socioeconomic representativeness in the modern military.* Research Institute of Industrial Economics, FN Working paper f#965. www.ifn.se/wfiles/wp/wp965.pdf. Accessed May 29, 2015.

Association of American Medical Colleges. (2016). *2016 physician specialty data report.* www.aamc.org/data/workforce/reports/457712/2016-specialty-databook.html. Accessed June 19, 2017.

Association of American Universities. (2015). *Report on the AAU climate survey on sexual assault and sexual misconduct.* www.aau.edu/sites/default/files/%40 Files/Climate Survey/AAU_Campus_Climate_Survey_12_14_15.pdf. Accessed June 14, 2017.

Astbury, J. (1996). *Crazy for you: The making of women's madness.* Melbourne, Victoria, Australia: Oxford University Press.

Auletta, K. (1982). *The underclass.* New York, NY: Random House.

Austen, I. (2012, November 23). Crackdown in Quebec: "Le Gap." *The New York Times.*

Austin, P. K. (2008). *One thousand languages: Living, endangered, and lost.* Berkeley: University of California Press.

Averett, S., & Korenman, S. (1999). Black and white differences in social and economic consequences of obesity. *International Journal of Obesity, 23,* 166–173.

Avert. (2017a). *HIV and AIDS in East and Southern Africa.* www.avert.org/professionals/hiv-around-world/sub-saharan-africa. Accessed June 28, 2017.

Avert. (2017b). *Women and girls, HIV and AIDS.* www.avert.org/professionals/hiv-socia-issues/key-affected-populations/women. Accessed June 20, 2017.

Avins, J. (2015, October 15). The dos and don'ts of cultural appropriation. *The Atlantic*.

Babbie, E. (1986). *Observing ourselves: Essays in social research*. Belmont, CA: Wadsworth.

Babbie, E. (1992). *The practice of social research*. Belmont, CA: Wadsworth.

Babbie, E. (2007). *The practice of social research* (11th ed.). Belmont, CA: Wadsworth.

Baby, and a car! Russians hold Conception Day. (2011, September 11). MSNBC Online. www.msnbc.msn.com/id/20730526/ns/world_news-europe/t/baby-car-russians-hold-conception-day/#.Tm4l8k_b8xk. Accessed September 12, 2011.

Baca Zinn, M., & Eitzen, D. S. (1996). *Diversity in families* (4th ed.). New York, NY: HarperCollins.

Bach, P. B., Cramer, L. D., Warren, J. L., & Begg, C. B. (1999). Racial differences in the treatment of early-stage lung cancer. *The New England Journal of Medicine, 341*, 119–205.

Bagdikian, B. H. (1991). Missing from the news. In J. H. Skolnick & E. Currie (Eds.), *Crisis in American institutions*. New York, NY: HarperCollins.

Bailey, B. L. (1988). *From front porch to back seat: Courtship in 20th century America*. Baltimore, MD: Johns Hopkins University Press.

Bailey, C. A. (1993). Equality with difference: On androcentrism and menstruation. *Teaching Sociology, 21*, 121–129.

Bailey, W. C. (1990). Murder, capital punishment, and television: Execution publicity and homicide rates. *American Sociological Review, 55*, 628–633.

Baird, J. (2013, July 6). In Australia, misogyny lives on. *The New York Times*.

Baker, A. (2013, January 5). Ergonomic seats? Most pupils squirm in a classroom classic. *The New York Times*.

Baker, A. (2016, March 9). The secret war crime. *The New York Times*.

Baker, A. (2017, May 30). Street stops by New York City police have plummeted, federal monitor finds. *The New York Times*.

Baker, P. (2017, August 2). Trump supports plan to cut legal immigration by half. *The New York Times*.

Baker, P., & Herszenhorn, D. M. (2010, April 23). Obama chastises Wall St. in call to stiffen rules. *The New York Times*.

Baker, P. L. (1997). And I went back: Battered women's negotiation of choice. *Journal of Contemporary Ethnography, 26*, 55–74.

Bald, M. (2000, December). Disputed dams. *World Press Review*.

Baldas, T. (2010). *Jurors may be swayed by a pretty face, study finds*. www.law.com/jsp/article.jsp?id=1202458388657&Jurors_May_Be_Swayed_by_a_Pretty_Face_Study_Finds&slreturn=1&hbxlogin=1. Accessed May 19, 2010.

Ball, J. (2014, May 16). More than 2.7 billion people live in countries where being gay is a crime. *The Guardian*.

Ballard, C. (1987). A humanist sociology approach to teaching social research. *Teaching Sociology, 15*, 7–14.

Bandura, A., & Walters, R. H. (1963). *Social learning and personality development*. New York, NY: Holt, Rinehart & Winston.

Banerjee, A. V., & Duflo, E. (2006). *The economic lives of the poor*. MIT Department of Economics Working Paper Series, #06-29. Cambridge, MA.

Banerjee, N. (2005, January 23). Aided by elders and Web, Iraq veterans turn critics. *The New York Times*.

Banfield, E. (1970). *The unheavenly city*. Boston, MA: Little, Brown.

Banks, J., Marmot, M., Oldfield, Z., & Smith, J. P. (2006). Disease and disadvantage in the United States and in England. *Journal of the American Medical Association, 295*, 2037–2045.

Barber, B. (1992, March). Jihad vs. McWorld. *Atlantic Monthly*, 53–65.

The Barna Group. (2016). *Most Americans believe in supernatural healing*. Research Release on Faith and Christianity. www.barna.com/research/americans-believe-supernatural-healing/. Accessed January 6, 2017.

Baron-Cohen, S. (2003). *The essential difference: Men, women, and the extreme male brain*. London, UK: Allen Lane.

Barone, E. (2014, September 8-15). Who we are. *Time*.

Barro, J. (2015, December 16). How unpopular is Trump's Muslim ban? Depends on how you ask. *The New York Times*.

Barro, R. J., & McCleary, R. M. (2003). Religion and economic growth across countries. *American Sociological Review, 68*, 760–781.

Barron, J. (2016, April 3). Segmented sleep. *The New York Times*.

Barry, D. (2017, January 26). In swirl of "untruths" and "falsehoods" calling a lie a lie. *The New York Times*.

Barry, E. (2016, January 19). Desperate for slumber on cold nights, homeless encounter sleep mafia. *The New York Times.*

Barry, E., & Davenport, C. (2016, October 13). A climate deal could push air-conditioning out of India's reach. *The New York Times.*

Barstow, D. (2003, December 22). U.S. rarely seeks charges for deaths in workplace. *The New York Times.*

Barth, E., Goldin, C., Kerr, S. P., & Olivetti, C. (2017, June 12). The average mid-forties male college graduate earns 55% more than his female counterparts. *Harvard Business Review.* hbr.org/2017/06/the-average-mid-forties-male-college-graduate-earns-55-more-than-his-female-counterparts. Accessed June 19, 2017.

Baruchin, A. (2011, August 30). Stigma is toughest foe in an epilepsy fight. *The New York Times.*

Basler, G. (2015, December 27). Catching up with child art prodigy Marla Olmstead. *Pressconnects.* www.press connects.com/story/news/local/2015/12/27/catching-up-child-art-prodigy-marla-olmstead/77668896/. Accessed December 28, 2016.

Bassok, D., & Reardon, S. F. (2013). "Academic redshirting" in kindergarten prevalence, patterns, and implications. *Education, Evaluation, and Policy Analysis, 35,* 283–297.

Baxter, V., & Kroll-Smith, S. (2005). Normalizing the workplace nap: Blurring the boundaries between public and private space and time. *Current Sociology, 53,* 33–55.

Bazelon, E. (2008, July 20). The next kind of integration. *The New York Times Magazine.*

Bazelon, E. (2010, July 18). The new abortion providers. *The New York Times Magazine.*

Bazelon, E. (2011, April 24). Trolls, the bell tolls for thee. *The New York Times Magazine.*

Beaman, A. L., Klentz, B., Diener, E., & Svanum, S. (1979). Objective self-awareness and transgression in children: A field study. *Journal of Personality and Social Psychology, 37,* 1835–1846.

Bearak, B. (2010, September 6). Dead join the living in a family celebration. *The New York Times.*

Beauboeuf-Lafontant, T. (2009). *Behind the mask of the strong black woman: Voice and the embodiment of a costly performance.* Philadelphia, PA: Temple University Press.

Beck, J. (2015a). Don't let them see your tampons. *The Atlantic.* www.theatlantic.com/health/archive/2015/06/don't-let-them-see-your-tampons/394376/. Accessed June 15, 2017.

Beck, J. (2015b, March). The growing risk of suicide in rural America. *The Atlantic.* www.theatlantic.com/health/archive/2015/03/the-growing-risk-of-suicide-in-rural-america/387313/. Accessed December 26, 2016.

Becker, H. S. (1963). *Outsiders: Studies in the sociology of deviance.* New York, NY: Free Press.

Becker, H. S. (2008). *Art worlds.* Berkeley: University of California Press.

Becker, H. S., & Geer, B. (1958). The fate of idealism in medical school. *American Sociological Review, 23,* 50–56.

Bedoya, A. M. (2017, June 21). Deportation is going high-tech under Trump. *The Atlantic.* www.theatlantic.com/technology/archive/2017/06/data-driven-deportation/531090/. Accessed June 26, 2017.

Begley, S. (2011, January 31). Why almost everything you hear about medicine is wrong. *Newsweek.*

Beinggirl.com. (2010). *Keeping it quick and quiet.* www.being girl.com/en_US/articledetail.jsp?ContentId=ART11906. Accessed June 25, 2010.

Belkin, L. (2003, May 11). Why is Jonathan Simms still alive? *The New York Times Magazine.*

Bell, I., & McGrane, B. (1999). *This book is not required.* Thousand Oaks, CA: Pine Forge Press.

Bell, S. T., Kuriloff, P. J., & Lottes, I. (1994). Understanding attributions of blame in stranger rape and date rape situations: An examination of gender, race, identification, and students' social perceptions of rape victims. *Journal of Applied Social Psychology, 24,* 1719–1734.

Bellah, R., Madsen, R., Sullivan, W. M., Swidler, A., & Tipton, S. M. (1985). *Habits of the heart.* New York, NY: Harper & Row.

Belluck, P. (2001, January 20). A nation's voices: Concern and solace, resentment and redemption. *The New York Times.*

Belluck, P. (2002, January 15). Doctors' new practices offer deluxe service for deluxe fee. *The New York Times.*

Belluck, P. (2004, November 14). To avoid divorce, move to Massachusetts. *The New York Times.*

Belluck, P. (2014, October 12). A promising pill, not so hard to swallow. *The New York Times.*

Belson, K. (2004, June 27). I want to be alone. Please call me. *The New York Times.*

Belson, K. (2014, September 12). Brain trauma to affect one in three players, N.F.L. agrees. *The New York Times.*

Benedict, H. (2009). *The lonely soldier: The private war of women serving in Iraq.* Boston, MA: Beacon Press.

Benen, S. (2015, June 17). RNC: Trump's immigration rhetoric "not helpful." *MSNBC Online.* www.msnbc.com/rachel-maddow-show/rnc-trumps-immigration-rhetoric-not-helpful. Accessed June 18, 2015.

Benko, J. (2015, June 7). Cloud atlas. *The New York Times Magazine.*

Benner, K. (2017, July 1). Women in tech reveal culture of harassment. *The New York Times.*

Bennett, G., Henson, R. K., & Zhang, J. (2003). Generation Y's perceptions of the action sports industry segment. *Journal of Sports Management, 17,* 95–115.

Bennett, J. (2010, July 28). The beauty advantage. *Newsweek.*

Benokraitis, N. V., & Feagin, J. R. (1993). Sex discrimination: Subtle and covert. In J. Henslin (Ed.), *Down-to-earth sociology* (7th ed.). New York, NY: Free Press.

Bentley, T. S. (2014, December). 2014 U.S. organ and tissue transplant cost estimates and discussion. *Milliman Research Report.* www.milliman.com/uploadedFiles/Insight/Research/health-rr/1938HDP_20141230.pdf. Accessed June 3, 2015.

Ben-Yehuda, N. (1990). *The politics and morality of deviance.* Albany: State University of New York Press.

Berenson, A. (2005, May 31). Despite vow, drug makers still withhold data. *The New York Times.*

Berenson, A. (2008, December 8). Weak patchwork of oversight lets bad hospitals stay open. *The New York Times.*

Berg, B. (1992). The guilt that drives working mothers crazy. In J. Henslin (Ed.), *Marriage and family in a changing society.* New York, NY: Free Press.

Berger, D. L., & Williams, J. E. (1991). Sex stereotypes in the United States revisited: 1972–1988. *Sex Roles, 24,* 413–423.

Berger, J. (2004, October 24). Pressure to live by an outmoded tradition is still felt among Indian immigrants. *The New York Times.*

Berger, P. L. (1963). *Invitation to sociology.* Garden City, NY: Anchor Books.

Berger, P. L., & Kellner, H. (1964). Marriage and the construction of reality: An exercise in the micro-sociology of knowledge. *Diogenes, 46,* 1–23.

Berger, P. L., & Luckmann, T. (1966). *The social construction of reality.* Garden City, NY: Anchor Books.

Bergner, D. (2014, March 19). Is stop-and-frisk worth it? *The Atlantic.*

Bernard, J. (1972). *The future of marriage.* New York, NY: Bantam Books.

Bernard, J. (1981). The good provider role: Its rise and fall. *American Psychologist, 36,* 1–12.

Bernard, T. S. (2010, July 19). Need a mortgage? Don't get pregnant. *The New York Times.*

Bernard, T. S. (2015, June 29). Fate of domestic partner benefits in question after marriage ruling. *The New York Times.*

Berndt, T. J., & Heller, K. A. (1986). Gender stereotypes and social inferences. *Journal of Social and Personality Psychology, 50,* 889–898.

Bernstein, J., & Ellison, J. (2011, June 5). Hotel confidential. *Newsweek.*

Bernstein, N. (2012, November 22). Chefs, butlers, and marble baths: Not your average hospital room. *The New York Times.*

Bernstein, R. (2003, June 29). Aging Europe finds its pension is running out. *The New York Times.*

Bertelsmann Stiftung. (2011). *Social justice in the OECD—How do the member states compare.* www.sqi-network.org/pdf/SGI-11_Social_Justice_OECD.pdf. Accessed June 3, 2013.

Bertenthal, B. I., & Fischer, K. W. (1978). Development of self-recognition in the infant. *Developmental Psychology, 14,* 44–50.

Bertocchi, G., & Dimico, A. (2010, November). *Slavery, education, and inequality.* Institute for the Study of Labor (IZA). Discussion Paper #5329.

Bertrand, M., & Mullainathan, S. (2004). Are Emily and Greg more employable than Lakisha and Jamal? A field experiment on labor market discrimination. *American Economic Review, 94,* 991–1013.

Bhattacharya, J., DeLeire, T., Haider, S., & Currie, J. (2003). Heat or eat? Cold-weather shocks and nutrition in poor American families. *American Journal of Public Health, 93,* 1149–1154.

Bianchi, S. M., Robinson, J. P., & Milkie, M. A. (2006). *Changing rhythms of American family life.* New York, NY: Russell Sage.

Bibbins-Domingo, K. (2009). Racial differences in incident heart failure among young adults. *The New England Journal of Medicine, 360,* 1179–1190.

Bidgood, J. (2013, December 31). Daunting calculus for Maine shrimpers as entire season is lost. *The New York Times.*

Bilefsky, D. (2015, June 11). Comments on women in the lab spur outcry. *The New York Times.*

Bilefsky D. (2017, March 15). E.U. court, in "bold step" allows banning head scarves at work. *The New York Times.*

Bilefsky, D., & Anderson, C. (2017, February 23). A paid hour a week for sex? Swedish town considers it. *The New York Times.*

Billings, A. C., Angelini, J. R., & Eastman, S. T. (2005). Diverging discourses: Gender differences in televised golf announcing. *Mass Communication and Society, 8,* 155–171.

Bingham, A. (2012). Half of Americans do not know the President's religion. *ABC News Online.* abcnews.go.com/blogs/politics/2012/07/half-of-americans-do-not-know-the- presidents-religion. Accessed June 13, 2013.

Bird: NBA "a black man's game." (2004). *ESPN Online.* http://sports.espn.go.com/nba/news/story?id=1818396. Accessed June 10, 2004.

Birenbaum, A., & Sagarin, E. (1976). *Norms and human behavior.* New York, NY: Praeger.

Blackmon, D. A. (2009). *Slavery by another name: The re-enslavement of black Americans from the Civil War to World War II.* New York, NY: Anchor.

Blakeslee, S. (1998, October 13). Placebos prove so powerful even experts are surprised. *The New York Times.*

Blakeslee, S. (2012, April 3). Mind games: Sometimes a white coat isn't just a white coat. *The New York Times.*

Blanton, K. (2007, March 16). A "smoking gun" on race, subprime loans. *The Boston Globe.*

Blass, T. (2004). *The man who shocked the world: The life and legacy of Stanley Milgram.* New York, NY: Basic Books.

Blau, F. D., & Kahn, L. M. (2013). Female labor supply: Why is the United States falling behind? *American Economic Review, 103,* 251–256.

Blau, P. M., & Meyer, M. W. (1987). The concept of bureaucracy. In R. T. Schaeffer & R. P. Lamm (Eds.), *Introducing sociology.* New York, NY: McGraw-Hill.

Bleyer, A., & Welch, G. (2012). Effect of three decades of screening mammography on breast cancer incidence. *New England Journal of Medicine, 367,* 1998–2005.

Blinder, A., & Robertson, C. (2016, March 4). Proposed bills would protect opponents of gay rights. *The New York Times.*

Block, F., Korteweg, A. C., & Woodward, K. (2013). The compassion gap in American poverty policy. In D. Newman & J. O'Brien (Eds.), *Sociology: Exploring the architecture of everyday life (Readings).* Thousand Oaks, CA: Sage.

Blow, C. M. (2010, June 12). Friends, neighbors, and Facebook. *The New York Times.*

Blow, C. M. (2013, April 27). The morose middle class. *The New York Times.*

Blow, C. M. (2015, January 5). Privilege of "arrest without incident." *The New York Times.*

The BlueGreen Alliance. (2015). *Jobs 21! Good jobs for the 21st century.* www.bluegreenalliance.org/news/publications/image/Platform-vFINAL.pdf. Accessed June 23, 2015.

Blum, S. D. (2009). *My word! Plagiarism and college culture.* Ithaca, NY: Cornell University Press.

Blumstein, P., & Schwartz, P. (1983). *American couples.* New York, NY: Morrow.

Blustein, P. (2005, June 12). Debt cut is set for poorest nations. *The Washington Post.*

Bocian, D. G., Ernst, K. S., & Li, W. (2006). *Unfair lending: The effect of race and ethnicity on the price of subprime mortgages.* Durham, NC: Center for Responsible Lending. www.responsiblelending.org. Accessed October 10, 2007.

Bollen, J., Gonçalves, B., Ruan, G., & Mao, H. (2012). Happiness is assertive in online social networks. *Artificial Life, 17,* 237–251.

Bonilla-Silva, E. (2003). *Racism without racists: Color-blind racism and the persistence of racial inequality in the United States.* Lanham, MD: Rowman & Littlefield.

Bonilla-Silva, E. (2008). "New racism," color-blind racism, and the future of whiteness in America. In S. J. Ferguson (Ed.), *Mapping the social landscape.* New York, NY: McGraw-Hill.

Bonnie, R. J., & Whitebread, C. H. (1974). *The marijuana conviction.* Charlottesville: University of Virginia Press.

Booth, A., Johnson, D. R., Branaman, A., & Sica, A. (1995). Belief and behavior: Does religion matter in today's marriage? *Journal of Marriage and the Family, 57,* 661–671.

Borghaei, H., Paz-Ares, L., Horn, L., Spigel, D. R., Steins, M., Ready, N. E., . . . Brahmer, J. R. (2015). Nivolumab versus Docetaxel in advanced nonsquamous non-small cell lung cancer. *New England Journal of Medicine, 373,* 1627–1639.

Bowen, F. (2016, June 22). Playing one sport year-round isn't smart, even for kids who want to go pro. *The Washington Post.*

Bowen, J. R. (1996). The myth of global ethnic conflict. *Journal of Democracy, 7,* 3–14.

Bowker, L. H. (1993). A battered woman's problems are social, not psychological. In R. J. Gelles & D. R. Loeske (Eds.), *Current controversies on family violence.* Newbury Park, CA: Sage.

Bowley, G. (2012, January 30). Afghan kin are accused of killing woman for not bearing a son. *The New York Times.*

Bradshaw, C. P., Waasdorp, T. E., O'Brennan, L. M., & Gulemetova, M. (2011). *Findings from the National Education Association's Nationwide Study of Bullying.* National Education Association. www.nea.org/assets/docs/Nationwide_Bullying_Research_Findings.pdf. Accessed July 15, 2015.

Bradsher, K. (1993, July 22). Mark Twain would understand the water crisis that's corrupting Iowans. *The New York Times.*

Bragg, R. (1998, January 4). Proposal to ban sofas from porches creates culture clash. *The Indianapolis Star.*

Bramlett, M. D., & Mosher, W. D. (2002). *Cohabitation, marriage, divorce, and remarriage in the United States.* Hyattsville, MD: National Center for Health Statistics. www.cdc.gov/nchs/data/series/sr_23/sr23_022.pdf. Accessed August 11, 2006.

Braun, D. (1997). *The rich get richer: The rise of income inequality in the United States and the world.* Chicago, IL: Nelson-Hall.

Breiding, M. J. (2014). Prevalence and characteristics of sexual violence, stalking, and intimate partner victimization—National Intimate Partner and Sexual Violence Survey, United States, 2011. *Morbidity and Mortality Weekly Report, 63,* 1–18.

Brescoll, V. L., & Uhlmann, E. L. (2008). Can an angry woman get ahead? Status conferral, gender, and expression of emotion in the workplace. *Psychological Science, 19,* 268–275.

Breslau, K. (2007, December 25). Majora Carter. *Newsweek.*

Brewis, A. A., Wutich, A., Falletta-Cowden, A., & Rodriguez-Soto, I. (2011). Body norms and fat stigma in global perspective. *Current Anthropology, 52,* 269–276.

Brint, S. (1998). *Schools and societies.* Thousand Oaks, CA: Pine Forge Press.

Brinton, C. (1965). *The anatomy of revolution.* New York, NY: Vintage Books.

Brizendine, L. (2006). *The female brain.* New York, NY: Broadway.

Broder, J. M. (2006, April 2). Immigrants and the economics of hard work. *The New York Times.*

Broderick, R. (2013, September 16). A lot of people are very upset that an Indian-American woman won the Miss America Pageant. *Buzzfeed.* www.buzzfeed.com/ryanhatesthis/a-lot-of-people-are-very-upset-that-an-Indian-American-woman. Accessed May 31, 2014.

Brodesser-Akner, T. (2014, April 6). It's time to get back in the pool. *The New York Times.*

Brodey, D. (2005, September 20). Blacks join the eating-disorder mainstream. *The New York Times.*

Bronner, E. (1998, January 10). Inventing the notion of race. *The New York Times.*

Bronner, E. (2012, July 3). Poor land in jail as companies add huge fees for probation. *The New York Times.*

Bronner, E. (2013, March 16). Right to lawyer can be empty promise for poor. *The New York Times.*

Bronson, P., & Merryman, A. (2010, July 19). The creativity crisis. *Newsweek.*

Brookings Institution. (2006). *From poverty, opportunity: Putting the market to work for lower income families.* www.brookings.edu/metro/pubs/20060718_PovOp.pdf. Accessed July 18, 2006.

Brooks, D. (2012, January 31). The great divorce. *The New York Times.*

Brooks, D. (2013, February 1). The easy problem. *The New York Times.*

Brooks, S. (2009). *Black men can't shoot.* Chicago, IL: University of Chicago Press.

Broverman, I., Vogel, S., Broverman, D., Clarkson, F., & Rosenkrantz, P. (1972). Sex role stereotypes: A current appraisal. *Journal of Social Issues, 28,* 59–78.

Brown, A. (2017). *5 key findings about LGBT Americans.* Pew Research Center. www.pewresearch.org/fact-tank/2017/06/13/5-key-findings-about-lgbt-americans/. Accessed June 14, 2017.

Brown, D. (2011, July 13). Two studies show that drugs used to treat AIDS can be used to prevent HIV infection too. *The Washington Post.*

Brown, P. (1998). Biology and the social construction of the "race" concept. In J. Ferrante & P. Brown (Eds.), *The social construction of race and ethnicity in the United States.* New York, NY: Longman.

Brown, P. L. (2011, March 6). Bill to ban Chinese delicacy has some fuming. *The New York Times.*

Brown, R. (1986). *Social psychology.* New York, NY: Free Press.

Brown, T. (2010, September 7). Learning to talk the talk in a hospital. *The New York Times.*

Browne, B. A. (1998). Gender stereotypes in advertising on children's television in the 1990s: A cross-national analysis. *Journal of Advertising, 27,* 83–96.

Brownmiller, S. (1975). *Against our will: Men, women, and rape*. New York, NY: Simon & Schuster.

Bruni, F. (2012, January 15). Running from millions. *The New York Times*.

Brutally Honest. (2004). *Jimmy Swaggart. Just. Shut. Up.* www.brutallyhonest.org/brutally_honest/2004/09/jimmy_swaggart_html. Accessed June 2, 2005.

Brutus, D. (1999). Africa 2000 in the new global context. In T. J. Gallagher (Ed.), *Perspectives: Introductory sociology*. St. Paul, MN: Coursewise.

Bryc, K., Durand, E. Y., Macpherson, J. M., Reich, D., & Mountain, J. L. (2015). The genetic ancestry of African Americans, Latinos, and European Americans across the United States. *American Journal of Human Genetics, 96,* 37–53.

Buchholz, T. G., & Buchholz, V. (2012, March 10). The go-nowhere generation. *The New York Times*.

Buckley, C. (2009, February 18). For uninsured young adults, do-it-yourself medical care. *The New York Times*.

Buckley, C. (2010, December 9). To test housing program, some are denied aid. *The New York Times*.

Buckley, C. (2015, October 30). China approves two-child policy to help economy. *The New York Times*.

Bullard, R. D. (1993). Anatomy of environmental racism and the environmental justice movement. In R. D. Bullard (Ed.), *Confronting environmental racism*. Boston, MA: South End Press.

Bullard, R. D. (2001). Decision making. In L. Westra & B. E. Lawson (Eds.), *Faces of environmental racism: Confronting issues of global justice*. Lanham, MD: Rowman & Littlefield.

Bullington, B. (1993). All about Eve: The many faces of United States drug policy. In F. Pearce & M. Woodiwiss (Eds.), *Global crime connections*. Toronto, Ontario, Canada: University of Toronto Press.

Bunk busters unravel the art of spin. (2007). *National Public Radio*. www.npr.org/templates/story/story.php?storyId=10416827. Accessed September 5, 2009.

Bureau of Transportation Statistics. (2012). *Number of U.S. aircraft, vehicles, vessels, and other conveyances*. www.rita.dot.gov/bts/sites/rita.dot.gov.bts/publications/national_transportation_statistics/html/table_01_11.html. Accessed December 31, 2012.

Burger, J. M. (2009). Replicating Milgram: Would people still obey today? *American Psychologist, 64,* 1–11.

Butler, R. (1989). A generation at risk: When the baby boomers reach Golden Pond. In W. Feigelman (Ed.), *Sociology full circle*. New York, NY: Holt, Rinehart & Winston.

Butterfield, F. (2000, April 26). Racial disparities seen as pervasive in juvenile justice. *The New York Times*.

Byrd, A., & Tharps, L. L. (2014, May 1). When black hair is against the rules. *The New York Times*.

Cahill, S. (1999). Emotional capital and professional socialization: The case of mortuary science students (and me). *Social Psychology Quarterly, 62,* 101–116.

Caldwell, C. (2005, January 23). The triumph of gesture politics. *The New York Times*.

California Legislative Information. (2014). *Senate Bill No. 967.* leginfo.legislature.ca.gov/faces/billNavClient.xhtml?bill_id=201320140SB967. Accessed September 7, 2014.

Camarota, S. A. (2004). *Economy slowed, but immigration didn't: The foreign-born population, 2000–2004*. Washington, DC: Center for Immigration Studies. www.cis.org. Accessed June 9, 2005.

Cambridge University Press. (2016). *Aesthetics or athletics?* www.cambridge.org/about-us/media/press-releases/aesthetics-or-athletics/. Accessed January 6, 2017.

Cameron, D. (2000). Styling the worker: Gender and the commodification of language in the globalized service economy. *Journal of Sociolinguistics, 4/3,* 323–347.

Cameron, D., & Berkowitz, B. (2016, June 14). The state of gay rights around the world. *Washington Post Online*. www.washingtonpost.com/graphics/world/gay-rights/. Accessed January 17, 2017.

Campbell, A. (1987). Self-definition by rejection: The case of gang girls. *Social Problems, 34,* 451–466.

Campos, P. F. (2017, July 29). White economic privilege is alive and well. *The New York Times*.

Caplan, B. (2011). *Selfish reasons to have more kids: Why being a great parent is less work and more fun than you think*. New York, NY: Basic Books.

Caplan, P. J. (1995). *They say you're crazy: How the world's most powerful psychiatrists decide who's normal*. Reading, MA: Addison-Wesley.

Caramenico, A. (2012, May 7). *Hospitals lose millions from cancelled surgeries*. Fierce Healthcare. www.fiercehealthcare.com/story/hospitals-lose-millions-cancelled-surgeries/2012-05-07. Accessed May 22, 2015.

Carey, B. (2007, January 14). Can Johnny come out and (be taught) to play? *The New York Times*.

Carey, B. (2012, January 19). New autism rule will trim many, a study suggests. *The New York Times*.

Carlson, E. (2009). 20th-century U.S. generations. *Population Bulletin, 64,* 1–17.

Carmichael, M. (2008, December 1). Katrina kids: Sickest ever. *Newsweek*.

Carnevale, A. P., & Rose, S. J. (2003). *Socioeconomic status, race/ethnicity, and selective college admissions*. Washington, DC: Century Foundation. www.tcf.org/Publications/Education/carnevale_rose.pdf. Accessed September 4, 2009.

Carothers, B. (2013, April 21). The tangle of the sexes. *The New York Times*.

Carr, D. (2011, April 17). Keep your thumbs still when I'm talking to you. *The New York Times*.

Carr, D., & Friedman, M. A. (2006). Body weight and the quality of interpersonal relationships. *Social Psychology Quarterly, 69,* 127–149.

Carter, B., Abnet, C. C., Feskanich, D., Freedman, N. D., Hartge, P., Lewis, C. E., . . . Jacobs, E. J. (2015). Smoking and mortality—Beyond established causes. *New England Journal of Medicine, 372,* 631–640.

Carter, H., & Glick, P. C. (1976). *Marriage and divorce: A social and economic study*. Cambridge, MA: Harvard University Press.

Carter, M. (2014, July 31). Man who set fire in Capitol Hill nightclub sentenced to 10 years. *Seattle Times*.

Case, A., & Deaton, A. (2015). Rising morbidity and mortality in midlife among white non-Hispanic Americans in the 21st century. *Proceedings of the National Academy of Sciences, 112,* 15078–15083.

Cashdan, E. (2008). Waist-to-hip ratio across cultures: Trade-offs between androgen- and estrogen-dependent traits. *Current Anthropology, 49,* 1099–1107.

Cashin, S. (2017, June 4). Interracial love is saving America. *The New York Times*.

Cast, A. D. (2004). Role taking and interaction. *Social Psychology Quarterly, 67,* 296–309.

Castle, S. (2015, December 16). Cleaning out the cupboard of British law. *The New York Times*.

Catalano, S. (2012). *Intimate partner violence, 1993–2010*. U.S. Bureau of Justice Statistics, NCJ239203. bjs.ojp.usdoj.gov/content/pub/pdf/ipv9310.pdf. Accessed January 16, 2013.

Catalyst. (2017). *Women CEOs of the S&P 500*. www.catalyst.org/knowledge/women-ceos-sp-500. Accessed January 26, 2017.

Catholic News Agency. (2013, June 10). *Chile proposes financial incentives for childbearing*. www.catholicnewsagency.com/news/chile-proposes-financial-incentives-for-childbearing/. Accessed June 27, 2013.

Center for American Progress. (2013). *Global wage trends for apparel workers, 2001-2011*. www.americanprogress.org/wp-content/uploads/2013/07/RealWageStudy-3.pdf. Accessed May 31, 2015.

Center for Public Integrity. (2008). *Iraq: The war card*. www.publicintegrity.org/projects/entry/276. Accessed May 3, 2009.

Center on Budget and Policy Priorities. (2016). *TANF cash benefits have fallen by more than 20 percent in most states and continue to erode*. www.cbpp.org/research/family-income-support/tanf-cash-benefits-have-fallen-by-more-than-20-percent-in-most-state. Accessed June 3, 2017.

Centers for Disease Control and Prevention. (1999). Ten great public health achievements in the United States, 1900–1999. *Mortality and Morbidity Weekly Report, 48,* 241–243.

Centers for Disease Control and Prevention. (2011). *The national intimate partner and sexual violence survey*. www.cdc.gov/violenceprevention/pdf/nisvs_report2010-a.pdf. Accessed June 26, 2014.

Centers for Disease Control and Prevention. (2013). Suicide among adults aged 35–64 years—United States, 1999–2010. *Morbidity and Mortality Weekly Report, 62,* 321–325.

Centers for Disease Control and Prevention. (2014a). *Antibiotic resistance threats in the United States, 2013*. www.cdc.gov/drugresistance/threat-report-2013/pdf/ar-threats-2013-508.pdf#page=6. Accessed June 28, 2015.

Centers for Disease Control and Prevention. (2014b). *Tobacco-related mortality*. www.cdc.gov/tobacco/data_statistics/fact_sheets/health_effects/tobacco_related_mortality/index.htm#cigs. Accessed June 24, 2014.

Centers for Disease Control and Prevention. (2015a). *Deaths, percent of total deaths, and death rates for the 15 leading causes of death: United States and each state: 2014*. www.cdc.gov/nchs/data/dvs/lcwk9_2014.pdf. Accessed December 26, 2016.

Centers for Disease Control and Prevention. (2015b). *2014 Ebola outbreak in West Africa—Case counts*. www.cdc.gov/vhf/ebola/outbreaks/2014-west-africa/case-counts.html. Accessed January 4, 2015.

Centers for Disease Control and Prevention. (2015c). *Occupational cancer*. www.cdc.gov/niosh/topics/cancer/. Accessed January 18, 2017.

Centers for Disease Control and Prevention. (2015d). *Preventing healthcare-associated infections*. CDC at Work. www.cdc.gov/washington/~cdcatWork/pdf/infections.pdf. Accessed January 21, 2015.

Centers for Disease Control and Prevention. (2015e). *Suicide: Facts at a glance*. www.cdc.gov/Violenceprevention/pdf/Suicide-DataSheet-a.pdf. Accessed December 26, 2016.

Centers for Disease Control and Prevention. (2015f). *Trends in the prevalence of sexual behaviors and HIV testing—National YRBS: 1991-2013.* www.cdc.gov/healthyyouth/yrbs/pdf/trends/us_sexual_trend_yrbs.pdf. Accessed June 17, 2015.

Centers for Disease Control and Prevention. (2016a). *Climate effects on health.* www.cdc.gov/climateandhealth/effects/default.htm. Accessed June 28, 2017.

Centers for Disease Control and Prevention. (2016b). *Current cigarette smoking among adults in the United States.* www.cdc.gov/tobacco/data_statistics/fact_sheets/adult_data/cig_smoking/index.htm. Accessed January 18, 2017.

Centers for Disease Control and Prevention. (2016c). *Health, United States, 2015.* www.cdc.gov/nchs/data/hus/hus15.pdf#specialfeature. Accessed June 5, 2017.

Centers for Disease Control and Prevention. (2016d). *Measles cases and outbreaks.* www.cdc.gov/measles/cases-outbreaks/html. Accessed December 28, 2016.

Centers for Disease Control and Prevention. (2016e). *Sickle Cell Disease (SCD): Data and statistics.* www.cdc.gov/ncbddd/sicklecell/data.html. Accessed June 13, 2017.

Centers for Disease Control and Prevention. (2017). *Cigarette smoking and tobacco use among people in low socio-economic status.* www.cdc.gov/tobacco/disparities/low-ses/indes.htm. Accessed June 16, 2017.

Chafetz, J. S. (1978). *A primer on the construction and testing of theories in sociology.* Itasca, IL: Peacock.

Chafetz, J. S., & Dworkin, A. G. (1987). In the face of threat: Organized anti-feminism in comparative perspective. *Gender & Society, 1,* 33–60.

Chambliss, D. F. (1989). The mundanity of excellence: An ethnographic report on stratification and Olympic swimmers. *Sociological Theory, 7,* 70–86.

Chambliss, W. (1964). A sociological analysis of the law of vagrancy. *Social Problems, 12,* 66–77.

Chapkis, W. (2010). Patients, "potheads," and dying to get high. In D. M. Newman & J. O'Brien (Eds.), *Sociology: Exploring the architecture of everyday life: Readings.* Thousand Oaks, CA: Pine Forge Press.

Charles, M. (2011, Spring). What gender is science? *Contexts.* http://contexts.org/articles/spring2011/what-gender-is-science/. Accessed June 21, 2011.

Charon, J. (1992). *Ten questions: A sociological perspective.* Belmont, CA: Wadsworth.

Charon, J. (1998). *Symbolic interactionism.* Upper Saddle River, NJ: Prentice Hall.

Chase-Dunn, C., & Rubinson, R. (1977). Toward a structural perspective on the world system. *Politics and Society, 7,* 453–476.

Chaudhry, L. (2006, April 7). Acting your race. *In These Times.*

Chen, E., Matthews, K. A., & Boyce, W. T. (2002). Socioeconomic differences in children's health: How and why do these relationships change with age? *Psychological Bulletin, 128,* 295–329.

Cherlin, A. J. (1992). *Marriage, divorce, remarriage.* Cambridge, MA: Harvard University Press.

Cherlin, A. J., Furstenberg, F. F., Jr., Chase-Lansdale, P. L., Kiernan, K. E., Robins, P. K., Morrison, D. R., & Teitler, J. O. (1991). Longitudinal studies of effects of divorce on children in Great Britain and the United States. *Science, 252,* 1386–1389.

Cherney, I. D., & London, K. (2006). Gender-linked differences in the toys, television shows, computer games, and outdoor activities of 5- to 13-year-old children. *Sex Roles, 54,* 717–726.

Chetty, R., Friedman, J. N., Saez, E., Turner, N., & Yagan, D. (2017). *Mobility report cards: The role of colleges in intergenerational mobility.* The Equality of Opportunity Project. www.equality-of-opportunity.org/papers/coll_mrc_paper.pdf. Accessed May 23, 2017.

Chetty, R., Stepner, M., & Abraham, S. (2016). The association between income and life expectancy in the United States. *JAMA, 315,* 1750-1766.

Child, L. (2016, May 16). Telling tales. *The New Yorker.*

CHILD, Inc. (2016). *Religious exemptions to medical treatment of children in state civil and criminal codes.* www.childrenshealthcare.org/?page_id=24#exemptions. Accessed December 27, 2016.

Child Rights International Network. (2014). *Child sexual abuse and the Holy See: the need for justice, accountability, and reform.* www.tbinternet.ohchr.org/Treaties/CAT/Shared Documents/VAT/INT_CAT_CSS_VAT_17113_E.pdf. Accessed January 20, 2015.

Children's Health Watch. (2013). *Punishing hard work: The unintended consequences of cutting SNAP benefits.* Policy report. www.childrenshealthwatch.org/publication/punishing-hard-work-unintended-consequences-cutting-snap-benefits/. Accessed July 3, 2014.

China changes death penalty law. (2006, October 31). *The New York Times.*

Ching, C. L., & Burke, S. (1999). An assessment of college students' attitudes and empathy toward rape. *College Student Journal, 33,* 573–584.

Chira, S. (2016, October 21). Men need help. Is Hillary Clinton the answer? *The New York Times.*

Chira, S. (2017, June 25). Jobs men don't want. *The New York Times.*

Choma, R. (2015). *One member of Congress=18 American households: Lawmakers' personal finances far from average.* Center for Responsive Politics. www.opensecrets.org. Accessed May 26, 2015.

Chopik, W. J., & O'Brien, E. (2016). Happy you, healthy me? Having a happy partner is independently associated with better health in oneself. *Health Psychology Advance Online Publication.* www.apa.org/pubs/journals/releases/hea-hea0000432.pdf. Accessed December 27, 2016.

Christakis, N. A., & Fowler, J. H. (2007). The spread of obesity in a large social network over 32 years. *The New England Journal of Medicine, 357,* 370–379.

Chua, A. (2011). *Battle hymn of the Tiger Mother.* New York, NY: Penguin.

Ciancanelli, P., & Berch, B. (1987). Gender and the GNP. In B. B. Hess & M. M. Ferree (Eds.), *Analyzing gender: A handbook of social science research.* Newbury Park, CA: Sage.

Clarity, J. F. (1999, March 14). Lost youth in Ireland: Suicide rate is climbing. *The New York Times.*

Clark, B. (1960). The "cooling out" function in higher education. *American Journal of Sociology, 65,* 569–576.

Clark, C. (1997). *Misery and company: Sympathy in everyday life.* Chicago, IL: University of Chicago Press.

Clark, L. P., Millet, D. B., & Marshall, J. D. (2014). National patterns in environmental injustice and inequality outdoor NO_2 air pollution in the United States. *PLoS ONE, 9(4):* e94431. www.journals.plos.org/plosone/article?id=10.1371/journal.pone.0094431. Accessed June 4, 2015.

Clausen, J. A. (1986). *The life course: A sociological perspective.* Englewood Cliffs, NJ: Prentice Hall.

Clemmitt, M. (2009). Extreme sports. *CQ Researcher, 19,* 297–320.

Clifford, S. (2011, April 24). One size fits nobody: Seeking a steady 4 or a 10. *The New York Times.*

Clifford, S. (2013, September 20). Textile plants humming, but not with workers. *The New York Times.*

Clifford, S., & Hardy, Q. (2013, July 15). Attention shoppers: Stores are tracking your cell. *The New York Times.*

Cluster, D. (1979). *They should have served that cup of coffee.* Boston, MA: South End Press.

CNN.com. (2009). *Most blacks say MLK's vision fulfilled, poll finds.* http://edition.cnn.com/2009/POLITICS/01/19/king.poll/. Accessed August 13, 2009.

Coates, T-N. (2014, June). The case for reparations. *The Atlantic.* www.theatlantic.com/features/2014/05/the-case-for-reparations/361631/. Accessed June 7, 2015.

Cohen, A. K. (1955). *Delinquent boys: The culture of the gang.* New York, NY: Free Press.

Cohen, A. K. (1966). *Deviance and control.* Englewood Cliffs, NJ: Prentice Hall.

Cohen, F. G. (1986). Treaties on trial: The continuing controversy over Northwest Indian fishing rights. Seattle: University of Washington Press.

Cohen, P. (2013, November 24). Jump-starting the struggle for equality. *The New York Times.*

Cohen, P. (2015, April 11). Middle class, or so they think. *The New York Times.*

Cohen, P. (2016, September 26). With pay rising, millions climb out of poverty. *The New York Times.*

Cohen, R. A., Martinez, M. E., & Zammitti, E. P. (2016). *Health insurance coverage: Early release of estimates from the National Health Interview Survey, January-March 2016.* National Center for Health Statistics. www.cdc.gov/nchs/data/nhis/earlyrelease/insur201609.pdf. Accessed May 31, 2017.

Cohn, D., Passel, J. S., Wang, W., & Livingston, G. (2011). *Barely half of U.S. adults are married—a record low.* Pew Research Center. www.pewsocialtrends.org/2011/12/14/barely-half-of-u-s-adults-are-married-a-record-low/. Accessed January 10, 2017.

Cohn, N. (2013, June 27). As a long-term political issue, gay marriage will be more like abortion than integration. *New Republic.*

Cohn, N. (2015, May 23). Lack of transparency a problem for pollsters. *The New York Times.*

Colby, S. L., & Ortman, J. M. (2014). The baby boom cohort in the United States: 2012 to 2060. *Current Population Reports.* P25-1141. www.census.gov/prod/2014pubs/p25-1141.pdf. Accessed June 16, 2015.

Colby, S. L., & Ortman, J. M. (2015). Projections of the size and composition of the U.S. population: 2014 to 2060. *Current Population Reports.* P25-1143. www.census.gov/content/dam/Census/library/publications/2015/demo/p25-1143.pdf. Accessed June 18, 2015.

Coll, S. (2017, June 26). The politics of anger. *The New Yorker.*

The College Board. (1998). *SAT and gender differences* (Research Summary RS-04). http://professionals.collegeboard.com/profdownload/pdf/rs04_3960.pdf. Accessed August 13, 2009.

The College Board. (2014). *The 10th annual AP report to the nation.* www.media.collegeboard.com/digitalServices/pdf/ap/rtn/10th-annual/10th-annual-ap-report-to-the-nation.single-page.pdf. Accessed June 4, 2015.

Collier, K. (2015, October 5). Texas' controversial social studies textbooks under fire again. *The Texas Tribune.*

Collins, G. (2011, April 7). Medicine on the move. *The New York Times.*

Collins, R. (1971). Functional and conflict theories of educational stratification. *American Sociological Review, 36,* 1002–1019.

Collins, R. (1981). On the microfoundations of macrosociology. *American Journal of Sociology, 86,* 984–1014.

Common Sense Media. (2013). *Zero to eight: Children's media use in America 2013.* www.commonsensemedia.org/research/zero-to-eight-childrens-media-use-in-america-2013. Accessed January 12, 2015.

The Commonwealth Fund. (2015). *U.S. health care from a global perspective.* www.commonwealthfund.org/publications/issue-briefs/2015/oct/us-health-care-from-a-global-perspective. Accessed January 2, 2017.

Congeni, J. (2009). Management of the adolescent concussion victim. *Adolescent Medicine: State of the Art Reviews, 20,* 41–56.

Congressional Budget Office. (2014). *The distribution of household income and federal taxes, 2011.* www.cbo.gov/sites/default/files/cbofiles/attachments/49440-Distribution-of-Income-and-Taxes.pdf. Accessed May 28, 2015.

Congressional Budget Office. (2017). *H.R. 1628, American Health Care Act of 2017.* www.cbo.gov/publication/52752. Accessed May 31, 2017.

Conrad, P. (1975). The discovery of hyperkinesis: Notes on the medicalization of deviant behavior. *Social Problems, 23,* 12–21.

Conrad, P. (2005). The shifting engines of medicalization. *Journal of Health and Social Behavior, 46,* 3–14.

Conrad, P., & Leiter, V. (2004). Medicalization, markets, and consumers. *Journal of Health and Social Behavior, 45,* 158–176.

Conrad, P., & Schneider, J. W. (1992). *Deviance and medicalization: From badness to sickness.* Philadelphia, PA: Temple University Press.

A continuing abomination. (2008, November 1). *The Economist.*

Conway, L. (2013). *How many of us are there? An investigative report.* Gender Centre. www.gendercentre.org/au/resources/polare-archive/archived-articles/how-many-of-us-are-there.htm. Accessed January 9, 2015.

Cook, B. (2013, August 22). Youth sports complex scores millions in Pepsi "pouring rights" deal. *Forbes.*

Cookson, P., & Persell, C. (1985). *Preparing for power.* New York, NY: Basic Books.

Cooley, C. H. (1902). *Human nature and social order.* New York, NY: Scribner.

Coolidge, S. (2005, August 20). Parents must pay $7M. *The Cincinnati Enquirer.*

Coontz, S. (1992). *The way we never were.* New York, NY: Basic Books.

Coontz, S. (2005). *Marriage, a history: From obedience to intimacy, or how love conquered marriage.* New York, NY: Viking.

Coontz, S. (2013a, June 23). The disestablishment of marriage. *The New York Times.*

Coontz, S. (2013b, February 17). Why gender equality stalled. *The New York Times.*

Coontz, S. (2017, April 2). Do millennial men want stay-at-home wives? *The New York Times.*

Cose, E. (2009, February 2). Revisiting "The rage of the privileged class." *Newsweek.*

Cose, E. (2011, May 23 & 30). Meet the new optimists. *Newsweek.*

Coser, R. L. (1960). Laughter among colleagues: A study of the social functions among staff of a mental hospital. *Psychiatry, 23,* 81–95.

Cosgrove, L., Bursztajn, H., & Krimsky, S. (2009). Developing unbiased diagnostic and treatment guidelines in psychiatry. *New England Journal of Medicine, 360,* 2035–2036.

Coulson, M. A., & Riddell, C. (1980). *Approaching sociology.* London, UK: Routledge & Kegan Paul.

Counterterrorism Communications Center. (2008, March 14). *Words that work and words that don't: A guide for counterterrorism communication.* www.investigativeproject.org/documents/misc/id/127. Accessed May 22, 2011.

Covert, B. (2017, September 3). Working women peaked two decades ago. *The New York Times.*

Cowan, R. (1991). More work for mother: The postwar years. In L. Kramer (Ed.), *The sociology of gender.* New York, NY: St. Martin's Press.

Cowell, A. (2007, March 8). Commons moves again to erode nobles' power in Britain. *The New York Times.*

Cowley, G. (2003, May 5). How progress makes us sick. *Newsweek.*

Coyle, M. (2003). *Race and class penalties in crack cocaine sentencing* (Sentencing Project Report No. 5077). www.sentencingproject.org/doc/publications/5077.pdf. Accessed September 4, 2009.

Crandall, M., Nathens, A. B., Kernic, M. A., Holt, V. L., & Rivara, F. P. (2004). Predicting future injury among women in abusive relationships. *Journal of Trauma: Injury, Infection, and Critical Care, 56,* 906–912.

Cranz, G. (1998). *The chair: Rethinking culture, body, and design.* New York, NY: Norton.

Crary, D. (2007, June 3). TB case raises ethical questions. *The Indianapolis Star.*

Crary, D. (2017, July 25). Pressure mounts to curtail surgery on intersex children. *Chicago Tribune.*

Crawford, S. P. (2011, December 4). The new digital divide. *The New York Times.*

Crocker, L. (2014, January 16). Virginia legislator running for congress says spousal rape should be legal. *The Daily Beast.* www.thedailybeast.com/virginia-legislator-running-for-congress-says-spousal-rape-should-be-legal. Accessed June 21, 2017.

Cross, G. (1997). *Kids' stuff: Toys and the changing world of American childhood.* Cambridge, MA: Harvard University Press.

Cross, J., & Guyer, M. (1980). *Social traps.* Ann Arbor: University of Michigan Press.

Crossette, B. (2001, February 28). Against a trend, U.S. population will bloom, UN says. *The New York Times.*

Croteau, D., & Hoynes, W. (2000). *Media/society: Industries, images, and audiences.* Thousand Oaks, CA: Pine Forge Press.

Crowder, K., Pais, J., & South, S. J. (2012). Neighborhood diversity, metropolitan constraints, and household migration. *American Sociological Review, 77,* 325–353.

Crystal, D. (2003). *English as a global language.* Cambridge, UK: Cambridge University Press.

CTIA-The Wireless Association. (2016). *Annual wireless industry survey.* www.ctia.org/industry-data/ctia-annual-wireless-industry-survey. Accessed December 30, 2016.

Cuevas, M. (2016, December 27). Suit: Versace used "secret code" for black customers. *CNN Online.* www.cnn.com/2016/12/27/us/versace-code-lawsuit-trnd/index.html. Accessed June 7, 2017.

Curra, J. (2000). *The relativity of deviance.* Thousand Oaks, CA: Sage.

Currie, J., DellaVigna, S., Moretti, E., & Pathania, V. (2009). *The effect of fast food restaurants on obesity* (Working Paper No. 14721). Cambridge, MA: National Bureau of Economic Research. www.nber.org/papers/w14721.pdf. Accessed May 15, 2009.

Currier, C. (2012). *The 24 states that have sweeping self-defense laws just like Florida's.* ProPublica. www.propublica.org/article/the-23-states-that-have-sweeping-self-defense-laws-just-like-floridas. Accessed January 21, 2013.

Curtin, J. S. (2004). Suicide also rises in land of rising sun. *Asia Times Online.* www.atimes.com/atimes/Japan/FG28Dh01.html. Accessed November 19, 2004.

Curtin, S. C., Warner, M., & Hedegaard, H. (2016). *Increase in suicide in the United States, 1999-2014.* National Center for Health Statistics Data Brief #241. www.cdc.gov/nchs/products/databriefs/db241.htm. Accessed December 26, 2016.

Cushing, R., & Bishop, B. (2005, July 20). The rural war. *The New York Times.*

Customs and Border Protection. (2016). *US border patrol fiscal year staffing statistics (FY1992-FY2016).* www.cbp.gov/sites/default/files/assets/documents/2016-Oct/BP Staffing FY1992-FY2016.pdf. Accessed June 26, 2017.

Dahrendorf, R. (1959). *Class and class conflict in industrial society.* Stanford, CA: Stanford University Press.

Daley, S. (1996, May 9). A new charter wins adoption in South Africa. *The New York Times.*

Daley, S. (2000, April 9). More and more, Europeans find fault with U.S. *The New York Times.*

Daniels, R. (1990). *Coming to America.* New York, NY: HarperCollins.

Dansky, K. (2014). *An MRAP is not a blanket.* American Civil Liberties Union. www.aclu.org/blog/criminal-law-reform-immigrants-rights-technology-and-liberty/mrap-not-blanket. Accessed January 6, 2015.

Danziger, S., & Gottschalk, P. (2004, December). *Diverging fortunes: Trends in poverty and inequality* (PRB Report). Washington, DC: Population Reference Bureau. www.prb.org. Accessed January 19, 2005.

Dao, J. (2010a, February 12). Single mother is spared court-martial. *The New York Times.*

Dao, J. (2010b, July 8). V.A. is easing rules to cover stress disorder. *The New York Times.*

Dao, J. (2011, May 14). Unfounded suspicions wreak havoc on lives of two Muslim soldiers. *The New York Times.*

Dao, J. (2013, June 24). When victims of military sex assaults are men. *The New York Times.*

Dargis, M. (2011, May 25). 3 men and a monkey-baby. *The New York Times.*

Davenport, C., & Robertson, C. (2016, May 3). Resettling the first American "climate refugees." *The New York Times.*

Davey, M. (2011, September 7). Families feel sharp edge of state budget cuts. *The New York Times.*

Davey, M. (2015, October 30). A new look at sex offenders and lockups than never end. *The New York Times.*

Davey, M. (2017, May 26). U.S. indicts 21 people in sex-trafficking ring. *The New York Times.*

Davidson, A. (2011, November 27). When did the rules change? *The New York Times Magazine.*

Davidson, A. (2013, January 13). A tax on annoying behavior? *The New York Times Magazine.*

Davidson, A. (2014, June 20). Hi mom, I'm home. *The New York Times Magazine.*

Davies, J. C. (1962). Toward a theory of revolution. *American Sociological Review, 27,* 5–19.

Davis, D. B. (2006). *Inhuman bondage: The rise and fall of slavery in the New World.* New York, NY: Oxford University Press.

Davis, F. J. (1991). *Who is black?* University Park: Pennsylvania State University Press.

Davis, G. (2013, February 7). UN condemns "normalization" surgery for intersexuality. *Ms. Magazine.*

Davis, K. (1937). The sociology of prostitution. *American Sociological Review, 2,* 744–755.

Davis, K. (1976). The world's population crisis. In R. K. Merton & R. Nisbett (Eds.), *Contemporary social problems.* New York, NY: Harcourt Brace Jovanovich.

Davis, K., & Moore, W. (1945). Some principles of stratification. *American Sociological Review, 10,* 242–247.

Davis, S. (2003). Sex stereotypes in commercials targeted toward children: A content analysis. *Sociological Spectrum, 23,* 407–424.

Dawes, R. M., & Messick, D. M. (2000). Social dilemmas. *International Journal of Psychology, 35,* 111–116.

Dean, C. (2017, July/August). Political science. *Brown Alumni Magazine.*

Deane, D. (2007, July 4). Justice is unequal for parents who host teen drinking parties. *The New York Times.*

Death Penalty Information Center. (2013). *Death penalty representation.* www.deathpenaltyinfo.org/death-penalty-representation. Accessed January 23, 2013.

Death Penalty Information Center. (2016). *The death penalty in 2016: Year end report.* www.deathpenaltyinfo.org/documents/2016YrEnd.pdf. Accessed December 22, 2016.

Death Penalty Information Center. (2017). *Facts about the death penalty.* www.deathpenaltyinfo.org/documents/FactSheet.pdf. Accessed January 17, 2017.

Deaux, K., & Kite, M. E. (1987). Thinking about gender. In B. B. Hess & M. M. Ferree (Eds.), *Analyzing gender: A handbook of social science research.* Newbury Park, CA: Sage.

DeCastro, J. M. (1994). Family and friends produce greater social facilitation of food-intake than other companions. *Physiology and Behavior, 56,* 445–455.

DeCastro, J. M. (2000). Eating behaviors: Lessons from the real world of humans. *Ingestive Behavior and Obesity, 16,* 800–813.

Decker, G. (2011, July 4). More Hispanics are identifying themselves as Indians. *The New York Times.*

Declaration of sentiments and resolutions, Seneca Falls Convention, 1848. (2001). In P. S. Rothenberg (Ed.), *Race, class, and gender in the United States.* New York, NY: Worth.

DeFronzo, J. (1991). *Revolutions and revolutionary movements.* Boulder, CO: Westview Press.

DeJean, A. (2017, May 8). Texas's governor just signed the most anti-immigrant bill in years. *Mother Jones.* www.motherjones.com/politics/2017/05/sanctuary-cities-outlawed-now-law-texas/. Accessed June 26, 2017.

de Bourmont, M. (2017, February 10). Roma's hope in education is hobbled in France. *The New York Times.*

de la Baume, M. (2013, May 24). Bid in France to add courses in English raises fear for language. *The New York Times.*

DeLeire, T. (2000). The unintended consequences of the Americans with Disabilities Act. *Regulation, 23,* 21–24.

Deming, D., & Dynarski, S. (2008). *The lengthening of childhood* (Working Paper No. 14124). Cambridge, MA: National Bureau of Economic Research. www.nber.org/papers/w14124.pdf?new_window=1. Accessed May 14, 2009.

DeNavas-Walt, C., Proctor, B. D., & Lee, C. H. (2006). *Income, poverty, and health insurance: Coverage in the United States: 2005* (U.S. Census Bureau, Current Population Reports, P60-231). Washington, DC: Government Printing Office.

DeNavas-Walt, C., Proctor, B. D., & Smith, J. C. (2008). *Income, poverty, and health insurance coverage in the United States: 2007* (U.S. Census Bureau, Current Population Reports, P60-235). www.census.gov/prod/2008pubs/p60-235.pdf. Accessed September 4, 2009.

DeNavas-Walt, C., Proctor, B. D., & Smith, J. C. (2010). *Income, poverty, and health insurance coverage in the United States: 2009* (U.S. Census Bureau, Current Population

Reports, P60-238). www.census.gov/prod/2010pubs/p60.238.pdf. Accessed September 16, 2010.

DeNavas-Walt, C., Proctor, B. D., & Smith, J. C. (2011). *Income, poverty, and health insurance coverage in the United States: 2010.* (U.S. Census Bureau, Current Population Reports, P60-239). www.census.gov/prod/2011pubs/p60-239.pdf. Accessed September 13, 2011.

DeNavas-Walt, C., & Proctor, B. D. (2014). *Income, poverty, and health insurance coverage in the United States: 2013.* (U.S. Census Bureau, Current Population Reports, P60-249). www.census.gov/content/dam/Census/library/publications/2014/demo/p60-249.pdf. Accessed July 3, 2015.

Denizet-Lewis, B. (2017, October 15). The kids who can't. *The New York Times Magazine.*

Denzin, N. (1977). *Childhood socialization: Studies in the development of language, social behavior, and identity.* San Francisco, CA: Jossey-Bass.

Denzin, N. (1989). *The research act: A theoretical introduction to sociological methods.* Englewood Cliffs, NJ: Prentice Hall.

DeParle, J. (2012, April 8). Welfare limits left poor adrift as recession hit. *The New York Times.*

DeParle, J., Gebeloff, R., & Tavernise, S. (2011, November 18). Meet the near poor: Older, married, suburban, & struggling. *The New York Times.*

DePaulo, B. (2007). *Singled out: How singles are stereotyped, stigmatized, and ignored, and still live happily ever after.* New York, NY: St. Martin's Press.

Derber, C. (1979). *The pursuit of attention.* New York, NY: Oxford University Press.

Deresiewicz, W. (2011). The end of solitude. In M. Bauerline (ed.), *The digital divide: Arguments for and against Facebook, Google, texting, and the age of social networking.* New York, NY: Tarcher/Penguin.

Dervarics, C. (2004, March). *Conspiracy beliefs may be hindering HIV prevention among African Americans* (PRB Report). Washington, DC: Population Reference Bureau. www.prb.org. Accessed March 16, 2005.

Desilver, D., & Bialek, K. (2017). *Blacks and Hispanics face extra challenges in getting home loans.* Pew Research Center. www.pewresearch.org/fact-tank/2017/01/10/blacks-and-hispanics-face-extra-challenges-in-getting-home-loans/. Accessed June 9, 2017.

Desmond, M., & Emirbayer, M. (2009). What is racial domination? *DuBois Review, 6,* 335–355.

DeSouza, R.-M. (2004, October). *In harm's way: Hurricanes, population trends, and environmental change* (PRB Report).

Washington, DC: Population Reference Bureau. www.prb.org. Accessed December 30, 2004.

Deutsch, K. W. (1966). *Nationalism and social communication.* Cambridge, MA: MIT Press.

Deutscher, G. (2010, August 29). You are what you speak. *The New York Times Magazine.*

Dewan, S. (2015, June 11). Poor, accused and punished by bail system. *The New York Times.*

Dey, J. G., & Hill, C. (2007). *Behind the pay gap.* Washington, DC: American Association of University Women Educational Foundation. www.aauw.org. Accessed April 1, 2007.

Diamond, J. (2005). *How societies choose to succeed or fail.* New York, NY: Viking.

Dickerson, C. (2015, June 22). *Secret World War II chemical experiments tested troops by race.* National Public Radio. www.npr.org/2015/6/22/415194765/u-x-troop-tested-by-race-in-secret-world-war-ii-chemical-experiments. Accessed June 23, 2015.

Diekman, A. B., & Murnen, S. K. (2004). Learning to be little women and little men: The inequitable gender equality of nonsexist children's literature. *Sex Roles, 50,* 373–385.

Diekmann, A., & Engelhardt, H. (1999). The social inheritance of divorce: Effects of parent's family type in postwar Germany. *American Sociological Review, 64,* 78–93.

Digital Insights. (2014). *Social media 2014 statistics—An interactive infographic you've been waiting for!* blog. digitalinsights.in/social-media-users-2014-stats-numbers/05205287.html. Accessed January 15, 2015.

Diller, L. H. (1998). *Running on Ritalin.* New York, NY: Bantam Books.

Dillon, S. (2011, July 6). Saving money means less time for school. *The New York Times.*

DiMaggio, P. J., & Powell, W. W. (1983). The iron cage revisited: Institutional isomorphism and collective rationality in organizational fields. *American Sociological Review, 48,* 147–160.

DiMaggio, P. J., & Powell, W. W. (1991). Introduction. In W. W. Powell & P. J. DiMaggio (Eds.), *The new institutionalism in organizational analysis.* Chicago, IL: University of Chicago Press.

Dion, K., Berscheid, E., & Walster, E. (1972). What is beautiful is good. *Journal of Personality and Social Psychology, 24,* 285–290.

Division for the Advancement of Women. (2009). *Convention on the elimination of all forms of discrimination* against women: Overview of the convention. New York, NY: Author. www.un.org/womenwatch/daw/cedaw/. Accessed June 4, 2009.

Dixon, T. L., & Linz, D. (2000). Race and the misrepresentation of victimization on local television news. *Communication Research, 27,* 547–573.

Dobash, R. E., & Dobash, R. P. (1979). *Violence against wives: A case against the patriarchy.* New York, NY: Free Press.

Dobie, K. (2016, January 10). To catch a rapist. *The New York Times Magazine.*

Do fines ever make corporations change? (2010, September 13). *Newsweek.*

Dokoupil, T. (2011, June 6). Mad as hell. *Newsweek.*

Dokoupil, T. (2012, July 16). Is the onslaught making us crazy? *Newsweek.*

Doleac, J. L. (2017). *New evidence that lead exposure increases crime.* The Brookings Institution. www.brookings.edu/blog/up-front/2017/06/01/new-evidence-that-lead-exposure-increases-crime/. Accessed June 11, 2017.

Domhoff, G. W. (1983). *Who rules America now? A view from the eighties.* Englewood Cliffs, NJ: Prentice Hall.

Domhoff, G. W. (1998). *Who rules America? Power and politics in the year 2000.* Mountain View, CA: Mayfield.

Domino's. (2016). *Domino's 101: Basic facts.* biz.dominos.com/web/public/about-dominos/fun-facts. Accessed January 1, 2017.

Dominus, S. (2004, February 22). Life in the age of old, old age. *The New York Times Magazine.*

Donadio, R. (2010a, April 5). Comments by cardinal on sexuality create a stir. *The New York Times.*

Donadio, R. (2010b, April 30). In abuse crisis, a church is pitted against society and itself. *The New York Times.*

Dorak, M. T., & Karpuzoglu, E. (2012, November 28). Gender differences in cancer susceptibility: An inadequately addressed issue. *Frontiers in Genetics.* www.ncbi.nim.nih.gov/pmc/articles/PMC3508426/. Accessed June 10, 2015.

Dougherty, C. (2015, July 12). Put down the phone. *The New York Times.*

Doyle, J. M., & Kao, G. (2007). Are racial identities of multiracials stable? Changing self-identification among single and multiple race individuals. *Social Psychology Quarterly, 70,* 405–423.

Draper, R. (2014, November 30). In the company of men. *The New York Times Magazine.*

Drucker, S. (1996, March 10). Who is the best restaurateur in America? *The New York Times Magazine.*

Drug Enforcement Administration. (2015). *Federal trafficking penalties for Schedules I, II, III, IV, and V (except marijuana).* www.dea.gov/druginfo/ftp_chart1.pdf. Accessed January 25, 2015.

Drug Policy Alliance. (2015). *The federal drug control budget: New rhetoric, same failed drug war.* www.drugpolicy.org/sites/default/files/DPA_Fact_sheet_Drug_War_Budget_Feb2015.pdf. Accessed January 18, 2017.

Dube, A. (2013, November 30). The minimum we can do. *The New York Times.*

Dugger, C. W. (1996, February 29). Immigrant cultures raising issues of child punishment. *The New York Times.*

Dugger, C. W. (1999, April 25). India's poorest are becoming its loudest. *The New York Times.*

Dugger, C. W. (2004, December 28). Supermarket giants crush Central American farmers. *The New York Times.*

Duncan, G. J. (2007). School readiness and later achievement. *Developmental Psychology, 43,* 1428–1446.

Duncan, G. J., & Chase-Lansdale, P. L. (2001). For better and for worse: Welfare reform and the well-being of children and families. In G. J. Duncan & P. L. Chase-Lansdale (Eds.), *For better and for worse.* New York, NY: Russell Sage.

Durkheim, É. (1947). *The division of labor in society* (G. Simpson, Trans.). Glencoe, IL: Free Press. (Original work published 1893)

Durkheim, É. (1951). *Suicide.* New York, NY: Free Press. (Original work published 1897)

Durkheim, É. (1954). *The elementary forms of religious life* (J. Swain, Trans.). New York, NY: Free Press. (Original work published 1915)

Durkheim, É. (1958). *Rules of sociological method* (G. E. G. Catlin, Ed.; A. Solovay & J. H. Mueller, Trans.). Glencoe, IL: Free Press. (Original work published 1895)

Durkin, J. D. (2016, August 11). New poll shows that 41% of Republicans STILL don't think Obama ws born in the U.S. *Mediaite.* www.mediaite.com/online/new-poll-shows-that-41-of-republicans-still-dont-think-obama-was-born-in-the-u-s/. Accessed December 28, 2016.

Durose, M. R., Cooper, A. D., & Snyder, H. N. (2014). *Recidivism of prisoners released in 30 states in 2005: Patterns from 2005 to 2010.* NCJ244205. U.S. Bureau of Justice Statistics. www.bjs.gov/content/pub/pdf/rprts05p5010.pdf. Accessed January 21, 2015.

Dye, J. L. (2008). *Fertility of American women: 2006* (U.S. Census Bureau, Current Population Reports, P20-558). www.census.gov/prod/2008pubs/p20-558.pdf. Accessed September 4, 2009.

Dynarski, S. (2015, June 2). For poor, getting to college is only half the battle. *The New York Times.*

Dzimiri, C. (2014). Marry the girl next door (endogamy). *Journal of Humanities and Social Science, 19,* 114–118.

Eagly, A. H., & Karau, S. J. (2002). Role congruity theory of prejudice toward female leaders. *Psychology Review, 109,* 573–598.

Eappen, S. (2013). Relationship between occurrence of surgical complications and hospital finances. *Journal of the American Medical Association, 309,* 1599–1606.

Eating Disorders Coalition. (2017). *Facts about eating disorders: What the research shows.* eatingdisorderscoalition. org.s208556.gridserver.com/couch.uploads/file/fact-sheet_2016.pdf. Accessed June 16, 2017.

Ebaugh, H. R. F. (1988). *Becoming an ex.* Chicago, IL: University of Chicago Press.

Eberhardt, J. L., Goff, P. A., Purdie, V. J., & Davies, P. G. (2004). Seeing black: Race, crime, and visual processing. *Journal of Personality and Social Psychology, 87,* 876–893.

Eckholm, E. (2011a, December 27). Battling anew over the place of religion in public schools. *The New York Times.*

Eckholm, E. (2011b, March 22). With few jobs, a single pastor points to a bias. *The New York Times.*

Eckholm, E. (2015a, June 27). Conservative lawmakers and religious groups seek exemptions after ruling. *The New York Times.*

Eckholm, E. (2015b, June 26). In a first, New Jersey jury says group selling gay cure committed fraud. *The New York Times.*

Eddy, M. (2013, January 19). German priests carried out sexual abuse for years. *The New York Times.*

Edelman, A. (2016, October 10). Donald Trump—who made and lost billions with help of millions in loans from rich daddy—claims he is a "blue collar worker." *Daily News.*

Edidin, P. (2005, March 6). How to shake hands or share a meal with an Iraqi. *The New York Times.*

Edney, J. J. (1979, August). Free riders en route to disaster. *Psychology Today,* 80–102.

Edney, J. J., & Harper, C. S. (1978). The commons dilemma: A review of contributions from psychology. *Environmental Management, 2,* 491–507.

Edwards, H. (1971, November). The sources of black athletic superiority. *The Black Scholar, 3,* 32–41.

Ehrenreich, B. (2002, June 30). Two-tiered morality. *The New York Times.*

Ehrenreich, B., & English, D. (1979). *For her own good: 150 years of the experts' advice to women.* Garden City, NY: Anchor Books.

Ehrlich, P. R., & Ehrlich, A. H. (1993). World population crisis. In K. Finsterbusch & J. S. Schwartz (Eds.), *Sources: Notable selections in sociology.* Guilford, CT: Dushkin.

Eisenberg, M. E., Wall, M., & Neumark-Sztainer, D. (2012). Muscle-enhancing behaviors among adolescent girls and boys. *Pediatrics, 130,* 1019–1026.

Eitzen, D. S., & Baca Zinn, M. (1991). *In conflict and order: Understanding society.* Boston, MA: Allyn & Bacon.

Elder, G. H., & Liker, J. K. (1982). Hard times in women's lives: Historical influences across 40 years. *American Journal of Sociology, 88,* 241–269.

Eligon, J. (2013, July 17). Florida case spurs painful talks between black parents and children. *The New York Times.*

Eligon, J. (2017, May 3). Praise for victim prompts a debate. *The New York Times.*

Eligon, J., & Gebeloff, R. (2016, August 20). Affluent and black and still trapped by segregation. *The New York Times.*

Eliot, L. (2010). *Pink brain, blue brain: How small differences grow into troublesome gaps and what we can do about it.* New York, NY: Mariner Books.

Elliott, C. (2003, June). American bioscience meets the American dream. *The American Prospect.*

Elliott, D., & Simmons, T. (2011). *Marital events of Americans: 2009.* (U.S. Bureau of the Census, American Community Survey Report ACS-13). www.census.gov/prod/2011pubs/acs-13.pdf. Accessed September 4, 2011.

Ellison, J. (2011, April 11). The military's secret shame. *Newsweek.*

Emont, J. (2017, May 18). In Indonesia, 2 men are sentenced to public lashing for homosexuality. *The New York Times.*

Enck, P., & Häuser, W. (2012, August 12). Beware the nocebo effect. *The New York Times.*

England, P. (2010). The gender revolution: Uneven and stalled. *Gender & Society, 24,* 149–166.

England, P., & Thomas, R. J. (2007). The decline of the date and the rise of the college hook-up. In A. S. Skolnick & J. H. Skolnick (Eds.), *Family in transition.* Boston, MA: Allyn & Bacon.

Enloe, C. (1993). *The morning after: Sexual politics at the end of the cold war*. Berkeley: University of California Press.

Entine, J. (2000). *Taboo: Why black athletes dominate sports and why we're afraid to talk about it*. New York, NY: PublicAffairs.

Epstein, C. F. (1989). Workplace boundaries: Conceptions and creations. *Social Research, 56,* 571–590.

Epstein, R., Blake, J. J., & González, T. (2017). *Girlhood interrupted: The erasure of black girls' childhood*. Center on Poverty and Inequality. www.law.georgetown.edu/academics/centers-institutes/poverty-inequality/upload/girlhood-interrupted.pdf. Accessed July 10, 2017.

Equality Now. (2017). *Sex trafficking fact sheet*. www.equalitynow.org/sites/default/files/Sex Trafficking Fact Sheet.pdf. Accessed May 24, 2017.

Erdely, S. R. (2012, February 4). One town's war on gay teens. *Reader Supported News*. Readersupportednews.org/news-section2/328-121/9792-one-towns-war-on-gay-teens. Accessed February 5, 2012.

Erikson, K. (1966). *Wayward Puritans*. New York, NY: Wiley.

Erlanger, S. (2000, April 2). Across a new Europe, a people deemed unfit for tolerance. *The New York Times*.

Erlanger, S. (2010, August 19). France intensifies effort to expel Roma, raising questions. *The New York Times*.

Eurostat. (2016a). *File: Crude divorce rate, selected years, 1960-2014*. Ec.europa.eu/ehavior/statistics-explained/index.php/File:crude_divorce_rate,_selected_years,_1960-2014_(¹)_(per_1_000_inhabitants)_YB16.png. Accessed January 15, 2017.

Eurostat. (2016b). *Pupils learning English*. Ec.europa.eu/Eurostat/tgm/table.do?tab=table&plugin=1&language=en&pcode=tps00057. Accessed January 2, 2017.

Evans, L., & Davies, K. (2000). No sissy boys here: A content analysis of the representation of masculinity in elementary school reading textbooks. *Sex Roles, 42,* 255–270.

Evans, T., & Nichols, M. (2009, March 22). Waiting for help in Indy. *The Indianapolis Star*.

Evans-Pritchard, E. E. (1937). *Witchcraft, oracles and magic among the Azande*. Oxford, UK: Oxford University Press.

Evered, R. (1983). The language of organizations: The case of the Navy. In L. R. Pondy, P. J. Frost, G. Morgan, & T. C. Dandridge (Eds.), *Organizational symbolism*. Greenwich, CT: JAI Press.

Fackler, M. (2011, March 24). Severed from the world, villagers survive on tight bonds and to-do lists. *The New York Times*.

Fairlie, R. W. (2012). *Immigrant entrepreneurs and small business owners, and their access to financial capital*. Small Business Administration. www.sba.gov/sites/default/files/rs396tot.pdf. Accessed July 3, 2013.

Falcone, M. (2009, February 13). 100,000 parents of citizens were deported over 10 years. *The New York Times*.

Faleiro, S. (2013, January 2). The unspeakable truth about rape in India. *The New York Times*.

Faludi, S. (1991). *Backlash: The undeclared war against women*. New York, NY: Crown.

Family of VCJD victim claim untried treatment is a success. (2003). *Vegsource Newsletter*. www.vegsource.com/talk/madcow/messages/422.html. Accessed June 30, 2003.

Farb, P. (1983). *Word play: What happens when people talk*. New York, NY: Bantam Books.

Farley, J. (1982). *Majority-minority relations*. Englewood Cliffs, NJ: Prentice Hall.

Farley, R. (2002). *Identifying with multiple races: A social movement that succeeded but failed?* (Population Studies Center Research Report No. 01-491). Ann Arbor: University of Michigan, Institute for Social Research.

Farmer, R. (2002, Spring). Same sex couples face post–September 11 discrimination. *National NOW Times*.

Farrar, L. (2010). Chinese companies "rent" white foreigners. *CNN Online*. www.cnn.com/2010/BUSINESS/06/29/china.rent.white.people/index.html. Accessed June 1, 2011.

Fausset, R., & Blinder, A. (2015, March 6). States weigh legislation to let businesses refuse to serve gay couples. *The New York Times*.

Fausto-Sterling, A. (1985). *Myths of gender: Biological theories about women and men*. New York, NY: Basic Books.

Feagin, J. R. (1975). *Subordinating the poor*. Englewood Cliffs, NJ: Prentice Hall.

Feagin, J. R., & McKinney, K. D. (2003). *The many costs of racism*. New York, NY: Rowman & Littlefield.

Feagin, J. R., & O'Brien, E. (2003). *White men on race: Power, privilege, and the shaping of cultural consciousness*. Boston, MA: Beacon Press.

Fearing demographic abyss, Putin promises mums more money. (2006, May 10). *Agence France Presse—English*.

Fears, D., & Deane, C. (2001, July 5). Biracial couples report tolerance. *The Washington Post*.

Federal Bureau of Investigation (2011). *Uniform crime report: Expanded homicide data*. ucr.fbi.gov/crime-in-the-u.s./crime-in-the-u.s.-2011/offenses-known-to-law-enforcement/expanded/expandhomicidemain.pdf. Accessed December 28, 2016.

Federal Bureau of Investigation. (2014). *Latest hate crime statistics report released.* www.fbi.gov/news/stories/2014/december/latest-hate-crime-statistics-report-released. Accessed June 9, 2015.

Federal Bureau of Investigation. (2017). *Historic sentencing for gang member who killed transgender woman.* www.fbi.org/news/stories/historic-hate-crime-sentencing. Accessed June 14, 2017.

Federal Communication Commission. (2013). *The dangers of texting while driving.* www.fcc.gov/guides/texting-while-driving. Accessed June 30, 2013.

Federal Highway Administration. (2016). *FWHA forecasts of vehicle miles traveled (VMT): Spring 2016.* www.fwha.dot.gov/policyinformation/tables/vmt/vmt_forecast_sum.pdf. Accessed January 1, 2017.

Federal Reserve. (2015). *Report on the economic well-being of U.S. households in 2014.* www.federalreserve.gov/econresdata/2014-report-economic-well-being-us-households-201505.pdf. Accessed May 30, 2015.

Fee, D. (2013). Covenant marriage: Reflexivity and retrenchment in the politics of intimacy. In D. Newman & J. O'Brien (Eds.), *Sociology: Exploring the architecture of everyday life (Readings).* Thousand Oaks, CA: Sage.

Feeding America. (2014). *Hunger in America—National Report.* help.feedingamerica.org/HungerInAmerica/hunger-in-america-2014-full-report.pdf. Accessed May 31, 2017.

Feldmann, L., Marlantes, L., & Bowers, F. (2003, March 14). The impact of Bush linking 9/11 and Iraq. *Christian Science Monitor.*

Felmlee, D., Sprecher, S., & Bassin, E. (1990). The dissolution of intimate relationships: A hazard model. *Social Psychology Quarterly, 53,* 13–30.

Fendrich, J. M. (2003). The forgotten movement: The Vietnam antiwar movement. *Sociological Inquiry, 73,* 338–358.

Ferree, M. M. (1992). The political context of rationality. In A. D. Morris & C. M. Mueller (Eds.), *Frontiers in social movement theory.* New Haven, CT: Yale University Press.

Festinger, L., Riecken, H., & Schacter, S. (1956). *When prophecy fails.* New York, NY: Harper & Row.

Fiese, B. H., & Skillman, G. (2000). Gender differences in family stories: Moderating influence of parent gender role and child gender. *Sex Roles, 43*(5/6), 267–283.

Figert, A. (1996). *Women and the ownership of PMS.* New York, NY: Aldine de Gruyter.

Filkins, D. (2016, May 13). "Do not resist" and the crisis of police militarization. *The New Yorker Online.* www.newyorker.com/news/news-desk/do-not-resist-and-the-crisis-of-police-militarization. Accessed December 28, 2016.

Fincham, F., & Bradbury, T. N. (1987). The impact of attributions in marriage: A longitudinal analysis. *Journal of Personality and Social Psychology, 53,* 510–517.

FindLaw.com. 2016. *Parental liability.* family.findlaw.com/parental-rights-and-liability/parental-liability.html. Accessed December 27, 2016.

Fine, C. (2010). *Delusions of gender: How our minds, society, and neurosexism create difference.* New York, NY: Norton.

Finer, J. (2005, August 12). The new Ernie Pyles: Sgtlizzie and 67shdocs. *The Washington Post.*

Fingerhut, H. (2016). *Support steady for same-sex marriage and acceptance of homosexuality.* Pew Research Center. www.pewresearch.org/fact-tank/2016/05/12/support-steady-for-same-sex-marriage-and-acceptance-of-homosexuality/. Accessed January 16, 2017.

Finn, P. J. (2012). Preparing for power in elite boarding schools and in working-class schools. *Theory into Practice, 51,* 57–63.

First, A. (2011). 14 most outdated pieces of baby advice. *Parenting.* Shine.yahoo.com/channel/parenting/14-most-outdated-pieces-of-baby-advice-2554194. Accessed September 27, 2011.

Fish, S. (2000). The nifty nine arguments against affirmative action in higher education. *Journal of Blacks in Higher Education, 27,* 79–81.

Flaherty, J. (2014, January 15). In Louisiana's "cancer alley," growing sinkhole creates more concerns. *Al-Jazeera America.* america.aljazeera.com/watch/shows/america-tonight/america-tonight-blog/2013/9/12/in-louisiana-s-canceralleyhugesinkholecreatesmoreconcerns.html. Accessed July 18, 2017.

Flores, A.R., & Barclay, S. (2013). *Public support for marriage for same-sex couples by state.* The Williams Institute. www.williamsinstitute.law.ucla.edu/research/marriage-and-couples-rights/public-support-for-marriage-for-same-sex-couples-by-state. Accessed June 25, 2014.

Flynn, J. (1999). Searching for justice: The discovery of IQ gains over time. *American Psychologist, 54,* 5–20.

Folbre, N., & Yoon, J. (2006, January 5). *The value of unpaid child care in the U.S. in 2003.* Paper presented at the meeting of the Allied Social Science Association, Boston, MA. (Cited with permission of author)

Foley, E. (2014, June 25). Deportation separated thousands of U.S.-born children from parents in 2013. *Huffington Post Politics*. www.huffingtonpost.com/2014/06/25/parents-deportation_n_5531552.html. Accessed June 22, 2015.

Food and Drug Administration. (2015). *Expanded access (compassionate use)*. www.fda.gov/NewsEvents/PublicHealthFocus/ExpandedAccessCompassionateUse/default.html. Accessed June 28, 2015.

Forbes Magazine. (2015). America's most promising companies—#22 Nitro Circus. www.forbes.com/companies/nitro-circus/. Accessed June 22, 2015.

Forbes Magazine. (2017). Celebrity 100. www.forbes.com/celebrities/#76da4f5c5947. Accessed May 24, 2017.

Forman, T. A., Williams, D., & Jackson, J. (1997). Race, place, and discrimination. *Perspectives on Social Problems, 9*, 231–261.

Foroohar, R. (2010, April 26). The Burqa revolution. *Newsweek*.

Fortune. (2017). Global 500 2016. Fortune.com/global500/list. Accessed June 4, 2017.

Fountain, H. (2005, June). Unloved, but not unbuilt. *The New York Times*.

Fouts, G., & Burggraf, K. (2000). Television situation comedies: Female weight, male negative comments, and audience reactions. *Sex Roles, 42*, 925–932.

Fowler, J. H., & Christakis, N. A. (2008). Dynamic spread of happiness in a large social network: Longitudinal analysis over 20 years in the Framingham Heart Study. *British Medical Journal, 338*, 23–31.

Fox, J. A. (2012). *Intimate partner violence: Down but far from out*. Boston College. boston.com/community/blogs/crime_punishment/2012/ 11/intimate_partner_violence_down.html. Accessed January 16, 2013.

Frank, A. G. (1969). *Capitalism and under-development in Latin America*. New York, NY: Monthly Review Press.

Frank, T. A. (2013, June 27). Why liberals should oppose the immigration bill. *The New Republic*. www.newrepublic.com/article/113651/liberal-opposes-immigration-reform. Accessed June 21, 2015.

Franke-Ruta, G. (2013, July 16). Listening in on "the talk": What Eric Holder told his son about Trayvon. *The Atlantic*.

Frankel, J. (2016, December 2). Reading literature won't give you super powers." *The Atlantic*.

Frankel, T. C. (2016, December 19). Tossed aside in the "white gold rush." *Washington Post*.

Frankenberg, E. (2006). *The segregation of American teachers*. Cambridge, MA: Civil Rights Project at Harvard University.

Franklin, D. (2006, August 15). Patient power: Making sure your doctor really hears you. *The New York Times*.

Franklin, J. (2010, September 9). Chilean miners: A typical day in the life of a subterranean miner. *The Guardian*.

Free Press. (2016). *Wave of mergers map*. www.freepress.nat/wave-mergers-map. Accessed December 28, 2016.

Freedom to Marry. (2014). *The freedom to marry internationally*. www.freedomtomarry.org/landscape/entry/c/international. Accessed June 24, 2014.

Freiberg, P. (1991). Self-esteem gender gap widens in adolescence. *APA Monitor, 22*, 29.

French, H. W. (1999, November 15). "Japanese only" policy takes body blow in court. *The New York Times*.

French, H. W. (2000, May 3). Japan unsettles returnees, who yearn to leave again. *The New York Times*.

French, H. W. (2007, March 22). China scrambles for stability as its workers age. *The New York Times*.

Freund, P. E. S., & McGuire, M. B. (1991). *Health, illness, and the social body: A cultural sociology*. Englewood Cliffs, NJ: Prentice Hall.

Friedman, B. (2012, January 28). Privacy, technology and law. *The New York Times*.

Friedman, H. L. (2015). Tiger girls on the soccer field. In D. M. Newman, J. O'Brien, & M. Robertson (Eds.), *Sociology: Exploring the architecture of everyday life (Readings)*. Thousand Oaks, CA: Sage.

Friend, T. (2017, January 9). California dreamin'. *The New Yorker*.

Fry, R. (2016a). *For first time in modern era, living with parents edges out other living arrangements for 18- to 34-year olds*. Pew Research Center. www.pewsocialtrends.org/2016/05/24/for-first-time-in-modern-era-living-with-parents-edges-out-other-living-arrangements-for-18-to-34-year-olds/. Accessed January 8, 2017.

Fry, R. (2016b). *Millennials overtake Baby Boomers as America's largest generation*. Pew Research Center. www.pewresearch.org/fact-tank/2016/04/256/millennials-overtake-baby-boomers/. Accessed June 21, 2017.

Fry, R. (2017). *It's becoming more common for young adults to live at home—and for longer stretches*. Pew Research Center. www.pewresearch.org/fact-tank/2017/05/05/its-becoming-more-common-for-young-adults-to-live-at-home-and-for-longer-stretches/. Accessed June 23, 2017.

Fryer, R. G. (2006, Winter). "Acting white": The social price paid by the best and brightest minority students. *Education Next,* pp. 53–59.

Furstenberg, F. F. (2011). Diverging development: The not-so-invisible hand of social class in the United States. In S. Ferguson (Ed.), *Shifting the center.* New York, NY: McGraw-Hill.

Furstenberg, F. F., & Harris, K. M. (1992). The disappearing American father? Divorce and the waning significance of biological parenthood. In S. J. South & S. E. Tolnay (Eds.), *The changing American family: Sociological and demographic perspectives.* Boulder, CO: Westview Press.

Fustos, K. (2010a, June). *Marriage and partnership turnover for American families.* Population Reference Bureau. http://www.prb.org/Articles/2010/usmarriagepolicyseminar.aspx. Accessed August 28, 2011.

Fustos, K. (2010b). *Marriage benefits men's health.* Population Reference Bureau. www.prb.org/Articles/2010/usmarriagemenshealth.aspx? P=1. Accessed June 5, 2011.

Fuwa, M. (2004). Macro-level gender inequality and the division of household labor in 22 countries. *American Sociological Review, 69,* 751–767.

Gabriel, T. (2010, July 6). To stop cheats, colleges learn their trickery. *The New York Times.*

Gaines, C. (2016, September 15). The 32 NFL teams are worth as much as every MLB and NBA team combined. *Business Insider.* www.businessinsider.com/nfl-teams-value-2016-9. Accessed December 27, 2016.

Gale, R. P. (1986). Social movements and the state: The environmental movement, countermovement and governmental agencies. *Sociological Perspectives, 29,* 202–240.

Galles, G. M. (1989, June 8). What colleges really teach. *The New York Times.*

Galliher, J. M., & Galliher, J. F. (2002). A "commonsense" theory of deterrence and the "ideology" of science: The New York State death penalty debate. *Journal of Criminal Law and Criminology, 92,* 307–333.

Gallup. (2014). *One-fifth of Americans worry about getting Ebola.* www.gallup.com/poll/178097/one-fifth-americans-worry-getting-ebola.aspx?version=print. Accessed January 4, 2015.

Gamson, W. A., Fireman, B., & Rytina, S. (1982). *Encounters with unjust authority.* Homewood, IL: Dorsey Press.

Gamson, W. A., & Wolfsfeld, G. (1993). Movements and media as interactive systems. *Annals of the American Academy of Political and Social Science, 528,* 114–125.

Gans, H. (1971, July/August). The uses of poverty: The poor pay for all. *Social Policy,* 20–24.

Gans, H. (1996). Positive functions of the undeserving poor: Uses of the underclass in America. In J. Levin & A. Arluke (Eds.), *Snapshots and portraits of society.* Thousand Oaks, CA: Pine Forge Press.

Gans, H. (2005). Race as class. *Contexts, 4,* 17–21.

Gao, G. (2015). *Why the former USSR has far fewer men than women.* Pew Research Center. www.pewresearch.org/fact-tank/2015/08/14/why-the-former-ussr-has-far-fewer-men-than-women/. Accessed January 10, 2017.

García, J. L., Heckman, J. J., Leaf, D. E., & Prados, M. J. (2016). *The life-cycle benefits of an influential early childhood program.* National Bureau of Economic Research, NBER Working paper #22993. www.nber.org/papers/w22993. Accessed May 22, 2017.

Garcia, M. (2014, April 30). Brunei phasing in antigay law; will soon allow death by stoning. *The Advocate.*

Garcia-Moreno, C., Jansen, H., Ellsberg, M., Heise, L., & Watts, C. H. (2006). Prevalence of intimate partner violence: Findings from the WHO multi-country study on women's health and domestic violence. *Lancet, 368,* 1260–1269.

Gardner, G. (2005, March/April). Yours, mine, ours—or nobody's? *World Watch.*

Gardner, P. (2007). *Parent involvement in the college recruiting process: To what extent?* Collegiate Employment Research Institute Research Brief 2-2007. ceri.msu.edu/publications/pdf/ceri2-07.pdf. Accessed June 23, 2017.

Garfinkel, J. (2003, February 24). Boutique medical practices face legal, legislative foes. *Cincinnati Business Courier.* www.bizjournals.com/cincinnati/stories/2003/02/24/focus2.html. Accessed July 12, 2004.

Garner, B. A. (2010, February 28). Webinar: What makes for a successful mash-up neologism. *The New York Times Magazine.*

Garrison, L. T. (2012). *6 modern societies where women rule.* Mental Floss. Mentalfloss.com/article/31274/6-modern-societies-where-women-literally-rule. Accessed June 13, 2017.

Garsd, J. (2015, March 4). *Is fighting racism in soccer "a lost cause?" FIFA president says no.* National Public Radio. www.npr.org/sections-the two-way/2015/03/04/390707630/is-fighting-racism-in-soccer-a-lost-cause-fifa-president-says-no. Accessed June 6, 2015.

Garson, B. (1988). *The electronic sweatshop.* New York, NY: Penguin Books.

Gates, H. L. (2007, November 18). Forty acres and a gap in wealth. *The New York Times.*

GBD 2015 Healthcare Access and Quality Collaborators. (2017, May 18). Healthcare access and quality index based on mortality from causes amenable to personal health care in 195 countries and territories, 1990-2015: A novel analysis from the Global Burden of Disease Study 2015. *The Lancet Online*. www.thelancet.com/pdfs/journals/lancet/PIIS0140-6736(17)30818-8.pdf. Accessed May 23, 2017.

Geena Davis Institute on Gender in Media. (2012). *Research facts*. www.seejane.org/research. Accessed January 9, 2013.

Geena Davis Institute on Gender in Media. (2014). *Gender bias without borders*. www.seejane.org/wp-content/uploads/gender-bias-without-borders-executive-summary.pdf. Accessed January 12, 2015.

Geena Davis Institute on Gender in Media. (2016). *The real truth: Women aren't seen or heard*. seejane.org/research-informs-empowers/data/. Accessed January 6, 2017.

Gelles, R. J., & Straus, M. A. (1988). *Intimate violence*. Newbury Park, CA: Sage.

Gentleman, A. (2007, June 3). Indian shepherds stoop to conquer caste system. *The New York Times*.

Gergen, K. J. (1991). *The saturated self*. New York, NY: Basic Books.

Gerlach, P., & Hine, V. H. (1970). *People, power, change: Movements of social transformation*. Indianapolis, IN: Bobbs-Merrill.

Getahun, D., Jacobsen, S. J., Fassett, M. J., Chen, W., Demissie, K., & Rhoads, G. G. (2013). Recent trends in childhood Attention-Deficit/Hyperactivity Disorder. *JAMA Pediatrics, January 21,* E1–E7.

Getlin, J., & Wilkinson, T. (2003, April 3). "Embedded" reporters are mixed blessing for the military. *The Seattle Times*.

Gettleman, J. (2011, December 28). For Somali women, pain of being a spoil of war. *The New York Times*.

Giddens, A. (1984). *The construction of society: Outline of the theory of structuration*. Berkeley: University of California Press.

Giddens, A. (2005). The global revolution in family and personal life. In A. S. Skolnick & J. H. Skolnick (Eds.), *Family in transition*. Boston, MA: Allyn & Bacon.

Gilbert, D. L. (2015). *The American Class Structure in an Age of Growing Inequality,* 9th ed. Thousand Oaks, CA: Sage.

Gillen, B. (1981). Physical attractiveness: A determinant of two types of goodness. *Personality and Social Psychology Bulletin, 7,* 277–281.

Gilligan, C. (1990). Teaching Shakespeare's sister: Notes from the underground of female adolescence. In C. Gilligan, N. P. Lyons, & T. J. Hanmer (Eds.), *Making connections*. Cambridge, MA: Harvard University Press.

Gilman, S. (2004). *Fat boys*. Lincoln: University of Nebraska Press.

Ginzel, L. E., Kramer, R. M., & Sutton, R. I. (2004). Organizational impression management as a reciprocal influence process: The neglected role of the organizational audience. In M. J. Hatch & M. Schultz (Eds.), *Organizational identity*. New York, NY: Oxford University Press.

Giridharadas, A. (2010, April 11). Where a cellphone is still cutting edge. *The New York Times*.

Gitlin, T. (1979). Prime time ideology: The hegemonic process in television entertainment. *Social Problems, 26,* 251–266.

Gittleson, B. (2016, April 15). John Kasich advises female student not to "go to parties where there's a lot of alcohol." *ABC News*. Abcnews.go.com/Politics/john-kasich-advises-female-student-parties-lot-alcohol/story?id=38429352. Accessed June 15, 2017.

GiveDirectly. (2016). *Research on cash transfers*. www.givedirectly.org/research-on-cash-transfers. Accessed January 2, 2017.

Gladstone, B. (2017). *The trouble with reality: A rumination on moral panic in our time*. New York, NY: Workman.

Gladwell, M. (2010, October 4). Small change. *The New Yorker*.

Glaeser, E., & Vigdor, J. (2012). *The end of the segregated century: Racial separation in America's neighborhoods, 1890–2010*. Manhattan Institute for Policy Research. Civic Report #66. www.manhattan-institute.org/html/cr_66.htm. Accessed June 14, 2013.

Glater, J. D. (2006, December 3). Straight "A" students? Good luck making partner. *The New York Times*.

Glick, P., & Fiske, S. T. (1996). The ambivalent sexism inventory: Differentiating hostile and benevolent sexism. *Journal of Personality and Social Psychology, 70,* 491–512.

Glynn, S. J. (2012). *The new breadwinners: 2010*. Center for American Progress. www.american progress.org/wp-content/uploads/issues/2012/04/pdf/breadwinners.pdf. Accessed January 16, 2013.

Godson, R., & Olson, W. J. (1995). International organized crime. *Society, 32,* 18–29.

Goffman, A. (2009). On the run: Wanted men in a Philadelphia ghetto. *American Sociological Review, 74,* 339–357.

Goffman, E. (1952). On cooling the mark out: Some aspects of adaptation to failure. *Psychiatry, 15,* 451–463.

Goffman, E. (1959). *The presentation of self in everyday life.* Garden City, NY: Doubleday.

Goffman, E. (1961). *Asylums.* Garden City, NY: Doubleday.

Goffman, E. (1963). *Stigma: Notes on the management of spoiled identity.* Englewood Cliffs, NJ: Prentice Hall.

Goffman, E. (1967). *Interaction ritual.* Chicago, IL: Aldine-Atherton.

Goldberg, S. (1999). The logic of patriarchy. *Gender Issues, 17,* 53–69.

Golden, L. (2016). *Still falling short on hours and pay.* Economic Policy Institute. www.epi.org/publications/still-falling-short-on-hours-and-pay-part-time-work-becoming-new-normal/. Accessed May 2, 2017.

Goldin, C. (2014). A grand gender convergence: Its last chapter. *American Economic Review, 104,* 1091–1119.

Goldin, C., & Katz, L. F. (2016). *Women working longer: Facts and some explanations.* National Bureau of Economic Research Working paper 22607. www.nber.org/papers/w22607.pdf. Accessed June 21, 2017.

Goldsmith, R. E. (2016). The big five, happiness, and shopping. *Journal of Retailing and Consumer Services, 31,* 52–61.

Goldstein, J. (2013, August 18). The crazy cash-giveaway experiment. *The New York Times Magazine.*

Goleman, D. (1989, October 10). Sensing silent cues emerges as key skill. *The New York Times.*

Goleman, D. (1990, December 25). The group and the self: New focus on a cultural rift. *The New York Times.*

Goleman, D. (1993, May 4). Therapists find some patients are just hateful. *The New York Times.*

Goleman, D. (2013, October 5). Rich people just care less. *The New York Times.*

Golway, T. (2004, August 2–9). Redrafting America. *America.*

Goode, Erica. (1999, January 12). Pediatricians renew battle over toilet training. *The New York Times.*

Goode, Erica. (2011, May 21). States seeking new registries for criminals. *The New York Times.*

Goode, Erica. (2012, March 22). Stronger hand for judges in the "bazaar" of plea deals. *The New York Times.*

Goode, Erich. (1989). *Drugs in American society.* New York, NY: McGraw-Hill.

Goode, Erich. (1994). *Deviant behavior.* Englewood Cliffs, NJ: Prentice Hall.

Goode, W. J. (1971). World revolution and family patterns. *Journal of Marriage and the Family, 33,* 624–635.

Goodman, J. C. (2005). *Aid to Katrina victims: A right/left consensus.* Dallas, TX: National Center for Policy Analysis. www.ncpa.org/pub/ba529. Accessed May 23, 2009.

Goodnough, A., & Atkinson, S. (2016, May 1). A potent side effect of the Flint water crisis: Mental health problems. *The New York Times.*

Goodstein, L. (2003, September 11). Survey finds slight rise in Jews' intermarrying. *The New York Times.*

Goodstein, L. (2009, April 3). Early alarm for church on abusers in the clergy. *The New York Times.*

Goodstein, L. (2013, October 1). Poll shows major shift in identity of U.S. Jews. *The New York Times.*

Goodstein, L. (2014a, December 7). In seven states, atheists push to end largely forgotten ban. *The New York Times.*

Goodstein, L. (2014b, June 20). Presbyterians vote to allow same-sex marriages. *The New York Times.*

Goodstein, L., & Eckholm, E. (2012, June 14). Church battles efforts to ease sex abuse suits. *The New York Times.*

Gootman, E. (2006, October 19). Those preschoolers are looking older. *The New York Times.*

Gorbis, E., & Kholodenko, Y. (2005, September 1). Plastic surgery addiction in patients with body dysmorphic disorder. *Psychiatric Times.*

Gordon, I., & Raja, T. (2012, March/April). 164 anti-immigration laws passed since 2010? A MoJo analysis. *Mother Jones.* www.motherjones.com/politics/2012/03/anti-immigration-law-database#database. Accessed June 19, 2015.

Gordon, M. M. (1964). *Assimilation in American life.* New York, NY: Oxford University Press.

Gordon, R. G. (2005). *Ethnologue: Languages of the world* (15th ed.). Dallas, TX: SIL International.

Gould, E., Schieder, J., & Geier, K. (2016). *What is the gender pay gap and is it real?* Economic Policy Institute. www.epi.org/publication/what-is-the-gender-pay-gap-and-is-it-real/#epi-toc-13. Accessed June 20, 2017.

Gould, S. J. (1981). *The mismeasure of man.* New York, NY: Norton.

Gould, S. J. (1997, June). Dolly's fashion and Louis's passion. *Natural History.*

Gove, W., Hughes, M., & Geerkin, M. R. (1980). Playing dumb: A form of impression management with undesirable effects. *Social Psychology Quarterly, 43,* 89–102.

Gove, W., Style, C. B., & Hughes, M. (1990). The effect of marriage on the well-being of adults. *Journal of Family Issues, 11*, 34–35.

Government Accountability Office. (2016). *K-12 education: Better use of information could help agencies identify disparities and address racial discrimination.* www.gao.gov/assets/680/676745.pdf. Accessed June 12, 2017.

Governors Highway Safety Association. (2016). *Distracted driving.* www.ghsa.org/issues/distracted-driving. Accessed July 13, 2017.

Gracey, H. L. (1991). Learning the student role: Kindergarten as academic boot camp. In J. Henslin (Ed.), *Down-to-earth sociology.* New York, NY: Free Press.

Grady, D. (2008, December 4). Parents torn over extra frozen embryos from fertility procedures. *The New York Times.*

Grady, D. (2009, May 24). Where life's start is a deadly risk. *The New York Times.*

Grady, D. (2013, January 16). When pills fail, this, er, option provides a cure. *The New York Times.*

Graham, L. O. (1999). Our kind of people: Inside America's black upper class. New York, NY: HarperCollins.

Grant, A. (2015, September 6). Friends at work? *The New York Times.*

Green, J. P. (2015, March 11). Working class discontent limned in new poll. *The Democratic Strategist.* Thedemocraticstrategist.org/2015/03/working_class_discontent_limned/. Accessed May 31, 2017.

Greenblatt, A. (2011). Aging population. *CQ Researcher, 21*, 577–600.

Greencastle Banner Graphic. (1992, March 7). [Letter to the editor].

Greene, M. F. (2004, November 28). Sandlot summer: Hyperscheduled, overachieving children learn how to play. *The New York Times Magazine.*

Greenhouse, L. (2007, June 29). Justices, 5–4, limit use of race for school integration plans. *The New York Times.*

Greenhouse, S. (2006, July 14). On dusty corner, laborers band together for more pay. *The New York Times.*

Greenhouse, S. (2009, May 16). Bill would guarantee up to 7 paid sick days. *The New York Times.*

Greenhouse, S. (2011, May 21). Sexual affronts a known hotel hazard. *The New York Times.*

Greenhouse, S. (2014, May 14). The age premium: Retaining older workers. *The New York Times.*

Greenhouse, S. (2015, July 4). Protests and progress on farmworker wages. *The New York Times.*

Greenhouse, S. (2016, April 3). $15 an hour? It's no longer crazy. *The New York Times.*

Greenwood, S., Perrin, A., & Duggan, M. (2016). *Social media update 2016.* Pew Research Center. www.pewinternet.org/2016/11/11/social-media-update-2016/. Accessed January 6, 2017.

Grieco, E. M., Acosta, Y. D., de la Cruz, G. P., Gambino, C., Gryn, T., Larsen, L. J., . . . Walters, N. P. (2012). *The foreign-born population in the United States: 2010.* ACS-19. U.S. Bureau of the Census. www.census.gov/prod/2012pubs/acs-19.pdf. Accessed June 17, 2015.

Griffin, S. (1986). *Rape: The power of consciousness.* New York, NY: Harper & Row.

Griffin, S. (1989). Rape: The all-American crime. In L. Richardson & V. Taylor (Eds.), *Feminist frontiers II.* New York, NY: Random House.

Griswold, W. (1994). *Cultures and societies in a changing world.* Thousand Oaks, CA: Pine Forge Press.

Gross, E., & Etzioni, A. (1985). *Organizations and society.* Englewood Cliffs, NJ: Prentice Hall.

Gross, E., & Stone, G. P. (1964). Embarrassment and the analysis of role requirements. *American Journal of Sociology, 70*, 1–15.

Gross, J. (2004a, February 24). Older women team up to face future together. *The New York Times.*

Gross, J. (2004b, May 31). Splitting up boys and girls, just for the tough years. *The New York Times.*

Gross, J. (2006, July 16). Checklist for camp: Bug spray. Sunscreen. Pills. *The New York Times.*

Gross National Happiness (2015). *Bhutan GNH Index.* www.grossnationalhappiness.com/articles/. Accessed January 7, 2015.

Grossbard, L. (2011, June 5). Does Twitter make you stupid? *The New York Times.*

The Guardian. (2016, January 24). IOC rules transgender athletes can take part in Olympics without surgery. *The Guardian.* www.theguardian.com/sport/2016/jan/25/IOC-rules-transgender-athletes-can-take-part-in-olympics-without-surgery. Accessed January 2, 2017.

Gunnell, J. J., & Ceci, S. J. (2010). When emotionality trumps reason: A study of individual processing style and juror bias. *Behavioral Sciences and the Law, 28*, 850–877.

Guttmacher Institute. (2017). *An overview of abortion laws*. www.guttmacher.org/state-policy/explore/overview-abortion-laws. Accessed June 28, 2017.

Hacker, A. (1992). Two nations: Black and white, separate, hostile, unequal. New York, NY: Scribner.

Hacker, A. (1994, October 31). White on white. *The New Republic*.

Hafferty, F. W. (1991). *Into the valley: Death and socialization of medical students*. New Haven, CT: Yale University Press.

Hagan, J. (1985). *Modern criminology: Crime, criminal behavior and its control*. New York, NY: McGraw-Hill.

Hagan, J. (2000). The poverty of a classless criminology: The American Society of Criminology 1991 presidential address. In R. D. Crutchfield, G. S. Bridges, J. G. Weis, & C. Kubrin (Eds.), *Crime readings*. Thousand Oaks, CA: Pine Forge Press.

Hagerty, B. B. (2011, May 23). Doomsday believers cope with an intact world. *NPR Online*. www.npr.org/2011/05/23/136560695/doomsday-believers-cope-with-an-intact-world. Accessed May 23, 2011.

Haider, A. H., Schneider, E. B., Kodadek, L. M., Adler, R. R., Ranjit, A., Torain, M., . . . Lau, B. D. (2017). Emergency department query for patient-centered approaches to sexual orientation and gender identity. *JAMA Internal Medicine, 177,* 819–828.

Hakim, D. (2015a, April 9). New topic in Europe's sex-ed classrooms: Making more babies. *The New York Times*.

Hakim, D. (2015b, July 1). U.S. chamber travels the world, fighting curbs on smoking. *The New York Times*.

Hall, P. (1990). The presidency and impression management. In J. W. Heeren & M. Mason (Eds.), *Sociology: Windows on society*. Los Angeles, CA: Roxbury.

Hall, W. (1986). Social class and survival on the *S.S. Titanic*. *Social Science and Medicine, 22,* 687–690.

Hallin, D. C. (1986). We keep America on top of the world. In T. Gitlin (Ed.), *Watching television*. New York, NY: Pantheon Books.

Hamilton, C., Anderson, K., Barnes, R., & Dorling, K. (2011). *Administrative detention of children: A global report*. UNICEF. www.unicef.org/protection/files/Administrative_detention_discussion_paper_April2011.pdf. Accessed June 29, 2011.

Hamilton, D., Goldsmith, A. H., & Darity, W. (2008). *Shedding "light" on marriage: The influence of skin shade on marriage for black females*. Globalisation and Development Centre Working Paper #16. Epublications.bond.edu.au/cgi/viewcontent.cgi?artivle=1015&context=gdc. Accessed June 10, 2014.

Hamilton, D. L. (1981). *Cognitive processes in stereotyping and intergroup behavior*. Hillsdale, NJ: Erlbaum.

Hamilton, J. A. (1996). Women and health policy: On the inclusion of women in clinical trials. In C. F. Sargent & C. B. Brettell (Eds.), *Gender and health: An international perspective*. Upper Saddle River, NJ: Prentice Hall.

Hamilton, V. L., & Sanders, J. (1995). Crimes of obedience and conformity in the workplace: Surveys of Americans, Russians, and Japanese. *Journal of Social Issues, 51,* 67–88.

Hampton, K., Sessions, L., Her, E. J., & Rainie, L. (2009). *Social isolation and new technology*. Pew Internet and American Life Project. www.pewinternet.org/~/media//Files/Reports/2009/PIP_Tech_and_Social_Isolation.pdf. Accessed June 3, 2011.

Haney López, I. E. (1996). *White by law: The legal construction of race*. New York, NY: New York University Press.

Hankiss, E. (2001). *Symbols of destruction: After September 11*. Brooklyn, NY: Social Science Research Council. http://essays.ssrc.org/sept11/essays/hankiss.htm. Accessed September 4, 2009.

Hannon, L., DeFina, R., & Bruch, S. (2013). The relationship between skin tone and school suspension for African Americans. *Race and Social Problems, 5,* 281–295.

Harbeck, J. (2013, April 10). How foreign languages mutate English words. *The Week*. www.theweek.com/article/index/242413/how-foreign-languages-mutate-english-words. Accessed January 7, 2015.

Harden, B. (2000, April 6). Africa's gems: Warfare's best friend. *The New York Times*.

Hardin, G., & Baden, J. (1977). *Managing the commons*. New York, NY: Freeman.

Hardy, Q. (2014, January 7). Webcams see all (tortoise, watch your back). *The New York Times*.

Hareven, T. K. (1978). Transitions: The family and the life course in historical perspective. New York, NY: Academic Press.

Hareven, T. K. (1992). American families in transition: Historical perspectives on change. In A. S. Skolnick & J. H. Skolnick (Eds.), *Family in transition* (7th ed.). New York, NY: HarperCollins.

Harjani, A. (2013, November 24). Domestic violence results in huge costs for economy. *CNBC Online*. www.cnbc.com/id/101224173#. Accessed June 26, 2014.

Harmon, A. (2009, May 17). Fighting for a last chance at life. *The New York Times*.

Harney, A. (2012, December 16). Without babies, can Japan survive? *The New York Times*.

Harper, S. R., Williams, C. D., & Blackman, H. W. (2013). *Black male student-athletes and racial inequalities in NCAA Division I college sports.* Center for the Study of Race and Equity in Education. Philadelphia: University of Pennsylvania.

Harrington, B., Van Deusen, F., & Ladge, J. (2010). *The new dad: Exploring fatherhood within a career context.* Boston College Center for Work & Family. http://www.bc.edu/content/dam/files/centers/cwf/pdf/BCCWF_Fatherhood_Study_The_New_Dad1.pdf. Accessed August 28, 2011.

Harris, D. R., & Sim, J. J. (2002). Who is multiracial? Assessing the complexity of lived race. *American Sociological Review, 67,* 614–627.

Harris, E. A. (2017, June 25). Same sex parents' hurdles: For those couples who choose to have children, custody issues can be daunting and contradictory. *The New York Times.*

Harris, G. (2005, August 6). F.D.A. responds to criticism with new caution. *The New York Times.*

Harris, G. (2006, September 30). F.D.A. says Bayer failed to reveal drug risk study. *The New York Times.*

Harris, G. (2009, January 12). F.D.A. is lax on oversight during trials, inquiry finds. *The New York Times.*

Harris, G. (2011a, October 2). Calling the nurse "doctor," a title physicians oppose. *The New York Times.*

Harris, G. (2011b, December 31). F.D.A. finds short supply of attention deficit drugs. *The New York Times.*

Harris, G. (2011c, October 7). U.S. panel says no to prostate test for healthy men. *The New York Times.*

Harris, G. (2012, November 30). Giving new life to vultures to restore a human ritual of death. *The New York Times.*

Harris, G. (2015, May 4). Nepal's bureaucracy blamed as quake relief supplies pile up. *The New York Times.*

Harris, M. C. (1996). Doctors implicated in Tutsi genocide. *Lancet, 347,* 684.

Harris, T. W. (2015, June 17). Black like who? *The New York Times.*

Harris Interactive. (2011). *Massive 6-to-1 majority favors tougher regulations of Wall Street.* www.harrisinteractive.com/vault/HI-Harris-Poll-Wall-Street-2011-05-20.pdf. Accessed June 2, 2013.

Harris-Perry, M. (2012, April 16). What it's like to be a problem. *The Nation.*

Hart, B., & Risley, T. R. (1995). *Meaningful differences in the everyday experience of young American children.* Baltimore, MD: Paul H. Brookes.

Hartlep, N. D. (2013). I refuse to be a pawn for whiteness: A Korean transracial adoptee speaks out. In C. Hayes & N. D. Hartlep (Eds.), *Unhooking from whiteness.* Boston, MA: Sense Publishers.

Hartmann, H., Kraut, R. E., & Tilly, L. A. (1989). Job content: Job fragmentation and the deskilling debate. In D. S. Eitzen & M. Baca Zinn (Eds.), *The reshaping of America.* Englewood Cliffs, NJ: Prentice Hall.

Hartocollis, A. (2006, June 24). Women have seen it all on subway, unwillingly. *The New York Times.*

Hartocollis, A. (2012a, April 10). For elderly, E.R.'s of their own. *The New York Times.*

Hartocollis, A. (2012b, January 8). Young, obese, and drawn to surgery. *The New York Times.*

Hartocollis, A. (2015, June 17). New girl in school: Transgender surgery at 18. *The New York Times.*

Hartzband, P., & Groopman, J. (2011). The new language of medicine. *New England Journal of Medicine, 365,* 1372–1373.

Hass, N. (1995, September 10). Margaret Kelly Michaels wants her innocence back. *The New York Times Magazine.*

Hathaway, B. (2016). *Implicit bias may help explain high preschool expulsion rates for black children.* Yale Child Study Center. news.yale.edu/2016/09/27/implicit-bias-may-help-explain-high-preschool-expulsion-rates-black-children. Accessed June 6, 2017.

Hatzenbuehler, M. L. (2011). The social environment and suicide attempts in lesbian, gay, and bisexual youth. *Pediatrics, 127,* 896–903.

Haub, C. (2010). *Recession putting brakes on increases in birth rates.* Population Reference Bureau. www.prb.org/Articles/2010/lowfertilitytfr.aspx?p=1. Accessed August 26, 2010.

Haub, C. (2011). *Birth rate trends in low-fertility countries.* Population Reference Bureau. www.prb.org/Articles/2011/low-fertility-countries-tfr.aspx?p=1. Accessed March 28, 2011.

Haub, C. (2012). *Changing the way U.S. Hispanics are counted.* Population Reference Bureau. www.prb.org/Articles/2012/us-census-and-hispanics.aspx?p=1. Accessed November 9, 2012.

Haub, C. (2013). *Rising trend of births outside marriage.* Population Reference Bureau. www.prb.org/Articles/2013/nonmarital-births.aspx?p=1. Accessed May 20, 2013.

Haub, C., & Gribble, J. (2011). The world at 7 billion. *Population Bulletin, 66,* 1–12.

Hauser, C. (2016, December 18). Salon workers in Illinois to train on signs of abuse. *The New York Times.*

Hauser, C. (2017, March 15). With backlog of rape kits, Texas turns to the crowd. *The New York Times.*

Haushofer, J., & Shapiro, J. (2016). The short-term impact of unconditional cash transfers to the poor: Experimental evidence from Kenya. *Quarterly Journal of Economics, 131,* 1973–2042.

Havrilesky, H. (2014, October 19). Never quit. *The New York Times Magazine.*

Health Grades. (2011). *Health Grades Patient Safety in American Hospitals Study.* www.cpmhealthgrades.com/CPM/assets/File/HealthGrades PatientSafetyInAmericanHospitalsStudy2011.pdf. Accessed May 28, 2013.

Healy, J. (2014, December 14). Montana dress code has female legislators sporting new look: Clenched jaws. *The New York Times.*

Heffernan, V. (2008, May 25). Narrow minded. *The New York Times Magazine.*

Hegewisch, A., & Williams-Baron, E. (2017). *The gender wage gap by occupation 2016; and by race and ethnicity.* Institute for Women's Policy Research. IWPR#C456. iwpr.org/publications/gender-wage-gap-occupation-2016-race-ethnicity/. Accessed June 20, 2017.

Heller, N. (2017, May 15). Is the gig economy working? *The New Yorker.*

Helmreich, W. B. (1992). The things they say behind your back: Stereotypes and the myths behind them. In H. E. Lena, W. B. Helmreich, & W. McCord (Eds.), *Contemporary issues in sociology.* New York, NY: McGraw-Hill.

Henderson, J. J., & Baldasty, G. J. (2003). Race, advertising, and prime-time television. *Howard Journal of Communication, 14,* 97–112.

Henley, N. (1977). *Body politics.* Englewood Cliffs, NJ: Prentice Hall.

Henning, P. J. (2012, September 17). Deferred prosecution agreements and cookie-cutter justice. *Dealbook/New York Times.* dealbook.nytimes.com/2012/09/17/deferred-prosecution-agreements-and-cookie-cutter-justice/. Accessed January 22, 2013.

Henrich, J., Heine, S. J., & Norenzayan, A. (2010). The WEIRDEST people in the world? *Behavioral and Brain Sciences, 33,* 61–135.

Henriques, D. B. (1999, August 24). New take on perpetual calendar. *The New York Times.*

Henriques, D. B. (2009, June 30). Madoff, apologizing, is given 150 years. *The New York Times.*

Henshaw, S. K., & Finer, L. B. (2003). The accessibility of abortion services in the United States, 2001. *Perspectives on Sexual and Reproductive Health, 35,* 16–24.

Henslin, J. (1991). *Down-to-earth sociology.* New York, NY: Free Press.

Herbert, B. (2009, February 21). The invisible war. *The New York Times.*

Herman, N. J. (1993). Return to sender: Reintegrative stigma-management strategies of ex-psychiatric patients. *Journal of Contemporary Ethnography, 22,* 295–330.

Herrnstein, R. J., & Murray, C. (1994). *The bell curve: Intelligence and class structure in American life.* New York, NY: Free Press.

Hertz, F. (2014). *Housing discrimination against unmarried couples.* NOLO. www.nolo.com/legal-encyclopedia/free-books/living-together-book/chapter5-2.html. Accessed January 16, 2015.

Hess, A. (2016, January 31). Fear factor. *The New York Times Magazine.*

Hess, A. (2017, June 18). Ice storm. *The New York Times Magazine.*

Hewitt, J. P. (1988). *Self and society: A symbolic interactionist social psychology.* Boston, MA: Allyn & Bacon.

Hewitt, J. P., & Hewitt, M. L. (1986). *Introducing sociology: A symbolic interactionist perspective.* Englewood Cliffs, NJ: Prentice Hall.

Hewitt, J. P., & Stokes, R. (1975). Disclaimers. *American Sociological Review, 40,* 1–11.

Heymann, J. (2013). *Children's chances: How countries can move from surviving to thriving.* Cambridge, MA: Harvard University Press.

Hibbler, D. K., & Shinew, K. J. (2005). The social life of interracial couples. In R. H. Lauer & J. C. Lauer (Eds.), *Sociology: Windows on society.* Los Angeles, CA: Roxbury.

Higginbotham, E., & Weber, L. (1992). Moving up with kin and community: Upward social mobility for black and white women. *Gender & Society, 6,* 416–440.

Hill, C., & Silva, E. (2006). *Drawing the line: Sexual harassment on campus.* Washington, DC: American Association of University Women. www.aauw.org/research/upload/DTLFinal.pdf. Accessed September 5, 2009.

Hill, M. E. (2000). Color differences in the socioeconomic status of African American men: Results from a longitudinal study. *Social Forces, 78,* 1437–1460.

Hill, N. E. (1997). Does parenting differ based on social class? African American women's perceived socialization for achievement. *American Journal of Community Psychology, 25,* 67–97.

Hills, S. (1980). *Demystifying social deviance.* New York, NY: McGraw-Hill.

Hinshaw, S. P., & Scheffler, R. M. (2014, February 24). Expand Pre-K. Not A.D.H.D. *The New York Times.*

Hirschi, T. (1969). *Causes of delinquency.* Berkeley: University of California Press.

Hitt, J. (2005, August 21). The new Indians. *The New York Times Magazine.*

Hochschild, A. R. (1983). *The managed heart.* Berkeley: University of California Press.

Hochschild, A. R. (1997). *The time bind: When work becomes home and home becomes work.* New York, NY: Metropolitan Books.

Hochschild, J. L., & Weaver, V. (2007). The skin color paradox and the American racial order. *Social Forces, 86,* 643–670.

Hodson, R. (1991). The active worker: Compliance and autonomy at the workplace. *Journal of Contemporary Ethnography, 20,* 47–78.

Hodson, R. (1996). Dignity in the workplace under participative management: Alienation and freedom revisited. *American Sociological Review, 61,* 719–738.

Hodson, R. (2001). *Dignity at work.* New York, NY: Cambridge University Press.

Hoffman, J. (2005, January 25). Sorting out ambivalence over alcohol and pregnancy. *The New York Times.*

Hollander, J. A., Renfrow, D. G., & Howard, J. A. (2011). *Gendered situations, gendered selves.* Lanham, MD: Rowman & Littlefield.

Holliday, C. (2014, June 5). American "Obruni": Black Americans considered Anglo in Ghana. *The Charlotte Post.*

Holmes, A. (2015, July 5). Background checks. *The New York Times Magazine.*

Holmes, S. A. (1995, December 31). The strange politics of immigration. *The New York Times.*

Holson, L. M. (2011a, January 25). For the funeral too distant, mourners gather on the Web. *The New York Times.*

Holson, L. M. (2011b, July 5). Who's on the family tree? Now it's complicated. *The New York Times.*

Holt-Lunstad, J., Smith, T. B., & Layton, J. B. (2010). Social relationships and mortality risk: A meta-analytic review. *PloSMed,* 7(7):e1000316. Journals.plos.org/plosmedicine/article?id=10.1371/journal.pmed.1000316. Accessed June 5, 2017.

Holtzworth-Munroe, A., & Jacobson, N. S. (1985). Causal attributions of married couples: When do they search for causes? What do they conclude when they do? *Journal of Personality and Social Psychology, 48,* 1398–1412.

hooks, b. (1992). Eating the other: Desire and resistance. In b. hooks (ed.), *Black looks: Race and representation.* Boston, MA: South End Press.

Hooks, G., & Smith, C. L. (2004). The treadmill of destruction: National sacrifice areas and Native Americans. *American Sociological Review, 69,* 558–575.

Horon, I. L., & Cheng, D. (2001). Enhanced surveillance for pregnancy-associated mortality—Maryland, 1993–1998. *Journal of the American Medical Association, 285,* 1455–1459.

Horowitz, A. (2012, December 16). Walk like a fish. *The New York Times.*

Horwitz, A. V. (2002). *Creating mental illness.* Chicago, IL: University of Chicago Press.

Hotez, P. J. (2012, August 19). Tropical diseases: The new plague of poverty. *The New York Times.*

Houppert, K. (2005, March 28). The new face of protest? *The Nation.*

House, J. (1981). Social structure and personality. In M. Rosenberg & R. H. Turner (Eds.), *Social psychology: Sociological perspectives.* New York, NY: Basic Books.

How many people in the world speak English 2013? (2013). Exploredia Team. www.exploredia.com/how-many-people-in-the-world-speak-english-2013/. Accessed January 9, 2015.

Hsiang, S., Kopp, R., Jina, A., Rising, J., Delgado, M., Mohan, S., . . . Houser, T. (2017). Estimating economic damage from climate change in the United States. *Science, 356,* 1362–1369.

Hu, W. (2011, June 16). Anti-homework rebels gain a new recruit: The principal. *The New York Times.*

Huber, J., & Form, W. H. (1973). *Income and ideology.* New York, NY: Free Press.

Hudson, V. M., & den Boer, A. (2004). *Bare branches: The security implications of Asia's surplus male population.* Cambridge, MA: MIT Press.

Huff, R., Desilets, C, & Kane, J. (2010). *The 2010 National Public Survey on White Collar Crime.* National White Collar Crime Center. Crimesurvey.nw3c.org/docs/nw3c2010survey.pdf. Accessed January 22, 2013.

Hughes, D., & Chen, L. (1997). When and what parents tell children about race: An examination of race-related socialization among African American families. *Applied Developmental Science, 1,* 200–214.

Hull, K. E., & Nelson, R. L. (2000). Assimilation, choice, or constraint? Testing theories of gender differences in the careers of lawyers. *Social Forces, 79,* 229–264.

Human Rights Campaign. (2014a). *Corporate equality index 2014: Rating American workplaces on lesbian, gay, bisexual, and transgender equality.* www.hrc.org/campaigns/corporate-equality-index. Accessed June 18, 2014.

Human Rights Campaign. (2014b). *The cost of the closet and the rewards of inclusion.* www.hrc.org/resources/entry/the-cost-of-the-closet-and-the-rewards-of-inclusion. Accessed June 18, 2014.

Human Rights Campaign. (2017a). *Corporate equality index 2017.* www.hrc.org/campaigns/coporate-equality-index. Accessed January 17, 2017.

Human Rights Campaign. (2017b). *Maps of state laws and policies.* www.hrc.org/state_maps. Accessed January 17, 2017.

Human Rights Watch. (2009a). *Testing justice: The rape kit backlog in Los Angeles City and County.* www.hrw.org/sites/default/files/reports/rape kit0309.pdf. Accessed May 4, 2009.

Human Rights Watch. (2009b). *Time to tear down the wall of caste.* www.hrw.org/en/news/2009/10/09/time-tear-down-wall-caste. Accessed June 15, 2011.

Human Rights Watch. (2011). *ILO: New landmark treaty to protect domestic workers.* www.hrw.org/mews/2011/06/16/ilo-new-landmark-treaty-protect-domestic-workers. Accessed June 23, 2013.

Human Rights Watch. (2012). *India: UN members should act to end caste discrimination.* www.hrw.org/news/2012/05/14/india-un-members-should-act-end-caste-discrimination. Accessed June 4, 2013.

Human Rights Watch. (2014). *Cleaning human waste.* www.hrw.org/reports/2014/08/25/cleaning-human-waste-0. Accessed May 30, 2015.

Humes, K. R., Jones, N. A., & Ramirez, R. R. (2010). *Overview of race and Hispanic origin: 2010* (2010 Census Briefs, C2010BR-02). www.census.gov/prod/cen2010/briefs/c2010br-02.pdf. Accessed April 1, 2011.

Humphreys, L. (1970). *The tearoom trade: Impersonal sex in public places.* Chicago, IL: Aldine-Atherton.

Hunt, J. (1985). Police accounts of normal force. *Urban Life, 13,* 315–341.

Hunter, M. L. (2005). *Race, gender and the politics of skin tone.* New York, NY: Routledge.

Hunter, T. W. (2011, August 2). Putting an antebellum myth to rest. *The New York Times.*

Hunter-Gault, C. (2012, May 28). Violated hopes. *The New Yorker.*

Hurley, L. (2016, June 23). *U.S. Supreme Court upholds race-based college admissions.* Reuters. www.reuters.com/article/us-usa-court-affirmativeaction-idUSKCN0Z91N3. Accessed June 12, 2017.

Hutchens, T. (2002, December 21). Coverdale gives IU its heart and soul. *The Indianapolis Star.*

Hvistendahl, M. (2011). *Unnatural selection: Choosing boys over girls, and the consequences of a world full of men.* New York, NY: PublicAffairs.

Hyde, J. S. (1984). How large are gender differences in aggression? A developmental meta-analysis. *Developmental Psychology, 20,* 722–736.

Ignatieff, M. (2005, June 26). Who are Americans to think that freedom is theirs to spread? *The New York Times Magazine.*

Ignatius, A. (1988, July 14). China's birthrate is out of control again as one-child policy fails in rural areas. *The Wall Street Journal.*

IMG Academy. (2015). *Tuition.* www.imgacademy.com/private-school/admissions/tuition. Accessed June 23, 2015.

IMS Health. (2012). *Trends in attention deficit hyperactivity disorder ambulatory diagnosis and medical treatment in the United States, 2000–2010.* www.imshealth.com/portal/site/ims. Accessed January 22, 2013.

Inciardi, J. A. (1992). *The war on drugs II.* Mountain View, CA: Mayfield.

Ingber, H. (2015, December 18). How Muslim parents talk to their children about extremism. *The New York Times.*

Institute for Women's Policy Research. (2016). *Pay equity & discrimination.* Iwpr.org/issue/employment-edcuation-economic-change/pay-equity-discrimination/. Accessed June 19, 2017.

Institute of Medicine. (1999). *To err is human: Building a safer health care system.* Washington, DC: Committee on Quality of Health Care in America, National Academy Press.

Institute of Medicine. (2003). *Preparing for the psychological consequences of terrorism: A public health strategy.* Washington, DC: National Academies Press. www.nap.edu. Accessed June 10, 2003.

Institute of Medicine. (2013). *U.S. health in international perspective: Shorter lives, poorer health.* Report Brief. www

.iom.edu/~/Media/Files/Report%20files/2013/US-Health-International-Perspective/USHealth_Intl_PerspectiveRB.pdf. Accessed February 14, 2013.

Institute on Taxation and Economic Policy. (2015). *Who pays? 5th edition.* www.itep.org/whopays/full-report.php#ExecutiveSummary. Accessed May 29, 2015.

International Center for Academic Integrity. (2015). *Statistics.* www.academicintegrity.org/icai/iintegrity-3.php. Accessed January 2, 2017.

International Centre for Prison Studies. (2017). Highest to lowest—Prison population rate. www.prisonstudies.org/highest-to-lowest/prison_population_rate?field_region_taxonomy_tid=All. Accessed January 17, 2017.

International Labour Organization. (2017). *World employment social outlook: Trends for women 2017.* www.ilo.org/wcmsp5/groups/public/—-dgreports/—-inst/documents/publication/wcms_557245.pdf. Accessed June 20, 2017.

International Society of Aesthetic Plastic Surgery. (2016). *ISAPS International survey on aesthetic/cosmetic procedures performed in 2015.* www.isaps.org/Media/Default/global-statistics/2016 ISAPS Results.pdf. Accessed January 7, 2016.

Internet World Stats. (2014). *Internet world users by language.* www.internetworldstats.com/stats7.htm. Accessed January 9, 2015.

Intersex Society of North America. (2008). *How common is intersex?* www.isna.org/faq/frequency. Accessed May 27, 2014.

Ioannidis, J. P. A. (2005). Contradicted and initially stronger effects in highly cited clinical research. *Journal of the American Medical Association, 294,* 218–228.

Irving, S. K., & Loveless, T. A. (2015). *Dynamics of economic well-being: Participation in government programs, 2009-2012: Who gets assistance?* U.S. Bureau of the Census. P70-141. www.census.gov/content/dam/Census/library/publications/2015/demo/p70-141.pdf. Accessed June 2, 2017.

Irwin, N. (2016, March 31). Job growth in past decade was in temp and contract. *The New York Times.*

Issenberg, S. (2007). *The sushi economy.* New York, NY: Gotham Books.

Is there a Santa Claus? (1897, September 21). *The New York Sun.*

Ito, M., Horst, H., Bittanti, M., Boyd, D., Herr-Stephenson, B., Lange, P. G., . . . Robinson, L. (2008). *Living and learning with new media: Summary of findings from the Digital Youth Project* (Reports on Digital Media and Learning). Chicago, IL: MacArthur Foundation. http://digitalyouth.ischool.berkeley.edu/files/report/digitalyouth-WhitePaper.pdf. Accessed June 7, 2009.

Jackall, R. (1988). *Moral mazes: The world of corporate managers.* New York, NY: Oxford University Press.

Jackson, S. (1995). The social context of rape: Sexual scripts and motivation. In P. Searles & R. J. Berger (Eds.), *Rape and society.* Boulder, CO: Westview Press.

Jacobs, A. (2009, April 5). Rural China's hunger for sons fuels traffic in abducted boys. *The New York Times.*

Jacobs, A. (2011, April 15). For many bachelors in China, no property means no dates. *The New York Times.*

Jacobs, A., & Century, A. (2012, September 6). As China ages, Beijing turns to morality tales to spur filial devotion. *The New York Times.*

Jain, R. (2015, June 1). Parents use "corrective rape" to "straighten gays." *The Times of India.* Timesofindia.indiatimes.com/life-style/relationships/parenting/Parents-use-corrective-rape-to-straighten-gays/articleshow/47489949.cms. Accessed June 15, 2017.

Jamail, D. (2007). *Another casualty: Coverage of the Iraq war.* New York, NY: Global Policy Forum. http://globalpolicy.org/component/content/article/168-general/36698.html. Accessed September 5, 2009.

Jamrisko, M., & Kolet, I. (2012). Cost of college degree in U.S. soars 12-fold: Chart of the day. *Bloomberg News.* www.bloomberg.com/news/2012-08-15/cost-fo-college-degree-in-u-s-soars-12-fold-chart-of-the-day.html. Accessed January 16, 2013.

Janoff-Bulman, R. (1979). Characterological versus behavioral self-blame: Inquiries into depression and rape. *Journal of Personality and Social Psychology, 37,* 1798–1809.

Jäntti, M. (2006). *American exceptionalism in a new light: A comparison of intergenerational earnings mobility in the Nordic countries, the United Kingdom, and the United States.* Discussion Paper #1938. Institute for the Study of Labor. ftp.iza.org/dp1938.pdf. Accessed June 2, 2013.

Japanese railways hope soothing lights will curb suicides. (2009, November 5). *The New York Times.*

Jardim, E., Long, M. C., Plotnick, R., van Inwegen, E., Vigdor, J., & Wething, H. (2017). *Minimum wage increases wages, and low-wage employment: Evidence from Seattle.* National Bureau of Economic Research Working Paper #23532. www.nber.org/papers/w23532?utm_campaign=ntw&utm_medium=email&utm_source=ntw. Accessed June 29, 2017.

Jarosz, B., & Mather, M. (2017). Losing ground: Young women's well-being across generations in the United States. Population Reference Bureau. *Population Bulletin, 72,* 1–24.

Jauhar, S. (2017, April 22). Executions need doctors. *The New York Times.*

Jefferson, T. (1955). *Notes on the State of Virginia*. Chapel Hill: University of North Carolina Press. (Original work published 1781)

Jenkins, H. (1999, July). Professor Jenkins goes to Washington. *Harper's Magazine*.

Jenkins, J. C., & Perrow, C. (1977). Insurgency of the powerless: Farm worker movements (1946–1972). *American Sociological Review, 42*, 249–268.

Jennings, D. (2010, March 16). With cancer, let's face it: Words are inadequate. *The New York Times.*

Jett, S., LaPorte, D. J., & Wanchisn, J. (2010). Impact of exposure to pro-eating disorder websites on eating behavior in college women. *European Eating Disorders Review, 18*, 410–416.

Jha, M. (2011). Trends in selective abortions of girls in India: Analysis of nationally representative birth histories from 1990–2005 and census data from 1991–2011. *The Lancet, 377*, 1921–1928.

Jian, M. (2013, May 22). China's brutal one-child policy. *The New York Times.*

Johnson, B. E., Kuck, D. L., & Schander, P. R. (1997). Rape myth acceptance and sociodemographic characteristics: A multidimentional analysis. *Sex Roles, 36*, 693–707.

Johnson, D. (2009, January 21). Trials loom for parents who embraced faith over medicine. *The New York Times.*

Johnson, G. (2015, August 25). The gradual extinction of accepted truths. *The New York Times.*

Johnson, I. (2013, June 16). China embarking on vast program of urbanization. *The New York Times.*

Johnson, J. (2013, May 23). Paul Tudor Jones: In macro trading, babies are a "killer" to a woman's focus. *The Washington Post.*

Johnson, J., & Hauslohner, A. (2017, May 20). "I think Islam hates us": A timeline of Trump's comments about Islam and Muslims. *Washington Post.*

Johnson, K. (2015, October 31). Costume correctness on campus: Feel free to be you, but not me. *The New York Times.*

Johnson, K., Pérez-Peña, R., & Eligon, J. (2015, June 17). At center of storm, a defiant "identify as black." *The New York Times.*

Johnson, P. A., Fitzgerald, T., Salganicoff, A., Wood, S. F., & Goldstein, J. M. (2014). *Sex-specific medical research: Why women's health can't wait*. Report of Brigham & Women's Hospital. www.brighamandwomens.org/Departments_and_Services/womenshealth/ConnorsCenter/Policy/ConnorgReportFINAL.pdf. Accessed June 15, 2015.

Johnson, R. (1987). *Hard time: Understanding and reforming the prison*. Pacific Grove, CA: Brooks/Cole.

Johnston, D. (2002, April 7). Affluent avoid scrutiny on taxes even as I.R.S. warns of cheating. *The New York Times.*

Jones, A. (2010). Your guide to dormcest: Avoiding the pitfalls, scoring the perks. *Her campus: A collegiate guide to life.* www.hercampus.com/love/your-guide-dormcest-avoiding-pitfalls-scoring-perks. Accessed June 6, 2011.

Jones, E. E., & Pittman, T. S. (1982). Toward a general theory of strategic self-presentation. In J. Suls (Ed.), *Psychological perspectives on the self* (Vol. 1). Hillsdale, NJ: Lawrence Erlbaum.

Jones, J. M. (1986). The concept of racism and its changing reality. In B. P. Bowser & R. G. Hunt (Eds.), *Impacts of racism on white Americans*. Beverly Hills, CA: Sage.

Jones, N. (2009). *Between good and ghetto: African American girls and inter-city violence*. New Brunswick, NJ: Rutgers University Press.

Jones, R. K., & Jerman, J. (2017). *Abortion incidence and service availability in the United States, 2014*. Guttmacher Institute. www.guttmacher.org/journals/prsh/2017/01/abortion-incidence-and-service-availability-united-states-2014. Accessed June 28, 2017.

Jordan, M. (2009, May 20). Pupils abused for decades in Irish schools; panel finds misconduct by priests, nuns until 1990. *The Washington Post.*

Jordan-Young, R., & Karkazis, K. (2012, June 18). You say you're a woman? That should be enough. *The New York Times.*

Joseph Rowntree Foundation. (2016). *Brexit vote explained: Poverty, low skills, and lack of opportunities*. www.jrf.org.uk/report/brexit-vote-explained-poverty-low-skills-and-lack-opportunities. Accessed June 26, 2017.

Joshi, N. (2015, January 5). Doctor, shut up and listen. *The New York Times.*

Jost, K. (2002). Sexual abuse and the clergy. *CQ Researcher, 12*, 393–416.

Joyful Heart Foundation. (2015). *The accountability project*. www.endthebacklog.org/backlog-where-it/accountability-project. Accessed June 10, 2015.

Juergensmeyer, M. (1996, November). Religious nationalism: A global threat? *Current History.*

Kaeble, D., & Glaze, L. (2016). *Correctional populations in the United States, 2015*. NCJ250374. U.S. Bureau of Justice Statistics. www.bjs.gov/content/pub/pdf/cpus15.pdf. Accessed January 17, 2017.

Kahlenberg, R. D. (2017, August 3). The walls we won't tear down. *The New York Times.*

Kahn, J. (2004, May 30). The most populous nation faces a population crisis. *The New York Times.*

Kahn, J. (2007, May 22). Harsh birth control steps fuel violence in China. *The New York Times.*

Kahn, J. (2012, May 11). Trouble, age 9. *The New York Times.*

Kahneman, D., Krueger, A. B., Schkade, D., Schwarz, N., & Stone, A. A. (2006). Would you be happier if you were richer? A focusing illusion. *Science, 312,* 1908–1910.

Kain, E. (1990). *The myth of family decline.* Lexington, MA: Lexington Books.

Kaiser Family Foundation. (2008). *Abortion in the U.S.: Utilization, financing, and access.* www.kff.org/womens health/upload/3269-02.pdf. Accessed September 5, 2009.

Kaiser Family Foundation. (2016). *Key facts about the uninsured population.* www.kff.org/uninsured/fact-sheet/key-facts-about-the-uninsured-population/. Accessed June 9, 2017.

Kalb, C. (2010, March 14). Culture of corpulence. *Newsweek.*

Kalmijn, M. (1994). Assortive mating by cultural and economic occupational status. *American Journal of Sociology, 100,* 422–452.

Kalmijn, M., & Flap, H. (2001). Assortive meeting and mating: Unintended consequences of organized settings for partner choices. *Social Forces, 79,* 1289–1312.

Kane, E. (2006). *We put it down in front of him, and he just instinctively knew what to do: Biological determinism in parents' beliefs about the origin of gendered childhoods.* Paper presented at Annual Meeting of American Sociological Association. Montreal.

Kane, E. (2009). I wanted a soul mate: Gendered anticipation and frameworks of accountability in parents' preferences for sons and daughters. *Symbolic Interaction, 34,* 372–389.

Kang, C. (2013, February 27). Survey finds gap in Internet access between rich, poor students. *The Washington Post.*

Kang, J. C. (2015, May 10). The witnesses. *The New York Times Magazine.*

Kanin, E. J. (1994). False rape allegations. *Archives of Sexual Behavior, 23,* 81–87.

Kanter, R. M. (1977). *Men and women of the corporation.* New York, NY: Basic Books.

Kanter, R. M., & Stein, B. A. (1979). *Life in organizations: Workplaces as people experience them.* New York, NY: Basic Books.

Kaptchuk, T. J., Friedlander, E., Kelley, J. M., Sanchez, M. N., Kokkotou, E., Singer, J. P., . . . Lembo, A. J. (2010). Placebos without deception: A randomized control trial in irritable bowel syndrome. *PloS ONE, 5,* 1–14.

Karabel, J. (1972). Community colleges and social stratification. *Harvard Educational Review, 42,* 521–559.

Karraker, K. H., Vogel, D. A., & Lake, M. A. (1995). Parents' gender stereotyped perceptions of newborns: The eye of the beholder revisited. *Sex Roles, 33,* 687–701.

Karush, S. (2001, May 6). Russia's population drain could open a floodgate of consequences. *Los Angeles Times.*

Katbamna, M. (2009, October 27). Half a good man is better than none at all. *The Guardian.*

Katel, P. (2005). Illegal immigration. *CQ Researcher, 15,* 393–420.

Katel, P. (2006). War on drugs. *CQ Researcher, 16,* 649–672.

Katel, P. (2008). Affirmative action. *CQ Researcher, 18,* 841–864.

Katz, J. (1975). Essences as moral identities: Verifiability and responsibility in imputations of deviance and charisma. *American Journal of Sociology, 80,* 1369–1390.

Kaufman, D. (2011, June 5). Does Twitter make you stupid? [Letter to the editor]. *The New York Times.*

Kearl, M. C. (1980). Time, identity and the spiritual needs of the elderly. *Sociological Analysis, 41,* 172–180.

Kearl, M. C., & Gordon, C. (1992). *Social psychology.* Boston, MA: Allyn & Bacon.

Keck, Z. (2014). Indian Supreme Court creates "third gender" category for transgenders. *The Diplomat.* April. Thediplomat.com/2014/04/indian-supreme-court-creates-third-gender-category-for-transgenders/. Accessed May 23, 2014.

Keith, V. M., & Herring, C. (1991). Skin tone and stratification in the black community. *American Journal of Sociology, 97,* 760–778.

Kelles, J. L. (2017, January 1). Click doctors. *The New York Times Magazine.*

Kelley, R. (2008, November 17). A letter to my son on election night. *Newsweek.*

Kelley, R. (2009, February 2). Beyond just black and white. *Newsweek.*

Kelty, R., Kleykamp, M., & Segal, D. R. (2010). The military and the transition to adulthood. *The Future of Children, 20,* 181–207.

Kennedy, P. (1993). *Preparing for the 21st century.* New York, NY: Random House.

Kennedy, S., & Ruggles, S. (2014). Breaking up is hard to count: The rise of divorce in the United States, 1980–2010. *Demography, 51,* 587–598.

Kent, M., & Lalasz, R. (2006, June). *In the news: Speaking English in the United States.* Washington, DC: Population Reference Bureau. www.prb.org. Accessed July 20, 2006.

Kerbo, H. R. (1991). *Social stratification and inequality.* New York, NY: McGraw-Hill.

Kershaw, S. (2005, January 26). Old law shielding a woman's virtue faces an updating. *The New York Times.*

Kershaw, S. (2008, October 30). Move over, my pretty, ugly is here. *The New York Times.*

Kessler, S. J., & McKenna, W. (1978). *Gender: An ethnomethodological approach.* Chicago, IL: University of Chicago Press.

Kessler-Harris, A. (1982). *Out to work: A history of wage-earning women in the United States.* New York, NY: Oxford University Press.

Kidd, D. C., & Castano, E. (2013). Reading literary fiction improves theory of mind. *Science, 342,* 377–380.

Kiefer, H. M. (2004). *Public on justice system: Fair, but still too soft.* Gallup. www.gallup.com/poll/10474/Public-Justice-System-Fair-Still-Too-Soft.aspx. Accessed January 21, 2015.

Kilgore, A. (2017, May 31). Being black in America is tough: LeBron James responds to racist vandalism incident. *Washington Post.*

Kim, D., & Leigh, J. P. (2010). Estimating the effects of wages on obesity. *Journal of Occupational and Environmental Medicine, 52,* 495–500.

Kim, K. H., & Van Tassel-Baska, J. (2010). The relationship between creativity and behavior problems among under-achieving elementary and high school students. *Creativity Research Journal, 22,* 185–193.

Kimmel, M. S. (2004). *The gendered society.* New York, NY: Oxford University Press.

King, J. B. (2016, November 22). *Letter to states calling for an end to corporal punishment in schools.* Office of the Secretary of Education. www2.ed.gov/policy/gen/guid/school-discipline/files/corporal-punishment-dcl-11-22-2016.pdf. Accessed January 5, 2017.

King, M. L., Jr. (1991). Letter from Birmingham City jail. In C. Carson, D. J. Garrow, G. Gill, V. Harding, & D. Clark Hine (Eds.), *The eyes on the prize civil rights reader.* New York, NY: Penguin Books.

Kirkwood, M. K., & Cecil, B. K. (2001). Marital rape: A student assessment of rape laws and the marital exemption. *Violence Against Women, 7,* 1234–1253.

Kirn, W. (2009, May 10). More than a numbers game. *The New York Times Magazine.*

Kirp, D. L. (2006, July 23). After the bell curve. *The New York Times Magazine.*

Klatch, R. (1991). Complexities of conservatism: How conservatives understand the world. In A. Wolfe (Ed.), *America at century's end.* Berkeley: University of California Press.

Kleck, R. (1968). Physical stigma and nonverbal cues emitted in face-to-face interaction. *Human Relations, 21,* 19–28.

Kleck, R., Ono, H., & Hastorf, A. (1966). The effects of physical deviance and face-to-face interaction. *Human Relations, 19,* 425–436.

Kleinfield, N. R. (2012, May 13). Why don't we have any white kids? *The New York Times.*

Klerman, J. A., Daley, K., & Pozniak, A. (2013). *Family and medical leave in 2012: Executive summary.* Abt Associates. www.dol.gov/asp/evaluation/fmla/FMLA-2012-Executive-Summary.pdf. Accessed January 15, 2017.

Knuckey, J., & Orey, B. D. (2000). Symbolic racism in the 1995 Louisiana gubernatorial election. *Social Science Quarterly, 81,* 1027–1035.

Kobrin, F. E. (1976). The fall in household size and the rise of the primary individual in the United States. *Demography, 31,* 127–138.

Koch, K. (1999, October 22). Rethinking Ritalin. *CQ Researcher* [Special issue].

Kochhar, R., & Fry, R. (2014). *Wealth inequality has widened along racial, ethnic lines since the Great Recession.* Pew Research Center. www.pewresearch.org/fact-tank/2014/12/12/racial-wealth-gaps-great-recession/. Accessed June 1, 2015.

Kocieniewski, D. (2006, October 10). A history of sex with students, unchallenged over the years. *The New York Times.*

Koenig, S. (2011, August 26). Gossip. *This American Life.* www.thisamericanlife.org/radio-archives/episode/444/gossip. Accessed January 14, 2013.

Koerth-Baker, M. (2013, October 15). The not-so-hidden cause behind the A.D.H.D. epidemic. *The New York Times.*

Kohn, D. (2015, May 17). Let the kids learn through play. *The New York Times.*

Kohn, M. L. (1979). The effects of social class on parental values and practices. In D. Reiss & H. A. Hoffman (Eds.), *The American family: Dying or developing.* New York, NY: Plenum Press.

Kohut, A. (2012, January 27). Don't mind the gap. *The New York Times.*

Kokopeli, B., & Lakey, G. (1992). More power than we want: Masculine sexuality and violence. In M. L. Anderson &

P. H. Collins (Eds.), *Race, class and gender: An anthology.* Belmont, CA: Wadsworth.

Kolata, G. (2011, February 6). Mysterious maladies. *The New York Times.*

Kolata, G. (2013, December 19). Hypertension guidelines can be eased, panel says. *The New York Times.*

Kolata, G. (2016, September 26). When doctors can't see past patients' weight. *The New York Times.*

Kolata, G., & Cohen, S. (2016, January 17). Drug overdoses propel rise in mortality rates of whites. *The New York Times.*

Kolbe, T., Partridge, M., & O'Reilly, F. (2015). *Time and learning in schools: A national profile.* National Center on Time & Learning. www.timeandlearning.org/publications/time-and-learning-schools-national-profile. Accessed May 22, 2015.

Kolbert, E. (2013, March 11). Up all night. *The New Yorker.*

Korean girls take poison to aid kin. (1989, March 3). *Hartford Courant.*

Kosmin, B. A., & Keysar, A. (2009). *American religious identification survey (ARIS 2008).* Hartford, CT: Trinity College. www.livinginliminality.files.wordpress.com/2009/03/aris_report_2008.pdf. Accessed May 6, 2009.

Kotkin, J. (2012, July 23 & July 30). Generation screwed. *Newsweek.*

Kovel, L. (1980). The American mental health industry. In D. Ingleby (Ed.), *Critical psychiatry.* New York, NY: Pantheon Books.

Krakauer, J. (2015). *Missoula: Rape and the justice system in a college town.* New York, NY: Random House.

Kramer, P. (1997). *Listening to Prozac.* New York, NY: Penguin Books.

Kraska, P. B. (2007). Militarization and policing—its relevance to 21st century police. *Policing, 1,* 501–513.

Kraus, M. W., Côte, S., & Keltner, D. (2010). Social class, contextualism, and empathetic accuracy. *Psychological Science, 21,* 1716–1723.

Kreider, R. M., & Ellis, R. (2011). *Number, timing, and duration of marriages and divorces: 2009* (U.S. Census Bureau, Current Population Reports, P70-125). www.census.gov/prod/2011pubs/p70-125.pdf. Accessed June 3, 2011.

Kress, M. (2005, April 20). Mormonism is booming in the U.S. and overseas. *The News-Sentinel.*

Kriner, D. L., & Shen, F. X. (2010). *The casualty gap: The causes and consequences of American wartime inequalities.* New York, NY: Oxford University Press.

Kristof, N. D. (1993, July 21). Peasants of China discover new way to weed out girls. *The New York Times.*

Kristof, N. D. (2010, May 22). Moonshine or the kids? *The New York Times.*

Kristof, N. D. (2012, October 28). Want a real reason to be outraged? *The New York Times.*

Kristof, N. D. (2014, November 16). When whites just don't get it, Part 4. *The New York Times.*

Kroeger, T., Cooke, T., & Gould. E. (2016). *The class of 2016: The labor market is still far from ideal for young graduates.* Economic Policy Institute. www.epi.org/files/pdf/103124.pdf. Accessed December 23, 2016.

Krogstad, J. M. (2014). *Census Bureau explores new Middle East/North Africa ethnic category.* Pew Research Center. www.pewresearch.org/fact-tank/2014/03/24/census-bureau-explores-new-middle-eastnorth-africa-ethnic-category/. Accessed October 15, 2017.

Krueger, A. B. (2002, November 14). The apple falls close to the tree, even in the land of opportunity. *The New York Times.*

Krugman, P. (2008, February 18). Poverty is poison. *The New York Times.*

Krugman, P. (2014, March 17). That old-time whistle. *The New York Times.*

Krugman, P. (2015, June 22). Slavery's long shadow. *The New York Times.*

Krysan, M., Couper, M. P., Farley, R., & Forman, T. (2009). Does race matter in neighborhood preferences? Results from a video experiment. *American Journal of Sociology, 115,* 527–559.

Kubany, E. S., Abueg, F. R., Owens, J. A., Brennan, J. M., Kaplan, A. S., & Watson, S. B. (1995). Initial examination of a multidimensional model of trauma-related guilt: Applications to combat veterans and battered women. *Journal of Psychopathology and Behavioral Assessment, 17,* 353–376.

Kulick, D., & Machado-Borges, T. (2005). Leaky. In D. Kulick & A. Meneley (Eds.), *Fat: The anthropology of an obsession.* New York, NY: Tarcher/Penguin.

Kulikowski, L. (2014, November 14). The 23 countries with the most extreme income inequality. *The Street.* www.thestreet.com/story/12916499/13/23-countries-where-income-inequality-has-become-the-worst-ever.html. Accessed May 29, 2015.

Kuperinsky, A. (2012, January 27). Trending. McDonald's Twitter fiasco. *The Star-Ledger.* www.nj.com/entertainment/index.ssf/2012/01/mcdonalds_twitter_jan_brewer_s.html. Accessed January 14, 2013.

Kurtz, L. R. (1995). *Gods in the global village*. Thousand Oaks, CA: Pine Forge Press.

Kurutz, S. (2008, December 14). Fast food zoning. *The New York Times*.

Kurutz, S. (2014, November 2). The "kind of, sort of" era. *The New York Times*.

Lacey, M. (2006, December 14). Rwandan priest sentenced to 15 years for allowing deaths of Tutsi in church. *The New York Times*.

Lacey, M. (2011, September 25). In Arizona, complaints that an accent can hinder a teacher's career. *The New York Times*.

LaCoste-Caputo, J. (2007, June 21). Academic ratings, teacher pay tied. *San Antonio Express-News*.

LaFraniere, S. (2007, July 4). Seeking to end an overfed ideal. *The New York Times*.

LaFraniere, S. (2011, April 24). For many Chinese, new wealth and a fresh face. *The New York Times*.

LaFraniere, S., & Levin, D. (2010, November 12). Assertive Chinese marooned in mental wards. *The New York Times*.

Lakoff, R. (1975). *Language and woman's place*. New York, NY: Harper & Row.

Lakshmi, R. (2005, February 27). India call centers suffer storm of 4-letter words. *The Washington Post*.

Lalami, L. (2015, November 29). For or against. *The New York Times Magazine*.

Lalasz, R. (2006). *Americans flocking to outer suburbs in record numbers*. Washington, DC: Population Reference Bureau. www.prb.org. Accessed May 9, 2006.

Lamont, M. (1992). *Money, morals and manners: The culture of the French and American upper middle class*. Chicago, IL: University of Chicago Press.

Lander, L. (1988). *Images of bleeding: Menstruation as ideology*. New York, NY: Orlando.

Landler, M. (2002, December 1). For Austrians, HoHoHo is no laughing matter. *The New York Times*.

Landrigan, C. P., Parry, G. J., Bones, C. B., Hackbarth, A. D., Goldmann, D. A., & Sharek, P. J. (2010). Temporal trends in rates of patient harm resulting from medical care. *New England Journal of Medicine, 363*, 2124–2134.

Lang, S. (1998). *Men as women, women as men: Changing gender in Native American cultures*. Austin: University of Texas Press.

Langman, L. (1988). Social stratification. In M. B. Sussman & S. K. Steinmetz (Eds.), *Handbook of marriage and the family*. New York, NY: Plenum Press.

Langston, D. (1992). Tired of playing monopoly? In M. L. Anderson & P. H. Collins (Eds.), *Race, class and gender: An anthology*. Belmont, CA: Wadsworth.

Lanvers, U. (2004). Gender in discourse behavior in parent-child dyads: A literature review. *Child: Care, Health, and Development, 30*, 481–493.

Lapchick, R. (2017). *The racial and gender report card*. The Institute for Diversity and Ethics in Sport. www.tidesport .org/reports.html. Accessed June 5, 2017.

Lapierre, M. A., Piotrowski, J. T., & Linebarger, D. L. (2012). Background television in the homes of US children. *Pediatrics, 130*, 839–846.

Lareau, A. (2003). *Unequal childhoods: Class, race, and family life*. Berkeley: University of California Press.

Lareau, A., & Weininger, E. B. (2008). Time, work and family life: Reconceptualizing gendered time patterns through the case of children's organized activities. *Sociological Forum, 23*, 419–454.

Larmer, B. (2015, January 4). Cram city. *The New York Times Magazine*.

Larson, L. E., & Goltz, J. W. (1989). Religious participation and marital commitment. *Review of Religious Research, 30*, 387–400.

Lasch, C. (1977). *Haven in a heartless world*. New York, NY: Basic Books.

Lathrop, D., & Flagg, A. (2017, August 23). In deeming a killing "justifiable," race is a factor. *The New York Times*.

Lauer, R., & Handel, W. (1977). *Social psychology: The theory and application of symbolic interactionism*. Boston, MA: Houghton Mifflin.

Lauzen, M. M. (2016). *Boxed in 2015-16: Women on screen and behind the scenes in television*. Center for the Study of Women in Television and Film. womenintvfilm.sdsu.edu/ files/2015-16-Boxed-in-Report.pdf. Accessed January 6, 2017.

Lavy, V., & Sand, E. (2015). *On the origins of gender human capital gaps: Short and long term consequences of teachers' stereotypical biases*. National Bureau of Economic Research Working Paper #20909. www.nber.org/papers/w20909. pdf. Accessed June 12, 2015.

Leape, L. L., & Bates, D. W. (1995). Systems analysis of adverse drug events. *Journal of the American Medical Association, 274*, 35–43.

LeBesco, K. (2004). *Revolting bodies? The struggle to redefine fat identity*. Amherst: University of Massachusetts Press.

Lee, B. Y. (2017, May 21). "Rib cage bragging": Beware of this new body trend. *Forbes Magazine*.

Lee, M. (2006). *The neglected link between food marketing and childhood obesity in poor neighborhoods.* Washington, DC: Population Reference Bureau. www.prb.org. Accessed July 12, 2006.

Lee, S. M. (1993). Racial classifications in the U.S. Census: 1890–1990. *Ethnic and Racial Studies, 16,* 75–94.

Lee-St. John, J. (2007, February 12). A time limit on rape. *Time.*

Legewie, J., & DiPrete, T. A. (2012). School context and the gender gap in educational achievement. *American Sociological Review, 77,* 463–485.

Lehman, E. J., Hein, M. J., Baron, S. L., & Gersic, C. M. (2012). Neurodegenerative causes of death among retired National Football League players. *Neurology, 79,* 1970–1974.

Lehrer, J. (2012). The fragile teenage brain. *Grantland*, ESPN. com. www.grantland.com/story/_/id/7443714/jonah-lehrer-concussions-adolscents-future-football. Accessed, December 22, 2012.

Leibovich, M. (2014, April 13). Did anyone wash dishes in this family? *The New York Times Magazine.*

Leinberger, P., & Tucker, B. (1991). *The new individualists: The generation after the organization man.* New York, NY: HarperCollins.

Lemert, E. (1972). *Human deviance, social problems, and social control.* Englewood Cliffs, NJ: Prentice Hall.

Leonhardt, D. (2013, July 22). In climbing income ladder, location matters. *The New York Times.*

Leonhardt, D. (2014, May 27). Is college worth it? *The New York Times.*

Leonhardt, D. (2016, December 11). The American dream quantified at last. *The New York Times.*

Lerner, M. (1970). The desire for justice and reactions to victims. In J. Macauley & L. Berkowitz (Eds.), *Altruism and helping behavior.* New York, NY: Academic Press.

Lesane-Brown, C. L. (2006). A review of race socialization within black families. *Developmental Review, 26,* 400–426.

Lesko, N. (2008). Our guys/good guys: Playing with high school privilege and power. In S. J. Ferguson (Ed.), *Mapping the social landscape.* New York, NY: McGraw-Hill.

Lester, W. (2005, January 8). Poll: 29% in U.S. give tsunami aid. *The Indianapolis Star.*

Leu, D. J., Forzani, E., Rhoads, C., Maykel, C., Kennedy, C., & Timbrell, N. (2015). The new literacies on online research and comprehension: Rethinking the reading achievement gap. *Reading Research Quarterly, 50,* 37–59.

Levine, H. G. (1992). Temperance cultures: Concern about alcohol problems in Nordic and English-speaking cultures.

In M. Lader, G. Edwards, & D. C. Drummond (Eds.), *The nature of alcohol and drug-related problems.* New York, NY: Oxford University Press.

Levitt, S. D., & Dubner, S. J. (2009). *Freakonomics: A rogue economist explores the hidden side of everything.* New York, NY: Harper Perennial.

Levy, A. (2006, May 29). Dirty old women. *The New York Magazine.* http://nymag.com/news/features/17064/index1 .html. Accessed September 5, 2009.

Lewin, T. (1998, December 13). How boys lost out to girl power. *The New York Times.*

Lewin, T. (2000, April 11). Disabled student is suing over test-score labeling. *The New York Times.*

Lewin, T. (2001, October 21). Shelters have empty beds: Abused women stay home. *The New York Times.*

Lewin, T. (2006, July 9). At colleges, women are leaving men in the dust. *The New York Times.*

Lewin, T. (2009, December 10). College dropouts cite low money and high stress. *The New York Times.*

Lewis, M. (1978). *The culture of inequality.* New York, NY: New American Library.

Lewis, M. (2016). *The undoing project: A friendship that changed our minds.* New York, NY: WW Norton.

Lewis, M. M. (1948). *Language in society.* New York, NY: Social Science Research Council.

Lewis, O. (1968). The culture of poverty. In D. P. Moynihan (Ed.), *On understanding poverty: Perspectives from the social sciences.* New York, NY: Basic Books.

Lewis, P. H. (1998, August 15). Too late to say "extinct" in Ubykh, Eyak or Ona. *The New York Times.*

Lewis, R., & Yancey, G. (1997). Racial and nonracial factors that influence spouse choice in black/white marriages. *Journal of Black Studies, 28,* 60–78.

Liazos, A. (1985). *Sociology: A liberating perspective.* Boston, MA: Allyn & Bacon.

Liben, L. S., & Bigler, B. R. (2002). The developmental course of gender differentiation: Conceptualizing, measuring, and evaluating constructs and pathways. *Monographs of the Society for Research in Child Development, 67,* 1–112.

Lichtblau, E. (2008, April 9). In justice shift, corporate deals replace trials. *The New York Times.*

Lichtblau, E. (2016, September 18). Hate crimes against American Muslims most since post-9/11 era. *The New York Times.*

Light, P. (1988). *Baby boomers.* New York, NY: Norton.

Lindesmith, A. R., Strauss, A. L., & Denzin, N. K. (1991). *Social psychology*. Englewood Cliffs, NJ: Prentice Hall.

Link, B. G., Mirotznik, J., & Cullen, F. T. (1991). The effectiveness of stigma-coping orientations: Can negative consequences of mental illness labeling be avoided? *Journal of Health and Social Behavior, 32,* 302–320.

Link, B. G., & Phelan, J. C. (2001). Conceptualizing stigma. *Annual Review of Sociology, 27,* 363–385.

Linneman, T. J. (2012). Gender in *Jeopardy!* Intonation variation on a television game show. *Gender & Society, 27,* 82–105.

Lino, M., Kuczynski, K., Rodriguez, & Schap, T. R. (2017). *Expenditures on children by families, 2015*. Misc. Report 1528-2015. U.S. Department of Agriculture. www.cupp .usda.gov/sites/default/files/crc2015.pdf. Accessed January 15, 2017.

Linton, R. (1937). One hundred percent American. *American Mercury, 40,* 427–429.

Lipka, M. (2014). *Young U.S. Catholics overwhelmingly accepting of homosexuality*. Pew Research Center. www .pewresearch.org/fact-tank/2014/10/16/ypung-u-s-cath olics-overwhelmingly-accepting-of-homosexuality/. Accessed January 16, 2015.

Lipka, M. (2015). *5 facts about abortion*. Pew Research Center. www.pewresearch.org/fact-tank/2015/06/11/5-facts-about-abortion/. Accessed June 25, 2015.

Lipka, M. (2017). *Muslims and Islam: Key findings in the U.S. and around the world*. Pew Research Center. www.pewre-search.org/fact-tank/2017/05/26/muslims-and-islam-key-findings-in-the-u-s-and-around-the-world/. Accessed June 6, 2017.

Lippmann, L. W. (1922). *Public opinion*. New York, NY: Harcourt Brace Jovanovich.

Lips, H. M. (1993). *Sex and gender: An introduction*. Mountain View, CA: Mayfield.

Lipson, C. (2004). *Doing honest work in college*. Chicago, IL: University of Chicago Press.

Liptak, A. (2003, June 3). For jailed immigrants, a presumption of guilt. *The New York Times*.

Liptak, A. (2004, March 17). Bans on interracial unions offer perspective on gay ones. *The New York Times*.

Liptak, A. (2014, December 1). Case seeking job protections for pregnant women heads to Supreme Court. *The New York Times*.

Lisak, D., Gardinier, L., Nicksa, S. C., & Cote, A. M. (2010). False allegations of sexual assault: An analysis of ten years of reported cases. *Violence Against Women, 16,* 1318–1334.

Little, A. G. (2007, September 2). Not in whose backyard? *The New York Times Magazine.*

Little Mommy. (2017). *About Little Mommy*. www.little mommy.com/en-us/brandinfo.aspx. Accessed January 5, 2017.

Livingston, G. (2014). *Four-in-ten couples are saying "I do," again*. Pew Research Center. www.pewsocialtrends.org/files/2014/11/2014-11-14_remarriage-final.pdf. Accessed January 15, 2017.

Livingston, G. (2016). *Among 41 nations, U.S. is the outlier when it comes to paid parental leave*. Pew Research Center. www.pewresearch.org/fact-tank/2016/09/26/u-s-lacks-mandated-paid-parental-leave/. Accessed January 15, 2017.

Lofland, L. H. (1973). *A world of strangers: Order and action in urban public space*. New York, NY: Basic Books.

Lohr, S. (2012, March 2). For impatient web users, an eye blink is just too long to wait. *The New York Times*.

Long, H. (2016). *U.S. has lost 5 million manufacturing jobs since 2000*. CNN Money. money.cnn.com/2016/03/29/news/economy/uw-manufacturing-jobs/index.html. Accessed June 4, 2017.

Longman, J., & Higgins, M. (2005, August 3). Rad dudes of the world, unite. *The New York Times*.

Longman, T. (2009). *Christianity and genocide in Rwanda*. Cambridge, UK: Cambridge University Press.

López, G., & Bialik, K. (2017). *Key findings about U.S. immigrants*. Pew Research Center. www.pewresearch.org/fact-tank/2017/05/03/key-findings-about-u-s-immigrants. Accessed June 26, 2017.

López, G., & Krogstad, J. M. (2017). *How Hispanic police officers view their jobs*. Pew Research Center. www.pewresearch .org/fact-tank/2017/02/15/how-hispanic-police-officers-view-their-jobs/. Accessed June 6, 2017.

Lorber, J. (1989). Dismantling Noah's Ark. In B. J. Risman & P. Schwartz (Eds.), *Gender in intimate relationships: A microstructural approach*. Belmont, CA: Wadsworth.

Lorber, J. (2000). *Gender and the social construction of illness*. Walnut Creek, CA: AltaMira Press.

Lovett, I. (2013, March 10). Neighborhoods seek to banish sex offenders by building parks. *The New York Times*.

Lowenstein, R. (2006, July 9). The immigration equation. *The New York Times*.

Lowrey, A. (2013a, May 5). Movin' on up. *The New York Times Magazine*.

Lowrey, A. (2013b, March 31). When problems start getting real. *The New York Times Magazine*.

Luhrmann, T. M. (2015, July 5). The appeal of piety. *The New York Times*.

Luker, K. (1984). *Abortion and the politics of motherhood*. Berkeley: University of California Press.

Luo, F., Florence, C., Quispe-Agnoli, M., Ouyang, L., & Crosby, A. (2011). Impact of business cycles on US suicide rates, 1928–2007. *American Journal of Public Health, 101*, 1139–1146.

Lutz, A. (2012, June 14). These 6 corporations control 90% of the media in America. *Business Insider*. www.businessinsider .com/these-6-corporations-control-90-of-the-media-in-america-2012-6. Accessed January 7, 2015.

Lyall, S. (2000, July 8). Irish now face the other side of immigration. *The New York Times*.

Lyall, S. (2012, July 12). Caitlin Moran has her sights set on blowing up feminism. *The New York Times Magazine*.

Lyman, R. (2015, April 21). Empty nest? In Slovakia, it may begin when the child is 35. *The New York Times*.

Lynch, T., Tompkins, J. E., van Driel, I. I., & Fritz, N. (2016). Sexy, strong, and secondary: A content analysis of female characters in video games across 31 years. *Journal of Communication, 66*, 564–584.

Lytton, H., & Romney, D. M. (1991). Parents' differential socialization of boys and girls: A metaanalysis. *Psychology Bulletin, 109*, 267–296.

Lytton, T. D. (2007, February 4). Legal legacy. *The Boston Globe*.

MacAndrew, C., & Edgerton, R. B. (1969). *Drunken comportment: A social explanation*. Chicago, IL: Aldine-Atherton.

MacDonald, K., & Parke, R. D. (1986). Parent-child physical play: The effects of sex and age on children and parents. *Sex Roles, 15*, 367–378.

Macgillivray, I. K. (2000). Educational equity for gay, lesbian, bisexual, transgendered, and queer/questioning students: The demands of democracy and social justice for America's schools. *Education and Urban Society, 32*, 303–323.

Macur, J. (2017, August 6). Who qualifies to compete as a woman? A fight resumes. *The New York Times*.

Madden, M. (2014). *Public perceptions of privacy and security in the post-Snowden era*. Pew Research Internet Project. www. pewinternet.org/2014/11/12/public-privacy-perceptions/. Accessed June 24, 2015.

Mahler, J. (2017, January 1). Search party. *The New York Times Magazine*.

Makary, M. A., & Daniel, M. (2016, May 3). Medical error—The third leading cause of death in the U.S. *The BMJ*. 353. www.bmj.com/content/353/bmj.i2139. Accessed January 26, 2017.

The Malala Fund. (2016). *What we do*. www.malala.org/ about. Accessed December 27, 2016.

Malik, K. (2017, June 14). In defense of cultural appropriation. *The New York Times*.

Mallory, C., & Sears, B. (2016). *Evidence of discrimination in public accommodations based on sexual orientation and gender identity*. The Williams Institute. williamsinstitute.law.ucla .edu/up-content/Public-Accommodations-Discrimination-Complaints-2008-2014.pdf. Accessed June 14, 2017.

Mandery, E. J. (2014, April 25). End college legacy preferences. *The New York Times*.

Mann, C. C. (1993, February). How many is too many? *Atlantic Monthly*.

Manning, L. (2007). Nightmare at the day care: The Wee Care case. *Crime Magazine*. www.crimemagazine.com/ nightmare-day-care-wee-care-case. Accessed June 7, 2011.

Manning, W. D., & Smock, P. J. (1999). New families and nonresident father-child visits. *Social Forces, 78*, 87–117.

Mannon, J. (1997). *Measuring up*. Boulder, CO: Westview Press.

Mansfield, H. (2006). *Manliness*. New Haven, CT: Yale University Press.

Marchant, J. (2016, January 10). A placebo treatment for pain. *The New York Times*.

Marger, M. N. (1994). *Race and ethnic relations: American and global perspectives*. Belmont, CA: Wadsworth.

Marger, M. N. (2005). The mass media as a power institution. In S. J. Ferguson (Ed.), *Mapping the social landscape*. New York, NY: McGraw-Hill.

Markoff, J. (2011, October 11). Government aims to build a "data eye in the sky." *The New York Times*.

Markoff, J. (2013, April 4). Software subs for professors on essay test. *The New York Times*.

Marla Olmstead. (2004). *About Marla*. www.marlaolmstead .com. Accessed November 23, 2004.

Marsh, B. (2005, January 2). The vulnerable become more vulnerable. *The New York Times*.

Martin, C. (2015, February 8). Good lovers lie. *The New York Times*.

Martin, C. L., & Ruble, D. (2004). Children's search for gender cues. *Current Directions in Psychological Science, 13*, 67–70.

Martin, C. L., & Ruble, D. (2009). Patterns of gender development. *Annual Review of Psychology, 61*, 353–381.

Martin, J. B. (2010). The development of ideal body image perceptions in the United States. *Nutrition Today, 45*, 98–100.

Martin, P., & Midgley, E. (2010). *Immigration in America 2010* (Population Bulletin Update). www.prb.org/pdf10/immigration-update2010.pdf. Accessed July 6, 2010.

Martinez-Alier, J. (2003). *The environmentalism of the poor.* Cheltenham, UK: Edward Elgar.

Marx, K. (1963). *The 18th Brumaire of Louis Bonaparte.* New York, NY: International. (Original work published 1869)

Marx, K., & Engels, F. (1982). *The communist manifesto.* New York, NY: International. (Original work published 1848)

Mascarenhas, A. (2016, February 4). Sex determination: An old law, a new debate. *The Indian Express.* www.indianexpress.com/article/explained/sex-determination-an-old-law-a-new-debate/. Accessed June 24, 2017.

Mateo, A., & Menza, K. (2017, March 27). The results of a 1976 survey of women about sexual harassment at work remain virtually unchanged in 2017. *Redbook.*

Mather, M. (2016). *Trends and challenges facing America's Latino children.* Population Reference Bureau. www.prb.org/Publications/Articles/2016/trends-and-challenges-facing-americas-latino-children.aspx. Accessed June 5, 2017.

Mather, M., & Adams, D. (2006). *The risk of negative child outcomes in low-income families.* Washington, DC: Population Reference Bureau. www.prb.org/pdf06/RiskNegOut_Families.pdf. Accessed July 27, 2006.

Mather, M., & Feldman-Jacobs, C. (2015). *Women and girls at risk of female genital mutilation/cutting in the United States.* Population Reference Bureau. www.prb.org/Publications/Articles/2015/us-fgmc.aspx. Accessed February 5, 2015.

Mather, M., & Jacobsen, L. A. (2010). *Hard times for Latino men in U.S.* Population Reference Bureau. www.prb.org/Articles/2010/latinomen.aspx. Accessed June 16, 2011.

Mather, M., & Jarosz, B. (2014). *The demography of inequality in the United States.* Population Reference Bureau. www.prb.org/pdf14/united-states-inequality.pdf. Accessed May 30, 2015.

Matthew, D. B. (2015). *Just medicine: A cure for racial inequality in American health care.* New York: NYU Press.

Mathews, L. (1996, July 6). More than identity rides on a new racial category. *The New York Times.*

Matthews, J. (2012, December 12). Cash incentives for students. *The Washington Post.*

McAdam, D. (1982). *Political process and the development of black insurgency, 1930–1970.* Chicago, IL: University of Chicago Press.

McAdam, D., McCarthy, J. D., & Zald, M. N. (1988). Social movements. In N. J. Smelser (Ed.), *Handbook of sociology.* Newbury Park, CA: Sage.

McAuliff, M. (2012, March 20). Paul Ryan wants "welfare reform round 2." *Huffington Post.* www.huffingtonpost.com/2012/03/20/paul-ryan-welfare-reform_n_1368277.html. Accessed June 17, 2014.

McCain, F. (1991). Interview with Franklin McCain. In C. Carson, D. J. Garrow, G. Gill, V. Harding, & D. Clark Hine (Eds.), *The eyes on the prize civil rights reader.* New York, NY: Penguin Books.

McCall, G. J., & Simmons, J. L. (1978). *Identities and interactions.* New York, NY: Free Press.

McCarthy, J. (2014, May 21). *Same-sex marriage support reaches new high at 55%.* Gallup. www.gallup.com/poll/169640/sex-marriage-support-reaches-new-high.aspx. Accessed July 17, 2015.

McCarthy, J. D., & Wolfson, M. (1992). Consensus movements, conflict movements, and the cooptation of civic and state infrastructures. In A. D. Morris & C. M. Mueller (Eds.), *Frontiers in social movement theory.* New Haven, CT: Yale University Press.

McCarthy, J. D., & Zald, M. N. (1977). Resource mobilization and social movements: A partial theory. *American Journal of Sociology, 82,* 1212–1241.

McCarthy, T. (2001, May 14). He makes a village. *Time.*

McCormick, J. S., Maric, A., Seto, M. C., & Barbaree, H. E. (1998). Rela tionship to victim predicts sentence length in sexual assault cases. *Journal of Interpersonal Violence, 13,* 413–420.

McDonaldization. (2015). *What is McDonaldization?* www.mcdonaldization.com/whatisit.shtml. Accessed May 20, 2015.

McDonald's Corporation. (2016). *2015 annual report.* corporate.mcdonalds.com/content/dam/About McDonalds/Investors 2/2015 Annual Report.pdf. Accessed January 26, 2017.

McEwan, J. (2005). Proving consent in sexual cases: Legislative change and cultural evolution. *International Journal of Evidence and Proof, 9,* 1–28.

McGee, C. (2010, August 23). The open road wasn't quite open to all. *The New York Times.*

McGeehan, P. (2012, February 8). For hotel staff, panic buttons and big raises. *The New York Times.*

McGill, A. (2016, December 20). Merry Christmas vs. Happy Holidays, Round 2,016. *The Atlantic.*

McHale, S. M., Crouter, A. C., & Whiteman, S. D. (2003). The family contexts of gender development in childhood and adolescence. *Social Development, 12,* 125–148.

McHugh, P. (1968). *Defining the situation.* Indianapolis, IN: Bobbs-Merrill.

McIntosh, P. (2001). White privilege: Unpacking the invisible knapsack. In P. Rothenberg (Ed.), *Race, class, and gender in the United States*. New York, NY: Worth.

McKenry, P. C., & Price, S. J. (1995). Divorce: A comparative perspective. In B. B. Ingoldsby & S. Smith (Eds.), *Families in multicultural perspective*. New York, NY: Guilford Press.

McKinley, J. (2010, March 13). Conservatives on Texas panel carry the day on curricular change. *The New York Times*.

McKinley, J. (2011, February 17). "Non-English" tip policy raises eyebrows, then fades. *The New York Times*.

McKinley, J., & Mueller, B. (2015, October 15). Glimpses at a secretive sect after teenager's fatal beating. *The New York Times*.

McLaren, L. M. (2003). Anti-immigrant prejudice in Europe: Contact, threat perception, and preferences for the exclusion of migrants. *Social Forces, 81*, 909–936.

McLean, R. (2005, January 12). Spaniards dare to question the way the day is ordered. *The New York Times*.

McLean, R. (2006, January 21). In the new year, a novel idea for Spanish government workers: A literal lunch hour. *The New York Times*.

McLoyd, V. C., Cauce, A. M., Takeuchi, D., & Wilson, L. (2000). Marital processes and parental socialization in families of color: A decade review of research. *Journal of Marriage and the Family, 62*, 1070–1094.

McNeil, D. G. (2010, June 20). The curse of plenty. *The New York Times*.

McNeil, D. G. (2011, May 23). AIDS: A price break for antiretroviral drugs in 70 of the world's poorest countries. *The New York Times*.

McNeil, D. G. (2015, December 22). F.D.A. ends lifetime ban on blood donations by gay men, but caveat draws scorn. *The New York Times*.

McPherson, M., Smith-Lovin, L., & Brashears, M. E. (2006). Social isolation in America: Changes in core discussion networks over two decades. *American Sociological Review, 71*, 353–375.

Mead, G. H. (1934). *Mind, self and society*. Chicago, IL: University of Chicago Press.

Medina, J. (2016, May 19). A website for neighbors faces claims of profiling. *The New York Times*.

Mehan, H., & Wood, H. (1975). *The reality of ethnomethodology*. New York, NY: Wiley.

Meier, B. (2004, June 15). Group is said to seek full drug-trial disclosure. *The New York Times*.

Mele, C. (2016, December 8). Libraries become unexpected sites of surging hate crimes. *The New York Times*.

Meltzer, M. (2014, May 22). Who is a feminist now? *The New York Times*.

Mental Health Channel. (2007). *"General anxiety disorder" and "social phobias."* Northampton, MA: Author. www.mentalhealthchannel.net. Accessed June 18, 2007.

Mercy Corps. (2017). *Quick facts: What you need to know about the Syria crisis*. www.mercycorps.org/articles/iraq-jordan-lebanon-syria-turkey/quick-facts-what-you-need-know-about-syria-crisis. Accessed July 21, 2017.

Merton, R. (1948). The self-fulfilling prophecy. *Antioch Review, 8*, 193–210.

Merton, R. (1957). *Social theory and social structure*. New York, NY: Free Press.

Messick, D. M., & Brewer, M. B. (1983). Solving social dilemmas: A review. In L. Wheeler & P. Shaver (Eds.), *Review of personality and social psychology*. Beverly Hills, CA: Sage.

Messner, M. (2002). Boyhood, organized sports, and the construction of masculinities. In D. M. Newman & J. O'Brien (Eds.), *Sociology: Exploring the architecture of everyday life (Readings)*. Thousand Oaks, CA: Pine Forge Press.

Meyer, J. W., & Rowan, B. (1977). Institutionalized organizations: Formal structure as myth and ceremony. *American Journal of Sociology, 83*, 340–363.

Mez, J., Daneshvar, D. H., & Kiernan, P. T. (2017). Clinicopathological evaluation of chronic traumatic encephalopathy in players of American football. *JAMA, 318*, 360–370.

Miall, C. E. (1989). The stigma of involuntary childlessness. In A. S. Skolnick & J. H. Skolnick (Eds.), *Family in transition*. Boston, MA: Little, Brown.

Michaels, K. (1993). Eight years in Kafkaland. *National Review, 45*, 36–38.

Michels, R. (1949). *Political parties*. Glencoe, IL: Free Press. (Original work published 1911)

Michener, H. A., DeLamater, J. D., & Schwartz, S. H. (1986). *Social psychology*. San Diego, CA: Harcourt Brace Jovanovich.

Mihm, S. (2009, December 13). Artificial car noise. *The New York Times Magazine*.

Mikolajczyk, R. T., Iannotti, R. J., Farhat, T., & Thomas, V. (2012). Ethnic differences in perceptions of body satisfaction and body appearance among U.S. schoolchildren: A cross-sectional study. *BMC Public Health, 12*, 1–9.

Milbank, D., & Deane, C. (2003, September 6). Hussein link to 9/11 lingers in many minds. *The Washington Post*.

Milgram, S. (1974). *Obedience to authority.* New York, NY: Harper & Row.

Miller, C. C. (2015, February 7). How teacher biases can sway girls from math and science. *The New York Times.*

Miller, C. C. (2017a, January 16). Job disconnect: Male applicants/ feminine language. *The New York Times.*

Miller, C. C. (2017b, July 4). Relief for families, but no thanks to Congress. *The New York Times.*

Miller, C. C. (2017c, January 19). Sexes differ on persistence of sexism. *The New York Times.*

Miller, C. C. (2017d, July 2). When job puts sexes together, works cringe. *The New York Times.*

Miller, C. C. (2017e, January 5). Why men don't want jobs done mostly by women. *The New York Times.*

Miller, C. C., & Bui, Q. (2016, February 28). Rise in marriage equals helps fuel divisions by class. *The New York Times.*

Miller, C. L. (1987). Qualitative differences among gender-stereotyped toys: Implications for cognitive and social development. *Sex Roles, 16,* 473–488.

Miller, E., & Almon, J. (2009). *Crisis in the kindergarten: Why children need to play in school.* College Park, MD: Alliance for Childhood.

Miller, L. (2011, July 25). How to raise a global kid. *Newsweek.*

Miller, M. V. (1985). Poverty and its definition. In R. C. Barnes & E. W. Mills (Eds.), *Techniques for teaching sociological concepts.* Washington, DC: American Sociological Association.

Millman, M. (1980). *Such a pretty face.* New York, NY: Norton.

Mills, C. W. (1940). Situated actions and vocabularies of motive. *American Sociological Review, 5,* 904–913.

Mills, C. W. (1956). *The power elite.* New York, NY: Oxford University Press.

Mills, C. W. (1959). *The sociological imagination.* New York, NY: Oxford University Press.

Mills, J. L. (1985, February). Body language speaks louder than words. *Horizons.*

Minder, R. (2017, August 4). Where villagers play dead for a day in gratitude for being spared. *The New York Times.*

Minton, T. D., & Zeng, Z. (2017). *Jail inmates in 2015.* NCJ250394. U.S. Bureau of Justice Statistics. www.bjs.gov/content/pub/pdf/ji15.pdf. Accessed June 28, 2017.

Mishel, L., Bivens, J., Gould, E., & Shierholz, H. (2013). *The state of working America.* Economic Policy Institute. stateofworkingAmerica.org/subjects/overview/?reader. Accessed May 31, 2013.

Mobius, M. M., & Rosenblat, T. S. (2006). Why beauty matters. *American Economic Review, 96,* 222–235.

Moeller, P. (2012, March 26). Top 10 reasons to hire older people. *US News & World Report.* money.usnews.com/money/blogs/the-best-life/2012/03/26/top-10-reasons-to-hire-older-people. Accessed June 28, 2013.

Mohamed, B. (2016). *A new estimate of the U.S. Muslim population.* Pew Research Center. www.pewresearch.org/fact-tank/2016/01/06/a-new-estimate-of-the-u-s-muslim-population/. Accessed January 6, 2017.

Mokhiber, R. (1999, July/August). Crime wave! The top 100 corporate criminals of the 1990s. *Multinational Monitor,* 1–9.

Mokhiber, R., & Weissman, R. (2004, December). The ten worst corporations of 2004. *Multinational Monitor,* 8–21.

Molloy, B. L., & Herzberger, S. D. (1998). Body image and self-esteem: A comparison of African-American and Caucasian women. *Sex Roles, 38,* 631–643.

Molotch, H., & Lester, M. (1974). News as purposive behavior: On the strategic use of routine events, accidents, and scandals. *American Sociological Review, 39,* 101–112.

Molotch, H., & Lester, M. (1975). Accidental news: The great oil spill as local occurrence and national event. *American Journal of Sociology, 81,* 235–260.

MomsRising.org. (2017). *About MomsRising.* www.momsrising.org/page/moms/aboutmomsrising. Accessed June 28, 2017

Monk-Turner, E., Kouts, T., Parris, K., & Webb, C. (2007). Gender role stereotyping in advertisements for three radio stations: Does musical genre make a difference? *Journal of Gender Studies, 16,* 173–182.

Moore, E. A. (2015, May 18). Droughtshaming: California's new class warfare. *USA Today.*

Moore, R. B. (1992). Racist stereotyping in the English language. In M. L. Anderson & P. H. Collins (Eds.), *Race, class and gender: An anthology.* Belmont, CA: Wadsworth.

Moore, S. A. D. (2003). Understanding the connection between domestic violence, crime, and poverty: How welfare reform may keep battered women from leaving abusive relationships. *Texas Journal of Women and the Law, 12,* 451–484.

Moore, T. J., & Mattison, D. R. (2016). Adult utilization of psychiatric drugs and differences by sex, age, and race. *JAMA Internal Medicine,* E1. Jamainternalmedicine.com. Accessed January 18, 2017.

Morgan, B. L. (1998). A three-generational study of tomboy behavior. *Sex Roles, 39,* 787–800.

Morgan, G. (1986). *Images of organizations.* Newbury Park, CA: Sage.

Morgan, M. (1982). Television and adolescents' sex role stereotypes: A longitudinal study. *Journal of Personality and Social Psychology, 48,* 1173–1190.

Morgan, M. (1987). Television sex role attitudes and sex role behavior. *Journal of Early Adolescence, 7,* 269–282.

Morgan, R. (1996). *Sisterhood is global.* New York, NY: Feminist Press at the City University of New York.

Morris, W. (2015, October 11). Who do you think you are? *The New York Times Magazine.*

Morrongiello, B. A., & Hogg, K. (2004). Mothers' reactions to children misbehaving in ways that can lead to injury: Implications for gender differences in children's risk taking and injuries. *Sex Roles, 50,* 103–118.

Moss-Racusin, A., Dovidio, J. F., Brescoll, V. L., Graham, M. J., & Handelsman, J. (2012). Science faculty's subtle gender biases favor male students. *Proceedings of the National Academy of Sciences.* www.pnas.org/cgi/doi/10.1073/pnas.1211286109. Accessed June 21, 2013.

Mottl, T. L. (1980). The analysis of countermovements. *Social Problems, 27,* 620–635.

Mouawad, J., & White, M. C. (2013, December 23). On jammed jets, sardines turn on one another. *The New York Times.*

Mui, Y. Q. (2012, July 8). For black Americans, financial damage from subprime implosion is likely to last. *The Washington Post.*

Mukherjee, S. (2016, May 2). Same but different. *The New Yorker.*

Mulrine, A. (2003, May 5). Echoes of a scandal. *U.S. News & World Report.*

Murdock, G. P. (1949). *Social structure.* New York, NY: Macmillan.

Murdock, G. P. (1957). World ethnography sample. *American Anthropologist, 59,* 664–687.

Murphy, C. (2015). *Most U.S. Christian groups grow more accepting of homosexuality.* Pew Research Center. www.pewresearch.org/fact-tank/2015/12/18/most-u-s-christians-grow-more-accepting-of-homosexuality. Accessed January 17, 2017.

Murphy, D. E. (2004, January 11). Imagining life without illegal immigrants. *The New York Times.*

Murphy, K. (2017, January 7). Yes, it's your parents' fault. *The New York Times Online.* www.nytimes.com/2017/01/07/opinion/sunday/yes-its-your-parents-fault.html? r=0. Accessed January 9, 2017.

Murphy, T. (2017, July/August). A new way to look at race. *Brown Alumni Magazine.*

Murray, C. J. L., & Ng, M. (2014). *Nearly one-third of the world's population is obese or overweight, new data show.* Institute for Health Metrics and Evaluation. www.healthdata.org/news-release/nearly-one-third-world's-population-obese-or-overweight-new-data-show. Accessed June 11, 2015.

Muscat, K. K. (2013). Black athletic superiority: Fact or fiction? *The Triple Helix,* Easter. www.camtriplehelix.com. Accessed June 14, 2013.

Mydans, S. (1995, February 12). A shooter as vigilante, and avenging angel. *The New York Times.*

Mydans, S. (2007, April 9). Across cultures, English is the word. *International Herald Tribune.*

Nanda, S. (1994). *Cultural anthropology.* Belmont, CA: Wadsworth.

Nasar, S., & Mitchell, K. B. (1999, May 23). Booming job market draws young black men into the fold. *The New York Times.*

National Academies of Sciences, Engineering, and Medicine. (2017). *The economic and fiscal consequences of immigration.* www.nap.edu/catalog/23550/the-economic-and-fiscal-consequences-of-immigration. Accessed October 17, 2017.

National Academy of Sciences. (2007). *Beyond bias and barriers: Fulfilling the potential of women in academic science and engineering.* Washington, DC: National Academies Press.

National Alliance on Mental Illness. (2013). *Mental Illness: Facts and numbers.* www2.nami.org/factsheets/mentalillness_factsheet.pdf. Accessed July 13, 2015.

National Alliance to End Homelessness. (2016). *State of homelessness in America 2016.* www.endhomelessness.org/library/entry/SOH2016. Accessed June 2, 2017.

National Assessment of Educational Progress. (2015). *The nation's report card: 2015—Mathematics and reading at grade 12.* nationsreportcard.gov/reading_math_g12_2015/#1. Accessed January 27, 2017.

National Association for Single Sex Public Education. (2013). *Single-sex schools/schools with single-sex classrooms/What's the difference?* www.singlesexschools.org/schools-schools.htm. Accessed June 23, 2013.

National Association for the Advancement of Colored People. (2016). *The NAACP real world guide to interacting* with law enforcement: The 411 on the Five-O. www.naacp.org/wp-content/uploads/2016/03/154904-NAACP-PROOF.pdf. Accessed January 4, 2017.

National Association of Colleges and Employers. (2016). *Hiring up for class of 2016 graduates but projections trimmed from last fall.* www.naceweb.org/about-us/press/2016/hiring-up-for-class-of-2016-graduates.aspx. Accessed December 23, 2016.

National Association of School Psychologists. (2013). *Youth gun violence fact sheet.* www.nasponline.org/resources/crisis_safety/youth_gun_violence_fact_sheet.pdf. Accessed June 28, 2015.

National Association to Advance Fat Acceptance. (2016). *News releases.* www.naafaonline.com/dev2/about-news.html. Accessed January 8, 2017.

National Center for Education Statistics. (2010). *Teachers' use of educational technology in U.S. public schools: 2009.* NCES2010-040.Nces.ed.gov/pubsearch/pubsinfo.asp?pubid=2010040. Accessed July 2, 2013.

National Center for Education Statistics. (2013a). *Adult skills in an international context.* www.nces.ed.gov/fastfacts/display.asp?id=683. Accessed May 22, 2015.

National Center for Education Statistics. (2013b). *Characteristics of public and private elementary and secondary school teachers in the United States: Results from the 2011-12 schools and staffing survey.* www.nces.ed.gov/pubs2013/2013314.pdf. Accessed June 6, 2015.

National Center for Education Statistics. (2014a). *Fast facts: Graduation rates, Table 326.10.* www.nces.ed.gov/programs/digest/d13/tables/dt13_326.10.asp. Accessed June 6, 2015.

National Center for Education Statistics. (2014b). *Performance of U.S. 15-year-old students in mathematics, science, and reading literacy in an international context.* www.nces.ed.gov/pubs2014/2014024rev.pdf. Accessed May 22, 2015.

National Center for Education Statistics. (2016). *Welcome to PISA 2015 results—International trends in average scores (Tables M1 and T2).* nces.ed.gov/surveys/pisa/pisa2015/index.asp. Accessed January 27, 2017.

National Center for Education Statistics. (2017a). *Digest of education statistics.* nces.ed.gov/programs/digest/current_tables.asp. Accessed June 16, 2017.

National Center for Education Statistics. (2017b). *Indicators of school crime and safety: 2016.* nces.ed.gov/pubs2017/2017064.pdf. Accessed June 28, 2017.

National Center for Fair and Open Testing. (2016). *SATs drop again, as test-optional movement surges.* www.fairtest.org/sats-drop-again-testoptional-movement-surges. Accessed May 24, 2017.

National Center for Health Statistics. (2014). *Health: United States: 2013.* www.cdc.gov/nchs/data/hus/hus13.pdf. Accessed January 2, 2015.

National Center for Health Statistics. (2015a). *Health: United States: 2015.* www.cdc.gov/nchs/data/hus/hus15.pdf. Accessed December 26, 2016.

National Center for Health Statistics. (2015b). *National marriage and divorce trends.* www.cdc.gov/nchs/nvss/marriage_divorce_tables.htm. Accessed January 15, 2017.

National Center for Missing and Exploited Children. (2017). *Missing children, state care, and child sex trafficking.* www.missingkids.org/en_US/publications/missingchildrenstatecare.pdf. Accessed May 24, 2017.

National Center on Time and Learning. (2013). *Mapping the field: A report on expanded time schools in America.* www.timeandlearning.org/mapping. Accessed May 28, 2013.

National Committee on Pay Equity. (2007). *Current legislation.* Washington, DC: Author. www.pay-equity.org/info-leg.html. Accessed July 11, 2007.

National Conference of State Legislatures. (2009). *State laws regarding marriage between first cousins.* Washington, DC: Author. www.ncsl.org/programs/cyf/cousins.htm. Accessed April 28, 2009.

National Consortium for the Study of Terrorism and Responses to Terrorism. (2016). *Patterns of Islamic state-related terrorism, 2002–2015.* www.start.umd.edu/pubs/START_IslamicStateTerrorismPatterns_BackgroundReport_Aug2016.pdf. Accessed December 26, 2016.

National Crime Records Bureau. (2016). *Crime in India: 2015.* ncrb.nic.in. Accessed June 20, 2017.

National Digestive Diseases Information Clearinghouse. (2011). *Hemochromatosis.* http://digestive.niddk.nih.gov/ddiseases/pubs/hemochromatosis. Accessed April 1, 2011.

National Eating Disorders Association. (2011). *Statistics: Eating disorders and their precursors.* www.nationaleatingdisorders.org/informationresources/general-information.php#factsstatistics. Accessed June 20, 2011.

National Eating Disorders Association. (2015). *Get the facts on eating disorders.* www.nationaleatingdisorders.org/get-facts-eating-disorders. Accessed June 11, 2015.

National Employment Law Project. (2015). *It's time to raise the minimum wage.* www.nelp.org/publication/time-raise-minimum-wage/. Accessed June 25, 2015.

National Fair Housing Alliance. (2015). *Where you live matters: 2015 Fair Housing Trends Report.* www.national fairhousing.org/LinkClick.aspx?fileticket=SYWmBgwpazA%3d&tabid=3917&mid=5321. Accessed June 3, 2015.

National Fair Housing Alliance. (2017). *The case for fair housing: 2017 fair housing trends report.* nationalfairhousing.org/wp-content/uploads/2017/05/TRENDS-REPORT-5-17-17-FINAL.pdf. Accessed June 9, 2017.

National Highway Traffic Safety Administration. (2017). *Distracted driving 2015.* crashstats.nhtsa.dot.gov/Api/Public/ViewPublication/812381. Accessed June 28, 2017.

National Human Trafficking Hotline. (2017). *Hotline statistics.* humantraffickinghotline.org/states. Accessed May 24, 2017.

National Institute of Mental Health. (2010). *Statistics.* www.nimh.nih.gov/statistics/index.shtml. Accessed June 9, 2011.

National Institute on Aging. (2006). *Dramatic changes in U.S. aging highlighted in new Census* (NIH report). Bethesda, MD: Author. www.nia.nih.gov/NewsAndEvents/PressReleases/PR2006030965PlusReport.htm. Accessed July 31, 2006.

National Institute on Aging. (2015). *Growing older in America: The health and retirement study.* hrs.isr.umich.edu/about/data-book. Accessed January 9, 2017.

National Institute on Alcohol Abuse and Alcoholism. (2015). *College drinking.* Pubs.niaaa.nih.gov/publications/CollegeFactSheet/CollegeFactSheet.pdf. Accessed January 18, 2017.

National Low Income Housing Coalition. (2016). *Out of reach 2016: No refuge for low income renters.* www.nlihc.org/sites/default/files/oor/OOR_2016.pdf. Accessed June 1, 2017.

The National Marriage Project. (2010). *When marriage disappears: The new middle America.* www.virginia.edu/marriageproject/pdfs/Union_11_12_10.pdf. Accessed September 4, 2011.

National Partnership for Women and Families. (2005). *Expecting better: A state-by-state analysis of parental leave programs.* Washington, DC: Author. www.nationalpartnership.org/site/DocServer/ParentalLeaveReportMay05.pdf?doc ID=1052. Accessed September 5, 2009.

National Partnership for Women and Families. (2014). *Paid family and medical leave: Good for business.* Fact Sheet. www.nationalpartnership.org/research-library/work-family/paid-leave/paid-leave-good-for-business.pdf. Accessed January 16, 2015.

National Public Radio. (2009). *In India, skin-whitening creams reflect old bia*ses. www.npr.org/templates/story/story.php?storyId=120340646. Accessed June 18, 2010.

National Public Radio. (2014). *Planet Money makes a t-shirt.* Apps.npr.org/tshirt/#/title. Accessed May 21, 2015.

National Sleep Foundation. (2008). *2008 sleep in America poll.* www.sleepfoundation.org/sites/default/files/2008 POLL SOF.pdf. Accessed January 5, 2015.

National Women's Law Center. (2006). *The Paycheck Fairness Act: Helping to close the wage gap for women.* Washington, DC: Author. www.pay-equity.org/PDFs/PaycheckFairnessActApr06.pdf. Accessed September 5, 2009.

Navarro, M. (2014, November 11). Homeless because they are abused at home. *The New York Times.*

NCAA. (2013). *Estimated probability of competing in athletics beyond the high school interscholastic level.* www.ncaa.org/sites/default/files/Probability-of-going-pro-methodology_Update2013.pdf. Accessed June 2, 2015.

Neilson, S. (2016, March 7). Prison uniforms make it harder to "go straight." *Newsweek.*

Nelkin, D., & Pollak, M. (1981). *The atom besieged.* Cambridge, MA: MIT Press.

Nestle, M. (2002). *Food politics.* Berkeley: University of California Press.

Neubeck, K. (1986). *Social problems: A critical approach.* New York, NY: Random House.

Neuman, W. L. (1994). *Social research methods: Qualitative and quantitative approaches.* Boston, MA: Allyn & Bacon.

Neumeister, L. (2015, June 22). Suit targets bias of post-9/11 US. *Lewiston Sun Journal.*

Newcomb, A. (2012). Oregon faith healer parents get probation in son's death. *Yahoo News.* Gma.yahoo.com/oregon/-faith-healer-parents-probation-sons-death-193833596-abc-news-topstories-html. Accessed January 9, 2013.

Newman, D. (2009). *Families: A sociological perspective.* New York, NY: McGraw-Hill.

Newman, D. (2017). *Identities and inequalities: Exploring the intersections of race, class, gender, and sexuality* (2nd ed.). New York, NY: McGraw-Hill.

Newman, K. (2005). Family values against the odds. In A. S. Skolnick & J. H. Skolnick (Eds.), *Family in transition* (13th ed.). Boston, MA: Allyn & Bacon.

Newport, F. (2011). *Americans prefer boys to girls, just as they did in 1941.* Gallup.www.gallup.com/poll/148187/americans-prefer-boys-girls-1941.aspx. Accessed July 17, 2015.

Newport, F. (2013). *In U.S. 87% approve of black-white marriage, vs. 4% in 1958.* Gallup. www.gallup.com/poll/163697/approve-marriage-blacks-whites.aspx. Accessed January 1, 2015.

Newport, F. (2015). *Americans continue to shift left on moral issues*. Gallup. www.gallup.com/poll/183413/americans-continue-shift-left-key-moral-issues.aspx. Accessed January 10, 2017.

Newswise. (2011). New research finds obesity negatively impacts income, especially for women. The George Washington University. www.newswise.com/articles/view/583521?print-article. Accessed January 14, 2013.

Niebuhr, G. (1998, April 12). Makeup of American religion is looking more like a mosaic, data say. *The New York Times.*

Nippon.com. (2014). *Suicide in Japan.* www.nippon.com/en/features/n00075/. Accessed January 3, 2015.

Nixon, R. (2013, February 2). U.S. releases new rules for school snack foods. *The New York Times.*

NoBullying.com (2015). *LGBT bullying statistics.* www.nobullying.com/lgbt-bullying-statistics/. Accessed June 9, 2015.

The nocebo response. (2005, March). *Harvard Mental Health Letter,* pp. 6–7.

Norton, M. I., & Ariely, D. (2011). Building a better America—one wealth quintile at a time. *Perspectives on Psychological Science, 6,* 9–12.

Norton, M. I., & Sommers, S. R. (2011). Whites see racism as a zero-sum game that they are now losing. *Perspectives in Psychological Science, 6,* 215–218.

Nossiter, A. (2014, February 9). Nigeria uses law and whip to "sanitize" gays. *The New York Times.*

Nossiter, A. (2015, May 19). Former captives in Nigeria tell of mass rapes. *The New York Times.*

O'Connell Davidson, J. (2002). The practice of social research. In D. M. Newman & J. O'Brien (Eds.), *Sociology: Exploring the architecture of everyday life (Readings).* Thousand Oaks, CA: Pine Forge Press.

Ody, E. (2012, March 16). Wealthy families skip waiting rooms with concierge medial plans. *Bloomberg Business.* www.bloomberg.com/news/articles/2012-03-16/wealthy-families-skip-waiting-rooms-with-concierge-medical-plans. Accessed May 27, 2015.

Office of Presidential Advance. (2002). *Presidential advance manual.* www.aclu.org/pdfs/freespeech/presidential_advance_manual.pdf. Accessed June 1, 2011.

Ogden, C. L., Carroll, M. D., Fryar, C. D., & Flegal, K. M. (2015). *Prevalence of obesity among adults and youth: United States, 2011-2014.* National Center for Health Statistics Data Brief #219. www.cdc.gov/nchs/data/databriefs/db219.pdf. Accessed January 6, 2017.

Ohgami, H., Terao, T., Shiotsuki, I., Ishii, N., & Iwata, N. (2009). Lithium levels in drinking water and risk of suicide. *British Journal of Psychiatry, 194,* 464–465.

O'Keefe, E. (2013, June 27). Senate approves comprehensive immigration bill. *Washington Post.*

Oldenburg, R., & Brissett, D. (1982). The third place. *Qualitative Sociology, 5,* 265–284.

Oliphant, B. (2016). *Support for death penalty lowest in more than four decades.* Pew Research Center. www.pewresearch.org/fact-tank/2016/09/29/support-for-death-penalty-lowest-in-more-than-four- decades/. Accessed January 17, 2017.

Olsen, M. (1965). *The logic of collective action.* Cambridge, MA: Harvard University Press.

Olsen-Phillips, P., Choma, R., Bryner, S., & Weber, D. (2015). *The political one percent of the one percent in 2014: Mega donors fuel rising cost of elections.* Center for Responsive Politics. www.opensecrets.org. Accessed May 26, 2015.

Omi, M., & Winant, H. (1992). Racial formations. In P. S. Rothenberg (Ed.), *Race, class and gender in the United States.* New York, NY: St. Martin's Press.

One child left behind. (2009, March/April). *UTNE Reader.*

Onishi, N. (2004, March 30). On U.S. fast food, more Okinawans grow super-sized. *The New York Times.*

Orenstein, P. (2008, February 10). Girls will be girls. *The New York Times Magazine.*

Orfield, G., Ee, J., Frankenberg, E., & Siegel-Hawley, G. (2016). *Brown at 62: School segregation by race, poverty, and state.* Civil Rights Project UCLA. www.civilrightsproject.ucla.edu/research/k-12-education/integration-and-diversity/brown-at-62-segregation-by-race-poverty-and-state/Brown-at-62-final-corrected-2.pdf. Accessed June 12, 2017.

Orfield, G., & Frankenberg, E. (2014). *Brown at 60: Great progress, a long retreat, and an uncertain future.* The Civil Rights Project. UCLA. www.civilrightsproject.ucla.edu/research/k-12-education/integration-and-diversity/brown-at-60-great-progress-a-long-retreat-and-an-uncertain-future/Brown-at-60-051814.pdf. Accessed June 4, 2015.

Organ Procurement and Transplantion Network. (2017). *National data.* optn.transplant.hrsa.gov/data/view-data-reports/national-data/. Accessed June 11, 2017.

Organization for Economic Cooperation and Development. (2014). *CO2.2: Child poverty.* www.oecd.org/els/soc/CO2_2_ChildPoverty_jan2014.pdf. Accessed May 31, 2015.

Organization for Economic Cooperation and Development. (2015a). *The ABC of gender equality in education: Aptitiude, behaviour, confidence.* www.oecd.org/pisa/

keyfindings/pisa-2012-results-gender-eng.pdf. Accessed March 11, 2015.

Organization for Economic Cooperation and Development. (2015b). *Gender wage gap.* www.data.oecd.org/earnwage/gender-wage-gap.htm. Accessed June 14, 2015.

Osnos, E. (2017, January 30). Survival of the richest. *The New Yorker.*

O'Sullivan-See, K., & Wilson, W. J. (1988). Race and ethnicity. In N. Smelser (Ed.), *Handbook of sociology.* Newbury Park, CA: Sage.

Outsports. (2016). *A record 56 out LGBT athletes compete in Rio Olympics.* www.outsports.com/2016/7/11/12133594/rio-olympics-teams-2016-gay-lgbt-athletes-record. Accessed January 16, 2017.

Padavic, I., & Reskin, B. (2002). *Women and men at work* (2nd ed.). Thousand Oaks, CA: Sage.

Padawer, R. (2012, August 8). What's so bad about a boy who wants to wear a dress? *The New York Times Magazine.*

Padawer, R. (2014, October 15). Sisterhood is complicated. *The New York Times Magazine.*

Palmer, B. (2012, November 15). Can we bring back the stockades? *Slate.* www.slate.com. Accessed July 3, 2013.

Pappas, A. (2013, May 22). Another lawmaker says Oklahoma disaster relief must be offset with spending cuts. *The Daily Caller.* dailycaller.com/2013/05/22/lawmaker-disaster-relief-must-be-offset-with-spending-cuts/. Accessed May 31, 2013.

Parenti, M. (1986). *Inventing reality.* New York, NY: St. Martin's Press.

Parenti, M. (1995). *Democracy for the few.* New York, NY: St. Martin's Press.

Parenti, M. (2006). Mass media: For the many, by the few. In P. S. Rothenberg (Ed.), *Beyond borders: Thinking critically about global issues.* New York, NY: Worth.

Parker, K., Wang, W., & Rohal, M. (2014). *Record share of Americans have never married.* Pew Research Center. www.pewsocialtrends.org/files/2014/09/2014-09-24_Never_Married_Americans.pdf. Accessed January 15, 2015.

Parker-Pope, T. (2011, March 31). Fat stigma is fast spreading around the globe. *The New York Times.*

Parker-Pope, T. (2012a, February 5). The kids are more than all right. *The New York Times.*

Parker-Pope, T. (2012b, August 28). Overtreatment is taking a harmful toll. *The New York Times.*

Parlee, M. B. (1989). Conversational politics. In L. Richardson & V. Taylor (Eds.), *Feminist frontiers II.* New York, NY: Random House.

Parsons, T. (1951). *The social system.* New York, NY: Free Press.

Parsons, T. (1971). Kinship and the associational aspect of social structure. In F. L. K. Hsu (Ed.), *Kinship and culture.* Chicago, IL: Aldine-Atherton.

Parsons, T., & Bales, R. F. (1955). *Family, socialization and interaction process.* Glencoe, IL: Free Press.

Parsons, T., & Smelser, N. (1956). *Economy and society.* New York, NY: Free Press.

Pascoe, C. J. (2010). Dude, you're a fag? In S. Ferguson (Ed.), *Mapping the social landscape.* New York, NY: McGraw-Hill.

Passel, J. S., & Cohn, D. (2011). *Unauthorized immigrant population: National and state trends, 2010.* http://pewhispanic.org/files/reports/133.pdf. Accessed June 24, 2011.

Passel, J. S., & Cohn, D. (2015). *Share of unauthorized immigrant workers in production, construction jobs falls since 2007.* Pew Research Center. www.pewhispanic.org/2015/03/26/share-of-unauthorized-immigrant-workers-in-production-construction-jobs-falls-since-2007/. Accessed June 19, 2015.

Passel, J. S., & Cohn, D. (2016). *Overall numbers of U.S. unauthorized immigrants holds steady since 2009.* Pew Research Center. www.pewhispanic.org/2016/09/20/overall-number-of-u-s-unauthorized-immigrants-holds-steady-since-2009/. Accessed June 26, 2017.

Pattani, A. (2017, August 28). Skin lightening procedure is short on evidence. *The New York Times.*

Pattillo-McCoy, M. (1999). *Black picket fences: Privilege and peril among the black middle class.* Chicago, IL: University of Chicago Press.

Paul, R. (2010, July 26). Perspectives. *Newsweek.*

Payer, L. (1988). *Medicine and culture.* New York, NY: Penguin Books.

Pear, R. (1992, December 4). New look at U.S. in 2050: Bigger, older and less white. *The New York Times.*

Pear, R. (2012, January 6). Report finds most errors at hospitals go unreported. *The New York Times.*

Pearce, D. (1979). Gatekeepers and homeseekers: Institutional patterns in racial steering. *Social Problems, 26,* 325–342.

Pearce, D. (2014, January). Competing poverty measures: An analysis. *ASA Footnotes.*

Pearce, L. D., & Axinn, W. G. (1998). The impact of family religious life on the quality of mother child relations. *American Sociological Review, 63,* 810–828.

Peck, B. M., & Conner, S. (2011). Talking with me or talking at me? The impact of status characteristics on doctor–patient interaction. *Sociological Perspectives, 54,* 547–567.

Pedrique, B., Strub-Weurgraft, Some, C., Olliaro, P., Trouiller, P., Ford, N., Pecoul, B., & Bradol, J-H. (2013, October 24). The drug and vaccine landscape for neglected diseases (2000-11): A systematic assessment. *The Lancet,* 1–9.

Peluchette, J. V. E., & Karl, K. (2007). The impact of workplace attire on employee self-perceptions. *Human Resource Development Quarterly, 18,* 345–360.

Pennington, B. (2003, November 12). As team sports conflict, some parents rebel. *The New York Times.*

Pérez-Peña, R. (2003, April 19). Study finds asthma in 25% of children in central Harlem. *The New York Times.*

Pérez-Peña, R. (2012a, August 20). More Hispanics are in college, report finds. *The New York Times.*

Pérez-Peña, R. (2012b, September 8). Studies find more students cheating, with high achievers no exception. *The New York Times.*

Pérez-Peña, R. (2013, May 31). Limited success as colleges seek to attract poor. *The New York Times.*

Pérez-Peña, R., & Bogdanich, W. (2014). In Florida, student assaults, an added burden on accusers. *The New York Times.*

Pérez-Peña, R. (2015, June 13). The odd case of the woman playing black. *The New York Times.*

Peri, G. (2009). *The effect of immigration on productivity: Evidence from U.S. states* (National Bureau of Economic Research Working Paper 15507). www.nber.org/papers/w15507.pdf?new_window=1. Accessed July 5, 2010.

Perlez, J. (1991, August 31). Madagascar, where the dead return, bringing joy. *The New York Times.*

Perlin, S. A., Sexton, K., & Wong, D. W. S. (1999). An examination of race and poverty for populations living near industrial sources of air pollution. *Journal of Exposure Analysis and Environmental Epidemiology, 9,* 29–48.

Perlman, D., & Fehr, B. (1987). The development of intimate relationships. In D. Perlman & S. Duck (Eds.), *Intimate relationships: Development, dynamics and deterioration.* Newbury Park, CA: Sage.

Pescosolido, B. A. (1986). Migration, medical care and the lay referral system: A network theory of role assimilation. *American Sociological Review, 51,* 523–540.

Pescosolido, B. A., Grauerholz, E., & Milkie, M. A. (1997). Culture and conflict: The portrayal of Blacks in U.S. children's picture books through the mid- and late-twentieth century. *American Sociological Review, 62,* 443–464.

Peterson, I. (2005, March 14). Casino with weight policy finds boon in controversy. *The New York Times.*

Peterson, P. (1991). The urban underclass and the poverty paradox. In C. Jencks & P. Peterson (Eds.), *The urban underclass.* Washington, DC: Brookings Institution.

Peterson, S. B., & Lach, M. A. (1990). Gender stereotypes in children's books: Their prevalence and influence in cognitive and affective development. *Gender and Education, 2,* 185–197.

Pethokoukis, J. (2014). *"The Bell Curve" 20 years later: Q&A with Charles Murray.* American Enterprise Institute. www.aei.org/publication/bell-curve-20-years-later-qa-charles-murray/. Accessed June 7, 2015.

Petts, R. J. (2014). Family, religious attendance, and trajectories of psychological well-being among youth. *Journal of Family Issues, 28,* 759–768.

Pew Charitable Trusts. (2013). *How much protection does a college degree afford?* www.pewstates.org/uploadedFiles/PCS_Assets/2013/Pew_college_grads_recession_report.pdf. Accessed January 10, 2013.

Pew Forum on Religion and Public Life. (2004). *The American religious landscape and politics, 2004.* Washington, DC: Pew Research Center. www.pewforum.org/publications/surveys/green.pdf. Accessed December 31, 2004.

Pew Forum on Religion and Public Life. (2008). *U.S. religious landscape survey: Religious affiliation, diverse and dynamic.* http://religions.pewforum.org/pdf/report-religious-landscape-study-full.pdf. Accessed May 30, 2011.

Pew Forum on Religion and Public Life. (2010). *U.S. religious knowledge survey.* http://pewforum.org/Other-Beliefs-and-Practices/U-S-ReligiousKnowledge-Survey.aspx. Accessed May 30, 2011.

Pew Forum on Religion and Public Life. (2014a). *Most say religious holiday displays on public property are OK.* www.pewforum.org/2014/12/15/most-say-religious-displays-should-be-allowed-on-public-property/. Accessed January 12, 2015.

Pew Forum on Religion and Public Life. (2014b). *Public sees religion's influence waning.* www.pewforum.org/2014/09/22-public-sees-religions-influence-waning-2/. Accessed January 12, 2015.

Pew Global Attitudes Project. (2012). *Chapter 2. Attitudes toward American culture and ideas.* www.pewglobal.org/2012/06/13/chapter-2-attitudes-toward-american-culture-and-ideas/. Accessed January 7, 2015.

Pew Hispanic Center. (2013). *A nation of immigrants.* www.pewhispanic.org/files/2013/01/statistical_portrait_final_jan_29.pdf. Accessed June 28, 2013.

Pew Research Center. (2007). *Muslim Americans: Middle class and mostly mainstream.* Washington, DC: Author. http://pewresearch.org/assets/pdf/muslim-americans.pdf. Accessed September 5, 2009.

Pew Research Center. (2010). *Millennials: A portrait of generation next.* http://pewsocialtrends.org/2010/12/20/files/2010/10/millennials-confident-connected-open-to-change.pdf. Accessed June 23, 2011.

Pew Research Center. (2011). *Pessimism about national economy rises, personal financial views hold steady.* http://people-press.org/2011/06/23/section-2-views-of-personal-finances/. Accessed June 27, 2011.

Pew Research Center. (2012a). *The rise of intermarriage.* www.pewsocialtrends.org/files/2012/02/SDT-Intermarriage-II.pdf. Accessed January 14, 2013.

Pew Research Center. (2012b). *Young, underemployed, and optimistic.* www.pewsocialtrends.org/2012/02/09/young-underemployed-and-optimistic/. Accessed June 26, 2013.

Pew Research Center. (2013a). *A survey of LGBT Americans: Attitudes, experiences, and values in changing times.* www.pewsocialtrends.org/2013/06/13/a-survey-of-lgbt-americans. Accessed June 14, 2013.

Pew Research Center. (2013b). *Teens and technology 2013.* www.pewinternet.org/Reports/2013/Teen-and-tech.aspx. Accessed January 12, 2015.

Pew Research Center. (2014a). *Beyond red vs. blue: The political typology.* www.people-press.org/files/2014/06/6-26-14-Political-Typology-release1.pdf. Accessed May 30, 2015.

Pew Research Center. (2014b). *Millennials in adulthood: Detached from institutions, networked with friends.* www.pewsocialtrends.org/files/2014/03/2014-03-07_generations-report-version-for-web.pdf. Accessed June 17, 2015.

Pew Research Center. (2014c). *Political polarization in the American public.* www.people-press.org/files/2014/06/6-12-2014-Political-Polarization-Release.pdf. Accessed June 22, 2015.

Pew Research Center. (2014d). *Religious landscape study.* www.pewforum.org/religious-landscape-study/. Accessed January 6, 2017.

Pew Research Center. (2015a). *The American middle class is losing ground.* www.pewsocialtrends.org/2015//12/09/the-american-middle-class-is-losing-ground/. Accessed May 25, 2017.

Pew Research Center. (2015b). *America's changing religious landscape.* www.pewforum.org/2015/05/12/americas-changing-religious-landscape/. Accessed May 18, 2015.

Pew Research Center. (2015c). *Broad public support for legal status for undocumented immigrants.* www.people-press.org/files/2015/06/6-4-15-immigration-release.pdf. Accessed June 19, 2015.

Pew Research Center. (2015d). *The future of world religions: Population growth projections, 2010–2050.* www.pewforum.org/2015/04/02/religions-projections-2010-2050/. Accessed January 29, 2017.

Pew Research Center. (2015e). *Modern immigration wave brings 59 million to U.S. driving population growth and change through 2065.* www.pewhispanic.org/2015/09/28/modern-immigration-wave-brings-59-million-to-u-s-driving-population-growth-and-change-through-2065/. Accessed June 26, 2017.

Pew Research Center. (2015f). *Multiracial in America: Proud, diverse, and growing in numbers.* www.pewsocialtrends.org/files/2015/06/2015-06-11_multiracial_in_america_final-updated.pdf. Accessed June 11, 2015.

Pew Research Center. (2015g). *Parenting in America.* www.pewsocialtrends.org/2015/12/17/parenting-in-america/. Accessed January 4, 2017.

Pew Research Center. (2015h). *Support for same-sex marriage at record high, but key segments remain opposed.* www.people-press.org/files/2015/06/6-8-15-Same-sex-marriage-release1.pdf. Accessed June 26, 2015.

Pew Research Center. (2017). *Attendance at religious services.* Religious Landscape Study. www.pewforum.org/religious-landscape-study/attendance-at-religious-services/. Accessed January, 2017.

Pew Research Social & Demographic Trends (2014). *Mapping the marriage market for young adults.* www.pewsocialtrends.org/interactives/marriage-market/. Accessed January 2, 2015.

Pfohl, S. J. (1994). *Images of deviance and social control.* New York, NY: McGraw-Hill.

Phillips, K. (2002). *Wealth and democracy.* New York, NY: Broadway Books.

Philpott, T. (2012, August 15). 80 percent of public schools have contracts with Coke or Pepsi. *Mother Jones.*

Piff, P. K., Stancato, D. M., Côté, S., Mendoza-Denton, R., & Keltner, D. (2012). Higher social class predicts increased unethical behavior. *Proceedings of the National Academy of Sciences, 109,* 4086–4091.

Pine Tree Legal Assistance. (2017). *Maine Parentage Act: Who can be a parent?* http://ptla.org/maine-parentage-act#. Accessed October 8, 2017.

Piper, A. (1992). Passing for white, passing for black. *Transition, 58,* 4–32.

Piven, F. F. (2013, February 18). Movements making noise. *The Nation.*

Piven, F. F., & Cloward, R. A. (1977). *Poor people's movements: Why they succeed, how they fail.* New York, NY: Vintage Books.

Pizza must go through: It's the law in San Francisco. (1996, July 14). *The New York Times.*

Planty, M., Langton, L., Krebs, C., Berzofsky, M., & Smiley-McDonald, H. (2013). *Female victims of sexual violence 1994–2010.* U.S. Bureau of Justice Statistics. NCJ240655. www.bjs.gov/content/pub/pdf/fvsv9410.pdf. Accessed June 18, 2013.

Polgreen, L. (2010, March 31). Suicides, some for separatist cause, jolt India. *The New York Times.*

Pollack, A. (2012, June 7). Tests of parents are used to map genes of a fetus. *The New York Times.*

Pollan, M. (2007, January 28). Unhappy meals. *The New York Times Magazine.*

Pollan, M. (2013, May 19). Some of my best friends are bacteria. *The New York Times Magazine.*

Pollard, K., & Scommegna, P. (2014). *Just how many baby boomers are there?* Population Reference Bureau. www.prb.org/Publications/Articles/2002/JustHowManyBabyBoomersAreThere.aspx. Accessed June 16, 2015.

Popenoe, D. (1993). American family decline, 1960–1990: A review and appraisal. *Journal of Marriage and the Family, 55,* 527–555.

Popenoe, R. (2005). Ideal. In D. Kulick & A. Meneley (Eds.), *Fat: The anthropology of an obsession.* New York, NY: Tarcher/Penguin.

Population Reference Bureau. (2010). China's rapidly aging population. *Today's Research on Aging, 20,* 1–5.

Population Reference Bureau. (2011). *The world's women and girls.* www.prb.org/pdf11/world-women-girls-2011-data-sheet.pdf. Accessed June 21, 2011.

Population Reference Bureau. (2012). *Status report: Adolescents and young people in sub-Saharan Africa.* www.prb.org/pdf12/status-report-youth-subsaharan-Africa.pdf. Accessed May 31, 2015.

Population Reference Bureau. (2013). *Ending female genital mutilation/cutting: Lessons from a decade of progress.* www.prb.org/pdf14/progress-ending-fgm.pdf. Accessed January 8, 2015.

Population Reference Bureau. (2014). *World population data sheet: 2014.* www.prb.org/pdf14/2014-world-population-data-sheet_eng.pdf. Accessed May 29, 2015.

Population Reference Bureau. (2016). *2016 world population data sheet.* www.prb.org/pdf16/prb-wpds2016-web-2016.pdf. Accessed June 3, 2017.

Porter, E. (2005, April 5). Illegal immigrants are bolstering Social Security with billions. *The New York Times.*

Porter, E. (2006, October 17). Law on overseas brides is keeping couples apart. *The New York Times.*

Porter, E. (2012, June 13). Motherhood still a cause of pay inequity. *The New York Times.*

Porter, E. (2016, October 29). Richer but not better off. *The New York Times.*

Powell, B., Bolzendahl, C., Geist, C., & Steelman, L. C. (2010). *Counted out: Same-sex relations and Americans' definitions of family.* New York, NY: Russell Sage.

Powell, M. (2009, May 31). On diverse force, blacks still face special peril. *The New York Times.*

Powell, M. (2012, January 24). In police training, a dark film on U.S. Muslims. *The New York Times.*

Powers, R. (2016). What about the children? *The Balance.* www.thebalance.com/what-about-the-children-3332640. Accessed January 10, 2017.

Prah, P. M. (2006). Domestic violence. *CQ Researcher, 16,* 1–24.

President's Council on Bioethics. (2003). *Beyond therapy: Biotechnology and the pursuit of happiness.* Washington, DC: Government Printing Office.

Preston, J. (2011, May 30). A crackdown on employing illegal workers. *The New York Times.*

Preston, J. (2013, October 7). Ailing cities extend hand to immigrants. *The New York Times.*

Preston, J., & Stelter, B. (2011, February 18). Cellphone cameras become the world's eyes and ears on protests across the Middle East. *The New York Times.*

Price, S. L. (1997, December 8). Whatever happened to the white athlete? *Sports Illustrated.*

Price paid in military lives equal to 9/11 toll. (2006, September 23). *Banner Graphic.*

Priestley, T. (2015, December 30). Why the next generation after Millennials will be "builders" not "founders." *Forbes.* www.forbes.com/sites/theopriestley/2015/12/30/why-the-next-generation-after-millennials-will-be-builders-not-founders/#362a1c8a5ccb. Accessed June 21, 2017.

Proctor, B. D., & Dalaker, J. (2002). *Poverty in the United States: 2001* (U.S. Census Bureau, Current Population Reports, P60–219). Washington, DC: Government Printing Office.

Proctor, B. D., Semega, J. L., & Kollar, M. A. (2016). *Income and poverty in the United States: 2015.* U.S. Bureau of the Census. P60-256(RV). www.census.gov/content/dam/Census/library/publications/2016/demo/p60-256.pdf. Accessed May 24, 2017.

Project for Excellence in Journalism. (2005). *Embedded reporters: What are Americans getting?* Washington, DC: Pew Research Center. www.journalism.org/sites/journalism.org/files/pejembedreport.pdf. Accessed September 5, 2009.

ProQuest Statistical Abstract. (2013). *Statistical abstract of the United States: 2013 Online edition.* si. Conquestsystems.com/sa/index.html?id=5d40ca75-82e1=4194-b9dc-44cd63428eaa#. Accessed January 16, 2013.

ProQuest Statistical Abstract. (2015). *Statistical abstract of the United States: 2015 Online edition.* http://statabs.proquest.com.ezproxy.depauw.edu/sa/index.html. Accessed July 2, 2015.

ProQuest Statistical Abstract. (2017). *Statistical abstract of the United States: 2017.* Statabs.proquest.com/sa/index.html. Accessed July 3, 2017.

Protect Our Defenders. (2017). *Facts on United States military sexual violence.* www.protectourdefenders.com/wp-content/uploads/2013/05/1.-MSA-Fact-Sheet-170508.pdf. Accessed June 14, 2017.

Prothero, S. (2007). *Religious literacy.* San Francisco, CA: Harper.

Provine, R. R. (2000). *Laughter: A scientific investigation.* New York, NY: Penguin Books.

Provine, R. R. (2012). *Curious behavior.* Cambridge, MA: Belknap Press.

Pugliesi, K. (1987). Deviation in emotion and the labeling of mental illness. *Deviant Behavior, 8,* 79–102.

Puhl, R., & Brownell, K. D. (2001). Bias, discrimination, and obesity. *Obesity Research, 9,* 788–805.

Pullella, P. (2014, July 7). Pope Francis calls clergy sex abuse "a leprosy," says 2 percent of priests are pedophiles in Eugenio Scalfari interview. *Huffington Post.* www.huffingtonpost.com/2014/07/13/pope-francis-priests-pedophiles-two-percent_n_5582157.html. Accessed January 20, 2015.

Putnam, R. D. (1995). Bowling alone: America's declining social capital. *Journal of Democracy, 6,* 65–78.

Quenqua, D. (2012a, October 2). In business, nondrinking can be a costly expense. *The New York Times.*

Quenqua, D. (2012b, November 19). Muscular body image lures boys into gym, and obsession. *The New York Times.*

Quinney, R. (1970). *The social reality of crime.* Boston, MA: Little, Brown.

Rabin, R. C. (2008, December 16). Living with in-laws linked to heart risks in Japanese women. *The New York Times.*

Rabin, R. C. (2014a, September 23). Health researchers will get $10.1 million to counter gender bias in studies. *The New York Times.*

Rabin, R. C. (2014b, May 15). Labs are told to start including a neglected variable: females. *The New York Times.*

Rabin, R. C. (2016, October 31). Offered breast reconstruction, more women opt to "go flat." *The New York Times.*

Rabinovitch, S. (2013, March 15). Data reveal scale of Chinese abortions. *Financial Times.*

Rainie, L. (2016). *The state of privacy in post-Snowden America.* Pew Research Center. www.pewresearch.org/fact-tank/2016/09/21/the-state-of-privacy-in-america/. Accessed June 28, 2017.

Raley, S., & Bianchi, S. (2006). Sons, daughters, and family processes: Does gender of children matter? *Annual Review of Sociology, 32,* 401–421.

Rampell, C. (2011, June 10). Companies spend on equipment, not workers. *The New York Times.*

Rampell, C. (2012, October 5). When job-creation engines stop at just one. *The New York Times.*

Rampell, C. (2013, April 7). Lean in, dad. *The New York Times Magazine.*

Rank, M. (2013, November 3). Poverty in America is mainstream. *The New York Times.*

Rank, M. (2014, April 20). From rags to riches to rags. *The New York Times.*

Rape, Abuse & Incest National Network. (2009). *Marital rape.* www.rainn.org/public-policy/sexual-assault-issues/marital-rape. Accessed July 8, 2013.

Rattner, S. (2014, June 22). Fear not the coming of the robots. *The New York Times.*

Rauch, J. (2017, July/August). The conservative case for unions. *The Atlantic.*

Raven, D. (2015, April 26). ISIS: Pregnant girls aged 9 having secret abortions after being raped by twisted Islamic State militants. *The Mirror.* www.mirror.co.uk/news/world-news/isis-pregnant-girls-aged-9-5587288. Accessed June 10, 2015.

Read, J. G., & Gorman, B. K. (2010). Gender and health inequality. *Annual Review of Sociology, 36,* 371–386.

Reardon, S. F., Fox, L., & Townsend, J. (2015). Neighborhood income composition by household race and income, 1990–2009. *The Annals of the American Academy of Political and Social Science, 660,* 78–97.

Reddy, G. (2005). *With respect to sex: Negotiating Hijra identity in South Asia.* Chicago, IL: University of Chicago Press.

Redstone, J. (2003). *The language of war.* Worldwatch. www.omegastar.org/worldwatch/America/Language_of_War.html. Accessed May 23, 2003.

Reeves, A., McKee, M., & Stuckler, D. 2014. Economic suicides in the Great Recession in Europe and North America. *British Journal of Psychiatry, 209,* 1–2.

Reich, L. (2014, August 17). Playing the numbers in digital dating. *The New York Times.*

Reilly, M. (2017, March 10). GOP congressman asks why men should have to pay for prenatal care. *Huffington Post.* www.huffingtonpost.com/entry/john-simkus-prenatal-care_us_58c1e4fae4b0ed71826b6e4e. Accessed June 15, 2017.

Reiman, J., & Leighton, P. (2013). *The rich get richer and the poor get prison.* Boston, MA: Allyn & Bacon.

Reinharz, S. (1992). *Feminist methods in social research.* New York, NY: Oxford University Press.

Reitzel, L. R., Regan, S. D., Nguyen, N., Cromley, E. K., Strong, L. L., Wetter, D. W., & McNeill, L. H. (2014). Density and proximity of fast food restaurants and body mass index among African Americans. *American Journal of Public Health, 104,* 110-116.

Rennison, C. M., & Welchans, S. (2000). *Intimate partner violence* (Special Report No. NCJ 178247). Washington, DC: United States Bureau of Justice Statistics.

Renzetti, C. M., & Curran, D. J. (2003). *Women, men and society: The sociology of gender.* Boston, MA: Allyn & Bacon.

Reskin, B., & Hartmann, H. (1986). *Women's work, men's work: Sex segregation on the job.* Washington, DC: National Academy Press.

Restaurant Opportunities Center of New York. (2009). *The great service divide: Occupational segregation & inequality in the New York City restaurant industry.* www.rocunited.org/files/GREATSERVICEDIVIDE.pdf. Accessed June 17, 2011.

Reuters. (2014, May 17). Attorney General Eric Holder: Persistent, subtle racism poses bigger threat than "outbursts of bigotry." *Newsweek.* www.newsweek.com/attorney-general-eric-holder-persistent-subtle-racism-poses-bigger-threat-outbursts-2513450. Accessed June 12, 2014.

Reyes, L., & Rubie, P. (1994). *Hispanics in Hollywood: An encyclopedia of film and television.* New York, NY: Garland Press.

Rhoden, W. C. (2006). *Forty million dollar slaves: The rise, fall, and redemption of the black athlete.* New York, NY: Crown.

Rice, A. (2009, April 12). Mission from Africa. *The New York Times Magazine.*

Rich, M. (2013, September 29). Creationists on Texas panel for biology textbooks. *The New York Times.*

Rich, M. (2014, December 1). Old tactic gets new use: Schools segregate boys and girls. *The New York Times.*

Rich, M. (2015, June 10). Kindergartens ringing the bell for play inside the classroom. *The New York Times.*

Rich, M. (2017, July 2). The crematory is booked? Japan offers corpse hotels. *The New York Times.*

Rich, M., Cox, A., & Bloch, M. (2016, May 3). In schools nationwide, money predicts success. *The New York Times.*

Richards, K. (2014, December 13). The 5 most embarrassing revelations from Sony's sprawling hack. *ADWeek.* www.adweek.com/news/advertising-branding/5-most-embarrassing-revelations-sonys-sprawling-hack-161937. Accessed January 13, 2015.

Richtel, M. (2011, December 14). Ban on cell use by drivers urged. *The New York Times.*

Richtel, M. (2016, April 28). On your phone at the wheel? Watch out for the textalyzer. *The New York Times.*

Ridgeway, C. L., & Smith-Lovin, L. (1999). The gender system and interaction. *Annual Review of Sociology, 25,* 191–216.

Rieff, D. (2005, November 6). Migrant worry. *The New York Times Magazine.*

Rieff, D. (2006, July 2). America the untethered. *The New York Times Magazine.*

Riesman, D. (1950). *The lonely crowd.* New Haven, CT: Yale University Press.

Riley, M. W. (1971). Social gerontology and the age stratification of society. *Gerontologist, 11,* 79–87.

Riley, M. W., Foner, A., & Waring, J. (1988). Sociology of age. In N. J. Smelser (Ed.), *Handbook of sociology.* Newbury Park, CA: Sage.

Rimer, S., & Arenson, K. W. (2004, June 24). Top colleges take more blacks, but which ones? *The New York Times.*

Risman, B., & Seale, E. (2010). Betwixt and between: Gender contradictions among middle schoolers. In B. Risman (Ed.), *Families as they really are.* New York, NY: Norton.

Rittner, C. (2004). *Genocide in Rwanda: Complicity of the churches*. St. Paul, MN: Paragon House.

Ritzer, G. (2008). *The McDonaldization of society*. Thousand Oaks, CA: Pine Forge Press.

Rivera, L. A. (2015, May 31). Guess who doesn't fit in at work. *The New York Times*.

Roach, M. (2013). *Gulp: Adventures on the alimentary canal* (Kindle version). New York, NY: Norton.

Robbins, A. (2004). *Pledged: The secret life of sororities*. New York, NY: Hyperion.

Robbins, A. (2015, May 28). We need more nurses. *The New York Times*.

Robbins, R. (2016, March 9). Drug makers now spend $5 billion a year on advertising. Here's what that buys. *Stat News*. www.statnews.com/2016/03/09/drug-industry-advertising/. Accessed January 18, 2017.

Robert Wood Johnson Foundation. (2012). *F as in fat: How obesity threatens America's future*. www.healthy americans.org/assets/files/TFAH2012FasinFatFnlRv.pdf. Accessed January 11, 2013.

Roberts, E. F. S. (2012). *God's laboratory: Assisted reproduction in the Andes*. Berkeley: University of California Press.

Roberts, S. (2008, August 17). A nation of none and all of the above. *The New York Times*.

Roberts, S. (2010, January 21). Census figures challenge views of race and ethnicity. *The New York Times*.

Roberts, S. (2011, May 19). A judicial rite: Suspects on parade (bring a raincoat). *The New York Times*.

Robinson, B. A. (1999). *Facts about inter-faith marriages*. www.religioustolerance.org/ifm_fact.htm. Accessed July 6, 2003.

Robinson, R. V., & Bell, W. (1978). Equality, success and social justice in England and the United States. *American Sociological Review, 43*, 125–143.

Robinson, R. V., & Kelley, J. (1979). Class as conceived by Marx and Dahrendorf: Effects on income inequality and politics in the United States and Great Britain. *American Sociological Review, 44*, 38–58.

Rodriguez, C. E., & Cordero-Guzman, H. (2004). Placing race in context. In C. A. Gallagher (Ed.), *Rethinking the color line: Readings in race and ethnicity*. New York, NY: McGraw-Hill.

Rodriguez, M. N., & Emsellem, M. (2011). *65 million "need not apply."* The National Employment Law Project. www.nelp.org/page/-/65_Million_Need_Not_Apply .pdf?nocdn=1. Accessed March 31, 2011.

Roehling, M. V. (1999). Weight-based discrimination in employment: Psychological and legal aspects. *Personnel Psychology, 52*, 969–1017.

Roethlisberger, E. J., & Dickson, W. J. (1939). *Management and the worker*. Cambridge, MA: Harvard University Press.

Roland, A. (1988). *In search of self in India and Japan*. Princeton, NJ: Princeton University Press.

Ronson, J. (2015). *So you've been publicly shamed*. New York, NY: Riverhead.

Rosato, D. (2004, August). Flights of fancy: Part 2. Airlines' class warfare. *Money*.

Roscigno, V. J., & Hodson, R. (2004). The organizational and social foundations of worker resistance. *American Sociological Review, 69*, 14–39.

Rose, M. (2004). *The mind at work*. New York, NY: Viking.

Rosenbaum, J. E., Deil-Amen, R., & Person, A. (2006). *After admission: From college access to college success*. New York, NY: Russell Sage.

Rosenbloom, S. (2014, June 1). In pursuit of the "pink dollar." *The New York Times*.

Rosenfeld, M. J. (2005). A critique of exchange theory in mate selection. *American Journal of Sociology, 110*, 1284–1325.

Rosenthal, E. (2002, November). Study links rural suicides in China to stress and ready poisons. *The New York Times*.

Rosenthal, E. (2012a, June 3). Let's (not) get physical. *The New York Times*.

Rosenthal, E. (2012b, April 15). Nigeria tested by rapid rise in population. *The New York Times*.

Rosenthal, R., & Jacobson, L. (1968). *Pygmalion in the classroom*. New York, NY: Holt, Rinehart & Winston.

Rosin, H. (2015, December). The Silicon Valley suicides. *The Atlantic*. www.theatlantic.com/magazine/archive/2015/12/ the-silicon-valley-suicides/413140/. Accessed December 26, 2016.

Rosner, S. (2013, May 5). New bills, similar faces. *The New York Times*.

Ross, C. E., Mirowsky, J., & Goldstein, K. (1990). The impact of family on health: The decade in review. *Journal of Marriage and the Family, 52*, 1059–1078.

Rossi, A. (1968). Transition to parenthood. *Journal of Marriage and the Family, 30*, 26–39.

Rossi, P., Waite, E., Bose, C. E., & Berk, R. E. (1974). The seriousness of crimes: Normative structure and individual differences. *American Sociological Review, 39*, 224–237.

Rothenberg, P. S. (Ed.). (1992). *Race, class and gender in the United States*. New York, NY: St. Martin's Press.

Rothman, B. K. (1984). Women, health and medicine. In J. Freeman (Ed.), *Women: A feminist perspective*. Palo Alto, CA: Mayfield.

Rothman, B. K. (1988). *The tentative pregnancy: Prenatal diagnosis and the future of motherhood*. London, UK: Pandora.

Rothman, B. K., & Caschetta, M. B. (1999). Treating health: Women and medicine. In S. J. Ferguson (Ed.), *Mapping the social landscape: Readings in sociology*. Mountain View, CA: Mayfield.

Rothman, D. J., & Edgar, H. (1992). Scientific rigor and medical realities: Placebo trials in cancer and AIDS research. In E. Fee & D. M. Fox (Eds.), *AIDS: The making of a chronic disease*. Berkeley: University of California Press.

Rothstein, R. (2001, December 12). An economic recovery will tell in the classroom. *The New York Times*.

Rothstein, R. (2014). *The racial achievement gap, segregated schools, and segregated neighborhoods—A constitutional insult*. Economic Policy Institute. www.epi.org/publication/the-racial-achievement-gap-segregated-schools-and-segregated-neighborhoods-a-constitutional-insult/. Accessed June 4, 2015.

Rothstein, R. (2017). *The color of law: A forgotten history of how our government segregated America*. New York, NY: Liveright.

Rousseau, B. (2017, January 13). Where talking to in-laws is tough. *The New York Times*.

Rubin, A. J. (2011, December 2). For Afghan women, justice runs into the static wall of custom. *The New York Times*.

Rubin, A. J. (2015, March 3). A thin line of defense against "honor killings." *The New York Times*.

Rubin, J. Z., Provenzano, F. J., & Luria, Z. (1974). The eye of the beholder: Parents' views on sex of newborns. *American Journal of Orthopsychiatry, 44*, 512–519.

Rubin, L. (1994). *Families on the fault line*. New York, NY: HarperCollins.

Rubinstein, S., & Caballero, B. (2000). Is Miss America an undernourished role model? *Journal of the American Medical Association, 283*, 1569.

Rucker, P. (2009, April 8). Some link economy with spate of killings. *The New York Times*.

Rudman, L. A., & Glick, P. (1999). Feminized management and backlash toward agentic women: The hidden costs to women of a kinder, gentler image of middle managers. *Journal of Personality and Social Psychology, 77*, 1004–1010.

Ruhl, J., & Ruhl, D. (2015, November 2). NCR research: Costs of sex abuse crisis to US church underestimated. *National Catholic Reporter*. www.ncronline.org/news/accountability/ncr-research-costs-sex-abuse-crisis-us-church-underestimated. Accessed January 17, 2017.

Rusbult, C. E., Zembrodt, I. M., & Iwaniszek, J. (1986). The impact of gender and sex-role orientation on responses to dissatisfaction in close relationships. *Sex Roles, 15*, 1–20.

Rushton, G. (2016, October 25). These eating disorder survivors want "Pro-Ana" sites outlawed in Australia. *Buzzfeed News*. www.buzzfeed.com/ginarushton/these-eating-disorder-survivors-want-pro-ana-sites-outlawed?utm_term=.eox3xN6MX#.mwq4mjyXa. Accessed June 16, 2017.

Russell Sage Foundation. (2016). *Percentage share of aggregate national income by quintile, and top 5%, 1967–2012*. www.russellsage.org/research/chart/book/percentage-share-aggregate-national-household-income-quintile-and-top-5-1967-2012. Accessed June 1, 2017.

Rwandan Stories. (2011). *With me, he behaved nicely*. www.rwandanstories.org/genocide/strangness_of_mind.html. Accessed May 19, 2011.

Rybczynski, W. (1999, April 18). One good turn. *The New York Times Magazine*.

Saad, L. (2012). *Majority in U.S. dissatisfied with next generation's prospects*. Gallup Politics. www.gallup.com/poll/155021/majority-dissatisfied-next-generations-prospects.aspx. Accessed June 26, 2013.

Saad, L. (2014). *The "40-hour" workweek is actually longer—by seven hours*. Gallup. www.gallup.com/poll/175286/hour-workweek-actually-longer-seven-hours.aspx. Accessed January 18, 2015.

Sack, K. (2009, March 14). Bad economy leads patients to put off surgery, or rush it. *The New York Times*.

Sadker, D., Sadker, M., & Zittleman, K. R. (2009). *Still failing at fairness: How gender bias cheats girls and boys in school and what we can do about it*. New York, NY: Scribner.

Sadker, M., Sadker, D., Fox, L., & Salata, M. (2004). Gender equity in the classroom: The unfinished agenda. In M. S. Kimmel (Ed.), *The gendered society reader*. New York, NY: Oxford University Press.

Saez, E., & Zucman, G. (2016). Wealth inequality in the United States since 1913: Evidence from capitalized income tax data. *The Quarterly Journal of Economics, 131*, 519–578.

Safire, W. (2006, January 15). Mideastisms. *The New York Times Magazine*.

Sagal, P. (2015, June). The fear factor. *Runner's World*.

Sage, G. H. (2001). Racial equality and sport. In D. S. Eitzen (Ed.), *Sport in contemporary society*. New York, NY: Worth.

Saint Louis, C. (2010, July 4). What big eyes you have, dear, but are those contacts risky? *The New York Times*.

Saint Louis, C. (2011, May 15). Dessert, laid-back and legal. *The New York Times*.

Saint Louis, C. (2017, May 2). Finding their voices. *The New York Times*.

Salganik, M. J., Dodds, P. S., & Watts, D. J. (2006). Experimental study of inequality and unpredictability in an artificial cultural market. *Science, 311,* 854–856.

Samuels, A. (2011, September 5). Reliving MLK's last hours. *Newsweek*.

Samuelson, R. J. (2012, August 5). The social and economic reasons for Generation Squeezed. *Washington Post*.

Sanborn, J. (2017, January 18). Flint's water crisis still isn't over. Here's where things stand a year later. *Time*. time.com/4634937/flint-water-crisis-criminal-charges-bottled-water/. Accessed June 11, 2017.

Sandstrom, A. (2017). *Faith on the hill*. Pew Research Center. www.pewforum.org/2017/01/03/faith-on-the-hill-115/. Accessed January 6, 2017.

Sanger-Katz, M. (2014, October 27). Number of Americans without health insurance is down by about 25 percent. *The New York Times*.

Saperstein, A., Penner, A. M., & Light, R. (2013). Racial formation in perspective: Connecting individuals, institutions and power relations. *Annual Review of Sociology, 39,* 359–378.

Sapir, E. (1929). The status of linguistics as a science. *Language, 5,* 207–214.

Sapir, E. (1949). *Selected writings* (D. G. Mandelbaum, Ed.). Berkeley: University of California Press.

Saul, L. (1972). Personal and social psychopathology and the primary prevention of violence. *American Journal of Psychiatry, 128,* 1578–1581.

Saulny, S. (2009, November 8). Overweight Americans push back with vigor in the health care debate. *The New York Times*.

Saulny, S. (2011, March 20). Black and white and married in the deep south: A shifting image. *The New York Times*.

Saunders, D. J. (2016, November 13). How "herding" blinded pollsters to Trump win. *Town Hall*. townhall.com/columnists/debrajsaunders/2016/11/13/how-herding-blinded-pollsters-to-trump-win-n2244791. Accessed January 27, 2017.

Saunders, J. M. (1991). Relating social structural abstractions to sociological research. *Teaching Sociology, 19,* 270–271.

Savacool, J. (2009). *The world has curves: The global quest for the perfect body*. New York, NY: Rodale.

Savage, D. (2008, November 12). Anti-gay, anti-family. *The New York Times*.

Save the Children. (2017). *Stolen childhoods: End of childhood report 2017*. www.savethechildren.org/site/c.8rKLIXMGIp14E/b.9525451/k.F8D9/End_of_Childhood_US.htm. Accessed June 1, 2017.

Sayer, L., Casper, L., & Cohen, P. (2004, October). *Women, men, and work* (PRB Report). Washington, DC: Population Reference Bureau. www.prb.org. Accessed December 30, 2004.

Sayre, S. (2012, August 31). Hopes raised, Roma in France still face a date with the bulldozer. *The New York Times*.

Scheiber, N. (2017, June 22). Welcome to the work force, will dad need a chair, too? *The New York Times*.

Schlesinger, A. (1992). *The disuniting of America*. New York, NY: Norton.

Schlosser, E. (2001). *Fast food nation*. New York, NY: Houghton Mifflin.

Schmitt, E., & Shanker, T. (2005, July 25). New name for "War on Terror" reflects wider U.S. campaign. *The New York Times*.

Schodolski, V. J. (1993, December 26). Funeral industry, pitching videos, 2-for-1 specials to baby boomers. *The Indianapolis Star*.

Schoenborn, C. A. (2004). Marital status and health: United States, 1999–2002. Centers for Disease Control and Prevention. *Vital and Health Statistics, 351*. http://www.cdc.gov/nchs/data/ad/ad351.pdf. Accessed September 5, 2009.

Schooler, C. (1996). Cultural and social structural explanations of cross-national psychological differences. *Annual Review of Sociology, 22,* 323–349.

Schreiber, N., Bellah, L. D., Martinez, Y., McLaurin, K. A., Strok, R., Garven, S., & Wood, J. M. (2006). Suggestive interviewing in the McMartin Preschool and Kelly Michaels day care abuse cases: A case study. *Social Influence, 1,* 16–47.

Schrobsdorff, S. (2006, October 17). Fashion designers introduce less-than-zero sizes. *Newsweek*.

Schulman, M. (2014, January 6). Hands down. *The New Yorker*.

Schultz, K. (2017, January 18). In Bhutan, happiness index as gauge for social ills. *The New York Times*.

Schuman, H., & Krysan, M. (1999). A historical note on Whites' beliefs about racial inequality. *American Sociological Review, 64,* 847–855.

Schutt, R. K. (2015). *Investigating the social world*. Thousand Oaks, CA: Sage.

Schwartz, C. (2016, October 16). Generation Adderall. *The New York Times Magazine.*

Schwartz, C. R., & Mare, R. D. (2005). Trends in educational assertive marriage from 1940 to 2003. *Demography, 42*, 621–646.

Schwartz, J. (2013, December 15). A Utah law prohibiting polygamy is weakened. *The New York Times.*

Schwartz, J., Revkin, A. C., & Wald, M. L. (2005, September 12). In reviving New Orleans, a challenge of many tiers. *The New York Times.*

Schwartz, N. D. (2016, April 24). In age of broad wealth gap, not everyone is in the same boat. *The New York Times.*

Schwartz, N. D. (2017, June 3). The doctor is in. Co-pay? $40,000. *The New York Times.*

Schwartzman, L. F. (2007). Does money whiten? Intergenerational changes in racial classification. *American Sociological Review, 72*, 940–963.

Schwarz, A. (2012, June 10). Risky rise of the good grade pill. *The New York Times.*

Schwarz, A. (2013, December 15). The selling of attention deficit disorder. *The New York Times.*

Schwarz, A. (2014, May 17). Among experts, scrutiny of attention deficit diagnoses in 2- and 3-year olds. *The New York Times.*

Schwarz, A. (2015a, April 19). Abuse of attention deficit pills graduates into the workplace. *The New York Times.*

Schwarz, A. (2015b, December 11). Still in a crib, yet being given antipsychotics. *The New York Times.*

Scommegna, P. (2012). *Dementia cases expected to triple by 2050 as world population ages*. Population Reference Bureau. www.prb.org/Articles/2012/global-dementia.aspx?p=1. Accessed June 27, 2013.

Scott, A. O. (2010, May 9). Gen X has a midlife crisis. *The New York Times.*

Scott, J., & Leonhardt, D. (2005, May 15). Class in America: Shadowy lines that still divide us. *The New York Times.*

Scott, L. D. (2003). The relation of racial identity and racial socialization to coping with discrimination among African American adolescents. *Journal of Black Studies, 33*, 520–538.

Scott, M., & Lyman, S. (1968). Accounts. *American Sociological Review, 33*, 46–62.

Scott, R. (1981). *The making of blind men: A study of adult socialization*. New Brunswick, NJ: Transaction Books.

Scull, A., & Favreau, D. (1986). A chance to cut is a chance to cure: Sexual surgery for psychosis in three nineteenth-century societies. In S. Spitzer & A. T. Scull (Eds.), *Research in law, deviance and social control* (Vol. 8). Greenwich, CT: JAI Press.

Searcey, D., & Gebeloff, R. (2015, January 26). More fall out as middle class shrinks further. *The New York Times.*

Seelye, K. Q., & Bidgood, J. (2016, November 5). Locker room talk becomes talk of Harvard. *The New York Times.*

Seemiller, C., & Grace, M. (2015). *Generation Z goes to college*. New York, NY: Jossey-Bass.

Segal, D. (2009, March 12). Financial fraud rises as target for prosecutors. *The New York Times.*

Sehgal, P. (2015, October 4). Takeover. *The New York Times Magazine.*

Sengupta, S. (2004, October 26). Relentless attacks on women in West Sudan draw an outcry. *The New York Times.*

Sengupta, S. (2012, May 18). Reticent rich: Preferred style in Silicon Valley. *The New York Times.*

Sengupta, S. (2016, March 6). The world's big problem: Young people. *The New York Times.*

Sennett, R. (1984). *Families against the city: Middle-class homes in industrial Chicago*. Cambridge, MA: Harvard University Press.

Sennett, R., & Cobb, J. (1972). *Hidden injuries of class*. New York, NY: Vintage Books.

Serrano, R. A. (2011, June 30). Federal panel OKs shorter sentences for crack offenders. *The Seattle Times.*

Sex offender's case denied in court. (2001, January 16). *Associated Press Online.* www.highbeam.com/doc/1P1-39751038.html. Accessed October 2, 2011.

Sexton, T. (2009). America's only winnable war: Invasion of the culture snatchers. *Yahoo voices.* Voices.yahoo.com/Americas-only-winnable-war-invasion-culture-2504076.html. Accessed December 31, 2012.

Shah, A. (2009). Poverty facts and statistics. *Global Issues.* www.globalissues.org/article/26/poverty-facts-and-stats#src1. Accessed May 28, 2009.

Shah, A. (2013a). Poverty facts and statistics. *Global Issues.* www.globalissues.org/article/26/poverty-facts-and-stats. Accessed May 29, 2015.

Shah, A. (2013b). Structural adjustments: A major cause of poverty. *Global Issues.* www.globalissues.org/article/3/structural-adjustment- a-major-cause-of-poverty. Accessed June 3, 2013.

Shakin, M., Shakin, D., & Sternglanz, S. H. (1985). Infant clothing: Sex labeling for strangers. *Sex Roles, 12,* 955–964.

Shane, S. (2017, January 18). How to make a masterpiece in fake news. *The New York Times.*

Shanker, T. (2004, December 8). Inquiry faults commanders in assaults on cadets. *The New York Times.*

Shapiro, T. M. (2008). The hidden cost of being African American. In S. J. Ferguson (Ed.), *Mapping the social landscape.* New York, NY: McGraw-Hill.

Shapo, H. S. (2006). Assisted reproduction and the law: Disharmony on a divisive social issue. *Northwestern University Law Review, 100,* 465–479.

Sharkey, J. (2014, October 20). For travel pros, Ebola fears create teaching moments. *The New York Times.*

Sharma, V. K., Rango, J. N., Connaughton, A., & Sabesan, V. J. (2014, March 14). *Incidence of head and neck injuries in extreme sports.* Paper #766 American Academy of Orthopedic Surgeons 2014 Annual Meeting.

Shenk, D. (2010, May/June). Are you a genius? *Brown Alumni Magazine.*

Shibutani, T. (1961). *Society and personality: An interactionist approach to social psychology.* Englewood Cliffs, NJ: Prentice Hall.

Shierholz, H., Davis, A., & Kimball, W. (2014). The class of 2014: The weak economy is idling too many young graduates. *Economic Policy Institute Briefing Paper #377.* www.epi.org/publication/class-of-2014/. Accessed January 2, 2015.

Shim, E. (2014, June 27). *The median age of marriage in every state in the U.S., in two maps.* News.mic. www.mic.com/articles/92361/the-median-age-of-marriage-in-every-state-in-the-u-s-in-two-maps. Accessed June 17, 2015.

Shipler, D. K. (2004). *The working poor: Invisible in America.* New York, NY: Knopf.

Short, K. (2015). The supplemental poverty measure: 2014. *Current Population Reports, P60-254.* www.census.gov/content/dam/Census/library/publications/2015/demo/P60-254.pdf. Accessed May 31, 2017.

Shorto, R. (2010, February 14). Founding father? *The New York Times Magazine.*

Shugart, H. A. (2003). She shoots, she scores: Mediated construction of contemporary female athletes in coverage of the 1999 U.S. Women's soccer team. *Western Journal of Communication, 67,* 1–31.

Shulevitz, J. (2012, September 9). Why fathers really matter. *The New York Times Magazine.*

Shulevitz, J. (2015a, May 10). Mom: The designated worrier. *The New York Times.*

Shulevitz, J. (2015b, June 28). Regulating sex. *The New York Times.*

Shweder, R. A. (1997, March 9). It's called poor health for a reason. *The New York Times.*

Sidel, R. (1986). *Women and children last.* New York, NY: Penguin Books.

Sidel, R. (1990). *On her own: Growing up in the shadow of the American dream.* New York, NY: Penguin Books.

Siegel, B. E. (2017, May 1). Shaming the children so parents will pay the school lunch bill. *The New York Times.*

Siegel, R. B. (2004). A short history of sexual harassment. In C. A. MacKinnon & R. B. Siegel (Eds.), *Directions in sexual harassment law.* New Haven, CT: Yale University Press.

Signorielli, N. (1990). Children, television, and gender roles. *Journal of Adolescent Health Care, 11,* 50–58.

Silber, J. H., Rosenbaum, P. R., Clark, A. S., Giantonio, B. J., Ross, R. N., Teng, Y., . . . Fox, K. R. (2013). Characteristics associated with differences in survival among black and white women with breast cancer. *JAMA, 310,* 389–397.

Silverman, D. (1982). *Secondary analysis in social research: A guide to data sources and methods with examples.* Boston, MA: Allen & Unwin.

Simmel, G. (1950). *The sociology of Georg Simmel* (K. Wolff, Ed.). New York, NY: Free Press. (Original work published 1902)

Simon, S. (2009, April 13). Education board in Texas faces curbs. *The Wall Street Journal.*

Simons, M. (2001, April 30). An awful task: Assessing 4 roles in death of thousands in Rwanda. *The New York Times.*

Simons, M. (2011, June 25). Official gets life sentence for genocide in Rwanda. *The New York Times.*

Simpson, I. H. (1979). *From student to nurse: A longitudinal study of socialization.* Cambridge, UK: Cambridge University Press.

Singer, N. (2009, August 5). Medical papers by ghostwriters pushed therapy. *The New York Times.*

Singer, N. (2010, August 13). Eat an apple (doctor's orders). *The New York Times.*

Sinha, P. (2014, September 5). Why do doctors commit suicide? *The New York Times.*

Sinozich, S., & Langton, L. (2014). *Rape and sexual assault victimization among college-age females, 1995–2013.* U.S. Bureau of Justice Statistics, NCJ248421. www.bjs.gov/content/pub/pdf/rsavcaf9513.pdf. Accessed January 6, 2015.

Skocpol, T. (1979). *States and social revolutions: A comparative analysis of France, Russia and China.* New York, NY: Cambridge University Press.

Skolnick, A. S. (1991). *Embattled paradise*. New York, NY: Basic Books.

Slackman, M. (2006, August 6). The fine art of hiding what you mean to say. *The New York Times*.

Slackman, M. (2007, May 26). A quiet revolution in Algeria: Gains by women. *The New York Times*.

Slepian, M. L., Ferber, S. N., Gold, J. M., & Rutchick, A. M. (2015). The cognitive consequences of formal clothing. *Social Psychological and Personality Science, 6,* 661–668.

Smith, A. (2010). *Neighbors online*. Pew Research Center. www.pewinternet.org/2010/08/09/neighbors-online. Accessed January 15, 2015.

Smith, A. (2011). *How Americans use text messaging*. Pew Research Center. www.pewinternet.org/2011/09/19/how-americans-use-text-messaging. Accessed December 30, 2016.

Smith, A. (2015). *U.S. smartphone use in 2015*. Pew Research Center. www.pewinternet.org/2015/04/01/us-smartphone-use-in-2015. Accessed January 2, 2017.

Smith, A. (2016). *15% of American adults have used online dating sites or mobile dating apps*. Pew Research Center. www.pewinternet.org/2016/02/11/15-percent-of-american-adults-have-used-online-dating-sites-or-mobile-dating-apps/. Accessed January 8, 2017

Smith, A., & Anderson, M. (2016). *5 facts about online dating*. Pew Research Center. www.pewresearch.org/fact-tank/2016/02/29/5-facts-about-online-dating/. Accessed January 8, 2017.

Smith, C. S. (2002, May 5). Risking limbs for height and success in China. *The New York Times*.

Smith, C. S. (2005, April 30). Abduction, often violent, a Kyrgyz wedding rite. *The New York Times*.

Smith, D. (1997, May 1). Study looks at portrayal of women in media. *The New York Times*.

Smith, E. (2010, April 26). The Texas curriculum massacre. *Newsweek*.

Smith, P. A. (2015, November 10). Waste as its own solution. *The New York Times*.

Smith, S. L., Choueiti, M., Prescott, A., & Pieper, K. (2012). *Gender roles and occupations: A look at character attributes and job-related aspirations in film and television*. Geena Davis Institute on Gender in Media. www.seejane.org/downloads/KeyFindings_GenderROles.pdf. Accessed January 9, 2013.

Snell, T. L. (2014). *Capital punishment, 2013—Statistical tables* (NCJ248448). U.S. Bureau of Justice Statistics. www.bjs.gov/content/pub/pdf/cp13st.pdf. Accessed January 20, 2015.

Snipp, C. M. (1986). American Indians and natural resource development. *American Journal of Economics and Sociology, 45,* 457–474.

Sokolove, M. (2005, February 13). Clang! *The New York Times Magazine*.

Soldo, B. J., & Agree, E. M. (1988). America's elderly. *Population Bulletin, 43,* 1–45.

Sommers, B. D., Long, S. K., & Baicker, K. (2014). Changes in mortality after Massachusetts health care reform: a quasi-experimental study. *Annals of Internal Medicine, 160,* 585–593.

Sorkin, A. R., & Thee-Brenan, M. (2014, December 11). Many feel American dream is out of reach. *The New York Times*.

South, S. J., & Lloyd, K. M. (1995). Spousal alternatives and marital dissolution. *American Sociological Review, 60,* 21–35.

Southern Poverty Law Center. (2016a). *The Trump effect: The impact of the 2016 presidential election on our nation's schools*. www.splcenter.org/20161128/trump-effect-impact-2016-presidential-election-our-nations-schools. Accessed June 5, 2017.

Southern Poverty Law Center. (2016b). *Update: 1,094 bias-related incidents in the month following the election*. www.splcenter.org/hatewatch/2016/12/16/update-1094-bias-related-incidents-month-following-election. Accessed June 5, 2017.

Spada, M. M. (2014). An overview of problematic internet use. *Addictive Behavior, 39,* 3–6.

Sports quiz: White men can't jump and other assumptions about sports and race (Assumption 6). (2007). Arlington, VA: American Anthropological Association. www.understandingrace.org/lived/sports/index.html. Accessed May 30, 2009.

Springen, K. (2006, February 27). States: Time to stub out smoking. *Newsweek*.

Srikameswaran, A. (2002, July 23). Minorities lag in receiving transplants and heart surgeries. *Pittsburgh Post-Gazette*.

Sroufe, L. A. (2012, January 29). Ritalin gone wrong. *The New York Times*.

Stacey, J. (1991). Backward toward the postmodern family. In A. Wolfe (Ed.), *America at century's end*. Berkeley: University of California Press.

Staggenborg, S. (1998). *Gender, family, and social movements*. Thousand Oaks, CA: Pine Forge Press.

Stagnitti, M. N. (2005). *Antidepressant use in the U.S. civilian noninstitutionalized population, 2002* (Brief No. 77). Rockville, MD: Medical Expenditure Panel Survey. www.meps.ahrq.gov. Accessed June 3, 2005.

Stainbrook, K. (2014, June 18). All about hikikomori: Japan's missing million. *Tofugu*. www.tofugu.com/2014/06/18/all-about-hikikomori-japans-missing-million/. Accessed January 9, 2015.

Staples, W. G. (2014). *Everyday surveillance: Vigilance and visibility in postmodern life*. Lanham, MD: Rowman & Littlefield.

Starbucks. (2016). *Starbucks company profile*. www.starbucks.com/about-us/company-information/starbucks-company-profile. Accessed January 1, 2017.

Stark, R., & Bainbridge, W. S. (1980). Networks of faith: Interpersonal bonds and recruitment in cults and sects. *American Journal of Sociology, 85,* 1376–1395.

Starr, P. (1982). The social transformation of American medicine. New York, NY: Basic Books.

The State of Obesity. (2014). *Special report: Racial and ethnic disparities in obesity*. www.stateofobesity.org/disparities/. Accessed January 13, 2015.

The State of Obesity. (2016). *The health care costs of obesity*. Stateofobesity.org/healthcare-costs-obesity/. Accessed January 6, 2017.

Statista. (2015). *Distribution of computer and video gamers in the United States from 2006 to 2015 by gender*. www.statista.com/statistics/232383/gender-split-of-us-computer-and-video-gamers/. Accessed May 19, 2015.

Statista. (2016a). *Annual net revenue of Amazon from 2006 to 2015, by region (in billion U.S. dollars)*. www.statista.com/statistics/266289/net-revenue-of-amazon-by-region/. Accessed January 1, 2017.

Statista. (2016b). *Number of monthly active Facebook users worldwide as of 3rd quarter 2016*. www.statista.com/statistics/264810/number-of-monthly-active-facebook-users-worldwide/. Accessed January 9, 2017.

Statistic Brain. (2014). *Online dating statistics*. www.statisticbrain.com/online-dating-statistics/. Accessed January 15, 2015.

Statistic Brain. (2017). *Women in the military statistics*. www.statisticbrain.com/women-in-the-military-statistics/. Accessed June 13, 2017.

Stein, R. (2007, May 27). Critical care without consent. *The Washington Post*.

Steinhauer, J. (2005, May 29). When the Joneses wear jeans. *The New York Times*.

Steinhauer, J. (2013, June 18). Elite units in military to admit women. *The New York Times*.

Steinhauer, J., & Rosenberg, M. (2016, September 9). Trump faulted for his notions about assaults. *The New York Times*.

Steinmetz, S. K., Clavan, R., & Stein, K. F. (1990). *Marriage and family realities: Historical and contemporary perspectives*. New York, NY: Harper & Row.

Stephan, C. W., & Stephan, W. G. (1989). After intermarriage: Ethnic identity among mixed heritage Japanese-Americans and Hispanics. *Journal of Marriage and the Family, 51,* 507–519.

Stephens, W. N. (1963). *The family in cross-cultural perspective*. New York, NY: University Press of America.

Stephens-Davidowitz, S. (2014, January 18). Google, tell me. Is my son a genius? *The New York Times*.

Steuerle, C. E. (2007). *Crumbs for children?* Washington, DC: Urban Institute. www.urban.org/publications/901068.html. Accessed June 24, 2007.

Stevens, M. (2017, June 10). Justice dept. calls killing in Kansas a hate crime. *The New York Times*.

Stevenson, B., & Wolfers, J. (2007). *Marriage and divorce: Changes and their driving forces* (Working Paper No. 12944). Cambridge, MA: National Bureau of Economic Research. http://bpp.wharton.upenn.edu/jwolfers/Papers/MarriageandDivorce(JEP).pdf. Accessed May 12, 2007.

Stewart, A. J., Copeland, A. P., Chester, A. L., Malley, J. E., & Barenbaum, N. B. (1997). *Separating together: How divorce transforms families*. New York, NY: Guilford Press.

Stewart, J. (2015, June 3). Brave New Girl, *The Daily Show*. Comedy Central.

St. George, D. (2007, May 13). Pushing the motherhood cause. *The Washington Post*.

Stiles-Shields, C., & Carroll, R. A. (2014). Same-sex domestic violence: Prevalence, unique aspects, and clinical implications. *Journal of Sex and Marital Therapy, 4,* 1–13.

Stille, A. (2001, December 15). Grounded by an income gap. *The New York Times*.

Stille, A. (2002, June 29). Textbook publishers learn to avoid messing with Texas. *The New York Times*.

Stinnett, N., & DeFrain, J. (1985). *Secrets of strong families*. Boston, MA: Little, Brown.

Stockard, J., & O'Brien, R. M. (2002). Cohort effects on suicide rates: International variation. *American Sociological Review, 67,* 854–872.

Stokes, R., & Hewitt, J. P. (1976). Aligning actions. *American Sociological Review, 41,* 837–849.

Stolberg, S. G. (1998, April 5). Live and let die over transplants. *The New York Times*.

Stolberg, S. G. (2004, March 21). When spin spins out of control. *The New York Times*.

Stone, D., & Colarusso, L. (2011, November 21). Welfare for millionaires. *Newsweek*.

Stone, G. P. (1981). Appearance and the self: A slightly revised version. In G. P. Stone & H. A. Farberman (Eds.), *Social psychology through symbolic interaction*. New York, NY: Wiley.

Stonington, J., & McIntyre, A. (2011, November 10). The best and worst states for getting divorced. *Bloomberg News*. www.bloomberg.com/money-gallery/2011-11-10/best-and-worst-states-for-getting-divorced.html#slide1. Accessed January 16, 2013.

Stover, L. (2014, April 22). Make them fit, please! *The New York Times*.

Stout, H. (2015, June 21). Oh, to be young, millennial, and so wanted by marketers. *The New York Times*.

Straus, M. A. (1977). A sociological perspective on the prevention and treatment of wife beating. In M. Roy (Ed.), *Battered women*. New York, NY: Van Nostrand Reinhold.

Straus, M. A., & Gelles, R. J. (1990). How violent are American families? Estimates from the National Family Violence Resurvey and other studies. In M. A. Straus & R. J. Gelles (Eds.), *Physical violence in American families*. New Brunswick, NJ: Transaction.

Streitfeld, D. (2013, April 8). Teacher knows if you've done the e-reading. *The New York Times*.

Strohschein, L. (2016). Do men really benefit more from marriage than women? *American Journal of Public Health, 106*, e2.

Strom, S. (2005, January 13). U.S. charity overwhelmed by disaster aid. *The New York Times*.

Strube, M. J., & Barbour, L. S. (1983). The decision to leave an abusive relationship: Economic dependence and psychological commitment. *Journal of Marriage and the Family, 45*, 785–793.

Stryker, J. (1980). *Symbolic Interactionism*. Menlo Park, CA: Benjamin/Cummings.

Stryker, J. (1997, July 13). The age of innocence isn't what it once was. *The New York Times*.

Student Loan Hero. (2017). *A look at the shocking student loan debt statistics for 2017*. studentloanhero.com/student-loan-debt-statistics/. Accessed July 2, 2017.

Suarez, Z. (1998). The Cuban-American family. In C. H. Mindel, R. W. Habenstein, & R. Wright (Eds.), *Ethnic families in America: Patterns and variations*. Upper Saddle River, NJ: Prentice Hall.

Sudarkasa, N. (2001). Interpreting the African heritage in Afro-American family organization. In S. Ferguson (Ed.), *Shifting the center: Understanding contemporary families*. Mountain View, CA: Mayfield.

Sudnow, D. (1965). Normal crimes: Sociological features of the penal code in a public defender's office. *Social Problems, 12*, 255–264.

Sullivan, P. (2015, October 10). Work-life balance is tricky all the way up the income ladder. *The New York Times*.

Sullivan, R. (2006, June 25). A slow-road movement. *The New York Times Magazine*.

Sullivan, T. A., Warren, E., & Westbrook, J. L. (2000). *The fragile middle class: Americans in debt*. New Haven, CT: Yale University Press.

Suls, R. (2016). *Deep divides between, within parties on public debates about LGBT issues*. Pew Research Center. www.pewresearch.org/fact-tank/2016/10/04/deep-divides-between-within-parties-on—public-debates-about-lgbt-issues/. Accessed January 10, 2017.

Sulzberger, A. G. (2011, February 11). Hospitals shift smoking bans to smoker bans. *The New York Times*.

Sulzberger, A. G., & Goodstein, L. (2011, October 14). Bishop indicted; charge is failing to report abuse. *The New York Times*.

Surowiecki, J. (2016, April 25). Unlikely alliances. *The New Yorker*.

Sutherland, E., & Cressey, D. (1955). *Criminology*. Philadelphia, PA: Lippincott.

Swanson, A. (2015, February 11). Big pharmaceutical companies are spending far more on marketing than research. *Washington Post*.

Swanson, G. (1992). Doing things together: On some basic forms of agency and structuring in collective action and on some explanations for them. *Social Psychology Quarterly, 55*, 94–117.

Swarns, R. L. (2001, April 20). Drug makers drop South Africa suit over AIDS medicines. *The New York Times*.

Swarns, R. L. (2008a, September 2). Bipartisan calls for new federal poverty measure. *The New York Times*.

Swarns, R. L. (2008b, August 25). Blacks debate civil rights risk in Obama's rise. *The New York Times*.

Swarns, R. L. (2016, December 19). Reckoning with a legacy of insuring slaves' lives. *The New York Times*.

Swartz, M. (2007, June 10). Shop stewards on Fantasy Island? *The New York Times Magazine*.

Swift, A. (2016). *Americans' trust in mass media sinks to new low*. Gallup. www.gallup.com/poll/195542/americans-trust-mass-media-sinks-to-new-low.aspx. Accessed December 30, 2016.

Swinburn, B. A., Sacks, G., Hall, K. D., McPherson, K., Finegood, D. T., Moodie, M. L., & Gortmaker, S. L. (2011). The global obesity pandemic: Shaped by global drivers and local environments. *The Lancet, 378,* 804–814.

Sykes, G., & Matza, D. (1957). Techniques of neutralization: A theory of delinquency. *American Sociological Review, 22,* 664–670.

Symmes, P. (2012, February 23). Hunted in Alabama. *Newsweek.*

Szoldra, P. (2014, August 12). This is the terrifying result of the militarization of police. *Business Insider.* www.businessinsider.com/police-militarization-ferguson-2014-8. Accessed January 6, 2015.

Tabuchi, H. (2011, January 3). Despite shortage, Japan keeps a high wall for foreign labor. *The New York Times.*

Tabuchi, H. (2012, July 5). Japan Fukushima nuclear crisis called "man made." *The New York Times.*

Tabuchi, H. (2014, March 16). Unskilled and destitute are hiring targets for Fukushima cleanup. *The New York Times.*

Takayama, H. (2003, January 13). The Okinawa way. *Newsweek.*

Talbot, M. (2000, January 9). The placebo prescription. *The New York Times Magazine.*

Tannen, D. (1990). *You just don't understand: Women and men in conversation.* New York, NY: Ballantine.

Tanenhaus, S. (2014, August 17). Generation nice. *The New York Times.*

Tapia, A. T. (1995, December). Christian faith in the age of Prozac. *Harper's Magazine.*

Tarrow, S. (1994). *Power in movement.* New York, NY: Cambridge University Press.

Tatlow, D. K. (2014, May 9). Cautious Chinese gain comfort with hugs. *The New York Times.*

Tauber, M. A. (1979). Parental socialization techniques and sex differences in children's play. *Child Development, 50,* 225–234.

Taubes, G. (2012, May 14). The new obesity campaigns have it all wrong. *Newsweek.*

Tavernise, S. (2011a, August 16). Parents skip marriage for cohabitation, report finds. *The New York Times.*

Tavernise, S. (2011b, September 19). Poor young families soared in '10, data show. *The New York Times.*

Tavernise, S. (2012, December 14). Life expectancy rises around world, study finds. *The New York Times.*

Tavernise, S. (2015, April 17). Teenagers pick up e-cigarettes, as old-school smoking declines. *The New York Times.*

Tavernise, S. (2016, February 12). Life spans of the rich leave the poor behind. *The New York Times.*

Tavris, C., & Offir, C. (1984). *The longest war: Sex differences in perspective.* New York, NY: Harcourt Brace Jovanovich.

Tax Foundation. (2017). *2017 tax brackets.* www.taxfoundation.org/2017-tax-brackets. Accessed June 2, 2017.

Taylor, P. (2014a). *The next America: Boomers, millennials, and the looming generational showdown.* New York, NY: Public Affairs.

Taylor, P. (2014b). *The next America: Two dramas in slow motion.* Pew Research Center. www.pewresearch.org/next-america/#Two-Dramas-in-Slow-Motion. Accessed June 1, 2015.

Taylor, S. J., & Bogdan, R. (1980). Defending illusions: The institution's struggle for survival. *Human Organization, 39,* 209–218.

Teachman, J. D. (1991). Contributions to children by divorced fathers. *Social Problems, 38,* 358–371.

Telhami, S. (2016). *American attitudes toward Muslims and Islam.* The Brookings Institution. www.brookings.edu/research/american-attitudes-toward-muslims-and-islam. Accessed June 6, 2017.

Terry, K. (2004). *The nature and scope of the problems of sexual abuse of minors by priests and deacons.* New York, NY: John Jay College of Criminal Justice. www.bishop-accountability.org/reports/2004_02_27_JohnJay/index.html#credits. Accessed May 21, 2009.

Tharps, L. L. (2016). *Same family, different colors: Confronting colorism in America's diverse families.* Boston, MA: Beacon Press.

This American Life. (2011). *The psychopath test.* www.thisamericanlife.org/radio-archives/episode/436/the-psychopath-test. Accessed June 8, 2011.

Thoits, P. (1985). Self-labeling process in mental illness: The role of emotional deviance. *American Journal of Sociology, 91,* 221–249.

Thomas, J. L. (2014, March 13). Settlements and legal fees escalate for the Kansas City-St. Joseph diocese. *Kansas City Star.*

Thomas, K. (2010, December 1). L.P.G.A. will allow transgender players to compete. *The New York Times.*

Thomas, K. (2015, February 25). Maker of drug to treat binge-eating first marketed the disease. *The New York Times.*

Thomas, K., & Schmidt, M. S. (2012, July 3). Drug firm guilty in criminal case. *The New York Times.*

Thomas, M. (2015). *The impact of mandated benefits on the gender differential in promotions.* Unpublished Manuscript, Cornell University. www.economics.cornell.edu/sites/default/files/files/events/Thomas_paper.pdf. Accessed June 12, 2015.

Thompson, D. (2013, September 16). Where Americans—rich and poor—spent every dollar in 2012. *The Atlantic.* www.theatlantic.com/business/archive/2013/09/where-americans-spent-rich-and-poor-spent-every-dollar-in-2012/279727/. Accessed May 27, 2015.

Thompson, K., & Clement, S. (2016, July 16). Poll: Majority of Americans think race relations are getting worse. *Washington Post.*

Thomson, D. S. (2000). The Sapir-Whorf hypothesis: Worlds shaped by words. In J. Spradley & D. W. McCurdy (Eds.), *Conformity and conflict.* Boston, MA: Allyn & Bacon.

Thomson-DeVeaux, A. (2013). *New survey illuminates differences among the world's Muslims.* Public Religion Research Institute. publicreligion.org/2013/05/new-survey-illuminates-differences-among-the-worlds-muslims/. Accessed June 17, 2013.

Thornton, M. (1997). Strategies of racial socialization among black parents: Mainstreaming, minority, and cultural messages. In R. Taylor, J. Jackson, & L. Chatters (Eds.), *Family life in black America.* Thousand Oaks, CA: Sage.

Thurn, S. (2012, April 27). U.S. firms add jobs, but mostly overseas. *Wall St. Journal.*

Tibet Society. (2015, January 9). *Police shoot into crowd of Tibetans following self-immolation.* www.tibetsociety.com/content/View/518. Accessed May 22, 2015.

Tietz, J. (2006, April 20). The killing factory. *Rolling Stone.*

Tilly, C. (1978). *From mobilization to revolution.* Reading, MA: Addison-Wesley.

Timms, E., & McGonigle, S. (1992, April 5). Psychological warfare. *The Indianapolis Star.*

Tobin, J. J., Wu, D. Y. H., & Davidson, D. H. (1989). *Preschool in three cultures: Japan, China and the United States.* New Haven, CT: Yale University Press.

Tönnies, F. (1957). *Community and society* [Gemeinschaft und Gesellschaft] (C. P. Loomis, Ed.). East Lansing: Michigan State University Press. (Original work published 1887)

Top antidepressant drugs in the United States based on revenue in 2011-2012(in million US dollars). 2015. Statista. www.statista.com/statistics/242644/revenues-of-top-depression-drugs-in-the-us-2011-2012/. Accessed January 22, 2015.

Towell, L. (2007, November 18). Patients without borders. *The New York Times Magazine.*

Trautner, H. M., Ruble, D. N., Cyphers, L., Kirsten, B., Behrendt, R., & Hartmann, P. (2005). Rigidity and flexibility of gender stereotypes in childhood: Developmental or differential? *Infant and Child Development, 14,* 365–381.

Trepagnier, B. (2013). Silent racism: Passivity in well-meaning white people. In D. M. Newman & J, O'Brien (Eds.), *Sociology: Exploring the architecture of everyday life (Readings).* Thousand Oaks, CA: Sage.

Triandis, H. C., McCusker, C., & Hui, C. H. (1990). Multimethod probes of individualism and collectivism. *Journal of Personality and Social Psychology, 59,* 1006–1020.

Trotsky, L. (1959). *The history of the Russian Revolution* (F. W. Dupee, Ed.). Garden City, NY: Doubleday. (Original work published 1930)

Trotter, R. T., & Chavira, J. A. (1997). *Curanderismo: Mexican American folk healing.* Athens: University of Georgia Press.

Truman, J. L., & Morgan, R. E. (2016). *Criminal victimization, 2015.* United States Bureau of Justice Statistics. www.bjs.gov/content/pub/pdf/cv15.pdf. Accessed December 28, 2016.

Trunk, P. (2007, July 16). What Gen Y really wants. *Time.*

Tsai, T. (2012a). *China has too many bachelors.* Population Reference Bureau. www.prb.org/Articles/2012/china-census-excess-males.aspx?p=1. Accessed December 21, 2012.

Tsai, T. (2012b). *Working mothers with college degrees see gains in paid maternity leave.* Population Reference Bureau. www.prb.org/Articles/2012/working-mothers-paid-leave.aspx?p=1. Accessed January 16, 2013.

Tsushima, T., & Gecas, V. (2001). Role taking and socialization in single-parent families. *Journal of Family Issues, 22,* 267–288.

Tugend, A. (2006, April 15). Pining for the kick-back weekend. *The New York Times.*

Tumin, M. (1953). Some principles of stratification: A critical analysis. *American Sociological Review, 18,* 387–393.

Turkheimer, E., Haley, A., Waldron, M., D'Onofrio, B., & Gottesman, I. I. (2003). Socioeconomic status modifies heritability of IQ in young children. *Psychological Science, 14,* 623–628.

Turkle, S. (2011). *Alone together: Why we expect more from technology and less from each other.* New York, NY: Basic Books.

Turkle, S. (2012, April 21). The flight from conversation. *The New York Times.*

Turner, A. (2015). Generation Z: Technology and social interest. *Journal of Individual Psychology, 71,* 103–113.

Turner, E. H., Matthews, A. M., Linardatos, E., Tell, R. A., & Rosenthal, R. (2008). Selective publication of antidepressant trials and its influence on apparent efficacy. *The New England Journal of Medicine, 358,* 252–260.

Turner, J. H. (1972). *Patterns of social organization*. New York, NY: McGraw-Hill.

Turner, R. W., & Killian, L. M. (1987). *Collective behavior*. Englewood Cliffs, NJ: Prentice Hall.

Twenge, J. (2017, September). Has the smartphone destroyed a generation's mental health? *The Atlantic*.

Twenge, J. M., Campbell, W. K., & Gentile, B. (2012). Increases in individualistic words and phrases in American books, 1960–2009. *PLoSONE, 7(7):* e40181. www.plosone.org/article/info%Adoi%2F10.1371%Fjournal.pone.0040181. Accessed May 28, 2013.

Twilley, N. (2016, November 28). Cold remedy. *The New York Times Magazine*.

Tyre, P. (2006, January 30). The trouble with boys. *Newsweek*.

Ubiñas, L. A., & Gabrieli, C. (2011, August 23). Shortchanged by the bell. *The New York Times*.

Uggen, C., & Blackstone, A. (2004). Sexual harassment as a gendered expression of power. *American Sociological Review, 69,* 64–92.

Ukraine bill proposes prison for positive gay depictions. (2012, July 24). *The New York Times*.

UNAIDS. (2016a). *Fact sheet November 2016*. www.unaids.org/sites/default/files/media_asset/UNAIDS_FactSheet_en.pdf. Accessed June 4, 2017.

UNAIDS. (2016b). *Global AIDS update 2016*. www.who.int/hiv/pub/arv/global-AIDS-update-2016_en.pd?ua=1. Accessed June 28, 2017.

Undersecretary of Defense. (2013). *Memorandum for secretaries of the military departments*. www.defense.gov/home/features/2013/docs/Further-Guidance-on-Extending-Benefits-to-Same-Sex-Spouses-of-Military-M.pdf. Accessed June 24, 2014.

UN Habitat. (2014). *Background paper*. unhabitat.org/wp-content/uploads/2014/07/WHD-2014-Background-Paper.pdf. Accessed June 26, 2017.

UNICEF. (2009). *The state of the world's children 2009*. Geneva, Switzerland: Author. www.unicef.org/sowc09/docs/SOWC09-FullReport-EN.pdf. Accessed September 5, 2009.

UNICEF. (2010). *Child protection from violence, exploitation, and abuse*. www.unicef.org/media/media_45451.html. Accessed July 1, 2013.

UNICEF. (2014a). *Children of the recession: The impact of the economic crisis on child well-being in rich countries*. Innocenti Report Card 12. www.unicef-irc.org/publications/pdf/rc12-eng-web.pdf. Accessed May 31, 2015.

UNICEF. (2014b). *Committing to child survival: A promise renewed*. data.unicef.org/corecode/uploads/document6/uploaded_pdfs/corecode/APR-2014-17Oct14-web_194.pdf. Accessed June 24, 2015.

UNICEF. (2014c). *Rapid acceleration of progress is needed to achieve universal primary education by 2015*. data.unicef.org/education/primary. Accessed June 14, 2015.

UNICEF. (2015). *An estimated 150 million children worldwide are engaged in child labour*. data.unicef.org/child-protection/child-labour. Accessed June 24, 2015.

UNICEF. (2016). *87 million children under 7 have known nothing but conflict-UNICEF*. www.unicef.org/media/media_90745.html. Accessed June 28, 2017.

UNICEF. (2017). *25 million children out of school in conflict zones-UNICEF*. www.unicef.org/media/media_95861.html. Accessed June 28, 2017.

United Nations. (2011). *World population prospects*. Department of Economic and Social Affairs. http://esa.un.org/unpd/wpp/index.htm. Accessed June 23, 2011.

United Nations. (2014a). *Demographic yearbook*. www.unstats.un.org/unsd/demographic/products/dyb/dyb2013.htm. Accessed January 18, 2015.

United Nations. (2014b). *World urbanization prospects: 2014 revision*. http://esa.un.org/unpd/wup/Highlights/WUP2014-Highlights.pdf. Accessed June 17, 2015.

United Nations. (2017). *World population prospects: Median age of population*. esa.un.org/unpd/wpp/Download/Standard/Population/. Accessed June 24, 2017.

United Nations General Assembly. (2016). *Racism, xenophobia, increasing globally, experts tell third committee, amid calls for laws to combat hate speech concerns over freedom of expression*. www.un.org/press/en/2016/gashc4182.doc.htm. Accessed June 12, 2017.

United Nations High Commissioner for Refugees. (2015). *Worldwide displacement hits all-time high as war and persecution increase*. www.unhcr.org/558193896.html. Accessed June 22, 2015.

United Nations High Commissioner for Refugees. (2016). *Global trends: Forced displacement in 2015*. www.unhcr.org/576408cd7. Accessed June 26, 2017.

United Nations Population Division. (2003). *World population prospects: The 2002 revision*. Geneva, Switzerland: Author. www.un.org/esa/population/publications/wpp2002/wpp2002-highlightsrev1.pdf. Accessed June 26, 2003.

United Nations Population Fund. (2016). *Migration*. www.unfpa.org/migration. Accessed June 26, 2017.

United Nations Treaty Collection. (2017). *Convention on the elimination of all forms of discrimination against women*.

treaties.un.org/Pages/ViewDetails.aspx?src=TREAT&mtdsg_no1V-8&chapter=4&clang=_en. Accessed June 20, 2017.

United States Bureau of Justice Statistics. (2013). *Sourcebook of criminal justice statistics*. www.albany.edu/sourcebook/. Accessed January 20, 2015.

United States Bureau of Justice Statistics. (2017). *NCVS victimization analysis tool (NVAT) report*. www.bjs.gov/index. cfm?ty=nvat. Accessed June 14, 2017.

United States Bureau of Labor Statistics. (2013). *Marriage and divorce patterns by gender, race, and educational attainment*. www.bls.gov/opub/mlr/2013/article/marriage-and-divorce-patterns-by-gender-race-and-educational-attainment.htm. Accessed January 18, 2015.

United States Bureau of Labor Statistics. (2015). *Numbers of non-fatal occupational injuries by identity and case types, 2013*. www.bls.gov/iif/oshwc/osh/os/ost63960.pdf. Accessed January 21, 2015.

United States Bureau of Labor Statistics. (2016a). *Consumer expenditures—2015*. USDL-16-1768. www.bls.gov/news .release/cesan.nr0.htm. Accessed May 31, 2017.

United States Bureau of Labor Statistics. (2016b). *Employee tenure in 2016*. USDL-16-1867. www.bls.gov/news.release/ tenure.nr).htm. Accessed June 26, 2017.

United States Bureau of Labor Statistics. (2016c). *Employment characteristics of families-2015*. USDL-16-0795. www.bls.gov/ news.release/famee_nr0.htm. Accessed January 15, 2017.

United States Bureau of Labor Statistics. (2016d). *Local area unemployment statistics*. www.bls.gov/web/metro/laum mtrk.htm. Accessed December 26, 2016.

United States Bureau of Labor Statistics. (2016e). *National census of fatal occupational injuries in 2015*. USDL-16-2304. www.bls.gov/news-release/pdf/cfoi.pdf. Accessed January 18, 2017.

United States Bureau of Labor Statistics. (2016f). *Occupational employment and wages, May 2016-Refuse and recyclable material collectors*. www.bls.gov/oes/current/ oes537081.htm. Accessed May 24, 2017.

United States Bureau of Labor Statistics. (2017a). *American time use survey—Tables A-1 & A-7A*. www.bls.gov/tus/#tables. Accessed June 16, 2017.

United States Bureau of Labor Statistics. (2017b). *Employed persons by class of worker and part-time status. Table A-8*. www.bls.gov/news.release/empsit.t08.htm. Accessed May 24, 2017.

United States Bureau of Labor Statistics. (2017c). *The employment situation—April 2017*. USDL-17-0551. www.bls. gov/news.release/empsit.nr0htm. Accessed May 23, 2017.

United States Bureau of Labor Statistics. (2017d). *The employment situation, Tables A-2 and A-3*. www.bls.gov/ news.release/empsit.toc.htm. Accessed June 9, 2017.

United States Bureau of Labor Statistics. (2017e). *Table 39: Median weekly earnings of full-time wage and salary workers by detailed occupation and sex*. www.bls.gov/cps/cpsaat39.htm. Accessed June 20, 2017.

United States Bureau of the Census. (2000). *Statistical abstract of the United States*. Washington, DC: Government Printing Office.

United States Bureau of the Census. (2002). *Statistical abstract of the United States*. Washington, DC: Government Printing Office.

United States Bureau of the Census. (2004). *Statistical abstract of the United States*. Washington, DC: Author. www.census.gov/prod/www/statistical-abstract-04.html. Accessed June 15, 2005.

United States Bureau of the Census. (2005). *Current population survey (CPS): Definitions and explanations*. Washington, DC: Author. www.census.gov/population/www/cps/cps def.html. Accessed September 21, 2005.

United States Bureau of the Census. (2006). *Special edition: 300 million*. Washington, DC: Author. www.census.gov/ Press-Release/www/releases/archives/facts_for_features_ special_editions/007276.htm. Accessed July 12, 2007.

United States Bureau of the Census. (2011a). *International data base*. www.census.gov/ipc/www/idb. Accessed June 23, 2011.

United States Bureau of the Census. (2011b). *Statistical abstract of the United States*. Washington, DC: Author. www. census.gov/compendia/statab/2011 edition.html. Accessed July 4, 2011.

United States Bureau of the Census. (2014). *2014 national population projections: Summary tables*. www.census.gov/ population/projections/data/national/2014/summaryta bles.html. Accessed June 21, 2015.

United States Bureau of the Census. (2015). *Total midyear population for the world: 1950–2050*. www.census.gov/popu lation/international/data/worldpop/table_population.php. Accessed June 17, 2015.

United States Bureau of the Census. (2016a). *Hello my name is. . .* www.census.gov/library/visualizations/2016/comm/ cb16-tps154_surnames_top15.html. Accessed June 5, 2017.

United States Bureau of the Census. (2016b). *Table HH-4: Households by size: 1960 to present*. www.census.gov/hhes/ families/data/households.html. Accessed January 10.

United States Bureau of the Census (2017). *Income, poverty and health insurance coverage in the United States: 2016*. Release

CB17-156. www.census.gov/newsroom/press-releases/2017/income-poverty.html. Accessed October 13, 2017.

United States Commission on Human Rights. (1992). Indian tribes: A continuing quest for survival. In P. S. Rothenberg (Ed.), *Race, class and gender in the United States*. New York, NY: St. Martin's Press.

United States Conference of Catholic Bishops. (2011). *The causes and context of sexual abuse of minors by Catholic priests in the United States, 1950–2010*. www.usccb.org/mr/causes-and-context-ofsexual-abuse-of-minors-by-catholic-priests-in-the-united-states-1950-2010.pdf. Accessed June 6, 2011.

United States Conference of Mayors. (2014). *Hunger and homelessness survey: A status report on hunger and homelessness in America's cities*. www.usmayors.org/pressreleases/uploads/2014/1211-report-hh.pdf. Accessed June 2, 2015.

United States Department of Education. (2017). *Every Student Succeeds Act (ESSA)*. www.ed.gov/essa?src=rn. Accessed July 13, 2017.

United States Department of Health and Human Services. (2006). *Sustaining state programs for tobacco control: Data highlights 2006*. www.cdc.gov/tobacco/data_statistics/state_data/data_highlights/2006/pdfs/dataHighlights06rev.pdf. Accessed September 5, 2009.

United States Department of Health and Human Services. (2015). *Child maltreatment 2014*. www.acf.hhs.gov/sites/default/files/cb/cm2014.pdf. Accessed January 16, 2017.

United States Department of Health and Human Services. (2017). *TANF caseload data 2017*. www.acf.hhs.gov/ofa/resource/tanf-caseload-data-2017. Accessed June 3, 2017.

United States Department of Homeland Security. (2014). *2013 yearbook of immigration statistics*. www.dhs.gov/sites/default/files/publications/ols_yb_2013_0.pdf. Accessed June 18, 2015.

United States Department of Justice. (2010). *Americans with Disabilities Act Title III Regulations-Section 36.105*. www.ada.gov/regs2010/titleIII_2010/titleIII_2010_regulations.htm. Accessed December 28, 2016.

United States Department of Justice. (2013). *A national protocol for sexual assault medical forensic examinations—2nd edition*. NCJ241903. www.safeta.org/associations/8563/files/SAFE_PROTOCOL_2012-508.pdf. Accessed April 27, 2013.

United States Department of Justice. (2014). *Re: Toyota Motor Corporation—Deferred prosecution agreement*. www.justice.gov/sites/default/diles/opa/legacy/2014/03/19/toyota-def-pros-agr.pdf. Accessed January 23, 2015.

United States Department of Labor. (2011). *Facts on Executive Order 11246—Affirmative action*. Office of Federal Contract Compliance Programs. www.dol.gov/OFCCP/regs/compliance/aa.htm. Accessed June 17, 2011.

United States Department of Labor. (2012). *Fact sheet #28A: Employee protections under the Family and Medical Leave Act*. www.dol.gov/whd/regs/compliance/whdfs28a.pdf. Accessed January 15, 2017.

United States Department of Labor. (2014). *FMLA is working*. www.dol.gov/whd/fmla/survey/FMLA_Survey_factsheet.pdf. Accessed January 18, 2015.

United States Equal Employment Opportunity Commission. (2017a). *Charges alleging sex-based harassment (charges filed with EEOC) FY2010-FY2016*. www.eeoc.gov/eeoc/statistics/enforcement/sexual_harassment_new. Accessed June 13, 2017.

United States Equal Employment Opportunity Commission. (2017b). *Pregnancy discrimination charges EEOC & FEPAs combined: FY1997-FY2011*. www.eeoc.gov/eeoc/statistics/enforcement/pregnancy.cfm. Accessed June 17, 2017.

United States Network for Global Economic Justice. (2000). *False profits: Who wins, who loses when the IMF, World Bank, and WTO come to town*. Washington, DC: Author. www.50years.org/april16/booklet.html. Accessed June 22, 2000.

United States Sentencing Commission. (2013). *Annual report 2013*. www.ussc.gov/research-and-publications/annual-reports-sourcebooks/2013/annual-report-2013. Accessed January 23, 2015.

United States Sentencing Commission. (2014a). *Quick facts: Crack cocaine trafficking offenses*. www.ussc.gov/sites/default/files/pdf/research-and-publications/quick-facts/Quick_Facts_Crack_Cocaine.pdf. Accessed January 22, 2015.

United States Sentencing Commission. (2014b). *Quick facts: Powder cocaine trafficking offenses*. www.ussc.gov/sites/default/files/pdf/research-and-publications/quick-facts/Quick_Facts_Powder_Cocaine.pdf. Accessed January 22, 2015.

United States Sentencing Commission. (2016). *Federal offenders in prison—March 2016*. www.ussc.gov/sites/default/files/pdf/research-and-publications/quick-facts/Quick-Facts_BOP_March2016.pdf. Accessed January 18, 2017.

United States Sentencing Project. (2014). *Facts about prison and people in prison*. sentencingproject.org/doc/publications/inc_Facts About Prisons.pdf. Accessed June 25, 2014.

United States Sentencing Project. (2016). *The color of justice: Racial and ethnic disparity in state prisons*. www.sentencingproject.org/wp-content/uploads/2016/06/The-Color-of-Justice-Racial-and-Ethnic-Disparity-in-State-Prisons.pdf. Accessed January 18, 2017.

United States Surgeon General. (2014). *The health consequences of smoking-50 years of progress: A report of the Surgeon General, 2014*. www.surgeongeneral.gov/library/reports/50-years-of-progress/. Accessed June 23, 2014.

University of Southern California Marshall School of Business. (2013, October 30). Media consumption to average 15.5 hours a day by 2015. *Science Daily*. www.science daily.com/releases/2013/10/131030111316.htm/. Accessed January 6, 2017.

UN Women (2015). *The Beijing Declaration and Platform for Action turns 20*. www.unwomen.org/~/media/headquar ters/attachments/sections/library/publications/2015/sg report_synthesis-en_web.pdf. Accessed March 10, 2015.

UN Women (2016). *Facts and figures: Ending violence against women*. www.unwomen.org/en-what-we-do/ending-vio lence-against-women/facts-and-figures. Accessed June 20, 2017.

Upton, R. L. (2010). "Fat eggs": Gender and fertility as important factors in HIV/AIDS prevention in Botswana. *Gender & Development, 18*, 515–524.

Urbina, I. (2006, November 5). Sites invite online mourning, but don't speak ill of the dead. *The New York Times*.

Urbina, I. (2009, February 25). In push to end death penalty, some states cite cost-cutting. *The New York Times*.

Urbina, I. (2013a, June 4). Blacks are singled out for marijuana arrests, federal data suggests. *The New York Times*.

Urbina, I. (2013b, December 23). In buying cheap clothes, U.S. flouts own counsel. *The New York Times*.

Useem, J. (2017, July/August). Power causes brain damage. *The Atlantic*.

U.S. English. (2016). *About U.S. English*. www.usenglish. org/history/. Accessed December 30, 2016.

Usgovernmentspending.com. (2017). *United States, federal, state, and local government spending*. www.govern mentspending.com/year_spending_2017USbn_18bs2n#u sgs302. Accessed June 3, 2017.

Ushomirsky, N., & Williams, D. (2015). *Too many states still spend less on educating students who need the most*. The Education Trust. www.edtrust.org/wp-content/ uploads/2014/09/FundingGaps2015_TheEducationTrust .pdf. Accessed May 28, 2015.

U.S. PIRG Education Fund. (2012). *Transportation and the new generation*. www.pirg.org/sites/pirg/files/ reports/Transportation%20%26%20the%20New%20 Generation%20vUS_0.pdf. Accessed December 31, 2012.

Utne, L. (2006, March/April). Soldiers for peace. *Utne Reader*.

Van Ausdale, D., & Feagin, J. R. (2001). *The first R: How children learn race and racism*. Lanham, MD: Rowman & Littlefield.

van den Haag, E. (1975). *Punishing criminals: Concerning a very old and painful question*. New York, NY: Basic Books.

Vanek, J. (1980). Work, leisure and family roles: Farm households in the United States: 1920–1955. *Journal of Family History, 5*, 422–431.

van Nood, E. (2013). Duodenal infusion of donor feces for recurrent *Clostridium difficile*. *New England Journal of Medicine, 368*, 407–415.

Van Ryn, M., & Burke, J. (2000). The effect of patient race and socio-economic status on physicians' perceptions of patients. *Social Science and Medicine, 50*, 813–820.

Vaughan, D. (1986). *Uncoupling*. New York, NY: Vintage Books.

Vaughan, H. (2016). *The feminization of God and gender-bender generation*. Christ Life Ministries. www.christlife min.org/home/blog/articles/the-feminization-of-god/. Accessed June 15, 2017.

Velázquez, N. (2002). In search of justice. In J. B. Schor & B. Taylor (Eds.). *Sustainable planet: Solutions for the Twenty-First century*. Boston, MA: Beacon Press.

Victor, D. (2016a, December 6). Freed at first, Louisiana man is charged in "road rage" killing of a football player. *The New York Times*.

Victor, D. (2016b, December 31). Transgender boy is told to leave the Cub Scouts. *The New York Times*.

Viets, E. (1992, November 29). Give a whistle, he'll love it. *St. Louis Post-Dispatch*.

Villarosa, L. (2017, June 11). America's hidden H.I.V. epidemic. *The New York Times Magazine*.

Villarreal, A. (2010). Stratification by skin color in contemporary Mexico. *American Sociological Review, 75*, 652–678.

Voyandoff, P. (1990). Economic distress and family relations: A review of the eighties. *Journal of Marriage and Family, 52*, 1099–1115.

Wahl, O. (1999). *Telling is risky business*. New Brunswick, NJ: Rutgers University Press.

Waite, L. J., & Gallagher, M. (2000). *The case for marriage: Why married people are happier, healthier, and better off financially*. New York, NY: Doubleday.

Waldman, A. (2003, March 28). Broken taboos doom lovers in an Indian village. *The New York Times*.

Waldman, A. (2005, May 8). Sri Lankan maids' high price for foreign jobs. *The New York Times*.

Waldrop, J. (2013, March 13). State medical boards trying to limit who can be called "Doctor." *Clinical Advisor*.

The Walk Free Foundation. (2016). *The Global Slavery Index 2016.* globalslaveryindex.org-assets.s3.amazonaws.com/downloads/GSI-2016-Full-Report.pdf. Accessed May 24, 2017.

Wal-Mart. (2016). *Our story.* www.corporate.walmart.com/our-story/. Accessed January 1, 2017.

Wallace, J. (2016, August 9). Even Cambodia's dead prefer dollars. *The New York Times.*

Walters, M. L., Chen, J., & Breiding, M. J. (2013). *The National Intimate Partner and Sexual Violence Survey (NISVS): 2010 findings on victimization by sexual orientation.* Centers for Disease Control and Prevention. www.cdc.gov/violence prevention/pdf/nisvs_sofindings.pdf. Accessed January 16, 2017.

Wang, A. B. (2017a, May 28). "Brave and selfless" Oregon stabbing victims hailed as heroes for standing up to racist rants. *Washington Post.*

Wang, A. B. (2017b, July 2). Trump brings up the war on Christmas—in July. *Washington Post.*

Wang, S. (2015, December 17). Indy Star poll: 70% of Hoosiers support LGBT protections. *Indianapolis Star.*

Wang, S., & Aamodt, S. (2011, September 25). Delay kindergarten at your child's peril. *The New York Times.*

Wang, W., & Morin, R. (2009). *Home for the holidays . . . and every other day.* Pew Research Center. http://pewsocial trends.org/2009/11/24/home-for-the-holidays-and-every-other-day/. Accessed June 6, 2011.

Wang, W., Parker, K., & Taylor, P. (2013). *Breadwinner moms.* Pew Research Center. www.pewsocialtrends.org/2013/05/29/breadwinner-moms/. Accessed June 18, 2013.

Wansink, B. (2006). *Mindless eating: Why we eat more than we think.* New York, NY: Bantam.

War Child. (2015). *Child soldiers.* www.warchild.org.uk/issues/child-soldiers. Accessed June 23, 2015.

Ward, L. M., & Friedman, K. (2006). Using TV as a guide: Associations between television viewing and adolescents' sexual attitudes and behavior. *Journal of Research on Adolescence, 16,* 133–156.

Warner, J. (2010, June 20). Dysregulation nation. *The New York Times.*

Warshaw, R. (1988). *I never called it rape.* New York, NY: Harper & Row.

Washington, H. A. (2006). *Medical apartheid: The dark history of medical experimentation on black Americans from Colonial times to the present.* New York, NY: Doubleday.

Washuk, B. (2015, June 16j). Ride calls attention to senior-driving problem. *Lewiston Sun Journal.*

Waters, M. C. (2008). Optional ethnicities: For Whites only? In D. Newman & J. O'Brien (Eds.), *Sociology: Exploring the architecture of everyday life (Readings).* Thousand Oaks, CA: Pine Forge Press.

Watson, C. M., Quatman, T., & Edler, E. (2002). Career aspirations of adolescent girls: Effects of achievement level, grade, and single-sex school environment. *Sex Roles, 46,* 323–335.

Wattenberg, E. (1986). The fate of baby boomers and their children. *Social Work, 31,* 20–28.

Watts, D. J. (2007, April 15). Is Justin Timberlake a product of cumulative advantage? *The New York Times Magazine.*

Watts, N., Adger, W. N., Agnolucci, P., Blackstock, J., Byass, P., Cai, W., . . . Costello, A. (2015, June 22). Health and climate change: Policy responses to protect public health. *The Lancet Online.* www.thelancet.com/pdfs/journals/lancet/PIIS0140-6736(15)60854-6.pdf. Accessed June 24, 2015.

Watzlawick, P. (1976). *How real is real?* Garden City, NY: Doubleday.

Watzlawick, P. (1984). Self-fulfilling prophecies. In P. Watzlawick (Ed.), *The invented reality: How do we know what we believe we know? Contributions to constructivism.* New York, NY: Norton.

Weaver, M. (2017, March 14). Burqa bans, headscarves, and veils: A timeline of legislation in the west. *The Guardian.* www.theguardian.com/world/2017/mar/14/headscarves-and-mus lim-veil-ban-debate-timeline. Accessed June 12, 2017.

Weber, M. (1946). Bureaucracy. In H. H. Gerth & C. W. Mills (Eds.), *From Max Weber: Essays in sociology.* New York, NY: Oxford University Press.

Weber, M. (1947). *The theory of social and economic organization.* New York, NY: Free Press.

Weber, M. (1970). *From Max Weber: Essays in sociology* (H. H. Gerth & C. W. Mills, Eds.). New York, NY: Oxford University Press.

Weber, M. (1977). *The Protestant ethic and the spirit of capitalism.* New York, NY: Macmillan. (Original work published 1904)

Weber, M. (1978). *Economy and society* (G. Roth & C. Wittich, Trans.). Berkeley: University of California Press. (Original work published 1921)

Weeks, J. (1995). *Population: An introduction to concepts and issues* (Rev. 5th ed.). Belmont, CA: Wadsworth.

Wehrfritz, G., & Cochrane, J. (2005, January 17). Charity and chaos. *Newsweek.*

Weil, A. (2011, November 7 & 14). Don't let chaos get you down. *Newsweek*.

Weil, E. (2006, September 24). What if it's (sort of) a boy and (sort of) a girl? *The New York Times Magazine*.

Weil, E. (2007, June 3). When should a kid start kindergarten? *The New York Times Magazine*.

Weinberg, D. H. (2007, July/August). Earnings by gender: Evidence from Census 2000. *Monthly Labor Review*, 26–34.

Weiser, M. (2014, July 15). California adopts $500 criminal penalty for water waste. *Sacramento Bee*.

Weitzman, L., Eifler, D., Hodada, E., & Ross, C. (1972). Sex-role socialization in picture books for preschool children. *American Journal of Sociology, 77*, 1125–1150.

Welch, H. G., Schwartz, L., & Woloshin, S. (2007, January 2). What's making us sick is an epidemic of diagnoses. *The New York Times*.

Wells, M. (2011, August 11). Mullin left indelible mark on Pacers over 3 seasons. *The Indianapolis Star*.

Whalen, C. K., & Henker, B. (1977). The pitfalls of politicization: A response to Conrad's "The discovery of hyperkinesis: Notes on the medicalization of deviance." *Social Problems, 24*, 590–595.

What is coltan? (2002, January 21). *ABCNews.com*. http://abcnews.go.com/Nightline/story?id= 128631&page=1. Accessed September 5, 2009.

White, J. E. (1997, May 5). Multiracialism: The melding of America. *Time*.

White, L., & Brinkerhoff, D. (1981). The sexual division of labor: Evidence from childhood. *Social Forces, 60*, 170–181.

White, R. (2014). Strict belief-based diet contributed to Calgary infant's death, parents face charges. CTV Calgary. www.calgary.ctvnews.ca/strict-belief-based-diet-con tributed-to-calgary-infant-s-death-parents-face-charges-1.2146526#ixzz3M6NRtpws. Accessed January 5, 2015.

The White House Blog. (2010). *A look behind the scenes of presidential advance*. www.white house.gov/blog/2010/01/21/ a-look-behindscenes-presidential-advance. Accessed June 1, 2011.

Whorf, B. (1956). *Language, thought and reality*. Cambridge, MA: MIT Press.

Whyte, M. K. (1990). *Dating, mating and marriage*. New York, NY: Aldine de Gruyter.

Whyte, W. H. (1956). *The organization man*. Garden City, NY: Doubleday.

Wiecha, J. L., Finkelstein, D., Troped, P. J., Fragala, M., & Peterson, K. E. (2006). School vending machine use and fast-food restaurant use are associated with sugar-sweetened beverage intake in youth. *Journal of the Academy of Nutrition and Dietetics, 10*, 1624–1630.

Wike, R. (2012). *Anti-Americanism down in Europe, but a values gap persists*. Pew Global Attitudes Project. www .pewglobal.org/2012/12/04/anti-americanism-down-in-europe-but-a-values-gap-persists/. Accessed January 9, 2015.

Wilcox, W. B. (2000). Conservative Protestant child discipline: The case of parental yelling. *Social Forces, 79*, 856–891.

Wildman, S. M., & Davis, A. D. (2002). Making systems of privilege visible. In P. S. Rothenberg (Ed.), *White privilege: Essential readings on the other side of racism*. New York, NY: Worth.

Wilkinson, L. C., & Marrett, C. B. (1985). *Gender influences in classroom interaction*. Orlando, FL: Academic Press.

Williams, A. (2015, September 18). Move over, millennials, here comes Generation Z. *The New York Times*.

Williams, C. L. (2006). *Inside toyland: Working, shopping, and social inequality*. Berkeley: University of California Press.

Williams, J. C., Blair-Joy, M., & Berdahl, J. L. (2013). Cultural schemas, social class and the flexibility of stigma. *Journal of Social Issues, 69*, 209–234.

Williams, S. J. (2011). Our hard days' nights. *Contexts, 10*, 26–31.

Williams, T. C. (2011, September 16). Racial bias seen in study of lead dust and children. *The New York Times*.

Williams, T. C. (2012, March 18). As black as we wish to be. *The New York Times*.

Williamson, R. C. (1984). A partial replication of the Kohn-Gecas-Nye thesis in a German sample. *Journal of Marriage and the Family, 46*, 971–979.

Wilmer, F. (2002). *The social construction of man, the state, and war: Identity, conflict, and violence in former Yugoslavia*. New York, NY: Routledge.

Wilper, A. P., Woolhandler, S., Lasser, K.E., McCormick, D., Bor, D. H., & Himmelstein, D. U. (2009). Health insurance and mortality in US adults. *American Journal of Public Health, 99*, 2289–2295.

Wilson, C. (2012, April 7). Courtesy charter outlaws rude behavior. *Abacus News*.

Wilson, D. (2009a, August 30). Race, ethnicity, and care. *The New York Times.*

Wilson, D. (2009b, June 12). Senate approves tight regulation over cigarettes. *The New York Times.*

Wilson, D. (2010, November 14). Cigarette giants in a global fight on tighter rules. *The New York Times.*

Wilson, J. L., Peebles, R., Hardy, K. K., & Litt, I. F. (2006). Surfing for thinness: A pilot study of pro-eating disorder website usage in adolescents with eating disorders. *Pediatrics, 118,* 1635–1643.

Wilson, M., & Baker, A. (2010, October 8). Lured into a trap, then tortured for being gay. *The New York Times.*

Wilson, W. J. (1980). *The declining significance of race.* Chicago, IL: University of Chicago Press.

Winerip, M., Schwirtz, M., & Gebeloff, R. (2016, December 5). For blacks facing parole, signs of broken system in New York. *The New York Times.*

Wingfield, N. (2011, December 3). Thinking aloud, endlessly. *The New York Times.*

Winter, G. (2002, May 19). Workers say Coke sold old soda. *The New York Times.*

Wise, T. (2002). Membership has its privileges: Thoughts on acknowledging and challenging whiteness. In P. S. Rothenberg (Ed.), *White privilege: Essential readings on the other side of racism.* New York, NY: Worth.

Witt, S. (2005). How television shapes children's gender roles. In R. H. Lauer & J. C. Lauer (Eds.), *Sociology: Windows on society.* Los Angeles, CA: Roxbury.

Wolf-Meyer, M. J. (2012). *The slumbering masses: Sleep, medicine, and modern American life.* Minneapolis: University of Minnesota Press.

Wolfe, A. (1991). *America at century's end.* Berkeley: University of California Press.

Wolfers, J., Quealy, K., & Leonhardt, D. (2015, April 21). 1.5 million black men, missing from daily life. *The New York Times.*

The Women's Media Center. (2011). *Statistics summary.* http://womensmediacenter.com/index.php?option=com_contents&view=article& id=157&Itemid=167. Accessed April 12, 2011.

The Women's Media Center. (2017). *The status of women in the U.S. media 2017.* wmc.3cdn.net/10c550d19ef9f3688f_mlbres2jd.pdf. Accessed June 16, 2017.

Wong, E. (2015, October 31). China's longtime one-child rule is gone, but trauma lingers. *The New York Times.*

Wood, M. (2014, May 15). How young is too young for a digital presence? *The New York Times.*

Wood, M. (2015, February 5). Led by Tinder, the mobile dating game surges. *The New York Times.*

Wood, N. (2005, February 6). Eight nations agree on plan to lift status of Gypsies. *The New York Times.*

Woolf, S. H., & Aron, L. (2013). *U.S. health in international perspective: Shorter lives, poorer health.* Washington, DC: National Academy Press.

Wootson, C. (2016a, March 19). A California waiter refused to serve 4 Latina women until he saw "proof of residency." *Washington Post.*

Wootson, C. (2016b, August 19). White supremacist stabs interracial couple after seeing them kiss at bar, police say. *Washington Post.*

Workers of the world. (1998, January 30). *Economist.*

World Bank. (2012). *Projects and lending.* www.worldbank.org. Accessed June 3, 2013.

World Bank. (2015). *Labor force participation rate, female (% of female population ages 15+) (modeled ILO estimate).* www.data.worldbank.org/indicator/SL.TLF.CACT.FE.ZS. Accessed June 15, 2015.

World Bank. (2017). *World development indicators: Size of the economy.* wdi.worldbank.org/table/WV.1. Accessed June 4, 2017.

World Health Organization. (2012). *Dementia: A public health priority.* apps.who.int/iris/bitstream/10665/75263/1/9789241564458_eng.pdf. Accessed June 27, 2013.

World Health Organization. (2013a). *Global and regional estimates of violence against women: Prevalence and health effects of intimate partner violence and non-partner sexual violence.* apps.who.int/iris/bitstream/10665/85239/1/9789241564625_eng.pdf. Accessed January 20, 2015.

World Health Organization. (2013b). *WHO report on the global tobacco epidemic 2013.* apps.who.int/iris/bistream/10665/85380/1/9789241505871_eng.pdf.

World Health Organization. (2015). *Tobacco control.* www.who.int/gho/tobacco/en/. Accessed January 22, 2015.

World Health Organization. (2016a). *Female genital mutilation.* www.who.int/mediacentre/factsheets/fs241/en/. Accessed January 2, 2017.

World Health Organization. (2016b). *Suicide rates data by country.* apps.who.int/gho/data/node.main.MHSUICIDE?lang=en. Accessed December 26, 2016.

World Hunger Education Service. (2015). *2015 world hunger and poverty facts and statistics*. www.worldhunger.org/articles/Learn/world hunger facts 2002.htm. Accessed May 29, 2015.

World Wildlife Fund. (2016). *Living planet report 2016*. www.worldwildlife.org/pages/living-planet-report-2016. Accessed June 23, 2017.

Worsnop, R. (1996). Getting into college. *CQ Researcher, 6*, 169–192.

Wortham, J. (2010, May 14). Everyone is using cellphones, but not so many are talking. *The New York Times*.

Wortham, J. (2011, December 14). The Facebook resisters. *The New York Times*.

Wortham, J. (2015, June 21). Our bodies, our feeds. *The New York Times*.

Worthen, M. (2009, January 11). Who would Jesus smack down? *The New York Times Magazine*.

Worthen, M. (2010, November 14). Housewives of God. *The New York Times Magazine*.

Wright, E. O. (1976). Class boundaries in advanced capitalist societies. *New Left Review, 98*, 3–41.

Wright, E. O., Costello, C., Hachen, D., & Sprague, J. (1982). The American class structure. *American Sociological Review, 47*, 709–726.

Wright, E. O., & Perrone, L. (1977). Marxist class categories and income inequality. *American Sociological Review, 42*, 32–55.

Wright, J. D., & Wright, S. R. (1976). Social class and parental values for children: A partial replication and extension of the Kohn thesis. *American Sociological Review, 41*, 527–537.

Wrong, D. (1988). *Power: Its forms, bases, and uses*. Chicago, IL: University of Chicago Press.

Wu, F. H. (2002). *Yellow: Race in America beyond black and white*. New York, NY: Basic Books.

WuDunn, S. (1996, September 11). A taboo creates a land of Romeos and Juliets. *The New York Times*.

Wuthnow, R. (1994). *Sharing the journey*. New York, NY: Free Press.

Wynia, M. K., VanGeest, J. B., Cummins, D. S., & Wilson, I. B. (2003). Do physicians not offer useful services because of coverage restrictions? *Health Affairs, 22*, 190–198.

Xu, X., Bishop, E. E., Kennedy, S. M., Simpson, S. A., & Pechacek, T. F. (2015). Annual health care spending attributable to cigarette smoking: An update. *American Journal of Preventative Medicine, 48*, 326–333.

Yardley, J. (2000, March 25). Unmarried and living together, till the sheriff do us part. *The New York Times*.

Yardley, J. (2011, May 25). As wealth and literacy rise in India, report says, so do sex-selective abortions. *The New York Times*.

Yardley, W. (2007, August 28). When wildfires threaten, wealthy get extra shield. *The New York Times*.

Yi, C.-C., Chang, C.-E., & Chang, Y.-H. (2004). The intergenerational transmission of family values: A comparison between teenagers and parents in Taiwan. *Journal of Comparative Family Studies, 35*, 523–545.

Yong, W. (2010, December 7). Divorce soars in Iran as women say no, and work the system. *The New York Times*.

Yoshino, K. (2006). *Covering: The hidden assault on our civil rights*. New York, NY: Random House.

Young, C. (2017, July 21). Rethinking campus rape policy. *The New York Times*.

Young, J. Q., Ranji, S. R., Wachter, R. M., Lee, C. M., Niehaus, B., & Auerbach, A. D. (2011). "July effect": Impact of the academic year-end changeover on patient outcomes: A systematic review. *Annals of Internal Medicine, 155*, 309–315.

Young, L. M., & Powell, B. (1985). The effects of obesity on the clinical judgments of mental health professionals. *Journal of Health and Social Behavior, 26*, 233–246.

Younis, M. (2011). *Muslim Americans identify with God and country*. Abu Dhabi Gallup Center. www.gallup.com/poll/148799/Muslim-Americans-Identify-God-Country.aspx. Accessed September 8, 2011.

Yudell, M., Roberts, D., DeSalle, R., & Tishkoff, S. (2016). Taking race out of human genetics. *Science, 351*, 564–565.

Yurkiewicz, I. (2012, June 12). Three bizarre tales of medical survivors, and what they can (and cannot) teach us about medicine. *Scientific American*.

Zak, D. (2016, June 29). Baby boomers are the zombie invasion we feared. *Washington Post*.

Zeigler, K., & Camarota, S. A. (2016). *Immigrants in the United States*. Center for Immigration Studies. cis.org/immigrants-in-the-United-States. Accessed June 26, 2017.

Zernike, K. (2003, January 20). 30 years after *Roe v. Wade*, new trends but the old debate. *The New York Times*.

Zernike, K. (2016, March 1). Testing for grit? Schools pushed on social skills. *The New York Times*.

Zhu, W. X., Lu, L., & Hesketh, T. (2009). China's excess males, sex selective abortion, and one child policy: Analysis of data from 2005 national intercensus survey. *British Medical Journal, 338,* 1211–1213.

Zimbardo, P. (2007). *The Lucifer effect: Understanding how good people turn evil.* New York, NY: Random House.

Zoepf, K. (2007, September 23). A dishonorable affair. *The New York Times Magazine.*

Zola, I. (1986). Medicine as an institution of social control. In P. Conrad & R. Kern (Eds.), *The sociology of health and illness.* New York, NY: St. Martin's Press.

Zoll, R. (2005, June 7). Poll reveals U.S. leads in religious devotion. *The Indianapolis Star.*

Zuckoff, M. (2000, June 8). Lawsuit accuses drug maker Eli Lilly of concealing Prozac data from trial. *The Boston Globe.*

Zuger, A. (1999, April 30). Take some strychnine and call me in the morning. *The New York Times.*

Zuger, A. (2005, October 30). For a retainer, lavish care by "boutique doctors." *The New York Times.*

Zurcher, L. A., & Snow, D. A. (1981). Collective behavior: Social movements. In M. Rosenberg & R. H. Turner (Eds.), *Social psychology: Sociological perspectives.* New York, NY: Basic Books.

Zweigenhaft, R. L. (1987). Minorities and women of the corporation. In G. W. Domhoff & T. R. Dye (Eds.), *Power elites and organizations.* Newbury Park, CA: Sage.

Zwerdling, D. (2004). U.S. military whistle blowers face retribution. *National Public Radio.* www.npr.org/templates/story/story.php?storyId=1905858. Accessed June 19, 2007.

• Index •